5 STEPS TO A 5™

AP U.S. History
2024

5 STEPS TO A 5™

AP U.S. History

2024

Daniel P. Murphy
Emily Lewellen

Mc Graw Hill

New York Chicago San Francisco Athens London Madrid
Mexico City Milan New Delhi Singapore Sydney Toronto

2 3 4 5 6 7 8 9   LOV   28 27 26 25 24
1 2 3 4 5 6 7 8 9   LHS   28 27 26 25 24 23 (Elite Student Edition)

ISBN   978-1-265-25933-4
MHID   1-265-25933-X

e-ISBN   978-1-265-26048-4
e-MHID   1-265-26048-6

ISBN   978-1-265-26164-1 (Elite Student Edition)
MHID   1-265-26164-4

e-ISBN   978-1-265-26197-9 (Elite Student Edition)
e-MHID   1-265-26197-0

Trademarks: McGraw Hill, the McGraw Hill logo, 5 Steps to a 5, and related trade dress are trademarks or registered trademarks of McGraw Hill and/or its affiliates in the United States and other countries and may not be used without written permission. All other trademarks are the property of their respective owners. McGraw Hill is not associated with any product or vendor mentioned in this book.

AP, Advanced Placement Program, and College Board are registered trademarks of the College Board, which was not involved in the production of, and does not endorse, this product.

The series editor was Grace Freedson, and the project editor was Del Franz.
Series design by Jane Tenenbaum.

McGraw Hill products are available at special quantity discounts to use as premiums and sales or for use in corporate training programs. To contact a representative, please visit the Contact Us pages at www.mhprofessional.com.

McGraw Hill is committed to making our products accessible to all learners. To learn more about the available support and accommodations we offer, please contact us at accessibility@mheducation.com. We also participate in the Access Text Network (www.accesstext.org), and ATN members may submit requests through ATN.

CONTENTS

PREFACE

So, you have decided to take AP U.S. History. Prepare to be continually challenged in this course: this is the only way you will attain the grade that you want on the AP exam in May. Prepare to read, to read a lot, and to read critically; almost all students successful in AP U.S. History say this is a necessity. Prepare to analyze countless primary source documents; being able to do this is critical for success in the exam as well. Most important, prepare to immerse yourself in the great story that is U.S. history. As your teacher will undoubtedly point out, it would be impossible to make up some of the people and events you will study in this class. What really happened is much more interesting!

This study guide will assist you along the journey of AP U.S. History. The chapter review guides give you succinct overviews of the major events of U.S. history. At the end of each chapter is a list of the major concepts, a time line, and multiple-choice and short-answer review questions for that chapter. In addition, a very extensive glossary is included at the back of this manual. All of the **boldface** words throughout the book can be found in the glossary (it would also be a good study technique to review the entire glossary before taking the actual AP exam).

The first five chapters of the manual describe the AP test itself and suggest some test-taking strategies. There are also two entire sample tests, with answers. These allow you to become totally familiar with the format and nature of the questions that will appear on the exam. On the actual testing day you want absolutely no surprises!

In the second chapter, you will also find time lines for three approaches to preparing for the exam. It is obviously suggested that your preparation for the examination be a year-long process; for those students unable to do that, two alternative calendars also appear. Many students also find that study groups are very beneficial in studying for the AP test. Students who have been successful on the AP test oftentimes form these groups very early in the school year.

It should also be noted that the AP U.S. History exam that you will be taking may be different from the one that your older brother or sister took in the past. The format of the exam changed in 2015. Further revisions were made to the 2018 exam. We will outline the test in detail in the first several chapters. Please do not use old study guides or review sheets that were used to prepare for prior tests; these do not work anymore!

We hope this manual helps you in achieving the "perfect 5." That score is sitting out there, waiting for you to reach for it.

INTRODUCTION: 5-STEP PROGRAM

The Basics

This guide provides you with the specific format of the AP U.S. History exam, three sample AP U.S. History tests, and a comprehensive review of major events and themes in U.S. history. After each review chapter, you will find a list of the major concepts, a time line, and several review multiple-choice and short-answer questions.

Reading this guide is a great start to getting the grade you want on the AP U.S. History test, but it is important to read on your own as well. Several groups of students who have all gotten a 5 on the test maintain that the key to success is to *read* as much as you possibly can on U.S. history.

Reading this guide will not guarantee you a 5 when you take the U.S. History exam in May. However, by carefully reviewing the format of the exam and the test-taking strategies provided for each section, you will definitely be on your way! The review section that outlines the major developments of U.S. history should augment what you have learned from your regular U.S. history textbook. This book won't "give" you a 5, but it can certainly point you firmly in that direction.

Organization of the Book

This guide conducts you through the five steps necessary to prepare yourself for success on the exam. These steps will provide you with many skills and strategies vital to the exam and the practice that will lead you toward the perfect 5.

In this introductory chapter we will explain the basic five-step plan, which is the focus of this entire book. The material in Chapter 1 will give you information you need to know about the AP U.S. History exam. In Chapter 2 three different approaches will be presented to prepare for the actual exam; study them all and then pick the one that works best for you. Chapter 3 contains a practice AP U.S. History exam; this is an opportunity to experience what the test is like and to have a better idea of your strengths and weaknesses as you prepare for the actual exam. Chapter 4 describes historical skills and themes emphasized in the exam. Chapter 5 contains a number of tips and suggestions about the different types of questions that appear on the actual exam. We will discuss ways to approach the multiple-choice questions, the short-answer questions, the document-based question (DBQ), and the long essay question. Almost all students note that knowing how to approach each type of question is crucial.

For some of you, the most important part of this manual will be found in Chapters 6 through 30, which contain a review of U.S. history from the European exploration of the Americas to the presidency of Joe Biden. Undoubtedly, you have studied much of the material included in these chapters. However, these review chapters can help highlight certain important material that you may have missed or forgotten from your AP History class. At the end of each chapter, you will also find a list of the major concepts, time line of important events discussed in the chapter, and multiple-choice and short-answer review questions.

After these review chapters you will find two complete practice exams, including multiple-choice questions, short-answer questions, and essays. Correct answers and explanations for these answers are also included. Take one of the exams and evaluate your success; review any material that you had trouble with. Then take the second exam and use the results to guide your additional study. At the back of the manual is a glossary that defines all of the **boldface** words found in the review chapters. Use this to find the meaning of a specific term you might be unfamiliar with; some students find reviewing the entire glossary a useful method of reviewing for the actual exam.

Five-Step Program

Step 1: Set Up Your Study Program

In Step 1, you will read a brief overview of the AP U.S. History exam, including an outline of the topics that might be covered on the test itself. You will also follow a process to help determine which of the following preparation programs is right for you:

- Full school year: September through May
- One semester: January through May
- Six weeks: Basic Training for the Exam

Step 2: Determine Your Test Readiness

Step 2 provides you with a diagnostic exam to assess your current level of understanding. This exam will let you know about your current level of preparedness and on which areas and periods you should focus your study.

- Take the diagnostic exam slowly and analyze each question. Do not worry about how many questions you get right. Hopefully the exam will boost your confidence.
- Review the answers and explanations following the exam, so that you see what you do and do not yet fully know and understand.

Step 3: Develop Strategies for Success

Step 3 provides strategies and techniques that will help you do your best on the exam. These strategies cover the multiple-choice, the short-answer, and the two different essay parts of the test. These tips come from discussions with both AP U.S. History students and teachers. In this section you will:

- Learn the skills and themes emphasized in the exam.
- Learn how to read and analyze multiple-choice questions.
- Learn how to answer multiple-choice questions, including whether or not to guess.
- Learn how to respond to short-answer questions.
- Learn how to plan and write both types of essay questions.

Step 4: Review the Knowledge You Need to Score High

Step 4 makes up the majority of this book. In this step you will review the important names, dates, and themes of American history. Obviously, not all of the material included in this book will be on the AP exam. However, this book is a good overview of the content studied in a "typical" AP U.S. History course. Some of you are presently taking AP courses that cover more material than is included in this book; some of you are in courses that cover less. Nevertheless, thoroughly reviewing the material in the content section of this book will significantly increase your chance of scoring well.

Step 5: Build Your Test-Taking Confidence

In Step 5, you will complete your preparation by taking two complete practice exams and examining your results on them. It should be noted that the practice exams included in this book do not include questions taken from actual exams; however, these practice exams do include questions that are very similar to the "real thing."

Graphics Used in This Book

To emphasize particular skills and strategies, we use several icons throughout this book. An icon in the margin will alert you that you should pay particular attention to the accompanying text. We use three icons:

The first icon points out a very important concept or fact that you should not pass over.

The second icon calls your attention to a problem-solving strategy that you may want to try.

The third icon indicates a tip that you might find useful.

Boldface words indicate terms that are included in the glossary at the end of the book. Boldface is also used to indicate the answer to a sample problem discussed in the test. Throughout the book, you will find marginal notes, boxes, and starred areas. Pay close attention to these areas because they can provide tips, hints, strategies, and further explanations to help you reach your full potential.

STEP 1

Set Up Your Study Program

CHAPTER 1

What You Need to Know About the AP U.S. History Exam

IN THIS CHAPTER

Summary: Learn about the test, what's on it, how it's scored, and what benefits you can get from taking it.

Key Ideas

✪ Most colleges will award credit for a score of 4 or 5. Even if you don't do well enough on the exam to receive college credit, college admissions officials like to see students who have challenged themselves and experienced the college-level coursework of AP courses.

✪ Since 2015, the exam has had a new format. The new exam de-emphasizes the simple memorization of historical facts. Instead, you have to demonstrate an ability to use historical analytical skills and think thematically across time periods in American history.

✪ In addition to multiple-choice and short-answer questions, the test contains a DBQ (document-based question) and one long essay question.

Advanced Placement Program

The Advanced Placement (AP) program was begun by the College Board in 1955 to administer standard achievement exams that would allow highly motivated high school students the opportunity to earn college credit for AP courses taken in high school. Today there are 38 different AP courses and exams, with well over 5 million exams administered each May.

There are numerous AP courses in the social studies besides U.S. History, including European History, World History, U.S. Government and Politics, Comparative Government, Psychology, and Micro and Macro Economics. The majority of students who take AP courses and exams are juniors and seniors; however, some schools offer AP courses to freshmen and sophomores (AP U.S. History is usually not one of those courses). It is not absolutely necessary to be enrolled in an AP class to take the exam in a specific subject; there are rare cases of students who study on their own for a particular AP examination and do well.

Who Writes the AP Exams? Who Scores Them?

AP exams, including the U.S. History exam, are written by experienced college and secondary school teachers. All questions on the AP exams are field tested before they actually appear on an AP exam. The group that writes the history exam is called the AP U.S. History Development Committee. This group constantly reevaluates the test, analyzing the exam as a whole and on an item-by-item basis.

As noted in the preface, the AP U.S. History exam has undergone a substantial transformation that took effect beginning with the 2015 test. New revisions were made to the 2018 exam. The College Board has conducted a number of institutes and workshops to ensure that teachers across the United States are well qualified to assist students in preparing for this new exam.

The multiple-choice section of each AP exam is graded by computer, but the free-response questions are scored by humans. A number of college and secondary school teachers of U.S. History get together at a central location or online in early June to score the free-response questions of the AP U.S. History exam administered the previous month. The scoring of each reader during this procedure is carefully analyzed to ensure that exams are being evaluated in a fair and consistent manner.

AP Scores

Once you have taken the exam and it has been scored, your raw scores will be transformed into an AP grade on a 1-to-5 scale. A grade report will be sent to you by the College Board in July. When you take the test, you should indicate the college or colleges that you want your AP scores sent to. The report that the colleges receive contains the score for every AP exam you took this year and the grades that you received on AP exams in prior years. In addition, your scores will be sent to your high school. (Note that it is possible, for a fee, to withhold the scores of any AP exam you have taken from going out to colleges. See the College Board website for more information.)

As noted above, you will be scored on a 1-to-5 scale:

- 5 indicates that you are extremely well qualified. This is the highest possible grade.
- 4 indicates that you are well qualified.
- 3 indicates that you are qualified.
- 2 indicates that you are possibly qualified.
- 1 indicates that you are not qualified to receive college credit.

Benefits of the AP Exam

If you receive a score of a 4 or a 5, you can most likely get actual college credit for the subject that you took the course in; a few colleges will do the same for students receiving a 3. Colleges and universities have different rules on AP scores and credit, so check with the college or colleges that you are considering to determine what credit they will give you for a good score on the AP History exam. Some colleges might exempt you from a freshman-level course based on your score even if they don't grant credit for the score you received.

The benefits of being awarded college credits before you start college are significant: You can save time in college (by skipping courses) and money (by avoiding paying college tuition for courses you skip). Almost every college encourages students to challenge themselves; if it is possible for you to take an AP course, do it! Even if you do not do well on the actual test—or you decide not to take the AP test—the experience of being in an AP class all year can impress college admissions committees and help you prepare for the more academically challenging work of college.

AP U.S. History Exam

Achieving a good score on the AP U.S. History exam will require you to do more than just memorize important dates, people, and events from America's history. To get a 4 or a 5 you have to demonstrate an ability to master primary and secondary sources, construct an argument, and utilize specific historical analytical skills when studying history. In addition, you will be asked to demonstrate your ability to think thematically and evaluate specific historical themes across time periods in American history. Every question on the AP U.S. History exam is rooted in these analytical skills and historical themes. You'll find more information about these analytical skills and historical themes in Chapter 4.

As far as specific content, there is material that you need to know from nine predetermined historical time periods of U.S. history. For each of these time periods, key concepts have been identified. You will be introduced to a concept outline for each of the historical periods in your AP course. You can also find this outline at the College Board's AP U.S. History website. These concepts are connected to the historical themes and analyzed using historical analytical skills.

To do well on this exam you have to exhibit the ability to do much of the work that "real" historians do. You must know major concepts from every historical time period. You must demonstrate an ability to think thematically when analyzing history, and you must utilize historical thinking skills when doing all of this. The simple memorization of historical facts is given less emphasis in the new exam. This does not mean that you can ignore historical detail. Knowledge of historical information will be crucial in explaining themes in American history. Essentially this exam is changing the focus of what is expected of AP U.S. History students. It is asking you to take a smaller number of historical concepts and to analyze these concepts very carefully. The ability to do this does not necessarily come easily; one of the major functions of this book is to help you "think like a historian."

Periods of U.S. History

As noted earlier, U.S. history has been divided into specific time periods for the purposes of the AP course. The creators of the AP U.S. History exam have established the following nine historical periods and have also determined approximately how much of the year should be spent on each historical era:

- **Period 1: 1491 to 1607.** Approximately 4 to 6 percent of instructional time should be spent on this period.
- **Period 2: 1607 to 1754.** Approximately 6 to 8 percent of instructional time should be spent on this period.
- **Period 3: 1754 to 1800.** Approximately 10 to 17 percent of instructional time should be spent on this period.
- **Period 4: 1800 to 1848.** Approximately 10 to 17 percent of instructional time should be spent on this period.
- **Period 5: 1844 to 1877.** Approximately 10 to 17 percent of instructional time should be spent on this period.

- **Period 6: 1865 to 1898.** Approximately 10 to 17 percent of instructional time should be spent on this period.
- **Period 7: 1890 to 1945.** Approximately 10 to 17 percent of instructional time should be spent on this period.
- **Period 8: 1945 to 1980.** Approximately 10 to 17 percent of instructional time should be spent on this period.
- **Period 9: 1980 to present.** Approximately 4 to 6 percent of instructional time should be spent on this period.

On the actual AP test that you will take:

- 4 to 6 percent of the exam will relate to issues concerning Period 1.
- 36 to 59 percent of the exam will relate to issues concerning Periods 2, 3, 4, and 5.
- 30 to 51 percent of the exam will relate to issues concerning Periods 6, 7, and 8.
- 4 to 6 percent of the exam will relate to issues concerning Period 9.

Many students are worried when their AP class doesn't get to the present day. As you can see, only 5 percent of the test is on material after 1980; therefore, not making it all the way to the 2020 victory of Joe Biden will not have a major impact on your score.

Structure of the AP U.S. History Exam

The AP U.S. History exam consists of two sections, each of which contains two parts. You'll be given 95 minutes to complete Section I, which includes multiple-choice questions (Part A) and short-answer questions (Part B). You'll have 100 minutes to complete Section II, which includes the document-based question (Part A) and the long essay question (Part B). Here is the breakdown:

Section I
- Part A: 55 multiple-choice questions—55 minutes recommended—40% of the exam score.
- Part B: Three short-answer questions—40 minutes recommended—20% of the exam score. Questions 1 and 2 are required; you can choose between 3 and 4. These questions will address one or more of the themes that have been developed throughout the course and will ask you to use historical thinking when you write about these themes.

Section II
- Part A: One document-based question (DBQ)—60 minutes (including a 15-minute reading period) recommended—25% of the exam score. In this section, you will be asked to analyze and use a number of primary-source documents as you construct a historical argument.
- Part B: One long essay question—40 minutes recommended—15% of the exam score. You will be given a choice between three options, addressing periods 1–3, 4–6, or 7–9. It will be critical to use historical analytical skills when writing your response.

This presents an overview. There will be more information about the different components of the exam later in this book.

Taking the AP U.S. History Exam

Registration and Fees

If you are enrolled in AP U.S. History, your teacher or guidance counselor is going to provide all of these details. However, you do not have to enroll in the AP course to take the

AP exam. When in doubt, the best source of information is the College Board's website: www.collegeboard.com.

There are also several other fees required if you want your scores rushed to you or if you wish to receive multiple score reports. Students who demonstrate financial need may receive a refund to help offset the cost of testing.

Night Before the Exam

Last-minute cramming of massive amounts of material will not help you. It takes time for your brain to organize material. There is some value to a last-minute review of material. This may involve looking at the fast-review portions of the chapters or looking through the glossary. The night before the test should include a light review and various relaxing activities. *A full night's sleep is one of the best preparations for the test.*

What to Bring to the Exam

Here are some suggestions:

- Several pencils and an eraser that does not leave smudges.
- Several black ballpoint pens (for the essays).
- A watch so that you can monitor your time. The exam room may or may not have a clock on the wall. Make sure you turn off the beep that goes off on the hour.
- Your school code.
- Your driver's license, Social Security number, or some other ID, in case there is a problem with your registration.
- Tissues.
- Something to drink—water is best.
- A quiet snack.
- Your quiet confidence that you are prepared.

What *Not* to Bring to the Exam

It's a good idea to leave the following items at home or in the car:

- Your cell phone and/or other electronic devices.
- Books, a dictionary, study notes, flash cards, highlighting pens, correction fluid, a ruler, or any other office supplies.
- Portable music of any kind (although you will probably want to listen as soon as you leave the testing site!).
- Panic or fear. It's natural to be nervous, but you can comfort yourself that you have used this book and that there is no need for fear on your exam.

Day of the Test

Once the test day has arrived, there is nothing further you can do. Do not worry about what you could have done differently. It is out of your hands, and your only job is to answer as many questions correctly as you possibly can. The calmer you are, the better your chances are of doing well.

Follow these simple commonsense tips:

- Allow plenty of time to get to the test site.
- Wear comfortable clothing.
- Eat a light breakfast and/or lunch.
- Think positive. Remind yourself that you are well prepared and that the test is an enjoyable challenge and a chance to share your knowledge.
- Be proud of yourself!

CHAPTER 2

Preparing for the AP U.S. History Exam

IN THIS CHAPTER

Summary: The right preparation plan for you depends on your study habits and the amount of time you have before the test. This chapter provides some examples of plans you can use or adapt to your needs.

Key Ideas

✪ Choose the study plan that is right for you.

✪ Begin to prepare for the AP exam at the beginning of the school year. Developing historical analytical skills, evaluating themes in U.S. history, and studying important concepts take far more time and effort than simply memorizing facts. The sooner you begin preparing for the test, the better.

Getting Started

You have made the decision to take AP U.S. History. Enjoy! You will be exposed to all of the fascinating stories that make up U.S. history. To be successful in this course, you will have to work much harder than you would in a "regular" high school U.S. history course. You will be required to read more, including reading and analyzing a wide variety of primary source documents throughout the year. In addition, you will be required to utilize historical thinking, to analyze history in a thematic way, and to be knowledgeable of specific concepts that help guide the study of American history. It cannot be stressed enough that the examination for this course that you will take in May is not a test that will simply measure what you "know" about U.S. history; instead, it is an examination that tests your ability to analyze major events, concepts, and themes in American history utilizing specific historical analytical skills.

Being able to utilize historical analytical skills, study history thematically, and develop conceptual thinking are not skills that develop overnight. In fact, it is difficult to develop these skills in the context of one specific course. If you are reading this before you are actually enrolled in an AP U.S. History course, you may want to take the most challenging history courses you can *before* you take AP U.S. History. Try to think conceptually in any history course that you take; it involves integrating historical facts into larger interpretive themes.

Creating a Study Plan

As has already been noted several times, preparing for this exam involves much more than just memorizing important dates, names, and events that are important in U.S. history. Developing historical analytical skills, evaluating themes in U.S. history, and studying important concepts take far more time and effort than simply memorizing facts. Therefore, it is strongly suggested that you take a year-long approach to studying and preparing for the test.

However, for some students this is not possible. Therefore, some suggestions for students who have only one semester to prepare for the exam and students who have only six weeks to prepare for the exam are included. In the end, it is better to do *some* systematic preparation for the exam than to do none at all.

Study Groups

Many students who have gotten a 5 on the U.S. History exam reported that working in a study group was an important part of the successful preparation that they did for the test. In an ideal setting, three to five students get together, probably once a week, to review material that was covered in class the preceding week and to practice historical, thematic, and conceptual thinking. If at all possible, do this! A good suggestion is to have study groups set a specific time to meet every week and stick to that time. Without a regular meeting time, study groups usually meet fewer times during the year, often cancel meetings, and so on.

THREE PLANS FOR TEST PREPARATION

Plan A:
Yearlong Preparation for the AP U.S. History Exam

This is the plan we highly recommend. Besides doing all of the readings and assignments assigned by your teacher, also do the following activities. (Check off the activities as you complete them.)

IN THE FALL

_____ Create a study group and determine a regular meeting time for that group.

_____ Coordinate the materials in this manual with the curriculum of your AP U.S. History class.

_____ Study the review chapters in Step 4 of this book that coincide with the material you are studying in class.

_____ Begin to do outside reading on U.S. history topics (either topics of interest to you or topics that you know you need more background in).

_____ In your study group, emphasize historical analysis and thematic and conceptual thinking.

FROM DECEMBER TO MARCH

_____ Continue to meet with your study group and emphasize historical analysis and thematic and conceptual thinking.

_____ Continue to study the review chapters in Step 4 of this book that coincide with the material you are studying in class.

_____ Take the diagnostic test in Step 2 of this book to see what the test will be like and assess your strengths and weaknesses.

_____ Learn the strategies discussed in Step 3 of this book. Practice applying them as you study and review for the AP U.S. History exam.

_____ Carefully study the format and approach to document-based questions (DBQs). You will probably have one on your midterm exam in class.

_____ Using the eras of U.S. history you have studied in class, create your own DBQ for two of the units and try to answer it.

_____ Intensify your outside reading of U.S. history topics.

_____ Take two U.S. history textbooks and compare and contrast their handling of three events of U.S. history. What do these results tell you?

DURING APRIL AND MAY

_____ Continue to meet with your study group and emphasize historical analysis and thematic and conceptual thinking. Many study groups meet at additional times in the weeks leading up to the test.

_____ Continue to study the review chapters in Step 4 of this book that coincide with the material you are studying in class.

_____ Practice creating and answering multiple-choice and short-answer questions in your study group.

_____ Develop and review worksheets of essential historical content with your study group.

_____ Highlight material in your textbook (and in this manual) that you may not understand, and ask your teacher about it.

_____ Write two or three essays as they would appear on the exam under timed questions and have a member of your study group (or a classmate) evaluate them.

_____ Take the practice tests provided in Step 5 of this book. Set a timer and practice pacing yourself.

You are well prepared for the test. Go get it!

Plan B:
One-Semester Preparation for the AP U.S. History Exam

 Besides doing all of the readings and assignments assigned by your teacher, you should do the following activities. (Check off the activities as you complete them.)

FROM JANUARY TO MARCH

———— Establish a study group of other students preparing in the same way that you are. In your study group you should review essential factual knowledge, but also analyze the essential themes and concepts in the course.

———— Study the review chapters in Step 4 of this book that coincide with the material you have studied or are studying in class.

———— Take the diagnostic test in Step 2 of this book to familiarize yourself with the test and assess your strengths and weaknesses.

———— Learn the strategies discussed in Step 3 of this book. Practice applying them as you study and review for the AP U.S. History exam.

———— Write two or three document-based and sample multiple-choice questions.

———— Read at least one outside source (historical essay or book) on a topic that you are studying in class.

———— In your study group, practice creating and answering short-answer and multiple-choice questions.

DURING APRIL AND MAY

———— Continue to meet with your study group, and review essential factual knowledge and essential themes and concepts of the course you have taken or are currently taking. Some study groups increase the amount of time that they meet together in the weeks right before the test.

———— Study the review chapters in Step 4 of this book that coincide with the material you have studied or are presently studying in class. Focus on weak areas you identified in the diagnostic test of Step 2 of this book.

———— Practice creating and answering sample essays with your study group.

———— Develop and review worksheets of essential historical content with your study group.

———— Ask your teacher to clarify things in your textbook or in this manual that you do not completely understand. If you have nagging questions about some specific historical details, get the answers to them!

———— Take the practice tests provided in Step 5 of this book. Set a timer and practice pacing yourself.

Plan C:
Four- to Six-Week Preparation for the AP U.S. History Exam

 Besides doing all of the reading and assignments assigned by your teacher, do the following activities. (Check off the activities as you complete them.)

IN APRIL

_____ Take the diagnostic test in Step 2 of this book to familiarize yourself with the test and assess your strengths and weaknesses.

_____ Study the review chapters in Step 4 of this book that coincide with any weak areas you identified from the diagnostic exam.

_____ Learn the strategies discussed in Step 3 of this book. Practice applying them as you study and review for the AP U.S. History exam.

_____ Write one sample document-based question (DBQ) as modeled by samples in this manual.

_____ Carefully review the sections of this manual that outline the essential content of each historical period.

_____ If possible, create or join a study group with other students to help prepare for the exam.

IN MAY

_____ Many teachers organize study sessions right before the actual exam. Go to them!

_____ With your study group or individually, review essential content from the course and major concepts of each unit.

_____ Complete another sample DBQ essay and analyze your results.

_____ Review the glossary of this manual another time to help review essential content.

_____ Be certain of the format of the test and the types of questions that will be asked.

_____ Take the practice tests provided in Step 5 of this book. Set a timer and practice pacing yourself.

STEP **2**

Determine Your Test Readiness

CHAPTER **3**   Take a Diagnostic Exam

CHAPTER 3

Take a Diagnostic Exam

IN THIS CHAPTER

Summary: In the following pages, you will find a diagnostic exam whose content and structure closely matches the "real" AP U.S. History exam. Use this test to familiarize yourself with the actual test and to assess your strengths and weaknesses.

How to Use the Diagnostic Exam

Section I of the AP U.S. History exam contains a multiple-choice section and a short-answer section.

Section II contains the document-based question (DBQ) and an essay question—you will need to pick one question to answer out of the three questions you are given.

55 minutes for 55 multiple-choice questions
40 minutes for three short-answer questions
60 minutes for one document-based question
40 minutes for one long essay question

The purpose of this chapter is to allow you to familiarize yourself with the test and to assess your test readiness in terms of both the skills and the content understanding needed. Try to take this test under testlike conditions; in other words, time yourself and do the test—or at least each section of the test—uninterrupted. Note that in Chapter 5 you will find strategies for each type of question that will allow you to more effectively and efficiently tackle the questions.

When to Use the Diagnostic Exam

This diagnostic test can be helpful to you regardless of whether you are following Plan A, B, or C. Those who choose Plan A should study this exam early in the year so that you will thoroughly understand the format of the test. Look for the types of multiple-choice and short-answer questions early, and carefully study the format of the essay questions. Go back and look at this exam throughout the year: Many successful test-takers maintain that knowing how to tackle the questions that will be asked on any exam is just as important as knowledge of the subject matter.

Plan B students (who are using one semester to prepare) should also analyze the format of the exam. Plan B folks: as you begin using this book you might also want to actually answer the multiple-choice and short-answer questions dealing with content you have already studied in class and answer the document-based question and the free-response question and evaluate your results. This will help you analyze the success of your previous preparation for the test.

Plan C students should take this diagnostic exam as soon as they begin working with this manual to analyze the success of their previous preparation for the actual exam.

Conclusion (After the Exam)

After you have studied or taken the diagnostic exam, you will continue to Step 3 of your 5 Steps to a 5. Chapter 5 will provide you with tips and strategies for answering all of the types of questions that you found on the diagnostic exam.

Don't be discouraged if you answered a lot of questions on the diagnostic exam incorrectly. At this point, the main thing is that you get a feel for the types of questions that you will encounter on the real AP U.S. History exam.

AP U.S. HISTORY DIAGNOSTIC EXAM

Answer Sheet for Multiple-Choice Questions

1 Ⓐ Ⓑ Ⓒ Ⓓ	16 Ⓐ Ⓑ Ⓒ Ⓓ	31 Ⓐ Ⓑ Ⓒ Ⓓ	46 Ⓐ Ⓑ Ⓒ Ⓓ
2 Ⓐ Ⓑ Ⓒ Ⓓ	17 Ⓐ Ⓑ Ⓒ Ⓓ	32 Ⓐ Ⓑ Ⓒ Ⓓ	47 Ⓐ Ⓑ Ⓒ Ⓓ
3 Ⓐ Ⓑ Ⓒ Ⓓ	18 Ⓐ Ⓑ Ⓒ Ⓓ	33 Ⓐ Ⓑ Ⓒ Ⓓ	48 Ⓐ Ⓑ Ⓒ Ⓓ
4 Ⓐ Ⓑ Ⓒ Ⓓ	19 Ⓐ Ⓑ Ⓒ Ⓓ	34 Ⓐ Ⓑ Ⓒ Ⓓ	49 Ⓐ Ⓑ Ⓒ Ⓓ
5 Ⓐ Ⓑ Ⓒ Ⓓ	20 Ⓐ Ⓑ Ⓒ Ⓓ	35 Ⓐ Ⓑ Ⓒ Ⓓ	50 Ⓐ Ⓑ Ⓒ Ⓓ
6 Ⓐ Ⓑ Ⓒ Ⓓ	21 Ⓐ Ⓑ Ⓒ Ⓓ	36 Ⓐ Ⓑ Ⓒ Ⓓ	51 Ⓐ Ⓑ Ⓒ Ⓓ
7 Ⓐ Ⓑ Ⓒ Ⓓ	22 Ⓐ Ⓑ Ⓒ Ⓓ	37 Ⓐ Ⓑ Ⓒ Ⓓ	52 Ⓐ Ⓑ Ⓒ Ⓓ
8 Ⓐ Ⓑ Ⓒ Ⓓ	23 Ⓐ Ⓑ Ⓒ Ⓓ	38 Ⓐ Ⓑ Ⓒ Ⓓ	53 Ⓐ Ⓑ Ⓒ Ⓓ
9 Ⓐ Ⓑ Ⓒ Ⓓ	24 Ⓐ Ⓑ Ⓒ Ⓓ	39 Ⓐ Ⓑ Ⓒ Ⓓ	54 Ⓐ Ⓑ Ⓒ Ⓓ
10 Ⓐ Ⓑ Ⓒ Ⓓ	25 Ⓐ Ⓑ Ⓒ Ⓓ	40 Ⓐ Ⓑ Ⓒ Ⓓ	55 Ⓐ Ⓑ Ⓒ Ⓓ
11 Ⓐ Ⓑ Ⓒ Ⓓ	26 Ⓐ Ⓑ Ⓒ Ⓓ	41 Ⓐ Ⓑ Ⓒ Ⓓ	
12 Ⓐ Ⓑ Ⓒ Ⓓ	27 Ⓐ Ⓑ Ⓒ Ⓓ	42 Ⓐ Ⓑ Ⓒ Ⓓ	
13 Ⓐ Ⓑ Ⓒ Ⓓ	28 Ⓐ Ⓑ Ⓒ Ⓓ	43 Ⓐ Ⓑ Ⓒ Ⓓ	
14 Ⓐ Ⓑ Ⓒ Ⓓ	29 Ⓐ Ⓑ Ⓒ Ⓓ	44 Ⓐ Ⓑ Ⓒ Ⓓ	
15 Ⓐ Ⓑ Ⓒ Ⓓ	30 Ⓐ Ⓑ Ⓒ Ⓓ	45 Ⓐ Ⓑ Ⓒ Ⓓ	

AP U.S. HISTORY DIAGNOSTIC EXAM

Section I

Time: 95 minutes

Part A (Multiple Choice)

Part A recommended time: 55 minutes

Directions: Each of the following questions refers to a historical source. These questions will test your knowledge about the historical source and require you to make use of your historical analytical skills and your familiarity with historical themes. For each question select the *best* response and fill in the corresponding oval on your answer sheet.

Questions 1–4 refer to the following cartoon.

Political cartoon from 1807

1. This cartoon criticizes which policy of President Thomas Jefferson?
   A. The Louisiana purchase
   B. The Embargo Act
   C. The War with Tripoli
   D. Reductions in government spending

2. Jefferson was responding to what situation?
   A. British interference with American shipping and trade
   B. British support for Indians in the West
   C. Aggressive actions by the French Emperor Napoleon
   D. Electoral losses to domestic opponents

3. Which of the following reflects the way many Americans responded to Jefferson's policy?
   A. Emigrating to other countries
   B. Advocating military involvement in the Napoleonic Wars
   C. Engaging in illicit trade with foreign countries
   D. Moving to the Western frontier

4. Which of the following most closely resembles Jefferson's policy?
   A. The Open Door in China
   B. The Good Neighbor Policy with South America
   C. Manifest Destiny of the 1840s
   D. Neutrality Laws of the 1930s

Questions 5–8 refer to the following quotation.

Yes, let us pray for the salvation of all those who live in that totalitarian darkness—pray that they will discover the joy of knowing God. But until they do, let us be aware that while they preach the supremacy of the State, declare its omnipotence over individual man, and predict its eventual domination of all peoples on the earth, they are the focus of evil in the modern world. ... But if history teaches anything, it teaches that simpleminded appeasement or wishful thinking about our adversaries is folly. It means the betrayal of our past, the squandering of our freedom. So, I urge you to speak out against those who would place the United States in a position of military and moral inferiority. ... So, in your discussions of the nuclear freeze proposals, I urge you to beware the temptation of pride—the temptation of blithely ... declaring yourselves above it all and label both sides equally at fault, to ignore the facts of history and the aggressive impulses of an evil empire, to simply call the arms race a giant misunderstanding and thereby remove yourself from the struggle between right and wrong and good and evil.

—Ronald Reagan, Address to the National Association of Evangelicals, March 8, 1983

5. The sentiments in the passage above most directly reflect which of the following?
   A. A religious revival in the 1980s
   B. An intensification of the cold war in the early 1980s
   C. A desire to limit the size of government
   D. A distrust of the American military

6. Which of the following would have been most likely to approve the sentiments expressed in the passage?
   A. An antinuclear activist
   B. An atheist
   C. A Democrat
   D. A Republican

7. The sentiments expressed in the passage are most closely linked to which of the following policies?
   A. Strategic Defense Initiative (SDI)
   B. Business deregulation
   C. Encouraging prayer in the public schools
   D. Military cutbacks

8. The sentiments in the passage best reflect which long-standing concern of American presidents?
   A. Support for civil rights
   B. Promoting the separation of church and state
   C. Containment of communism
   D. Expanding the welfare state

Questions 9–12 refer to the following quotation.

They were smart and sophisticated, with an air of independence about them, and so casual about their looks and manners as to be almost slapdash. I don't know if I realized as soon as I began seeing them that they represented the wave of the future, but I do know I was drawn to them. I shared their restlessness, understood their determination to free themselves of the Victorian shackles of the pre-World War I era and find out for themselves what life was all about.

—Colleen Moore, movie star, writing about the 1920s

9. In this passage, Moore is writing about which of the following?
   A. The Ku Klux Klan
   B. Prohibitionists
   C. Flappers
   D. The Model T

10. Many young women of the 1920s expressed their freedom through which of the following?
   A. Political activism
   B. "Mannish" haircuts, new clothing styles, and cosmetics
   C. Living amongst the poor in settlement houses
   D. Rejection of marriage and child-rearing

11. The new freedoms for women in the 1920s were supported by which of the following?
   A. Widespread economic prosperity
   B. Growth in fundamentalist Christianity
   C. A massive movement of women into political offices
   D. Moral reforms like the temperance movement

12. The passage by Moore most directly reflects which of the following continuities in U.S. history?
   A. Concerns about economic inequality
   B. Efforts to expand civil rights
   C. Worries about political radicalism
   D. Concerns for individual liberty and self-expression

Questions 13–16 refer to the following quotation.

I am for doing good to the poor, but … I think the best way of doing good to the poor, is not making them easy in poverty, but leading or driving them out of it. I observed … that the more public provisions were made for the poor, the less they provided for themselves, and of course became poorer. And, on the contrary, the less was done for them, the more they did for themselves, and became richer.

—Benjamin Franklin, *Autobiography*

13. In this passage, Franklin takes a position similar to which of the following?
   A. Advocates of a market-driven economy like Adam Smith
   B. Supporters of the First Great Awakening
   C. Opponents of British rule in America
   D. Believers in an extensive social welfare system

14. The idea that Franklin expresses in this passage most directly reflects which of the following continuities in U.S. history?
   A. Concern about a religious foundation for society
   B. Belief in individual self-reliance
   C. A distrust of politicians
   D. A desire to expand Social Security

15. Which of the following helped Franklin justify his position?
   A. Strong class distinctions in colonial America
   B. British efforts to tax Americans
   C. A decline in religious beliefs
   D. Social mobility in colonial America

16. Which of the following presidents would be most likely to share Franklin's position?
   A. Barack Obama
   B. Lyndon Baines Johnson
   C. Calvin Coolidge
   D. Franklin D. Roosevelt

Questions 17–20 refer to the following cartoon.

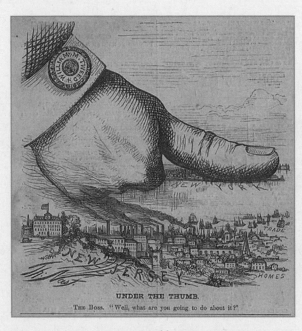

Thomas Nast, *Harper's Weekly*, June 10, 1871

17. Which of the following *best* expresses Nast's perspective in this cartoon?
   A. New York City is benefiting from the leadership of Tammany Hall boss William M. Tweed.
   B. New Jersey is unfairly exploiting New York City.
   C. The federal government is oppressing New York City.
   D. Tammany Hall boss William M. Tweed wields too much power in New York City.

18. Urban political machines like Tammany Hall derived most of their support from which of the following?
   A. Immigrants and lower-class voters
   B. The wealthier classes of society
   C. Patronage from the federal government
   D. Rural voters from outside the city

19. Urban political machines endured for many years because they provided which of the following?
    A. Honest and efficient government
    B. Help and services for the poor
    C. Rights and privileges unavailable outside the city
    D. Opposition to the encroachments of the federal government

20. Nast's journalistic perspective can *best* be compared to which of the following?
    A. Progressive muckrakers exposing the business practices of the Standard Oil Company
    B. Yellow journalists during the period of the Spanish-American War
    C. Reporters investigating President Richard M. Nixon during the Watergate scandal
    D. Newspaper coverage of World War II

Questions 21–24 refer to the following quotation.

At last they brought him [John Smith] to Werowocomoco, where was Powhatan, their emperor. Here more than two hundred of those grim courtiers stood wondering at him, as he had been a monster; till Powhatan and his train had put themselves in their greatest braveries. Before a fire upon a seat like a bedstead, he sat covered with a great robe, made of raccoon skins, and all the tails hanging by. On the other hand did sit a young wench of sixteen or eighteen years, and along on each side of the house, two rows of men, and behind them as many women, with all their heads and shoulders painted red, many of their heads bedecked with the white down of birds, but every one with something, and a great chain of white beads about their necks. At his entrance before the king, all the people gave a great shout. ... Having feasted him after their best barbarous manner they could, a long consultation was held, but the conclusion was, two great stones were brought before Powhatan; then as many as could laid hands on him, dragged him to them, and thereon laid his head, and being ready with their clubs to beat out his brains, Pocahontas, the king's dearest daughter, when no entreaty could prevail, got his head in her arms, and laid her own upon his to save his from death; whereat the emperor was contented he should live to make him hatchets, and her bells, beads, and copper; for they thought him as well of all occupations as themselves. For the king himself will make his own robes, shoes, bows, arrows, pots; plant, hunt, or do anything so well as the rest.

—John Smith, *The General Historie of Virginia*, 1624

21. Which of the following *best* describes the perspective of Captain John Smith?
    A. Powhatan and his followers were a backward people.
    B. Europeans unfairly looked down on Indians.
    C. Indians lacked the vices of the more technologically advanced Europeans.
    D. Indian women were the dominant force in their society.

22. Smith's account makes clear which of the following?
    A. The people of Powhatan's Confederacy were divided by strong class distinctions.
    B. Powhatan's people made important decisions by consensus.
    C. Powhatan enjoyed the same sorts of power as a European king.
    D. Powhatan's people lived in poverty.

23. Smith's story *best* illustrates which of the following?
    A. Indians were unusually cruel.
    B. Europeans were usually deceitful in dealing with Indians.
    C. The English were foolish to venture into the American wilderness.
    D. Indian-European relations often suffered from misunderstanding and suspicion.

24. In the context of this story, Pocahontas can *best* be compared to which of the following women?
    A. Susan B. Anthony
    B. Sally Ride
    C. Jane Addams
    D. Amelia Earhart

Questions 25–28 refer to the following quotation.

Let us not wallow in the valley of despair, I say to you today, my friends.

And so even though we face the difficulties of today and tomorrow, I still have a dream. It is a dream deeply rooted in the American dream.

I have a dream that one day this nation will rise up and live out the true meaning of its creed: "We hold these truths to be self-evident, that all men are created equal."

I have a dream that one day on the red hills of Georgia, the sons of former slaves and the sons of former slave owners will be able to sit down together at the table of brotherhood.

I have a dream that one day even the state of Mississippi, a state sweltering with the heat of injustice, sweltering with the heat of oppression, will be transformed into an oasis of freedom and justice.

I have a dream that my four little children will one day live in a nation where they will not be judged by the color of their skin but by the content of their character.

I have a *dream* today!

—Martin Luther King, Jr., "I Have a Dream" speech, Lincoln Memorial, August 28, 1963

25. Martin Luther King, Jr., in this passage is calling for which of the following?
  A. Economic justice for the poor
  B. Renewed commitment to the cold war struggle against communism
  C. Equal rights for African Americans
  D. Special privileges for African Americans

26. In this passage, King points out which of the following?
  A. A contradiction between American ideals and American practice
  B. A need to create new American ideals
  C. The superiority of African American values
  D. The futility of hoping for change

27. At the time of King's speech, which of the following would be likely to oppose King's message?
  A. A Midwestern Republican senator
  B. A Southern Democratic senator
  C. A Northern liberal
  D. A member of the Southern Christian Leadership Conference (SCLC)

28. In this passage, King is addressing which continuity in U.S. history?
  A. The struggle for greater economic opportunity
  B. A fear of sectionalism in the United States
  C. Concerns about moral decline
  D. The struggle for individual liberty

Questions 29–32 refer to the following cartoon.

War Department cartoon, 1943
Credit: U.S. Army

29. The message of the cartoon can be *best* described by which of the following?
A. The invasion of Europe is endangered by inferior weapons.
B. The war is being lost.
C. Too many American supplies have been given to allied nations.
D. Civilians play a vital role in the war effort.

30. Viewing this cartoon would encourage Americans to do which of the following?
A. Avoid the wasteful use of metal products
B. Plant a victory garden
C. Volunteer for military service
D. Build fewer ships and construct more tanks

31. This cartoon most directly refers to which aspect of the American war effort during World War II?
A. American efforts to launch a second front in Europe as early as possible
B. Military operations in the Mediterranean in 1942 and 1943
C. American industrial production
D. Efforts to create new and improved weapons systems

32. The message of the cartoon for Americans can *best* be compared to which of the following?
A. The environmental movement of the 1970s
B. The boycotts of British goods in the 1760s and 1770s
C. Abolitionism in the nineteenth century
D. Consumerism in the 1950s

Questions 33–36 refer to the following quotation.

That whereas your poor and humble Petition(er) being condemned to die, do humbly beg of you to take it into your Judicious and pious considerations that your poor and humble petitioner knowing my own innocence Blessed be the Lord for it and seeing plainly the wiles and subtlety of my accusers by my self can not but Judge charitably of Others that are going the same way of my self if the Lord steps not mightily in I was confined a whole month upon the same account that I am condemned now for and then cleared by the afflicted persons as some of your honors know and in two days time I was cried out upon by them and have been confined and now am condemned to die the Lord above knows my innocence then and likewise does now at the great day will be known to men and Angels I petition your honors not for my own life for I know I must die and my appointed time is set but the Lord he knows it is that if be possible no more Innocent blood may be shed which undoubtedly cannot be avoided In the way and course you go in I Question not but your honors does to the utmost of your Powers in the discovery and detecting of witchcraft and witches and would not be guilty of Innocent blood but for the world but by my own innocence I know you are in the wrong way the Lord in his infinite mercy direct you in this great work if it be his blessed will that no more innocent blood be shed.

—Mary Easty, petition to her judges, Salem, Massachusetts, 1692

33. Mary Easty in this passage is asking her judges to do which of the following?
   A. Stop condemning innocent persons to death for witchcraft
   B. Redouble their efforts to find the real witches in Salem
   C. Separate church from state in their deliberations
   D. Stop their oppression of women

34. Most historians believe that the Salem Witch Trials were the result of which of the following?
   A. The activities of a coven of witches in Salem
   B. Social tensions in Salem
   C. English efforts to enforce religious conformity in Massachusetts
   D. The ideas of the English political philosopher John Locke

35. The religious convictions of Mary Easty and the rest of Salem were shaped by which of the following?
   A. Roman Catholicism
   B. Anglicanism
   C. Quakerism
   D. Puritanism

36. Writers and intellectuals have often compared the Salem Witch Trials to which of the following?
   A. The mistreatment of slaves in the South
   B. Anti-immigrant rioting in the nineteenth century
   C. Government actions in the Red Scares of the twentieth century
   D. The suppression of strikers in the late nineteenth century

Questions 37–40 refer to the following quotation.

Companions in Arms!! These remains which we have the honor of carrying on our shoulders are those of the valiant heroes who died in the Alamo. Yes, my friends, they preferred to die a thousand times rather than submit themselves to the tyrant's yoke. What a brilliant example! Deserving of being noted in the pages of history. The spirit of liberty appears to be looking out from its elevated throne with its pleasing mien and pointing to us saying: "These are your brothers, Travis, Bowie, Crockett, and others whose valor places them in the rank of my heroes." Yes soldiers and fellow citizens, these are the worthy beings who, by the twists of fate, during the present campaign delivered their bodies to the ferocity of their enemies; who barbarously treated as beasts, were bound by their feet and dragged to this spot, where they were reduced to ashes. The venerable remains of our worthy companions as witnesses, I invite you to declare to the entire world, "Texas shall be free and independent or we shall perish in glorious combat."

—Colonel Juan N. Seguin, Alamo Defenders' Burial Oration,
Columbia Telegraph and Texas Register, April 4, 1837

37. Colonel Juan N. Seguin honored the memory of the defenders of the Alamo because
   A. they fought to the death for their cause.
   B. they defeated an invading Mexican army.
   C. they saved New Orleans from the British.
   D. they saved San Antonio from a large war band of Comanche.

38. Colonel Seguin's oration makes it clear that
   A. he thought the defense of the Alamo was a strategic mistake.
   B. many Tejanos (Texans of Mexican descent) favored Texan independence.
   C. he thought the United States was imposing a tyranny on Texas.
   D. he opposed the movement of American settlers into Texas.

39. The defenders of the Alamo gave their lives for what continuity in American history?
   A. The quest for racial justice
   B. The desire for political liberty
   C. The search for social security
   D. Opposition to gun control

40. A dispute over the boundary of Texas led to which of the following conflicts?
   A. The War of Jenkins' Ear
   B. The Quasi-War with France
   C. The Spanish-American War
   D. The Mexican War

Questions 41–44 refer to the following quotation.

When we stormed the Pentagon, my wife and I we leaped over this fence, see. We were really stoned, I mean I was on acid flying away, which of course is an antirevolutionary drug you know, you can't do a thing on it. I've been on acid ever since I came to Chicago. It's in the form of honey. We got a lab guy doin' his thing. I think he might have got assassinated, I ain't seen him today. Well, so we jumped this here fence, see, we were sneaking through the woods and people were out to get the Pentagon. We had this flag, it said NOW with a big wing on it, I don't know. The right-wingers said there was definitely evidence of Communist conspiracy 'cause of that flag. . . . So we had Uncle Sam hats on, you know, and we jumped over the fence and we're surrounded by marshals, you know, just closin' us in, about 30 marshals around us. And I plant the . . . flag and I said, "I claim this land in the name of free America. We are Mr. and Mrs. America. Mrs. America's pregnant." And we sit down and they're goin' . . . crazy. I mean we got arrested and unarrested like six or seven times.

—Abbie Hoffman, Yippie Workshop Speech, 1968

41. Abbie Hoffman and the Yippies were protesting which of the following?
    A. McCarthyism
    B. The Great Society
    C. Legal acid
    D. The Vietnam War

42. Which of the following most directly influenced the ideas of Hoffman and the Yippies?
    A. Muckrakers
    B. The New Deal
    C. The New Left
    D. The New Conservatism

43. Which of the following most directly influenced the tactics of Hoffman and the Yippies?
    A. The Civil Rights Movement
    B. The House Un-American Activities Committee
    C. The Tea Party Movement
    D. The Social Gospel

44. The counterculture of the 1960s sought which of the following?
    A. Economic security for the Baby Boom generation
    B. Political and military security against the threat of Communism
    C. Greater freedom for personal self-expression
    D. A return to traditional religious and family values

Questions 45–48 refer to the following image.

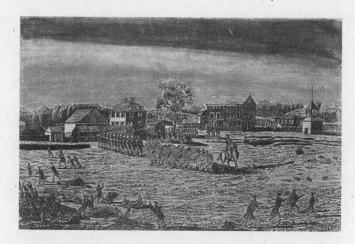

Amos Doolittle, "The Battle of Lexington," 1775

45. The British decision to fire on American militiamen at Lexington, Massachusetts, on April 19, 1775, led to which of the following?
A. A controversial court case
B. A series of uprisings against the British government across the colonies
C. A collapse in the support for the Sons of Liberty
D. An invasion by the French in Canada

46. British military commanders always assumed that they would benefit from which of the following?
A. Command of the sea
B. The support of the other European powers
C. Superior air power
D. The support of a majority of Americans for Parliament's legislation

47. When the Americans rebelled against Great Britain, they benefited from which of the following?
A. The enormous industrial productivity of the United States
B. Weapons that were technologically superior to those of the British
C. The support of most Native American peoples
D. The great geographical extent of the country

48. Militiamen played a key role during the American Revolutionary War by
A. repeatedly routing British Regulars in battle.
B. waging a spectacular campaign of sabotage and commando raids.
C. controlling populations not under the direct supervision of the British Army.
D. buying out the contracts of Britain's Hessian mercenaries.

Questions 49–52 refer to the following quotation.

I arrived at Wichita the 28th, the raid was postponed until the 29th. I took hatchets with me and we also supplied ourselves with rocks, meeting at the M. E. church, where the W. C. T. U. Convention was being held. I announced to them what we intended doing and asked them to join us. Sister Lucy Wilhoite, Myra McHenry, Miss Lydia Muntz, and Miss Blanch Boies, started for Mahan's wholesale liquor store. Three men were on the watch for us, we asked to go in to hold gospel services as was our intention before destroying this den of vice, for we wanted God to save their souls, and to give us ability and opportunity to destroy this soul damning business. They refused to let us come near the door. I said, "Women, we will have to use our hatchets," with this I threw a rock through the front, then we were all seized, and a call for the police was made. There was of course, a big crowd. Mrs. Myra McHenry was in the hands of a ruffian who shook her almost to pieces. One raised a piece of a gas pipe to strike her, but was prevented from doing so. We were hustled into the hoodlum wagon, and driven through the streets amid the yell, execrations and grimaces of the liquor element.

—Carry A. Nation, *The Use and Need of the Life of Carry A. Nation, Written by Herself*, 1905

49. For which of the following causes was Carry A. Nation famous as an activist?
A. Temperance
B. Women's suffrage
C. Trust busting
D. Muckraking

50. Nation can be compared most directly to which of the following?
A. Tecumseh
B. Abraham Lincoln
C. Rosa Parks
D. Hillary Clinton

51. Nation's cause would attain a great victory with the enactment of
A. the Nineteenth Amendment, giving women the right to vote.
B. the Sherman Antitrust Act.
C. the Social Security Act.
D. Prohibition.

52. The major event that helped pave the way for the triumph of Nation's cause was
A. the assassination of William McKinley.
B. World War I.
C. The Great Depression.
D. World War II.

Questions 53–55 refer to the following quotation.

Be it enacted by the Senate and House of Representatives of the United States of America in Congress assembled, That there be granted to the several States, for the purposes hereinafter mentioned, an amount of public land, to be apportioned to each State a quantity equal to thirty thousand acres for each senator and representative in Congress to which the States are respectively entitled under the census of eighteen hundred and sixty. . . . *And be it further enacted,* That all moneys derived from the sale of the lands aforesaid . . . and the interest of which shall be inviolably appropriated by each State which may take and claim the benefit of this act, to the endowment, support, and maintenance of at least one college where the leading object shall be, without excluding other scientific and classical studies, and including military tactics, to teach such branches of learning as are related to agriculture and the mechanic arts, in such manner as the legislatures of the States may respectively prescribe, in order to promote the liberal and practical education of the industrial classes in the several pursuits and professions of life.

—Morrill Land-Grant Act, July 2, 1862

53. Which of the following was a major purpose of the Morrill Land-Grant Act?
  A. To stimulate the excellence of American literature
  B. To provide higher education to women
  C. To provide support to farmers and working men
  D. To address worries about the low educational level of soldiers in the Union Army

54. The Morrill Land-Grant Act reflected the governing philosophy of which political party?
  A. The Federalist Party
  B. The Republican Party
  C. The Democratic Party
  D. The Populist Party

55. The Morrill Land-Grant Act can be compared most directly to which of the following?
  A. The Homestead Act
  B. The Kansas-Nebraska Act
  C. The Pure Food and Drug Act
  D. The Agricultural Adjustment Act

Go on to Part B ➜

Part B (Short Answer)

Part B recommended time: 40 minutes

Directions: Answer three questions. You must answer questions 1 and 2, and you can choose to answer either 3 or 4. Carefully read and follow the directions for each question. Some will refer to historical sources. These questions will require you to make use of your historical analytical skills and your familiarity with historical themes. These questions do *not* require you to develop a thesis in your responses.

Question 1 is based on the following passage:

The sixteen years of Jefferson and Madison's rule furnished international tests of popular intelligence upon which Americans could depend. The ocean was the only open field for competition among nations. Americans enjoyed there no natural or artificial advantages over Englishmen, Frenchmen, or Spaniards; indeed, all these countries possessed navies, resources, and experience greater than were to be found in the United States. Yet the Americans developed, in the course of twenty years, a surprising degree of skill in naval affairs. ... Not only were American vessels better in model, faster in sailing, easier and quicker in handling, and more economical in working than the European, but they were also better equipped. The English complained as a grievance that the Americans adopted new and unwarranted devices in naval warfare; that their vessels were heavier and better constructed, and their missiles of unusual shape and improper use. The Americans resorted to expedients that had not been tried before, and excited a mixture of irritation and respect in the English service, until "Yankee smartness" became a national misdemeanor.

—Henry Adams, *History of the United States During the Administrations of Thomas Jefferson and James Madison*, 1889–1891

1. Using the excerpt, answer A, B, and C.
   A. Briefly describe Adams's perspective on the American navy during the War of 1812.
   B. Briefly explain ONE historical event or development that supports Adams's perspective.
   C. Briefly explain ONE historical event or development that would challenge Adams's perspective.

Question 2 is based on the following cartoon:

Clifford Berryman, 1936

2. Using the 1936 image, answer A, B, and C.
   A. Briefly explain the subject matter of the image.
   B. Briefly explain the political point of view of the image.
   C. Briefly explain ONE example of a political perspective opposed to the political point of view of the image.

Answer EITHER Question 3 OR Question 4.

3. Answer A, B, and C.
   A. Briefly explain ONE example illustrating the transportation situation in the United States before the advent of the railroads.
   B. Briefly explain ONE example of a transportation advantage provided by railroads.
   C. Briefly explain ONE example of how railroads influenced American economic, political, or military history.

4. Answer A, B, and C.
   A. Briefly explain how ONE of the following was important for African Americans.
   Dred Scott v. Sandford
   Plessy v. Ferguson
   Brown v. Board of Education of Topeka, Kansas
   B. Briefly explain how a SECOND of these options was important for African Americans.
   C. Briefly explain ONE example of how the Supreme Court's attitude to African American civil rights changed over time.

STOP. End of Section I.

Section II

Time: 100 minutes

Part A (Document-Based Question)

Part A recommended time: 60 minutes

Directions: Use the documents to answer the question. You may want to spend up to 15 minutes outlining your response and 45 minutes writing the essay that answers the question.

Provide a thesis that responds to all elements of the question with a historically plausible argument. This thesis of one or more sentences must be in the introduction or conclusion.

Connect historical evidence supporting your argument to a broader historical context that reaches beyond the time frame of the question.

Use at least three of the documents to address the topic of the question.

Support your argument with evidence from at least six of the seven documents.

Support your argument by analyzing historical evidence that comes from outside the documents.

Base your analysis of no less than three documents on at least one of the following: the point of view of the author, the purpose of the author, the intended audience of the document, or the historical context of the document.

Demonstrate a complex understanding of the subject of the question, using historical evidence to modify, qualify, or confirm your argument.

1. To what extent did the Federalist administrations of George Washington and John Adams promote national unity and advance the authority of the federal government?

Document A
Source: George Washington's First Inaugural Address, April 30, 1789

> *I behold the surest pledges that as on one side no local prejudices or attachments, no separate views or party animosities, will misdirect the comprehensive and equal eye which ought to watch over [Congress] so . . . that the foundation of our national policy will be laid in the pure and immutable principles of private morality, and the preeminence of free government be exemplified by all the attributes which can win the affections of its citizens and command the respect of the world.*

Document B
Source: Virginia Resolutions on the Assumption of State Debts, December 16, 1790

> *The General Assembly of the Commonwealth of Virginia . . . represent [that] . . . in an agricultural country like this . . . to perpetuate a large monied interest, is a measure which . . . must in the course of human events produce . . . the prostration of agriculture at the feet of commerce, or a change in the present form of federal government, fatal to the existence of American liberty.*

Document C
Source: Thomas Jefferson's Opinion on the Constitutionality of the Bank, February 15, 1791

> *I consider the foundation of the Constitution as laid on this ground—that all powers not delegated to the United States, by the Constitution, nor prohibited by it to the states, are reserved to the states, or to the people. To take a single step beyond the boundaries thus specially drawn around the powers of Congress, is to take possession of a boundless field of power.*

Document D

Source: Alexander Hamilton's Opinion on the Constitutionality of the Bank, February 23, 1791

> *This restrictive interpretation of the word necessary is also contrary to this sound maxim of construction; namely, that the powers contained in a constitution of government, especially those which concern the general administration of the affairs of a country, its finances, trade, defense, etc., ought to be construed liberally in advancement of the public good.*

Document E

Source: George Washington's Proclamation on the Whiskey Rebellion, August 7, 1794

> *Whereas combinations to defeat the execution of the laws laying duties upon spirits distilled within the United States . . . have . . . existed in some of the western parts of Pennsylvania; and whereas the said combinations, proceeding in a manner subversive equally of the just authority of government and the rights of individuals; . . . it is in my judgement necessary under the circumstances to take measures for calling forth the militia in order to suppress the combinations aforesaid, and to cause the laws to be duly executed.*

Document F

Source: The Sedition Act, July 14, 1798

> *That if any person shall write, print, utter, or publish, any false, scandalous, and malicious writing or writings against the government of the United States . . . with the intent to defame the said government, . . . then such person, being convicted before any court of the United States having jurisdiction thereof, shall be punished by a fine not exceeding two thousand dollars, and by imprisonment not exceeding two years.*

Document G

Source: Kentucky Resolutions, November 16, 1798

> *Resolved, that the several States composing the United States of America, are not united on the principle of unlimited submission to their general government; . . . that [the States] retain to themselves the right of judging how far the licentiousness of speech and press may be abridged without lessening their useful freedom . . . therefore [the Sedition Act], which does abridge the freedom of the press, is not law but is altogether void.*

Go on to Part B ➜

Part B (Long Essay)

Part B recommended time: 40 minutes

Directions: Answer *one* of the following questions.

Provide a thesis that responds to all elements of the question with a historically plausible argument. This thesis of one or more sentences must be in the introduction or conclusion.

Connect historical evidence supporting your argument to a broader historical context that reaches beyond the time frame of the question.

Provide examples of historical information that are relevant to the question.

Use well-chosen examples of historical information that support your argument.

Use historical reasoning to construct an argument that answers the question.

Demonstrate a complex understanding of the subject of the question, using historical evidence to modify, qualify, or confirm your argument.

2. Evaluate the extent to which British imperial policy stimulated a desire for independence in America during the eighteenth century.

3. Evaluate the extent to which Manifest Destiny and the Mexican War affected sectional differences in the United States.

4. Evaluate the extent to which the role of the United States as a world power changed between the Spanish-American War and the Cold War.

STOP. End of Section II.

ANSWERS TO THE DIAGNOSTIC EXAM

Multiple Choice

1. B	15. D	29. D	43. A
2. A	16. C	30. A	44. C
3. C	17. D	31. C	45. B
4. D	18. A	32. B	46. A
5. B	19. B	33. A	47. D
6. D	20. C	34. B	48. C
7. A	21. A	35. D	49. A
8. C	22. B	36. C	50. C
9. C	23. D	37. A	51. D
10. B	24. C	38. B	52. B
11. A	25. C	39. B	53. C
12. D	26. A	40. D	54. B
13. A	27. B	41. D	55. A
14. B	28. D	42. C	

Count the number you got correct and enter this number on the scoring worksheet on page 56.

Explanations for the Multiple-Choice Questions

1. B. The cartoon criticizes President Thomas Jefferson's 1807 Embargo Act. Following a British naval attack on the American frigate U.S.S. *Chesapeake* that forced the ship to surrender and resulted in removal of four alleged British deserters, many Americans called for war. President Jefferson wanted to avoid war with Great Britain and believed that economic pressure could force the British to change their policy of interfering with American trade and ships. Jefferson persuaded Congress to pass the Embargo Act, which cut off the export of American goods to Europe. The embargo devastated American trade and was very unpopular with many Americans.

2. A. President Jefferson was responding to British interference with American shipping and trade. The British were at war with Napoleonic France and were trying to cut off trade with French-controlled parts of Europe. The British seized American ships that they thought were trading with their enemy, and they also impressed American sailors to serve in their navy. Americans deeply resented these policies, which showed no respect for American rights or the flag of the United States.

3. C. Many Americans responded to Jefferson's Embargo Act by ignoring it and engaging in illicit trade, especially with Canada. Jefferson convinced Congress to pass legislation rigorously enforcing the embargo. This made it even more unpopular.

4. D. The Neutrality Laws of the 1930s most closely resemble Jefferson's policy. These laws also regulated American trade to achieve foreign policy objectives. The authors of the Neutrality Laws hoped to keep the United States out of another war by avoiding the conditions that led to American involvement in World War I. The Neutrality Laws stated that, once the president recognized the existence of a foreign war, Americans could not make loans to or sell munitions to warring powers, or take passage on belligerent ships.

5. B. President Ronald Reagan's "Evil Empire" speech reflected an intensification of the cold war in the early 1980s. Concerned about Soviet actions in the 1970s, such as the 1979 invasion of Afghanistan, Reagan intensified an arms buildup begun by President Jimmy Carter. Convinced of the essential criminality of the Soviet Union's totalitarian system, Reagan believed that the United States needed to wage the cold war from a position of strength.

6. D. A Republican would have been most likely to support President Reagan's position. Ronald Reagan was a champion of conservative Republican ideas in both domestic and foreign policy.

7. A. The sentiments of the passage are most closely linked to the passage of the Strategic Defense Initiative (SDI), popularly known as the "Star Wars" program. The SDI was a missile defense program proposed by President Reagan and intended to defend the United States by shooting down incoming nuclear missiles. Many critics thought the plan impractical, expensive, and too provocative to the Soviets. President Reagan believed that it offered a way out of the menace of nuclear annihilation. The SDI program, along with Reagan's military buildup, put more pressure on the Soviet Union.

8. C. The sentiments in the passage best reflect the long-standing concern of American presidents to contain communism. The containment of communism had been a cornerstone of American foreign policy since the late 1940s. President Reagan was determined to halt and reverse what he believed was an expansion of Communist influence in the 1970s.

9. C. In this passage Colleen Moore is writing about flappers. Flappers were young women in the 1920s who cut their hair short in a bobbed style, wore shorter dresses, and often experimented with makeup and cigarettes. The flappers represented the growing freedom of women in the United States in the years after World War I and the passage of the Nineteenth Amendment giving women the right to vote.

10. B. Many young women of the 1920s expressed their freedom through "mannish" haircuts, new clothing styles, and cosmetics. Rather than focusing on politics and social reform, many young women of this period explored their growing independence through an emphasis on social freedoms and self-expression.

11. A. The new freedoms for women in the 1920s were supported by widespread economic prosperity.

Growing economic security gave many people more leisure time and the opportunity to explore greater personal freedoms. The general prosperity stimulated a vibrant cultural life that opened up new ways for women to express themselves.

12. **D.** The passage by Moore most directly reflects concerns for individual liberty and self-expression. Women in the 1920s took advantage of new opportunities to expand their personal freedoms and express themselves more openly.

13. **A.** In this passage, Benjamin Franklin takes a position similar to advocates of a market-driven economy like Adam Smith. The author of *The Wealth of Nations*, Adam Smith defended the principles of modern capitalism. Like Smith, Franklin believed that individuals operating freely in the market can accomplish more than paternalistic government policies can. Franklin believed that the best way to help the poor is to encourage them to help themselves.

14. **B.** The idea that Franklin expresses in this passage most directly reflects a belief in individual self-reliance. Franklin was himself a self-made man. He articulated the self-reliant ethos that became a long-standing American value.

15. **D.** A high degree of social mobility in colonial America helped Franklin justify his position. Most Americans were farmers, or in the few cities, businesspeople or artisans. The ready availability of land and a prospering economy opened up many avenues for social advancement. The absence of a privileged aristocracy, along with plentiful avenues to accumulate wealth, made America a land of opportunity.

16. **C.** The president most likely to share Franklin's position was Calvin Coolidge. A man who rose from modest circumstances to the presidency, Coolidge was a believer in hard work and thrift. He insisted on reducing government expenses and resisted interfering with business and the markets.

17. **D.** In this cartoon, Thomas Nast expresses his conviction that Tammany Hall boss William M. Tweed wields too much power in New York City. As the leader of the Tammany Hall political machine that dominated politics in New York City, Boss Tweed used his power to enrich himself and his cronies. Nast was a longtime opponent of Tweed and helped publicize the political boss's misdeeds through his cartoons. Tweed eventually was sentenced to prison because of his crimes.

18. **A.** Urban political machines like Tammany Hall derived most of their support from immigrants and lower-class voters. When they controlled the political structure of a city, machines prospered through the control of city contracts for improvements like sewers and streets. Machine politicians would pocket kickbacks from contractors eager for the work. This money, in turn, funded a hierarchical machine structure that reached into every neighborhood. Local precinct captains would help turn out the vote on election day, keeping the machine in power.

19. **B.** Urban political machines endured for many years because they provided help and services for the poor. In an era before extensive social services and welfare, urban political machines assisted the poor with gifts of food and shelter, and sometimes jobs. In return, the machines expected these people to vote in their favor.

20. **C.** Nast's journalistic perspective can best be compared to reporters investigating President Richard M. Nixon during the Watergate scandal. Nixon, like Tweed, was accused of misusing his office. As with Nast, reporters like Bob Woodward and Carl Bernstein of the *Washington Post* played a key role in exposing a political leader's wrongdoing.

21. **A.** From the perspective of Captain John Smith, Powhatan and his followers were a backward people. Smith sees the Indians as "barbarous." They wear animal skins and paint, and are cruelly ready to execute Smith. The fact that Powhatan makes his own clothes and tools would also lead Smith to see this as a primitive society.

22. **B.** Smith's account makes clear that Powhatan's people made decisions by consensus. After a feast, Powhatan consults with his people and there is a long discussion about what to do with Smith. When the decision is made to kill Smith, only the determined intervention of Pocahontas saves him.

23. **D.** Smith's story illustrates that Indian-European relations often suffered from misunderstanding and suspicion. Smith did not appreciate the concerns of Powhatan's people, and the Indians clearly were hostile to the newly arrived English. Only Pocahontas in this story attempts to bridge the divide between the Indians and the English.

24. **C.** In the context of this story, the peace-making Pocahontas can best be compared to Jane Addams. In addition to being a founder of Hull

House in Chicago and a pioneering social worker, Addams was also a vocal peace activist. Addams was awarded the Nobel Peace Prize in 1931.

25. **C.** Martin Luther King, Jr., in this passage is calling for equal rights for African Americans. King gave his "I Have a Dream" speech during the August 28, 1963, march on Washington, when 250,000 people congregated in the nation's capital to express their support for proposed civil rights legislation.

26. **A.** In this passage, King points out a contradiction between American ideals and American practice caused by racial discrimination. Invoking the Declaration of Independence and Constitution of the United States, King in this speech called for all Americans, regardless of their color, to enjoy the inalienable rights of life, liberty, and the pursuit of happiness.

27. **B.** A Southern Democratic senator would be likely to oppose the message of King's speech. The Democratic Party in the South had dominated the region for over a century and for the most part strongly supported the Jim Crow laws upholding racial segregation. The civil rights laws of the 1950s and 1960s were passed with the overwhelming support of Northern Democrats and Republicans.

28. **D.** In this passage, King is addressing the struggle for greater individual liberty in American history. As King pointed out in his "I Have a Dream" speech, Americans since the founding of the United States have been striving to achieve greater individual liberty for themselves and their families. King saw the civil rights movement as a continuation of that struggle.

29. **D.** The message of the cartoon can be best described as civilians playing a vital role in the war effort. Americans on the home front during World War II were encouraged to see themselves as active participants in the conflict. Food products like meat and sugar and consumer goods like gasoline were rationed. People raised victory gardens and bought war bonds. Many women and African Americans took jobs in war industries. What people did at home was seen as crucial to supporting the fighting men overseas.

30. **A.** Viewing this cartoon would encourage Americans to avoid the wasteful use of metal products. Metals were vital for the manufacture of weapons and ammunition. Civilians collected scrap metal that could be melted down

and used for the war effort. Many consumer goods made of metal, most notably new automobiles, were not available during the war as industries focused on war production.

31. **C.** The cartoon most directly refers to American industrial production during World War II. The United States became what President Franklin D. Roosevelt called the "Arsenal of Democracy" during the war, producing enough weapons and military supplies to equip Americans fighting a global war, while also providing great quantities of Lend-Lease aid to American allies. American industrial output was a major factor in winning World War II.

32. **B.** The message of the cartoon can be best compared to the boycotts of British goods in the 1760s and 1770s. In both cases, Americans were asked to give up goods and make sacrifices to help further a larger cause. In the 1760s and 1770s Americans gave up British goods to exert pressure on British policymakers. In World War II, Americans made sure most metals went to war production to ensure the defeat of Nazi Germany and Imperial Japan.

33. **A.** Mary Easty in this passage is asking her judges to stop condemning innocent people to death for witchcraft. In 1692, a group of girls in Salem, Massachusetts, began acting as if they were possessed. They claimed that they were bewitched. This led to a witch-hunting hysteria that resulted in 20 executions, including the death of Mary Easty. Eventually, the governor of Massachusetts put an end to the witchcraft prosecutions. Years later, the convictions of the people executed and imprisoned during this hysteria were officially overturned.

34. **B.** Most historians believe that the Salem Witch Trials were the result of social tensions in Salem. Massachusetts was undergoing rapid political and social change in the early 1690s. Most of those accused of being witches came from more prosperous families associated with business and trade, while the accusers came from less well-off farming families. Fears about witchcraft probably also reflected anxieties about the shifting social and economic status of people in Salem.

35. **D.** The religious convictions of Mary Easty and the rest of Salem were shaped by Puritanism. Massachusetts was settled in the 1630s by Calvinist Puritans escaping the religious domination of the Anglican Church in England. They

saw their new colony as an opportunity to create a truly godly community. Initially only members of Puritan congregations could vote. Concern that people were falling away from strict Puritan belief probably played a part in the Salem witch hysteria.

36. **C.** Writers and intellectuals have often compared the Salem Witch Trials to government actions in the Red Scares of the twentieth century. The investigations of Senator Joseph McCarthy in the early 1950s were often compared to witch hunts. Arthur Miller's play about the events in Salem, *The Crucible* (1953), was a critique of McCarthyism.

37. **A.** Colonel Juan N. Seguin honored the memory of the defenders of the Alamo because they had died for their cause. Seguin had served with Lieutenant Colonel William B. Travis at the Alamo. Seguin was sent with a message asking for help and so was not present when the Alamo garrison was overwhelmed on March 6, 1836.

38. **B.** Colonel Seguin's oration makes it clear that many Tejanos favored Texan independence. Seguin was a native of San Antonio and had been active in politics. He favored a federal structure for Mexico and opposed the centralizing policies of Mexican President Antonio Lopez de Santa Anna. Federalist Tejanos joined with American settlers to resist the Mexican government. After the Battle of the Alamo, Seguin organized a company of Tejano cavalry that helped protect the Texan army of Sam Houston and fought at the Battle of San Jacinto on April 21, 1836, which secured Texan independence.

39. **B.** The defenders of the Alamo gave their lives for the desire for political liberty. They were opposed to the efforts of Mexican President Antonio Lopez de Santa Anna to impose a stronger central government on the country. They wanted a return to the Mexican Constitution of 1824, which granted more powers to the Mexican states.

40. **D.** A dispute over the boundary of Texas led to the Mexican War. The Mexican government refused to recognize Texan independence and was deeply angered when the United States annexed Texas as a state in 1845. The Texans claimed that their southern boundary was the Rio Grande river; Mexico vehemently disputed this. In early 1846, President James K. Polk ordered an American army, under General Zachary Taylor, to the Rio Grande. Mexican troops attacked a detachment of American dragoons on April 25, 1846. The United States responded with a declaration of war.

41. **D.** Abbie Hoffman and the Yippies were protesting the Vietnam War. Hoffman helped lead the October 21, 1967, March on the Pentagon that drew some 50,000 protesters. Hoffman's actions there were described in Norman Mailer's book *The Armies of the Night* (1968). In August 1968, Hoffman and his Youth International Party (the Yippies) played a prominent role in protests at the Democratic National Convention. When police attacked protesters, riots broke out. Hoffman was one of seven protest leaders, known collectively as the Chicago Seven, who were subsequently indicted for conspiracy and incitement to riot. Hoffman's conviction for incitement to riot was later overturned.

42. **C.** The New Left most directly influenced the ideas of Hoffman and the Yippies. Central to the formation of the New Left in the United States was the Students for a Democratic Society (SDS) movement organized in 1962. The SDS rejected the old-style authoritarian leftism of the Communist Party. In the 1962 Port Huron Statement, the SDS called for "participatory democracy" that would build a broad social movement for change. Over time, the New Left in the United States would grow increasingly receptive to the countercultural ideals of personal self-expression.

43. **A.** The Civil Rights Movement most directly influenced the tactics of Hoffman and the Yippies. Civil rights protesters directly challenged racial discrimination by taking nonviolent actions, such as staging sit-ins at segregated drugstore lunch counters. Hoffman and the Yippies engaged in protest theater, such as tossing fake money from a balcony onto the floor of the New York Stock Exchange. What distinguished the Yippies from other protesters was their offbeat sense of humor, which involved such actions as nominating a pig for president in 1968.

44. **C.** The counterculture of the 1960s sought greater freedom for personal self-expression. Fueled by the great number of young people resulting from the Baby Boom and the disillusionment with authority born of the Civil Rights Movement and the Vietnam War, the counterculture of the 1960s emphasized antiestablishment attitudes. People influenced by the counterculture looked for new ways to live

a fulfilling life. Famously, the "hippies" rejected conventional middle class mores, growing their hair long, dressing differently, and experimenting with drugs to expand their consciousness. Books that influenced the counterculture were Jack Kerouac's *On the Road* (1957) and Ken Kesey's *One Flew Over the Cuckoo's Nest* (1962).

45. B. The British decision to fire on American militiamen on April 19, 1775, led to a series of uprisings against the British government across the colonies. As word of the fighting at Lexington and Concord spread across the colonies, British authority collapsed, and American rebels took control of governments, forcing out royal officials. The Second Continental Congress convened in Philadelphia in May and in June appointed George Washington commander of the newly created Continental Army.

46. A. British commanders always assumed that they would benefit from command of the sea. The British Navy was the most powerful in the world. Command of the sea gave the British the strategic flexibility to range up and down the Atlantic coast of the colonies. Until near the end of the war, this was a great advantage. The successful intervention of a French fleet at the Battle of the Chesapeake on September 5, 1781, made possible the isolation and defeat of Lord Charles Cornwallis's British Army at the Battle of Yorktown. Cornwallis's surrender on October 19, 1781, was decisive in convincing the British government to end the war.

47. D. When the Americans rebelled against Great Britain, they benefitted from the great geographical extent of the country. By European standards, the American colonies covered an enormous territory. Much of it was underdeveloped or wilderness. The British did not have the troops to cover all this ground. The British could control some major cities, but they often were isolated and defeated when they ventured into the countryside. A good example of this is the isolation and defeat of General John Burgoyne's army at Saratoga on October 17, 1777.

48. C. Militiamen played a key role during the American Revolutionary War by controlling populations not under the direct supervision of the British Army. While the battlefield performance of militias could be spotty, the militias were very important in maintaining the authority of the American government wherever the British were not present, which meant most of the country. The militias intimidated Loyalists and ensured support for American policies.

49. A. Carry A. Nation was famous as an activist for temperance. After her first husband died of alcoholism, she became a supporter of temperance. Eventually, her methods became more direct and violent as she attacked saloons and their stocks of liquor with rocks and her trademark hatchet.

50. C. Nation can be compared most directly to Rosa Parks. They both took direct action to further their beliefs. While Parks did not act violently, as Nation did, she did sit in the whites-only section of a bus in Montgomery, Alabama, sparking a famous civil rights struggle.

51. D. Nation's cause would attain a great victory with the enactment of Prohibition. A resolution calling for a constitutional amendment prohibiting intoxicating liquor in the United States passed Congress in December 1917 and was ratified by the states in January 1919. Congress passed the Volstead Act in October 1919, which provided an enforcement mechanism for the new amendment. The Eighteenth Amendment went into effect in January 1920.

52. B. The major event that helped pave the way for the triumph of Nation's cause was World War I. The use of grain for alcoholic beverages was restricted by Congress as a war measure because the grain was needed for food. Thus, the consumption of intoxicating liquors was reduced through government action during the war. The spirit of wartime idealism and self-sacrifice also helped spur support for the passage of the Eighteenth Amendment.

53. C. A desire to provide support to farmers and working men was a major purpose of the Morrill Land-Grant Act. The act was the culmination of an effort to give practical assistance to farmers and various types of workers by giving them the most advanced technical education. Most land-grant universities sponsored programs in agriculture and engineering. Examples include Cornell University, Iowa State University, and the Massachusetts Institute of Technology.

54. B. The Morrill Land-Grant Act reflected the governing philosophy of the Republican Party. The Republican Party, with its slogan of "free labor, free land, and free men," not only opposed the extension of slavery but also inherited the Whig Party's willingness to use the government to stimulate economic opportunities. An earlier version of the Morrill Act was vetoed by Democratic President James Buchanan. In the absence of many Southern Democrats during the Civil War, the Republican-dominated Congress passed the Morrill Act. President Abraham Lincoln willingly signed the measure into law.

55. A. The Morrill Land-Grant Act can be compared most directly to the Homestead Act. Republicans supported the Homestead Act, which gave 160 acres of land in the west to Americans willing to settle on it and work it for five years as a way of offering opportunity to "free men." Southern Democrats opposed the Homestead Act because they feared it would block the expansion of slavery. Like the Morrill Act, an early version of the Homestead Act was vetoed by Democratic President James Buchanan. Also like the Morrill Act, the Homestead Act was passed in 1862 and signed into law by President Abraham Lincoln.

Explanations for the Short-Answer Questions

Each short-answer question is worth three points. Give yourself one point for each part of the question (A, B, and C) that you get right. Then enter your score on the scoring worksheet on page 56.

1. A. Adams is arguing that during the early nineteenth century and during the War of 1812 the U.S. Navy distinguished itself. Despite a relative lack of resources and experience, the American navy compared very favorably to its larger competitors. American frigates were more heavily constructed and better armed than comparable ships in European navies. Americans were willing to innovate in naval and military technology. This earned them the grudging respect of their English opponents in the War of 1812. Adams sees this as a sign of "popular intelligence" in the American people.
B. During the War of 1812, American warships like the USS *Constitution*, "Old Ironsides," won a number of famous ship-to-ship battles with British warships. Daring American naval captains like Stephen Decatur became national heroes. American naval forces on the Great Lakes won decisive victories over their British competitors. A fleet commanded by Oliver Hazard Perry won the Battle of Lake Erie on September 10, 1813. Perry reported his victory with the memorable words, "We have met the enemy and they are ours." A fleet commanded by Thomas Macdonough won the Battle of Lake Champlain on September 11, 1814, helping turn back a British invasion of the United States from Canada.
C. Though American naval vessels performed well in individual encounters, the small American navy could not prevail against the numerical superiority of the British navy. By the end of the War of 1812, most of the surviving American warships were blockaded in ports. The British navy was able to land armies that attacked and burned Washington in 1814, and that threatened New Orleans in late 1814 and early 1815.

2. A. This cartoon concerns the "Alphabet Soup" of agencies that emerged during President Franklin Roosevelt's New Deal. Early in the New Deal, Roosevelt and Congress launched a number of new programs and agencies to promote economic recovery from the Great Depression and provide relief to jobless Americans. Pictured in the cartoon are the AAA, the Agricultural Adjustment Administration, which attempted to raise farm prices by paying farmers to take land out of production, the PWA, the Public Works Administration, which launched a series of public works to provide jobs, and the WPA, the Works Progress Administration, which directly hired unemployed workers and set them to work on projects ranging from construction to the creation of murals and plays.
B. The cartoon is sympathetic to Roosevelt and the New Deal, showing the various "Alphabet Soup" agencies as happy children dancing around a smiling father-figure president. The early New Deal was popular, leading to Roosevelt's Democratic Party winning a victory in the 1934 Congressional elections. Despite this, there were challenges to the New Deal coming from both the right and left in American politics. In 1935, the Supreme Court struck down as unconstitutional the National Recovery Administration (NRA) which had attempted to get industries to cooperate in setting standards on such things as prices and wages. Roosevelt

responded with the Second New Deal and the passage of such laws as the Social Security Act (1935), which set up a system to provide pensions to the elderly, and the National Labor Relations Act (1935), which made it easier for workers to organize unions.

C. There were a number of critics of the New Deal. The Supreme Court invalidated some of the legislation of the First New Deal. Only after a bruising political battle in Roosevelt's second term, during which he lost a lot of political support attempting to pass legislation that would have "packed" the Court with his supporters, did the Supreme Court begin upholding New Deal legislation. Many conservatives opposed the New Deal. Former Democratic New York governor Al Smith was a member of the Liberty League, which believed that the New Deal undermined property rights. From the left, Louisiana Senator Huey Long did not believe that the New Deal was going far enough. He promoted a "Share the Wealth" plan that would give every American a home and a $2,500 income. The money for this would come from confiscating wealth from millionaires.

3. A. Before railroads, transportation in the United States was often very difficult. Roads were poor and often badly maintained. Some roads, like the Lancaster Turnpike, completed in Pennsylvania in the 1790s, were exceptions to this rule and economically important. Opposition to federal road construction on state's rights constitutional grounds limited roadbuilding. The best way to travel and transport goods was by water, by sea along the coast and by river in the interior. The Ohio and Mississippi Rivers were major transportation routes, especially after the invention of the steamboat, which allowed movement both up and down stream. By 1860, over a thousand steamboats were operating in the Mississippi River Valley. Canals offered a way to bring waterways to areas not blessed with a convenient river. New York Governor DeWitt Clinton's Erie Canal, completed in 1825, connected the Hudson River and New York City to the Great Lakes. This inaugurated a canal-building craze. By 1840, over 3,300 miles of canals had been constructed.

B. The advantage of railroads was that they were cheaper to build than canals, and tracks could be laid in almost any type of terrain.

The first railroad was constructed in 1828, and by the 1830s railroads were spreading rapidly. In the next two decades the gauges for tracks were standardized, making possible a national railway network. Safety devices improved. In 1859, the Pullman sleeper car appeared, providing a new level of comfort for travelers. Increasingly speedy, safe, and economical, by the 1850s, railroads were becoming the dominant transportation mode in the United States.

C. Before 1840, most Midwestern grain was shipped south down the Mississippi River to the port of New Orleans. With the rise of a thriving railroad network in the Northeast and Northwest, Midwestern grain was increasingly shipped to the big cities of the east. The west and east became increasingly economically interdependent. The growing economic ties between west and east would prove decisive in the Civil War. American expansionists dreamed of a railroad connection between the settled areas of the United States and the Pacific coast. Senator Stephen Douglas of Illinois wanted a transcontinental railroad to start west from Chicago. This northern transcontinental route would have to run through the Kansas and Nebraska Territories. Kansas and Nebraska would have to be organized politically to facilitate railroad construction. The only way that Douglas could win Southern votes for this in the Senate was to overturn the Missouri Compromise, which banned slavery in these territories. Douglas's 1854 Kansas-Nebraska Act provided for the settlers in Kansas and Nebraska to decide the issue of slavery in their territories through popular sovereignty. The Kansas-Nebraska Act outraged many people in the North, who saw it as potentially allowing slavery into what should have been free territory. Popular sovereignty in Kansas devolved into violence, as proslavery and antislavery settlers fought each other. Douglas's scheme to promote a railroad helped bring on the Civil War. During the Civil War, railroads were often vital lines of communication and supply. Occasionally, troops were shipped from one front to another by railroad. As the war went on, the Northern advantage in miles of railroad became increasingly important as the growing industrial might of the North was mobilized for the Union war effort. Railroads became strategic targets during the war. Atlanta, Georgia, was vital to the South as an industrial center and railroad hub. This made it a key target for Union General William Tecumseh Sherman in 1864. When Sherman left Atlanta for his famous march to the sea, his troops made sure to destroy railroad tracks along the way. The Confederacy lacked the industrial capacity to replace these tracks.

4. A, B. Dred Scott was a slave in Missouri whose masters had taken him to live in the free state of Illinois and the Wisconsin Territory for several years. Scott went to court to ask for his freedom, arguing that residence in free territory had made him free. In 1857, the Supreme Court in *Dred Scott v. Sandford* ruled that, as a black slave, Scott could not be a citizen and therefore could not sue in the courts. The Court also ruled that, since Scott was the property of his masters, residence in a free state did not make him free; private property could not be taken from citizens without due process. This reasoning led the Court to rule the Missouri Compromise unconstitutional, opening up the possibility of slaveholders freely taking their slaves anywhere in the country. The Dred Scott decision outraged many Northerners and intensified sectional differences in the 1850s. Following the end of Reconstruction in 1877, Southern states began to institutionalize discrimination against African Americans. Measures such as poll taxes and literacy laws were enacted to keep African Americans from voting. Jim Crow laws segregated whites and blacks in public and private facilities. The 1896 Supreme Court decision in *Plessy v. Ferguson* responded to a challenge against segregation in railroad accommodations in Louisiana. The Court held that segregation was lawful as long as the segregated accommodations were "separate but equal." This decision helped institutionalize segregation in the South; the stipulation that segregated facilities should be equal was ignored. Overturning *Plessy v. Ferguson* became a longstanding goal of the National Association for the Advancement of Colored People (NAACP). The NAACP and its lead lawyer, Thurgood Marshall, took the case of Oliver Brown to the Supreme Court. Brown was unhappy that his daughter could not attend a local school in Topeka, Kansas,

but was instead bussed to an all-black school. In 1954, the Supreme Court in *Brown v. Board of Education of Topeka, Kansas* unanimously ruled that segregated schools were "inherently unequal" and thus unconstitutional. This effectively overruled *Plessy v. Ferguson* and overturned the legal foundations of racial segregation in the United States.

C. Over time the attitude of the Supreme Court moved from hostility to African American rights to support for the African American civil rights movement. In *Dred Scott v. Sandford*, Chief Justice Roger Taney of Maryland, along with Southern and pro-slavery justices, hoped to resolve the slavery issue dividing the nation. Instead of making a narrow, technical ruling in the case, they intentionally attempted to mount a constitutional defense of slavery. Though Taney had freed his own slaves, he argued that blacks were so inferior to whites they had no claim to the rights of citizens. The Supreme Court, in the aftermath of Reconstruction, helped Southerners establish the Jim Crow regime in the South. In the 1883 *Civil Rights Cases*, the Court struck down the 1875 Civil Rights Act that had given African Americans equal access to accommodations like hotels and restaurants. The Court argued that African Americans were only accorded Fourteenth Amendment protections against discrimination in public facilities; privately owned businesses could constitutionally discriminate in choosing their customers. *Plessy v. Ferguson* continued the process of narrowing the social gains made by African Americans during Reconstruction by offering a constitutional defense of segregation. For years the NAACP chipped away at *Plessy v. Ferguson* in the courts. A victory came in 1944, when in *Smith v. Allwright* the Supreme Court declared all-white political primaries unconstitutional. This was an opening in the effort to end segregation. Earl Warren, who became Chief Justice in 1953, after being nominated by President Dwight Eisenhower, was determined to take a stand against legalized discrimination. He played a leading role in organizing a unanimous decision in *Brown v. Board of Education*. From this point on, the Supreme Court was a supporter of African American civil rights. Fittingly, Thurgood Marshall, who argued the *Brown* case, joined the Supreme Court in 1967, becoming the first African American Supreme Court Justice.

Explanation for the Document-Based Question

To do well on this question, be sure to follow all the directions! Provide a historically plausible thesis that addresses all aspects of the prompt. Your thesis should respond to and go beyond the prompt. Restating or paraphrasing the prompt is not an acceptable thesis. Your thesis can be at the beginning or the end of your essay; it will not be counted if it is anywhere else. Put your response in a broader context, referring to historical factors preceding, following, or taking place at the same time as the subject of the prompt. Be sure to use at least six of the documents. You need to explain the historical significance of the documents; simply referring to or quoting them will not count for points. For at least three of the documents, explain how the point of view of the author, the intended audience, or the document's historical context is relevant to your larger argument. Bring in as much evidence beyond the documents as you can. Evidence that you use to provide context or to deepen discussion of at least three of the documents will not be applied to the overall outside evidence point; you can't double-dip on these evidence points! The more historical information outside the documents that you can provide, the better. Finally, show a complex understanding of the subject matter of the prompt. You can do this in a variety of ways. For instance, you can connect this subject matter to similar historical events in another period. Other possibilities include highlighting differing perspectives on the subject matter, or exploring differing interpretations of the causes of the historical event that you are discussing. Relate this to your larger argument; an off-hand reference will not be counted.

Here is some information to help with this.

1. Although the Federalists intended to unify the nation and strengthen the federal government, their political and economic policies split the nation into rival partisan factions. You might note that debates over ratification of the Constitution set the stage for the emergence of political parties by the end of the 1790s. You could briefly discuss the supporters and opponents of ratification, the anti-Federalists, and *The Federalist Papers,* particularly *The Federalist,* no. 10. You should examine the ideological conflict between loose and strict interpretations of the Constitution, as well as federal versus state authority. You should identify the leading Federalists (Washington, Adams, Hamilton) and Republicans (Jefferson, Madison, Randolph). Document A indicates Washington's desire that Congress may set policy without party division. You may note, however, that friction stemmed from Hamilton's financial program. You should examine his intention to establish a sound financial foundation for the new nation by creating a national bank, addressing the public debt (Assumption Act, Funding Bill), and raising revenue (excise taxes, tariffs). While Hamilton's program strengthened the federal government, it fostered dissent among the Republicans. Document B reflects Virginia's opposition to the assumption of state debts. You should note that the conflict over the Bank of the United States in Documents C and D reflects Jefferson and Hamilton's interpretations of the "necessary and proper clause" of the Constitution. You may also contrast the Republican view of an agricultural economy in Document B, with Federalist support for the Tariff of 1789 and Hamilton's Report on Manufactures. You may note that opposition to the excise tax led to the Whiskey Rebellion. In Document E, Washington states his intention to enforce federal law and implement powers granted under the Constitution. Washington demonstrated federal authority by calling forth the militias from three states to suppress the rebellion. You may refer to Shays' Rebellion. You may begin a discussion of diplomatic policy with Washington's Neutrality Proclamation (1793) and Neutrality Act (1794). You might explain how the neutrality policy survived the challenge of "Citizen Genet." However, Great Britain challenged the policy by seizing American

ships. You should discuss partisan perceptions of Jay's Treaty. You may note that it achieved some of its nationalistic goals regarding the Northwest Territory and promoting commerce with Great Britain. However, you should also address Republican views of its shortcomings. You may address Pinckney's Treaty. You should discuss Washington's views on parties in his Farewell Address. You should also note how the election of 1796 yielded a Federalist president (Adams) and a Republican vice president (Jefferson). You should also note how the strife in the executive office reflected party differences in the United States. A discussion of the undeclared naval war with France will reveal the pro-British views of Federalists and pro-French sympathies of the Republicans. You should discuss how opposing perceptions of the war and the XYZ Affair led to the Alien and Sedition Acts of 1798 (Document F).

You should observe how Madison and Jefferson penned the Virginia and Kentucky Resolutions (Document G), which asserted the theory of nullification. You might conclude how the problems of the Adams's administration led to the election of Jefferson in 1800.

Scoring for the Document-Based Question

TASKS	POINTS
Give yourself 1 point if you wrote a thesis that responds to the question with a historically plausible argument. You can't just restate or repeat the question. Your thesis can be expressed in one or more sentences in the introduction or conclusion of your essay.	
Give yourself 1 point if you put the question into a wider historical context. To do this, you should connect the topic of the question to events, developments, or processes that take place before, during, or after the period immediately covered in the question. A brief reference or phrase will not earn you this point.	
There are 2 points possible here. Give yourself 1 point for providing the historical content of at least three of the documents to address the question. Give yourself another point if you supported your argument by using the historical content of at least six of the documents. You must explain the historical significance of these documents. Simply quoting documents does not count. To get the second point you must relate the six documents to your argument.	
Give yourself 1 point if you used at least one piece of historical information that goes beyond the evidence in the documents. A brief reference to a piece of information will not earn a point. You must describe the how this historical information relates to the question. The historical information for this point must be different from information that you use to earn the point for placing the question in a wider historical context.	
Give yourself 1 point if you explained the point of view of the author, the purpose of the author, or a document's intended audience or historical context for at least three documents. You must explain how or why these are relevant for your argument.	
Give yourself 1 point if you demonstrated a complex understanding of the subject of the question, using historical evidence to modify, qualify or confirm your argument. This understanding must be used to develop your argument, and can't merely be a brief reference or phrase.	
TOTAL (7 points possible)	

Explanations for the Long Essay Questions

To do well on this question, be sure to follow all the directions! Provide a historically plausible thesis that addresses all aspects of the prompt. Your thesis should respond to and go beyond the prompt. Restating or paraphrasing the prompt is not an acceptable thesis. Use your historical analytical skills to construct your argument, emphasizing such aspects of the subject matter as cause and effect or change and continuity. Your thesis can be at the beginning or the end of your essay; it will not be counted if it is anywhere else. Put your response in a broader context, referring to historical factors preceding, following, or taking place at the same time as the subject of the prompt. Provide as much historical evidence as you can. You want to do this both to provide information that is relevant to the subject matter and to support your argument. Finally, show a complex understanding of the subject matter of the prompt. You can do this in a variety of ways. For instance, you can connect this subject matter to similar historical events in another period. Other possibilities include highlighting differing perspectives on the subject matter, or exploring differing interpretations of the causes of the historical event that you are discussing. Relate this to your larger argument; an off-hand reference will not be counted.

Here is some information to help with this.

2. You can begin this essay with a discussion of the French and Indian War, which drove the French off the North American continent, and gave Great Britain control of the eastern seaboard from Canada to Florida. The defeat of the French vastly improved the security of the American colonists. Neither the western Native Americans nor the Spanish in Louisiana posed much of a threat to them. They no longer needed significant British military protection. Ironically, this was just what the British wanted to give them. The French and Indian War had been the American phase of the Seven Years War, a genuine world war that saw fighting from America to Europe to India. The war had been enormously expensive, and Britain had accumulated an enormous debt that had to be paid down. At the same time, members of the British government wanted to reorganize and rationalize their expanded empire. It seemed reasonable to these men that the Americans help pay for a war that had given them such benefits. The first move in this new policy on the part of the British government came with the 1765 Quartering and Stamp Acts. The Quartering Act required the Americans to provide quarters and support for garrisons the Americans did not feel they needed. The Stamp Act imposed a tax on various transactions and paper products. The Stamp Act outraged Americans because it imposed a tax on them without representation. During the long period of "salutary neglect" which had run from the seventeenth century to the 1760s, the British government had allowed the colonists to largely govern themselves. All colonies had elected legislatures that voted in any needed taxes. Americans conceded the right of the British government to regulate trade, but drew the line at "internal" taxes. In response to the Stamp Act, groups such as the Sons of Liberty appeared to oppose the law. A meeting of representatives from nine colonies at the Stamp Act Congress demonstrated growing colonial unity. In the face of American resistance, Parliament repealed the Stamp Act, but passed the Declaratory Act which asserted Parliament's power to legislate for the colonies. In 1767, Parliament passed the Townshend Acts. These all represented "external" taxes, putting duties on such American imports as glass, paper, and tea. Violators of the acts could be tried in British admiralty courts. Americans were not favorably impressed by these "external" taxes. They were not for regulating commerce, but were clearly intended to raise revenue without American consent. In addition, trying Americans in naval courts and not before

juries of their peers was seen as an act of tyranny. Americans resisted the taxes with nonimportation drives. This decreased the amount of American imports from Britain, hurting British merchants. In 1770, all the taxes were dropped but that on tea. That same year a scuffle between a mob of Americans and some British soldiers led to the Boston Massacre. Though the soldiers were acquitted of murder charges, and this further poisoned American attitudes toward the British military. In 1773, in an ill-advised attempt to assist the ailing East India Company, the British government gave the East India Company a monopoly on tea sales in America. The sweetener for Americans was that the East India Company tea would be cheaper. This did not assuage the Americans, who saw this as a plot to reconcile them to the tea tax. They resented the imposition of a monopoly on them. Committees of Correspondence organized resistance. In Boston, a group of Americans dressed as Mohawk Native Americans dumped East India Company tea into the harbor. The outraged British government imposed the "Intolerable Acts," closing the port of Boston until the tea was paid for, giving more power to the royal governor, and limiting the freedom of town meetings. The unrelated Quebec Act angered Americans by giving privileges to the French Catholics in Canada, and seemingly cutting off American expansion to the west. The First Continental Congress denounced the "Intolerable Acts." Much of Massachusetts was defying the authority of the royal governor in Boston. Both sides made preparations for war. On April 19, 1775, British troops attempting to capture an American arsenal exchanged shots with militia, beginning the American Revolutionary War. War came because the British authorities insisted on changing the way that they governed the colonies, and because the Americans insisted on defending what they believed were their traditional rights.

To do well on this question, be sure to follow all the directions! Provide a historically plausible thesis that addresses all aspects of the prompt. Your thesis should respond to and go beyond the prompt. Restating or paraphrasing the prompt is not an acceptable thesis. Use your historical analytical skills to construct your argument, emphasizing such aspects of the subject matter as cause and effect or change and continuity. Your thesis can be at the beginning or the end of your essay; it will not be counted if it is anywhere else. Put your response in a broader context, referring to historical factors preceding, following, or taking place at the same time as the subject of the prompt. Provide as much historical evidence as you can. You want to do this both to provide information that is relevant to the subject matter and to support your argument. Finally, show a complex understanding of the subject matter of the prompt. You can do this in a variety of ways. For instance, you can connect this subject matter to similar historical events in another period. Other possibilities include highlighting differing perspectives on the subject matter, or exploring differing interpretations of the causes of the historical event that you are discussing. Relate this to your larger argument; an off-hand reference will not be counted.

Here is some information to help with this.

3. You could begin by briefly looking at the way sectional differences and concerns over slavery had shaped American politics since the Missouri Compromise of 1820. The annexation of Texas was held up for years because many Northern politicians did not want to add to the power of the slave states. President John Tyler finally had to resort to the expedient of joint resolutions in Congress to bring Texas into the Union in 1845. A discussion of Manifest Destiny could reference the Louisiana Purchase of 1803, which gave the United States a claim to territories touching on the Pacific Ocean. The journalist John O'Sullivan coined the term "Manifest Destiny" in an 1845 editorial promoting the annexation of more territory. O'Sullivan's call for the United States to overspread the North American continent captured a popular mood

supporting American expansionism. James K. Polk campaigned for the presidency in 1844 as an expansionist, calling for the annexation of Texas as well as for all of Oregon in a territorial dispute with the British. His campaign caught the spirit of Manifest Destiny, and his victory was a mandate for American expansion. Polk compromised with the British over Oregon, but a boundary dispute with Mexico led to war. Militarily the conflict was a triumph for the United States, and in the peace the United States gained California and much of the southwest, increasing the size of the United States by one third. Yet Polk's great achievement also sowed the seeds of disaster. The question of whether slavery would be allowed in the new territories soon arose and helped polarize American politics in the crucial decade of the 1850s. Victory in the Mexican war helped set the stage for the Civil War. Even as the war was in its early stages, in August 1846, a Democratic representative from Pennsylvania named David Wilmot submitted an amendment to an appropriations bill barring slavery from any territory taken from Mexico. The Wilmot Resolution passed the House of Representative twice, and was killed in the Senate. It infuriated Southerners and set the stage for debate in the election of 1848. With Polk declining to run for a second term, the Democrats nominated Lewis Cass of Michigan. Cass first popularized the theory of "popular sovereignty" in the territories. This took the slavery issue out of the halls of Congress, and left the question to be decided by the people of the territories. For many, this seemed a reasonable compromise, and popular sovereignty would later be taken up by Stephen Douglas in the 1850s. The Whigs fell back on an old formula in 1848, and nominated Zachary Taylor, a popular commander in the Mexican War, who had no overt political philosophy. They kept their platform as vague as possible. A third force in the election was the Free Soil Party, composed of Northern antislavery men. Some were abolitionists who opposed slavery as a moral issue. Others believed that slavery hurt the prospects of free labor. The Free-Soilers nominated Martin Van Buren for president. Their slogan of "Free soil, free speech, free labor, and free men" would reverberate over the next decade. Taylor's heroic appeal won him the election. The Free-Soilers won almost 300,000 votes and may have cost Cass the electoral votes in New York and the election. By the time Taylor took office, the discovery of gold had transformed California. Tens of thousands of people poured into the territory. In 1849, the Californians asked for admission to the Union as a free state. This set off a political crisis. Southerners opposed this rapid move to statehood, and the prospect of another free state crystallized their fears over abolitionist agitation and the Underground Railroad. President Taylor supported the admission of California and asked that discussions of slavery be avoided. This did not have any effect other than angering Southerners. Some Southern "fire-eaters" even talked of secession. Stepping in to avert this danger to the Union was the "Great Pacificator" Henry Clay. Seventy-three years of age and a veteran engineer of compromises since that of 1820, Clay proposed a series of measures designed to offer something to everyone. California would be admitted as a free state. The New Mexico Territory would be organized without reference to slavery. The boundary between Texas and New Mexico would be adjusted. The United States would assume the debt of the Republic of Texas. Slavery would be left alone in the District of Columbia. The slave trade would be banned in the District of Columbia. A fugitive slave law would be enacted. Congress would disavow any authority to interfere with the interstate slave trade. Clay made an impassioned speech on behalf of his compromise. Two other legislative giants also weighed in. The dying John C. Calhoun argued that the compromise did not go far enough in protecting the South. Daniel Webster made one of his most eloquent speeches supporting the compromise. Younger men spoke up. William Seward opposed the compromise because of its provisions protecting slavery. Stephen Douglas played a crucial role lining up votes behind the compromise. The prospects for the compromise improved when President Taylor died suddenly on July 9, 1850. His successor, Millard Fillmore, was a strong supporter of Clay's program. In September the compromise was passed in a series of five bills, with Clay and Douglas putting together different combinations of votes to pass each. In the short run, the Compromise of 1850 saved the Union and seemed to settle sectional differences. But tensions remained strong under surface comity. The Fugitive Slave Act, which opened the North to slave-hunters and which fined and jailed Northerners who helped fugitive slaves, was very unpopular in the North, and fueled antislavery sentiment. The political landscape would shift in the 1850s as the Whig Party disappeared, eventually to be replaced by the antislavery Republican Party. When Stephen Douglas passed his Kansas-Nebraska Act in 1854, the passions raised by the Mexican war would reemerge, and the United States would be set on a course to Civil War.

To do well on this question, be sure to follow all the directions! Provide a historically plausible thesis that addresses all aspects of the prompt. Your thesis should respond to and go beyond the prompt. Restating or paraphrasing the prompt is not an acceptable thesis. Use your historical analytical skills to construct your argument, emphasizing such aspects of the subject matter as cause and effect or change and continuity. Your thesis can be at the beginning or the end of your essay; it will not be counted if it is anywhere else. Put your response in a broader context, referring to historical factors preceding, following, or taking place at the same time as the subject of the prompt. Provide as much historical evidence as you can. You want to do this both to provide information that is relevant to the subject matter and to support your argument. Finally, show a complex understanding of the subject matter of the prompt. You can do this in a variety of ways. For instance, you can connect this subject matter to similar historical events in another period. Other possibilities include highlighting differing perspectives on the subject matter, or exploring differing interpretations of the causes of the historical event that you are discussing. Relate this to your larger argument; an off-hand reference will not be counted.

Here is some information to help with this.

4. Before the Spanish American War, the United States did not play a prominent role as a great power, despite its burgeoning economic strength. Beginning in the 1880s, the United States did begin building up a modern navy, leading to an interest in coaling stations in places like Pearl Harbor in Hawaii and Pago Pago in Samoa. Despite this, as late as 1893, President Grover Cleveland would refuse an opportunity to annex the Hawaiian Islands. The Spanish American War of 1898 ushered the United States onto the world stage. After rapidly defeating the obsolescent naval forces of Spain, the United States became an imperial power. Though Cuba, the occasion of the war with Spain, would be given a measure of independence, the United States retained control of Puerto Rico, Guam, and the Philippines. The Philippines, with the magnificent harbor at Manila Bay, were seen as a way station to China, which many Americans hoped would become a major market for American goods. This interest in China led the United States in 1900 to join in the suppression of the antiforeigner Boxer Rebellion. The United States, through its "Open Door" notes, attempted to keep the Chinese market from being closed by colonial powers. This would be the keystone of American foreign policy in China through World War II. In the early twentieth century the United States exerted its power in the western hemisphere, building the Panama Canal and, through President

Theodore Roosevelt's corollary to the Monroe Doctrine, asserting a right to police the small republics of the Caribbean and Central America. American troops would be repeatedly sent to restore order in countries like Haiti and Nicaragua through the early 1930s. Under Theodore Roosevelt, the United States was accepted into the club of great powers. Roosevelt won a Nobel Peace Prize for helping negotiate an end to the Russo-Japanese War of 1904-1906, and American delegates took part in the 1906 Algeciras Conference. The United States attempted to remain neutral during World War I, while maintaining a profitable trading relationship with Britain and France. Germany's unrestricted submarine campaign brought the United States into the war in 1917. American troops helped turn the tide against Germany on the Western Front. President Woodrow Wilson's Fourteen Points became, for many people around the world, a blueprint for a better postwar world. For a time, as the Treaty of Versailles was being negotiated at Paris in 1919, Woodrow Wilson seemed to be the most influential figure in the world. This power evaporated quickly. Wilson did not prevent the imposition of harsh peace terms on the Germans. His League of Nations failed to win ratification in the United States Senate. The United States did not become isolationist in the 1920s. President Warren Harding hosted the 1921–1922 Washington Disarmament Conference. The 1924 Dawes Plan helped stabilize German and European finances. The Great Depression turned the United States inward. President Hoover did little to oppose Japanese aggression in Manchuria in 1931. President Franklin Roosevelt "torpedoed" the London Economic Conference, attempting to stabilize the international economy so he could focus on fighting the Depression in the United States. Both Hoover and Roosevelt improved relations with Latin America through the "Good Neighbor" policy, which rejected the role of the United States as "policeman" of the Western Hemisphere. The mid-1930s saw the height of American isolationism with the passage of the 1935, 1936, and 1937 Neutrality Laws, essentially designed to prevent another World War I by forbidding Americans to trade with warring countries or travel on belligerent ships. During the late 1930s, President Roosevelt became increasingly alarmed at the aggressions of Japan, Italy, and Germany. Following the outbreak of World War II in 1939, he took steps to allow trade with Britain and France, and began a major rearming program. This military buildup intensified after the defeat of France in 1940. Roosevelt assisted Britain with the Destroyers for Bases Deal, giving Britain old American destroyers in exchange for leases on British bases in the Western Hemisphere. In 1941, Roosevelt persuaded Congress to pass the Lend-Lease Act, allowing him to give military supplies to Britain and other countries fighting Germany. The United States was waging an undeclared naval war on the Atlantic Ocean by late 1941, as the United States Navy helped protect British convoys from German submarines. In the Pacific, Japan launched an all-out war on China in 1937. Following the defeat of France in 1940, the Japanese moved into French Indochina. In 1941, the Japanese established more definite control over Indochina. The United States finally halted its trade in metals and oil with Japan, and demanded that the Japanese end the war in China. The Japanese preferred to fight, hoping to conquer the resources they needed in the British and Dutch colonies of Malaysia and Indonesia. To do this safely, they had to neutralize the American fleet at Pearl Harbor. The December 7, 1941, Japanese attack on Pearl Harbor brought the United States into World War II. American military and industrial power proved crucial in defeating Japan and Germany. American policymakers, remembering the failure of Woodrow Wilson at the end of World War I, were determined that the United States would play a constructive role in the postwar world. The United States hosted the new United Nations. The United States played a key role in the 1944 Bretton Woods Conference that laid the foundations of the World Bank, the International Monetary Fund (IMF), and the postwar international economic order. Complicating a postwar settlement was a growing conflict with the Soviet Union, an ally during World War II, but a Communist totalitarian state run by the dictator Josef Stalin. At the end of World War II, the Soviets brutally established their control in Eastern Europe. There was fear that they might try and subvert the pro-American governments of Western Europe. The American policy of containment began to take shape. In 1947, President Harry Truman used a bill to provide support to Greece and Turkey to announce what became known as the Truman Doctrine: the United States would assist any nation threatened by Communism, either by external attack or internal subversion. In 1949, after an abortive Soviet attempt to blockade West Berlin, the United States and 11 other countries formed the North Atlantic Treaty Organization (NATO). NATO gave the signatories collective security against a Soviet attack. The United States, for the first time since the end of the French alliance in 1800, had entered into an alliance with other countries. The United States was now committed to the defense of Western Europe. This would be a cornerstone of American policy for decades to come.

Scoring the Long Essay Question

TASKS	POINTS
Give yourself 1 point if you wrote a thesis that responds to the question with a historically plausible argument. You can't just restate or repeat the question. Your thesis can be expressed in one or more sentences in the introduction or conclusion of your essay.	
Give yourself 1 point if you put the question into a wider historical context. To do this, you should connect the topic of the question to events, developments, or processes that take place before, during, or after the period immediately covered in the question. A brief reference or phrase will not earn you this point.	
You can earn up to 2 points for providing evidence in your essay. Give yourself 1 point if you provided examples of historical information that are relevant to the question. This will increase to 2 points if you used well-chosen examples of historical information that support your argument.	
Give yourself 1 point if you used your historical analytical skills, such as identifying cause and effect, in constructing an argument that addresses the question.	
Give yourself 1 point if you demonstrated a complex understanding of the subject of the question, using historical evidence to modify, qualify, or confirm your argument. This understanding must be used to develop your argument, and can't merely be a brief reference or phrase.	
TOTAL (6 points possible)	

AP U.S. HISTORY DIAGNOSTIC TEST

Scoring Conversion

You can get a rough approximation of your score on the AP U.S. History exam. Use the answer explanations to award yourself points on the free-response questions. Then compute your raw score using the worksheet below. Finally, refer to the table below to translate your raw score to an AP score of 1 to 5.

Section I: Multiple Choice

Number of questions answered correctly (55 possible) _____ × 1.31 = _____

Section I: Short Answer

Question 1 (3 points possible): _____ × 4 = _____

Question 2 (3 points possible): _____ × 4 = _____

Question 3 or 4 (3 points possible): _____ × 4 = _____

Section II: Document-Based Question

Question 1 (7 points possible) _____ × 6.43 = _____

Section II: Long Essay Question

Question 2, 3, or 4 (6 points possible) _____ × 4.5 = _____

RAW SCORE: Add your points in the column above (180 possible): _____

Conversion Table

RAW SCORE	APPROXIMATE AP SCORE
Low 110s to 180	5
Mid-90s to low 110s	4
Mid-70s to mid-90s	3
Mid-50s to mid-70s	2
Below the mid-50s	1

STEP 3

Develop Strategies for Success

CHAPTER 4

Mastering Skills and Understanding Themes for the Exam

IN THIS CHAPTER

Summary: The exam emphasizes historical analytical skills and a thematic approach to U.S. history. You will need to familiarize yourself with the specific skills and themes listed in this chapter and then be able to apply these skills and interpret these themes using your knowledge of U.S. history.

Key Ideas

✪ Just memorizing facts will not be enough to do well on the new exam.

✪ You should become familiar with the two historical practices and four historical analytical skills.

✪ You should also become familiar with seven historical themes.

✪ All the questions on the new exam will be based on one or more of these skills and themes.

The AP U.S. History Exam

If you have taken the diagnostic exam, it should be clear that the questions on the exam—multiple choice, short answer, document-based question (DBQ), and long essay—require you to think in terms of specific historical practices, historical analytical skills, and historical themes. To do well, it is essential that you have a thorough understanding of the two historical practices, four historical analytical skills, and seven historical themes. You should try to regularly utilize them throughout your study of U.S. history. Your teacher will provide you with many activities that will allow you to work with these skills and themes. Whether you are part of a study group or studying alone, you should find additional opportunities to use them while reviewing major events in U.S. history. These skills and themes are the tools you should use to analyze—not just memorize—the information that you are introduced to in your classwork and reading.

Reasoning Skills, Historical Analytical Skills, Historical Themes, and Exam Questions

Reasoning Skills

Doing well with questions on the AP U.S. History exam will involve mastering three reasoning skills.

1. **Comparing historical developments.** This involves relating and contrasting events across time and space, creating contexts by which to evaluate them.
2. **Identifying cause and effect.** This involves establishing the relationships between events, determining the ways historical actions and forces influence each other.
3. **Differentiating between change and continuity.** This involves identifying patterns over periods of time and demonstrating how changes and continuities are related to broad historical forces.

Historical Analytical Skills

Questions on the AP U.S. History exam will all involve one or more of the historical analytical skills in the following list. Be sure you practice these skills as you review for the exam.

1. **Processes and developments.** Be able to identify and analyze historical processes and developments.
2. **Sources and context.** Be able to identify, analyze, and put into context primary and secondary sources.
3. **Arguments in sources.** Be able to identify and analyze arguments found in primary and secondary sources.
4. **Historical context.** Be able to identify and analyze the context of historical events.
5. **Finding connections.** Be able to identify and analyze connections and patterns linking historical events.
6. **Making an argument.** Be able to explain an argument and support it with historical evidence.

Historical Themes

All questions on the AP U.S. History exam will relate in some way to the following overarching themes of U.S. History. You'll need to use your historical analytical skills to explain, interpret, and apply these themes of U.S. history.

1. **American identities.** This addresses the development of American nationalism, and within this larger national identity, the emergence of various group identities during the course of U.S. history.
2. **American economies and technology.** This addresses the ways that Americans have structured their economic systems over time, and how technological change has affected economic development in the United States.

3. **American populations.** This addresses the movements to and within the United States by various groups of people.
4. **Political power in the United States.** This addresses the role of government in American history, the understandings Americans have had about the nature of government, and the ways people in the United States have organized themselves to shape the political process.
5. **The United States in world affairs.** This addresses the ways in which the American colonies and the United States interacted with other peoples and governments, in North America and around the world.
6. **The influence of American geography and environment.** This addresses the ways the physical environment and geography of America, including such factors as climate, plants, animals, and natural resources, helped shape the history of the United States.
7. **American culture and conviction.** This addresses the significance of ideas, religious beliefs, and cultural values as formative influences In American history.
8. **Social systems and structures.** This addresses the ways changing modes of social organization have influenced American history.

To illustrate the ways in which the questions on the new exam expect you to make use of these historical analytical skills and historical themes, let's look at a few examples.

Sample Multiple-Choice Questions

Multiple-choice questions on the exam will often begin with a look at some historical document that you will be asked to read, analyze, and interpret. Following the document below, we'll try some sample multiple-choice questions like those you'll find on the actual test.

> Everybody is talkin' these days about Tammany men growin' rich on graft, but nobody thinks of drawin' the distinction between honest graft and dishonest graft. There's all the difference in the world between the two. Yes, many of our men have grown rich in politics. I have myself. I've made a big fortune out of the game, and I'm gettin' richer every day, but I've not gone in for dishonest graft—blackmailin' gamblers, saloonkeepers, disorderly people, etc.—and neither has any of the men who have made big fortunes in politics.
>
> There's an honest graft, and I'm an example of how it works. I might sum up the whole thing by sayin': "I seen my opportunities and I took 'em."
>
> Just let me explain by example. My party's in power in the city, and it's goin' to undertake a lot of public improvements. Well, I'm tipped off, say, that they're goin' to lay out a new park in a certain place.
>
> I see my opportunity and I take it. I go to that place and I buy up all the land I can in the neighborhood. Then the board of this or that makes its plan public, and there is a rush to get my land, which nobody cared for particular before.
>
> Ain't it perfectly honest to charge a good price and make a profit on my investment and foresight? Of course, it is. Well, that's honest graft.
>
> —William Riordan, *Plunkitt of Tammany Hall*, 1905

Let's look at a sample multiple-choice question based on this passage:

1. The perspective of George Washington Plunkitt expressed in the passage above most directly reflected the attitudes of which of the following?
   A. Progressive political reformers
   B. The owners of big businesses and trusts
   C. Supporters of the Social Gospel
   D. Urban machine politicians

The correct answer is D. George Washington Plunkitt was a leader in New York City's Tammany Hall political machine, and his questionable distinction between "dishonest" and "honest" graft is a justification of the fact that, like many machine politicians, he used his position and insider knowledge to make money at the taxpayers' expense. Note that you have to use historical practices and historical analytical skills to answer the question, including evaluating and interpreting historical data as you interpret the meaning of the passage, and comparing historical events as you weigh the correct answer against responses reflecting contemporary events, such as the rise of progressivism, the growth of big business, and the efforts of social workers and reformers to ameliorate conditions in the cities, including the Protestant leaders preaching the Social Gospel. The question also asks you to reflect on historical themes, such as political power in the United States, because of its obvious political content, and American populations, because the movement of masses of people into rapidly growing American cities in the late nineteenth century was the essential backdrop to the rise of the great urban political machines.

Let's try another multiple-choice question:

2. Given the perspective expressed by George Washington Plunkitt in the preceding passage, which of the following reforms would he be most likely to oppose?
   A. Civil service reform
   B. Abolitionism
   C. Dechartering the Bank of the United States
   D. Creating Social Security

The correct answer is A. As a machine politician who used his position in the city to feather his nest, George Washington Plunkitt vehemently opposed civil service reform, which would replace machine workers on the city payroll with civil servants who would not owe their livelihood and loyalty to political bosses. A historical analytical skill useful in answering the question is connecting events to broader historical trends, necessary in relating Plunkitt's concerns to the movement for civil service reform in the late nineteenth and early twentieth centuries. Grouping events into periods is essential because the other responses to the question date from other times in American history. Correctly answering the question requires you to connect Plunkitt to what was for him a contemporary reform movement. Historical themes that are important for this question are political power in the United States, because once again we are dealing with politics, and American culture and conviction, because this question asks you to reflect on important social ideas in U.S. history.

Sample Short-Answer Question

Now let's try a short-answer question.

1. Answer A, B, and C.
   A. Briefly explain ONE example of a group that contributed to the rapid settlement of the Trans-Mississippi West in the period 1865–1890.
   B. Briefly explain a SECOND example of a group that contributed to the rapid settlement of the Trans-Mississippi West in the period 1865–1890.
   C. Briefly explain ONE example of a way one of these groups influenced the activity of another of these groups during the rapid settlement of the Trans-Mississippi West.

This question asks you to discuss factors in the rapid opening of the West in the period following the Civil War. You can treat the impact of railroads, the emergence of the great open-range cattle empire, and the rise of a new farming frontier. To answer it, you need to use such historical analytical skills as differentiating between change and continuity when you relate one of the options to a broader historical pattern, and identifying cause and effect, as you explore how one of the options affected another. Relevant historical themes are American economies and technology and the influence of American geography and environment as you analyze economic development in the very distinctive climactic environment of the West in the late nineteenth century. The historical theme of American identities would come into play as you discussed the emergence of distinctive cultures among cattlemen and western farmers.

Sample Essay Question

Long essay questions, including DBQs, can draw on all the historical analytical skills, but they often especially test your skill in the historical practices of evaluating and interpreting historical data and creating and assessing historical arguments. Consider a DBQ that begins with the following statement:

Evaluate the extent to which US involvement in World War I was the result of an unrealistic understanding of the freedom of the seas.

In an essay dealing with this position, the historical practices identified above would need to be heavily utilized. Creating and assessing historical arguments and interpreting the past would be important putting it into context and evaluating its strengths and weaknesses. As you do this, you will also rely on the historical theme concerning the United States in world affairs.

In Conclusion

What should be clear by now is that the historical practices, historical analytical skills, and historical themes discussed in this chapter are the intellectual framework of the AP U.S. History exam. You ought to be as familiar with these practices, skills, and themes as you are with the facts of U.S. history. Mastery of them will enable you to respond effectively to the questions that you will encounter on the test next spring.

CHAPTER 5

Strategies for Approaching Each Question Type

IN THIS CHAPTER

Summary: Knowing how to most efficiently and effectively attack each type of question on the test will help you score higher on the exam. Learn the question-answering strategies in this chapter and practice applying them to the test questions.

Key Ideas

Multiple-Choice Questions

- Multiple-choice questions relate to prompts such as historical texts and images.
- The questions test analytical and interpretive skills as well as factual knowledge.
- Intelligent guessing will improve your score on the test; there is no penalty for guessing.
- There may be more than one possible "right" answer.
- Memorizing the facts is *not* enough.

Short-Answer Questions

- Short-answer questions ask you to make use of your historical analytical skills and thematic knowledge.
- For short-answer questions, it is *not* necessary to develop a thesis statement.

Document-Based Essay Question

- Use an appropriate organizational approach: create a thesis and support it.
- It is not necessary to spend the entire time writing your answer.
- There must be logic to your answer.

✪ Make your essay as readable as possible.

✪ Make sure to comment on all the documents you include in your essay.

✪ It is not necessary to use every single document, but you must use at least six of the seven documents to construct your argument in order to get the maximum number of points possible.

✪ For at least three documents, address one of the following: the point of view of the author, the purpose of the author, the intended audience of the document, the historical context of the document.

✪ The document-based question will ask you to use your historical analytical skills and thematic knowledge while explaining and interpreting events over longer periods of time.

✪ No document-based question will concentrate on material from before 1607 or after 1980.

Long Essay Question

✪ Use an appropriate organizational approach: create a thesis and support it.

✪ Make an outline before you begin to write.

✪ Pick the question you know the most about.

✪ Watch your time!

✪ The long essay question will ask you to use your historical analytical skills and thematic knowledge while explaining and interpreting events over longer periods of time.

✪ No long essay question will concentrate on material from before 1607 or after 1980.

Reading and Interpreting Primary Source Documents

✪ Be prepared to analyze a variety of primary source documents.

Taking the Exam

✪ Come to the exam prepared but relaxed.

Multiple-Choice Questions

All multiple-choice questions will be tied to a prompt. These prompts may be primary source texts, secondary source texts, or images. For each prompt there will be two to six questions. These questions will require you to interpret source material and analyze it in conjunction with your broader historical knowledge. Remember, you will have 55 minutes to answer 55 questions. This does not give you a lot of time to ponder each question.

All questions on the test will have four possible answers. The following question is an example of the format of questions you may encounter on the exam:

The peace, the freedom and the security of ninety percent of the population of the world is being jeopardized by the remaining ten percent who are threatening a breakdown of all international order and law. ... When an epidemic of physical disease starts to spread, the community approves and joins in a quarantine of the patients in order to protect the health of the community against the spread of the disease. ... War is a contagion, whether it is declared or undeclared. It can engulf states and peoples remote from the original scene of hostilities. We are determined to keep out of war, yet we cannot insure ourselves against the disastrous effects of war and the dangers of involvement. We are adopting such measures as will minimize our risk of involvement, but we cannot have complete protection in a world of disorder in which confidence and security have broken down. … Most important of all, the will for peace on the part of peace-loving nations must express itself to the end that nations that may be tempted to violate their agreements and the rights of others will desist from such a course. There must be positive endeavors to preserve peace.

—Franklin D. Roosevelt, "Quarantine" Address, October 5, 1937

1. In the passage above, Franklin D. Roosevelt is expressing concern about which of the following?
A. The economic consequences of the Great Depression
B. The explosion of the U.S.S. *Maine*
C. American interventions in Central America and the Caribbean
D. Aggressive actions by Japan, Italy, and Germany

The correct answer is D. In the "Quarantine" Address, President Franklin D. Roosevelt was warning his fellow Americans about the dangers posed by the military actions taken by Japan in China, Italy in Ethiopia, and Germany in the Rhineland and Spain. Note that to correctly answer this, you have to understand what President Roosevelt is saying in the passage and put it into the historical context of the 1930s, a time when war clouds were gathering because of the aggressions of the totalitarian states.

Sometimes multiple-choice questions will ask you to make connections between the topic discussed by a source and another historical period. Here is an example:

2. The policy being proposed by Franklin D. Roosevelt in the passage above can *best* be compared to which of the following?
A. The Monroe Doctrine
B. The containment policy
C. George Washington's policy of "no entangling foreign alliances"
D. Isolationism

The correct answer is B. President Roosevelt was calling for a policy in which the "peace-loving nations" combined to "quarantine" the warlike states, dissuading them from further aggressive action. This is similar to the containment policy of the cold war, in which the United States and its allies attempted to halt or "contain" the expansion of communism. Note that the question asks you to compare policies from a wide range of U.S. history.

Useful Hints for the Multiple-Choice Section

• **Carefully consider the document used in the prompt:** Identifying the source and context of the prompt can help in recognizing the correct answer.

• **Guessing:** On the multiple-choice portion of the test, no points are deducted for incorrect responses. Therefore it is to your advantage to guess on every question when you are not sure of the correct answer.

• **There may be more than one possible right answer.** The directions ask you to "select the one that is *best* in each case." Get rid of one or two responses that are obviously incorrect, and focus on the others. For example:

3. Which of the following would be most likely to support the perspective of Franklin D. Roosevelt in the passage above?
  A. A believer in Manifest Destiny
  B. An Isolationist
  C. A supporter of collective security
  D. A Democrat

Looking at the possible answers, let's eliminate those that are obviously incorrect. Manifest Destiny was an ideology of American continental expansionism that flourished in the mid-nineteenth century; it is inapplicable to the situation Roosevelt was describing. Isolationists opposed American interventionism abroad; this runs counter to what Roosevelt was proposing. This leaves C and D. Roosevelt was a Democrat and obviously could normally expect heavy support from members of his party. But a number of Democrats were Isolationists. Supporters of collective security, regardless of party affiliation, believed that the United States should act with other countries to preserve international peace. Therefore, though D is a plausible answer, C is the *best* response.

- **Memorizing the facts is *not* enough.** Although you do need to have a good knowledge of the facts of U.S. history, these questions place a heavy emphasis on analysis and a thematic understanding of the American past.
- **Don't overlook the obvious.** Questions on the AP U.S. History test emphasize major themes in U.S. history. Don't overthink the question. If you think an answer is so obvious that it has to be right, it probably is! The questions in this exam are not designed to test you on obscure trivia.
- **Use a good pencil with a good eraser.** We know that this may seem a little far-fetched, but I have a colleague who is convinced that this is an approach to be emphasized. He maintains that many students get marked off because they don't entirely fill in the bubbles or totally erase when they change their answers. He claims to have proof of this. Don't take this lightly; be sure you don't lower your score just because your eraser left a lot of smudges.

Short-Answer Questions

Short-answer questions require you to prepare brief responses to questions that ask you to address themes in U.S. history and utilize your historical analytical skills. Very important, short-answer questions do *not* require thesis statements. Short-answer questions may relate to prompts similar to those in the multiple-choice questions, or they may ask you to evaluate broad assertions about U.S. history. You will have 40 minutes to answer three short-answer questions. You must answer the first two short-answer questions. You may choose between the third and fourth questions. The first two questions will cover periods 3–8. The third question will cover periods 1–5, and the fourth will cover periods 6–9.

The following question is an example of the format of questions you may encounter on the exam.

1. Answer Parts A, B, and C.
  A. Briefly explain how ONE of the following reform movements transformed American life during the late nineteenth and early twentieth centuries.
  - Populism
  - Progressivism
  - Feminism

B. Explain how your choice affected *one* of the other options.

C. Provide an example of opposition in the late nineteenth and early twentieth centuries to *one* of the options.

Useful Hints for the Short-Answer Section

- **Don't waste time!** You should answer three of these in 40 minutes. Don't get bogged down with an elaborate response—remember that these are *short*-answer questions.
- **Just answer the question.** You don't have to develop a persuasive argument.
- **Be sure to provide supporting facts.** The directions may ask for ONE example or piece of evidence, but it would be to your advantage to provide a few more facts.
- **Write in full sentences.** To properly answer the question, responses need to be in the form of sentences. Fragments and phrases won't cut it.
- **Keep your response inside the box on the answer sheet.** Many short-answer questions are scanned and scored online. Readers scoring online cannot see any writing that is outside the box.

Document-Based Question (DBQ)

During this essay section of the exam, you are required to use a number of documents and previously learned knowledge to answer a question. This question tests your historical analytical skills, your ability to interpret a variety of sources, and your ability to synthesize what you know into an effective response. You will need to craft a thesis that addresses a historical theme or a significant period in U.S. history. *Not all of the information needed to earn a 5 is included in the documents.* You need to bring what you know about the subject of the question to the table as well. In a typical question, you might be presented with a political cartoon, a graph, extracts from speeches and letters, and part of an editorial from the 1850s and asked to discuss the causes of the Civil War. By the time of the AP exam, your teacher will have probably provided you with numerous document-based questions. For a specific example of a DBQ, refer to the DBQ in the diagnostic test in the previous chapter. On the exam, the DBQ will contain no more than seven documents. The document-based question will focus on topics from periods 3–8.

You'll be given a total of 100 minutes to complete both Parts A and B of Section II. It is recommended that you spend 60 of the 100 minutes completing Part A, which is the document-based question.

The rubric used by the readers who will score your exam breaks the scoring into four parts with a possible highest score of 7 points:

A. You will earn 1 point for a thesis that responds to the question with a historically plausible argument. You can't just restate or repeat the question. Your thesis can be expressed in one or more sentences in the introduction or conclusion of your essay. It is always best to put your thesis in the introduction where the reader is more likely to look for it.

B. You will earn 1 point for putting the question into a wider historical context. To do this, you should connect the topic of the question to events, developments, or processes that take place before, during, or after the period immediately covered in the question. A brief reference or phrase will not earn you this point.

C. You can earn up to 3 points for using evidence from within and outside the documents. You will earn 1 point for using the historical content of at least three of the documents to address the question. This will increase to 2 points if you support your argument by using the historical content of at least six of the documents. You must explain the historical significance of these documents. Simply quoting documents does not count. To get the second point, you must relate the six documents to your argument.

You can earn 1 point if you use at least one piece of historical information that goes beyond the evidence in the documents. A brief reference to a piece of information will not earn a point. You must describe how this historical information relates to the question. The historical information for this point must be different from information that you use to earn the point for placing the question in a wider historical context.

D. You can earn 1 point for explaining the point of view of the author, the purpose of the author, or a document's intended audience or historical context for at least three documents. You must explain how or why these are relevant for your argument.

You can earn 1 point for showing a complex understanding of the subject of the question, using historical evidence to modify, qualify, or confirm your argument. This understanding must be used to develop your argument, and it can't be merely a brief reference or phrase. This can be done in a variety of ways, including:

Exploring the complexities of an issue by analyzing multiple variables

Discussing both similarity and difference, both continuity and change, both cause and effect, or multiple causes

Demonstrating relevant and meaningful connections across and within historical periods

Demonstrating the strength of an argument by corroborating multiple perspectives across themes

Modifying or qualifying your argument by examining diverse or alternative perspectives or evidence

The detailed instructions concerning the DBQ that you will get when you take the AP U.S. History exam will remind you to address the points above in your essay. Note that all of these parts emphasize your mastery of historical practices and historical analytical skills. You can place your thesis in the introduction or the conclusion of your essay, though it is usually a good idea to place it in your introduction.

Useful Hints for the DBQ

- **Be aware of the skills needed for the DBQ.** The DBQ will focus on one of the following historical analytical skills: identifying cause and effect, differentiating between change and continuity, comparing historical events, and connecting events to broader historical trends. Answering the DBQ will test your effectiveness with the following historical practices: evaluating and interpreting historical data and creating and assessing historical arguments.
- **Use the standard essay format.** This is the format that you have used for all historical essays. Start off with a thesis and then use analysis of individual documents to prove your thesis. If the documents are presented chronologically, then write about them in the same way. Don't place your discussions of documents on separate pages; keep your paragraphs close together so the reader knows that there is more to come.

- **You don't have to use all the documents, but it might be a good idea.** According to the DBQ instructions, you must use at least six of the seven documents. If possible, use all seven. This way, if you use one document inaccurately you won't lose a point. Also remember to provide information on the author's point of view or intention, the audience, or the historical context of at least three of the documents. Doing this for more than three documents will help you avoid losing a point if you make a mistake "sourcing" one of the documents.
- **You don't need to keep writing on and on.** It is not necessary to spend every second of the 60 minutes writing the essay. Answer the question, including what the documents say and what you can say about them, and be done with it. Remember, some of what you already know has to be included in your answer. You might want to spend up to 15 minutes outlining your answer and 45 minutes writing.
- **There must be logic to your answer.** Organization as well as knowledge is important. Please remember that there is no "right answer" to the DBQ.
- **Spelling:** Many students ask whether spelling counts. The answer is generally, no. Scorers know that you are rushed on these essays; in all probability, if you think your handwriting is bad they have likely seen worse. Nevertheless, do what you can to make your presentation as readable as possible. Avoid writing with a pencil. Avoid messiness—lots of scratch-outs, arrows going off in different directions pointing to material you forgot to insert—as much as is possible under the circumstances. Don't write using extremely small script. It is hard to give a high score to a student if you can hardly read what the student wrote. Also, if you write small, don't use gel pens, because their thick lines blur your script together making it almost impossible to read.
- **Don't waste time with direct quotes from the documents.** It will not help your score to spend time or space including direct quotes from the sources in your DBQ essay. If you are going to quote your sources, it is perfectly acceptable to paraphrase your quote. It is much more important to be sure to comment on any and all quotes that you include in your essay.
- **Answer the question.** This generally involves analysis and interpretation. Simply quoting the documents without analyzing them is not answering the question. You need to relate the documents to each other and their time periods. You should craft a sophisticated argument that explains historical complexity and places the material covered by the question into a broader historical context.
- **Demonstrate your historical knowledge.** To excel on the DBQ you must bring in outside information—the more the better. Don't just mention nouns or proper nouns. This information must be put in context and used to support your argument. Also don't put all your outside information in a prologue with your thesis; instead spread this information throughout your discussion of the documents.
- **Watch the time!** Don't get so wrapped up in the DBQ that you forget that you still have to do a long essay question.

Long Essay Question

Immediately after writing the DBQ essay, you will have to answer a long essay question. You will get to choose which of three questions you will answer. The long essay question asks you to utilize higher-level thinking skills, which means you will be asked to analyze and interpret events and themes of the past rather than simply give some historical facts. It is recommended that you spend 40 of the 100 minutes you are given for Section II of the exam to answer the long essay question.

The following question is an example of the format of questions you may encounter on the exam:

1. Evaluate the extent to which the development of different economic systems in the North and South was a major cause of the Civil War.

The rubric used by the readers who will score your exam breaks the scoring into four parts with a possible highest score of 6 points:

A. You will earn 1 point for a thesis that responds to the question with a historically plausible argument. You can't just restate or repeat the question. Your thesis can be expressed in one or more sentences in the introduction or conclusion of your essay.

B. You will earn 1 point for putting the question into a wider historical context. To do this, you should connect the topic of the question to events, developments, or processes that take place before, during, or after the period immediately covered in the question. A brief reference or phrase will not earn you this point.

C. You can earn up to 2 points for providing evidence in your essay. You will earn 1 point if you provide examples of historical information that are relevant to the question. This will increase to 2 points if you use well-chosen examples of historical information that support your argument throughout the essay.

D. You can earn up to 2 points for analysis and reasoning. You will earn 1 point if you use your historical analytical skills, such as identifying cause and effect, in constructing an argument that addresses the question. This will increase to 2 points if you show a complex understanding of the subject of the question, using historical evidence to modify, qualify, or confirm your argument. This understanding must be used to develop your argument, and it can't merely be a brief reference or phrase. This can be done in a variety of ways, including:

Exploring the complexities of an issue by analyzing multiple variables

Discussing both similarity and difference, both continuity and change, both cause and effect, or multiple causes

Demonstrating relevant and meaningful connections across and within historical periods

Demonstrating the strength of an argument by corroborating multiple perspectives across themes

Modifying or qualifying your argument by examining diverse or alternative perspectives or evidence

The prompt for the question will indicate what historical analytical skills are being emphasized. Use of these historical analytical skills is just as important as the effective use of factual evidence. You will pick the long essay that you answer from three options, focusing on periods 1–3, 4–6, and 7–9.

Useful Hints for the Long Essay Question

Use the organizational approach that you have probably utilized in answering long essay questions all year. Specifically this means you should:

- **Create a thesis.** What will your essay say? Decide the position you will take and then clearly state that position.
- **Write an effective opening statement.** This is crucial. Your thesis should be part of your opening statement.
- **Support your opening statement with historical facts.** Don't include facts for the sake of including them: make sure you use the historical facts you mention to support your opening argument throughout the essay.

- **If you can, include a discussion of counterarguments.** This shows that you thoroughly understand the issue at hand. This is usually done after you have supported your opening statement with sufficient evidence. This section often begins with "However, some historians believe ..." and discusses and evaluates evidence that contradicts your thesis.
- **Don't forget a conclusion.** An effective conclusion includes a restatement of your thesis.
- **Make a rough outline before you begin to write.** Make sure to answer the question. Don't just go around in circles with information you know about the topic in question.
- **Be sure to pick the question that you know the most about.** I have known students who said they chose a specific question because it "looked easier." Avoid that approach. You'll do your best on the question about which you have the most historical knowledge.
- **Watch your time!** Finally, don't spend too much time on your outline. If you decide to do the long essay before the DBQ, don't forget that you still have that task before you.

Using Primary Source Documents

As a student of AP U.S. History, you will undoubtedly be spending a lot of time this year analyzing primary source documents. Your teacher will probably give you a number of them to read during the year. The document-based question (DBQ) that is on every AP examination will most likely ask you to read and interpret a number of primary sources and then to make a historical argument based upon them.

Historical documents, accounts, and books can be either primary or secondary sources. A secondary source is an account written after the fact. A chapter in your textbook is a secondary source, as is a biography, for example, of Franklin D. Roosevelt written in 2005. However, when historians write secondary source accounts, their research should include a thorough study of the available primary sources. A primary source is a document from the era or person in question. A primary source relating to George Washington might be a letter that George Washington wrote when he was at Valley Forge, an account on Washington written by someone who knew him personally, or a portrait of Washington that was done when he was alive. Primary sources relating to the 1950s might be a speech made by Senator Joseph McCarthy, a recording of the song "Hound Dog" by Elvis Presley, or an episode of the television show *The Adventures of Ozzie and Harriet*. (Note that primary source documents are not limited to written documents.) Secondary source accounts such as your textbook usually have excerpts from various primary source accounts scattered throughout the chapters.

Analyzing primary source documents allows you to study history as a historian does. When you are analyzing, for example, the actual text of a fireside chat given by Franklin D. Roosevelt in 1933, you are the one doing the historical analysis; no other historian or author is doing the work for you.

Types of Primary Source Documents

Types of primary source documents that you will be reading will likely include:

- **Documents published during the time period.** These will include magazine articles, newspaper accounts, official government documents, posters, Supreme Court decisions, novels written during the era, and countless other sources.
- **Resources published after the fact.** These will include letters and diaries written by historical (and nonhistorical) figures that were not originally meant for publication.

These can be incredibly revealing; many politicians, for example, are much more honest in their diary entries than they are when they are giving speeches to the public. Oral histories are also very valuable and can be found at many local historical societies. A wonderful primary source, for example, would be the transcript (or audiotape) of a "common person" telling about the effects of the Great Depression on his or her family and community.

- **Visual documents.** Paintings and photographs can provide incredibly revealing details about any time period you may be studying. Recently, the photographs of people waiting for help after Hurricane Katrina told more about the suffering of New Orleans than a thousand-word article could have. In 1945, photographs from recently liberated Nazi concentration camps shocked the world. Newsreel and television footage of historical events can be invaluable.

- **Films.** Movies from any era can provide a fascinating window into the values and beliefs of that period. By watching a film from, for example, the 1980s, you can get an idea of how people talked, what they wore, and what they believed in that era. A 1967 movie, *Bonnie and Clyde*, glorified the lives of Bonnie Parker and Clyde Barrow, two small-time gangsters who continually flouted authority during the Great Depression. Although this film was about the 1930s, it perfectly reflected the disrespect for authority of many young people in the late 1960s.

- **Songs, recordings, etc.** Sources that one can listen to can also be valuable. As with films, songs are very valuable windows into the culture and values of a time period, whether it is "Fight the Power" by Public Enemy or "Masters of War" by Bob Dylan. Listening to speeches given by historical figures can also be a valuable historical tool.

Analyzing Primary Source Documents

It should be remembered that virtually every single primary source document contains some amount of bias. Memoirs written by many historical figures are generally self-serving and do not dwell on mistakes and problems from the writer's past. It is virtually impossible to write about anything without bias; therefore, it is critical to consider this when evaluating primary sources. A source in which an observer discusses the impact that Theodore Roosevelt had on people when he met them would be influenced by preexisting judgments and opinions the author already had about Theodore Roosevelt. As a result, it is necessary to use a number of primary sources when evaluating a historical figure, event, or era.

There are many methods that historians and students can utilize when studying primary source documents. When looking at a document, try to find some information about its producer. What was the relationship of the author to the person or event being described? Did the producer have preexisting biases toward the subject of the document? How far after the events being described was the document written? Another important question is the audience; the historian/student should identify the target group at which the document was aimed, and whether or not this might have influenced what was stated by the author.

Students wanting more specific information on analyzing primary source documents can go to the Teacher Resources page at the Library of Congress and the Primary Sources and Research Tools page at the Wisconsin Historical Society.

Review the Knowledge
You Need to Score High

CHAPTER 6

Settling of the Western Hemisphere (1491–1607)

IN THIS CHAPTER

Summary: There were several reasons why Europeans became interested in the Americas during this period. Economic, political, and religious factors were most important. The Spanish originally viewed the Americas as a barrier to a direct route to the Indies. However, soon they developed a large empire in South and Central America and viewed the region as a potential source of tremendous wealth. Some Native American tribes had developed complex civilizations in the years before the Europeans arrived. The ecosystem of the Americas was drastically altered by the arrival of the Europeans.

Key Concept

On the North American continent, contact among the peoples of Europe, the Americas, and West Africa created a new world.

Keyword

Columbian Exchange: exchange of crops, animals, diseases, and ideas between Europe and colonies of the Western Hemisphere that developed in the aftermath of the voyages of Columbus.

Native America

The Europeans did not encounter a cultural or political vacuum when they arrived in the Americas. North and South America were populated by a great number of peoples, ranging in social complexity from hunter-gatherer groups to city-based empires. In Mexico, the warlike Aztecs carved out an empire centered on their magnificent city of Tenochtitlan, crisscrossed with canals and adorned with great temples and palaces. Here flowed the tribute of their subject peoples, and also long lines of captives fated to be bloodily sacrificed to appease the Aztecs' gods. The Inca created the largest empire in the Americas; with its capital in Cusco, Peru, the Inca Empire stretched south to parts of what are now Chile and Argentina, and north to portions of modern Colombia. The Inca Empire was a highly organized state, held together by the most impressively developed road system in the Americas. Parts of this extensive network of roads still exist today.

In North America, the Mississippian culture arose in the Mississippi River Valley and then spread into what is now the Midwestern and southeastern United States. The Mississippian culture flourished from around A.D. 800 to 1600 and was notable for its urban development and the mounds it built, upon which temples and other buildings were erected. The great city of Cahokia, in Illinois, at its peak in the 1200s may have been home to 20,000 people. As in the Mississippi River Valley, the cultures of the Northeast and Atlantic seaboard consisted of communities with mixed agricultural and hunter-gatherer lifestyles. This contributed to the establishment of more permanent villages. In the Southwest, the Puebloans built villages and towns, sometimes in the faces of cliffs for greater protection. The peoples of the Southwest relied heavily on the cultivation of maize, which spread northward from Mexico. This hearty crop contributed to the settlement of these civilizations, as they could plant and harvest their food in one place, creating a more sedentary lifestyle. This allowed for greater economic development as well as social diversification within the communities. The Pueblo people also developed advanced irrigation tactics to help combat the area's arid conditions. These complex irrigation systems allowed for the increased cultivation of maize, as well as squash and beans. Collectively, these crops were known as the "three sisters." Many other North American peoples did not live in permanent settlements; instead they lived a nomadic existence, following the movement of fish and game. Some people lived in villages that moved from time to time as resources were depleted. This was especially true of the peoples of the Great Basin and the grasslands of the Western Plains, who were forced to follow their food sources due to the aridity of the region. While the natives in these regions also planted the "three sisters," they were not successful unless planted along a river. Instead, these tribes focused on collecting a wide variety of plant resources and hunting wild game. In the Western Plains, the main food source was the American buffalo. Tribes followed the migration patterns of the buffalo, and after hunting them using spears and bows and arrows, they used all parts of the animal.

In the Northwest and present-day California, nomadic lifestyles were common. The abundance of resources meant they did not need to develop agriculture to survive. In the Northwest, tribes became skilled fishermen, as they learned how to utilize the waterways of the region. Californian tribes were prosperous due to the diversity of plant and animal life available to them. They hunted and gathered on a seasonal basis, thereby practicing a subsistence economy. Some areas, however, supported permanent villages due to the plentiful resources provided by the ocean.

The first English settlers in North America encountered people collectively known as Woodland Indians. The Woodland Indians lived on the bounty of the eastern forests, hunting, gathering, and often planting their food. Two of the major language groups among the Woodland Indians were Algonquian and Iroquoian. The Native peoples of North America were divided into many distinctive tribal groupings.

The Europeans Arrive

In the late 1400s and early 1500s, Europe was going through a period of intense intellectual ferment. The Renaissance saw renewed interest in Europe's Classical Greek and Roman heritage; this rediscovery of the past stimulated new ideas and perspectives on the world. The

Scientific Revolution encouraged an exciting new experimental approach to the acquisition of knowledge about the natural environment; with more knowledge came the power to begin to alter that environment. The Reformation and Catholic Counter-Reformation inaugurated a period of religious upheaval leading to a flowering of religious fervor but also to intense religious conflict that would dominate international relations in Europe for more than a century. This period saw the inventions of technologies crucial to exploration. The Portuguese developed the caravel, a sailing ship capable of long ocean voyages. Improved navigational aids, such as the **astrolabe** and compass, made such voyages more practicable. Ever since the **Crusades**, which reintroduced Europeans to the markets of the East, demand had escalated for spices and other Asian goods. European merchants, blocked from the sources of these goods by the Islamic powers of the Middle East, yearned for different routes to Asia. As the medieval period drew to a close, states were growing more powerful; kings had the resources to finance overseas expeditions. All the pieces were coming together for an explosion of European exploration around the world.

Columbus

In this period of expanding intellectual horizons, many Europeans were looking beyond their traditional boundaries to the wider world. Prince Henry the Navigator of Portugal sponsored voyages of discovery to the Azores in the Atlantic and along the coast of Africa in the mid-1400s. After Henry's death, Portuguese mariners continued their explorations along the African coastline, reaching the Cape of Good Hope at the southern tip of Africa in 1488. A decade later, the Portuguese explorer Vasco da Gama led an expedition around the Cape of Good Hope and sailed on to India. Da Gama was the first person to succeed in opening a direct link between Europe and the markets of Asia.

Christopher Columbus was a Genoese navigator with a dream. He believed that by sailing due west across the Atlantic Ocean, he would reach China and open a trade route that would allow the treasures of the East to flow into Europe. He was not the first person to think of this. No serious scholar or navigator in the 1400s thought that the Earth was flat. But most scholars correctly believed that the Earth was so big that any ship sailing west into the Atlantic would run out of provisions before it reached Asia. Columbus's enthusiasm for this voyage was based on a mistake; he believed that the globe was smaller than it actually is. Hoping to find a sponsor for his voyage, Columbus first approached the Portuguese. Confident in the prospects opening up as a result of their discovery of a sea route to India, the Portuguese turned him down. Columbus turned next to King Ferdinand and Queen Isabella of Spain, who had just unified their country. These monarchs decided to take a chance on this persuasive visionary and provided Columbus with the resources to outfit and crew three small ships. After a long voyage, Columbus sighted land on October 12, 1492. Columbus landed on an island in the Bahamas, which he named San Salvador. Believing that he had reached the East Indies, Columbus called the native people he met "Indians." To his dying day, Columbus believed that he had reached the outer regions of Asia. In fact, he had reached a New World and had launched a new epoch in human history.

Columbus was a man of his time, not a modern anthropologist or social worker. He claimed his discoveries for Spain and regarded himself as the governor of the lands he had found. He hoped to convert the native people to Christianity; he also expected them to accept their new lot as subjects of the king and queen of Spain. Beginning with Columbus, the Spanish colonists forced Native Americans to work for them. The **encomienda** system forced Native Americans onto Spanish plantations in exchange for the dubious benefit of Spanish "protection." Those who refused were hunted down and often killed. However, many more Native Americans died of the diseases that the Europeans inadvertently brought with them. These diseases were the most lethal dimension of an immense transfer of plants and animals back and forth between the continents of Europe and North America. This flow of products across the Atlantic, known as the **Columbian Exchange**, permanently altered both continents. Another exchange was initiated in the 1500s. As new cash crops like sugar developed in the Americas, the European colonizers ran out of Native American labor. Beginning in the 1540s, African slaves were sold to colonists. This was the origin of the great African diaspora in the Americas.

Cortes in Mexico

The people whom Columbus first encountered lived in relatively simple societies. They possessed small amounts of gold, which greatly intrigued the Spanish, who wanted to find the source of this precious metal. The Spanish learned that on the mainland of Mexico, great Native American states existed, some possessing immeasurable wealth. In 1519, Hernando Cortes led a small army of 500 men from Cuba to Mexico. Here he encountered representatives of the great Aztec Empire. The Aztecs did not know what to make of Cortes; some thought that he was a god. Through a ruthless combination of force and diplomacy, Cortes made his way to the Aztec capital of Tenochtitlan. Here he was treated as a guest by the Aztec ruler, Montezuma. Relations soon deteriorated between the Spanish and the Aztecs. In the ensuing violence, Montezuma was killed, and Cortes and remnants of his army were forced from the city. Cortes rebuilt his forces and organized a coalition of tribes who hated their Aztec overlords for requiring them to supply victims for sacrifice. He besieged and overran Tenochtitlan in 1521, destroying the Aztec Empire. Cortes was one of the first and greatest of the Spanish conquistadors to overthrow the native states of Mexico, Central America, and Peru. The conquistadors incorporated the subjugated Native Americans into a vast new empire that was soon sending a glittering stream of gold and silver back home to Spain.

After finding wealth in Mexico, the Spanish hoped to continue expansion into the present-day Southwest. It was here they encountered the Pueblo people. Establishing a political center in Santa Fe, New Mexico, the Spanish sent Catholic missionaries to build churches and convert natives to Christianity. The Pueblo people grew tired of the demand for food and labor by the Spanish, as well as the attempts at conversion by the missionaries. In 1680, led by their leader Pope, they revolted against the Spanish in what became known as the Pueblo Revolt, or Pope's Rebellion. After successfully driving Spanish settlers out of New Mexico, the Pueblo enjoyed 12 years of independence before the Spanish returned and took control of the area once again.

As more Spanish conquistadores flocked to the New World searching for gold and glory, the Spanish developed a caste system for their expanding empire. At the top of this new societal pyramid were the peninsulares, or those who had full Spanish blood and were born in Spain. Next were criollos, who were Spaniards born in the Americas. Following criollos were mestizos, descendants of a Spaniard and a Native American, and mulattoes, descendants of a Spaniard and an African slave. At the bottom of the pyramid were Native Americans and slaves.

Chapter Review

Rapid Review

- Economic difficulties in Europe, the desire for geographic knowledge, the desire to acquire lands, riches, and raw materials, and the desire to spread Christianity all caused Europeans to become interested in the Americas.
- Cortes, Francisco Pizarro, and other Spanish conquistadors entered much of Central America, South America, the southeastern section of North America, and the area now known as Florida, conquering the Aztecs, the Incas, and other Native American tribes.

Guns, horses, and diseases brought from Europe all aided the Spanish in their efforts to defeat the native tribes.
- The Columbian Exchange was the exchange of animals, plants, diseases, and ideas that took place between the Western Hemisphere and Europe as a result of initial Spanish and Portuguese exploration.

Time Line

2500 BCE: Migration of Asians to the Americas across the Bering Strait begins

1492: Voyage of Columbus to the Americas

1519: Cortes enters Mexico

1520–1530: Smallpox epidemic devastates Native American populations in many parts of South and Central America, virtually wiping out some tribes

1542: Spanish explorers travel through southwestern United States

› Review Questions

Fact Check

Check your knowledge of the historical period covered in this chapter.

1. Which of the following was *not* an initial result of interaction between Spanish explorers and Native Americans?
   A. Diseases that killed many of the Native Americans
   B. Domestication by Native Americans of animals brought by Spanish explorers
   C. Spread of Catholicism among Native Americans
   D. Plants from South and Central America being sent back to Europe

2. Slave labor was brought to the Western Hemisphere by colonists because
   A. the region was lightly populated when the Spanish arrived.
   B. Native Americans were unfamiliar with the tools and methods necessary to harvest sugarcane.
   C. Aztec and Inca leaders had already begun to import slaves even before Spanish explorers arrived.
   D. there was a lack of manpower to do the labor-intensive work of harvesting sugarcane.

3. North American Native American tribes
   A. displayed a uniformity of lifestyle.
   B. modeled themselves after tribes from Central America and Mexico.
   C. were greatly varied in lifestyle and economic systems.
   D. formed alliances on numerous occasions to fight competing tribes.

4. One factor *not* responsible for European expansion into the Western Hemisphere was
   A. desire for economic expansion.
   B. desire to expand Christianity.
   C. democratization of European society.
   D. better shipbuilding and navigational tools.

5. The very first Americans
   A. were nomadic wanderers.
   B. lived in permanent sites.
   C. were subsistence farmers.
   D. predated Spain's arrival in the New World by only two centuries.

Multiple-Choice Questions

Here are multiple-choice questions like the ones on the AP U.S. History exam.

Questions 6–8 refer to the quotation below.

There are three halls in this grand temple, which contain the principle idols; . . . leading from the halls are chapels with very small doors, to which the light is not admitted, nor are any persons except the priests, and not all of them. In these chapels are the images or idols, . . . ; the principal ones, in which the people have greatest faith and confidence, I precipitated from their pedestals, and cast them down the steps of the temple, purifying the chapels in which they had stood, as they were all polluted with human blood, shed in the sacrifices. In the places of these I put images of our Lady and the Saints, which excited not a little feeling in Muteczuma and the inhabitants, who at first remonstrated, declaring that if my proceedings were known throughout the country, the people would rise against me; for they believed that their idols bestowed on them all temporal good, and if they permitted them to be ill-treated, they would be angry and withhold their gifts. . . . I answered, through the interpreters, that they were deceived in expecting any favors from idols, the work of their own hands, formed of unclean things; and that they must learn there was but one God, the universal Lord of all, who had created the heavens and earth, and all things else, and had made them and us. . . .

—Second Letter of Hernando Cortes to Charles V, October 30, 1520

6. This quotation from Cortes's letter to Charles V reflects which of the following attitudes?
   A. A sense of European racial superiority to Native Americans
   B. A desire to Christianize the Native Americans
   C. An intention to extract gold from the Native Americans
   D. A growing European appreciation for the values of other cultures

7. Cortes's actions in Mexico City contributed to which of the following results?
   A. The Spanish conquest of the Aztec Empire
   B. The failure of Cortes's expedition
   C. The cooperation of the Spanish and Aztecs in creating a new society in Mexico
   D. Spanish disinterest in the New World

8. Cortes's expedition to Mexico can best be compared to which of the following?
   A. General Custer at the Battle of the Little Big Horn
   B. The liberation of Europe during World War II
   C. The American Civil War
   D. The American conquest of the Philippines in 1899–1902

Short-Answer Question

The short-answer question below is similar to the ones you'll encounter on the AP U.S. History exam.

9. Answer Parts A, B, and C.
   A. Briefly explain ONE example of how Christopher Columbus's 1492 voyage of discovery transformed life for Native Americans and Europeans.
   B. Briefly explain a SECOND example of how Christopher Columbus's 1492 voyage of discovery transformed life for Native Americans and Europeans.
   C. Briefly explain ONE example of another consequential European voyage of discovery in the period 1480 to 1600.

› Answers and Explanations

1. B. It would take a long time before these animals were used by Native Americans; Native Americans were terrified of them and the Spanish explorers who rode on them.

2. D. Harvesting sugar took a massive amount of manpower. Since the Spanish had killed off a large number of native laborers and many more died from European diseases, slaves were needed.

3. C. There was a tremendous variety in the lifestyles and economic systems of Native Americans living in North America.

4. C. European expansion into the Western Hemisphere was supported and financed by European monarchs; no democratization of society or government was taking place at this time.

5. A. Almost all early Native American tribes were nomadic in nature.

6. B. A major goal of the Spanish colonizers was to Christianize the native peoples of America. The Spanish crown made it clear early in the sixteenth century that this was important, though some conquistadores chose to ignore this in their desire to exploit the people they were conquering.

7. A. The Aztec residents of Tenochtitlan grew angry at Cortes's high-handed actions and rose up in rebellion, expelling him and his troops from the city in 1520. Cortes responded by raising another army, made up mostly of contingents of native peoples hostile to the Aztecs. In 1521, Cortes reconquered the city, ending the Aztec Empire.

8. D. Cortes's expedition can best be compared to the American conquest of the Philippines in 1899–1902. Commodore George Dewey's 1898 victory in the Battle of Manila Bay during the Spanish-American War gave the United States a claim to the Philippines. As part of the Treaty of Paris ending the war, the United States purchased the Philippines from Spain. In the meantime, a Filipino government had been organized with Emilio Aguinaldo at its head. In the 1899–1902 Philippine War, the United States imposed its authority on the Filipinos.

9. Parts A and B: Columbus's voyage opened up lands with vast resources to the Europeans. The Spanish found great supplies of silver and gold in Central and South America. The Europeans also found new crops such as potatoes, maize, and tobacco. For the Native Americans, Columbus's voyage brought dramatic and often disastrous change. European diseases ravaged Native American populations. Europeans began conquering Native American lands, sometimes enslaving conquered populations. European missionaries brought Christianity to the New World. The Europeans also introduced new animals such as horses, pigs, and cattle.

Part C: The Portuguese explorer Bartolomeu Dias sailed around the Cape of Good Hope in Southern Africa in 1488. His countryman Vasco da Gama followed this route and sailed on to India in 1497 to 1499. Ferdinand Magellan led a Spanish expedition that in 1519 to 1522, eventually circumnavigated the globe. In 1497, John Cabot led an English expedition that landed somewhere in modern Canada. The French explorer Jacques Cartier led expeditions that explored the Gulf of St. Lawrence and the St. Lawrence River in Canada.

CHAPTER 7

Colonial America (1607–1650)

IN THIS CHAPTER

Summary: The French settled in Canada and eventually turned to trapping and fur trading. Overcrowding in England and religious persecution were both factors in driving some Englishmen toward America. In the Jamestown colony indentured servants and the first slaves brought to the Americas made up a majority of the workforce. The Massachusetts Bay Colony was established in 1629 by the Puritans; Governor John Winthrop envisioned the colony as a "city upon a hill." Religious dissent led to the founding of several more New England colonies.

Keywords

Puritans: group of religious dissidents who came to the New World so they would have a location to establish a "purer" church than the one that existed in England.
Separatists: religious group that also opposed the Church of England; this group first went to Holland, and then some went on to the Americas.
Indentured servants: individuals who exchanged compulsory service for free passage to the American colonies.

New France

French explorer Jacques Cartier sailed up the St. Lawrence River in what is now Canada in the 1530s. Despite this early start, the French did little to colonize Canada until the arrival of Samuel de Champlain in the early 1600s. The "Father of New France," Champlain founded the settlement of Quebec in 1608. Canada never attracted many French colonists. The wintry climate was uncongenial, and the prospect of living in a wilderness amidst tribes of sometimes hostile Native Americans did not appeal to most inhabitants of Ancien

Régime France. Some of those who might have been willing to move to New France, such as members of the dissident Protestant **Huguenot** minority, were forbidden to settle there by the king. As a result, although farming communities did develop along the St. Lawrence River, key roles in New France were played by Catholic missionaries, fur traders, and soldiers.

Sometimes these missionaries, fur traders, and soldiers did double duty as explorers, striking out deeply into the interior of the continent. The Jesuit priest Jacques Marquette teamed with Louis Jolliet to discover the upper reaches of the Mississippi River. Robert La Salle expanded on these discoveries in the Great Lakes region and along the Mississippi River, establishing a series of forts that laid claim to the Mississippi River Valley for France.

For the most part, the French got along better with the Native American peoples than did the English or Dutch. The French did not need large amounts of land for farming, thus avoiding disputes over land with their Native American neighbors. The French were mainly interested in converting the Native Americans to Christianity and trading for furs. Beyond that, they were generally more respectful of Native American customs and traditions; many French traders and explorers married Native American women. The sometimes heroically self-sacrificing **Jesuit** missionaries were often keen students of Native American culture. As a result, the Jesuit missions were great successes. The Jesuits did better than their **Franciscan** competitors in Spanish North America; the Franciscans' efforts were hurt by Spanish forced labor laws. With the important exception of the Iroquois Confederacy, most Native American tribes allied with the French in their wars with the British in the seventeenth and eighteenth centuries.

At the same time that Samuel de Champlain was pioneering New France, the commercially entrepreneurial Dutch were laying the foundations of their own colonial experiment in North America. Henry Hudson explored the river that would be named after him in 1609. He set up the first Dutch trading posts on Manhattan Island and the site that would eventually become Albany. Here the Dutch bartered for beaver pelts. The settlement of New Amsterdam was officially established on Manhattan in 1625. Though the Dutch prospered with the fur trade, the struggling colony of New Netherland never attracted many settlers and territorially was hemmed in by hostile Native American tribes. Ultimately it was the power of England's Royal Navy that doomed the Dutch colony. In 1664, New Amsterdam surrendered to an English fleet. From that time on, the bustling commercial center on Manhattan was known as New York.

English Interest in America

Population growth in England was spurring colonization. The government saw overseas settlements as a social safety valve, where jobless workers or landless farmers who might otherwise pose a threat to the established order might find new lives. Close to half the white immigrants to the British colonies before the American Revolution arrived as indentured servants, working for a set number of years in return for the price of their passage. A minority of these people were convicts, exported by the authorities to the colonies as a way of reducing the expense of confining them at home.

Another major impetus for English colonization was the quest of religious minorities to find a place where they could practice their faith undisturbed. During the English Reformation of the sixteenth century, the Church of England was established as the officially supported church of the kingdom. While the Church of England rejected the spiritual authority of the Pope in Rome and distanced itself from some Roman Catholic doctrines, it maintained an episcopal structure and liturgical practices rooted in the Catholic past. English **Puritans**, who adhered to the more radically Protestant doctrines of John Calvin intensely disliked what they saw as the Catholic tendencies of the Church of England. Under Queen Elizabeth I, the Puritans had been allowed to worship in their own way. Following the accession of James I to the English throne, the government began to crack down on the Puritan dissidents. By the 1620s and 1630s, many Puritans were looking to America as a refuge from the authorities.

Akin to the Puritans as religious dissenters were the **Separatists**. The Separatists were small groups of Calvinists who went beyond the practice of most Puritans by rejecting any association with the Church of England. One band of Separatists moved to the Netherlands hoping to find religious freedom but soon grew disillusioned as their children began to blend in with their Dutch neighbors.

Jamestown and the Chesapeake Colonies

In 1606, the **London Company** was given a charter by King James I to establish colonies in North America. The investors in this joint-stock company hoped to make a profit from the natural riches of the New World. In 1607, an expedition dispatched by the London Company founded Jamestown, the first permanent English settlement in North America. Unfortunately, the site of Jamestown was swampy and unhealthy; disease and the distaste for agriculture on the part of the adventurers who made up the bulk of the early settlers led to the Starving Time, a period of starvation resulting in the deaths of almost two-thirds of the population. Arguably, only the leadership of Captain John Smith saved the struggling colony.

Relations with the nearby Native American Powhatan Confederacy were difficult. At one point, Smith was captured by the Powhatans and later claimed that he had been saved from execution by Pocahontas, the daughter of the chief. Smith eventually established trade relations with the Powhatans, which helped sustain Jamestown. Pocahontas later married John Rolfe, one of the ablest English settlers. Rolfe played a decisive role in the history of what would become the colony of Virginia by systematizing the cultivation of tobacco. Despite the opposition of King James, who abhorred smoking, tobacco became a highly lucrative cash crop, and guaranteed the future prosperity of the colony.

Tobacco was a labor-intensive crop that dominated the economies of the Chesapeake colonies of Virginia and Maryland. Initially, **indentured servants** were sent to Virginia to work on tobacco plantations. In 1619, a passing Dutch ship paid for a load of supplies with 19 African slaves. Because these slaves had been baptized, they were treated as indentured servants and freed after a period of service. Later in the seventeenth century, more Africans were brought to English America, and slavery became a vital economic institution in the Southern colonies.

As the colonies grew, their need for government did as well. The distance from Great Britain combined with the lack of attention from the king led the colonies to self-govern. In Virginia, the House of Burgesses was established in 1619 and was the first democratically elected legislative assembly in what would become the United States.

Massachusetts and the New England Colonies

While a desire for riches drove the colonization of Virginia, a search for religious freedom spurred the initial settlement of New England. The Separatists who had settled in the Netherlands and grown unhappy there received a charter from the London Company to settle in America. In 1620, a group of them, led by William Bradford, set sail in the

Mayflower. Because they were looking for a place to practice their faith, the settlers saw this voyage as a pilgrimage and became known to history as the "Pilgrims."

After a stormy voyage, the Pilgrims made landfall at Cape Cod in Massachusetts. Before going ashore at a place they called Plymouth Rock, the men among the Pilgrims drew up and signed the Mayflower Compact, which established a representative government for the new colony. This is an early example of a social contract. Because the Pilgrims arrived late in the year and were unused to their new environment, they suffered many hardships and much loss of life. Eventually, with the help of Native Americans like Samoset and Squanto, the Pilgrims' colony of Plymouth became self-sustaining. Though Plymouth endured, it never became a great economic success, and in 1691, it was absorbed into the larger Massachusetts Bay Colony.

Puritans anxious about the deteriorating political and religious situation in England founded the Massachusetts Bay Colony. In America, they hoped to create a truly godly commonwealth, what their leader John Winthrop called a "city upon a hill." In 1629, a large, well-financed, and well-organized expedition sailed to Massachusetts with more than 700 people. They suffered no "starving times" and soon were joined by thousands more settlers. By 1640, over 20,000 people had moved to Massachusetts, which had become a thriving colony with numerous chartered towns, such as Boston and Salem. In addition to small-scale subsistence farming, settlers engaged in lumbering, shipbuilding, and fishing. The Massachusetts Bay Colony was different from Virginia as most of its founders came over as members of family groups rather than as individual adventurers. Given its very different economy, slavery never took root in Massachusetts the way that it did in Virginia.

Most of the colonists were Puritans, and the only men who could vote were freemen who belonged to a Puritan congregation. The elected legislature was called the General Court. John Winthrop was elected governor in 1629 and would hold that office for 20 years. In some ways, Massachusetts was a democratically representative theocracy. While the Puritans were seeking religious freedom for themselves, they were not necessarily interested in it for others. They were creating a polity that reflected their vision of God's commandments; this did not leave room for dissent.

Anne Hutchinson believed that she and others could experience direct revelations from the Holy Spirit and challenged the teaching authority of most of the colony's ministers. This unorthodox position attracted the attention of Governor Winthrop. After a trial, Hutchinson was expelled from the colony. She and her family settled in what would become Rhode Island. Roger Williams criticized the religious establishment in Massachusetts and was forced to leave. He also settled in what would become the more theologically unconstrained colony of Rhode Island. Other offshoots of Massachusetts also sprang up. Thomas Hooker and John Davenport founded settlements that eventually merged in the colony of Connecticut.

New Southern Colonies

In the seventeenth century, English kings sometimes gave grants of land in America to individuals or groups of individuals. In 1632, King Charles I gave a charter to the Calvert family to found the colony that would become Maryland. The Calverts hoped that Maryland would become a refuge for Catholics, who were persecuted in England. Despite some difficulties with Puritan settlers, Maryland became a place where Catholics could worship in peace. Carolina, which later split into North and South Carolina, was a proprietary colony given by King Charles II to a group of aristocrats in the 1660s. Maryland and the Carolinas developed plantation-dominated economies dependent upon slave labor.

Effects of European Settlement

The advent of the Europeans had dramatic consequences for North America. The diseases inadvertently brought by the Europeans devastated the Native Americans. One reason that the Pilgrims were able to easily move into the lands that became Plymouth is that the previous inhabitants had been killed off by maladies brought by earlier visitors. The Europeans brought new plants and animals that reshaped the ecology of North America. The need for labor in the South contributed to an Atlantic slave trade primarily focused on the Caribbean and South America. In the English colonies, the growth of self-government and the gradual emergence of genuine freedom of religion created a society very different from Europe and the rest of the world.

Chapter Review

Rapid Review

To achieve the perfect 5, you should be able to explain the following:

- French settlers in Canada were less oppressive than the Spanish. Jesuit priests converted thousands of Native Americans to Christianity. French settlers became increasingly interested in fur trading.
- Puritans and other religious dissidents came to the Americas because they felt the Church of England was too close to Catholicism.
- The first English settlement in America was the Jamestown colony, founded in 1607. Tobacco became the main crop in Jamestown, and the first slaves arrived in 1619.
- A group of religious Separatists arrived in Plymouth, Massachusetts, in 1620. The first year of settlement was difficult for these Pilgrims, who had to rely on help from the Native Americans to survive.
- The Massachusetts Bay Colony was established in 1629 by the Puritans. This colony was established as a "city upon a hill," where the will of God could be manifested. A limited representative government was established. Religious dissent was not tolerated in this colony: Dissenters were thrown out, and they founded new colonies in Rhode Island, Connecticut, and Portsmouth.
- The ecosystem of the Americas was tremendously altered by European settlement.

Time Line

1534–1535: French adventurers explore the St. Lawrence River
1607: The English settle in Jamestown
1619: Virginia establishes House of Burgesses (first colonial legislature)
1620: Plymouth colony founded
1629: Massachusetts Bay Colony founded
1634: Maryland colony founded
1636: Roger Williams expelled from Massachusetts Bay Colony and settles in Providence, Rhode Island; Connecticut founded by John Hooker
1642: City of Montreal founded by the French

› Review Questions

Fact Check
Check your knowledge of the historical period covered in this chapter.

1. Which colonists enjoyed the best relations with the Native Americans?
   A. The Spanish
   B. The French
   C. The Dutch
   D. The English

2. Who of the following was *not* a religious dissenter in Massachusetts Bay?
   A. William Bradford
   B. Roger Williams
   C. Anne Hutchinson
   D. Thomas Hooker

3. A colony designated as a refuge for English Catholics was
   A. Pennsylvania.
   B. South Carolina.
   C. Maryland.
   D. Virginia.

4. English people came to the New World because of
   A. their dislike for the Church of England.
   B. overcrowding in English cities.
   C. economic opportunity.
   D. All of the above.

5. Most early English colonies were different from those of Spain and France because they
   A. were not directly ruled by the crown.
   B. granted rights to Indians.
   C. were economic failures.
   D. were more sparsely populated.

Multiple-Choice Questions
Here are multiple-choice questions like the ones on the AP U.S. History exam.

Questions 6–8 refer to the quotation below.

We, whose names are underwritten, the Loyal Subjects of our dread Sovereign Lord King *James* . . . Having undertaken for the Glory of God, and Advancement of the Christian Faith, and the Honour of our King and Country, a Voyage to plant the first Colony in the northern Parts of *Virginia*; Do by these Presents, solemnly and mutually, in the Presence of God and one another, covenant and combine ourselves together into a civil Body Politick, for our better Ordering and Preservation, and Furtherance of the ends aforesaid; And by Virtue herof do enact, constitute, and frame, such just and equal Lawes, Ordinances, Acts, Constitutions, and Officers, from time to time, as shall be thought most meet and convenient for the general Good of the Colony; unto which we promise all due Submission and Obedience.

—From the Mayflower Compact, November 11, 1620

6. The Mayflower Compact can best be compared to which of the following documents?
   A. The Declaration of Independence
   B. The Gettysburg Address
   C. The Constitution
   D. The Fourteen Points

7. The people aboard the *Mayflower* were searching for which of the following?
   A. New sources of gold
   B. A better route to the Indies
   C. Religious freedom
   D. A refuge from royal justice

8. How did English colonies of the seventeenth century differ from those of France and Spain?
   A. They enjoyed greater self-government.
   B. Their economies were weaker.
   C. They were richer.
   D. They enjoyed better relations with the Native Americans.

Short-Answer Question

The short-answer question below is similar to the ones you'll encounter on the AP U.S. History exam.

9. Answer Parts A, B, and C.
   A. Briefly explain ONE reason why English colonies in the New World proved successful.
   B. Briefly explain a SECOND reason why English colonies in the New World proved successful.
   C. Briefly explain ONE advantage enjoyed by the rival French colonies.

❯ Answers and Explanations

1. **B.** The French were mainly interested in fur trading rather than farming, and so they posed less of a threat to Native American lands. French missionaries and fur traders were more respectful of Native American culture.

2. **A.** Bradford was a governor of Massachusetts Bay for 20 years; all of the others left for religious reasons and founded colonies elsewhere.

3. **C.** George Calvert settled this colony in 1632 for exactly that purpose.

4. **D.** The overcrowding of cities was an additional factor in convincing some English people to "try their lot" in the New World.

5. **A.** Most of the early English colonies were governed by companies or proprietors granted charters by the king.

6. **C.** The Mayflower Compact can best be compared to the Constitution. Although not a detailed outline of a government, the Mayflower Compact was a form of social contract that laid the foundations for the self-government of the Plymouth Colony.

7. **C.** The people aboard the *Mayflower* were searching for religious freedom. The Pilgrims were Separatists, Calvinist Puritans at odds with the practices of the Church of England. Leaving England, they lived for a time in the Netherlands. Worried that their children would become Dutch and lose important elements of their faith, the Pilgrims moved to America, where they hoped to live and hold their beliefs without interference.

8. **A.** The English colonies of the seventeenth century enjoyed greater self-government. The French and Spanish colonies were ruled by governors reporting directly to their monarchs. The English colonies, many of them established through private enterprise or as efforts to find religious freedom, were largely ignored for many years as the English worked out a balance between the powers of the monarch and Parliament.

9. **Parts A and B**: The English colonies early on developed institutions of self-government, such as the Virginia House of Burgesses in 1619. The English colonists discovered and exploited valuable crops and natural resources such as tobacco, corn, fish, furs, and timber. The English colonies often provided refuges for religious dissenters from back home—Puritans settled in Massachusetts and the New England colonies, Catholics in Maryland, and Quakers in Pennsylvania. Colonies such as Rhode Island and Pennsylvania were notable for their respect for religious freedom.

Part C: The French were more interested in converting the Native Americans to Christianity and in fur trading than taking land for agriculture. As a result the French generally got along better with the Native Americans than the English. This proved an advantage to the French in times of war with the English. The centralization of power in the hands of the governor of New France also often proved an advantage during wars with the English.

CHAPTER 8

British Empire in America: Growth and Conflict (1650–1750)

IN THIS CHAPTER

Summary: The economic theory of mercantilism, which held that a state should be as economically self-sufficient as possible, helped to motivate England and other European powers to discover and develop colonies, as colonies could provide raw materials. The triangular trade system tied together the economies of Europe, the Americas, and Africa and brought slaves to the Americas. The Salem Witch Trials in Massachusetts were a result of social unrest existing in the Massachusetts colony. Wars between the European powers spilled over into the Americas during this period, with Native American tribes cultivated as allies by either the English or the French.

Keywords

Mercantilism: economic system practiced by European powers in the late seventeenth century stating that economic self-sufficiency was crucial; as a result, colonial empires were important for raw materials.

Navigation Acts (1660): acts passed by the British Parliament increasing the dependence of the colonies on the English for trade; these acts caused great resentment in the American colonies but were not strictly enforced.

Triangular trade system: complex trading system that developed in this era between Europe, Africa, and the colonies; Europeans purchased slaves in Africa and sold them to the colonies, raw materials from the colonies went to Europe, while European finished products were sold in the colonies.

Middle Passage: voyage taken by African slaves on horribly overcrowded ships from Africa to the Americas.

Salem Witch Trials (1692): trials in Salem, Massachusetts, after which 19 people were executed as witches; historians note the class nature of these trials.

Salutary neglect: early eighteenth-century British policy relaxing the strict enforcement of trade policies in the American colonies.

Part of an Empire

European leaders in the seventeenth and eighteenth centuries expected colonies to generate wealth for the mother country. Most European statesmen subscribed to the economic theory of **mercantilism**. The proponents of mercantilism believed that a state's economic health depended upon a favorable balance of trade. Governments promoted this by regulating commerce, encouraging the export of goods while discouraging imports through high tariffs. Colonies served as the producers of cheap raw materials and staple products and as consumers of the mother country's finished goods. An operative assumption of mercantilists was that the wealth of the world was finite and that a state had to maximize its share of that wealth through government action. The American colonies played their part in this mercantilist scheme by supplying England with valuable commodities like tobacco, rice, fish, and lumber.

The first law regulating American trade was passed by Parliament in 1651. Under King Charles II, the **Navigation Acts** were passed in 1660 and 1663, with later revisions in the 1670s. These acts were designed to strengthen English trade, while hurting that of competitors like the Dutch. These acts required that English goods be transported only on English ships with majority-English crews. Colonial products such as tobacco, sugar, and rice intended for European markets had to be shipped to England first where they would be taxed. European goods intended for the American colonies also had to first be shipped to England and taxed.

The Navigation Acts increased the cost of living and the cost of doing business for the colonists. Many colonists colluded with the Dutch and other trading partners to evade these regulations. This led to some of the first conflicts between the colonies and the government in London. Disregard for English trade regulations was so extensive in New England that, in 1684, an English court convicted the Massachusetts Bay Colony of violating the Navigation Acts. This, along with Puritan resistance to the royal government, led to the revocation of the colony's charter. In 1686, King James II merged the New England colonies, New York, and New Jersey into the **Dominion of New England**. This new administrative structure increased royal authority under the king's hand-picked governor, Sir Edmund Andros.

Trouble also flared up in the south. When the price of tobacco began to fall in the 1660s, many planters blamed the unpopular Navigation Acts. This grievance was joined by others. Virginians living in the western part of the colony believed that the well-connected royal governor Sir William Berkeley was more concerned with the profits that he reaped from his office than protecting the colonists from raids by Native Americans. In 1676, a landowner named Nathaniel Bacon raised the standard of rebellion. He gathered an army of between 400 and 500 men to attack Native American settlements, some of which, such as those of the Pamunkey and Occoneechee, had been living at peace with the colonists; this army was also used to overawe the colonial government in what became known as Bacon's Rebellion. At one point, Bacon's men burned down Jamestown. Bacon died of dysentery shortly thereafter, and Governor Berkeley routed the remainder of the rebels, hanging 23 of them. In later years, some historians chose to interpret this discreditable episode as a rising of the "little man" against the colonial elite. Royal reinforcements arrived after Berkeley had crushed the rebellion. The governor was recalled to England.

In subsequent years, the power of the larger landowners grew relative to that of the royal governors. Believing that white indentured servants were more politically fractious, the landowners increased the proportion of powerless slaves in their workforces.

Interactions Between Native Americans and Europeans

Bacon's Rebellion served as one example of how interactions between Native Americans and Europeans resulted in conflict and violence. All European groups in the Americas encountered Native Americans, and many of them formed alliances with certain tribes in an effort to avoid violence. The French were well-known for their positive relations with Native tribes, having a working relationship with them regarding the fur trade. Many French settlers married into Native families as well, to be incorporated into the kinship system and allowed access to certain trade routes.

Other European groups did not have as positive of a relationship with the Native Americans close to their settlements. While all Europeans saw themselves as superior to Native Americans, the British acted on this feeling to take land and resources away from the tribes nearest to them. This resulted in frequent military confrontations, the most famous being Metacom's War, or King Philip's War.

Known as King Philip to the British, Metacom was the chief of the Wampanoag Indians in New England. As the British settlers continued to encroach on his people's land in their effort to accommodate the increasing British population, Metacom realized that the ancestral ways of the Wampanoag were being threatened. The only solution was to drive the British out. Realizing that the Wampanoag could not do this alone, Metacom allied his tribe with others in the area to form a Native alliance. This group then launched an all-out war against the British in 1675, burning their fields, killing their men, and capturing their women and children. The British fought back, and called upon their allies, the Mohawks and Mohegans, to help fight against Metacom and his followers. After a bloody 14 months, Metacom was shot and killed, thus bringing an end to the war.

Growth of Slavery

African slavery became increasingly widespread and institutionalized in the Chesapeake colonies during the 1670s and 1680s. In 1662, a law was passed in Virginia declaring that the child of a slave mother was also a slave. This nullified the English common law practice that one's legal status came from that of the father and ensured that children born into slavery remained in that condition. The number of indentured servants decreased because of doubts of their political reliability after Bacon's Rebellion and because fewer were willing to endure the hardship of agricultural labor in the south when more attractive working conditions could be found in the northern colonies. The Dutch had dominated the slave trade for many years. The end of their monopoly in 1682 led to lower prices for slaves in the English colonies. A labor force of enslaved Africans became increasingly attractive to prosperous planters. So as the number of indentured servants in the south dwindled, the number of African slaves greatly increased.

Europeans began to participate in the African slave trade when Portuguese explorers and merchants developed business contacts along the west coast of Africa in the 1440s. Once the Americas were opened up to European settlement in the sixteenth century and labor-intensive cash crops like sugar became enormously lucrative, African slaves became a valuable commodity. The burgeoning slave trade of the seventeenth and eighteenth centuries was an essential component of the **triangular trade system**. This was an Atlantic-wide system of trade and economic interdependence that knitted together Africa, the Caribbean islands, both South and North America, and Europe. Finished goods from Europe were traded for slaves in Africa, who were sold in the Western Hemisphere, where they helped produce staple products that were in turn shipped to Europe. The transportation of slaves from Africa to the Americas was known as the **Middle Passage**. Conditions for the people chained in the holds of the relatively primitive sailing ships of the day were horrifying. Disease in these confined quarters made the voyages deadly for both the slaves and the ships' crews. The mortality rate among the imprisoned slaves often rose as high as 20 percent.

Only about 6 percent of the Africans shipped across the Atlantic arrived in the British colonies in North America. Most African slaves were sent to South America or the Caribbean. A healthier climate and a better balance between the sexes meant that slave populations in the British North American colonies grew through natural reproduction, unlike the situation in the Caribbean islands where high death rates demanded a continuous importation of new slaves. Until the rise of larger plantations in the south from the 1730s forward, most slaves worked on small farms in groups of two or three with their master. Over time, the slaves developed a unique culture that blended both African and European elements. Their religious beliefs also sometimes exhibited a syncretic merger of African traditions and Christianity.

Slaves sometimes rose up against their owners, and slave rebellions were a major fear for colonists in the south. The largest slave uprising in the British colonies was the **Stono Rebellion**, which took place in South Carolina in 1739. A group of about 100 slaves rose up and began killing isolated planters. They lost a pitched battle against a force of militiamen, and eventually most of the rebels were killed in the fighting or were executed after being captured. In the aftermath of this rebellion, regulations concerning the control and treatment of slaves were tightened. Most slaves did not launch violent but futile revolts; instead they protested their treatment through work slow-downs, breaking tools, and other acts of minor sabotage. Although most slaves lived in the southern colonies, slavery existed in the north as well, where slaves worked as farmhands and servants.

Political Unrest in the Colonies

Massachusetts and the other New England colonies resented the loss of their authority to Sir Edmund Andros, the governor of the newly created Dominion of New England. King James II was overthrown during the **Glorious Revolution** of 1688 in England. The new English monarchs, William of Orange and Mary, the daughter of James II, gained power by agreeing to respect the prerogatives of Parliament. This was the beginning of constitutional monarchy in England. The Glorious Revolution inspired political upheaval in the colonies. In Massachusetts, Governor Andros was turned out of office and jailed. Protestant rebels overthrew the Catholic leaders of Maryland. In New York, a militia officer named Jacob Leisler took control of the colony.

The rebellious colonists declared their loyalty to William and Mary. The new monarchs abolished the Dominion of New England and restored most representative institutions in Massachusetts, though it became a royal colony with a royally appointed governor. Because William and Mary were Protestants, whereas James II had been a Catholic, the new English government supported the Protestants in Maryland. Jacob Leisler ran afoul of the new regime and was hanged as a rebel. This was a sign that the royal government intended to continue to play an important role in colonial affairs.

Salem Witch Trials

Rapid political change was only one of the stresses the colony of Massachusetts underwent during the late seventeenth century. The dominance of traditional Puritanism began to break down. Economic tensions developed between small farmers and a flourishing class of merchants and business entrepreneurs. For many, John Winthrop's godly commonwealth seemed to be a thing of the past. Anxieties associated with this religious and social change probably played a key role in the still controversial **Salem Witch Trials** of 1692.

Accused witches had been prosecuted and executed before in the colonies, but never on the scale that exploded in Salem, Massachusetts. A group of girls began to experience inexplicable seizures and complained of attacks by invisible forces. The girls accused people of persecuting them through witchcraft, which began an expanding series of judicial investigations. Before the hysteria abated, over 100 people had been jailed and 20 executed. Nineteen men and women were hanged, and one man was pressed to death. Five other people, including an infant, died in prison. Eventually, the accusers began to lose their credibility, and people began to question the likelihood that so many people were engaged in witchcraft. A new governor put an official end to the proceedings. Historians have noted that social tensions may have fueled the accusations of witchcraft; the accusers came from economically marginal farming families, whereas the accused were members of the better-off "commercial" class.

Imperial Wars

Louis XIV, the "Sun King" of France, attempted to establish his nation as the dominant power in Europe in the late seventeenth and early eighteenth centuries. England, a growing maritime power, resisted this. Beginning in 1689, the English and French fought a long series of wars that would culminate in the Battle of Waterloo in 1815. Early on, the American colonies of England and France became involved in these wars. The War of the League of Augsburg was known as King William's War in America and lasted from 1689 to 1697. War parties of French and Native Americans raided the frontier and destroyed the town of Schenectady, New York. In turn, colonists assisted the Iroquois tribe in attacking Canada. A force largely recruited in Massachusetts captured the French base of Port Royal in Acadia. The war ended without any decisive results in America.

Just a few years later, England and France were at war again. The War of the Spanish Succession, called Queen Anne's War in America, was waged from 1702 to 1713. Because Spain was allied with France, an English force from South Carolina attacked and burned St. Augustine in Florida. They armed local Native Americans, who then attacked Spanish missions. In the north, it was the English who suffered from Native American raids on the frontier. The most spectacular of these raids occurred in 1704, when a force of French and Native Americans devastated the town of Deerfield, Massachusetts, killing 48 people and taking 112 into captivity. As in King William's War, no decisive battles took place in America. English victories in Europe, under the great general the Duke of Marlborough, compelled the French to surrender Newfoundland, Acadia, and other territories in America through the Treaty of Utrecht.

American Self-Government

England and Scotland were formally united with the Acts of Union of 1706 and 1707. From this point on, the united kingdoms were known as Great Britain. In the early eighteenth century, the British encountered some limits to their control of the North American colonies. Because of the various ways the colonies had been formed, there was no consistent method of governance across the colonies. While most colonies were royal colonies with governors appointed by the monarch, some, such as Connecticut and Rhode Island, elected their own governors; in **proprietorships**, such as the Carolinas, Maryland, and Pennsylvania, governors were appointed by the proprietors who held title to the colony.

Despite this, everywhere in British North America, the principle of self-government had taken hold. However governors were appointed, **colonial assemblies** were elected by the people. The "people" of this time were men who owned a certain amount of property. This electorate was broader than that back in Great Britain or in any other of the great European powers, however. Though the assemblies were usually composed of substantial landowners, to some degree they did reflect public opinion, especially in New England, with its vital institution of town meetings. The colonial assemblies, beginning with Massachusetts in the 1720s, resisted pressure from Great Britain to regularize the payment of salaries to royal governors. This gave the assemblies powerful financial leverage in disputes with their governors and familiarized the assemblies with "the power of the purse."

Salutary Neglect

During the reigns of George I (1714–1727) and George II (1727–1760), the British government was preoccupied with international relations and the balance of power in Europe. Having come from the Electorate of Hanover, these kings were especially concerned with affairs in Germany and central Europe. The British government's chief goal in dealing with its colonies was furthering Great Britain's economic interests. Pursuant to their mercantilist worldview, British officials attempted to prevent Americans from manufacturing their own textiles (1699), hats (1732), and iron goods (1750). Because the Navigation Acts allowed the colonists as Englishmen to own ships and carry on trade, a vibrant merchant class emerged in America. These merchants followed their own interests, evading the Navigation Acts by doing business with the French West Indies and other non-British colonies. The British government became so concerned about the American sugar trade with the French in the Caribbean that Parliament passed the **Molasses Act** of 1733, raising duties on foreign sugar. Many American shippers continued to ignore British regulations. By 1750, a new generation of British colonial administrators was anxious to tighten the government's control over its insubordinate American subjects.

First Great American Religious Revival

The **First Great Awakening** was a religious revival that profoundly influenced spiritual and intellectual values in America. Beginning in the 1720s and lasting through the 1740s, the First Great Awakening challenged the established religious authorities and called for a personal and more emotional approach to divine worship. Exponents of the Great Awakening criticized traditional, overly intellectual sermonizing by ministers. Jonathan Edwards reduced his congregation to tears by preaching on "Sinners in the Hands of an Angry God," vividly describing the yawning pit of hell and the horrors awaiting sinners there. The dynamic Anglican preacher George Whitefield attracted crowds of thousands to his sermons as he travelled through the colonies in the 1740s.

By scorning the "establishment" and emphasizing fervor over traditional ministerial learning, the Great Awakening encouraged a greater sense of personal equality in the American colonies. A growing number of people became accustomed to thinking for themselves rather than deferring to authority. A people willing to question religious leaders soon proved ready to challenge political figures as well.

Chapter Review

Rapid Review

To achieve the perfect 5, you should be able to explain the following:

- The dominant economic theory of the era was mercantilism; British mercantilist measures such as the Navigation Acts created resentment in the American colonies.
- The importation of African slaves became increasingly important for the continued economic growth of several southern colonies.
- The Salem Witch Trials demonstrated the social conflict present in the American colonies.
- Eighteenth-century European wars between the British and the French spilled over into the Americas, with British and French colonies becoming involved.
- In the early eighteenth century, colonial assemblies became increasingly powerful and independent in several colonies, including Massachusetts.
- Even during the era of "salutary neglect," the British attempted to increase their economic control over the colonies.
- The religious revival called the Great Awakening caused some colonists to question many of the religious, social, and political foundations on which colonial life was based.

Time Line

1651: First of several Navigation Acts approved by British parliament
1676: Bacon's Rebellion takes place in Virginia
1682: Dutch monopoly on slave trade ends, greatly reducing the price of slaves coming to the Americas
1686: Creation of Dominion of New England
1688: Glorious Revolution in England; James II removed from the throne
1689: Beginning of the War of the League of Augsburg
1692: Witchcraft trials take place in Salem, Massachusetts
1702: Beginning of the War of the Spanish Succession
1733: Enactment of the Molasses Act
1739: Stono (slave) Rebellion in South Carolina
1740: George Whitefield tours the American colonies—the high point of the Great Awakening

› Review Questions

Fact Check

Check your knowledge of the historical period covered in this chapter.

1. The creation of the Dominion of New England
   A. increased democracy in the colonies.
   B. increased the power of the governor of the area.
   C. allowed New England colonies to discuss common grievances.
   D. guaranteed direct control of the king over affairs in the New England colonies.

2. A major effect of the Stono Rebellion was
   A. an increase in the number of slaves brought into the Southern colonies.
   B. increased fortifications around several southern cities.
   C. an attempt by slave owners to lessen the horrors of the Middle Passage.
   D. harsher treatment of slaves in many parts of the South.

3. The growth of colonial assemblies alarmed the British for all of the following reasons *except*
   A. assemblies holding the "power of the purse" could ultimately undermine British control.
   B. assemblies increased democratic tendencies in the colonies.
   C. assemblies occasionally ignored or resisted instructions from Great Britain.
   D. governors appointed in Britain had little control over these assemblies in most colonies.

4. For the British, the major economic role of the American colonies was
   A. to produce manufactured goods the English did not want to produce.
   B. to produce crops such as tobacco.
   C. to produce raw materials such as lumber.
   D. B and C above.

5. What changes in the slave system of the southern colonies began in the 1730s?
   A. The Dutch lost the monopoly on slave trading, thus increasing the number of slaves being brought into the Americas.
   B. Conditions during the Middle Passage began to slightly improve.
   C. More slaves began to live and work on larger plantations.
   D. A series of slave rebellions created much harsher treatment for slaves.

Multiple-Choice Questions

Here are multiple-choice questions like the ones on the AP U.S. History exam.

Questions 6–8 refer to the quotation below.

For the increase of shipping and encouragement of the navigation of this nation, wherein, under the good providence and protection of God, the wealth, safety, and strength of this kingdom is so much concerned; be it enacted by the King's most excellent majesty, and by the lords and commons in this present parliament assembled, and by the authority thereof, That from and after the first day of *December* 1660, and from thenceforward, no goods or commodities whatsoever shall be imported into or exported out of any lands, islands, plantations or territories to his Majesty belonging or in his possession . . . in Asia, Africa, or America, in any other ship or ships, vessel or vessels whatsoever, but in such ships or vessels as do truly and without fraud belong only to the people of England or Ireland . . . and whereof the master and three fourths of the mariners at least are *English* . . . .

—Navigation Act of 1660

6. The Navigation Act of 1660 expressed which of the following economic perspectives?
   A. Socialism
   B. Laissez faire
   C. Progressivism
   D. Mercantilism

7. The enactment of the Navigation Act of 1660 reflected which of the following?
   A. Growing English disinterest in the American colonies
   B. The desire of the English government to exert greater control over colonial trade
   C. The belief of the king and Parliament that it would be economically foolish for the government to interfere with private enterprise
   D. The English government's concern over religious and political dissidents moving to America

8. The Navigation Act of 1660 can best be compared to which of the following?
   A. The tariff in the late nineteenth-century United States
   B. Thomas Jefferson's opposition to the First Bank of the United States
   C. The creation of the Federal Reserve System in 1914
   D. William Jennings Bryan's campaign for free silver in 1896

Short-Answer Question

The short-answer question below is similar to the ones you'll encounter on the AP U.S. History exam.

9. Answer Parts A, B, and C.
   A. Briefly explain ONE way the British imperial system affected the colonies.
   B. Briefly explain a SECOND way the British imperial system affected the colonies.
   C. Briefly explain ONE way the colonies resisted greater British control.

〉 Answers and Explanations

1. **B**. This occurred after resistance in Massachusetts to the Navigation Acts, and it gave increased power to Sir Edmund Andros.

2. **D**. Many plantation owners were fearful of additional rebellions and felt that harsh treatment of slaves would prevent rebellious behavior.

3. **B**. These assemblies were in no way democratic, as in every colony they were dominated by the landowning elite.

4. **D**. The role of the colonies under mercantilism was to provide England with crops and raw materials.

5. **C**. Before the 1730s, most slaves worked on small farms. The Dutch lost their monopoly on slave trading back in 1682. The Stono Rebellion was the first major slave rebellion and occurred in 1739.

6. **D**. The Navigation Act of 1660 expressed the economic perspective of mercantilism. The supporters of mercantilism believed that there was a finite amount of wealth in the world; it was the job of government through the regulation of trade to increase a state's share of that trade.

7. **B**. The enactment of the Navigation Act of 1660 reflected the desire of the English government to exert greater control over colonial trade. This law tightened up and extended an earlier Navigation Act of 1651, which had been largely ignored by the colonies. The English government was increasingly determined to derive mercantilist benefits by funneling American trade through England.

8. **A**. The Navigation Act can best be compared to the tariff in the late nineteenth century United States. Like the Navigation Acts, the tariff was a government policy intended to promote economic prosperity by limiting competition. A high tariff in the late nineteenth century promoted the sale of American-made goods by making imported goods more expensive.

9. **Parts A and B**: The American colonies were affected by the British government's mercantilist policies. In 1660 and 1663 Parliament passed Navigation Acts compelling colonists to ship tobacco, rice, sugar, and other crops to England. Goods bound to the colonies had to go through English ports. The British continued to pass other financial regulations for the colonies, such as the 1733 Molasses Act. At times, the English attempted political reorganizations of the colonies, revoking their charters, as with Massachusetts in 1684. In 1686, the English government attempted to group New York, New Jersey, and the New England colonies into the Dominion of New England. This fell apart in 1689 after the overthrow of King James II. Another way the British imperial system affected the colonies was by involving them in imperial wars with the French and Spanish. Americans were involved in King William's War (1689–1697) and Queen Anne's War (1702–1713).

Part C: Colonists resisted greater British control by violating the Navigation Acts and later economic regulations. The colonists overthrew the Dominion of New England. In the period of "salutary neglect" colonial legislatures increased their independence and resisted efforts to strengthen the power of royal governors.

CHAPTER 9

Resistance, Rebellion, and Revolution (1750–1775)

IN THIS CHAPTER

Summary: Tensions between the British and the French intensified in the 1740s; a result of this tension was the Seven Years' War, in which colonial forces were involved. The French were defeated in this war, essentially ending their political influence on the American continent. During and after this war the British imposed a number of taxes and duties on their colonies, creating unrest. The Stamp Act created great resentment in the colonies. The results of this resentment included the Stamp Act Congress of 1765, the Boston Massacre of 1770, and the Boston Tea Party of 1773. The First Continental Congress met in 1774 and resolved that the colonies would resist efforts to tax them without their consent.

Keywords

French and Indian War (1756–1763): also known as the Seven Years' War, a conflict between the British and the French that also involved Native Americans and colonial forces. French defeat in this war greatly decreased their influence in the colonies.

Stamp Act (1765): imposed by the British, this act dictated that all legal documents in the colonies had to be issued on officially stamped paper. This act created strong resentment in the colonies and was later repealed.

Townshend Acts (1767): British legislation that forced colonies to pay duties on most goods coming from England; these duties were fiercely resisted and finally repealed in 1770.

Boston Massacre (1770): conflict between British soldiers and Boston civilians on March 5, 1770; five colonists were killed and six wounded.

Sons of Liberty: radical group that organized resistance against British policies in Boston in the 1760s and 1770s. This was the group that organized the Boston Tea Party.

Committees of Correspondence: created first in Massachusetts and then in other colonies, these groups circulated grievances against the British to towns within their colonies.

Boston Tea Party (1773): in response to British taxes on tea, Boston radicals disguised as Native Americans threw 350 chests of tea into Boston Harbor on December 16, 1773; important symbolic act of resistance to British economic control of the colonies.

First Continental Congress (1774): meeting in Philadelphia at which colonists vowed to resist further efforts to tax them without their consent.

War in the West

In 1750, the lands west of the Appalachian Mountains were inhabited by Native American tribes eager to trade with the Europeans but determined to maintain their independence. Both the British and French wanted to lay claim to this expansive territory. Ambitious speculators from Virginia began to purchase land in the Ohio Valley. The French, resolved to uphold their own interests in the area and to protect the tenuous lines of communication between Canada and Louisiana, responded by beginning construction on Fort Duquesne on the site of what is now Pittsburgh, Pennsylvania.

Now it was the turn of the British to be concerned about developments in the Ohio Valley. In 1754, Governor Robert Dinwiddie of Virginia dispatched a small force to the Ohio Territory to uphold British interests and persuade the French to leave. This detachment was commanded by a young militia officer named George Washington. After an initial success, Washington and his men were defeated and captured. The next year, the British responded by sending General Edward Braddock and a large force of British Regular troops to destroy Fort Duquesne. The French and Native American allies ambushed and destroyed Braddock's army near the fort. The frontier fighting of 1754 and 1755 began the **French and Indian War**, merging in 1756 with the much larger European Seven Years' War.

As fighting began with the French, the colonies and the British government found it difficult to coordinate their policies. In 1754, delegations from seven of the more northern colonies gathered for the **Albany Congress**. Benjamin Franklin and others hoped that the colonies and the British government could work out common measures for dealing with the Native Americans and the threat posed by the French. Franklin proposed a plan of union that would have created a colonial council with a president appointed by the king. Franklin's plan was rejected by both the colonial assemblies and the British government.

Defeat of New France

Despite the British and American advantages in numbers and sea power, the French won a series of impressive victories in North America from 1756 to 1758. The Native American allies of the French ravaged the western frontier. The turning point in the war came in 1757, when William Pitt rose to power in the British government. Pitt devised a strategy that focused on capturing French colonial possessions around the world. He poured resources into North America, including a fleet and 25,000 Redcoats. Willing to spend freely to get what he wanted, Pitt paid all expenses in raising colonial troops. Eventually 24,000 Americans fought with the British against the French. Faced with such overwhelming force, the French retreated back into Canada. The British followed them there in 1759, and at the Battle of the Plains of Abraham on September 13 defeated their main army and captured the city of Quebec. Montreal fell in 1760, completing the British conquest of Canada.

The war between Great Britain and France ended officially with the Treaty of Paris in 1763. The war made Britain the dominant power in North America. Britain retained Canada and had conquered Florida from Spain; thus, the British controlled the entire eastern seaboard. The war also eliminated France as a power in North America; driven from Canada, France gave Louisiana to its ally, Spain, as compensation for the loss of Florida.

The American colonists took pride in the important role that they had played in defeating the French. They were proud to be part of the victorious British Empire. At the same time, the French and Indian War had exposed differences between the colonists and the British. Many British soldiers and officials believed that the colonists could have done more to contribute to the war effort, both financially and in terms of fighting. In turn, many colonists resented what they believed was British condescension directed toward them. They disliked what they saw as the brutal and authoritarian behavior of the British military. They were outraged when British troops were quartered in their homes. The seeds had been planted for later divisions.

The British Need Money

Wars are expensive. War in the wilderness of America was especially expensive. William Pitt had focused on victory, not finances. Now his successors in office had to find the money to pay off an enormous government debt.

In 1763, King George III supported the rise of George Grenville to the position of prime minister. Grenville knew that one of his most important tasks as the head of the government would be to address the debt. He believed that the American colonies should pay a greater share of the cost of maintaining the empire. Like a growing number of British leaders, he was angered by American defiance of the Navigation Acts and wanted to bring an end to the period of salutary neglect in the British administration of the colonies.

Grenville began his campaign to bring the colonies to heel with the **Currency Act** of 1764. This act prohibited the colonies from issuing their own paper money. This forced the cash-strapped American colonists to pay British merchants in hard currency. Grenville followed this up with the **Sugar Act**, which lowered the duties on molasses imported to the colonies but strengthened the measures taken to ensure that the colonists would pay what they owed. Both laws added to the economic woes of the colonists, who were suffering from a postwar business slump. Many colonists criticized Grenville's acts, and some began to question the nature of the relationship between the colonies and their mother country.

Stamp Act Crisis

Grenville overplayed his hand with the **Stamp Act** of 1765. This was the first time that Parliament imposed a direct tax on the colonies, rather than a customs duty on imported goods. Colonists now had to purchase paper with a revenue stamp for such common documents and printed items as wills, newspapers, and playing cards. To pay this tax, the colonists had to use scarce hard currency rather than local issues of paper money. Not only was the British government raising money from the colonies, something Americans grudgingly accepted when it came to trade regulation, but the British revenue service was now reaching into the colonists' domestic affairs, taxing elements of their everyday lives. Americans across the colonies reacted to the Stamp Act with fury. They were being taxed without representation, in violation of more than a century of precedent during which they had managed their own internal finances. In July 1765, Samuel Adams played a leading role organizing the **Sons of Liberty** in Boston. Riots led by the Sons of Liberty intimidated the stamp agent for Massachusetts into surrendering his office. Branches of the Sons of Liberty sprang up in other colonies, and other stamp agents were compelled to resign. In the Virginia House of Burgesses, Patrick Henry made a name for himself denouncing the tyranny of George III.

Men were not the only ones who took action during this time; women did as well, forming the Daughters of Liberty. The actions of these women did not take the form of political protests, riots, and tarring and feathering government officials, however. Instead, women who pushed back against the new policies of the British Crown did so by organizing boycotts of British goods. As the main consumers of the household, women's purchasing power was incredibly powerful during this time. This was a boycott British merchants felt. Many women also pledged to stop buying and drinking British tea, and began creating their own herbal teas. On top of this, when Americans merchants signed non-importation agreements thereby swearing to stop the import of goods from Great Britain, women hosted spinning bees to help produce textiles locally. These actions greatly helped further along the cause of the colonists.

Across the colonies, leaders looked for a constructive response to what they regarded as the overreaching of the British government. Since the colonies were being taxed without representation, James Otis in Massachusetts and Benjamin Franklin in Pennsylvania argued that Americans should be elected to Parliament. In October 1765, delegates from nine colonies gathered at the **Stamp Act Congress** held in New York City. The Congress issued a Declaration of Rights and Grievances affirming that, as Englishmen, the colonists could not be taxed by a body that did not represent them. Colonists began talking about economic boycotts against British goods as a way of protesting against the Stamp Act.

Adding to the anger of the colonists was the passage of the **Quartering Act** requiring that the colonies house and feed the British troops stationed in America. Supporting soldiers whose only role after the defeat of the French seemed to be as enforcers of unpopular laws struck Americans as the height of tyranny.

Grenville left office in July 1765 and was replaced by Lord Rockingham. The new prime minister was anxious to calm the uproar in the colonies. British business owners, worried about a loss of trade with the colonies, lobbied effectively against the Stamp Act. Rockingham persuaded Parliament to repeal the Stamp Act early in 1766. Repeal of the Stamp Act delighted Americans and led to celebrations in the colonies. This self-congratulatory mood ended, however, when word came that Parliament, as a face-saving measure, had also passed the **Declaratory Act**, which asserted its right to legislate for the colonies "in all cases whatsoever."

Townshend Acts

In 1766, an ailing William Pitt returned as prime minister. Charles Townshend, the **Chancellor of the Exchequer**, became the dominant figure in formulating policy toward the colonies. Like Grenville before him, Townshend was driven by the need to raise revenue. As the Americans had objected to the Stamp Act because it taxed transactions within the borders of the colonies, Townshend assumed that the colonists would not object to taxes on British goods that they imported. In 1767, the **Townshend Acts** placed new duties on lead, paper, glass, and tea, all goods that the colonists bought from British merchants. In order to strengthen the position of the British authorities in America, Townshend used some of the money raised by the taxes to pay the salaries of royal governors and other British office holders, which weakened the power of the colonial assemblies. Townshend also tightened up the enforcement of British tax collection and trade regulations with the creation of an American Customs Board and new admiralty courts whose purpose was to try smugglers.

Townshend soon learned that the distinction that he made between "internal" and "external" taxes did not wash with most American colonists. The Americans believed that Parliament could not tax them without their consent. Soon a number of American leaders eloquently expressed this point of view. In his *Letters from a Farmer in Pennsylvania* (1767), John Dickinson argued that Parliament could regulate the empire's trade but lacked the authority to raise revenue from colonists. When some defenders of the Townshend Acts pointed out that the taxes were low, Dickinson responded, "If they have a right to levy a tax of one penny upon us, they have a right to levy a *million* upon us; for where does their right stop?" In an article about American opposition to taxation without representation, Benjamin Franklin warned British readers that "this unhappy new system of politics tends to dissolve those bands of union and to sever us forever."

Samuel Adams organized opposition to the Townshend Acts in Massachusetts. Early in 1768, he wrote a letter urging other colonies to join Massachusetts in resisting Parliament. In the letter, he opposed taxation without representation, declaring "that what a man has honestly acquired is absolutely his own, which he may freely give, but cannot be taken from him without his consent." The Massachusetts Assembly endorsed this **Circular Letter** and forwarded it to the other colonial assemblies. The British authorities were outraged, and the colonial secretary urged royal governors to dissolve any assemblies that joined with Massachusetts. Despite this, five other colonies issued similar documents. Boycotts of British goods became widespread across the colonies. Once again, American economic power made itself felt in Britain. Lord North became prime minister in 1770. He led Parliament in repealing all Townshend duties except that on tea, which was left as a reminder that the British government maintained its power to tax the colonies.

Boston Massacre

Boston, Massachusetts, became a flashpoint for tensions between British officials and colonists. Boston merchants defied British trade regulations, much to the fury of customs officers. In 1768, the British seized a smuggling ship belonging to John Hancock. American mobs retaliated by assaulting British officials. The British responded to this by stationing two regiments of British soldiers in Boston. The Redcoats soon became very unpopular as a symbol of British repression. Many working-class Bostonians hated the soldiers because, in their spare time, they took on part-time jobs that had once gone to local workers. Harassing soldiers became a sport for some Bostonians. On March 5, 1770, a mob started throwing snowballs laced with ice and rocks at a group of soldiers standing guard. The infuriated soldiers fired a volley at their tormentors, killing five men and wounding eight others. Samuel Adams turned the **Boston Massacre** into a public relations disaster for the British, propagandizing the event as a demonstration of British brutality. Despite this, many Americans who opposed British policy also deplored mob violence. John Adams undertook the defense of the British soldiers when they went on trial; of the eight accused, six were acquitted and two received the relatively mild punishment of a brand on their thumbs.

Tensions between the colonies and Britain seemed to subside a bit between 1770 and 1773. Business appeared to go on as usual. But fundamental issues had not been resolved. Samuel Adams formed a **Committee of Correspondence** in Boston to share news and coordinate protests against the British. Committees of Correspondence quickly spread across Massachusetts and throughout the colonies. These committees provided an essential organizational framework for American resistance to British policy.

Boston Tea Party

One British tax still remained, that on tea. Some Americans expressed their opposition to the tax by boycotting British tea. The boycott had an effect, hurting the British East India Company, which was in dire financial straits because of troubles in India. In an effort to provide assistance to the East India Company, Lord North's government sponsored the **Tea Act** of 1773. This legislation allowed the East India Company to market its tea to the Americans without having to go through middlemen in England; the tea tax stayed the same, but the price of high-quality British tea went down.

Lord North thought that the Tea Act was a win for everyone; the East India Company would be saved and the Americans would get cheaper tea, despite the tax. The Americans saw things differently. They saw the Tea Act as an insidious way of reaffirming Parliament's power to tax the colonies. They distrusted the special privilege granted the well-connected East India Company. At several ports, popular gatherings ensured that the East India Company tea stayed aboard ship. Things went further in Boston. On the evening of December 16, 1773, men dressed as Mohawk Indians swarmed onto the East India Company's ships and tossed some 350 chests of tea into the dirty waters of the harbor. The **Boston Tea Party** was an act of defiance that quickly focused the wrath of the British government on the city.

Intolerable Acts

The **Intolerable Acts**, also known as the Coercive Acts, were passed by Parliament early in 1774. They were designed to punish Massachusetts for the Boston Tea Party. The British closed the port of Boston to all but military or officially approved traffic. The British took control of government in Massachusetts, giving the royal governor the authority to appoint most officials in the state and limiting town meetings to just once a year. Finally, the unpopular Quartering Act was reimposed on all colonies. Although Massachusetts was the focus of the Intolerable Acts, Americans living elsewhere recognized that the British could just as easily impose coercive laws in their own colonies. Spontaneously, legislators in different colonial legislatures began calling for a gathering of colonial representatives to address the crisis in Massachusetts.

The passage of the Quebec Act of 1774 was associated in the minds of American colonists with the Intolerable Acts. In many ways an enlightened approach to governing the French population of Canada, the Quebec Act angered Americans because it included the western territories in an expanded province of Quebec and guaranteed freedom of worship to French Catholics. To the American colonists, it seemed as if the British were cutting them off from the west and surrounding them with their hereditary enemies.

First Continental Congress

The Continental Congress convened in Philadelphia on September 5, 1774. Fifty-six delegates from every colony but Georgia took part. The delegates were undecided about what to do. Samuel Adams wanted a complete boycott of British trade, whereas others urged a diplomatic approach to Parliament. John Adams united Congress with his **Declaration of Rights and Grievances**, which reiterated the American position that Parliament could regulate the trade of the colonies but could not tax the colonies without representation.

Congress also adopted the **Suffolk Resolves**, a declaration that originated in Massachusetts. The Suffolk Resolves defied the Intolerable Acts by refusing to recognize the changes that the British had made to the Massachusetts government. They also imposed a boycott of British products. Recognizing the increasing seriousness of the political situation, the Suffolk Resolves called on the colonies to see to the readiness of their militias.

Before adjourning on October 26, 1774, Congress drew up a petition to George III requesting the repeal of the Intolerable Acts. Congress also set May 10, 1775, as the date for the convening of a Second Continental Congress. As 1774 drew to a close, Americans pondered what the British government would do next.

Chapter Review

Rapid Review

To achieve the perfect 5, you should be able to explain the following:

- Tensions between the British and the French intensified in the 1740s when land speculators from English colonies began to acquire land in the Ohio Valley.
- The Seven Years' War (the French and Indian War in American textbooks) was between the English and colonial forces and the French; Native Americans fought on both sides.
- The defeat of the French in this war largely ended their influence in the Americas; after the war, the British attempted to make the colonies pay their fair share for the war effort.
- Parliamentary efforts during this era to produce money for Great Britain by imposing various taxes and duties on the colonies resulted in great unrest in the colonies.
- The impact of the Stamp Act on the colonies was great; as a result, nine colonies met at the 1765 Stamp Act Congress and the Sons of Liberty formed in Boston.
- Boston remained a center of opposition to British policy; the Boston Massacre in 1770 and the Boston Tea Party in 1773 helped to create resistance to the Crown in other colonies as well.
- The 1774 Intolerable Acts that closed the port of Boston and curtailed freedom of speech in Massachusetts outraged many in the colonies.
- The 1774 First Continental Congress passed a resolution stating that the colonies would firmly resist measures that taxed them without their consent. At this meeting it was also decided that individual colonies should start to raise and train state militias.

Time Line

1754: Representatives of colonies meet at Albany Congress to coordinate further Western settlement

1756: Beginning of Seven Years' War

1763: Signing of Treaty of Paris ending Seven Years' War

1764: Parliament approves Sugar Act, Currency Act

1765: Stamp Act approved by Parliament; Stamp Act Congress occurs and Sons of Liberty is formed, both in opposition to the Stamp Act

1766: Stamp Act repealed, but in Declaratory Act, Parliament affirms its right to tax the colonies

1767: Passage of the Townshend Acts

1770: Boston Massacre occurs

1773: Boston Tea Party takes place in December in opposition to the Tea Act

1774: Intolerable Acts adopted by Parliament
First Continental Congress held in Philadelphia

› Review Questions

Fact Check

Check your knowledge of the historical period covered in this chapter.

1. William Pitt was able to convince the colonies to fight in the Seven Years' War by
   A. threatening military reprisals by the British army.
   B. threatening to make the colonists fight the French by themselves.
   C. putting the recruiting of troops in the colonies totally in the hands of the colonies themselves.
   D. paying colonial soldiers generous bonuses to fight against the French.

2. The Stamp Act created great fury in the colonies because
   A. it imposed massive duties on the colonies.
   B. it was the first time Parliament had imposed a duty on the colonies.
   C. it took badly needed revenue away from colonial legislatures.
   D. this was the first time that Parliament imposed a direct tax on the colonies.

3. Who declared that British taxes on the colonists were "infringements of their natural and constitutional rights" because they were not represented in Parliament?
   A. Benjamin Franklin.
   B. John Hancock.
   C. Samuel Adams.
   D. Patrick Henry.

4. After the Seven Years' War, resentment between the British and the colonists existed for all of the following reasons *except*
   A. the British resented the fact that few colonists had actually helped them in the war against the French.
   B. British soldiers had been quartered in colonial homes.
   C. the British resented the fact that some colonists continued to trade with the French at the beginning of the war.
   D. colonial militiamen felt the British exhibited a patronizing attitude toward them.

5. Most delegates at the First Continental Congress of 1774
   A. felt that there should be a total boycott of British goods by the colonies.
   B. felt that the colonies should firmly resist measures to tax them without their consent.
   C. felt that it was time to seriously consider military measures against the British.
   D. wanted the British to totally refrain from regulating trade to the colonies.

Multiple-Choice Questions

Here are multiple-choice questions like the ones on the AP U.S. History exam.

Questions 6–8 refer to the quotation below.

A perpetual *jealousy*, respecting liberty, is absolutely requisite in all free states. The very texture of their constitution, in *mixed* governments, demands it. For the *cautions* with which power is distributed among the several orders, *imply*, that *each* has its share which is proper for the general welfare, and therefore that any further acquisition must be pernicious. . . . But of all states that have existed, there never was any, in which this jealousy could be more proper than in these colonies. For the government here is not only *mixed*, but *dependent*, which circumstance occasions *a peculiarity in its form*, of a very delicate nature.

> —John Dickinson, *Letters from a Farmer in Pennsylvania*, Letter XI, 1767–1768

6. In the passage above, what line of policy is Dickinson recommending to his fellow Americans?
   A. Greater trust in the British government
   B. Stronger central authority in London
   C. Greater attention to American liberties
   D. Secession from the British Empire

7. Dickinson was writing because of debates about
   A. British policies during the French and Indian War.
   B. British taxes imposed on the colonies.
   C. the rise of royal absolutism in Britain.
   D. Religious differences with Britain caused by the First Great Awakening.

8. The concerns addressed by Dickinson were most directly shared by those who drafted which of the following?
   A. The Constitution
   B. The Monroe Doctrine
   C. The Seneca Falls Declaration
   D. The Four Freedoms

Short-Answer Question

The short-answer question below is similar to the ones you'll encounter on the AP U.S. History exam.

9. Answer Parts A, B, and C.
   A. Briefly explain ONE reason for conflict between the colonies and the British government in the 1760s and 1770s.
   B. Briefly explain a SECOND reason for conflict between the colonies and the British government in the 1760s and 1770s.
   C. Briefly explain ONE way the colonists expressed their opposition to the actions of the British government.

› Answers and Explanations

1. **C.** Pitt put the recruiting of colonial troops totally in local hands and agreed to reimburse the colonies for all their expenses during the war.

2. **D.** All previous taxation of the colonies had been self-imposed.

3. **C.** This statement was first made by Adams in 1768 in an article he wrote opposing the Townshend Acts.

4. **A.** The colonies contributed nearly 24,000 men to the war effort—while the British contributed 25,000.

5. **B.** Although some, including Sam Adams, wanted a boycott of all British goods, John Adams crafted a compromise that called for the colonies to oppose "taxation without representation."

6. **C.** John Dickinson is recommending that his readers pay greater attention to American liberties. He saw the taxes imposed by the British in the 1760s as a direct threat to the rights of the American colonists. He was a leader in urging his fellow Americans to resist British interference with their self-government.

7. **B.** John Dickinson was writing because of concern about the taxes that the British government was imposing on the colonies. In particular, he was responding to the British Parliament's passage of the Townshend Acts in 1767 and 1768 that taxed imports into the colonies, such as paper, lead, and tea, and also tightened up the enforcement of these measures. Dickinson believed that the British government could regulate colonial trade, but it had no right to raise revenues in America.

8. **A.** The concerns addressed by Dickinson were most directly shared by those who drafted the Constitution. The framers of the Constitution knew that Americans were very aware that government could pose a threat to their jealously guarded liberties. This inspired the system of checks and balances in the Constitution, making it difficult for any branch of the government to impose itself on the others or the people.

9. **Parts A and B**: Victory in the French and Indian War eliminated the serious military threat posed by the French. The colonists now had much less need for the military security provided by Great Britain. The French and Indian War had been enormously expensive for the British government. The British attempted to meet a budget deficit by taxing the American colonies. This conflicted with the American opposition to taxation without representation; the Americans believed that they should be taxed only by their own elected representatives.

Successive British taxes—the Sugar Act (1764), the Stamp Act (1765), the Townshend Acts (1767), the Tea Act (1773)—were opposed and resisted by the colonists. The Americans also resented the Quartering Act (1765), which forced them to find housing and provisions for British troops stationed in their colonies. Many Americans were outraged by the Intolerable Acts (1774), imposed on Massachusetts following the Boston Tea Party; the port of Boston was shut down, and British officials were given the power to appoint all officials in the colony, and citizens had to ask British permission to hold town meetings.

Part C: Americans expressed their opposition in a variety of ways. A Stamp Act Congress composed of representatives from nine colonies organized resistance to the Stamp Act. Sam Adams founded the Sons of Liberty in 1765. In 1768, Sam Adams issued the Circular Letter opposing the Townshend Acts. Other colonists published works criticizing British policy, such as John Dickinson's *Letters from a Farmer in Pennsylvania* (1767). Sam Adams set up a Committee of Correspondence in Boston; soon similar Committees of Correspondence appeared across the colonies to exchange ideas and information. The 1773 Boston Tea Party was a protest against the Tea Act; men dressed as Indians dumped British tea into Boston Harbor. Following the imposition of the Intolerable Acts on Massachusetts in 1774, the First Continental Congress met in Philadelphia to coordinate resistance to British policy. It issued the Declaration of Rights and Grievances. The Suffolk Resolves called for a boycott of British goods until the Intolerable Acts were repealed. Militias began training across the American colonies.

CHAPTER 10

American Revolution and the New Nation (1775–1787)

IN THIS CHAPTER

Summary: The Second Continental Congress, meeting in May 1775, began to prepare the American colonies for war. The impact of *Common Sense* by Thomas Paine and other documents continued to fan anti-British sentiment in the colonies, although there were still a number of Loyalists who supported British policies. As commander of the colonial army, George Washington practiced a defensive strategy, which, along with invaluable assistance from the French, helped to defeat the British army. The first government of the new nation was established by the Articles of Confederation, which created a weak national government.

Keywords

Second Continental Congress (May 1775): meeting that authorized the creation of a Continental army; many delegates still hoped that conflict could be avoided with the British.

Common Sense **(1776):** pamphlet written by Thomas Paine attacking the system of government by monarchy; this document was very influential throughout the colonies.

Battle of Yorktown (1781): defeat of the British in Virginia, ending their hopes of winning the Revolutionary War.

Treaty of Paris (1783): treaty ending the Revolutionary War; by this treaty Great Britain recognized American independence and gave Americans the territory between the Appalachian Mountains and the Mississippi River.

Articles of Confederation (ratified 1781): document establishing the first government of the United States; the states retained much power and little power was given to the federal government.

Northwest Ordinances (1784, 1785, 1787): bills authorizing the sale of lands in the Northwest Territory to raise money for the federal government; bills also laid out procedures for these territories to eventually attain statehood.

Lexington and Concord

King George II and the British government headed by Lord North did not respond favorably to the petition of the First Continental Congress. The British government saw no reason to compromise with the American colonists. They failed to comprehend that events were moving out of their control. The Americans were rapidly establishing a unified front against the Intolerable Acts and British attempts to weaken colonial self-government. In Massachusetts, the assembly met in defiance of the orders of General Thomas Gage, the acting governor; it became in effect a shadow government, exerting its influence over most of the colony outside of Boston, where Gage sat with his small army of Redcoats.

Pursuant to the Suffolk Resolves' call for the colonies to upgrade their militias, the Massachusetts assembly created a militia system independent of General Gage's control. Arms and munitions for these men were stored at the town of Concord. In February 1775, the British government declared Massachusetts to be in a state of rebellion. On the night of April 18–19, Gage sent a force of 700 men to destroy the militia arsenal at Concord. Word of this expedition soon leaked to the Americans, and Paul Revere and William Dawes rode out of Boston to spread the word that the Redcoats were coming. As the sun rose on April 19, the British vanguard encountered a force of 80 militiamen gathered on the town common at **Lexington**. The British ordered the militia to disperse; the American militia commander ordered his men to fall back, but not everyone heard him. At this moment of uncertainty, someone fired a shot. More shots followed, and the British charged with bayonets. Within minutes, eight colonists were dead and ten wounded.

The British continued their advance to **Concord**. The Americans were ready for them; more and more militiamen were gathering. The British found and destroyed some military supplies but did little significant damage. A large group of militiamen advanced on the British troops guarding the North Bridge on the outskirts of the town and after an exchange of fire drove them away. The British began to march back to Boston; along the way, they were attacked by groups of angry militiamen. Only the timely arrival of reinforcements sent by Gage saved the column. In this fighting, 275 British soldiers were killed, wounded, or reported missing, while the Americans suffered 93 casualties.

In May, Ethan Allen and his Vermont Green Mountain Boys seized Fort Ticonderoga from its tiny British garrison. Almost a year later, in March 1776, cannon dragged through the snow from Ticonderoga would persuade the British to evacuate Boston.

Second Continental Congress

When the **Second Continental Congress** assembled in May, it faced unprecedented challenges; the colonies were in rebellion and engaged in a war with the greatest maritime empire in the world. As word of Lexington and Concord spread, British authority in the colonies rapidly collapsed. Colonial legislatures assumed local power, but the Second Continental Congress would have to guide the united destinies of the colonies in the coming conflict.

Congress acted with decisiveness. It created the Continental Army and appointed the experienced soldier George Washington of Virginia its commander. Congress created a committee to formulate and conduct foreign policy; it also began issuing paper money to finance the war.

Even as it prepared for military operations, Congress made a last effort at peace. Congress sent the "Olive Branch Petition" to George III, asking the king to mediate a "happy and permanent reconciliation" to the conflict between the colonies and the British government. George II was in no mood to offer concessions to the Americans. He and his government were determined to quell the rebellion in the colonies by force. British intransigence forced even political moderates in the colonies to consider the possibility of American independence.

Thomas Paine's *Common Sense*

Although Thomas Paine had only emigrated to America from England in 1774, he warmly embraced the cause of the colonists. In January 1776, he published ***Common Sense***, one of the most influential political works in American history. Paine's pamphlet struck a nerve and sold phenomenally. Within three months, over 100,000 copies were printed, and by the end of the Revolutionary War, some 500,000 copies had been distributed in a country with a population of around two million. Paine managed to reach almost everyone who was literate in America; it was an extraordinary mass media success for the eighteenth century.

Paine wanted the colonies to separate themselves from Great Britain. He argued that the colonies would prosper once freed from the political and economic shackles imposed by the British. He attacked the institution of the monarchy, to which many Americans were still attached. He declared that "monarchy and hereditary succession have laid the world in blood and ashes." Paine's *Common Sense* played an important role in persuading many Americans of the necessity of independence. The **Loyalist** minority recognized the power of Paine's pamphlet; one New Yorker observed that "the unthinking multitude are mad for it. . . ."

Declaration of Independence

On June 7, 1776, Richard Henry Lee of Virginia placed a motion before Congress resolving "that these United Colonies are, and of right ought to be, free and independent States. . . ." Lee also called for Congress to consider a government framework through which the states could address continental issues. While the congressional delegates discussed independence with each other and communicated with the legislatures in their home states, a committee including Benjamin Franklin, John Adams, and Thomas Jefferson was appointed to draft a declaration of independence. The committee gave Thomas Jefferson the task of producing a first draft. Jefferson had a reputation of being a gifted writer, and he was well read in the writings of the great political philosophers of the **Enlightenment**.

Jefferson's text evoked the natural rights theory of John Locke, asserting that men have "certain unalienable rights," and "that among these are life, liberty, and the pursuit of happiness." Jefferson also echoed Locke in arguing that when a government "becomes destructive of these ends it is the right of the people to alter or abolish it." Jefferson embraced the notion of government as a social contract, writing that governments derive "their just powers from the consent of the governed." The bulk of Jefferson's text was a long list of the wrongs that the colonies had suffered at the hands of the British. Jefferson attributed these to George III rather than Parliament, accentuating a tyrannical view of British rule. After some changes at the hands of the committee and in Congress, the Declaration of Independence was debated on July 1. The next day, July 2, Congress voted for independence. This decision was announced on July 4.

Reactions to Independence

The Declaration of Independence was greeted with celebrations throughout the newly minted states. While supporters of independence were in the ascendency and controlled the state governments, not all Americans wanted to renounce their allegiance to the mother country. Although sometimes caricatured as wealthy grandees with close economic and political ties to the British colonial administration, Loyalists in fact came from all economic strata. Many valued the economic and cultural connections to Great Britain; others doubted the legality and good sense of challenging Great Britain's power.

Many African Americans greeted the Declaration of Independence with hope. The strong affirmation of natural rights in the document seemed to challenge the institution of slavery. (In fact, Jefferson had blamed American slavery on the British in his first draft; this section of the text was removed by Congress.) While the ideals laid out in the Declaration of Independence highlighted the inequalities in society, it did not lead to the emancipation of slaves. It did, however, inspire some to push for the end of slavery, giving rise to the abolitionist movement that gained footing in the 1800s. During the war, some slaves fled to the British, and a few were recruited into special "Ethiopian" units fighting with the British Army. Some slaves in the northern states won their freedom by serving in the militia or the Continental Army. Free blacks saw the ideals of the American Revolution as supporting their attempts to claim their rights as citizens.

Native Americans saw nothing for themselves in the Declaration of Independence or a free United States. While some Native Americans fought with the Americans, most supported the British because they feared the land hunger of the new nation.

Women were also inspired by the revolutionary ideals portrayed in the Declaration of Independence and throughout the consequent war. During the war, some women followed their husbands to the front, serving as camp followers who cooked and did laundry for the men. Martha Washington even spent part of the winter at Valley Forge with General Washington. Other women took up arms themselves, like Deborah Sampson, who passed as a man for over a year and fought for the patriot cause before an illness caused her to be discovered as a woman. Women on the home front took on additional roles without question. They ran family farms and businesses, all while providing food and clothes for their families. All of these women served to further the patriot cause, and, in doing so, played an important role in the development of the concept of "republican motherhood." After the revolution, women were seen as an integral part of the education of their sons to maintain the revolutionary ideals that were fought for during the war. As such, these "republican mothers" needed to be educated themselves. Women needed this education to be able to teach their sons to be citizens of the new republic. While this role was seen as an incredibly important one, women were still seen as inferior to men during this time.

Balance of Forces

Great Britain possessed an overwhelming military advantage over the colonies. The British Navy controlled the seas. The British Army was a highly regarded professional force. The British supplemented their Redcoat Regulars with thousands of German troops, known collectively as **Hessians**. The British could also rely on the services of American Loyalists, many of whom joined the British army or formed their own military units. In contrast, the Americans had no navy at the outset of the war. The Continental Army was poorly paid and supplied by Congress and the states; it had to address an initial lack of discipline and training while engaging in military operations against the British. The Continental Army was supported in the field by units of inexperienced militiamen who often proved unreliable under fire.

Despite their military superiority, the British faced serious problems in combatting the American rebellion. British forces were a long way from home, at the end of a supply line that stretched across the Atlantic Ocean. Because it could take months to sail back and forth between America and Great Britain, it was very difficult for British commanders to communicate with the government in London. America was a vast place, much of it wilderness; the British could not hope to occupy it all with the troops that they had available, and they ended up occupying only a few cities along the coast. The new United States had no capital or decisive point at which capture would force an American surrender. British armies would march through the American countryside hoping to force a battle that would end the war; sometimes they would not return.

On the other hand, the Americans were fighting on their home ground. George Washington proved to be an able strategist, who realized that the United States would win the war if it simply avoided defeat; as a result, he made the survival of his army a priority, making it a rallying point for American resistance. American spirits were lifted early in the war when, in June 1775, American militiamen fought the British at **Bunker Hill** outside Boston. The Americans were forced from their position, but before this happened, they shot down almost 1,000 British soldiers. This gave the impression that American citizen soldiers could easily defeat British Regulars. However, subsequent experience would demonstrate that this was not the case.

The War in the North

The British were forced out of Boston in March 1776, when cannon dragged from Fort Ticonderoga threatened their ships in Boston Harbor. The British retreated to Halifax, Nova Scotia, to regroup. At the end of June, the British general William Howe arrived at New York City with a massively reinforced army. That summer, Howe defeated Washington's army and maneuvered it out of New York, chasing the Americans across New Jersey into Pennsylvania.

That winter, the prospects for the American cause seemed bleak. Washington's army suffered from low morale and was dwindling due to desertions and expiring enlistments. Washington retrieved the situation with a brilliant counterstroke. On the evening of December 25, he led his men across the Delaware River, surprising and capturing the Hessian garrison of Trenton, New Jersey. A few days later, Washington defeated a British detachment at Princeton. As a result, the British hastily evacuated their outposts in New Jersey, surrendering much of the gains of their summer campaign. Washington had reversed the momentum of the war and given American morale a much needed boost.

The Saratoga Campaign

The fighting of 1776 resulted in failure for the British. The following year, they attempted to cripple the rebellion with an ambitious strategy of cutting the colonies in two. British forces from Canada, New York City, and the Great Lakes would drive toward Albany, New York, and the Hudson River. With the Hudson River Valley under firm British control, the New England colonies would be divided from the colonies to the south. With different sections of the country isolated, the British believed that they could then suppress the rebellion.

Unfortunately for the British, difficulties in communication and the ambitions of generals upset the plan before it began. Instead of marching up the Hudson River to Albany, General Howe in New York City set sail for Philadelphia, hoping to capture the American capital and destroy Washington's army. Howe defeated Washington and captured Philadelphia, but as Washington demonstrated with an attack on British forces in the Philadelphia suburb of Germantown, his army was anything but destroyed. Howe's Philadelphia gambit not only failed to achieve any decisive results, but it deprived General John Burgoyne's army, advancing toward Albany from Canada, of desperately needed support. Burgoyne's army bogged down in the New York wilderness and was surrounded at Saratoga by hard-fighting American forces. Burgoyne surrendered on October 17, 1777.

This defeat was disastrous for the British. Not only was an entire British army eliminated, but the American victory at Saratoga convinced the French to declare war on Great Britain in 1778. Until this point, the French had been assisting the Americans only with covert shipments of arms and military supplies. The French did this not because of any love for the Americans or their principles, but because they wanted to weaken their long-time enemy, Great Britain. Saratoga convinced the French government that the Americans could win and that the British were vulnerable. French intervention changed the nature of the war, which now became an international conflict with French and British forces clashing around the world. Later, the Spanish and Dutch would join the fight against Great Britain. French naval and military support would prove crucial for the Americans in the final campaign of the war.

While American men served in militias or the Continental Army, American women also played a vital role in sustaining the war effort. They ran farms and businesses while men were away and provided many needed services for the Army. Some women hoped that revolutionary ideals would lead to an improvement in their legal status. In March 1776, Abigail Adams urged her husband, John Adams, to "remember the ladies. . . . Do not put such unlimited power in the hands of the husbands."

The War in the South

Facing a new war after Saratoga and the American alliance with France, the British reassessed their strategy. A new British commander, General Henry Clinton, abandoned Philadelphia and marched overland to New York City. Along the way he encountered Washington's Continental Army. During the winter of 1777–1778, Washington's men suffered terribly from cold and famine at **Valley Forge**. Washington supported the efforts of a German officer, Baron von Steuben, to improve the training of his troops. Steuben's labors paid off when Washington's and Clinton's armies faced each other at the Battle of Monmouth in June 1778. Although Clinton was able to continue his retreat to New York, Washington's Continental troops more than held their own in very hard fighting.

The British now decided to focus their increasingly stretched military resources on the south, which they believed to be a hotbed of colonists with Loyalist sympathies. Initially, all went well for the British. They reoccupied Georgia, and Clinton forced the surrender of Charleston and a garrison of 5,000 men in May 1780. After General Charles Cornwallis defeated the remaining American army in the south a few months later, it appeared that the British southern strategy had succeeded.

The tide soon turned. George Washington sent General Nathanael Greene south to rally what was left of the Continental forces. Although he never won a battle, Greene waged a brilliant campaign that left British forces in the Carolinas confined to a few cities and outposts.

After winning a bloody battle with Greene, General Cornwallis marched his battered Redcoats into Virginia to rest and resupply. He stationed his army at **Yorktown**. Learning of this, Washington marched his army and a force of French troops, led by the Comte de Rochambeau, south. The British hoped to evacuate Cornwallis's army by sea, but a French fleet, under the Comte de Grasse, arrived in Chesapeake Bay before them. On September 5, 1781, the French fleet held off the British at the Battle of the Virginia Capes. This left Cornwallis trapped. Late in September, Washington began a formal siege of Yorktown. His situation hopeless, Cornwallis surrendered on October 19. Yorktown was the last major battle of the war; with another army captured, the British realized that they had lost America.

The Treaty of Paris

Peace negotiations began in Paris in 1782. Benjamin Franklin, John Adams, and John Jay represented the United States in these talks. Negotiations were protracted because fighting was still going on between the British and the French and their allies. Finally, the American delegation signed a treaty with the British on September 3, 1783.

In the Treaty of Paris, Great Britain recognized the independence of the United States. The British retained Canada but ceded to the United States the lands between the Appalachian Mountains and the Mississippi River. For the new nation, the western boundary of the Mississippi River in part reflected the wartime victories of George Rogers Clark in the Ohio River Valley. The Americans won lucrative fishing rights off Newfoundland and Nova Scotia, while promising the British that prewar debts to British merchants would be paid and that Loyalists would have confiscated property returned.

New State Constitutions and the Articles of Confederation

Independence meant that old colonial charters had to be replaced by new state constitutions. Ten states had drawn up new constitutions by the end of 1777. These documents reflected a suspicion of executive power borne of the years of struggle with Great Britain, so most governors were given limited authority. All states but Pennsylvania and Vermont instituted **bicameral legislatures**. Many states ensured the freedoms of their citizens with bills of rights. Most states broadened their electorates by lowering the property qualification to vote.

The Continental Congress completed work on a constitution for a limited national government by the fall of 1777. The **Articles of Confederation** were sent to the state legislatures for ratification. As with the state constitutions, this constitution for the new nation was a reaction against the overly powerful government the Americans had rebelled against. The Articles of Confederation created a very weak continental government.

The centerpiece of the new government was a **unicameral legislature** in which each state would have one vote. Limited executive authority was vested in a Committee of Thirteen, in which each state would have a representative. There was no national judiciary. To ratify the Articles of Confederation or to amend them, all 13 state legislatures would have to vote affirmatively. This held up ratification for almost four years. Because of disputes over western lands, Maryland did not ratify the Articles of Confederation until 1781, finally allowing the new form of government to take hold.

As a government framework designed to avoid government tyranny, the Articles of Confederation gave Congress few powers. The national government could carry on foreign relations, manage the western territories, and make treaties with Native Americans. The national government could not regulate trade or interstate commerce or impose taxes; it remained financially dependent upon financial contributions from the states.

Financial Problems

During the Revolution, Congress never found a way to effectively finance the war effort. The government resorted to issuing large amounts of unsecured paper money. Rampant inflation soon ate away the value of these so-called **Continentals.** Because of its financial embarrassment, Congress never paid many soldiers who had served in the Continental Army. Only loans from France and other European countries kept the government operating. Conditions did not improve for the government after the war; it had many debts and no way to raise enough money to pay them. Efforts to place tariffs on imports failed to get a unanimous vote in Congress. The nation's financial woes were multiplied by a postwar economic depression.

Northwest Ordinances

The government did have one potential source of income open to it, the sale of western lands. Settlers were pouring into the territories west of the Appalachian Mountains. By 1790, 110,000 Americans had moved into Kentucky and Tennessee. The **Northwest Ordinances** of 1784, 1785, and 1787 established regulations for the sale of land and territorial organization of the Northwest Territory, which would become the foundation for the government's policy toward all western lands that it acquired in the future.

The 1784 Ordinance determined that the western territories would be organized as new states. The Land Ordinance of 1785 established a system for selling western lands and also ensured that a section of land in every township would be reserved for the support of public education. The Ordinance of 1787 ceded all state claims to western lands to the national government; created the Northwest Territory, a jurisdiction expected to eventually be divided into three to five states; and established a procedure for a territory to apply for statehood. The Ordinance prohibited slavery in the Northwest Territory, making the Ohio River a dividing line between eventual slave and free states. Taken together, the Northwest Ordinances were the most consequential legislation passed during the period of the Articles of Confederation.

Shays' Rebellion

Farmers in western Massachusetts had suffered in the bad economic times that followed the Revolution. Many suffered from heavy loads of debt and the scarcity of hard currency that creditors demanded. Adding to their burdens were heavy taxes imposed by the Massachusetts legislature. In 1786, groups of protesters began to forcibly stop foreclosures on bankrupt farms and disrupt court proceedings. The rebellion was named for Daniel Shays, a veteran of the Continental Army who had experienced the financial hardships that drove the uprising.

At one point, it seemed as if a force led by Shays might seize the unguarded national armory at Springfield. However, a force of privately funded militia dispersed the rebels. A timely decrease in taxes helped pacify the situation. The most important result was that Shays' Rebellion highlighted for many people the need for a stronger central government in the United States.

Chapter Review

Rapid Review

To achieve the perfect 5, you should be able to explain the following:

- The first armed resistance to the British army occurred at Lexington and Concord.
- The Second Continental Congress began to prepare the American colonies for war against the British, but by passing the Olive Branch Petition, they tried to accommodate colonial interests with those of the Crown.
- The impact of the message presented in *Common Sense* by Thomas Paine was widespread throughout the colonies.
- Many Loyalists lived in the colonies at the outbreak of the Revolutionary War; many were members of the economic elite, though supporters of the British cause came from all classes.
- Blacks and women played large roles in the war effort of the colonies.
- The defensive tactics of George Washington as leader of the Continental forces proved decisive, since a longer war was disadvantageous to the British army.
- French assistance to the Continental war effort proved invaluable; the French navy proved to be especially critical as the war progressed.
- The Treaty of Paris ended the Revolutionary War. In this treaty, American independence was recognized by the British and large amounts of territory west of the Appalachians became American territory.
- The Articles of Confederation created a weak national government, partially to avoid replicating the "tyranny" of the Crown in England.
- To many colonial observers, Shays' Rebellion demonstrated that a stronger national government was needed.

Time Line

1775: Battles of Lexington and Concord
      Meeting of Second Continental Congress
1776: *Common Sense* published by Thomas Paine
      Declaration of Independence approved
      Surrender of British forces of General Burgoyne at Saratoga
1777: State constitutions written in 10 former colonies

1777–1778: Continental army encamped for the winter at Valley Forge
French begin to assist American war efforts
1781: Cornwallis surrenders at Yorktown
Articles of Confederation ratified
1783: Signing of the Treaty of Paris
1786–1787: Shays' Rebellion in Massachusetts
1787: Northwest Ordinance establishes regulations for settlement of territories west
of the Appalachian Mountains

› Review Questions

Fact Check

Check your knowledge of the historical period covered in this chapter.

1. The purpose of the Olive Branch Petition was to
   A. rally colonial support for war against Great Britain.
   B. petition the king for redress of economic grievances suffered by the colonies.
   C. ask the king to craft a solution to end the tensions between Great Britain and the colonies.
   D. ask the king to grant independence to the colonies.

2. At the beginning of the Revolutionary War, the British were extremely confident of victory because all of the following reasons *except*
   A. they had outstanding generals that would be commanding British forces in the Americas.
   B. there were many Loyalists throughout the American colonies.
   C. the Continental army suffered from poor discipline.
   D. the British had an outstanding navy.

3. All of the following were contained in the Treaty of Paris of 1783 *except*
   A. territory west of the Appalachian Mountains was ceded to the Americans.
   B. American independence was recognized by Great Britain.
   C. Quebec and the area immediately surrounding it was ceded to the Americans.
   D. former Loyalists in the colonies could retrieve property seized from them during the Revolutionary War.

4. Women were important in the war effort because they
   A. provided much of the financial backing for the colonial cause.
   B. wrote influential articles in colonial newspapers urging the colonies to resist the British.
   C. provided clothing and blankets for the frozen troops at Valley Forge.
   D. maintained economic stability in the colonies by managing households across the colonies while men were off fighting the British.

5. The weakness of the national government created by the Articles of Confederation was demonstrated by the fact that it was *not given the power to*
   A. mediate disputes between states.
   B. raise an army.
   C. conduct foreign relations.
   D. print money.

Multiple-Choice Questions

Here are multiple-choice questions like the ones on the AP U.S. History exam.

Questions 6–8 refer to the quotation below.

I feel myself exceedingly obliged to you for the full & friendly communications in your letters . . . and shall (critically as matters are described in the latter) be extremely anxious to know the issue of the movements of the forces that were assembling, the one to support, the other to oppose the constitutional rights of Massachusetts. —The moment is, indeed, important! —If government shrinks, or is unable to enforce its laws; fresh maneuvers will be displayed by the insurgents—anarchy and confusion must prevail—and every thing will be turned topsey turvy in that State; where it is not probable the mischiefs will terminate.

> —George Washington, Letter to Henry Knox, February 3, 1787, concerning Shays' Rebellion

6. Shays' Rebellion in Massachusetts attracted a lot of attention across America because it revealed which of the following?
   A. The decline of Puritan religious fervor in New England
   B. The strength of popular resistance to British rule
   C. Growing concern over Indian attacks
   D. The weakness of the national government

7. The attitude expressed by Washington in his letter to Knox strengthened calls for
   A. a Declaration of Independence.
   B. a Great Awakening.
   C. a Constitutional Convention.
   D. no entangling foreign alliances.

8. Like many of the Founding Fathers, Washington feared an excess of
   A. socialism.
   B. Puritanism.
   C. republicanism.
   D. democracy.

Short-Answer Question

The short-answer question below is similar to the ones you'll encounter on the AP U.S. History exam.

9. Answer Parts A, B, and C.
   A. Briefly explain ONE reason for American victory in the Revolutionary War.
   B. Briefly explain a SECOND reason for American victory in the Revolutionary War.
   C. Briefly explain ONE advantage that the British enjoyed in the Revolutionary War.

› Answers and Explanations

1. **C.** Although the Second Continental Congress began to prepare the colonies for war against Great Britain, the delegates also voted to send this petition to George III, asking him to create harmony between Great Britain and the colonies.

2. **A.** Several of the main generals commanding British troops in the Revolutionary War proved early on to be quite ordinary in tactical and leadership skills.

3. **C.** None of the British territory in Canada was taken from them as a result of the treaty.

4. **D.** Although women assisted the war effort in many ways, they made an important contribution by managing estates and farms while their husbands were serving in the colonial forces or in the Continental Army.

5. B. The national government was not given the power to issue taxes, regulate commerce, or raise an army.

6. D. Shays' Rebellion in Massachusetts attracted a lot of attention across America because it revealed the weakness of the national government. Shays' Rebellion took place in late 1786 and early 1787. Cash-strapped farmers angered by the state's strict policies concerning debts forcibly shut down courts enforcing the laws. In January 1787 a rebel force approached the federal government's Springfield Armory. No national forces were available to defend the armory. The rebels were dispersed by a privately raised militia. Shays' rebellion demonstrated that the national government could not defend its own installations.

7. C. The attitude expressed by Washington in his letter to Knox strengthened calls for a Constitutional Convention. Concerns over the weakness of the national government under the Articles of Confederation had been growing. The failure of the Annapolis Convention in 1786 to produce improvements in trade regulations led to a call for a more ambitious convention to reform the government. The social unrest that produced Shays' Rebellion and the inability of the national government to protect the Springfield Armory helped convince Congress to authorize the 1787 convention at Philadelphia that drafted the Constitution.

8. D. Like many of the Founding Fathers, Washington feared an excess of democracy. Uprisings like Shays' Rebellion demonstrated to Washington and others that popular movements could also be a threat to liberty. The Constitution reflected this concern. Only the members of the House of Representatives were directly elected by the people. The senators were elected by the state legislatures, and the president was elected by the Electoral College.

9. Parts A and B: America was a very big place, much of it wilderness, with few roads and major cities. This made it difficult for British armies to win decisive victories against the Americans. The United States under the Second Continental Congress and then the Articles of Confederation was able to create a government that maintained an impressive degree of unity among the states while waging the war. The United States brought forward skillful military commanders like George Washington and Nathanael Greene. Despite many hardships, thousands of Americans served bravely in the Continental Army and militias. Thanks to the training efforts of men like the Baron von Steuben, the Continental Army eventually became capable of meeting the British army on equal terms. The United States conducted an effective foreign policy, bringing France into the war in 1778. Spain and the Netherlands also joined in the war against Great Britain. French naval and military support helped George Washington win the decisive victory at Yorktown in 1781.

Part C: The British enjoyed the advantage of possessing a large professional military. To supplement these forces, the British were able to hire the services of thousands of German troops, known collectively as Hessians. The British were able to rally many Native American tribes to their side. They were also able to count on the loyalty of about a fifth of the American population, and many loyalists served in British military units. The royal navy gave the British the command of the sea.

CHAPTER 11

Establishment of New Political Systems (1787–1800)

IN THIS CHAPTER

Summary: During the late 1780s the Articles of Confederation were discarded and the Constitution of the United States was created, establishing a stronger federal government. The Constitution established a bicameral legislature, three branches of government, and the division of power between the states and the federal government. The Bill of Rights also established many basic freedoms central to the identity of the United States. During the presidency of George Washington, different visions of America were expressed by Thomas Jefferson and Alexander Hamilton.

Keywords

Virginia Plan: during debate over the Constitution, the plan proposing a bicameral legislature with representatives determined by proportional representation.

New Jersey Plan: during debate over the Constitution, the plan proposing one legislative body for the country, with each state having one vote.

Great Compromise: Connecticut plan that stated that one house of the Congress would be based on population (the House of Representatives) while in the other house all states would have equal representation (the Senate).

Electoral College: procedure for electing the president and vice-president of the United States as outlined in the Constitution; electors from each state, and not the popular vote, ultimately elect the president.

Three-Fifths Compromise: as the Constitution was being created, the plan that stated that slaves would be counted as three-fifths of a free person when determining a state's population for tax purposes and electing members of the House of Representatives.

Federalists: party in the first years of the republic that favored a larger national government; was supported by commercial interests. Federalists were opposed by Jeffersonians, who wanted a smaller national government. **Alien and Sedition Acts:** proposed by President John Adams, gave the president power to expel "dangerous" aliens and outlawed "scandalous" publications against the government.

The Constitutional Convention

The financial frustrations of the national government and episodes like Shays' Rebellion convinced a number of American leaders that a stronger national government was a necessity. They believed that the loose system of the Articles of Confederation was inadequate to the needs of a potentially powerful nation. Some of the advocates for changes, such as Alexander Hamilton, had served in the army during the Revolutionary War and had developed a "continental" perspective that transcended loyalties to particular states.

In the wake of Shays' Rebellion, the nationalists were able to persuade Congress to authorize a convention to explore revisions to the Articles of Confederation. On May 25, 1787, delegates from all 13 states gathered in Philadelphia. Among the delegates were George Washington, who was elected president of the convention; Benjamin Franklin; Alexander Hamilton; and James Madison. Two prominent leaders who missed the convention were John Adams and Thomas Jefferson, both of whom were serving as ambassadors in Europe. Early on, it was decided to abandon efforts to reform the Articles of Confederation and instead craft a new governing document.

A consensus emerged that the new government needed more powers, such as the ability to tax, regulate trade and interstate commerce, and create a military. Where the delegates disagreed was on just how powerful the central government should be. Although the current government was clearly too weak, the delegates did not want to lay the foundations of a tyranny, in which small cliques of men could wield influence at the expense of the majority.

A major division emerged between the large states and small states over representation in a prospective national legislature. Small states wanted to retain the practice of the Articles of Confederation, wherein each state received one vote in Congress. Large states wanted representation determined by population. Sectional divisions between north and south over issues such as slavery came to the fore. Also controversial was the proper balance of power between the central government and the states.

Contention and Compromise

The basis for much of the discussion at the Constitutional Convention was the **Virginia Plan** devised by James Madison. Madison's framework called for a federal government with three branches: legislative, executive, and judicial. He also proposed a bicameral Congress, with its membership determined by **proportional representation**. Madison played a leading role at the Convention and is often called the "Father of the Constitution." Madison's notes on the debates at the Convention are a vital historical source for understanding the constitutional thinking of the founding fathers.

The delegates from smaller states opposed the Virginia Plan because they feared that the larger states would dominate the national government. Instead, they rallied behind the **New Jersey Plan**, which proposed a Congress similar to that of the Articles of Confederation: unicameral and with each state having one vote. Arguments between the advocates of the two competing plans continued until delegates from Connecticut outlined a third possibility that became known as the **Great Compromise**. The Connecticut proposal stipulated that each state would have two members in the upper house of the new legislature, while the members of the lower house would be chosen through proportional representation.

The delegates at the Constitutional Convention were not believers in pure democracy. They believed that an unchecked majority could be just as tyrannical as a king. To guard against this, they decided that the president would be elected by an **Electoral College**, the composition of which would be determined by the states. State legislatures elected senators; only the members of the House of Representatives would be directly elected by the people. The framers of the Constitution were intent on creating a government that would be strong enough to do the nation's business, but not so mighty that it could oppress the people. As a result of this, they crafted a government of checks and balances, carefully balancing the powers of the three branches of government.

Slavery

The issue of slavery was debated at the Constitutional Convention. Many Americans in the 1780s believed that, for economic reasons, the institution of slavery would gradually disappear. Many southerners, still heavily invested in slaves and dependent on them for their livelihood, defended slavery.

The delegates compromised on the slavery issue to ensure southern support for the Constitution. The ability of the federal government to regulate or outlaw the slave trade was postponed for 20 years, until 1808. Southerners wanted slaves to count toward congressional representation; northern delegates resisted this. In the end, the delegates agreed to the **Three-Fifths Compromise**, counting three-fifths of a state's slave population when allocating seats in the House of Representatives.

The Ratification Battle

The finished Constitution was signed on September 17, 1787. The delegates decided that the new Constitution would go into effect if **ratifying conventions** in nine states approved the document. Because the Constitution increased the strength of the national government, its supporters became known as **Federalists**. The Federalists were confident that the new federal structure of the government would meet the needs of the nation, while the balance of powers among the three branches of government would protect American liberties. **Anti-Federalists** were unwilling to trust a stronger central government. They remembered the tyrannical behavior of the British and believed that a powerful national government would inevitably diminish the authority of the states, which they saw as the best defenders of the people's rights.

The anti-Federalists highlighted the fact that the proposed Constitution lacked a bill of rights. The two sides were well matched, and the voting in some state conventions was quite close. To win in crucial states like Virginia and New York, Federalists signaled a willingness to accept amendments to the Constitution protecting the rights of American citizens.

When New York voted to ratify the Constitution on July 26, 1788, it was the eleventh state to throw its support behind the new governing document. On September 13, Congress certified the ratification of the Constitution. Rhode Island, the last state to ratify the Constitution, did so on May 29, 1790.

George Washington was the inevitable choice to be the first president. He was elected unanimously by the Electoral College. Washington established crucial precedents as chief executive, helping define the role of president in the new government. He upheld the dignity of his office and emphasized his duties as an administrator of government policies.

The Bill of Rights

While helping draft the Constitution, James Madison did not believe that it needed a bill of rights; he thought its outline of powers sufficiently protected people's liberties. During the ratification debates, however, he changed his mind. While running for a seat in the first Congress, he promised to sponsor a bill of rights as a series of amendments to the Constitution. This way, Madison could both address the fears of the anti-Federalists and protect his constitutional handiwork. Once in Congress, he submitted 12 amendments; by 1791, 10 of these had been ratified by the states.

The **Bill of Rights** reconciled anti-Federalists to the Constitution. Over time, the Bill of Rights has become a cherished guarantee of such fundamental American values as freedom of religion, freedom of speech, and freedom of assembly. The Bill of Rights ensured the right to bear arms and prohibited the quartering of soldiers in citizens' homes. It also ensured crucial protections to people caught up in the judicial system, such as trial by jury and a ban on "cruel and unusual punishments."

The last two amendments of the Bill of Rights offered broad support to the Revolutionary War principle that rights reside in the people and the vitality of federalism in the new government system. The Ninth Amendment states that the listing of rights in the Constitution does not "disparage" any others held by the people. The Tenth Amendment reserves all powers not given to the federal government by the Constitution, or forbidden to the states by it, for the states and the people. Taken together, the Amendments of the Bill of Rights reinforced the balance of powers so important to Madison and the other Founding Fathers.

The Birth of the Party System

Washington staffed his cabinet with brilliant men. Thomas Jefferson served as secretary of state and Alexander Hamilton as secretary of the treasury. These two men had competing visions of America's future. Out of their differences would come the first party system in the United States.

Alexander Hamilton wanted the United States to become a great commercial and manufacturing power. He wanted to emulate British economic practices, including **mercantilist policies** to support American trade. To do this, he supported a "loose" interpretation of the Constitution, which argued that the federal government had powers not specified in the document.

Thomas Jefferson favored an agrarian America, predominantly made up of independent yeoman farmers. He believed that manufacturing would be economically secondary in America, "a handmaid to agriculture." Instead of Hamilton's system of protective tariffs, he supported **free trade**, which would keep the price of manufactured goods low for farmers. Jefferson called for a "strict" interpretation of the Constitution, which held that the federal government had only the powers listed in its text. James Madison joined Jefferson in his opposition to Hamilton's program.

As Hamilton and Jefferson articulated their disagreements and gathered supporters, a two-party system emerged. Hamilton's followers called themselves Federalists. Jefferson's followers called themselves Democratic-Republicans, or simply Republicans. Federalists argued for an activist government that created a favorable economic climate for business. Commercially expansive cities and ports provided the strongest support for the Federalists. Republicans focused on agriculture and defended **laissez-faire economic principles**. Their appeal was especially strong in the rural areas of the south and west.

Hamilton's Economic Program

Hamilton realized that, if the United States was going to become a great commercial and manufacturing power, the nation's chaotic finances had to be addressed. He laid out an ambitious program to put the United States on a sound financial footing in his **Report on the Public Credit**. Hamilton proposed that all notes issued by the national government under the Articles of Confederation be redeemed at face value. He also proposed that the federal government assume the outstanding debts of the states. He argued for the formation of a **national bank**; this would both facilitate financial transactions with the federal government and stimulate investment in American businesses. Hamilton wanted the federal government to actively support business expansion through its policies. He proposed a high tariff on foreign goods to pay for his economic program.

Jefferson and Madison were repelled by Hamilton's activist vision of government and disliked his partiality for business. They believed that Hamilton was sacrificing America's agrarian majority to commercial interests. They were able to block some of Hamilton's initiatives, but Hamilton was still able to set up his system of public credit with a national bank and tariffs.

Effects of the French Revolution

The French Revolution erupted in the summer of 1789, just a few months after George Washington took office as president. Americans watched the evolution of the French Revolution from a constitutional monarchy to the Reign of Terror with a mixture of fascination and horror. Jefferson and the Republicans tended to favor the progress of the revolutionaries because of their professions of support for democracy and their celebration of Enlightenment ideals. Hamilton and the Federalists disdained the Revolution's contempt for established authorities and its descent into mass violence. By 1793, revolutionary France was at war with most of Europe. Great Britain was once again France's most implacable foe. British and French naval forces fought each other at sea, endangering American shipping. President Washington issued a **Declaration of Neutrality**. He hoped that the United States could avoid entanglement in what had become a world war.

Washington also faced troubles at home. The easiest way for western farmers to get their grain to market in a period of poor roads and difficult transportation was to distill it into alcohol. Hamilton placed a tax on whiskey to help pay for his economic program. This angered the western farmers, who already sympathized with Jefferson's agrarian outlook. A group of farmers in western Pennsylvania rebelled, evoking the egalitarian principles of the French Revolution. Angered and alarmed, Washington gathered a large force of militia and easily suppressed the rebellion.

Washington's Foreign Policy

Professing neutrality, American merchants attempted to trade with both Great Britain and France; this angered both combatants. In 1794, the British began searching and seizing American ships trading with the French West Indies. The British were also plotting with Native Americans in the Northwest Territory.

Washington attempted to settle these problems by sending Chief Justice John Jay on a diplomatic mission to London. The British were not in the mood to make concessions on American trade; they refused to recognize the principle of the freedom of the seas and insisted on removing French products from American ships. The British did agree to withdraw from military posts that they held in the American west. These posts were soon rendered untenable anyway by General Anthony Wayne's defeat of a Native American coalition at the Battle of Fallen Timbers. **Jay's Treaty** proved to be widely unpopular in the United States. The Senate ratified the treaty after a protracted debate and much political maneuvering in its favor by Alexander Hamilton.

Thomas Pinckney negotiated a treaty with Spain that opened up the Mississippi River to American navigation. Pinckney's Treaty proved popular because it gave western and southern farmers a vital waterway to transport their crops to the markets of New Orleans.

Washington decided against running for a third term as president, establishing a long-lasting precedent. Before he left office, he released his Farewell Address. In it, he gave policy advice to his fellow citizens. Washington was dismayed by the intensifying acrimony between Federalists and Republicans and warned against the divisive dangers of political parties. He also urged the United States to avoid "foreign entanglements" and alliances with other nations. For 150 years, America would follow Washington's advice on foreign affairs.

The Presidency of John Adams

John Adams served two terms as Washington's vice-president. In the election of 1796, he ran as a Federalist. His opponent was Thomas Jefferson, the Republican candidate. Adams received the most votes in the Electoral College, but under the rules of the time, Thomas Jefferson, who came in second, became the vice-president. This created an awkward situation in which the president and vice-president belonged to different political parties.

Adams lacked Washington's public stature, but he proved to be an effective president who successfully managed a major crisis during his term of office. Adams spent many months of his presidency at his home in Quincy, Massachusetts, leading by letter. In 1800, he would be the first president to take up residence in the Executive Mansion.

Crisis with France

The French resented the fact that the United States did not maintain the 1778 alliance that had been signed with the royal government that was overthrown in the French Revolution. Jay's Treaty led the French government to believe that the Americans were tilting toward the British. The French responded by capturing American ships. In 1798, Adams sent three diplomats to France to attempt a negotiated settlement. The French foreign minister, Talleyrand, was notoriously corrupt. He sent three agents to the Americans demanding a bribe before he would talk with them. The Americans indignantly refused and were supported by public opinion back in the United States. This became known as the "XYZ Affair" after the code names of Talleyrand's emissaries.

The breakdown in diplomacy led to limited hostilities. The Washington administration had begun the construction of a small but efficient navy. From 1798 to 1800, the United

States and France fought an undeclared naval war. American vessels won most of the war's ship-to-ship battles. By 1800, Napoleon Bonaparte had taken control of France, and diplomacy resumed. In the Convention of 1800, the French compensated the Americans for the merchant ships that they had seized, and the alliance of 1778 was officially terminated.

The Alien and Sedition Acts

Partisan politics continued unabated during the undeclared war with France. Some Republican journalists still sympathetic to the French Revolution published virulently worded attacks on the Adams administration. A few French immigrants joined in the verbal assault. Many Federalists saw the conflict with France as an opportunity to crush the Republican Party. They reacted to the intemperate journalism of their opponents with two laws in 1798. The **Alien Act** gave the president the authority to imprison or deport any alien who was thought to be "dangerous to the peace and safety of the United States." The **Sedition Act** enabled the president to prosecute persons who published "malicious" criticisms of his administration.

These laws proved very controversial. The Sedition Act led to the prosecution and jailing of a number of journalists and other citizens. Republicans denounced the Alien and Sedition Acts. The state legislatures of Kentucky and Virginia passed the **Kentucky and Virginia Resolves**, which maintained that states had no obligation to respect unconstitutional laws. Thomas Jefferson authored the Kentucky Resolves, and James Madison wrote the Virginia Resolves. These resolves helped lay the foundation for the doctrines of nullification and states' rights that would play an important role in later American history. The Alien and Sedition Acts became an important issue in the election of 1800. Their unpopularity hurt the candidacy of John Adams.

Chapter Review

Rapid Review

To achieve the perfect 5, you should be able to explain the following:

- The 1787 meeting on amending the Articles of Confederation turned into a historical session when the Constitution of the United States was drafted.
- The importance of James Madison in the formulation of the Constitution cannot be overemphasized.
- The format of the bicameral legislature, the branches of power established at the federal level, and the division of powers between federal and state governments made the U.S. Constitution a unique document for its time.
- The division between Federalists and anti-Federalists demonstrated that very different visions of America and the scope of the federal government existed in the United States at this time.
- The Bill of Rights enunciated the basic freedoms that Americans cherish today.
- During the Washington administration, very different visions of America were expressed by Alexander Hamilton and Thomas Jefferson. The ideas of Hamilton helped spur American economic growth during the Washington administration.
- The United States experienced a great deal of trouble from the British and French during this era.
- Many critics viewed the Alien and Sedition Acts of John Adams as gross overextensions of the power given to the federal government by the Constitution.

Time Line

1787: Constitutional Convention ratifies U.S. Constitution

1788: U.S. Constitution ratified by states

1789: Washington sworn in as first president

1790: Hamilton issues plans proposing to protect infant U.S. industries

1791: Establishment of First National Bank
Ratification of the Bill of Rights

1793: Democratic-Republican clubs begin to meet ·

1794: Whiskey Rebellion begins

1795: Jay's Treaty with England/Pinckney's Treaty with Spain

1796: John Adams elected president, Thomas Jefferson, vice-president (each from a different political party)

1798: XYZ Affair
Sedition Act of John Adams issued
Kentucky and Virginia Resolves

1800: Convention of 1800
Thomas Jefferson elected president

› Review Questions

Fact Check

Check your knowledge of the historical period covered in this chapter.

1. The Connecticut Plan presented to the Constitutional Convention of 1787 was a
   A. proposal for a two-house legislature based on proportional representation.
   B. proposal for a one-house legislature based on proportional representation.
   C. proposal for a two-house legislature, with one house based on proportional representation.
   D. proposal for a balance of power between executive, legislative, and judicial branches.

2. The Kentucky and Virginia Resolves
   A. expressed support for the new U.S. Constitution.
   B. stated that individual states do not have to enforce laws the states consider unconstitutional.
   C. were written to support John Adams's support of the Sedition Act.
   D. were written in opposition to the economic policies of Alexander Hamilton.

3. Many in America felt that the English and the French failed to treat the United States as a major power in this era. All of the following are evidence of that *except*
   A. the Convention of 1800.
   B. Jay's Treaty.
   C. the treatment of American ships by the British during the 1790s.
   D. the XYZ Affair.

4. Thomas Jefferson and Alexander Hamilton had different views on all of the following *except*
   A. the amount of power the federal government should have.
   B. the tariff policy of the United States.
   C. the importance of a national bank.
   D. their belief in the power of the U.S. Constitution.

5. Under the Electoral College system
   A. voters directly elect the president of the United States.
   B. voters approve electors, who elect the president of the United States.
   C. it is possible to win the popular vote and lose the election in the Electoral College.
   D. B and C above.

Multiple-Choice Questions

Here are multiple-choice questions like the ones on the AP U.S. History exam.

Questions 6–8 refer to the quotation below.

1. *Resolved,* That the several States composing, the United States of America, are not united on the principle of unlimited submission to their general government; but that, by a compact under the style and title of a Constitution for the United States, and of the amendments thereto, they constituted a general government for special purposes—delegated to that government certain definite powers, reserving, each State to itself, the residuary mass of right to their own self-government; and that whensoever the general government assumes undelegated powers, its acts are unauthoritative, void, and of no force . . . .

—The Kentucky Resolutions of 1798

6. The Kentucky Resolutions of 1798, written by Thomas Jefferson, were an eloquent expression of which of the following political ideas?
   A. Libertarianism
   B. States' rights
   C. Progressivism
   D. Nationalism

7. The Kentucky Resolutions of 1798 were a reaction to the passage of which of the following?
   A. The Alien and Sedition Acts
   B. The Constitution
   C. The Northwest Ordinance
   D. The Missouri Compromise

8. The Kentucky Resolutions of 1798 most directly influenced the actions of important political figures during
   A. the struggle for Texan independence.
   B. the removal of the Cherokees across the Mississippi.
   C. the Nullification Crisis.
   D. the struggle to regulate big business trusts.

Short-Answer Question

The short-answer question below is similar to the ones you'll encounter on the AP U.S. History exam.

9. Answer Parts A, B, and C.
   A. Briefly explain ONE example of debate over constitutional principles in the United States in the period 1786 to 1800.
   B. Briefly explain a SECOND example of debate over constitutional principles in the United State in the period 1786 to 1800.
   C. Briefly explain ONE example of a political leader taking a policy stance based on constitutional principle.

› Answers and Explanations

1. C. The Connecticut Plan, also called the Great Compromise, was ratified by the delegates. Under this plan, representation in the House of Representatives would be by population, while all states would have equal representation in the Senate.

2. B. After the passage of the Sedition Act, legislatures in Kentucky and Virginia passed resolutions stating that states do not have to enforce laws they consider to be unconstitutional.

3. A. As a result of the Convention of 1800, the French agreed to compensate the United States for ships seized during the previous decade. Events mentioned in all of the other choices demonstrate that the French and English had little respect for American rights in diplomatic matters and on the high seas during this era.

4. D. Both believed in the power of the Constitution, although their interpretations of the Constitution were different. Jefferson believed in a strict interpretation of the Constitution, while Hamilton believed in a broad interpretation.

5. D. As demonstrated in the presidential election of 2016, it is possible to get the most number of votes nationwide but to lose the presidential election in the Electoral College. This also occurred in the presidential elections of 1876, 1888, and 2000.

6. B. The Kentucky Resolutions of 1798 were an eloquent expression of the principle of states' rights. Thomas Jefferson, the author of the Kentucky Resolutions of 1798, here argued that states could declare acts of Congress that violated their rights unconstitutional. Though the Kentucky Resolutions of 1798 did not explicitly call for this, Jefferson believed that states could then refuse to enforce these laws.

7. A. The Kentucky Resolutions of 1798 were a reaction to the Alien and Sedition Acts. These acts were passed by the Federalist-dominated Congress in 1798, during a time of heightened tension with France, when full-scale war seemed imminent. These acts increased the residency requirement for naturalization, gave the president power to imprison or deport aliens, and outlawed extreme journalistic criticisms of the government. The Democratic-Republican opposition saw these laws as an outrageous attack on them and American liberties.

8. C. The Kentucky Resolutions of 1798 most directly influenced the actions of important political figures during the Nullification Crisis. In 1832, a state convention in South Carolina declared the tariffs of 1828 and 1832 unconstitutional. The convention declared that the tariffs were nullified and would not be enforced in the state. The South Carolinians believed that these tariffs unfairly protected northern manufacturers at the expense of southern agriculture. President Andrew Jackson threatened to use force against the recalcitrant South Carolinians until a compromise reduction in the tariff passed Congress and reduced tensions. The South Carolinians rescinded their Nullification Ordinance in 1833; they did not abandon their states' rights principles.

9. Parts A and B: Delegates debated constitutional principles at the 1787 Constitutional Convention. Issues included the type of state representation in Congress; this was resolved by the Great Compromise, which provided for two senators for each state, while members of the House of Representatives were allocated by population. A debate over ratification ensued. *The Federalist Papers*, authored by James Madison, Alexander Hamilton, and John Jay, made a powerful case for ratifying the new Constitution. Once the new government was launched, there were debates over the powers of the new central government and about how to interpret the Constitution. The Bank of the United States became a centerpiece of this debate, with supporters of a limited government and strict interpretation of the Constitution opposing the Bank, and supporters of a stronger government and a looser interpretation of the Constitution in favor of it. In 1798, the Federalist-dominated federal government passed the Alien and Sedition Acts giving the president power to deport certain immigrants and to regulate the press. Democratic-Republican critics of these measures passed the Kentucky and Virginia Resolves, arguing that the states could nullify laws that they believed were unconstitutional.

Part C: George Washington staked his prestige in supporting the new Constitution. James Madison fulfilled promises made during the ratification debate by sponsoring the amendments that became the Bill of Rights. Secretary of the Treasury Alexander Hamilton built his economic program, including the Bank of the United States, around his vision of a strong central government. Thomas Jefferson led the opposition to Hamilton's plans. Thomas Jefferson wrote the Kentucky Resolves, and James Madison wrote the Virginia Resolves.

CHAPTER 12

Jeffersonian Revolution (1800–1820)

IN THIS CHAPTER

Summary: The election of Thomas Jefferson in 1800 was a critical election in American history; Jefferson's view of America differed greatly from that of the Federalists. Alexander Hamilton and other Federalists envisioned America as a future industrial power. For Jefferson, the independence and pride of the yeoman farmer would guide America into the future. During the time when John Marshall was chief justice of the Supreme Court, the power of the federal courts increased. The overall size of America also increased in this era as a result of the Louisiana Purchase. The War of 1812 was fought over continued tensions between the Americans and the British. Many Americans in this era envisioned massive economic growth in the United States; this was the focus of Henry Clay's "American System."

Keywords

Marbury v. Madison **(1803):** critical Supreme Court decision that established the principle of judicial review, stating that the Supreme Court has the right to review all federal laws and decisions and declare whether or not they are constitutional.

Louisiana Purchase (1803): massive land purchase from Emperor Napoleon of France that virtually doubled the size of the United States.

Lewis and Clark Expedition (1804): expedition that discovered much about the western part of the North American continent and the economic possibilities there.

War of 1812: war between the British and the Americans over British seizure of American ships, connections between the British and Native American tribes, and other tensions. The British sacked Washington, DC, in 1814. The treaty ending the war merely restored diplomatic relations between the two countries.

American System: plan proposed by Senator Henry Clay and others to make America economically independent by increasing industrial production in the United States and by the creation of a Second National Bank.

Missouri Compromise (1820): political solution devised to keep the number of slave states and free states equal; Missouri entered the Union as a slave state and Maine entered as a free state. Potential states in the northern part of the Louisiana territory would also come in as free states in the future.

Election of 1800

John Adams decided to run for a second term as president in 1800. Charles Pinckney of South Carolina ran as the Federalist candidate for vice-president. Thomas Jefferson was again the Republican candidate for president. Aaron Burr of New York was the Republican running for the vice-presidency. Jefferson edged out Adams in the Electoral College with 73 votes to Adams's 65. However, because the Constitution made no distinction in the Electoral College between presidential and vice-presidential candidates, Aaron Burr also received 73 votes, throwing the election to the House of Representatives for a decision. Burr was an ambitious and unscrupulous politician and did not concede to Jefferson. Instead, he garnered substantial votes from Federalists who detested Jefferson. The election in the House of Representatives, where each state cast one vote, was a cliffhanger, with the voting going through 35 ballots without a victor. Ironically, Jefferson owed his victory on the thirty-sixth ballot to Alexander Hamilton, who told supporters that Burr was "the most unfit man in the United States for the office of president." This political crisis led to the adoption of the **Twelfth Amendment** in 1804, which allowed members of the Electoral College to cast separate ballots for the president and vice-president.

The election of 1800 was the first time that control of the presidency passed from one party to another. Because of this, it has sometimes been called the "Revolution of 1800." Thomas Jefferson brought remarkable abilities and a wealth of experience to the presidency. He was an Enlightenment man, fascinated by the latest scientific and political ideas, and a gifted writer. He was an able political leader who had built a successful party, yet as a former diplomat and secretary of state, he also had extensive experience in foreign affairs.

As a strict constitutional constructionist, Jefferson was determined to reverse the policies of the Federalists and scale back the reach of the federal government. Once in office, he and his secretary of the treasury, Albert Gallatin, cut taxes like that on whiskey. He allowed the hated Alien and Sedition Acts to lapse. Jefferson did not wipe out all the legislative achievements of the Washington and Adams administrations, however. At his inaugural, he had reached out to the political opposition by declaring, "We are all Republicans; we are all Federalists." Jefferson had opposed the creation of Hamilton's national bank; once in office, he accepted its economic usefulness and left it alone.

An Assertive Supreme Court

Until the 1930s, there was a long interval between presidential elections and the new president's inauguration in March of the following year. In 1801, the outgoing Federalists took advantage of this period to pass the **Judiciary Act**, creating many new federal circuit and district courts. Outgoing president Adams appointed Federalist judges to these courts. These were known as **"midnight appointments,"** because President Adams was erroneously believed to be signing these many commissions on his last night in office.

Jefferson and his partisans were outraged by this effort to pack the federal bench with Federalists. The new Republican Congress promptly repealed the Judiciary Act and launched the impeachment of a pair of Federalist judges. One of John Adams's last-minute judicial appointees was John Marshall, whom Adams nominated to be chief justice of the Supreme Court. Marshall was an able lawyer and Federalist politician who served as secretary of state in the last year of Adams's presidency. Marshall would become the longest-serving chief justice, heading the Court from 1801 to 1835. He would also be the most influential. His judicial rulings profoundly shaped American law. Federalist in principle, he asserted the supremacy of federal over state law. Marshall also elevated the stature and political significance of the Supreme Court.

One of Marshall's most important rulings came early, in the 1803 *Marbury v. Madison* decision. William Marbury was a Federalist whom John Adams appointed to be a justice of the peace in the District of Columbia. Marbury's letter of appointment was not delivered to him, and James Madison, secretary of state in the new Jefferson administration, refused to deliver it to him. Marbury sued for his letter. Marshall disliked Madison's action but ruled against Marbury anyway, arguing that the provision of the Judiciary Act of 1789 that enabled Marbury to sue was itself unconstitutional. This established the principle of **judicial review**, which gives the courts the ability to rule on the constitutionality of legislation. Marshall's assertion of judicial prerogative laid the foundation for the Supreme Court's later political influence.

A New Frontier

Thomas Jefferson envisioned a republic of independent farmers. He believed that only self-sufficient, property-owning citizens would be able to resist corruption and tyranny. To ensure such a future for the United States, Jefferson needed land. He became fascinated with the west. Settlers were already streaming into the lands west of the Appalachian Mountains. By 1800, one million Americans lived there. The Jefferson administration encouraged western settlement by easing the terms to purchase land; a down payment of $80 gave a purchaser rights to 160 acres of land. The movement west accelerated.

This massive influx of settlers inevitably led to conflict with the Native Americans who lived and hunted on these western lands. Jefferson believed that the Native American way of life must inevitably give way to the march of American civilization. He hoped that the Native Americans would eventually assimilate into American society and become farmers themselves, but he doubted that this would happen anytime soon. As a result, Jefferson believed that the best thing for the Native Americans would be to remove them to a more distant territory, where, over time, they could adapt to American ways. Jefferson thus laid the foundation of the policy of Native American removal that would come to a head in the later presidencies of Andrew Jackson and Martin Van Buren. Unsurprisingly, many Native Americans resisted American expansionism, including the brilliant Shawnee diplomat and soldier Tecumseh and his brother Tenskwatawa, a religious visionary called the "Prophet" by the Americans.

The Louisiana Purchase

The French dictator Napoleon Bonaparte forced the Spanish government to secretly cede Louisiana to France in 1800. Napoleon was hoping to re-create a French empire in the Americas. The American government learned that the French intended to return to Louisiana in 1801. The prospect of a militarily powerful and aggressive neighbor bordering the United States worried President Jefferson. He decided to attempt a diplomatic resolution to the problem and sent William Livingstone to France with an offer to purchase New Orleans. Livingston was later joined by James Monroe. In the meantime, Napoleon's dreams of a North American empire faded as an army dispatched to recapture the Caribbean island of Haiti perished of disease. War also loomed between France and Great Britain, and Napoleon knew that any French possessions in North America would be cut off by the British Navy. In 1803, Napoleon startled Livingston and Monroe by offering to sell the entire Louisiana Territory for $15 million. The **Louisiana Purchase** was a financial bargain for the United States. The Americans had been willing to offer $10 million for New Orleans alone; the purchase price for the entire territory worked out to roughly 3 cents an acre. The acquisition of the Louisiana Territory doubled the size of the United States.

Jefferson had some legal scruples about the federal government's ability to purchase such an expanse of territory since no such power is explicitly mentioned in the Constitution; he set these concerns aside because the Louisiana Purchase was so obviously in the interest of the United States and because the accession of so much new land in the west greatly strengthened his dream of an agrarian republic. Although some Federalists opposed the Louisiana Purchase because it reinforced Jefferson's political base in the west, the Senate ratified the treaty with France, and the House of Representatives quickly approved the expenditure of the purchase price.

Jefferson was anxious to know more about the interior of the North American continent, its flora and fauna, the peoples living there, and its economic potentialities. Even before the Louisiana Purchase, he had been contemplating sending mapping expeditions west. Once Louisiana was acquired, Jefferson sponsored the **Lewis and Clark Expedition** to explore the new lands that had been added to the United States. Meriwether Lewis and William Clark left St. Louis with a party of nearly 50 men in 1804. Over the course of a two-year journey, they made their way to the Pacific Ocean and back. The voluminous records of Lewis and Clark's trip provided Americans with a wealth of information about the lands that the pair had traversed and whetted the appetite for further western exploration and settlement.

Burr's Conspiracy

Political strife did not abate during Jefferson's presidency. The Federalists were declining but continued to oppose Jefferson's policies. The **Essex Junto**, a group of extreme Federalists based in New England, denounced what they saw as a "decline in public virtue" with Jefferson in office. Massachusetts senator Timothy Pickering believed that the president was a "Parisian revolutionary monster." In 1804, the Federalists nominated Charles C. Pinckney to run against Jefferson, but the Federalist candidate was overwhelmed in the election, winning only 14 electoral votes.

More problematic for Jefferson than the Federalist opposition was the challenge posed by his vice-president. After demonstrating his disloyalty during the electoral crisis of 1800, Aaron Burr recognized that he had lost any hope of playing an influential role in the

Jefferson administration. A wily schemer, Burr was accused of negotiating with secessionist Federalists. Alexander Hamilton believed the charge and criticized Burr in a letter. Learning of this, Burr challenged Hamilton to a duel. Hamilton agreed to the encounter, and on July 11, 1804, he was shot and killed by Burr.

Under indictment for murder in New York and New Jersey, Burr completed his term as vice-president and then traveled to the West. Here he launched a conspiracy with the equally unscrupulous general James Wilkinson and others to foment a rebellion against Spanish rule in Mexico. Burr hoped to restore his fortunes by conquering lands for himself in the southwest. Wilkinson betrayed Burr's scheme to both the Spanish and American governments. President Jefferson ordered Burr's arrest on a charge of treason. Jefferson hoped to see the conviction of his old rival, but Chief Justice John Marshall, who presided over the trial, was unsympathetic to the arguments of the prosecution, and Burr was acquitted.

Renewal of War in Europe

The resumption of war between France and Great Britain in 1803 had far-reaching effects on the United States. Once again, the United States attempted to maintain its neutrality while finding itself caught between the competing ambitions of two great powers. American merchants hoped to trade freely with all countries, but Great Britain imposed a blockade on all French-controlled Europe, seizing ships that did not have expensive British licenses. Napoleon created his Continental System, which placed an embargo on trade with Great Britain. As a result, the French Navy captured American ships doing business with the British. In addition to interfering with American commerce, the British Navy, short on manpower, instituted the practice of **impressment**. After stopping American ships on the high seas, British naval officers kidnapped American sailors and forced them to serve on their ships. The British claimed that the men they seized were British subjects; some probably were, but many were naturalized or American-born citizens. British warships ranged up and down the American seacoast, interfering with American shipping and impressing American sailors. The most notorious incident occurred in 1807, when a British warship fired on the unsuspecting U.S.S. *Chesapeake*, forcing it to strike its colors before taking off four members of its crew.

Most Americans were outraged by the *Chesapeake* incident. President Jefferson could have led a largely united nation to war. Instead, he decided to try a peaceful means of resolving the crisis. Jefferson believed that the United States could change British and French policy through an economic boycott. He persuaded the Republican-dominated Congress to pass the **Embargo Act of 1807**, which prohibited American exports. Unfortunately, the Embargo Act at first seemed to have a greater effect on the American economy than on the British and French. Seaborne trade largely dried up, hurting merchants and putting sailors out of work. Planters and farmers were hurt because they could not get their products to foreign markets. Economically disastrous, the Embargo Act became deeply unpopular, especially in the Federalist bastion of New England, where ocean-going commerce was especially important. Jefferson's economic policy failed to have its intended effect and divided the American people.

The Democratic-Republican Party was still strong enough to elect James Madison as president in 1808. Madison recognized that the Embargo Act had to be abandoned in order to restore American prosperity. As a replacement, he supported the **Non-Intercourse Act**, which allowed Americans to trade with all countries except Great Britain and France. Congress continued to pass bills through 1810, attempting to put enough economic pressure on Great Britain and France to compel them to stop interfering with American trade.

The War of 1812

Years of humiliation at the hands of the British led a group of young Republicans in Congress to call for war. Henry Clay of Kentucky was one of the leaders of these "War Hawks." He believed that if the United States did not resist British policies, it could not honorably call itself an independent nation. The War Hawks were also concerned about the situation in the west. Tecumseh and the Prophet were rallying the Native Americans of the trans-Appalachian region against further American settlement. Tecumseh hoped to organize a confederacy of tribes powerful enough to resist the American military. The Americans believed that Tecumseh was allied with the British in Canada. In 1811, the governor of Indiana, William Henry Harrison, led a force of 1,000 men against Prophetstown, which had been built by Tecumseh and his brother. Tecumseh was away, and the Prophet unwisely attacked the Americans who ultimately defeated the Prophet at the Battle of Tippecanoe. Harrison's army burned Prophetstown and dispersed its inhabitants, dealing Tecumseh's cause a severe blow. The War Hawks believed that a war with Britain would enable the United States to break what was left of Tecumseh's power. They also hoped to conquer new lands in Canada.

President Madison asked for war in June 1812. The enthusiasm of the War Hawks was not matched by everyone in the country. Many Federalists loathed Napoleonic France and believed that it would be economically advantageous to reach a diplomatic accommodation with Great Britain. Federalist New England would show little support for the war, and many New Englanders traded with the British in Canada.

Despite their bellicosity, the War Hawks had done little to ready the United States for a war against Great Britain. The army was tiny and untried, and the navy possessed just 17 ships. The weaknesses in the American army were exposed as attempts to invade Canada ended in ignominious failure. The navy did better, winning a number of ship-to-ship combats, but the British soon bottled up most American warships in their harbors. In 1813, an American naval victory on Lake Erie paved the way for William Henry Harrison to defeat a force of British and Native Americans at the Battle of the Thames near Detroit. The most significant result of the battle was the death of Tecumseh. In the south, members of the Creek tribe, allied with the British, attacked American settlers. Andrew Jackson at the head of a force of Tennessee militiamen crushed the Creeks in a series of bloody battles.

The End of the War

Napoleon's enemies forced him to abdicate in 1814. This freed up large numbers of British troops who were then deployed to America. The United States had to withstand major British attacks. A British invasion from Canada was turned back by an American naval victory on Lake Champlain. Another British army landed in Chesapeake Bay and captured the city of Washington, burning the Presidential Mansion and the Capitol. A follow-up attack on Baltimore was repulsed, inspiring Francis Scott Key to write "The Star-Spangled Banner." Andrew Jackson became a national hero in January 1815, when he handily defeated a British army attempting to seize the city of New Orleans. Jackson's victory actually took place *after* a peace treaty had been signed between the United States and Great Britain, but that news hadn't yet reached New Orleans.

In late 1814, negotiators gathered in Ghent, in what is now Belgium. Both sides were tired of the war, and the defeat of Napoleon put an end to the British blockade and impressment. The **Treaty of Ghent** ended the war on the basis of the status quo ante, the situation before the war. Aside from breaking the power of the Native Americans living east of the

Mississippi, the United States gained nothing tangible from the war. Militarily, the war had been at best a draw with the British. But the culminating victory at New Orleans and the fact that the United States held its own against Great Britain enabled Americans to see the war as a success, a veritable second war of American independence.

A Federalist Debacle and the Era of Good Feelings

During the war, many Federalists remained outspoken in their opposition to the conflict. While American diplomats were negotiating at Ghent, a number of New England Federalists gathered at the **Hartford Convention**. Here they denounced the war and debated topics including the **nullification** of laws, such as the embargo that they regarded as unconstitutional. Some delegates advocated the **secession** of New England from the union, although the convention as a whole never endorsed this.

The timing of these Federalists was bad. The end of the war and Jackson's victory at New Orleans left them looking both unwise and unpatriotic. The Federalist party never recovered from this embarrassment and faded away over the next few years. For a time, the triumphant Democratic-Republicans led a unified country in which they faced no significant political opposition. James Monroe was easily elected president in 1816 and served for two terms. The period from 1816 to 1823 became known as the **Era of Good Feelings**.

Henry Clay and the American System

Taking advantage of the confident postwar mood, Henry Clay publicized an economic program that he termed the **American System**. Clay expressed the reinvigorated nationalist spirit of the time by aiming to make the United States economically independent of Europe by encouraging American industry. President Madison and then President Monroe supported the plan. The failures of the War of 1812 had convinced many Republicans that the government should play a more vigorous role in the economy; in effect, they adopted important elements of Alexander Hamilton's economic vision.

In 1816, Congress created the **Second National Bank** to facilitate credit and financial transactions across the United States. The **Tariff of 1816** increased the tariff rate on foreign goods to 22 percent in order to encourage domestic manufacturers. The revenue from the tariff was earmarked for roads and other internal improvements to help American farmers, industrialists, and merchants get their products to markets. These policies helped spur a postwar economic boom that lasted until the onset of an economic depression in 1819.

Missouri Compromise

Slavery became a major political issue for the first time in 1819, when Missouri asked to enter the Union as a slave state. At this time, the number of free and slave states was equal at 11 each. In earlier years, slavery had seemed to be a declining institution. The Northwest Ordinance barred slavery from the Northwest Territory. In 1808, the importation of slaves from overseas was outlawed. But Eli Whitney's invention of the cotton gin had made cotton a lucrative cash crop. The demand for slave labor increased, making slaves much more valuable to their masters.

The expansion of slavery into the western territories suddenly became a heated issue. The balance of slave and free states gained new political urgency. The possibility of Missouri tipping this balance in favor of the slave states outraged many in the north. Acrimonious political debate ensued. Henry Clay, the speaker of the house, resolved the issue in 1820 with the **Missouri Compromise**. Clay paired the admission of Missouri to the Union with the admission of Maine as a free state. To prevent further disputes, he drew a line through the Louisiana Territory at 36 degrees, 30 minutes; states admitted south of that line would be slave states, whereas states admitted north of the line would be free states. Clay and many contemporaries hoped that the Missouri Compromise had put an end to the contentious issue of slavery.

Chapter Review

Rapid Review

To achieve the perfect 5, you should be able to explain the following:

- The election of Thomas Jefferson in 1800 is called the "Revolution of 1800," as the new president had a completely different vision of America from the Federalists whom he replaced.
- Thomas Jefferson was one of the most brilliant men ever to serve as president, and he instituted many "Republican" policies during his eight years in office.
- The role of the federal courts was greatly strengthened during the tenure of John Marshall as chief justice of the Supreme Court.
- The Louisiana Purchase more than doubled the size of the United States and allowed the "empire of liberty" to continue to expand.
- The case of Aaron Burr showed the deep political divisions that existed in the United States during this period.
- The Napoleonic Wars greatly impacted the relationship between the United States, England, and France.
- America entered the War of 1812 because President Madison convinced the nation that America's rights as a neutral power had been violated and because many in Congress felt that the British were encouraging the resistance by Native American tribes.
- The American System of Henry Clay and others was proposed after the War of 1812 and outlined a plan for broad economic growth for the United States.
- The Missouri Compromise temporarily solved the issue of the number of slave states versus the number of free states.

Time Line

1800: Thomas Jefferson elected president in "Revolution of 1800"
1801: John Marshall named chief justice of the Supreme Court
   Alien and Sedition Acts not renewed
1803: Louisiana Purchase
   Marbury v. Madison established federal judicial review
1804: Alexander Hamilton killed in duel with Aaron Burr
   Thomas Jefferson reelected
   Twelfth Amendment ratified (separate voting for president, vice president)
   Beginning of Lewis and Clark expedition
1807: Embargo Act greatly harms foreign trade

1808: James Madison elected president
      Further importation of slaves into the United States made illegal
1812: Beginning of the War of 1812
1814: British army sacks Washington
      Treaty of Ghent formally ends the War of 1812
      Native American removal from Southern territories begins in earnest
1814–1815: Hartford Convention (meeting of Federalists)
1815: Victory of Andrew Jackson at the Battle of New Orleans (after the War of
        1812 was officially over)
      Henry Clay proposes the American System
1816: James Monroe elected president
1816–1823: Era of Good Feelings
1820: Missouri Compromise

› Review Questions

Fact Check

Check your knowledge of the historical period covered in this chapter.

1. The *Marbury v. Madison* decision
   A. gave powers to the president that the Republicans of Thomas Jefferson claimed he didn't have.
   B. gave broad judicial power to the state courts.
   C. declared that the Alien and Sedition Acts were constitutional.
   D. established the principle of judicial review.

2. As a result of the election of Thomas Jefferson in 1800,
   A. more assistance was given to the commercial sector.
   B. American foreign policy became more pro-British.
   C. the federal debt rose dramatically.
   D. federal excise taxes were eliminated.

3. All of the following are reasons why America entered the War of 1812 *except*
   A. the impressment of American naval crews.
   B. the existence of a strong American navy ready to demonstrate its capabilities.
   C. the relationship between the British and Native American tribes in the western territories of North America.
   D. the desire of American leaders to acquire additional western territories.

4. The Hartford Convention demonstrated that
   A. the Federalist party had remained a dominant party in American political life.
   B. the War of 1812 brought political union to the United States.
   C. the concept of nullification was not exclusively a Southern one.
   D. the Treaty of Ghent was a controversial treaty.

5. The American System of Henry Clay
   A. favored strong economic growth and a Second National Bank.
   B. wanted to make the United States the military equivalent of Great Britain or France.
   C. favored lowering tariffs so that more goods could be purchased from abroad.
   D. advocated the elimination of slavery.

Multiple-Choice Questions

Here are multiple-choice questions like the ones on the AP U.S. History exam.

Questions 6–8 refer to the quotation below.

Brother, since the peace was made, you have killed some of the Shawnees, Winnebagoes, Delawares, and Miamis, and you have taken our land from us, and I do not see how we can remain at peace if you continue to do so. You try to force the red people to do some injury. It is you that are pushing them on to do mischief. You endeavor to make distinctions. You wish to prevent the Indians doing as we wish them—to unite, and let them consider their lands as the common property of the whole; you take tribes aside and advise them not to come into this measure; and until our design is accomplished we do not wish to accept of your invitation to go and see the President.

—Tecumseh, Speech to Governor William Henry Harrison at Fort Vincennes, 1810

6. Tecumseh argued that Native Americans should respond to the westward expansion of American settlement by
   A. embracing the culture of American settlers.
   B. forming a Native American confederacy.
   C. retreating westward across the Mississippi River.
   D. launching attacks against American cities in the East.

7. The disagreement between Tecumseh and William Henry Harrison most directly concerned which of the following?
   A. The injustice of racial prejudice
   B. The British impressments of American sailors
   C. Poor conditions on Native American reservations
   D. The American belief that tribal leaders could sell Native Amercian land

8. The death of Tecumseh and American victories in the War of 1812 led most directly to which of the following government policies?
   A. Citizenship for Native Americans
   B. Native American removal
   C. The enlistment of Native American scouts in the U.S. Army
   D. The passage of the Dawes Severalty Act of 1887, breaking up reservations

Short-Answer Question

The short-answer question below is similar to the ones you'll encounter on the AP U.S. History exam.

9. Answer Parts A, B, and C.
   A. Briefly explain ONE example of the influence of foreign wars on American policy during the period 1801 to 1812.
   B. Briefly explain a SECOND example of the influence of foreign wars on American policy during the period 1801 to 1812.
   C. Briefly explain ONE consequence of the War of 1812.

› Answers and Explanations

1. **D**. The decision stated that the Supreme Court had the right to decide on the constitutionality of federal rulings and laws.

2. **D**. All of the remaining answers would have been true if a Federalist had been elected president. Jefferson favored lessening the power of the federal government, and eliminating federal excise taxes was one way in which he did so.

3. **B**. The United States had an army of 6,000 men and 17 ships when war began. All the other choices are reasons why Americans supported the War of 1812.

4. C. Kentucky and Virginia spoke of nullification after the Sedition Act. New England Federalists saw the War of 1812 as a disaster and at the Hartford Convention also spoke of nullification.

5. A. The American System favored American economic growth, a National Bank, and increased tariffs to protect American businesses and finance new transportation systems within the United States.

6. B. Tecumseh argued that Native Americans should respond to the westward expansion of American settlement by forming a Native American confederacy. He attempted to maximize Native American strength by forming a military alliance of a number of tribes in what is now Indiana, Michigan, and Illinois. He hoped to add southern tribes to this alliance as well.

7. D. The disagreement between Tecumseh and William Henry Harrison most directly concerned the American belief that tribal leaders could sell Native American land. Harrison as the governor of the Indiana Territory was aggressive in purchasing Native American lands. Tecumseh held that these lands were owned by all Native Americans in common and that no individuals or tribe could transfer these lands to American settlers.

8. B. The death of Tecumseh and American victories in the War of 1812 led most directly to the government policy of Native American removal. The War of 1812 was a disaster for the Native Americans living east of the Mississippi River. Harrison defeated and killed Tecumseh in the north, and Andrew Jackson crushed the Creeks in the south. The Native Americans no longer had the power to resist American expansion. American settlers wanted Native American lands. American officials decided the easiest course of action would be to remove the eastern tribes to the west bank of the Mississippi River. The Indian Removal Act passed Congress in 1830.

9. Parts A and B: The 1803 Louisiana Purchase was made possible by the imminence of foreign war. Napoleon Bonaparte's hopes of reviving a French empire in America were foiled by the failure of a French army to subdue the slave rebellion in Haiti and by the prospect of renewed war in Europe. Napoleon knew that the British navy would cut Louisiana off from France, so he decided to sell the territory to the United States and acquire some funds for the coming war. Once the European war resumed in 1803, both the British and French interfered with American trade. The British sometimes stopped American ships and seized sailors, forcing them to serve in the British navy. This practice was known as impressment. In 1807, a British warship suddenly fired on the American warship the USS *Chesapeake,* before boarding it and taking away four sailors. President Thomas Jefferson responded with the Embargo Act of 1807, which cut off American trade with Europe. This effort at economic coercion failed to hurt the British and French, but badly hurt American shippers and traders. The Embargo Act was repealed in 1809 and was replaced by the Non-Intercourse Act, which prohibited trade just with Britain and France. Tired of British interference with American trade, the United States declared war in 1812.

Part C: Though essentially a military draw, the War of 1812 did have important consequences. The military power of the Native American tribes living east of the Mississippi River was broken. The great Shawnee military leader and orator Tecumseh was killed in the war. The remains of the Federalist party was discredited by the 1814 Hartford Convention, which had briefly discussed the secession of New England. Following the conclusion of the war and the great 1815 victory at the Battle of New Orleans, a renewed spirit of nationalism dominated the country. This period of political dominance by the Democratic-Republican party became known as the Era of Good Feelings. In 1816, the government created the Second Bank of the United States and passed the Tariff of 1816 to foster American business growth.

CHAPTER 13

Rise of Manufacturing and the Age of Jackson (1820–1845)

IN THIS CHAPTER

Summary: Large-scale textile production began in the United States during this era of factories in places like Lowell, Massachusetts. As America grew economically, it also began to assert its authority in the Western Hemisphere. The Monroe Doctrine boldly stated that the hemisphere was offlimits to European intervention. Beginning in 1824, the United States began the resettlement of Native American tribes east of the Mississippi. The era of "Jacksonian Democracy" was one where many say that the values of the "common man" reigned supreme. In the 1830s, the Whig Party emerged as an opposition party to the Democratic Party of Jackson. Several state legislatures began to claim that they could nullify federal laws that were not in the interests of their individual states.

Keywords

Monroe Doctrine (1823): proclamation that countries of the Western Hemisphere "are not to be considered as subjects for future colonization by any European powers."

Removal Act of 1830: Congressional act that authorized the removal of all Native American tribes east of the Mississippi to the west. The Trail of Tears and other forced migrations caused the deaths of thousands.

The Liberator: abolitionist newspaper begun by William Lloyd Garrison in 1831.

Spoils system: system used heavily during the presidency of Andrew Jackson whereby political supporters of the winning candidate are given jobs in the government.

Nullification: in reaction to tariff legislation passed in 1828, the South Carolina legislature explored the possibility of nullification, by which individual states could rule on the constitutionality of federal laws. Other Southern legislatures later discussed the idea of nullifying federal laws in their own states.

Whig Party: political party that emerged in the 1830s in opposition to the Democratic Party; Whigs favored policies that promoted commercial and industrial growth.

The Rise of Manufacturing

The end of the War of 1812 saw efforts to boost American manufactures and stimulate the economy. Henry Clay's American System was a conspicuous manifestation of this. The Tariff of 1816 protected domestic industries by placing a 25 percent duty on imports. States took the lead in internal improvements to spur commerce. New York State constructed the Erie Canal between 1817 and 1825, providing a waterway to allow goods to be easily transported between New York City and the Great Lakes.

At the beginning of the nineteenth century, most manufacturing was done through the **putting-out system**. Merchants provided raw materials to families, who then did the manufacturing work in their homes. A merchant might have dozens or hundreds of families working for him, producing textiles or making shoe components, for example.

The factory system in the United States began in the 1790s. The beginning of the Industrial Revolution in Great Britain had seen the creation of power-driven machinery to produce textiles. Manufacturers in New England used this new technology to turn southern cotton into cloth. Eli Whitney's cotton gin made it possible for southern planters to greatly increase their production of cotton. This in turn spurred an acceleration of the Industrial Revolution in the United States and Great Britain. Over 75,000 workers, nearly half of whom were women, were employed in American textile mills by the early 1840s. The increasing number of factory workers meant that many Americans no longer relied on semi-subsistence agriculture and instead supported themselves by producing goods for distant markets. This is a significant shift in the economy of the United States.

Lowell, Massachusetts, was a center of the American textile industry. Here mill owners developed the **"Lowell System."** They drew their workforce from young women in the surrounding areas. These young women worked in the mills for up to a few years, living in dormitories provided by the mill owners. Though the wages were poor, the employment gave these young women an income they might not otherwise have had. Some of them saw their time in the mills as an opportunity to build up a small nest egg before they returned home and married. The mill owners in turn benefited from a low-cost and continually replenished supply of workers. In Lowell and other industrial towns, a new middle class of white-collar workers associated with the factories emerged. They joined the manufacturers and bankers in bringing a new commercial prosperity to these cities. The emergence of this larger middle class and small, business elite took place alongside a growing population of working lower class Americans.

A **labor movement** among industrial workers was slow to develop. The Panic of 1819 was a financial crisis caused by changes in the international economy following the Napoleonic Wars and inflationary policies spurred by branches of the Second Bank of the United States speculating in land sales. Labor unrest emerged later, in the 1830s, with a call for state legislatures to limit working hours. In the 1840s, the textile industry saw increased demands by workers for better pay and working conditions.

The Monroe Doctrine

In the early 1820s, President James Monroe and Secretary of State John Quincy Adams became concerned that Spain and its ally France would attempt to reconquer the Latin American republics that had gained independence during the Napoleonic Wars. The British, worried about the loss of new markets in South America, shared this concern. The British proposed that they and the United States jointly guarantee the sovereignty of the new Latin American states. Reluctant to be seen acting in the shadow of the British, Monroe and Adams instead issued their own statement in 1823. The Monroe Doctrine declared that the United States would resist new European colonization in the Western Hemisphere. In turn, Monroe pledged that the United States would not interfere in European affairs. The Monroe Doctrine became a key tenet of American foreign policy for more than a century.

Native American Removal

Since the presidency of Thomas Jefferson, American political leaders had been convinced that the only solution to conflict with the Native Americans was to move all tribes to new lands west of the Mississippi. In 1824, the last year of his presidency, James Monroe called for the implementation of this removal policy. Monroe, like Jefferson before him, convinced himself that this exile to unfamiliar territory in the west would be good for Native Americans, giving them time to learn how to farm and adjust to the ways of the "white man" without interference by land-hungry settlers. Monroe ignored the fact that some Native Americans, such as the Cherokee, were already successfully adapting to a settled agricultural lifestyle.

The pressure to remove the Native Americans intensified during the presidency of Andrew Jackson. Congress passed and Jackson signed the **Removal Act of 1830**, which enabled the federal government to negotiate the removal of tribes living east of the Mississippi. Jackson had made his reputation as a military commander fighting Native Americans during the War of 1812, crushing the powerful Creek tribe and forcing the remaining Creeks to cede to the United States 60 percent of their land. Although professing to have no animus toward Native Americans, Jackson moved against them as efficiently and brutally as he had in the days when he had been a soldier.

The Cherokee fought removal in the courts. In 1831, in the Supreme Court case ***Cherokee Nation v. Georgia***, Chief Justice John Marshall raised questions about the legal standing of the Cherokee in American courts. A year later, in *Worcester v. Georgia*, Marshall nevertheless confirmed the right of the Cherokee to the land they held by treaty with the United States. President Jackson responded by refusing to implement Marshall's ruling. Jackson declared, "John Marshall has made his decision; let him enforce it."

Tribes began to be moved west in 1831. The Cherokee were compelled to leave their land in 1838, during the presidency of Jackson's chosen successor Martin Van Buren. The Cherokee were rounded up and escorted west by detachments of the Army. Along the way, the Cherokee suffered great privations from disease and inadequate provisions. About a third perished. In Florida, the Seminole resisted removal in a series of wars that lasted into the 1850s.

The Transportation Revolution and Religious Revival

Following the War of 1812, the American economy was transformed by rapid urbanization, the growth of industry, and the rapid settlement of the west. Facilitating this economic expansion was a transportation revolution. The federally constructed National Road connected the Potomac and Ohio Rivers. Steamboats traveled up and down America's great rivers. The construction of the Erie Canal inspired a spurt of canal building. Some states drove themselves into bankruptcy financing the construction of ill-conceived canals. Challenging the economic viability of canals in the 1840s was the rapid expansion of railroads. The transportation revolution stimulated American commercial development and ensured that more and more Americans were participants in a growing market economy.

While the economy of the United States expanded, a tremendous outpouring of religious feeling was shaping American culture. The **Second Great Awakening** stressed a personal, more emotional approach to traditional religion. The fervor that it stirred strengthened many existing Christian denominations, among them the Baptists and Methodists, and led to the creation of others such as the Adventist movement. Popular preachers such as Charles Grandison Finney and Timothy Dwight traveled the country spreading their evangelism to large gatherings. **Revival meetings** flourished throughout the country, where fervent sermonizing inspired some congregants to engage in public conversions, emotional outbursts, and speaking in tongues. The Second Great Awakening flourished in both the countryside and cities. Women played a growing role in their churches as volunteers in evangelical Christianity's "Benevolent Empire" of missionary organizations. The need to read and understand scripture stimulated efforts to provide women with education.

An Age of Reform

Economic and religious upheaval spurred an era of reform. Often motivated by religious ideas, reformers attempted to address a wide range of social problems. Dorothea Dix became famous in the 1830s and 1840s for her efforts to persuade states to provide better treatment for the mentally ill. Horace Mann campaigned for universal public education and improvements in teacher training. Other activists worked to improve prisons and conditions for the urban poor. One of the most influential reform causes was the **temperance movement** which attempted to combat the widespread problem of alcoholism. Temperance crusaders persuaded many localities to go "dry."

The evangelical Christian fervor that drove the temperance movement also empowered a growing opposition to the institution of slavery. The **Abolitionist movement** became a major social and political force in the 1820s and 1830s. One of the most conspicuously vocal abolitionists was William Lloyd Garrison, the founder and editor of the *Liberator*, an uncompromisingly abolitionist newspaper. Some abolitionists opposed slavery because they believed that it was sinful for people to own other human beings. Other abolitionists were motivated by concerns about the perceived dangers of racial mixing and conflict in the United States. The **American Colonization Society**, founded in 1817, encouraged the settlement of freed slaves in Africa.

African Americans played a leading role in abolitionism and the resistance to slavery. Frederick Douglass, a former slave from Maryland, became a powerful abolitionist speaker and in 1845 published his antislavery memoir *Narrative of the Life of Frederick Douglass*.

Very different was Nat Turner, a slave in Virginia who led a violent slave insurrection that killed 60 white men, women, and children. White citizens and state authorities responded by killing some 200 African Americans. Turner and 56 others were captured and executed. Frightened by the rebellion, slave owners imposed harsh **Black Codes** that further restricted the activities of their slaves.

Jacksonian Democracy

Politically, the 1820s inaugurated an era of the "common man." By the 1820s, property qualifications for voting had been eliminated or lowered in most states. In 1800, only five states allowed the selection of electors to the Electoral College by popular vote; in 1824, 18 of 24 states did so. By the end of the Era of Good Feelings in 1824, politics had become a popular pastime, complete with parades, buttons, and posters.

Alexis de Tocqueville, an aristocratic visitor from France, noted this egalitarian spirit and was inspired to write his classic *Democracy in America* (1835, 1840). Andrew Jackson dominated this period politically and encouraged the ascendency of the "common man." As a result, these years are often termed the era of "Jacksonian democracy."

The Election of 1824

Four **Democratic-Republican** leaders contended for the presidency in 1824. John Quincy Adams was secretary of state, William Crawford was secretary of the treasury, Henry Clay was speaker of the house, and Andrew Jackson was the leading military hero of the War of 1812. In the four-way race, Jackson won the most popular votes but failed to get a majority in the Electoral College. This threw the election to the House of Representatives. Henry Clay, effectively out of the race, instructed his supporters to vote for John Quincy Adams, who had come in second place to Jackson. This enabled Adams to edge out Jackson and win the presidency.

Adams promptly appointed Clay his secretary of state. Andrew Jackson was outraged at losing the election after having won the most popular and electoral votes. He denounced what he believed was a "corrupt bargain" between Adams and Clay. Jackson immediately began preparing the ground for a rematch in 1828, becoming a spokesman for the democratic assault on "privilege" in American politics.

The Election of 1828

John Quincy Adams was an able chief executive, but his presidency was blighted by the implacable opposition of the Jacksonians, who were coming to be known as the **Democratic Party**. The election of 1828 was bitterly contested, with defamation and mudslinging on both sides. The Jacksonians portrayed Adams as a thief who had stolen the election of 1824 and as an aristocrat with effete habits. Adams's supporters described Jackson, who had fought duels, as a violent killer. Because Jackson and his wife had unwittingly married before her divorce had become finalized, they were condemned as adulterers. Mrs. Jackson died soon after the election, and Jackson blamed her demise on the attacks on her character. Jackson decisively won the election, inaugurating a new political era.

President Jackson

Andrew Jackson had been born in a log cabin, but by the time he became president, he was a wealthy landowner and slaveholder in Tennessee. Although famous as a general, he had been active in politics for decades and had served as a congressman and senator from Tennessee. Positioning himself as the political champion of the people, Jackson cultivated an aura of stern democratic rectitude. He was affectionately called "Old Hickory" by his followers.

As both a Democrat and a democrat, Jackson believed that his supporters should take over federal offices held by the partisans of John Quincy Adams. He did not believe that any special expertise was necessary to hold a government job; he believed that any reasonably capable and well-informed citizen could perform these duties. Jackson consequently became a champion of the **spoils system**, appointing loyal Democrats to positions in the federal government. Jackson came to distrust his cabinet; instead he relied on the advice of his "**Kitchen Cabinet**," a group of his most trusted political cronies.

Jackson subscribed to the Jeffersonian ideal of a United States dominated by self-sufficient yeoman farmers. He was also a traditional Jeffersonian, believing in limited government and opposing federal involvement in the economy. He repeatedly vetoed bills calling for federal support for internal improvements. As a slave owner, Jackson opposed the abolitionist ferment in the country. Following the death in 1835 of John Marshall, Jackson appointed Roger B. Taney as chief justice of the Supreme Court. The Taney Court would become a stalwart defender of states' rights. Although Jackson advocated limited government, by sheer force of personality, he paradoxically strengthened the presidency. He would take actions that led his opponents to call him "King Andrew I."

The Nullification Controversy

The first crisis Jackson faced ironically forced him to assert the primacy of federal over state power. In 1828, during the waning days of the Adams administration, Congress passed a tariff bill designed to protect northern manufacturing interests. The increase in the cost of imported manufactured goods hurt southern and western farmers confronted with higher prices. Southern leaders termed the Tariff of 1828 the "Tariff of Abominations." The South Carolina legislature asserted the right of **nullification**, whereby states could refuse to enforce federal laws that they held to be unconstitutional. The chief theorist behind this new version of nullification was John C. Calhoun, a South Carolinian who had been elected Jackson's vice-president. Calhoun believed that the states needed a defense against the power of the federal government. He was worried that the more populous north would eventually force abolitionism on the south.

In 1830, a famous debate over nullification erupted in the U.S. Senate. In the **Webster-Hayne Debate**, Daniel Webster eloquently declared that if nullification were allowed, the consequence would be "states dissevered, discordant, belligerent; on a land rent with civil feuds, or drenched . . . in fraternal blood!"

President Jackson supported states' rights but resolutely opposed nullification. He took decisive action to demonstrate this. In 1832, after the passage of new tariffs, a convention in South Carolina voted to nullify this legislation. Jackson responded by preparing to send troops and federal marshals to South Carolina to enforce the law. Congress passed a **Force Act** supporting this action. Calhoun resigned as vice-president, while Jackson told confidantes that he would cheerfully send his former running mate to the gallows. The crisis was defused when Henry Clay helped engineer a bill that lowered the tariffs. Satisfied by this, the South Carolinians rescinded their act of nullification.

The Bank War

President Jackson's next great crisis involved the Second Bank of the United States, which had been chartered in 1816. The Bank was a vital component of Henry Clay's American System; it issued bank notes that served as a de facto national paper currency and played a key role in regulating credit and the activities of the state banks. The Bank was partly owned by the U.S. government and partly owned by private investors. Nicholas Biddle had managed the Bank since 1823. As a Jeffersonian, Jackson disliked the Bank on principle. He believed that the Bank had helped bring on the Panic of 1819. He was convinced that Biddle and the directors of the Bank enjoyed a power that was both unchecked and undemocratic.

Henry Clay ran against Jackson in the election of 1832. He used the Bank as an election issue, calling for it to be rechartered early. Clay saw to the passage of a rechartering bill, which Jackson promptly vetoed. Clay misjudged public opinion, believing that the electorate would support the Bank because of its obvious economic utility. Instead, Jackson portrayed the Bank as a sinister special interest. His attack on economic privilege resonated with voters, and he easily won reelection.

By now, Jackson regarded Biddle as a personal enemy and the Bank as a corrupt institution that had to be destroyed. In 1833, he withdrew federal money from the Bank and placed the funds in state banks, which were termed "pet banks" by his opponents. Biddle responded by calling in loans in an effort to keep his bank afloat. Jackson's **Bank War** and economic policies like the Specie Circular, which required gold or silver coins to purchase federal land, contributed to the onset of the **Panic of 1837**. This in turn led to an economic depression that carried into the 1840s.

The Whig Party and the Second Party System

In the 1830s, the opponents of Andrew Jackson gradually coalesced into the **Whig Party**. The Whigs would form the primary opposition to the Democrats into the 1850s. This period of party politics is known as the Second Party System.

While the Democrats maintained the Jeffersonian tradition of standing by limited government, the Whigs believed in a more active government. The Whigs supported Henry Clay's vision of the American System and supported a national bank, tariffs, and internal improvements. The Whigs wanted a government that would foster commerce, industry, and better markets for farmers. Because of their belief in the efficacy of government action, Whigs were more likely to favor reform legislation than were the Democrats. More oriented to business and commerce, Whigs were less land hungry and expansionist than the Democrats, and the Whigs were more cautious about calls for America's Manifest Destiny. Many wealthy businessmen and planters supported the Whig Party, but so too did many young men anxious to better themselves, such as Abraham Lincoln.

Andrew Jackson's chosen successor, Martin Van Buren, won the election of 1836. The Panic of 1837 undermined support for Democratic economic policy. In 1840, the Whigs nominated William Henry Harrison, another hero of the War of 1812, as their candidate for president. After a colorful campaign, which included the catchy slogan "Tippecanoe and Tyler Too," Harrison was elected. Harrison died a month after taking office, the victim of pneumonia contracted after being caught in the rain while on a walk. John Tyler became the first vice-president to succeed to office after the death of a president.

Chapter Review

Rapid Review

To achieve the perfect 5, you should be able to explain the following:

- A new production system developed in textile mills such as those that existed in Lowell, Massachusetts, in the early nineteenth century.
- The Monroe Doctrine boldly proclaimed that the Western Hemisphere was off limits to European intrusion.
- Beginning in 1824, it was official American policy to move Native American tribes west of the Mississippi; the horrors of many of these relocations are well documented.
- The Second Great Awakening influenced many to become involved in reform movements, including the Abolitionist movement.
- The presidency of Andrew Jackson is celebrated as an era when the "common man" reigned supreme, although Jackson greatly expanded the powers of the presidency.
- The Democratic Party of Andrew Jackson was the first highly organized political party in American history.
- Congress's tariff policy caused a renewal of interest in the policy of nullification in several Southern state legislatures.
- In the 1830s, the Whig Party emerged as the major party opposing the Democratic Party of Jackson.

Time Line

1790s: Beginning of Second Great Awakening
1816: Second Bank of United States chartered
Tariff of 1816 imposes substantial import tariffs
Election of James Monroe
1819: Panic of 1819 (high unemployment lasts until 1823)
1820: Missouri Compromise
Reelection of James Monroe
1820s: Growth of New England textile mills
1823: Monroe Doctrine
1824: Proposal by President Monroe to move Native Americans west of the
Mississippi River
1825: John Quincy Adams elected president by House of Representatives (no candidate
had won a majority in Electoral College)
1828: Andrew Jackson elected president
1830: Passage of Indian Removal Act in Congress
Webster-Hayne Debate
1830s: Growth of the Whig Party
1831: Cherokee nation goes to court to defend tribal rights in
Cherokee Nation v. Georgia
First issue of William Lloyd Garrison's *The Liberator* published
1832: Andrew Jackson reelected
Nullification crisis after nullification of tariffs by South Carolina
1834: First strike of women textile workers in Lowell, Massachusetts
1836: Democrat Martin Van Buren elected president
1840: Whig William Henry Harrison elected president
1841: William Henry Harrison dies after one month in office, and Vice President
John Tyler becomes president.

› Review Questions

Fact Check

Check your knowledge of the historical period covered in this chapter.

1. President Monroe claimed that westward relocation of Native Americans would be to the advantage of the Native Americans because
   A. they would not be bothered west of the Mississippi.
   B. the American military would protect them during the journey.
   C. they would be well compensated for the tribal lands that they were leaving.
   D. settlers west of the Mississippi were receptive to Native American settlement there.

2. The concept of nullification became an issue during this period when
   A. Georgia opposed congressional legislation concerning slavery.
   B. South Carolina nullified congressional legislation concerning the removal of Native Americans.
   C. South Carolina nullified congressional tariff bills.
   D. Southern representatives to the Electoral College switched their votes in the 1824 election.

3. Critics of Andrew Jackson would make all of the following claims *except* that
   A. he was a very common man and not fit to be president.
   B. he gave too much power to the presidency.
   C. he lacked experience in government affairs.
   D. he relied too much on his "Kitchen Cabinet."

4. The following are *true* about the textile mills of New England in the early nineteenth century *except*
   A. a large percentage of their workforce was made up of women.
   B. they depended on water for power.
   C. they used a system called the putting-out system.
   D. there was little labor unrest in the mills until the 1830s and 1840s.

5. Horace Mann is associated with
   A. abolitionism.
   B. the temperance movement.
   C. prison reform.
   D. educational reform.

Multiple-Choice Questions

Here are multiple-choice questions like the ones on the AP U.S. History exam.

Questions 6–8 refer to the cartoon below.

GENERAL JACKSON SLAYING THE MANY HEADED MONSTER.

[cartoon from http://www.loc.gov/pictures/item/2008661279/]

6. Andrew Jackson attacked the Second Bank of the United States because he believed that it
   A. embodied an undemocratic financial monopoly.
   B. interfered in debates over slavery.
   C. gave the president too much financial power.
   D. refused to finance internal improvements.

7. Which of the following would be most likely to oppose Jackson's bank policy?
   A. A southern planter
   B. A western farmer
   C. An urban laborer
   D. A northern businessman

8. As a government policy, Andrew Jackson's "Bank War" can best be compared to which of the following?
   A. Henry Clay's "American System"
   B. William McKinley's "Full Dinner Pail"
   C. Theodore Roosevelt's "trust-busting"
   D. Lyndon Baines Johnson's "Great Society"

Short-Answer Question

The short-answer question below is similar to the ones you'll encounter on the AP U.S. History exam.

9. Answer Parts A, B, and C.
   A. Briefly explain ONE example of how Andrew Jackson fostered the growth of "Jacksonian democracy" in the United States.
   B. Briefly explain a SECOND example of how Andrew Jackson fostered the growth of "Jacksonian democracy" in the United States.
   C. Briefly explain ONE policy promoted by Andrew Jackson's political opponents.

❯ Answers and Explanations

1. A. Monroe stated that Native Americans could not avoid being continually harassed if they lived east of the Mississippi, but that this would not happen after they moved.

2. C. Because the tariff bills increased the prices of cloth and iron, the South Carolina legislature first nullified the Tariff of 1828.

3. C. All of the other criticisms were often made against Jackson. However, he did have an impressive background: before becoming president, he had served as a congressman and a senator from Tennessee and as the territorial governor of Florida.

4. C. It was the putting-out system that these mills replaced.

5. D. Horace Mann wrote and spoke about the need to improve schools and to improve teacher training methods.

6. A. Andrew Jackson attacked the Second Bank of the United States because he believed that it embodied an undemocratic financial monopoly. He believed that the bank, which was partly government owned but independently operated, put too much power in private hands. He thought such an institution violated the Constitution and threatened states' rights. Jackson argued that the power of wealthy financiers such as those who ran the Second Bank of the United States threatened the liberties of the common man.

7. D. A northern businessman would be most likely to oppose Jackson's bank policy. The bank notes issued by the Second Bank of the United States were accepted everywhere and facilitated business. The check a national bank provided against inflation and the overextension of credit promoted stable business conditions.

8. C. As a government policy, Andrew Jackson's "Bank War" can best be compared to Theodore Roosevelt's "trust-busting." The campaign against the trusts was also seen as a campaign against privileged business interests that wielded too much control over American life.

9. Parts A and B: Andrew Jackson supported the lowering of property qualifications that allowed more men to vote. In 1824, Jackson won the popular vote and the largest number of electors, but not enough to claim the presidency; after the election was thrown into the House of Representatives, he was defeated by John Quincy Adams when Henry Clay gave his support to the former secretary of state. Jackson denounced what he called a "corrupt bargain," and called for more democratic and anti-elitist politics. As a Jeffersonian, he opposed government intervention in the economy, believing that "big" government would favor special interests. Once elected to the presidency in 1828, Jackson filled government jobs with his supporters. He defended this "spoils system" by arguing that any man should be able to carry out the duties of a government post. At his inauguration, Jackson invited the public to a reception at the White House, a gesture never made before. Jackson vetoed a bill re-chartering the Bank of the United States. He believed that the bank served the interests of the moneyed elite rather than the common man. Initially, Jackson's "Bank War" enhanced his image as a champion of the "common man."

Part C: President Jackson's opponents coalesced into the Whig Party. Whigs tended to support a greater government role in the economy. Most opposed Jackson's "Bank War." Many subscribed to Henry Clay's "American System," which called for a national bank to facilitate commerce, internal improvements to help farmers and businessmen get their goods to markets, and a tariff to help protect American industry.

CHAPTER 14

Union Expanded and Challenged (1835–1860)

IN THIS CHAPTER

Summary: Guided by the principle of "Manifest Destiny," Americans began to stream westward in the 1830s. By the mid-1840s settlers were entrenched in the Oregon and California territories. Americans also settled in Texas and helped the Texans defeat the Mexican army in 1836. The Mexican-American War took place between 1846 and 1847. By the terms of the treaty ending this war the United States paid Mexico $15 million; in return the United States acquired the northern part of the Texas territory and New Mexico and California. The pivotal issue for Americans remained whether newly acquired territories would enter the Union as slave states or as free states. Under the Missouri Compromise a line was drawn westward to the Pacific Ocean; all territories north of the line would enter the Union as free states and all territories south of the line would come in as slave states. The issue of whether California would enter the Union as a free or slave state necessitated the Compromise of 1850. The Kansas-Nebraska Act of 1854 stated that settlers living in those territories could vote on whether they would become slave states or free states. The *Dred Scott* Supreme Court decision of 1857 stated that Congress had no right to prohibit slavery in the territories and that even though Scott, an ex-slave, had spent time in a free state and a free territory this did not make him a free man. Tensions between the North and the South remained high. In the 1860 presidential election, former Illinois Congressman Abraham Lincoln campaigned on the need to contain slavery in the territories. After his election, representatives of seven Southern states met to create the Confederate States of America, with Jefferson Davis as the first president of the Confederacy.

Keywords

Manifest Destiny: concept that became popularized in the 1840s stating that it was the God-given mission of the United States to expand westward.

Mexican-American War: war fought over possession of Texas, which was claimed by both Mexico and the United States; the settlement ending this war gave the United States the northern part of the Texas territory and the territories of New Mexico and California.

Compromise of 1850: temporarily ending tensions between the North and the South, this measure allowed California to enter the Union as a free state but also strengthened the Fugitive Slave Act.

Fugitive Slave Act: part of the Compromise of 1850, legislation that set up special commissions in northern states to determine if accused runaway slaves were actually that. Commissioners were given more money if the accused was found to be a runaway than if he/she was not. Many northern state legislatures attempted to circumvent this law.

Kansas-Nebraska Act (1854): compromise that allowed settlers in Kansas and Nebraska to vote to decide if they would enter the Union as free states or slave states. Much violence and confusion took place in Kansas as various types of "settlers" moved into this territory in the months before the vote in an attempt to influence it.

***Dred Scott* case:** critical Supreme Court ruling that stated that slaves were property and not people; as a result they could not seek a ruling from any court. The ruling also stated that Congress had no legal right to ban slavery in any territory.

The Society of the South

In the South, although the majority of Southerners did not own slaves themselves, most leaders argued that slavery was part of the Southern way of life. The "peculiar institution" as they called it, was widespread throughout the region, particularly in the Deep South. While slaves were not given agency by their slave owners, they still found ways to resist and rebel. Some slaves rebelled outright, like Nat Turner whose organized attack led to the death of 55 white people and was violently put down. These rebellions struck fear into the slave owners, who then placed harsher restrictions onto their slaves. Some slaves ran away, either on their own or by using the Underground Railroad, an organization of safe houses from the South to the North led by conductors like Harriet Tubman. Most others resisted in covert ways by slowing their work down or intentionally breaking their tools. Enslaved people also created communities and strategies to protect their dignity and family structures.

In the South, cotton was king. Most plantations focused on planting and harvesting this lucrative cash crop. Cotton led to a huge increase in the number of slaves in the South, who made up to 75 percent of the population in some parts of the Deep South. The identity of the South was entangled with slavery, and many Southerners refused to entertain the idea of the abolition of slaves. As more and more people began to question the morality of slavery, Southerners dug their heels in and justified their practice using the Bible and history. They also intensified laws to further limit the education and movement of slaves as the abolitionist movement gained momentum and as the United States continued to expand.

Manifest Destiny

Americans had always dreamed of expanding their settlements westward. The acquisition of new lands to the west had been a core component of Thomas Jefferson's vision of an agrarian republic. In the 1840s, the age-old American urge to push against the line of the frontier became a clearly articulated ideology. In 1845, the journalist John O'Sullivan coined the term **Manifest Destiny**. He called for the United States "to overspread the continent allotted by Providence for free development of our yearly multiplying millions."

In the 1830s Americans began taking the long and arduous **Oregon Trail** west to the Williamette Valley of the Oregon territory. Tales of rich soil, plentiful wildlife, and a salubrious climate attracted settlers from the east. In the early 1840s people talked of "Oregon Fever." More than 5,000 Americans had made their way to Oregon by 1845. Among them was the missionary Marcus Whitman. He, his family, and 12 others were murdered by Native Americans in 1847. Despite the dangers, Americans were determined to settle and control the Oregon territory. The United States shared sovereignty in Oregon with Great Britain. American expansionists demanded all of Oregon, making their rallying cry "Fifty-four Forty or Fight." President James K. Polk decided to pursue diplomacy rather than conflict with the British. The **Oregon Treaty** of 1846 awarded most, though not all of the Oregon territory to the United States. Proponents of Manifest Destiny also called for the United States to acquire California. American settlers began to arrive in California in the 1830s. Like expansion into Oregon, expansion into California became a political issue in the 1840s.

The Alamo and Texas Independence

American expansionism helped spur conflict with Mexico. Mexico won its independence from Spain in 1821, but entered into a protracted period of political instability. Hoping to develop its underpopulated northern province of Texas, Mexican officials encouraged an influx of American settlers, who in return for accepting Mexican citizenship and adopting the Roman Catholic religion were provided with extensive grants of land. By 1836, there were 30,000 American settlers in Texas.

These American settlers soon found themselves at odds with the Mexican authorities. In the early 1830s they became caught up in Mexican political struggles between supporters of a federal system of government and those who wanted a stronger central government. The Texans favored the federalist cause. Centralizers won control of the Mexican government and began tightening their control over Texas. Most of the American settlers and many Mexicans in Texas responded by revolting. On March 2, 1836, the rebels proclaimed Texan independence. The Mexican president, General Antonio López de Santa Anna led an army into Texas. On March 6, his troops overwhelmed a garrison of 180 to 250 men, including Davy Crockett and Jim Bowie, at the Alamo in San Antonio. All the defenders of the Alamo died, but their heroic resistance inspired the Texan war-cry "Remember the Alamo!" The remaining Texan forces, aided by volunteers from the United States, rallied under General Sam Houston. On April 21, Houston's army surprised and routed Santa Anna's command at San Jacinto. Santa Anna was captured and forced to order all Mexican soldiers out of Texas.

The newly independent Texas became the Lone Star Republic, with Sam Houston as its president. Most Texans wanted their republic to be annexed by the United States. The politics of slavery prevented this. Many Northerners opposed the acquisition of a territory that would become another slave state. The admission of Texas into the Union would also lead to inevitable conflicts with Mexico, which refused to officially recognize the independence of Texas. President Andrew Jackson sympathized with the aspirations of the Texans, but was unwilling to risk the electoral prospects of his protégé Martin Van Buren in the presidential election that fall. He contented himself with extending diplomatic recognition to the Lone Star Republic.

The American annexation of Texas remained a political nonstarter until 1844. President John Tyler and his secretary of state, John C. Calhoun, both Southerners, worked to negotiate a treaty that would bring Texas into the Union as a slave state. Until the election of 1844, their efforts proved unavailing in the Senate.

Expansion and the Election of 1844

The election of 1844 proved to be the political high tide of Manifest Destiny. James K. Polk won the Democratic nomination for the presidency. He was the first American **dark horse candidate** to win a major party nomination; he was not put forward as a candidate until the Democratic nominating convention. Polk was hardly a political nonentity. A protégé of Andrew Jackson, he had served as Speaker of the House and as governor of Tennessee. Polk warmly embraced American expansionism. He called for the annexation of Texas and of all of the Oregon Territory. The nomination of Polk also demonstrated the growing dominance of the South in the Democratic Party. Polk would later sign the 1846 Walker Tariff that angered Northern manufacturing interests by lowering the tariff on imported products.

The Whig nominee in 1844 was Henry Clay, making his third run for the presidency. In an effort to conciliate all sectional interests, Clay refused to embrace expansionism. He hoped that his long experience in American politics and personal popularity would carry him through to victory. Clay's hopes would be frustrated by political abolitionism. The new anti-slavery Liberty party ran James Birney for the presidency in 1844. Though the Liberty party failed to attract widespread support (only 62,000 votes in total), its presence on the ballot probably cost Clay the electoral votes of New York and the election.

Polk's expansionism proved popular enough for him to win a close election. Before Polk's inauguration in March 1845, the outgoing president, John Tyler, secured the annexation of Texas through the unusual method of a joint resolution of Congress. Once in office, Polk began the diplomatic negotiations with Great Britain that resulted in the successful resolution of the Oregon boundary dispute. Polk's efforts to acquire more land from the Mexicans would not be resolved peacefully.

The Mexican War

Polk hoped to obtain all of his expansionist goals with Mexico through diplomacy. He wanted the Mexicans to accept the Rio Grande River as the southern boundary of Texas, rather than the more northerly Nueces River, which the Mexicans argued was the Texas border. Dreaming of trade on the Pacific Ocean, Polk wanted the superb harbor of San Francisco and all the California Territory around it. In October 1845, he sent the diplomat John Slidell to Mexico with a proposal to purchase the territory between the Nueces and Rio Grande rivers for $5 million, California for $25 million, and $5 million for the Mexican lands between Texas and California. The Mexican government refused to see Slidell. It took more emphatic action against an army led by General Zachary Taylor that Polk had provocatively posted along the Rio Grande River. In April 1846, Mexican troops attacked a patrol of American soldiers. This began hostilities between Mexico and the United States. Once Polk learned of the outbreak of fighting, he asked Congress for a declaration of war. The United States declared against Mexico on May 13, 1846.

The Mexican War was controversial, and it was opposed by many Americans. Many Whigs believed that Polk had forced the war on Mexico, without fully exploring a diplomatic solution. Many Northerners assumed that the war was a scheme by Southern Democrats to conquer new territories for the institution of slavery.

Although some contemporary observers predicted a Mexican victory because of the large number of men Mexico had under arms, the American army soon proved its military superiority. General Taylor defeated the Mexican forces confronting them along the Rio Grande and advanced into Northern Mexico. There he repulsed a Mexican counterattack at the hard-fought Battle of Buena Vista. In California, the United States fomented an uprising of American settlers. Supported by a small force of soldiers led by the explorer John C. Fremont, the rebels declared California independent on July 4, 1846, renaming the province as the **Bear Flag Republic**. Detachments of American troops conquered New Mexico and the rest of the Mexican lands Polk wanted for the United States. Territorially satisfied, Polk was ready to make peace. The Mexicans spurned his overtures, refusing to submit. To compel a Mexican surrender, Polk dispatched an army led by General Winfield Scott to the Mexican port of Vera Cruz. On March 8, 1847, Scott supervised the first major amphibious landing in American military history. Scott abandoned his lines of communication and supply and marched into the heart of Mexico. After winning several battles, Scott's army captured Mexico City on September 13, 1847. This effectively ended the war, though Mexican partisans continued to harass American troops.

Political Consequences of the Mexican War

The Mexican War was ended by the **Treaty of Guadalupe Hidalgo**, signed in Mexico on February 2, 1848. The United States paid Mexico $15 million for the territory in Texas north of the Rio Grande, New Mexico, and California. The United States also agreed to pay all the claims that American citizens had against the Mexican government. While some Americans criticized the treaty for being too lenient with the Mexicans and argued that even more Mexican territory should have been taken, the spoils of the Mexican War increased the territory of the United States by one-third. Much of the dream of Manifest Destiny had been realized. The United States now truly was a continental nation.

The expansion of American territory inevitably raised the question of the expansion of slavery. In the summer of 1846, David Wilmot, a Democratic representative from Pennsylvania, ignited a political firestorm. He attached an amendment to a military appropriations bill that prohibited slavery in any territory taken from Mexico during the war. The **Wilmot Proviso** outraged Southerners. It was passed by the House four times, but was defeated in the Senate. Wilmot's amendment forced a political debate that further polarized sectional tensions over slavery. Northerners argued that slavery should not be introduced where it had been illegal under Mexican rule. John C. Calhoun eloquently articulated the Southern position that an institution that was legal in many American states could not be prohibited in federal territories held in common by all the states. President Polk attempted to forge a compromise settlement by extending the **Missouri Compromise** line to the Pacific Ocean.

Both major parties attempted to avoid the issue of slavery in the election of 1848. The Whigs attempted to replicate their previous winning strategy of running a war hero and nominated General Zachary Taylor. Lacking a suitably famous general, the Democrats nominated Lewis Cass, a senator from Michigan. Members of the Liberty party and dissident Whigs and Democrats coalesced into the Free-Soil party dedicated to opposing the extension of slavery into the western territories. Former president Martin Van Buren accepted the Free-Soil nomination and received 10 percent of the popular vote. Taylor's military charisma trumped all other considerations and he won the election.

The Political Crisis of 1850

The need to organize the territories won from Mexico would not allow the issue of slavery to be set aside or postponed. Americans had to make a decision about slavery in the West. Heightened passions over the morality of slavery made normal political compromises more difficult to achieve.

In January 1848, gold was discovered in California. Within a year, the ensuing California "Gold Rush" brought more than 80,000 "forty-niners" into the territory. By late 1849 there were enough settlers in California to apply for statehood. Settlers in New Mexico also petitioned for statehood. Gatherings in both territories drafted constitutions that prohibited slavery. President Taylor encouraged the Californians in their efforts and was willing to allow them to enter the Union as a free state. In doing this, he roused the anger of many Southerners. Much of California lay below the extended Missouri Compromise line. Both the western territories and the balance of power in the Senate seemed to be slipping away from the South. Calls were made for a convention in the South to discuss secession. John C. Calhoun spoke for many Southerners when he declared, "I trust we shall persist in our resistance until restoration of all our rights or disunion, one or the other, is the consequence."

Henry Clay criticized talk of Southern secession. Known as the "great pacificator" for having engineered the Compromise of 1820, the aging Clay hoped to fashion one more great compromise to hold the Union together. He packaged a series of resolutions designed to give both Northern and Southern legislators victories to take home to their constituents. The provisions of the **Compromise of 1850** included the admission of California as a free state, the freedom of the residents of New Mexico and Utah to decide if they wanted slavery in their territories, the ending of slave-trading in the District of Columbia, and a strengthened **Fugitive Slave Act**. Clay could not get his compromise passed as an omnibus bill because of the opposition of President Taylor and the unwillingness of congressmen to vote for elements of the bill that went against their sectional interests. Following Taylor's unexpected death, his successor Millard Fillmore expressed support for the compromise. Senator Stephen A. Douglas, a Democrat from Illinois, shepherded the compromise through Congress, passing each element separately with the crucial support of moderate Southern Whigs and Northern Democrats.

Aftermath of the Compromise of 1850

For a time the Compromise of 1850 brought a degree of sectional harmony. However, beneath the surface profound differences between Northern and Southern interests simmered. The entrance of California into the Union tilted the balance of the Senate against the South. The admission of Minnesota and Oregon later in the decade made the South's dwindling legislative influence more worrisome to extremist defenders of slavery. The Fugitive Slave Act, which increased the federal role in apprehending runaway slaves, was deeply unpopular in the North. African Americans accused of being escaped slaves were denied normal judicial due process, making it obvious that the new federal system was stacked against anyone with a dark skin. Northerners who were caught helping escaped slaves were heavily fined. The Fugitive Slave Act proved counterproductive for Southern interests by inflaming abolitionist sentiment in the North. The most powerful expression of this was Harriet Beecher Stowe's novel *Uncle Tom's Cabin* (1852), which powerfully dramatized the evils of slavery. Stowe's novel helped crystallize antislavery feelings in the North, selling almost 275,000 copies within a year.

In the election of 1852, the major political parties hoped that the slavery issue had been laid to rest. The Whigs nominated yet another war hero, General Winfield Scott. The Democrats turned to another **dark horse candidate**, Franklin Pierce. The strength of the Democratic Party carried Pierce to victory.

Franklin Pierce in the White House

Pierce reverted to the expansionist policies of James K. Polk. His administration negotiated the **Gadsden Purchase** from Mexico, which gave the United States a strip of territory that would facilitate the construction of a transcontinental railroad routed through the South. Pierce sent a naval expedition commanded by Commodore Matthew C. Perry to open up trade and diplomatic relations with Japan. The president fostered Northern suspicions that he was Southern in his sympathies by attempting to buy Cuba from Spain. When this failed, members of his administration discussed a military occupation of the island. The main impetus behind talk of acquiring Cuba, and also behind privately run expeditions to seize territory in Central America, was a Southern desire to open up new lands to slavery.

Following its failure in 1852, the Whig Party fell apart. Many Whigs drifted into the newly emergent American or **Know-Nothing Party,** which capitalized on anti-immigrant feeling. Large numbers of Irish and German immigrants had flooded into the United States during the 1840s. This spurred a **nativist** reaction. The Know-Nothings were especially hostile to the Roman Catholicism practiced by many of the immigrants. During its brief moment of popularity the Know-Nothing Party tried to restrict further immigration and prevent recent immigrants from voting. The Know-Nothing Party faded away when slavery once again became the leading political issue.

The Kansas-Nebraska Act

Stephen A. Douglas reignited sectional conflict because of his dream of running a transcontinental railroad from Chicago to California. To do this, the territories of Kansas and Nebraska had to be politically organized. According to the terms of the Missouri Compromise, slavery was banned in these territories. Douglas needed Southern support to begin the process of organizing Kansas and Nebraska. The price for this support was abandoning the Missouri Compromise and allowing the people living in Kansa and Nebraska to decide whether they would allow the introduction of slavery. Douglas embraced the bargain and became a spokesman for popular sovereignty in the territories. In 1854, President Pierce signed Douglas's **Kansas-Nebraska Act** into law.

The immediate result was a political uproar in the North. Many Northerners regarded the bill as an outrageous attempt to spread slavery into free territory. Free-Soilers, former Whigs, and defecting Democrats joined in launching the **Republican party**. Drawing its strength from the North and West, the new party vehemently opposed the extension of slavery into the western territories. The Republican party swiftly replaced the Know-Nothings as the most significant political rival to the Democrats.

"Bleeding Kansas"

There was never any realistic prospect that Nebraska would become a slave state. Kansas, with its long border with Missouri, was another story. Elections in Kansas were scheduled for 1855. Knowing this, supporters and opponents of slavery worked to send settlers into the territory. When the election was held, illegal voting by Missourians who flocked across the border helped the proslavery side to victory. The resulting proslavery legislature crafted the "Lecompton Constitution" that legalized slavery in Kansas. Outraged antislavery settlers elected their own legislature and wrote a constitution that banned slavery. With two legislatures and two constitutions, Kansas was locked into conflict. The differences between the two sides escalated into bloodshed. In 1856, a band of proslavery gunmen shot up or burned much of Lawrence, Kansas, a community founded by abolitionists. In retaliation, the fiercely antislavery fanatic John Brown led a gang that butchered five proslavery settlers. The ongoing violence led newspapermen to term the stricken territory **"Bleeding Kansas."**

In the 1856 presidential election the Democrat, James Buchanan, won in a three-way race with John C. Fremont, the first Republican presidential candidate, and former president Millard Fillmore running as a Know-Nothing. Buchanan won 45 percent of the popular vote and only triumphed because of his support in the "Solid South."

The *Dred Scott* Decision

Dred Scott was a slave in Missouri who went to court and sued for his freedom. Scott's master had taken him to live for several years in the free state of Illinois and the free territory of Wisconsin. Scott argued that his residence for a time in free territory made him free. Scott's case made its way to the Supreme Court in 1856. In the ***Dred Scott* case**, the Supreme Court ruled that Scott was still a slave. The Court majority went beyond the specifics of the case and declared that African Americans were inherently inferior and could not be granted citizenship. It also ruled that Congress could not prohibit slavery in the territories because this violated constitutionally protected property rights.

The *Dred Scott* decision further inflamed sectional tensions. Southerners felt vindicated by the Supreme Court's ruling on slavery in the territories. Northerners were infuriated at the prospect of a panel of mostly Southern judges justifying the spread of slavery throughout the Union.

President Buchanan proved just as politically tone deaf as the Supreme Court. Ignoring the illegality surrounding the Lecompton Constitution, and a growing majority of free-soil settlers in Kansas, he urged Congress to recognize the territory as a slave state. Congress refused his recommendation. Kansas would enter the Union as a free state in 1861.

The Lincoln-Douglas Debates

Stephen A. Douglas ran for reelection to the Senate in 1858. He was opposed by Abraham Lincoln, the candidate of the Republican party. Lincoln had been an admirer of Henry Clay and a longtime Whig. He had served a term in Congress in the 1840s and had criticized the Mexican War. Lincoln was drawn back into politics by the Kansas-Nebraska Act and the *Dred Scott* decision. Because of Douglas's political prominence, his series of debates with Lincoln received national attention. These debates became a landmark of political oratory. They all centered on the issue of slavery and the territories. At the debate at Freeport,

Illinois, Lincoln asked Douglas how he could continue to promote popular sovereignty after the *Dred Scott* decision. Douglas replied with what came to be known as the **Freeport Doctrine**. He argued that the people of a territory could keep out slavery by legislating rules and regulations that would make it too difficult to maintain slaves. Douglas's position satisfied enough voters in Illinois, ensuring the retention of his Senate seat in the fall, but it won him many enemies in the South. Lincoln's brilliant performance during the debates marked him as a rising leader of the Republican party.

John Brown and Harpers Ferry

John Brown left Kansas and returned to the East dreaming of leading a great slave insurrection. He persuaded a few wealthy Northern abolitionists to fund his scheme. On October 16, 1859, Brown and 18 followers attacked the federal arsenal at Harpers Ferry, Virginia. He hoped to use the rifles that he captured there to arm slaves. Brown's raid proved to be a fiasco. He and his men were quickly surrounded and then captured by federal troops led by Colonel Robert E. Lee. Brown was convicted of treason and publically hanged. Some Northerners saw Brown as a martyr. Henry David Thoreau called him "the bravest and humanest man in all the country." Southerners were appalled by this sympathy for a man they regarded as a terrorist.

The Election of 1860

As the presidential election of 1860 approached, the Democratic Party divided along sectional lines. Stephen A. Douglas was the frontrunner for the nomination, but many Southern Democrats could not forgive him for the Freeport Doctrine. These Southerners walked out of the Democratic convention and nominated John Breckinridge. In the ensuing election campaign, Douglas defended the principle of popular sovereignty, while Breckinridge took the position that slavery should be allowed in all the territories. The Democratic split helped persuade John Bell, a former Whig from Tennessee, to run as the candidate of a new Constitutional Union party that appealed to sectional moderates. The divided political field opened up an electoral opportunity for the Republicans. Out of a crowded field of candidates, Abraham Lincoln emerged as the Republican nominee. He attempted to reassure Southerners that slavery would not be molested in the slave states, but adamantly opposed permitting the introduction of slavery into the western territories. When the final votes were tallied, Lincoln received 40 percent of the popular vote, but won decisively in the Electoral College, carrying all the Northern and Western states.

The election of Abraham Lincoln was a Southern nightmare come true. Lincoln had triumphed at the head of a party that received virtually no votes in much of the South. Southerners now faced the prospect of a party hostile to slavery controlling Congress and the presidency.

South Carolina led the way in seceding from the Union on December 20, 1860. Within six weeks Mississippi, Georgia, Florida, Alabama, Texas, and Louisiana followed. Representatives from the seceded states met at Montgomery, Alabama, in February 1861. They formed the **Confederate States of America**. The men gathered at Montgomery elected Jefferson Davis as the president of the new Confederacy. Davis's experience as a soldier and secretary of war were points in his favor. Few expected the Union to break up peacefully.

Chapter Review

Rapid Review

To achieve the perfect 5, you should be able to explain the following:

- The concept of Manifest Destiny spurred American expansion into Texas and the far West.
- American settlers much more loyal to the United States than to Mexico entered Texas in large numbers and encouraged Texas to break away from Mexico and eventually become an American state.
- The issue of slavery in the territories came to dominate American political debate more and more in the 1840s and 1850s.
- California entered the Union as a free state as a result of the Compromise of 1850.
- The Kansas-Nebraska Act created violence in the Kansas Territory as it "decided" on whether it would be slave or free; both Abolitionists and proslavery forces shipped in supporters to help sway the elections in this territory.
- The *Dred Scott* decision only intensified tensions between the North and the South.
- The election of 1860 was seen as an insult to many in the South, and after its results were announced, the secession of Southern states from the Union was inevitable.

Time Line

1836: Texas territory rebels against Mexico; independent republic of Texas created
1841: Beginning of expansion into Oregon territory
1844: James K. Polk elected president
1845: Texas becomes a state of the United States
1846: Oregon Treaty with Britain gives most of Oregon to United States
War with Mexico begins
Wilmot Proviso passed
1848: Gold discovered in California; beginning of California Gold Rush
Treaty of Guadalupe Hidalgo
Formation of Free-Soil party
Zachary Taylor elected president
1850: Passage of Compromise of 1850
1852: Franklin Pierce elected president
Uncle Tom's Cabin by Harriet Beecher Stowe published
1854: Kansas-Nebraska Act passed
Formation of the Republican party
1856: Democrat James Buchanan elected president
"Bleeding Kansas"
1857: *Dred Scott* decision announced
1858: Lincoln-Douglas debates
Freeport Doctrine issued by Stephen Douglas
1859: Harper's Ferry raid of John Brown
1860: Abraham Lincoln elected president
South Carolina secedes from the Union (December)

› Review Questions

Fact Check

Check your knowledge of the historical period covered in this chapter.

1. Northerners approved all of the provisions of the Compromise of 1850 *except*
   A. the section of the document concerning slavery in California.
   B. the section of the document concerning the Fugitive Slave Act.
   C. the section of the treaty on slave trading in Washington, DC.
   D. the section of the document concerning slavery in New Mexico.

2. During the presidential election of 1860
   A. the Democratic Party had split and was running two candidates.
   B. the new president was someone whom almost no one in the South had voted for.
   C. the issue of the future of slavery in the territories was a major issue.
   D. all of the above.

3. According to the concept of Manifest Destiny
   A. it was primarily economic factors that caused Americans to expand westward.
   B. it was primarily political factors that caused Americans to expand westward.
   C. westward expansion was the fulfillment of America's destiny.
   D. overpopulation on the eastern seaboard forced westward expansion.

4. American settlers first came to Mexico in the early 1830s
   A. to avenge the attack on the Alamo.
   B. for political reasons; most who came were disenchanted with American policy toward Native Americans.
   C. out of personal loyalty to Davey Crockett or Jim Bowie.
   D. because they could receive a large plot of land for next to nothing.

5. The political party of the era that supported nativist policies was the
   A. Free-Soil Party.
   B. Democratic Party.
   C. Know-Nothing Party.
   D. Whig Party.

Multiple-Choice Questions

Here are multiple-choice questions like the ones on the AP U.S. History exam.

Questions 6–8 refer to the quotation below.

The object of these sketches is to awaken sympathy and feeling for the African race, as they exist among us; to show their wrongs and sorrows, under a system so necessarily cruel and unjust as to defeat and do away the good effects of all that can be attempted for them, by their best friends, under it. In doing this, the author can sincerely disclaim any invidious feeling toward those individuals who, often without any fault of their own, are involved in the trials and embarrassments of the legal relations of slavery. Experience has shown her that some of the noblest of minds and hearts are often thus involved; and no one knows better than they do, that what may be gathered of the evils of slavery from sketches like these is not the half that could be told of the unspeakable whole.

—Harriet Beecher Stowe, Preface, *Uncle Tom's Cabin*, 1852

6. Harriet Beecher Stowe wrote *Uncle Tom's Cabin* in order to
A. encourage African American men to passively submit to injustice.
B. discourage criticisms of Southern plantation society.
C. argue that Northern wage laborers were just as oppressed as Southern slaves.
D. demonstrate the evil effects of slavery on both slaves and slave owners.

7. Readers sympathetic to Stowe's point of view would most likely have opposed which of the following?
A. The Wilmot Proviso
B. The Fugitive Slave Act
C. The Homestead Act
D. The Republican Party

8. The ideals Stowe expressed in *Uncle Tom's Cabin* were most directly reflected in which of the following legislative acts?
A. The Sherman Antitrust Act
B. The Immigration Act of 1924
C. The Civil Rights Act of 1964
D. The USA Patriot Act of 2001

Short-Answer Question

The short-answer question below is similar to the ones you'll encounter on the AP U.S. History exam.

9. Answer Parts A, B, and C.
A. Briefly explain ONE example of an issue leading to sectional hostility between the North and South in the period 1840 to 1860.
B. Briefly explain a SECOND example of an issue leading to sectional hostility between the North and South in the period 1840 to 1860.
C. Briefly explain ONE example of an effort to achieve compromise between the North and South in the period 1840 to 1860.

› Answers and Explanations

1. B. In the Compromise of 1850, provisions of the Fugitive Slave Act were made tougher. California was to enter the Union as a free state, the residents of New Mexico and Utah could decide if they wanted to be slave or free, and slave trading was outlawed in Washington, DC.

2. D. All of the factors mentioned concerning the 1860 election are true.

3. C. The concept of Manifest Destiny stated that social, political, and economic factors all came together to encourage western expansion, and that western expansion was actually "God's plan" for America.

4. D. Settlers who came and became Mexican citizens and Catholics could receive very large plots of land for almost nothing. The incident at the Alamo did not occur until 1836.

5. C. The Know-Nothing Party, a popular party in the early 1850s, supported a number of anti-immigrant and anti-Catholic policies.

6. D. Harriet Beecher Stowe wrote *Uncle Tom's Cabin* in order to demonstrate the evil effects of slavery on both slaves and slave owners. Stowe emphasized the moral evils of slavery; she believed that slavery violated the tenets of Christianity. She was especially disturbed at the way slave families could be broken up when individual members were sold.

7. B. Readers sympathetic to Stowe's point of view would most likely have opposed the Fugitive Slave Act. The Fugitive Slave Act was a component of the Compromise of 1850. It required officials in the North to arrest escaped slaves and return them to their masters in the South. This act enraged many in the North.

8. **C.** The ideals Stowe expressed in *Uncle Tom's Cabin* were most directly reflected in the Civil Rights Act of 1964. The Civil Rights Act of 1964 made it illegal to discriminate against people on the basis of their race, sex, religion, or national origin. This act was a major milestone in the struggle of African Americans for equal rights.

9. **Parts A and B**: The rise of abolitionism in the North angered many in the South. The House of Representatives imposed a gag rule on antislavery petitions that lasted from 1836 to 1844. Many opponents of slavery believed that the expansionism that resulted in the Mexican War of 1846 to 1848 was an attempt to create more slave states. The 1846 Wilmot Proviso in the House of Representatives calling for the prohibition of slavery in territory taken from Mexico angered many Southerners. The Fugitive Slave Act, part of the Compromise of 1850, offended Northerners who did not want escaping slaves hunted in their states. Harriet Beecher Stowe's *Uncle Tom's Cabin* (1852) was a powerful literary indictment of slavery. The 1854 Kansas-Nebraska Act inflamed sectional tensions by overturning the Missouri Compromise and raising the prospect of slavery in these two territories. Kansas became known as "Bleeding Kansas" because of the violence between proslavery and antislavery settlers. The 1856 *Dred Scott v. Sandford* Supreme Court decision, which ruled that Congress could not prohibit slavery in the territories, outraged many in the North. John Brown's unsuccessful attempt to start a slave rebellion by attacking the Harpers Ferry federal arsenal in 1859 terrified many Southerners. The election of the Republican candidate Abraham Lincoln to the presidency in 1860 on a purely sectional vote convinced many Southerners that they had to secede from the Union.

Part C: President James K. Polk tried to ensure both Northern and Southern support for American expansionism by seeing to it that both sections benefitted. In his 1844 presidential campaign he called for the annexation of slaveholding Texas and all of the Oregon Territory. Henry Clay tried to solve sectional tensions with his Compromise of 1850, which, among other provisions, saw California enter the Union as a free state and imposed a strong Fugitive Slave Act. During the 1850s, Senator Stephen A. Douglas believed he could reconcile sectional disputes over the western territories with his doctrine of "popular sovereignty," which would allow the settlers of territories decide whether they wanted slavery or not.

CHAPTER 15

Union Divided:
The Civil War (1861–1865)

IN THIS CHAPTER

Summary: The Civil War was the culmination of nearly 40 years of tensions between the North and the South. Northern Abolitionists looked forward to the war with great anticipation: victory over the South would finally allow the dreaded institution of slavery to be eliminated. The majority of Southerners rejoiced at the onset of war; they perceived that victory would allow the "Southern way of life" to continue without constant criticism from the North. As in many wars, politicians and generals on both sides predicted a quick victory. Newspapers in both the North and the South declared that the war would be over by Christmas of 1861.

To state that the Civil War was just about slavery is an oversimplification. Certainly, criticism by Northern Abolitionists of the "peculiar institution" of slavery, and Southern responses to that criticism, were important factors. However, other tensions between the North and the South also existed. The future of the American economy as seen by Northern industrialists differed drastically from the desires and needs of the leaders of Southern plantation societies. Most important, the Southern view of "states' rights" differed most dramatically from the view of the Union held in the North. By 1861, many political leaders in the South fervently espoused the views that John C. Calhoun had formulated decades earlier. It was up to the individual state to decide on the validity of any federal law or federal action for that state. This position was intolerable to President Lincoln and most political leaders in the North. If anything, it was debate over the states' rights issue that made the Civil War inevitable.

Other factors increased the animosity between the North and the South. By this point, slavery was synonymous with Southern identity; in Southern eyes, any attack on slavery was an attack on the South as a whole. The fact that this struggle between the North and the South had gone on for 40 years served to harden positions on both sides. In addition, by this point the population of the North was greater than the population of the South, and the number of free states was greater than the number of slave states. As a result, Southerners knew that Northern antislave interests would control the Congress (and the ability to influence Supreme Court appointments) and the Electoral College for the foreseeable future.

Keywords

First Battle of Bull Run (1861): early Civil War engagement ending in defeat for the Union army; this battle convinced many in the North that victory over the Confederacy would not be as easy as they first thought it would be.

Emancipation Proclamation: January 1, 1863, proclamation that freed slaves in Southern territories was controlled by the Union army.

Battle of Gettysburg (1863): bloodiest overall battle of the Civil War; many historians claim that the Southern defeat in this battle was the beginning of the end for the Confederacy.

Appomattox: Virginia courthouse where General Robert E. Lee surrendered Confederate forces on April 9, 1865.

North and South on the Brink of War

The North brought a number of advantages to a military struggle with the seceded states. Most of the nation's wealth was concentrated in the North. The North housed the largest banks and financial markets in great cities like New York and Chicago. The Northern states were far more industrialized and were connected together by an extensive network of railroads. The North was in a much better position to manufacture and transport weapons and other war supplies. The North also had an edge in manpower, with a population three times that of the South. Despite this, Southern supporters of the Confederacy still believed that they could win a war with the North. Many in the agrarian South overvalued the importance of cotton to international markets, believing that the great European powers of Great Britain and France would intervene to protect their textile industries. Southerners also saw themselves as enjoying a moral advantage; they would be fighting a defensive war to protect their homes and institutions. Southerners also realized that geography posed a problem for the North; the South was a huge territory that would require an enormous expenditure of resources to capture and hold.

Searching for Compromise

In the aftermath of the creation of the **Confederate States of America** in February 1861, there was no immediate rush of slave states in the upper South to secede. They had fewer slaves and were reluctant to leave the union. Leaders in these states attempted to formulate a compromise that would end the secession crisis. Congressional representatives from

Kentucky and Maryland urged the passage of legislation that would guarantee the continued existence of slavery in states and territories where it was already established. President James Buchanan, very much a lame duck, provided little leadership. In December 1860, he declared that secession was illegal, but he also believed that there were no constitutional grounds to compel states to remain in the Union.

The leaders of the Confederacy grew confident that they had nothing to fear from Buchanan. Confederates occupied most federal installations in the seceded states. In South Carolina, the new authorities demanded that federal troops evacuate **Fort Sumter**, a fortress situated on an island in Charleston harbor. In January 1861, Buchanan attempted to resupply the fort by sending south an unarmed merchant ship. When the Confederates drove the supply ship off with gunfire, Buchanan refused to use the navy to protect another supply run. This emboldened the Confederates in Charleston.

While Fort Sumter was the center of most Americans' attention, Senator John Crittenden of Kentucky proposed another compromise. The **Crittenden Plan** called for an assurance of federal protection of slavery where it already existed, and the formal extension of the Missouri Compromise line to the Pacific; territory to the south of the line would be open to slavery, while that north of the line would be free. Crittenden's compromise failed because Republicans refused to surrender their free-soil position on slavery in the territories that had just won them the national election.

Gunfire at Fort Sumter

Abraham Lincoln had to be politically circumspect in the long interval between his election in November 1860 and his inauguration in March 1861. Though all looked to him, he was not yet the president. He attempted to reassure Southerners that he would not interfere with slavery in the slave states, while holding firm to his position on slavery in the territories. He affirmed federal authority, while saying nothing to provoke a war. At his inauguration, Lincoln stated his desire for conciliation with the seceded states, but declared that if necessary he would use the military to restore the Union.

Lincoln knew that to rally opinion for a war against the secessionists he could not fire the first shots. He used the Fort Sumter crisis to maneuver the Confederates into doing that. In April 1861, Lincoln dispatched another supply ship toward Fort Sumter. Aware of the ship's impending arrival, Jefferson Davis and the Confederate authorities in Charleston decided to strike. The Confederates began a bombardment of the fort on April 12, and two days later the federal garrison surrendered.

Davis hoped that the attack on Fort Sumter would demonstrate Confederate strength and rally support for the secessionist cause. Once Lincoln issued a call for 75,000 volunteers to put down the rebellion, Virginia, North Carolina, Tennessee, and Arkansas did secede and join the Confederacy. But by various means Lincoln was able to keep the slave states of Maryland, Delaware, Kentucky, and Missouri in the Union; control of these states greatly improved the strategic position of the federal government.

Opening Strategies

Southerners sincerely claimed to be defending the principle of **states' rights**. What drove this concern was a resolute attachment to the institution of slavery, despite the fact that the great majority of Southerners owned no slaves. The centrality of slavery to secession undercut Confederate attempts to use cotton to win diplomatic support from Britain and France. These European powers were not particularly friendly to the U.S. government, and they wanted Southern cotton. But both Britain and France had long since outlawed slavery and were wary of being seen as supporting the "peculiar institution." Early in the war, a Confederate decision to embargo cotton exports to Europe backfired. President Davis and his advisors hoped that this would hurt Britain and France enough economically that their governments would be pressured into offering diplomatic recognition to the Confederacy. Instead, the Europeans discovered other sources of cotton, with disastrous long-term consequences for the South.

In 1861, great numbers of volunteers joined the Union and Confederate armies. In the first flush of enthusiasm, both sides predicted a quick and easy victory. President Lincoln rallied Northern public opinion for a war to preserve the Union; he argued that to allow the rebellion to succeed would be to undermine the foundations of representative government. The Confederate capital was moved to Richmond, Virginia, once that populous and prestigious state seceded. Northern newspapers editorialized "On to Richmond!" because they believed that the capture of this city within striking distance of Washington D.C. would end the war. The only important official who believed that the war would be long and hard was General Winfield Scott, the elderly commander of the U.S. Army. Lincoln urged the federal forces gathering outside Washington to attack. A half-trained army set off for Richmond. On July 21, 1861, this force was defeated by an equally green Confederate army at the **First Battle of Bull Run**. The Union troops retreated to Washington in disorder. The victorious Confederates were too disorganized to pursue them.

The Loss of Illusions

The heavy casualties at First Bull Run shocked both sides. President Lincoln began to realize that the war would be a hard one and studied the strategy proposed by General Scott. Termed the **Anaconda Plan** by uncomprehending journalists, Scott proposed a strict blockade of the southern coastline and the seizure of the Mississippi River; the Confederacy would be economically strangled before well-trained federal armies moved in to finish it off. Lincoln ordered the Navy to close off all Southern ports. This took time, but as the war went on, the blockade grew increasingly effective. By the end of the conflict, the South was economically crippled; it could not export cotton or import manufactured goods. The U.S. Navy captured New Orleans in April 1862, a vital first step in closing off the Mississippi River to the Confederacy.

Jefferson Davis also realized that he faced a long and difficult war. In April 1862, he persuaded the Confederate Congress to institute the first national draft in American history. Davis's efforts to bring more focus and efficiency to the war effort were hampered by the states' rights principles built into the Confederacy. Southern governors resisted the president's efforts to get more control over their states' troops and resources. Davis never solved the economic challenges facing the Confederacy. Repeating the mistake made by American leaders during the Revolutionary War, he printed paper money with no gold reserves to back the currency. The result was an inflation that eventually made Confederate money worthless.

Union Victories in the West

While often frustrated militarily in the East, the Union armies made steady progress in the West. In February 1862, a promising young federal general named Ulysses S. Grant captured Fort Henry and Fort Donelson in Tennessee, taking many prisoners and driving back Confederate forces in the Mississippi Valley. On April 6, the Confederates counterattacked Grant at Shiloh. The fighting was the bloodiest yet seen in the war, but in the end the Confederates were forced to retreat. Federal forces advanced further south after Shiloh, leaving them poised to attack Vicksburg, the last important Confederate bastion in the Mississippi River.

General George McClellan was appointed commander of the Union army in November 1861, displacing General Scott. McClellan was an able strategist, but proved extremely cautious; he always believed, erroneously, that the enemy outnumbered him. His job was to take Richmond, and he tried President Lincoln's patience with many delays. He finally moved in the spring of 1862, approaching Richmond from a different direction than Bull Run. Unfortunately for his army, he moved so slowly that the Confederates, under a new commander named Robert E. Lee, drove him back in a series of hard-fought battles. Lee proved his mastery of battle tactics by whipping another federal army at the **Second Battle of Bull Run**.

In an innovative attempt to frustrate the Union blockade, the Confederates constructed an **ironclad ship**, originally named the *Merrimack.* In March 1862, after sinking some federal ships, it fought an inconclusive battle with the *Monitor*, a hastily launched federal ironclad. The Confederates could not construct enough ironclads to make a difference in the war, but the new ships pointed the way to the future of all navies.

The Home Fronts

The states' rights ethos of the South posed challenges for the men charged with running the war. Many Southerners volunteered to serve for a year in 1861. By 1862, these men were looking forward to returning home. Concern about the effects of these departures upon the muster rolls of the Confederate armies led Jefferson Davis and Robert E. Lee to support the **conscription** law. This Confederate draft required three years of military service from all white men between the ages of 18 to 35. The ages were later extended from 17 to 50. The draft proved to be very unpopular. The exemptions granted to some large slave owners to keep a watch on their slaves led to cries that the conflict was "a rich man's war and a poor man's fight." Efforts to obstruct the law by state leaders meant that in parts of the Confederacy up to 60 percent of the military aged men did not serve in the army.

Southerners began to experience serious economic hardships in late 1862. Inflation drove up prices. Food shortages became common. Desertion from the army became a problem as men headed home to provide support for their families. In another measure that defied states' rights principles, the Confederate government imposed an income tax. This effort to bring in much-needed revenue met limited success in an increasingly poverty-stricken South; by the end of the war, the government was accepting payments in grain and livestock rather than money.

Unlike the South, the North prospered economically during the war. A positive balance sheet could not alleviate all the tensions resulting from the waging of a bloody and destructive war. Northern leaders were also worried about military manpower. In 1863, Congress passed a draft law that called up men between the ages of 20 and 45. The law was intended to stimulate voluntary enlistments, often accompanied by financial bounties. Relatively few men were drafted. Despite this, the law was widely condemned. Especially reviled was a provision that allowed wealthier citizens to avoid the draft by hiring a substitute or buying themselves out by paying the government a $300 fee. In July 1863, the law led to riots in New York City. Irish immigrants and others who felt threatened by the draft went on a rampage that destroyed property and resulted in 200 deaths; many of the victims were African Americans whom the rioters unfairly blamed for the war.

Though much more financially secure than the South, the North also faced challenges in funding an expensive war. The federal government passed an income tax law in 1861. The next year, the government issued **"greenbacks,"** paper money that was not backed by gold. Because of the superior credit of the United States, this paper money was accepted by the people and worked well through the end of the war.

President Lincoln expanded the power of the presidency during the war. He issued an executive order that put portions of Kentucky under **martial law**. He took vigorous action against Northern Democrats who publicly opposed the war. These antiwar Democrats were popularly known as **Copperheads**. During the war, 14,000 Copperheads were imprisoned without facing trial. Three men were deported into the Confederacy. Several times Lincoln suspended the **writ of habeas corpus** when Copperheads were arrested.

The Emancipation Proclamation

At the outset of the war, President Lincoln's only goal was to restore the Union. He resisted abolitionist appeals, fearing that talk of freeing slaves would cost the government support in the crucial border states. As the war dragged on, Lincoln realized that slavery was helping sustain the Southern war effort. He decided to free the slaves in the territories still controlled by the Confederacy as a war measure. He realized that he had to do this after a federal victory, to avoid it seeming an act of political desperation. Lincoln received his victory on September 17, 1862, where on the bloodiest single day of the Civil War, General McClellan's army turned back an invasion of Maryland by Robert E. Lee at the Battle of Antietam.

The **Emancipation Proclamation** went into effect on January 1, 1863. It changed the nature of the war. For the North the war was now about extending freedom as well as ending a rebellion. Initially, many Northerners were dubious about this, and the Democrats did well in the 1862 elections. Over time, the logic of ending slavery proved more compelling. This new moral purpose of liberating slaves ended any possibility of the European powers intervening to save the Confederacy. The problem of slaves living in Union territory remained to be settled at the end of the war. Southerners were outraged by the Emancipation Proclamation and vowed defiance.

The Turn of the Tide

The Confederacy remained formidable in late 1862 and early 1863. Robert E. Lee won impressive victories on December 13, 1862, at the **Battle of Fredericksburg**, and on May 1 to 3, 1863, at the **Battle of Chancellorsville**. For all his battlefield successes, Lee realized that Northern superiority in men and material could not be resisted forever. He convinced President Davis that the best way to end the war would be to crush the enemy's morale by winning a great victory on Northern soil.

In June 1863, Lee led his army north. A federal army commanded by General George Meade moved to intercept him. The two armies grappled with each other in a small town in Pennsylvania at the **Battle of Gettysburg**. From July 1 to July 3, Lee unsuccessfully attacked Meade's well-sited defenses. He was forced to retreat, having lost 28,000 men, a third of his army. The federal forces lost 24,000 men, and were too bloodied to quickly follow up on their victory. Lee was still a masterful tactician and his weakened army remained dangerous, but never again would he be able to take the initiative in the fighting. The war had reached a turning point.

That the balance of the war had shifted against the Confederacy was reinforced by important events in the West. Even as combat raged at Gettysburg, General Ulysses S. Grant was completing a long-drawn-out campaign to isolate and capture Vicksburg. The **Battle of Vicksburg** culminated in the surrender of the city on July 4, 1863. This gave Union forces control of the entire span of the Mississippi River, splitting the Confederacy. In November, President Lincoln gave his **Gettysburg Address** while dedicating a national cemetery at the battle site. This famous speech changed the focus of the war from the preservation of the Union to the moral cause of ending slavery. After Confederates defeated an army invading southeastern Tennessee at the September 18-20 Battle of Chickamauga, federal reinforcements were rushed to the area. On November 23 to 25, forces under General Grant won a series of battles around the city of Chattanooga that opened an invasion route into Georgia. Because of his outstanding successes, Grant was put in charge of the Union army in early 1864. He brought a new sense of energy and direction to federal military strategy. He devised a coordinated assault on the Confederacy. In May 1864, Grant traveled with Meade's army as it advanced toward Richmond, while General William Tecumseh Sherman aimed another army at the vital Southern railroad hub of Atlanta, Georgia.

War Weariness

Already by early 1864 some Confederate officials were calling for peace talks. Economic conditions continued to deteriorate. The Confederate army fought on, but under enormous strain. Once Grant's forces attacked in Virginia, they never broke contact with Lee's army. Showing his customary brilliance, and well-acquainted with the terrain, Lee inflicted heavy casualties on the invaders, but suffered irreplaceable losses as well. Grant knew that he could sustain an unequal exchange of casualties; he also knew that as he tied down and wore down Lee's army, other federal forces were knifing into the overstretched Confederacy. In Georgia, Sherman slowly maneuvered toward Atlanta, held back by a determined Confederate defense.

1864 was an election year. As the death toll mounted, President Lincoln's reelection prospects dimmed. The Democrats nominated General George McClellan, proclaiming their patriotism while hoping to capitalize on antiwar sentiment. By late summer, even Lincoln thought that he would be defeated. Battlefield victories changed the momentum of the campaign. Dissatisfied with the defense of Atlanta, Jefferson Davis appointed a more aggressive commander. The Confederates attacked Sherman and were badly defeated. Their losses were so great they had to evacuate Atlanta. The fall of Atlanta was a clear indication that the Confederacy was tottering. In Virginia, Grant forced Lee into a sustained defense of the town of Petersburg outside Richmond. Both sides settled down to trench warfare. Lee's devoted army was all but trapped. With victory in sight, Lincoln won reelection.

The End of the War

Determined to wreck what was left of Southern morale, General Sherman burned the militarily useful parts of Atlanta in November 1864. Then, living off the land, he marched an army across Georgia and captured the port of Savannah on the coast. Along the way, his men left a swathe of destruction. This made it clear that the Confederate army could no longer protect civilians in the Southern heartland. Desertions from Confederate forces mounted as men went home to protect their families. In early 1865, Sherman launched an equally devastating invasion of the Carolinas. In Virginia, Lee's position at Petersburg gradually grew worse. In early April, Grant threatened to encircle his army. Lee tried to escape but was cornered by Grant at **Appomattox**. On April 9, Lee surrendered his army. By the beginning of June, all other Confederate forces had laid down their arms.

President Lincoln hoped for a peace of reconciliation. On April 14, he was assassinated while attending a performance of *Our American Cousin* at Ford's Theater. The assassin was John Wilkes Booth, a failed actor and Southern fanatic who organized a conspiracy to kill Lincoln, the vice president, and the secretary of state. Booth was the only conspirator to succeed in his mission. He escaped, but was hunted down and killed a few days later by federal troops. Most of the other conspirators were captured, and after a trial by a military tribunal, several were hanged. For the 1864 election, Lincoln had chosen Andrew Johnson, a rough-hewn Unionist Democrat, to be his running mate. Now president, Johnson would have to lead the nation as it attempted to heal the wounds of a civil war.

Chapter Review

Rapid Review

To achieve the perfect 5, you should be able to explain the following:

- By 1861, various social, political, economic, and cultural factors made conflict between the North and the South inevitable.
- The North had numerous industrial, transportation, and financial advantages that they utilized throughout the Civil War.
- The Confederate States of America was created in February 1861; the fact that these states were organized as a confederacy had several disadvantages that would become obvious as the war progressed.
- Success for the Confederacy depended on European aid; Southerners overestimated the dependence of Europe on Southern crops.
- By late 1862, the war had produced severe effects on the home fronts; food shortages were occurring in the South, and President Lincoln imposed martial law in several locations and suspended the writ of habeas corpus in the cases of some of his political opponents.
- The Emancipation Proclamation provided a moral justification for Northerners to continue the war.
- The war shifted decisively in favor of the North in 1863, with the battles at Gettysburg and Vicksburg proving to be critical victories for the North.
- The surrender of the Confederacy in April 1865 was caused by a severe lack of morale, manpower, and economic stability in the South.

Time Line

1860: Lincoln elected president
       South Carolina secedes from Union
1861: Confederate States of America created
       Attack on Fort Sumter
       First Battle of Bull Run
       Union begins blockade of Southern ports
1862: New Orleans captured by Union navy
       Battle of Shiloh
       Conscription begins in Confederate states
       Emancipation of slaves in Southern states begins
       Battle of Antietam
       British announce they will not aid the Confederacy in any substantial way

1863: Emancipation Proclamation
Conscription begins in the North; draftees may hire "replacements"
First black soldiers enlist in Union army
Crucial Union victory at Gettysburg
Crucial Union victory at Vicksburg
Draft riots in New York City
1864: Abraham Lincoln reelected
General Sherman carries out his "march to the sea"
Desertion becomes a major problem in the Confederate army
1865: General Lee surrenders at Appomattox
Abraham Lincoln assassinated

› Review Questions

Fact Check

Check your knowledge of the historical period covered in this chapter.

1. The North held many advantages at the beginning of the Civil War *except*
   A. the North occupied more territory than the South.
   B. the North had more railroad lines.
   C. the North had more factories.
   D. the North had a larger population.

2. European states did not diplomatically recognize the Confederacy in the Civil War because
   A. there were alternative sources of cotton and other crops that they could turn to.
   B. they opposed the Confederacy's position on slavery.
   C. they did not believe that the Confederacy could win.
   D. all of the above.

3. The military draft was unpopular to many in the North because
   A. the draft allowed blacks to enter the armed forces.
   B. the draft allowed Irish-American immigrants to enter the army.
   C. the draft allowed those drafted to hire "replacements."
   D. martial law was needed in many locations to enforce the draft provisions.

4. The Battle of Vicksburg was an important victory for the Union because
   A. it reversed several Union defeats in the same year.
   B. it gave the Union a pathway to Atlanta.
   C. it gave the Union virtual control of the Mississippi River.
   D. it demonstrated that General Lee could, in fact, be beaten.

5. Copperheads were
   A. Democrats in the North who opposed the war.
   B. Republicans in the North who suggested that Lincoln be replaced.
   C. Democrats in the North who switched alliance to Lincoln.
   D. Southern Democrats who wanted negotiations with the North as early as 1863.

Multiple-Choice Questions

Here are multiple-choice questions like the ones on the AP U.S. History exam.

Questions 6–8 refer to the quotation below.

We rely greatly on the sure operation of a complete blockade of the Atlantic and Gulf ports soon to commence. In connection with such a blockade we propose a powerful movement down the Mississippi to the ocean, with a cordon of posts at proper points, and the capture of Forts Jackson and Saint Philip [at New Orleans —ed.]; the object being to clear out and keep open this great line of communication in connection with the strict blockade of the seaboard, so as to envelop the insurgent states and bring them to terms with less bloodshed than by any other plan.

—General Winfield Scott, Letter to General George B. McClellan, May 3, 1861

6. General Winfield Scott's "Anaconda Plan" proposed defeating the Confederacy by
   A. launching an immediate attack on the army defending the Confederate capital of Richmond.
   B. wearing down the Confederate armies through a policy of attrition.
   C. using superior federal resources to isolate and economically cripple the South.
   D. destroying Southern homes and businesses until the Southern people surrendered.

7. Which of the following was a major military advantage for the South during the Civil War?
   A. The geographical size of the Confederacy
   B. A numerical superiority in troops
   C. The loyalty of Southern slaves
   D. The willingness of Southern women to work in arms factories

8. General Scott was unusual among Northern leaders in 1861 because he believed that
   A. the war would not be won quickly.
   B. the Confederacy was vulnerable to Northern attacks.
   C. the war would be won quickly.
   D. the North needed to prepare for Confederate attacks.

Short-Answer Question

The short-answer question below is similar to the ones you'll encounter on the AP U.S. History exam.

9. Answer Parts A, B, and C.
   A. Briefly explain ONE example of why the Civil War went on longer than people initially expected.
   B. Briefly explain a SECOND example of why the Civil War went on longer than people initially expected.
   C. Briefly explain ONE example of an important turning point in the Civil War.

› Answers and Explanations

1. **A.** All of the others were major advantages for the Union war effort.

2. **D.** All of the reasons given helped convince the Europeans not to assist the Confederacy. The Confederacy's position on slavery proved to be especially troublesome, since slavery had long been outlawed in Europe.

3. **C.** The fact that replacement soldiers, usually immigrants, could be hired or that a payment of $300 to the government could get a man out of the draft made the system very unpopular to many.

4. **C.** The six-week Battle of Vicksburg occurred in 1863 and helped turn the war in the Union's favor. As a result of Vicksburg, the Mississippi River was virtually in the hands of the Union. Lee did not command the Confederate forces at Vicksburg.

5. A. Copperheads were Democrats in the North who claimed that the war would bring economic ruin to the North, with freed slaves taking jobs that whites now had. Some were arrested and deported.

6. C. General Winfield Scott's "Anaconda Plan" proposed defeating the Confederacy by using superior federal resources to isolate and economically cripple the South. Scott was one of the few leaders in Washington who thought that defeating the South would not be easy and would take time. Newspapers derided his strategy to cut off the South by imposing a naval blockade and seizing control the Mississippi River, naming it the "Anaconda Plan." In the end, the North followed the general outline of Scott's strategy.

7. A. A major military advantage for the South during the Civil War was the sheer size of the Confederacy. The North would be forced to mobilize massive forces to seize and control large swathes of the South while battling determined Confederate resistance.

8. A. General Scott was unusual among Northern leaders in 1861 because he believed that the war would not be won quickly. At the beginning of the war President Abraham Lincoln asked the states for just 75,000 men enlisted for three months. Many leaders thought that one battlefield victory would overcome Confederate resistance. This led to a premature federal advance on the Confederate capital of Richmond, Virginia, and a defeat at the First Battle of Bull Run on July 21, 1861.

9. Parts A and B: Although the North had significant advantages going into the war, such as a larger population, more railroads and industry, and greater financial resources, the South also possessed advantages. The South was a very large territory with 3,500 miles of coastline. To effectively occupy this territory and blockade this coastline would require large Northern army and naval forces. Technology helped prolong the war. Weapons such as the rifled musket made close encounters between troops more deadly. The rifled musket, and later repeating rifles, gave the defense an advantage over the offense. Battles became longer range firefights and less decisive. Both sides developed excellent generals whose skill helped frustrate the strategies of their opponents. Great Southern generals included Robert E. Lee and Thomas "Stonewall" Jackson. Great Northern generals included Ulysses S. Grant, William Tecumseh Sherman, and Philip Sheridan. Another factor that prolonged the war was the political determination of citizens on both sides to support their cause; the Civil War was a conflict between two popularly supported governments.

Part C: The Battle of Antietam on September 17, 1862, was enough of a Northern victory to enable President Abraham Lincoln to issue the Emancipation Proclamation, which made freeing slaves a federal war objective. General George Meade's defeat of General Lee at Gettysburg on July 1 to 3, 1863, ended the last major Southern offensive of the war. General Grant's victory at Vicksburg on July 4, 1863, gave the North control over the Mississippi River, splitting the Confederacy. General Sherman's capture of Atlanta on September 2, 1864, led Northerners to believe that the end of the war was in sight and ensured the reelection of President Lincoln. Sherman's subsequent "March to the Sea" from November 15 to December 21 demonstrated the inability of the Confederate government to prevent federal forces from operating in the heartland of the South.

Era of Reconstruction (1865–1877)

IN THIS CHAPTER

Summary: Postwar plans for assimilating the South back into the Union provoked strong resentment among many white Southerners. In addition, the plans of President Abraham Lincoln, the Radical Republicans in the Congress, and President Andrew Johnson all contained significant differences. Policies enacted that improved the political and economic position of former slaves were opposed by many Southern whites. The impeachment of Andrew Johnson demonstrated the disagreements over Reconstruction policy between Johnson and the Radical Republicans. Congressional passage of the Thirteenth, Fourteenth, and Fifteenth Amendments outlawed slavery, established the rights of blacks, and defined the framework by which Southern states could rejoin the Union. Passage of these amendments, profits made by carpetbaggers and scalawags, and the increased economic and political power held by some Southern blacks all caused some elements of traditional Southern society to feel long-lasting anger and resentment. The Compromise of 1877 ended Reconstruction, bringing another reordering of the political, economic, and social structures of the South.

Keywords

Reconstruction Era (1865–1877): period after the Civil War during which Northern political leaders created plans for the governance of the South and a procedure for former Southern states to rejoin the Union; Southern resentment of this era lasted well into the twentieth century.

Radical Republicans: congressional group that wished to punish the South for its secession from the Union; pushed for measures that gave economic and political rights to newly freed blacks in the South and that made it difficult for former Confederate states to rejoin the Union.

Reconstruction Act (1867): act placing Southern states under military rule and barring former supporters of the Confederacy from voting.

Carpetbaggers: northerners who moved to the South during the Reconstruction Era; traditional elements of Southern society were deeply resentful of profits made by carpetbaggers during this period.

Scalawags: term of derision used in the South during the Reconstruction Era for white Southerners who joined the Republican Party or supported Northern Reconstruction policies.

Ku Klux Klan: this group was founded in Tennessee in 1866; its oftentimes violent actions during the Reconstruction Era represented the resentments felt by many Southern whites toward the changing political, social, and economic conditions of the Reconstruction Era.

Compromise of 1877: political compromise ending the disputed presidential election of 1876. By the terms of this compromise Republican candidate Rutherford B. Hayes was awarded the electoral votes of Florida, Louisiana, and South Carolina, thus giving him the presidency; in return, all federal troops were removed from the South.

"Some men are born great, some achieve greatness and others lived during the Reconstruction period."

—Paul Laurence Dunbar, 1903

Lincoln and Reconstruction

The end of the Civil War raised difficult questions about what to do with the defeated South. On what terms would the seceded states be reintegrated into the Union? What would be done with Confederate military and political leaders? What should be done for the newly liberated slaves? Issues such as these tested a federal government that up to the Civil War had played a limited role in most Americans' lives.

Adding to the difficulty of rehabilitating the South was wartime devastation. Virtually the entire Southern railway net had been destroyed. Countless farms and plantations had been ruined. Several cities had been sacked and burned. Almost one-third of adult white males had been killed or wounded. Southern landowners lacked the capital to restore their property. Freed slaves and poor whites needed employment. The white workers feared economic competition from the **freedmen**, the name given to the former slaves.

The murder of Abraham Lincoln further confused the situation. Lincoln had long pondered the problem of restoring the Union. He laid the foundations of the **Reconstruction Era**. In 1863, Lincoln formulated the **Ten Percent Plan**. This plan allowed Southerners who had not held important Confederate military or political positions to swear their allegiance to the United States. Once 10 percent of registered voters in a seceded state did this, they could form a new state government loyal to the Union.

Radical Republicans in Congress opposed this plan. When Tennessee, Louisiana, and Arkansas attempted to resume their participation in the government on Lincoln's terms, the politically powerful Radical Republicans turned them down. The Radical Republicans included congressmen and senators who had been ardent abolitionists. They were determined to protect the freed slaves and push for their social and political equality. The Radical Republicans did not believe that the Southern states could truly be reintegrated into the Union until the freedmen participated politically in Reconstruction. They were well aware that the freedmen offered an enormous pool of Republican votes in the South. The Radical Republicans also hated and distrusted the old Southern political elite, and they thought that the South should be punished for its rebellion. They countered Lincoln's plan with their own. The **Wade-Davis Act** passed Congress in 1864. It required a majority of voters in the Southern states to take an "ironclad" oath proclaiming their current and past loyalty to the Union. The only way that a Southern state could reenter the Union on these terms would be by enfranchising large numbers of African American voters. President Lincoln contained this congressional challenge to his policy with a **pocket veto**.

The Southern legislatures later fed the Radical Republican's suspicions of them by passing **Black Codes,** which imposed such strict regulations of the freedmen that they appeared to be a step back toward slavery. The Black Codes denied African Americans free choice in employment, restricted their movements, and outlawed interracial marriage.

Andrew Johnson and Reconstruction

Andrew Johnson attempted to continue what he believed were the policies of his predecessor. He offered lenient terms to the South. Most Southerners would receive "amnesty and pardon" for swearing an oath to defend the Union and the Constitution. The exceptions would be former Confederate leaders and people whose property was valued over $20,000. As a man who had worked his way up from poverty, Johnson was hostile to the old planter elite and blamed them for secession. All that he demanded of states to resume their place in the Union was to acknowledge the illegality of secession, repudiate Confederate debt, and recognize the abolition of slavery. A Southerner himself, he turned a blind eye to the Black Codes that had emerged by 1866.

The Southern states had reorganized themselves on these terms by the end of 1865. The prospect of Southern representatives, many of them ex-Confederates, swiftly returning to Congress dismayed many in the North. The indifference of the Southern state legislatures to the rights of the freedmen outraged the Radical Republicans.

Efforts to Help the Freedmen

The Radical Republicans rejected President Johnson's Reconstruction program. Though they had many leaders, they were united by their desire to improve conditions for the freedmen in the South. In early 1865, Congress passed a bill establishing the Freedman's Bureau. This federal agency was responsible for assisting the freed slaves, helping them get an education and find employment. The Freedman's Bureau faced a daunting task. By 1866, most freed slaves were working on the plantations of their former masters as **tenant farmers** through the system of sharecropping, where the landowners provided the seed and land while the newly freed slaves worked the land to pay them for rent.

Opinions varied on the best way to help the freedmen. Senator Charles Sumner of Massachusetts believed that the surest guarantee of a better status for the freedmen would be the vote and political influence. Congressman Thaddeus Stevens argued that the freedmen needed economic independence, and he advocated confiscating land from wealthy Confederates and distributing it to their former slaves. In late 1865, Congress created a Joint Committee on Reconstruction to investigate conditions in the South and make recommendations on the reintegration of the Southern states.

The Joint Committee persuaded Congress to renew the authorization of the Freedman's Bureau. It also proposed a Civil Rights bill. Unhappy with Congressional interference with his Reconstruction policies, Johnson vetoed both these bills, declaring them unconstitutional. Johnson's sympathy for former Confederates and growing political combativeness began to alienate moderates in Congress and across the North. He did not help himself by giving a Washington's Birthday speech in which he denounced the Radical Republicans as traitors and charged that they wanted to murder him.

Moderate Republicans joined with their radical colleagues to override Johnson's vetoes. The life of the Freedman's Bureau was extended, and the **Civil Rights Act of 1866** granted the rights of citizenship to the freedmen. The freedmen could look to the federal courts and the U.S. military to enforce these rights. This act also provided support for the **Thirteenth Amendment**. Ratified in December 1865, this amendment to the Constitution outlawed slavery and involuntary servitude. The Thirteenth Amendment confirmed the effects of Lincoln's Emancipation Proclamation and freed all the slaves living in what had been Union territory.

Congress also passed the **Fourteenth Amendment**. This amendment defined national citizenship and gave the federal government the responsibility to protect equal rights for all Americans. It also contained measures aimed at the Southern states. Former Confederate leaders could not hold federal office, and states that denied freedmen the vote would have their congressional representation reduced. Anti-black riots in New Orleans and Memphis helped the amendment pass Congress. President Johnson spoke out against the Fourteenth Amendment. He was rebuked by Northern voters in the 1866 congressional elections, which returned a Radical Republican majority.

Radical Reconstruction

The Radical Republicans now had the political power to assert their Reconstruction agenda. They could override any presidential veto. In 1867, Congress passed a **Reconstruction Act** that put the former Confederacy under military rule. The South was divided into five regions, and an army general was placed in command of each. The Southern states had to hold new constitutional conventions. They were required to provide freedmen equal rights and the vote. Former Confederates lost their franchise. To be officially recognized, the Southern states had to ratify the Fourteenth Amendment. Congress also enacted two laws designed to weaken the recalcitrant President Johnson. The Army Act limited his ability to interfere with the army in the South. The **Tenure of Office Act** removed the power of the president to dismiss a cabinet secretary without the concurrence of the Senate. This measure was designed to protect the position of Secretary of War Edwin Stanton, an ally of the Radical Republicans.

The Impeachment of Andrew Johnson

President Johnson believed that the Tenure of Office Act was an unlawful infringement of his powers. In the fall of 1867, he attempted to fire Secretary Stanton. This precipitated a constitutional crisis. The Radical Republicans, anxious to be rid of Johnson, declared that he had violated the Constitution and launched an **impeachment** process. The House of Representatives voted articles of impeachment on February 24, 1868. No president had been impeached before. In May, Johnson was tried in the Senate. A vote of two-thirds of the Senate was necessary to convict him and remove him from office. He escaped conviction and removal by a one vote margin.

Though Johnson remained as president, he had become politically irrelevant. (He would briefly return to Washington as a senator from Tennessee before his death in 1875.) In the presidential election of 1868, the Republicans nominated General Ulysses S. Grant, the preeminent Union hero of the Civil War, who swept to an easy victory.

Final Phase of Radical Reconstruction

President Grant supported the goals of Radical Reconstruction. He advocated for the passage of the **Fifteenth Amendment**, which was ratified in March 1870. The Fifteenth Amendment protected African American voting rights, stating that no American could be prevented from voting "on account of race, color, or previous condition of servitude." In the elections of 1870, many freedmen voted for the first time. They helped elect 630 African Americans to Southern state legislatures. Sixteen African Americans were elected to the House of Representatives, and one was elected to the Senate. P.B.S. Pinchback was elected governor of Louisiana.

It is important to note that the Fifteenth Amendment only prohibited voter discrimination on the basis of race when it came to voting. It said nothing of gender discrimination. As a result, the women's rights movement was divided over its passage since women still did not have the right to vote. Within the women's rights movement, proponents of its passage argued that it brought women one step closer to gaining the right to vote themselves. Opponents argued that any amendment that did not grant women suffrage was unacceptable.

Grant had to deploy federal troops to protect African American voters in this election. White Southerners profoundly resented a political milestone that challenged their deeply held beliefs. They regarded the Reconstruction authorities as an oppressive and illegitimate occupation. Many did not bother to vote because of their anger over the process. They called Northerners who had moved south to assist with Reconstruction **carpetbaggers**. They dismissed Southerners who cooperated with the Republicans as **scalawags**.

Some Southerners resisted Reconstruction through violence. The **Ku Klux Klan** was founded in Tennessee in 1866. The Klan terrorized freedmen and their white allies, intimidating voters and burning schools. Their vigilante actions included torture and murder. Congress passed "Force" acts to make the interference with voting a crime. President Grant sent soldiers and federal marshals to pursue the Klan, and in parts of the South a low-intensity guerilla war festered for years.

The End of Reconstruction

Grant was reelected in 1872. He continued to support the rights of the freedmen and signed the Civil Rights Act of 1875 that called for equal treatment for African Americans in public accommodations, public transportation, and on juries. Despite this Northern enthusiasm for Reconstruction waned in the face of obdurate Southern opposition. A major recession in 1873 focused most peoples' attention on economic concerns. Scandals in the Grant Administration further diverted attention away from the South. Federal troops were gradually withdrawn from the South, allowing Southern whites to begin recapturing control of state governments.

In the presidential election of 1876, the Democrats nominated Samuel Tilden, the governor of New York. Tilden had become famous for his opposition to the Tammany Hall political machine in New York City and its corrupt boss William M. Tweed. The Republican candidate was Rutherford B. Hayes, the governor of Ohio. Hayes had served as a Union general during the Civil War. The election was close. Tilden won the popular vote, and once voting concluded, he seemed just one vote short of an Electoral College majority. The electoral votes of Florida, Louisiana, and South Carolina remained in dispute. These Southern states were still controlled by Republican reconstruction administrations. If Hayes received these electoral votes, he would win the election by one vote. To resolve this situation, Congress created a special commission with an equal number of Democrats and Republicans, and one independent. When the independent resigned to run for office, he was replaced by a Republican. The commission duly awarded all the contested electoral votes to Hayes, making him the prospective president. Democrats in and out of Congress protested loudly. To ease the contention and smooth Hayes's path to power, Democratic and Republican leaders worked out the **Compromise of 1877**. The Democrats did not attempt to block Hayes from becoming president. In return, the Republicans pulled the last federal troops out of the South and withdrew support for the remaining Republican state governments. Democratic "redeemer" regimes took over across the South. African Americans were quickly deprived of hard-won social and political rights. Southerners would write an early and highly critical history of Reconstruction that portrayed it as a colossal and misguided failure. The "Solid South" would remain Democratic and starkly racially segregated for almost a century.

Chapter Review

Rapid Review

To achieve the perfect 5, you should be able to explain the following:

- Any plan to assimilate the Southern states back into the Union after the Civil War would have major difficulties; a problem was determining the appropriate postwar status of former supporters of the Confederacy.
- The plans for Reconstruction proposed by Abraham Lincoln, the Radical Republicans, and Andrew Johnson all varied dramatically.
- Radical Republicans instituted policies to improve the political and economic status of former slaves; this created great resentment in other segments of Southern society.
- The impeachment of Andrew Johnson went forward because of major disagreements over policy between Johnson and the Radical Republicans in Congress.
- The Thirteenth, Fourteenth, and Fifteenth Amendments outlawed slavery, established the rights of blacks, and established the framework by which Southern states could rejoin the union.
- Profits made by carpetbaggers and scalawags further angered the traditional elements of Southern society. Many in the South, including members of the Ku Klux Klan, felt great resentment toward the carpetbaggers and scalawags and toward the political and economic power now held by some Southern blacks.

- The Compromise of 1877 ended Reconstruction in the South; as Union troops left, blacks were again reduced to the status of second-class citizens.

Time Line

1865: Andrew Johnson institutes liberal Reconstruction plan

Whites in Southern legislatures pass Black Codes

Thirteenth Amendment ratified

1866: Civil Rights Act, Freedmen's Bureau Act approved by Congress (vetoed by Johnson)

Fourteenth Amendment passes Congress (fails to be ratified in Southern states)

Antiblack riots in New Orleans, Memphis

Republicans who favor Radical Reconstruction win congressional elections, in essence ending Johnson's Reconstruction plan

Ku Klux Klan founded

1867: Tenure of Office Act approved by Congress (Congress had to approve presidential appointments, dismissals)

Reconstruction Act approved by Congress (Southern states placed under military rule)

Constitutional conventions called by former Confederate states

Johnson tries to remove Edwin Stanton as secretary of war, leading to cries for his impeachment

1868: Impeachment of Andrew Johnson: Johnson impeached in the House of Representatives, not convicted in the Senate

Southern states return to Union under policies established by Radical Republicans

Final ratification of Fourteenth Amendment

Former Civil War General Ulysses S. Grant elected president

1870: Amendment ratified

Many blacks elected in Southern state legislatures

1872: Confederates allowed to hold office

Ulysses S. Grant reelected

1876: Disputed presidential election between Tilden, Hayes

1877: Compromise of 1877 awards election to Hayes, ends Reconstruction in the South

› Review Questions

Fact Check

Check your knowledge of the historical period covered in this chapter.

1. Radical Republicans favored all of the following *except*
   A. the governing of the South by military generals.
   B. the impeachment of Andrew Johnson.
   C. the return of former Confederate leaders to positions of power in the South.
   D. the election of newly enfranchised blacks to positions in Southern state legislatures.

2. The official reason for impeachment proceedings against Andrew Johnson was
   A. he had violated the Tenure of Office Act.
   B. he had violated the Reconstruction Act.
   C. his Reconstruction policies were much too lenient to the South.
   D. he had failed to enforce the Civil Rights Act of 1866.

3. Black Codes were instituted to
   A. increase black participation in Southern politics during Reconstruction.
   B. increase the effectiveness of the Freedmen's Bureau.
   C. prevent blacks from having certain jobs.
   D. maintain slavery in some sections of the Deep South.

4. Reconstruction ended as a result of the Compromise of 1877 because
   A. a presidential mandate ordered that Reconstruction end.
   B. by the provisions of the compromise, the U.S. Army was removed from Southern states.
   C. the new president, Rutherford B. Hayes, was strongly against the existing Reconstruction policy.
   D. many blacks were now in positions of power in the South, and Reconstruction policies were no longer needed.

5. The Fifteenth Amendment
   A. allowed Southern states to reenter the Union.
   B. outlawed slavery.
   C. stated that a person could not be denied the vote because of his color.
   D. said that former Confederate officials could not hold public office.

Multiple-Choice Questions

Here are multiple-choice questions like the ones on the AP U.S. History exam.

Questions 6–8 refer to the quotation below.

I have confidence, not only in this country and her institutions, but in the endurance, capacity, and destiny of my people. We will, as opportunity offers and ability serves, seek our places, sometimes in the field of letters, arts, sciences, and the professions. More frequently mechanical pursuits will attract and elicit our efforts; more still of my people will find employment and livelihood as cultivators of the soil. The bulk of this people—by surroundings, habits, adaption, and choice—will continue to find their homes in the South, and constitute the masses of its yeomanry."

> —Senator Blanche K. Bruce, "Speech Before the Senate to Introduce a Resolution Appointing a Committee to Investigate Election Practices in Mississippi," March 31, 1876

6. Senator Blanche K. Bruce could express optimism about the future of his people because of changes brought about by
   A. the Industrial Revolution.
   B. the "New" Immigration.
   C. progressivism.
   D. Reconstruction.

7. As an African American, Senator Bruce would most likely have been a member of which of the following political parties?
   A. Democratic
   B. Republican
   C. Black Panther
   D. Populist

8. The ideas expressed by Senator Bruce most directly resemble those of
   A. Booker T. Washington.
   B. George Washington.
   C. Marcus Garvey.
   D. Barack Obama.

Short-Answer Question

The short-answer question below is similar to the ones you'll encounter on the AP U.S. History exam.

9. Answer Parts A, B, and C.
   A. Briefly explain ONE example of a way that the federal government attempted to assist African Americans in the South during Reconstruction.
   B. Briefly explain a SECOND example of a way that the federal government attempted to assist African Americans during Reconstruction.
   C. Briefly explain ONE example of a way white Southerners resisted the federal government's attempts to assist African Americans during Reconstruction.

› Answers and Explanations

1. **C.** All of the other choices were favored by Radical Republicans. The Reconstruction Act of 1867 placed the former Confederate states under military rule.

2. **A.** By attempting to remove Edwin Stanton as secretary of war, many in Congress stated that Johnson had knowingly violated the Tenure of Office Act, thus violating provisions of the U.S. Constitution.

3. **C.** Black Codes were adopted by Southern legislatures in 1866 and limited movement by blacks, prevented them from having certain jobs, and prohibited interracial marriage.

4. **B.** After Hayes was given the presidency by the Compromise of 1877, the U.S. Army left control of the South to the South. Without the army present to enforce Reconstruction policies, these policies ended. Blacks were soon second-class citizens again.

5. **C.** The Fifteenth Amendment stated that no American could be denied the right to vote "on account of race, color, or previous condition of servitude."

6. **D.** Senator Blanche K. Bruce could express optimism about the future of his people because of changes brought about by Reconstruction. The Thirteenth, Fourteenth, and Fifteenth Amendments to the Constitution freed the slaves, then made the freedmen citizens, and gave African American males the right to vote. During Reconstruction in the South, freedmen were able to exercise some liberties and take part in politics. Blanche Bruce was the first African American to be elected to a full term in the U.S. Senate. Things grew worse for African Americans in the South once Reconstruction ended in 1877.

7. **B.** As an African American, Senator Bruce would most likely have been a member of the Republican Party. The Republicans were the party of Lincoln, and they had pushed through the Thirteenth, Fourteenth, and Fifteenth Amendments. Hostile to Southern secessionists, Republicans were more likely to be sym-

pathetic to the aspirations of the freedmen. The Democratic Party in the South represented the interests of those anxious to restore white supremacy. Most African Americans would be Republicans until the era of the New Deal.

8. A. The ideas expressed by Senator Bruce most directly resemble those of Booker T. Washington. The founder of the Tuskegee Institute, which focused on training African Americans for jobs, Washington believed that his people should strive for economic success before agitating for social and political equality.

9. Parts A and B: Congress passed and the states ratified the Thirteenth Amendment in 1865, which ended slavery. In 1865, Congress also created the Freedmen's Bureau, which was charged with helping the freed slaves get employment and an education. The Fourteenth Amendment, ratified in 1868, guaranteed the citizenship rights of African Americans. The Radical Republicans in Congress passed the 1867 Reconstruction Act, putting the Southern states under military rule until they revised their state constitutions and recognized the Fourteenth Amendment. In 1870, the Fifteenth Amendment was ratified giving African American men the right to vote.

Part C: Many white Southerners resisted Reconstruction policies designed to help the freedmen. Shortly after the end of the Civil War, Southern legislatures passed Black Codes, which severely restricted the ability of African Americans to move about and freely contract for their labor. Interracial marriages were prohibited. In addition, Southerners elected many former Confederate officials and military leaders to high office, helping inspire Radical Reconstruction. Beginning in 1866, some Southerners joined the Ku Klux Klan and other secret organizations to terrorize African Americans and keep them from voting and asserting their rights. Once Reconstruction ended in 1877, Southerners gradually stripped African Americans of most of the rights that they had won after the Civil War.

Western Expansion and Its Impact on the American Character (1860–1895)

IN THIS CHAPTER

Summary: Settlers were encouraged to move westward after the Civil War by federal legislation such as the Homestead Act, which gave 160 acres of land to American citizens who were committed to settling on the land and who could pay the $10 registration fee. However, farming on the Plains proved much more difficult than many settlers thought it would be. Thousands of blacks moved west after the Civil War to escape life in the South; mining, ranching, and lumbering also attracted settlers to the West. This westward expansion greatly affected the lives of Native Americans, who were removed to reservations. Farmers in the West began to organize; Farmers' Alliances and the Grange were established to protect farmers' rights. The 1893 Turner Thesis (a well-known theory promulgated by a distinguished historian) proposed the idea that settlers had to become more adaptable and innovative as they moved westward and that these characteristics would slowly become ingrained into the very fabric of American society.

KEY IDEA

Keywords

Homestead Act (1862): bill that did much to encourage settlers to move west; 160 acres of land were given to any settler who was an American citizen or who had applied for citizenship, who was committed to farming the land for six months of the year, and who could pay the $10 registration fee for the land.

Massacre at Wounded Knee (1890): battle that was the last large-scale attempt by Native Americans to resist American settlement in the Great Plains region. Federal soldiers opened fire on Native Americans, killing more than 200.

Dawes Act (1887): act designed to break up Native American tribes by offering individual Native Americans land to be used for either farming or grazing.

Farmers' Alliances: organization that united farmers at the statewide and regional levels; policy goals of this organization included more readily available farm credits and federal regulation of the railroads.

Populist party: formed in 1892 by members of the Farmers' Alliances, this party was designed to appeal to workers in all parts of the country. Populists favored a larger role of government in American society, a progressive income tax, and more direct methods of democracy.

Turner Thesis (1893): thesis by the historian Frederick Jackson Turner suggesting that the innovations practiced by western settlers gradually became ingrained into the fabric of American society; democracy and self-improvement were also central to western expansion, Turner claimed. In short, Turner suggested that many of the characteristics of the "American character" were created by westward expansion. Later historians questioned parts of this thesis.

Government Encouragement of Western Settlement

Americans were moving into the lands west of the Mississippi River well before the Civil War. Beginning in 1862, actions taken by the federal government spurred a surge of settlement that rapidly transformed the West.

The **Homestead Act** encouraged farmers to move west. This legislation provided a settler 160 acres of land; to be eligible for this land, the settler had to be an American citizen, or, if an immigrant, to have applied for American citizenship; the settler had to be the head of a family and at least 21 years old; the settler had to commit to improving the property, building a house or other structures there, and residing on the property for at least six months during the year; and the settler needed to be able to pay a $10 registration fee for the land. The farmer would receive the title to the 160 acres after working it for five years. Homesteaders flooded into the western lands. By 1900, 610,000 plots of land had been distributed to settlers; this resulted in the transfer of 85 million acres of public land into private hands. Also passed in 1862 was the **Morrill Land-Grant Act**. This bill was intended to stimulate higher education in the states. The federal government gave hundreds of thousands of acres of public land to state governments; this land was sold to support the establishment of "land-grant" colleges. This land was often sold to settlers and **land speculators** for 50 cents an acre or less.

The federal government strongly supported the expansion of railroads into the western territories. Congress passed bills in 1862 and 1864 to assist the Union Pacific and Central Pacific railways in constructing a transcontinental railroad. These companies received 10 square miles of land on either side of every mile of track that they laid down. The railroads often sold some of this land to settlers.

Challenges for Western Farmers

The yeoman farmer had long been celebrated by Thomas Jefferson and others as the backbone of the American nation. The farmer was seen as the paradigmatic citizen, self-sufficient and independent. This idealized vision of the farmer would be severely tested on the Great Plains.

Conditions on the western plains were harsh. Winters were bitterly cold, and in the summers temperatures frequently rose above 100 degrees. Because of the lack of trees and wood, many settlers had to build their homes out of sod. These sod houses were less comfortable than more traditionally constructed homes, both in the winter and summer. Water was often in short supply, and tainted sources of water spread diseases such as typhoid. The pleasantly bucolic image of western farming purveyed by Currier and Ives prints and other popular media sources in the East was very different from the experience of settlers battling hordes of locusts, dust storms, and deadly blizzards. Most homesteaders failed. By 1900, two-thirds had given up on their farms. Many former homesteaders headed to a new life in the cities or returned East.

The only way to survive the conditions farmers faced on the arid Great Plains was to cooperate with neighbors. Barn-raising and fencing were collective enterprises. Farm women helped each other with chores and children. Rugged individualism was not a recipe for success on this new agricultural frontier.

Agricultural Innovation

The farmers who thrived on the Great Plains relied on new technologies and business methods. The U.S. Department of Agriculture was established in 1862, and it distributed information on new agricultural developments to farmers. The 1860s and 1870s saw the introduction of new and better plows and threshers, some of them steam-powered.

In many places on the Great Plains, small family farms were displaced by much more extensive **bonanza farms**. These larger agricultural concerns grew only one or two cash crops. Genuine agribusinesses, bonanza farms benefited from economies of scale, and sold produce in bulk to Eastern or foreign markets. The owners of bonanza farms could afford the latest and best technologies to help maximize their yields.

The growing prevalence of bonanza farms by the 1870s reflected larger changes in the American economy. They were the agricultural equivalent of the big businesses that were beginning to dominate American industry. Bonanza farms operated more efficiently than smaller farms and helped account for a significant rise in agricultural production. Because of these larger farms, the number of farmers fell, even as agricultural output rose. Between 1860 and 1900, the percentage of Americans working on farms fell from 60 percent to 37 percent.

The productivity of American agriculture led to problems for farmers, both big and small. An oversupply of grain at different points in the 1880s and 1890s led to sharp drops in price. Most farmers responded to this decrease in their income by increasing their crop production, which just exacerbated the problem. Many farmers fell into debt. Those who could not pay their mortgages had their farms foreclosed by banks. Distressed farmers looked for explanations of their difficulties and began to organize politically.

Women and Minorities on the Agricultural Frontier

Most farms on the Great Plains were worked by families. While the men labored in the fields, diaries and letters left by western women show that they were often beset by loneliness in a world where neighbors might be miles away. O. E. Rolvaag's novel *Giants in the Earth* (1927) describes how the bitter struggle for existence on the prairie drives the wife of an immigrant settler to insanity and death. Willa Cather's *O Pioneers!* (1913) provides a more positive picture of farming life in Nebraska. Though the immigrant protagonists of the novel suffer many hardships as they build up their farms, they eventually prosper and partake of the American dream. A female character holds the family together and guides them to their material success.

Perhaps because of the important role played by women on the farm, it was in the West that they first began to receive the right to vote. In 1887, two towns in Kansas allowed women to vote in local elections, and one elected a woman mayor. Wyoming led the way in giving women the right to vote in statewide elections.

Following the Civil War, many African Americans moved west to escape the oppressive life that they faced in the South. Few of these African American emigrants were able to start profitable farms; they often lacked financial reserves and still encountered racial discrimination. Some African Americans did become successful western farmers. The most famous group of African Americans to leave the South for the West were the **Exodusters**. These people modeled their journey on the exodus of the Israelites from Egypt to the Promised Land. Unfortunately the West did not prove to be a land of milk and honey for most of the Exodusters; fewer than 20 percent were able to establish themselves as farmers.

The Mining and Lumbering Frontier

Farmers were not the only people traveling west. People hoping to strike it rich flocked to the many places where gold and silver were reputed to have been discovered. Miners sought gold at Pike's Peak, Nevada, or the Black Hills of the Dakota Territory, and silver at Comstock, Nevada. A heterogeneous group of people, including Chinese laborers who had abandoned their jobs working on the railroads, crowded into mining towns that boomed for a time and often went bust. These towns had a deserved reputation for extravagance and lawlessness. Most prospectors never found anything of value. Those who did rarely had the means to fully exploit and profit from what they found. Eventually mining came to be dominated by large Eastern-based mining corporations like the **Anaconda Copper Company**. Like Anaconda, these firms discovered that they could profit just as much by mining copper and tin for industrial purposes as digging up precious metals.

Lumber companies moved into the Northwest in the 1870s. These companies reaped great rewards from the 1878 **Timber and Stone Act**, which allowed them to purchase government land that was unsuitable for farming at bargain rates. Lumber companies also hired front men to buy up woodlands inexpensively and then transfer the land titles to them. Fortunes were made providing lumber to a nation that was building at a frantic pace.

The Ranching Frontier

Western settlers inherited a cattle-ranching culture from the Mexicans. Following the Civil War, Texas ranchers had plenty of cattle, but no easy way of getting them to Eastern markets. In 1866, some Texas ranchers drove their herds of cattle overland to the nearest railroad in Kansas. This began the era of the "long drive" celebrated in countless westerns, as bands of cowboys, up to a third of whom may have been Mexican or African American, braved bandits, hostile Native Americans, stampedes, and bad weather, and moved vast numbers of cattle across the Plains to an ever-growing number of rail depots. The cattle were then shipped by rail to Chicago or other cities where they were slaughtered and processed. The beef could then be sent on for marketing in cities further east because of newly invented refrigerated rail cars.

Cattlemen grazed their animals on the "open range," unsettled public lands. As homesteaders moved into these lands, conflicts arose between farmers and ranchers. Farmers were planting crops on land where ranchers wanted to drive their cattle. Joseph Glidden's invention of barbed wire in 1873 enabled farmers to protect their land. The weather dealt another blow to traditional "open range" ranching. The exceptionally severe winters of 1885 to 1887 killed up to 85 percent of the cattle grazing on the Plains. The ranchers who survived this disaster turned to new methods, enclosing their land and utilizing scientific techniques of improving their stock.

The End of Native American Independence

The Native American tribes that lived west of the Mississippi River were overwhelmed in a very short period of time. Within two decades of the end of the Civil War the Plains tribes had lost their independence.

The completion of the transcontinental railroad in 1869 helped facilitate a massive wave of western settlement. Native American tribes could not pursue their traditional way of life as farmers, miners, and ranchers encroached on their lands. Whether tribes cooperated with the settlers or attacked them, the results were the same; they lost most of their lands and were relegated to reservations and government supervision. The federal government did not aim for the extermination of the Plains tribes, but it did not intend to allow them to stand in the way of settlement and economic development. The government hoped that a combination of missionaries and schools would "civilize" the Native Americans and integrate them into American society.

The tribe that most famously fought back against the tide of settlers was the **Sioux**. In 1865, the government declared that it was going to build a road through Sioux lands. This started a war that the Sioux waged very effectively. In one engagement in 1866, they killed 88 soldiers who fell into an ambush. The government began negotiations. In 1868, the Sioux accepted a reservation in the Black Hills of South Dakota. Unfortunately for them, gold was discovered in the Black Hills and miners poured into their lands. This led to a resumption of war. Chiefs including Sitting Bull and Crazy Horse led the Sioux off the reservation. The government dispatched columns of federal troops to round up the Sioux and their Cheyenne allies. One of these columns, a force of the Seventh Cavalry led by General George Custer, found the main Sioux encampment in June 1876. Not realizing how many Sioux warriors had gathered there, Custer attacked without waiting for reinforcements. He and more than 200 of his men were killed at the **Battle of the Little Bighorn**. This unusually decisive victory did not change the outcome of the war. More soldiers arrived, forcing the Sioux back onto their reservation. Other tribes such as the **Nez Perce** attempted to escape their reservations, but invariably were defeated and compelled to return.

Even had the Native Americans won more battlefield victories, they would have been forced to rely on government support because of the disappearance of the buffalo. The Plains tribes depended on the buffalo for food and much else; their lives were organized around the pursuit of buffalo herds. With government approval and support, settlers hunted the buffalo to near extinction. In doing so, they destroyed the foundation of Native American life on the Great Plains.

By the late 1880s, most Native Americans in the West lived on reservations, subsisting on rations provided by the government. Eastern humanitarians, hoping to improve the lot of these people and help them become self-sufficient, provided the impetus behind the passage of the 1887 **Dawes Act**. This legislation assumed that Native Americans would be better off if they emulated their white neighbors and became farmers. The Dawes Act broke up the reservations and divided the land among the individual members of the tribes. Ironically, this well-intentioned bill hurt the Native Americans. Few Native Americans became thriving farmers. Many sold their farms to settlers or land speculators. Much Native American land was permanently lost as a result.

The despair of the Plains Indians was reflected in a religious movement that emerged in 1890. Participants believed that **Ghost Dances** would lead to the disappearance of white settlers, the return of the buffalo, and the resurrection of dead warriors. The military authorities grew alarmed when Sitting Bull sponsored the Ghost Dance religion among the Sioux. Sitting Bull was killed when Indian Police attempted to arrest him. A band of Ghost Dancers fled the reservation. They were surrounded by troops of the Seventh Cavalry. As soldiers disarmed the Sioux camp, someone fired a shot. The troops unleashed a barrage of fire that killed over 200 men, women, and children in what came to be known as the **Massacre at Wounded Knee**.

On April 22, 1889, the "Indian territory" of Oklahoma was opened to settlement. A great land rush took place as "boomers" raced to place their stakes on unclaimed land. People who had entered Oklahoma a day early to grab land were called "sooners." The opening of Oklahoma was the last act in a process that saw settlers displace the Native Americans on the Great Plains.

Agrarian Anger and Populism

By the 1880s many Western farmers faced severe economic problems. Many Southern farmers were in a similar situation. These farmers blamed government policies for their troubles. Since the Civil War, the federal government had imposed high tariffs on imported goods to protect American industries. The farmers believed that these high tariffs hurt their ability to export their products abroad. Farmers were also angered by government fiscal policy and the state of the currency.

The Gold Standard

After the Civil War, the federal government took the wartime "greenbacks" out of circulation and pursued a **"tight money"** policy. The men driving government economic policy believed in a solid and stable currency, which they believed was best for business. They put the United States on the **gold standard**, where every dollar in circulation could in theory be exchanged for an equivalent value in gold held in reserve by the government. This restricted the amount of money available in the country and prevented inflation. In fact, as the country grew, the currency saw some deflation, as its limited supply made it more relatively valuable. Distressed farmers saw their debts grow more expensive because of deflation at the same time that the prices for their crops declined. They called for various measures to increase the money supply and drive up the price of their produce. Fiscally conservative presidents did little to expand the amount of currency.

The Grange and Farmers' Alliances

Western farmers founded the **Grange** in 1867. By 1875, over 800,000 farmers had joined the organization. Grangers formed farmer cooperatives to enable members to enjoy economies of scale by buying and marketing products. Members of the Grange also organized politically and sponsored state legislation to regulate railroads and grain elevators. In 1878, many of these farmers supported the **Greenback party**, which called for the printing of paper money to inflate the currency. The Greenback party elected some congressmen and local officials, but was unable to change American fiscal policy.

The Grange usually organized farmers on the local level. The **Farmers' Alliances** linked farmer associations on a statewide and regional level. In 1889, the Southern Alliance represented a million members. An African American association, the Colored Farmers National Alliance also had a million members. Two million farmers joined Farmers' Alliances in the Plains states. The Farmers' Alliances demanded federal regulation of the railroads, currency reform, easily accessible farm credits, and agriculture departments in every state. Another proposal called for federal warehouses where farmers could store grain for credit when prices were too low. In 1890, this program was summarized in the **Ocala Platform**, which was issued at an Alliance Convention held in Ocala, Florida.

By 1890, leaders of the Farmers' Alliances were exploring ways to exert their political power on the national level. In the South, the Alliance had helped elect four governors and forty-seven congressmen. In the West the Farmers' Alliances were flexing their political muscles as well. Women played an important role in the Farmers' Alliances. Mary Lease became a popular speaker, telling farmers to "raise less corn and more hell."

The federal government did respond to the unrest amongst farmers. The **Interstate Commerce Act** of 1887 created the Interstate Commerce Commission to regulate railroads, though initially, this did not prove effective. The **Sherman Antitrust Act** of 1890 outlawed any business that exercised a "restraint of trade." As with the Interstate Commerce Act, it would take some time for this legislation to produce results.

The Populist Revolt

On July 4, 1892, a convention of Farmers' Alliances launched the People's Party. Supporters of the party became known as Populists. Its founders hoped that the **Populist Party** would unite all working people across the country. Breaking from a century of tradition, Populists argued that because of the powerful forces transforming the economy, the federal government had to play a more active role in American life. The Populist platform called for increasing the amount of currency, a progressive income tax aimed at the wealthy, the direct election of senators, government ownership of railroads, as well as the telegraph and telephone systems, the eight-hour day for workers, and restrictions on immigration. James Weaver, who had served as a Union general during the Civil War and long been involved in the currency issue, was nominated for president.

The Populists received a million popular and 22 electoral votes in the 1892 election. Most of these came from the West. The Populists could not make headway in the Northeast, and the Democrats still dominated the South.

Populism and the Election of 1896

The Populists remained a political force after 1892. They opposed President Grover Cleveland because he was a strong defender of the gold standard. The great depression that began in 1893 spread deep hardship across the country. The Populists responded by continuing their criticism of government fiscal policy and the influence of Eastern business interests.

In 1896, the Republicans nominated William McKinley, who aligned himself with the industrial economy, calling for the gold standard, a high tariff, and a "full dinner pail" for industrial workers. The Democratic candidate was William Jennings Bryan, who won the nomination after giving an eloquent speech at the convention when he declared, "You shall not crucify mankind upon a cross of gold!" Bryan's fervent support for coining more silver to expand the currency won him the Populist nomination as well. In a bellwether election, Bryan won the South and West but lost to McKinley, who carried the Northeast and Midwest. The new urban and industrial order had triumphed over the agrarian vision of Bryan and the Populists.

Prosperity returned in the late 1890s. The economic problems of the farmers eased. It became clear that American society was changing as the great cities grew in population. The Populist party faded away, but most planks of their 1892 platform were eventually enacted into law.

The Idea of the West

The settlement of the trans-Mississippi West coincided with the growth of the modern mass media. Inexpensive and popular dime novels made millions familiar with western figures such as trappers, miners, and cowboys. One of the most prolific dime novel authors was Edward L. Wheeler. In works such as *Deadwood Dick: The Prince of the Road*, Wheeler romanticized a Wild West of gamblers and gunmen. Traveling Wild West shows started touring the country in 1883. Buffalo Bill Cody, a former buffalo hunter and Army scout, became world famous as the impresario of a show that featured cowboys doing rodeo tricks, staged battles between Native Americans and cavalry, and trick shooting by stars like Annie Oakley. Cody even persuaded Sitting Bull to tour with his show for a season. The West that Cody and others dramatized would be immortalized in the movies and on TV.

Another influential interpretation of the West would be provided by the historian Frederick Jackson Turner. In an 1893 paper he asserted that the American national character was shaped by the move west. He argued that American democracy and self-reliance were products of the frontier experience. The **Turner Thesis** proved to be enormously influential. It also raised serious questions for Turner's contemporaries. The 1890 census had recently declared the frontier closed. How, wondered some, could Americans maintain their democratic traditions in an increasingly urban and industrial nation?

Neither Cody nor Turner fully captured the full range of the Western experience. They both left out important perspectives and voices as they strove to explain the West. Yet they were correct in highlighting the historical importance of what was passing away.

Chapter Review

Rapid Review

To achieve the perfect 5, you should be able to explain the following:

- The Homestead Act and the Morrill Land-Grant Act encouraged thousands to go westward to acquire land for farming.
- Farming on the Great Plains proved to be very difficult and was oftentimes accomplished by help from one's neighbor; many farmers were not successful on the Great Plains.
- Bonanza farms were part of a transformation of agriculture that began in the late 1860s.
- Western states were the first states where women received the vote.
- Mining and lumbering also attracted many settlers to the West.
- Native American tribes were gradually forced off their lands because of American expansion to the West; some resistance to this by Native Americans did take place, such as at the Battle of the Little Bighorn and through the Ghost Dances.
- The 1887 Dawes Act did much to break up the remaining Native American tribal lands.
- American farmers organized beginning in the late 1860s through the Grange, through the Farmers' Alliances, and eventually through the Populist party.
- Dime-store novels of the era and the Turner Thesis presented contrasting views of western settlement and its overall impact on American society.

Time Line

1848: California Gold Rush
1859: Silver discovered in Comstock, Nevada
1862: Homestead Act, Morrill Land-Grant Act
       Department of Agriculture created by Congress
1867: Founding of the Grange
1869: Transcontinental Railroad completed
1870s: Popularity of *Deadwood Dick* stories by Edward L. Wheeler and other dime-store
       novels on the West
1874: Barbed wire invented by Joseph Glidden
1876: Battle of the Little Bighorn
1879: Exoduster movement leaves the South for the Great Plains
1880s: Large movement of immigrants westward
1883: "Buffalo Bill's Wild West Show" begins
1886: Beginnings of harsh weather that would help destroy the cattle industry
1887: Dawes Act
1889: Native American territories open for white settlement
1890: Massacre at Wounded Knee
       Wyoming women get the vote
       High point of political influence of the Farmers' Alliances
1893: Beginning of great depression of the 1890s
       Publication of the Turner Thesis
1896: William Jennings Bryan's "Cross of Gold" speech

❯ Review Questions

Fact Check

Check your knowledge of the historical period covered in this chapter.

1. Those farmers who were successful on the Great Plains
   A. came to the West as single men, without families.
   B. utilized many farming techniques they had learned in the East.
   C. personified the spirit of rugged individualism.
   D. relied on the assistance of other settlers around them.

2. Exodusters were
   A. newly arrived miners in Oregon.
   B. Southern blacks who went west to settle.
   C. those who "dusted" or cleaned crops on bonanza farms.
   D. immigrants who went west to farm.

3. The Dawes Act
   A. tried to turn Native Americans into farmers who would farm their own individual plots only.
   B. protected Native American land from further encroachment.
   C. broke up large Native American reservations into smaller ones.
   D. made Ghost Dances illegal.

4. The organization that expressed the views of farmers to the largest national audience was the
   A. Greenback party.
   B. Populist party.
   C. Grange.
   D. Farmers' Alliances.

5. The Turner Thesis
   A. agreed with accounts of the West in the dime-store novels of the 1870s concerning the character of western expansion.
   B. took into account the massacre of Native Americans.
   C. noted the impact of western expansion on the American character.
   D. emphasized the "hard living" that went on in many western settlements.

Multiple-Choice Questions

Here are multiple-choice questions like the ones on the AP U.S. History exam.

Questions 6–8 refer to the illustration below.

The Union Pacific and Central Pacific Railroads meet at Promontory Point, Utah, May 10, 1869

[from http://upload.wikimedia.org/wikipedia/commons/e/e4/1869-Golden_Spike.jpg]

6. The federal government encouraged the building of a transcontinental railroad with generous land grants because
   A. it wanted to encourage western settlement.
   B. it needed to transfer troops East and West during the Civil War.
   C. powerful senators wanted to help their supporters in the steel industry.
   D. politicians hoped the construction project would relieve unemployment.

7. Which of the following best describes what happened in the West in the 25 years following the conclusion of the Civil War?
   A. The West remained a largely unexplored wilderness.
   B. The frontier rapidly disappeared.
   C. The United States conquered new territories from the Mexicans and the British.
   D. The West became a major center of manufacturing.

8. Farmers valued access to railroads, but they often also feared them because
   A. railroads could be run through their lands according to the principle of eminent domain.
   B. railroads favored the interests of cattle ranchers.
   C. railroads brought waves of immigrants to their lands.
   D. railroads controlled their profits through the rates they charged for transporting their crops.

Short-Answer Question

The short-answer question below is similar to the ones you'll encounter on the AP U.S. History exam.

9. Answer Parts A, B, and C.
   A. Briefly explain ONE example of a way that American settlement rapidly transformed the West in the 25 years following the Civil War.
   B. Briefly explain a SECOND example of a way that American settlement rapidly transformed the West in the 25 years following the Civil War.
   C. Briefly explain ONE example of a way that Native Americans attempted to resist American settlement in the West in the 25 years following the Civil War.

> Answers and Explanations

1. D. Almost every diary from individuals who lived on the Plains noted that rugged individualism was not enough to be successful.

2. B. This group went west to farm in 1879 and modeled their journey after the journey of the Israelites fleeing Egypt to the Promised Land.

3. A. The Dawes Act tried to "civilize" Native Americans and destroy their tribal lands.

4. B. The Populist party platform was intended to appeal to all workers in society, including those in the city. The policies of the Populist party were heard nationwide in the 1892 presidential election; however, because of the power of the Democratic Party in the South, the Populist presidential candidate received only 1 million votes in the election.

5. C. Turner himself would later revise his thesis based on some of the characteristics of western expansion noted in the other possible answers.

6. A. The federal government encouraged the building of a transcontinental railroad with generous land grants because it wanted to encourage western settlement. Congress passed the Pacific Railroad Act in 1862. The Central Pacific Railroad starting from San Francisco, California, and the Union Pacific Railroad starting from Omaha, Nebraska, finally met at Promontory Point, Utah, in May 1869.

7. B. In the 25 years following the conclusion of the Civil War, the frontier largely disappeared. Native American tribes were rapidly displaced; cattlemen, farmers, miners, and others developed and exploited the resources of the West. Following the 1890 Census, a census official noted that the United States no longer possessed a traditional frontier line.

8. D. Farmers valued access to railroads, but they often feared them because railroads controlled their profits through the rates they charged for transporting their crops. Farmers believed that they faced discriminatory pricing from railroads that offered cheaper rates to larger businesses shipping goods over longer distances. The agrarian Grange and Farmers' Alliances movements, and later the Populist Party, called for government regulation of the railroads.

9. Parts A and B: The federal government provided support for western settlement by encouraging the building of a transcontinental railroad. The Union Pacific and Central Pacific Railroads finally met at Promontory Summit, Utah, on May 10, 1869. The rapid expansion of railroads in the west facilitated settlement. The federal government encouraged farmers to move west with the 1862 Homestead Act, which gave 160 acres to farm families that worked this land for five years. In addition to many family farms, large bonanza farms expanded through the west. Bonanza farms were an early form of agribusiness and grew only a few staple crops for the market. The lumber industry benefitted from the 1878 Timber and Stone Act, which offered land unsuitable for agriculture in the Northwest to "settlers." Miners followed strikes of gold at places like Pike's Peak Nevada and the Black Hills in the Dakota Territory, and silver at Comstock, Nevada. Individual prospectors were replaced by large corporations. The Anaconda Copper Company became powerful mining minerals other than gold and silver. In the postwar years ranching became a big business in the west, raising cattle to feed people in the Eastern cities. Beginning with a cattle drive from Texas to Sedalia, Kansas, in 1866, cowboys drove herds across the open range to towns with railroads that enabled the cattle to be shipped east. The era of the great cattle drives ended in the middle 1880s, as ranchers turned to new ways of raising and marketing their herds.

Part C: Many Native Americans attempted to resist American settlement by waging war against the newcomers. The Battle of the Little Bighorn was a notable victory won by the Sioux against a force of U.S. Cavalry commanded by General George A. Custer on June 25 to 26, 1876. Ultimately the Native Americans could not prevail militarily against the U.S. government, and they were forced onto reservations. Some Native Americans hoped for a miracle to restore their old way of life. In 1889, a Paiute prophet named Wovoka began preaching that if the Native Americans danced Ghost Dances they could bring back their dead ancestors, and the great herds of buffalo; the white men would also disappear from the West. The Ghost Dance phenomenon disturbed federal authorities. An attempt by U.S. Cavalry to round up Sioux Ghost Dancers leaving their reservation led to the tragic Wounded Knee Massacre on December 29, 1890.

CHAPTER 18

America Transformed into the Industrial Giant of the World (1870–1910)

IN THIS CHAPTER

Summary: During this era, there was massive industrial growth in the United States, making America the major industrial producer of the world. This growth was largely a product of the expansion of heavy industry; steel was an important component of this industrial growth. The development of the assembly line and Taylorism, which encouraged efficiency in the workplace, created a factory setting where skilled workmanship was de-emphasized. Horizontal and vertical integration allowed major American businesses such as Standard Oil and United States Steel to expand greatly. American workers began to unionize in this era through labor organizations such as the Knights of Labor, the American Federation of Labor, and the Industrial Workers of the World. "New" immigrants from eastern and southern Europe took unskilled jobs in many of the expanding factories but were not wanted by some labor organizations. The American city was also greatly transformed in this era. Political machines dominated many city governments, although efforts took place at the federal level to create a professional civil service system.

Keywords

Taylorism: following management practices of the industrial engineer Frederick Winslow Taylor, the belief that factories should be managed in a scientific manner, utilizing techniques that would increase the efficiency of the individual workers and the factory process as a whole.

Horizontal integration: strategy of gaining as much control over a single industry as possible, often by creating trusts and holding companies; this strategy was utilized by John D. Rockefeller and Standard Oil.

Vertical integration: strategy of gaining as much control over a single industry as possible by controlling the production, marketing, and distribution of the finished product. Andrew Carnegie and United States Steel are the best examples from the era of this approach.

"Gospel of Wealth": philosophy of Andrew Carnegie who believed that wealthy industrialists had an obligation to help local communities and philanthropic organizations.

Knights of Labor: established in the 1880s, this was the major union of that decade. It was made up of unions of many industries and accepted unskilled workers.

American Federation of Labor: national labor union formed by Samuel Gompers in 1886; original goal was to organize skilled workers by craft.

Industrial Workers of the World: more radical than the American Federation of Labor, this union was formed in 1905 and attempted to unionize unskilled workers not recruited by the AFL. Members of this union were called "Wobblies."

Gilded Age: depiction of late nineteenth-century America that emphasizes a surface of great prosperity hiding problems of social inequality and cultural shallowness.

Pendleton Civil Service Act (1883): federal act that established a civil service system at the federal level. For the first time, not all government jobs would be political appointments.

Tammany Hall: political machine that ran New York City Democratic and city politics became a model for other urban political machines in the late 1800s.

An Industrial Revolution

By the early 1890s the United States had supplanted Great Britain as the leading industrial nation in the world. American industrial growth after the Civil War was spectacular. In 1860, almost one out of four Americans worked in industry; by 1900, it was one out of two. The size of the factories in which these workers were employed changed dramatically; by the turn of the century some industrial plants were huge, with thousands of laborers. This rapid industrialization had profound effects on people's ordinary lives. Large numbers of Americans left their farms for the cities. They left behind rural rhythms of life and had to grow accustomed to time clocks and whistles indicating changing shifts. Instead of being able to wander from place to place and task to task, they had to stay put in a work station, engaged in the same repetitive motions for hours.

These Americans were part of the **Second Industrial Revolution**, which saw the emergence of new industries such as steel and chemicals, new sources of power such as electricity and petroleum, and new forms of business organization such as the trusts. Something that facilitated the early growth of American industry was a lack of involvement by the government. In the late nineteenth century, most American leaders believed in laissez-faire economics and left American business development to the "invisible hand" of the market.

Changes in American Industry

American industrial expansion was driven by the growth of **heavy industry**. Before the Civil War, American factories turned out consumer goods such as food products and textiles. These industries continued to be important, but in the postwar years industries emerged that produced goods for other industries, such as steel, petroleum products, and machinery. The steel industry thrived by supplying railroads, builders, and other industries. The oil industry provided fuel to factories as well as homes. High-grade machine products enabled businessmen to launch new industries.

In 1860, most American factories relied on water power. The opening of anthracite coal mines in Pennsylvania and West Virginia led to a drop in coal prices that made possible a speedy transition to steam power.

Industrial development occurred outside the Northeast and Midwest. Apostles of the **New South** promoted industrialization in their predominantly agrarian region. Steel production flourished around Birmingham, Alabama. Textile mills with modernized machinery took advantage of the proximity to raw materials and the availability of cheap labor in the South. The American Tobacco Company produced machine-made cigarettes, launching a new industry in the land of Dixie.

A Changing Workplace

As business became bigger in America, industrialists looked for ways to compete more efficiently and maximize profits. Consultants known as efficiency experts advised factory owners on the best ways to produce their goods. The most famous of these was Frederick W. Taylor, a mechanical engineer who pioneered a discipline that he called "scientific management." He timed the movements of workers and machines, and redesigned work spaces to eliminate unnecessary and time-consuming motions. He had no use for traditional ways of working that got in the way of speedy and efficient production. **Taylorism** could be hard on workers. Some jobs were lost as tasks were combined for efficiency. Taylor advocated paying workers "by the piece" so they would be incentivized to produce more.

One expression of the drive for efficiency was the development of the assembly line. The assembly line embodied the combination of new business organization and the application of new technologies that made the United States the world's industrial leader. Henry Ford founded the Ford Motor Company in 1903. In 1910, using a more traditional "craft" approach to manufacturing automobiles, his company turned out 12,000 vehicles. Ford introduced the assembly line to his factories in 1913; that year his company produced 250,000 cars. New manufacturing methods led to similar bursts of productivity in other industries.

The role of workers changed in this period. Most no longer needed to be skilled craftsmen. Instead, as critics of the new industrial order put it, they became "one more cog in the machine." Workers in Henry Ford's assembly line might spend their entire day repeating the same task, such as attaching a door or a lamp. Ford compensated his workers for the monotony of their labor by paying them the groundbreaking wage of $5 a day. Few other assembly line workers did so well at that time.

Since most factory jobs came to involve the repetition of simple motions, they could be easily learned by unskilled workers. Immigrants became a major source of industrial labor in the late nineteenth century. In some industries such as textiles, women continued to make up a large part of the workforce. Many children were employed in factories, especially in shoe manufacturing and in textile mills. In 1900, 20 percent of children aged 10 to 15 worked. Some states attempted to regulate child labor, but with limited results.

Employers saw no reason to pay men and women the same wages. Men were paid more because they were often regarded as the heads of households, and they were believed to be stronger and able to work harder. Unskilled male workers might make $8 a week, compared to $5 a week for skilled female workers. Despite these inequities, many working class women regarded factory work as preferable to the even lower pay of maids and household servants. Some women with educational attainments found work in offices. Others worked as shop clerks. The difficulty of supporting themselves on low wages drove many women into prostitution.

The cultural expectation of the time was that women would leave their jobs once they married; they and their children would be supported by the husband. This was more an ideal than a reality for poor women. Some married women continued to work outside the home, or they supplemented their family incomes by sewing or laundering for others.

Big Business

The period after the Civil War saw a period of intense creativity in business organization as new industries emerged and all industries grew larger. A dynamic generation of business tycoons built huge companies that required new corporate structures to be effectively managed. Some of these entrepreneurs became enormously wealthy and world famous. Andrew Carnegie embodied the classic American success story; arriving in the United States as a penniless eight-year old, he made his fortune manufacturing steel and retired one of the richest men in the world. John D. Rockefeller founded Standard Oil and at one time had a near monopoly of the American oil business.

Some of these industrialists could be quite ruthless in their pursuit of wealth. They saw themselves operating in a business climate where only the strong survived. Sometimes companies attempted to reduce this competition by agreeing to fix prices and production quotas. This collusion amongst businesses could hurt consumers and was outlawed by the **Interstate Commerce Act** of 1887. This act was primarily intended to regulate the railroads, but proved ineffective for many years because the Interstate Commerce Commission that it established was staffed by men sympathetic to business interests.

As businesses grew larger in the postwar years, they faced legal complications because state laws made it difficult to run interstate businesses or for corporations to own other corporations. An early legal response to this was the formations of **trusts**. This form of corporate organization was pioneered by John D. Rockefeller and Standard Oil. The creation of a trust allowed the stockholders of a subsidiary company to place control of their shares of that company "in trust" to the corporate board of Standard Oil. This organizational technique made it possible for Rockefeller to expand Standard Oil through **horizontal integration** by purchasing control of many smaller oil companies.

Trusts were eventually declared illegal. This led to the emergence of **holding companies**. In 1889, New Jersey became the first state to allow businesses incorporated there to own the stock of other corporations. This allowed the shareholders of Standard Oil to buy up the stock, and thus control of other oil companies. Rockefeller and his management team used the holding company model to merge 43 oil companies into Standard Oil of New Jersey. By the 1890s, Rockefeller produced 90 percent of the oil used in the United States. Rockefeller next aimed at **vertical integration** by buying up oil fields and moving from the refining and distribution of oil products into marketing them. He would then be able to control every phase of the oil business, from drilling for crude oil to selling refined oil products in stores and gas stations. Other practitioners of vertical integration were Gustavus Swift in meat-packing and Andrew Carnegie in steel.

The gap between rich and poor grew dramatically as great industrialists accumulated vast fortunes. The wealth of these businessmen was justified by the popular and influential ideology of **Social Darwinism**. Proponents of Social Darwinism, such as the philosopher William Graham Sumner, believed that human interactions reflected Charles Darwin's evolutionary principle of "natural selection." Those better suited to succeed because of intelligence, determination, and strength would thrive, while those less fit would fall behind. By this logic, the money and power accumulated by the rich was the just reward of their superiority and a manifestation of the working out of nature's plan. Andrew Carnegie softened some of the harder edges of Social Darwinism with his **"Gospel of Wealth."** He wrote that the great industrialists were the "guardians" of American wealth. He believed that the industrialists should not pass on all their fortunes to their children but should devote much of it to improving the community. One manifestation of this on Carnegie's part was his enthusiasm for building libraries across the country so that able young people could improve themselves and rise in the world. Both Carnegie and Rockefeller created foundations that over the years have dispensed over $650 million to educational and artistic causes. Carnegie and Rockefeller were not alone. Many industrialists endowed universities and museums. Despite this record of charitable giving, many of the industrialists of this period have been criticized as "Robber Barons" because of their Social Darwinist attitude toward their workers.

The Emergence of Labor Unions

Craft unions existed before the Civil War. Because of the relatively small size of businesses, they did not have a major impact on society. As industry grew, so did the unions. Strife between workers and industrialists became a major issue in the postwar years. In July 1877, railroad workers launched the first nationwide strike. Because of hard economic times the railroads were cutting back at their workers' expense, and the strikers were protesting layoffs and reduced wages. Violence marred the strike. Railroad property was destroyed in various parts of the country. In Pittsburgh, Pennsylvania, 30 strikers were killed in clashes with militiamen. President Hayes eventually deployed federal troops to stop the violence and break the strike. Though he sided with the owners, the president did call on them to "remove the distress which afflicts laborers."

The most influential union to arise in the 1870s was the **Knights of Labor**. Instead of being a craft union that protected the interests of one type of worker, such as shoemakers, the Knights of Labor attempted to represent all workers, skilled and unskilled. They encouraged immigrants, African Americans, and women to join their union. At its height in the mid-1880s, the Knights of Labor had 750,000 members. The leaders of the Knights of Labor dreamed of a more cooperative society in which working people would more fully share in the fruits of their labor. Their peaceableness made them reluctant to call strikes; this, in turn, made them less effective in dealing with hard-nosed employers. The Knights of Labor faded away as more confrontational labor unions captured the loyalties of workers.

The Knights of Labor were also blamed for radical actions over which they had no control. In the spring of 1886, workers went on strike at the McCormick reaper plant in Chicago. On May 1, 100,000 people gathered at a rally to show their solidarity with the workers. The next day, a smaller demonstration was scheduled at **Haymarket Square.**

A few of the people supporting the strike were radicals and anarchists influenced by violent social strife in Europe. When police arrived to break up the demonstration, someone set off a bomb. Seven policemen were killed. In the chaotic aftermath of the explosion, a gun battle erupted that left four civilians dead. Scores of police and citizens were injured by the bomb and bullets. Eight anarchists were arrested and convicted of the bombing. The Haymarket Square tragedy convinced many Americans that labor organizations like the Knights of Labor were breeding grounds for violent extremism. It fed antipathy toward immigrants and radical political beliefs.

The **American Federation of Labor (AFL)** proved more successful than the Knights of Labor. The AFL was an association of craft unions composed of skilled workers. For many years, the AFL was headed by Samuel Gompers, a tough and wily leader who carefully dissociated his unions from political or social radicalism. Instead, Gompers emphasized "bread and butter issues," and focused on achieving higher wages and shorter hours rather than remaking American society. The AFL was prepared to use strikes to attain its goals. A strike against the Carnegie Steel Company at Homestead, Pennsylvania, in 1892, and the American Railway Union's strike against the Pullman Palace Car Company in 1894 received national attention. The leader of the American Railway Union was Eugene V. Debs. The suppression of the Pullman strike convinced him to embrace socialism. Debs would run for president several times as head of the Socialist Party. Despite the failure of some strikes, the AFL grew more powerful and influential; by 1917, the AFL claimed 2.5 million members.

A very different labor organization was the **Industrial Workers of the World (IWW)**. This union originated amongst industrial miners in the West, who faced very difficult working conditions. The IWW embraced a radical social vision; it called for revolutionary violence and the imposition of socialism. Members of the IWW were nicknamed "Wobblies." The leader of the IWW was Big Bill Haywood of the Western Federation of Miners. "Mother" Jones worked with coal miners. The IWW did not shy away from strikes and bloodshed. Because of its extremist reputation, the union was brutally quashed by the federal government during World War I.

Unions helped some workers raise their wages and improve their working conditions. Many workers were unable to effectively organize themselves. The most successful labor organization, the AFL, focused only on skilled workers. The AFL resisted organizing women, African Americans, and other unskilled workers, believing that the presence of these groups in the workforce undercut the bargaining power of its members. Some women formed their own unions. In 1909, the International Ladies Garment Workers Union launched a notable strike in New York City.

Organized labor faced other challenges. Most industrialists discouraged their workers from joining unions. Many people associated unionism with radicalism, while others thought that unions weakened American individualism and self-reliance. The government generally supported business owners during strikes and occasionally used the military to break up strikes. Businessmen could also usually rely on the support of state and local governments and their police forces. Factory owners could also hire Pinkerton detectives to guard their plants and intimidate strikers.

Uneven Affluence

Many Americans prospered in the new industrial economy. They were able to take part in the emergence of a **consumer society** in which ordinary Americans were able to buy goods such as tea and silk stockings that had earlier been luxury items for the rich.

This period saw the rise of a large and growing middle class. This included members of the traditional professions, such as doctors, lawyers, educators, and the clergy, now enjoying heightened prestige because of more rigorous accrediting, as well as a new category of business employee that worked with their heads rather than their hands, shuffling paper rather than manipulating tools. Many men took their places in the expanding ranks of corporate managers, while a horde of men and women filled a rapidly proliferating variety of clerical and sales positions. These so-called white-collar workers were often products of a rapidly enlarging and improving educational system. More and more people graduated from high school, and a small but influential minority of men and women attended college. Middle-class Americans benefitted from modern housing outfitted with indoor plumbing and electricity. They were able to partake of a rich literary culture made possible by a burgeoning mass media. Popular and readily accessible magazines brought stories and articles by writers like Mark Twain, William Dean Howells, Sarah Orne Jewett, and Henry James into their homes. Appreciative audiences supported serious stage productions and an increasing number of symphony orchestras. Less intellectual amusement was provided by wild west shows and Vaudeville reviews in popular theaters that included acts by comedians, musicians, dancers, and acrobats. Sports were increasingly seen as important for a healthy life. Both sexes took up riding the bicycle. New sports like football and basketball attracted players and fans. Baseball was widely recognized as the national pastime, and professional teams and the National League emerged in the 1870s. Middle-class tastes dominated American culture. The proliferation of department stores symbolized the new possibilities for American consumers. Many middle-class Americans could buy what they wanted, not just what they needed. The average life expectancy increased by six years between 1900 and 1920. A growing number of middle-class homes now benefited from indoor plumbing and electricity.

Not all shared in this new affluence. Large numbers of Americans, from rural sharecroppers to immigrants living in overcrowded urban neighborhoods, could not afford to join in the new consumer society. A majority of working-class homes did not get flush toilets until the 1920s and 1930s. Higher wages were counterbalanced by increases in the cost of living that kept many consumer goods priced out of the reach of most workers.

The New Immigration

The late 1880s and early 1890s saw a significant change in the pattern of immigration to the United States. Prior to this period, most immigrants came from Northern Europe, usually from the British Isles and Germany. Assimilation was easier for the Irish and English because they shared a common language with Americans; Germans may have spoken a different language, but they came from a society with many cultural similarities to the United States. This was not the case with the **"new immigrants"** who began pouring into the United States in the late 1880s. These people came from Italy, Eastern Europe, and Russia. They did not speak English. Most were very poor, and looked and sounded very different from the Northern European immigrants Americans had grown used to. Many were Roman Catholic or Jewish, which made them seem even more alien in what was still a largely Protestant America.

This new immigration was alarming to some Americans because of the sheer numbers of arriving immigrants. Between 1870 and 1920, 28 million immigrants entered the United States. The high point of this immigration came between 1900 and 1910. The federal government opened Ellis Island in New York City harbor as a reception center in 1892. Here immigrants had to pass rudimentary health and security testing. Angel Island in San Francisco was opened as a similar reception center for the Pacific Coast.

14,000 Chinese workers were brought to the United States to help complete the construction of the transcontinental railroad. These Asian immigrants faced intense hostility from "native" workers who feared that they would depress wages by working for less. This anti-Chinese sentiment found political expression in the Chinese Exclusion Act of 1882, which restricted the entrance of Chinese laborers into the United States. To protect themselves from racial animosity, many Chinese moved to ethnically homogenous "Chinatowns" in large cities. The annexation of Hawaii in 1898 opened the way for Japanese living there to move to California and work on farms. This Japanese immigration reignited the same sorts of concerns and prejudices that the Chinese had encountered. In 1906, the San Francisco Board of Education segregated Asian students in separate schools. In 1913, the persistently anti-Japanese Californians passed the **Webb Alien Land Law** which prohibited Asians who were noncitizens from owning land in the state. Because Japan was a proud and powerful nation, these initiatives in California caused severe diplomatic trouble for the United States.

Most immigrants at first settled in the big coastal cities. Many of the Eastern and Southern European immigrants were fleeing religious persecution and economic hardship at home. They faced a wrenching process of acculturation in the United States as most of them transitioned from rural to urban life and found work in large factories. Like the Chinese, many sought the comfort of living with their compatriots in ethnic neighborhoods in the cities, where they could speak their language and more easily practice their religion. There they were jammed into teeming tenement houses. At the end of the nineteenth century, the Lower East Side of New York City was the most densely populated place in the world.

Many immigrants planned to work in the United States for a period of years and then return to their homelands. Some did go home, but most remained and played a critical role in American economic expansion. Many of the new immigrants worked in factories on the East Coast and in the Midwest. A number of immigrants joined the movement west and farmed. Some became miners. The one region that did not see a significant influx of immigrants was the South, where its relatively depressed agrarian economy offered newcomers few opportunities.

The Rise of the Modern American City

American cities grew dramatically after the Civil War because of industrialization and immigration. The newcomers to the cities were not all from overseas. Many people were leaving their farms as mechanization encouraged consolidation in agriculture. The booming cities beckoned as sources of economic opportunity. Not everyone in the cities prospered, and the poor found themselves crowded into slums.

Before the Civil War, most American cities were small enough that people could walk to where they wanted to go. As the cities grew, new forms of transportation allowed people to traverse the growing urban landscape. New York City unveiled elevated trains in 1867, and Boston opened a subway in 1897. Many cities installed cable cars and electric trolleys. This public transportation made it possible for upper- and middle-class commuters to live farther away from their workplaces in the city. In the early nineteenth century, the well-to-do built their homes in the center of town; now they began a movement to **suburbia**. City centers became business districts, dominated by banks, department stores, and office buildings. Factories and warehouses were located just outside the central business district. Blocks of inexpensive housing clustered around the factories, so workers could easily get to their jobs. The rich and the poor were increasingly far apart, geographically as well as in their incomes.

Housing was often in short supply for the working class. Older middle-class apartment buildings were divided and subdivided to house more and more poor families. Tenement houses were specially constructed to provide rooms for large numbers of people. They afforded their residents few amenities. Bathrooms were located outdoors. Many rooms had no windows for ventilation, much less a view. There were no elevators. These buildings were dingy and dirty. Because of poor plumbing and inadequate sewers, disease was rampant. Poverty bred crime, and gangs often terrorized neighborhoods. Gradually conditions improved. Building codes helped clean up the worst tenements. Some buildings began to offer running water, gas, and electricity.

The skylines of American cities changed dramatically. Before the Civil War, buildings rarely rose above four of five stories. New construction materials and methods led to an architectural revolution. The production of strong and durable **Bessemer steel** girders allowed builders to construct taller buildings around a steel framework. The introduction of elevators in the early 1880s provided a practical means to move people up and down these taller buildings. Architects like Chicago's Louis Sullivan began designing the first "skyscrapers." The Home Insurance Company building in Chicago, completed in 1885, was an early example of the new style of office building. It was ten stories high and had four elevators conveying passengers up and down.

American cities in the late nineteenth and early twentieth centuries were ongoing construction sites. In addition to office buildings, factories, and apartments, public works such as schools, roads, sewers, and parks were being built or extended. City planners began to seek ways to bring some order to the frantic pace of development.

Gilded Age Politics

Mark Twain popularized the term **"Gilded Age,"** which refers to the period between 1875 and 1900. For Twain, it was an expression that satirized the political corruption and crude money-grubbing that he thought characterized contemporary American society. (Something that is gilded has only a thin layer of gold over a baser metal.) It was an era of striking contrasts, politically and economically, that left many observers bewildered.

Modern commentators often criticize the politics of the Gilded Age as being much ado about nothing much. They find debates over the tariff and the currency superficial, and condemn the politicians of the day for not intervening more actively as the country industrialized and urbanized. What these commentators forget is that nineteenth-century Americans had different ideas about politics and government. They believed that the role of government was strictly limited, and after the crisis of the Civil War and Reconstruction, they wanted to restore what they believed was a more normal political equilibrium. President Grover Cleveland was widely commended for saying that "the lesson should be constantly enforced that though the people support the Government the Government should not support the people."

Politics was a popular avocation for Americans in the Gilded Age. They took a deep interest in political issues and party identification was high. Often nearly 75 percent of registered voters participated in presidential elections, a far higher rate than today.

The Democratic and Republican parties were very evenly balanced. Elections were close and control of Congress regularly passed back and forth. This had a moderating effect on political positions because the parties feared alienating swing voters. The Republicans could usually count on the support of the industrial Northeast, while the Democrats relied on the "Solid South." Most elections hinged on the results in a few swing states like New York, Indiana, and Ohio.

In the postwar period, Congress grew more important as presidents took a more restrained view of their powers. An issue that came to the forefront was the **spoils system**. This practice dated back to the days of Andrew Jackson and held that after an election the victorious party should reward its supporters by giving them government jobs. This often meant turning members of the opposing party out of their government positions and became a major burden for presidents as heads of the office-rich executive branch.

President Rutherford B. Hayes tried to reform this patronage system. He attempted to appoint officials for their qualifications rather than their political connections. He angered his own party's political bosses in Congress by removing some men from office who had benefited from the spoils system, including Chester A. Arthur, the Collector of the Port of New York.

Hayes's actions led to divisions in the Republican Party and ensured that he would not be renominated for the presidency in 1880. The eventual Republican nominee, Congressman James Garfield of Ohio, also called for reform of the spoils system. Garfield won the election, but in July 1881, only a few months after taking office, he was assassinated by a deranged man who believed that he should have been given a government job.

Garfield's assassination convinced Congress that something had to be done about the spoils system. President Chester A. Arthur, ironically a man associated with the spoils system, threw his support behind reform. In 1883, Congress passed the **Pendleton Civil Service Act**, which took a number of government jobs out of political control. It established the **Civil Service Commission**, which administered these positions. Applicants for these jobs had to demonstrate their fitness by passing examinations. The Pendleton Act also prohibited government officials from contributing to political campaigns, a practice that had been routine when officeholders were openly political functionaries. These reforms were the beginning of a **professional bureaucracy** in the legislative and executive branches. Initially only a few jobs were covered by the new civil service regulations, but the number grew over time. Today most jobs are covered by civil service regulations, although there are still many managerial positions in the federal bureaucracy that are filled by political appointees.

The election of 1884 was dominated by the personal issues of the candidates. The Republicans nominated Senator James Blaine of Maine. He was accused of taking gifts of stock in exchange for supporting bills favorable to railroads. The Democrats nominated Grover Cleveland, the governor of New York. As a younger man, Cleveland had accepted responsibility for an illegitimate child. During the election, Republicans chanted, "Ma, Ma, where's my Pa!" Despite this scandal, Cleveland won a close election.

Along with concerns about the currency, tariffs were one of the most prominent political issues of the Gilded Age. Generally Republicans supported high tariffs to protect American industry and jobs. Most Democrats, with their party base in the agrarian South and West, wanted to lower tariffs. Complicating matters were Eastern Democrats and Western Republicans who voted with the economic interests of their region. President Cleveland wanted to lower tariffs and made this the central issue of the 1888 presidential campaign. The results showed how closely divided Americans were politically. Cleveland won the popular vote, but lost in the Electoral College. His Republican opponent Benjamin Harrison became president. Cleveland came back to defeat Harrison in 1892, becoming the only president elected to two nonconsecutive terms.

Soon after Cleveland's second inauguration, the United States fell into one of the worst depressions in its history. Many factories closed their doors and millions of workers lost their jobs. The economic downturn aggravated the problems facing farmers. The Populists took the lead in calling for government relief. A Populist leader in Ohio named

Jacob Coxey led a column of unemployed workers to Washington. President Cleveland and Congress ignored **Coxey's Army**. Pressure intensified to loosen the currency supply by coining more silver. Cleveland, an economic conservative, held to the gold standard.

This currency debate framed the election of 1896. William McKinley's decisive victory ended the period of political parity between the Democrats and Republicans and began an era of Republican electoral dominance. McKinley was an able president, who is seen by some historians as the first "modern" chief executive because of the way that he organized and concentrated authority in his office. McKinley's campaign manager, Mark Hanna, is credited with pioneering the modern presidential campaign.

The governments of many cities were controlled by **political machines**. These were highly structured organizations designed to keep a leader, the "boss," and his associates in political power. Machines often relied on immigrants for their electoral strength; they provided working class citizens jobs, loans, and other favors in exchange for their votes. Once in control of city hall, the machine generated funds by extorting kickbacks from contractors doing city business. Machine operatives who received city jobs often paid back a percentage of their salary to the organization. This cash helped provide the funds that kept the machine well oiled and running smoothly. The most famous political machine was **Tammany Hall** in New York City. In the 1860s and 1870s, the Tammany boss William M. Tweed, and an unscrupulous group of officials embezzled millions of dollars from City Hall. Tweed was mercilessly lampooned by the political cartoonist Thomas Nast and eventually was investigated and jailed for his crimes. Despite Tweed's incarceration, Tammany Hall lived on and dominated New York City politics for decades. Though corrupt, machines did provide rudimentary social relief for the poor. Some machine politicians supported reforms in education and social services.

Social Criticism in the Gilded Age

Beginning with Mark Twain, a number of writers criticized American society during the Gilded Age. Edward Bellamy achieved a surprising literary success with *Looking Backward* (1888), which envisioned a socialist future for the United States. The hero of the book finds himself transported to Boston in 2000 and learns that peaceful economic "nationalism" has replaced the unfettered capitalism of his day. The journalist Jacob Riis published a groundbreaking study of the poor in New York City entitled *How the Other Half Lives* (1890). Riis described the appalling conditions in the tenement houses of the Lower East Side and documented this with evocative photographs that pioneered modern photojournalism. Upton Sinclair created a sensation in 1906 with *The Jungle*, a searing indictment of conditions in Chicago's meatpacking industry. Sinclair hoped to make the case for socialism, but most readers focused on his graphic descriptions of unsanitary practices in the meatpacking plants.

Chapter Review

KEY IDEA

Rapid Review

To achieve the perfect 5, you should be able to explain the following:

- The industrial growth that occurred in the United States during this era made the United States the major industrial producer of the world.

- The industrial growth was largely based on the expansion of heavy industry; the availability of steel was critical to this expansion.
- Taylorism and the assembly line created major changes in the workplace for factory workers.
- Horizontal and vertical integration allowed businesses to expand dramatically during this era; Standard Oil (John D. Rockefeller) and United States Steel (Andrew Carnegie) are the best examples of this type of expansion.
- Andrew Carnegie's "Gospel of Wealth" proclaimed it was the duty of the wealthy to return large amounts of their wealth back to the community.
- American workers began to unionize in this era by joining the Knights of Labor, the American Federation of Labor, and the Industrial Workers of the World. Because of intimidation by company bosses and the publicity that came from several unsuccessful strikes, union membership remained low, even into the twentieth century.
- The impact of the "new immigrants" from eastern and southern Europe on American cities and in the workplace was immense.
- The American city became transformed in this era, with new methods of transportation allowing many from the middle and upper classes to move to suburbia and still work in the city.
- Political life at the state and city levels during this era was dominated by various political machines, although reforms were instituted at the federal level and in some states to create a professional civil service system.

Time Line

1869: Knights of Labor founded in Philadelphia

1870: Beginning of Tammany Hall's control over New York City politics

1877: Major strike of railroad workers; President Hayes sends in federal troops to break up strike in Pittsburgh

1879: Publication of *Progress and Poverty* by Henry George

1881: Assassination of President James Garfield

1882: Chinese Exclusion Act passed by Congress

1883: Pendleton Civil Service Act enacted

1885: Completion of Home Insurance Company building in Chicago, America's first skyscraper

1886: Haymarket Square demonstration and bombing in Chicago

1887: Interstate Commerce Act enacted

1888: New Jersey passes legislation allowing holding companies
Publication of *Looking Backward* by Edward Bellamy

1890: Publication of *How the Other Half Lives* by Jacob Riis

1892: Ellis Island opens to process immigrants on the East Coast

1893: Beginning of major depression in America

1894: March of Coxey's Army on Washington, DC
United States becomes world's largest manufacturing producer

1896: Decisive victory of Republican William McKinley breaks decades-long deadlock between Democrats and Republicans
America begins to recover from great depression of early 1890s

1897: America's first subway begins regular service in Boston

1901: Assassination of President William McKinley

1903: Ford Motor Company established

1905: Industrial Workers of the World formed

1906: Publication of *The Jungle* by Upton Sinclair
1909: Strike of International Ladies Garment Workers Union in New York City
1910: Angel Island opens to process immigrants on West Coast
Number of American children attending school nears 60 percent
1913: Webb Alien Land Law enacted, prohibiting aliens from owning farmland in California
Ford Motor Company begins to use assembly line techniques; 250,000 automobiles produced in one year

› Review Questions

Fact Check

Check your knowledge of the historical period covered in this chapter.

1. The practices championed by Frederick W. Taylor that were championed by many factory owners of the era
   A. made it easier for immigrant workers to assimilate into the American working class.
   B. ensured that all workers would receive higher wages and conditions in the factories would improve.
   C. emphasized the need for greater efficiency in factory operations.
   D. reemphasized the need for extensive training before the worker could do almost any job in the factory.

2. Many citizens became involved in the political process by actively supporting the Republican and Democratic parties for all of the reasons listed *except*
   A. the parades, rallies, and campaigns of the era provided an exciting entry into the American political system.
   B. the strength of the two parties was roughly identical in this era, thus creating close and interesting races.
   C. the expansion and spread of newspapers in this era made more people aware of political developments.
   D. candidates for president from both parties in almost every race of this era were dynamic and very popular campaigners, thus energizing the forces of both parties.

3. An analysis of the march on Washington by Coxey's Army in 1894 demonstrates that
   A. large segments of the unemployed in America were willing to become involved politically to protest their situation.
   B. all classes in American society were deeply affected by the depression of the early 1890s.
   C. the policies of dealing with the depression in the 1890s were somewhat similar to policies championed by Herbert Hoover from 1929 to 1932.
   D. the march was extremely well covered by the press.

4. The following statements are true about the new industrial city of the late nineteenth century *except*
   A. the working class lived around the factories, usually somewhat near the center of the city.
   B. the factories of the city were almost always found near a source of water, since water power was common.
   C. the central area of the city usually consisted of offices, banks, and insurance buildings.
   D. many saloons existed in working-class neighborhoods.

5. Evidence that the standard of living for the working class improved in this era could be found by carefully analyzing all of the following *except*
   A. a comparison of increased wages with increased living costs for factory workers.
   B. an analysis of the increased diversity of foods available for purchase by factory workers.
   C. an analysis of the growth of amusement parks, sporting events, and movie theaters in the major cities.
   D. a comparison of the wages of most immigrant workers with the wages of workers who remained to work in the "old country."

Multiple-Choice Questions

Here are multiple-choice questions like the ones on the AP U.S. History exam.

Questions 6–8 refer to the quotation below.

The profits of the present Standard Oil Company are enormous. For five years the dividends have been averaging about forty-five million dollars a year, or nearly fifty per cent. on its capitalisation, a sum which capitalised at five per cent. would give $900,000,000. . . . When we remember that probably one-third of this immense annual revenue goes into the hands of John D. Rockefeller, that probably ninety per cent. of it goes to the few men who make up the "Standard Oil family," and that it must every year be invested, the Standard Oil Company becomes a much more serious public matter than it was in 1872, when it stamped itself as willing to enter into a conspiracy to raid the oil business—as a much more serious concern than in the years when it openly made warfare of business, and drove from the oil industry by any means it could invent all who had the hardihood to enter it.

—Ida Tarbell, *The History of the Standard Oil Company*, 1904

6. As a reporter, Ida Tarbell best exemplified which of the following?
   A. Know-Nothings
   B. Grangers
   C. Muckrakers
   D. Yellow journalists

7. John D. Rockefeller expanded the Standard Oil Corporation through a process known as
   A. vertical integration.
   B. scientific management.
   C. supply-side economics.
   D. horizontal integration.

8. The presidents of the Gilded Age did little about the rise of great corporations like Standard Oil because
   A. they were preoccupied with foreign policy.
   B. they believed that the federal government should not interfere with business.
   C. they were on the payroll of the great corporations.
   D. they could not persuade voters to take an interest in the activities of big business.

Short-Answer Question

The short-answer question below is similar to ones you'll encounter on the AP U.S. History exam.

9. Answer Parts A, B, and C.
   A. Briefly explain ONE example of a way in which American political leaders responded to rapid industrial growth in the late nineteenth century.
   B. Briefly explain a SECOND example of a way in which American political leaders responded to rapid industrial growth in the late nineteenth century.
   C. Briefly explain ONE example of a way that American workers responded to rapid industrial growth in the late nineteenth century.

› Answers and Explanations

1. **C.** Taylorism made efficiency in the workplace a science and set the stage for assembly line production techniques.

2. **D.** Most of the presidential candidates—and presidential winners—of this era were nondescript men, thus allowing much power to go over to Congress.

3. **C.** The march had little effect on government policy. Coxey's Army was relatively small by the time it got to Washington. Official policy of the time was that it was not the job of the federal government to actively intervene during hard times, a policy similar to that supported by Herbert Hoover in the first years of the Great Depression.

4. **B**. By 1890, most American industry had converted to steam power.

5. **A**. Many diverse foods were available for purchase by factory workers, but few could afford them. For many workers, wages did go up in this period; however, increased living costs often outstripped higher wages.

6. **C**. As a reporter, Ida Tarbell best exemplified the muckrakers. Getting their name from Theodore Roosevelt, the muckrakers were investigative journalists who exposed corruption in various aspects of American life. The muckrakers began to write at the end of the Gilded Age and flourished during the Progressive Era of the early twentieth century when their reporting helped inspire political reforms.

7. **D**. John D. Rockefeller expanded the Standard Oil Corporation through a process known as horizontal integration. He either bought out or drove out of business most of his competitors in the oil business. Vertical integration involved controlling an entire manufacturing process from the collection of raw materials to the production of a finished product. Andrew Carnegie practiced vertical integration in building up his steel empire.

8. **B**. The presidents of the Gilded Age did little about the rise of great corporations like Standard Oil because they believed that the federal government should not interfere with business. Nineteenth-century political leaders had a more restricted view of the role of government than would become prevalent in the twentieth century. Most presidents of this era were Republicans who favored a high tariff to protect American business and American jobs. Grover Cleveland, the only president of this period who was a Democrat, favored a lower tariff, but he was still very friendly to business.

9. **Parts A and B**: Most American political leaders did very little about the rapid industrial growth in the late nineteenth century. They believed in laissez-faire economics and did not believe in extensive government regulation of business. Popular concerns about the differences between what railroads charged individual consumers and big businesses led Congress to pass the Interstate Commerce Act in 1887. This created the Interstate Commerce Commission, which was charged with monitoring railroad rates. The emergence of "trusts," large businesses that owned more than one company, worried many people. Congress responded by passing the Sherman Antitrust Act in 1890, which outlawed trusts. Big business found a way around this. In 1888, the New Jersey legislature passed a law legalizing holding companies. A holding company owned a controlling interest in the stock of other companies. Soon many big corporations such as Standard Oil had reorganized themselves as holding companies.

Part C: One way that American workers responded to rapid industrial growth and the rise of large corporations was by organizing unions. The Knights of Labor was founded in 1869 and by the mid-1880s had a membership of 750,000 people. The Knights of Labor had both skilled and unskilled workers in its membership. It declined after being blamed for radical outrages like the 1886 Haymarket Square Bombing. The American Federation of Labor (AFL) was a grouping of unions that organized skilled workers. Under its longtime president Samuel Gompers, the AFL became the leading labor organization in the United States, with a membership of 2.5 million in 1917. The Industrial Workers of the World (IWW) was founded in 1905. The IWW was a radical union that emphasized class conflict. It organized skilled and unskilled workers.

CHAPTER 19

Rise of American Imperialism (1890–1913)

IN THIS CHAPTER

Summary: Beginning in the 1890s, the United States began to practice some of the same imperialistic policies that it had previously criticized major European powers for. Spurred on by sugar planters, America expanded its influence in Hawaii and in 1898 annexed the islands. Americans also pushed for an "Open Door" trading policy with China. Efforts to expand American influence abroad were motivated by economic, political, religious, and social factors; the "white man's burden" argument was influential in both Europe and the United States. There were also opponents to imperialism who often based their opposition on moral grounds. American imperialistic impulses flourished during the Spanish-American War; newly created American naval power was one important factor in the defeat of Spain. After contentious debate within the United States, America finally decided to annex the Philippines; it took three years for American forces to defeat Filipino rebels, who, instead of fighting the Spanish now resisted their new occupiers, the Americans. Americans finished building the Panama Canal in 1914; the Roosevelt Corollary to the Monroe Doctrine further increased American influence in Latin America.

Keywords

Open Door policy: policy supported by the United States beginning in 1899 that stated that all major powers, including the United States, should have an equal right to trade with China.

Social Darwinism: philosophy that emerged from the writings of Charles Darwin on the "survival of the fittest"; this was used to justify the vast differences between the rich and the poor in the late nineteenth century as well as American and European imperialistic ventures.

Spanish-American War: war that began in 1898 against the Spanish over treatment of Cubans by Spanish troops that controlled the island. As a result of this war, the United States annexed the Philippines, making America a major power in the Pacific.

Yellow journalism: method of journalism that utilized sensationalized accounts of the news to sell newspapers. This approach helped to whip up nationalistic impulses that led to the Spanish-American War.

U.S.S. *Maine*: U.S. naval ship that sank in Havana harbor in February 1898 following an explosion. The incident was used to increase calls for war against Spain. It was never definitively determined why or how the ship was sunk.

Panama Canal: canal across the Panama isthmus that was begun in 1904 and completed in 1914; its opening enabled America to expand its economic and military influence.

Roosevelt Corollary (1904): policy that warned Europeans against intervening in the affairs of Latin America and that claimed the right of the United States to intervene in the affairs of Latin American nations if "chronic wrongdoing" was taking place.

Dollar Diplomacy: foreign policy supported by President William Howard Taft and others that favored increased American investment in the world as a way of increasing American influence.

Postwar Diplomacy

Even before the Civil War, the U.S. government was interested in opening up new overseas markets for American goods and seeking sources of raw materials for American factories. These efforts continued in the postwar years. In 1867, Secretary of State William Henry Seward successfully orchestrated the purchase of Alaska from Russia. Initially termed "Seward's Folly," it soon became recognized that Alaska was rich in resources. Also in 1867, the United States acquired the Midway Islands in the Pacific Ocean. Midway could serve as a stopping point on the way to China and Japan. Changes in marine technology during this period saw ships shift from sails to coal-powered steam engines. The United States began seeking coaling stations in the Pacific, where American ships could refuel.

Initially, the United States did not join the great European powers in establishing colonies in Africa and Asia. Americans were still busy filling in the western frontier. Rapid industrialization and urbanization also absorbed much American energy. Only when the frontier was declared closed in the 1890s did a new generation of leaders like Theodore Roosevelt and Henry Cabot Lodge begin calling for American expansion overseas. These men were too young to have experienced the horrors of the Civil War and were willing to fight to secure the United States an empire of its own.

The United States was not prepared for imperial adventures. The State Department employed fewer than 100 people in the 1870s and early 1880s. The army was tiny by European standards; most of its troops were scattered across the West in small forts and engaged in patrolling the frontier. The navy had been allowed to deteriorate after the Civil War. Only during the presidency of Chester Arthur was there an effort to rebuild the navy, equipping it with modern all-steel ships.

Acquiring Hawaii

American missionaries arrived in Hawaii during the 1820s. The island chain was a port of call for American whalers and merchant ships. American entrepreneurs began cultivating sugar cane on the islands, and their plantations became highly lucrative businesses. In 1887, Congress allowed the importation of Hawaiian sugar duty-free. This enhanced the influence of the sugar planters in Hawaii, and they pressured King Kalakaua into promulgating a constitution that gave them greater political power.

In 1891, Queen Liliuokalani ascended to the Hawaiian throne. She was determined to reassert royal control over Hawaii and resist the political encroachments of people she saw as outsiders, such as the American planters. For their part, the sugar magnates feared the queen's nationalist program and wanted to convert Hawaii into a protectorate of the United States. This embrace of the U.S. flag was also spurred by changes in American trade policy; only if Hawaii was an American colony could its sugar be considered domestic produce and compete effectively in American markets. In 1893, the planters staged a coup that overthrew the queen. They were assisted by a small detachment of Marines provided by an American diplomat. The planters proclaimed a Hawaiian republic and immediately asked to be annexed by the United States.

Despite the intervention of the diplomat, Washington was not a party to the coup. President Cleveland sent a commission to Hawaii to investigate the attitudes of the Hawaiian people toward the new regime. When the commission reported back that a majority still supported Queen Liliuokalani, Cleveland refused to annex the islands. The United States took no action to restore the queen and eventually extended diplomatic recognition to the Republic of Hawaii. William McKinley did not share Cleveland's qualms about acquiring Hawaii and in the 1896 election declared that it was America's **"Manifest Destiny"** to possess the islands. Congress finally approved the annexation of Hawaii in 1898, against the backdrop of the Spanish-American War. American policymakers realized that Pearl Harbor provided the Navy with a strategically valuable base on the Pacific Ocean.

The New Imperialism

In the 1890s, American attitudes toward imperialism began to change. Though industrialists and businessmen generally feared that war would disrupt markets, they did begin to worry that they would need to find places to sell their goods overseas. Some sought sources of raw materials, such as rubber, that were unavailable in the continental United States.

Strategists such as the naval officer Captain Alfred Thayer Mahan argued that the United States needed to expand in order to protect its international position as a major economic and political power. One of history's most influential military theorists, Mahan published **_The Influence of Sea Power upon History_** in 1890. In this work, Mahan persuasively made the case that naval power was necessary to acquire markets overseas and to protect continued access to them. Mahan's writings were studied by naval officers around the world. They inspired the naval enthusiasms of American leaders like Theodore Roosevelt and helped justify legislation like the **Naval Act of 1900** that rapidly expanded the U.S. Navy.

The idea of **Social Darwinism** that rationalized economic inequality in the United States was also used to justify imperialism. This view of international relations held that nations, like people, struggled for survival, and the strong would rule the weak. Social Darwinism was easily harmonized with contemporary racial ideas and convictions about the superiority of the Anglo-Saxon "race." In 1885, the well-known minister Josiah Strong asserted that God had made the Anglo-Saxons their "brother's keepers" in his book *Our Country*. This same vision was conveyed in Rudyard Kipling's poem **"White Man's Burden,"** in which he urged Americans to accept the mission of ruling and civilizing "inferior races." American missionaries embraced imperialism because it offered them an opportunity to convert "heathens" in Africa and Asia. Some intellectuals like the scholarly Senator Albert J. Beveridge of Indiana saw imperialism overseas as a way for Americans to open a new frontier and recapture the pioneer spirit of their forebears.

The Spanish-American War

The United States burst onto the world scene as an imperial power in the **Spanish-American War**. Short, and relatively bloodless, this "splendid little war" ended a century of American noninvolvement in overseas affairs. The issue that brought on the war began close to home. The island of Cuba lies 90 miles off the coast of Florida. In 1868, some Cuban colonists launched a revolt against the Spanish authorities that governed the island. Though the revolt failed, it began a long period of unrest in Cuba. In 1895, an economic depression caused by falling sugar prices led to another revolt. Many Americans owned sugar plantations or had other financial investments in Cuba; they did not support the revolutionaries.

The U.S. government was initially indifferent to the situation in Cuba. This began to change when the Spanish government used ruthless methods to quell the insurrection. The Spanish sent 150,000 troops to Cuba and began a policy of **reconcentration**, which attempted to deny the rebels support by rounding up rural civilians and placing them in government-controlled camps. The Spanish concentration camps bred disease, and 225,000 people died. Cuban exiles in the United States implored Presidents Cleveland and McKinley to intervene in the war and end Spanish rule. Neither president showed any enthusiasm for a war in Cuba. McKinley had fought in the Civil War and had vivid memories of the human cost of battle. The rebels began burning American-owned plantations and sugar mills to intensify interventionist pressure on the U.S. government.

An emerging mass media pushed public opinion in favor of war. Large circulation newspapers like Joseph Pulitzer's *New York World* and William Randolph Hearst's *New York Morning Journal* attracted readers with boldly headlined news stories that privileged sensationalism over accuracy. This new style of newspapering became known as **yellow journalism**. Both Pulitzer and Hearst sent teams of reporters to Cuba charged with getting stories that would sell newspapers. Soon these papers were publicizing lurid, and often fanciful, accounts of Spanish misdeeds. These stories were widely reprinted across the United States and outraged Americans who believed what they read. The yellow press encouraged **jingoism**, a belligerent patriotism that demanded war with Spain.

President McKinley recognized the political power of the anti-Spanish sentiment whipped up by the newspapers. War became inevitable after the **U.S.S. *Maine*** exploded and sank in Havana Harbor on February 15, 1898. The *Maine* had been sent to Cuba after riots in the capital seemed to threaten American lives and property. The *Maine* probably blew up because of a failure with its boilers; the yellow journalists loudly declared that the Spanish had sunk the ship and demanded that readers "Remember the *Maine*!" A subsequent naval investigation failed to conclusively explain the explosion; the naval authorities were reluctant to blame a technical fault with their own ship. A foolish gaffe by a Spanish diplomat further inflamed American public opinion. In a letter stolen by Cuban revolutionaries the diplomat called McKinley "weak."

Combat in the Philippines and Cuba

Theodore Roosevelt, the assistant secretary of the navy, was an ardent imperialist who assumed that the United States would go to war with Spain. On February 25, while the secretary of the navy was out for the day, Roosevelt cabled American commanders in the Pacific to be ready to strike against the Spanish. President McKinley and the navy secretary later confirmed that in the event of war, Commodore George Dewey should attack the Spanish fleet in the Philippines.

By April, both expansionists dreaming of empire, and humanitarians shocked by newspaper reports of Cuban suffering were calling for war. McKinley attempted to defuse the crisis with diplomacy. The Spanish were prepared to meet most of McKinley's conditions for a settlement in Cuba. The Spanish concessions were not enough. McKinley decided that war had become a political necessity. He sent a message to Congress recommending an intervention in Cuba. The next day, Congress authorized the use of force to drive the Spanish from the island.

While the small but modern American navy was ready for war, the army was not. It took time to gather an invasion force at Tampa, Florida. The war would be over before the army's supply services fully organized themselves. Fortunately for the Americans, the Spanish in Cuba were equally disorganized and had become demoralized by years of guerilla warfare. A small American army landed in Cuba in June. The main fighting took place on July 1, when the Americans seized high ground outside the city of Santiago. Theodore Roosevelt, who had resigned his post in the Navy Department, became a national hero because of the courage he showed leading his regiment of volunteer "**Rough Riders**" up San Juan Hill. Two days later, the aged Spanish warships in Santiago harbor made a dash for the open sea and were annihilated by better-armed American warships. This ended the fighting in Cuba. The war cost 2,500 American lives, most of them to disease. Fewer than 400 Americans died in combat.

On the other side of the world, the U.S. Navy seemed to justify Mahan's theories about the importance of maritime power. Commodore Dewey sailed a small American squadron into Manila Harbor on May 1 and destroyed the decrepit Spanish fleet anchored there. This one-sided battle gave the United States a claim to the Philippines. The war officially ended with the **Treaty of Paris**. Spain granted Cuba independence and for $20 million ceded the Philippines, Guam, and Puerto Rico to the United States.

The Cuban Conundrum

Almost immediately after ensuring Cuban independence, some American policymakers began to have doubts about the ability of the Cubans to govern themselves and safeguard American interests. Concerns about imperial temptations had led a majority in Congress to insert the **Teller Amendment** in the April war resolution. This amendment declared that the United States had no intention of annexing Cuba. Postwar reconsiderations led Congress to soften its support for full Cuban autonomy.

Immediately following the defeat of the Spanish, President McKinley created a military government to rule Cuba. This regime lasted until 1901 and had some notable successes in improving public health and combating yellow fever. In the meantime the Cubans worked on a constitution. Reflecting the new imperial mood in Washington, the American government compelled the Cubans to integrate the **Platt Amendment** into their new constitution. This prohibited the Cubans from making treaties without American approval. It also gave the United States the power to intervene in Cuban politics "when necessary." The Platt Amendment limited full Cuban independence until the United States withdrew it in the 1930s.

The Debate over Empire

Cuba was next door to the United States. The acquisition of the Philippines, an extensive and heavily populated island chain thousands of miles away, spurred controversy. This debate was intensified as the Filipinos organized a government and demanded independence. Americans prided themselves on their revolutionary struggle for independence against Great Britain. Did traditional American political values sanction the United States becoming a colonial power?

The **Anti-Imperialist League** was founded in 1898 to oppose a colonial adventure in the Philippines. Eminent Americans such as Mark Twain, Andrew Carnegie, and William Jennings Bryan spoke out against imperialism. Arguments against empire ranged from the idealistic to the practical. Anti-imperialists condemned the hypocrisy of Americans forcing their rule on peoples overseas, while the United States still faced many social and economic challenges at home. Some opposed imperialism for racial reasons, fearing that it would facilitate a flood of "inferior races" into the United States.

The defenders of American policy in the Philippines had their own arguments. An empire was an extension of the American frontier, allowing modern-day Americans to maintain pioneer virtues. Control of the Philippines helped establish the United States in Asian markets. There was a strong likelihood that if the United States withdrew from the Philippines, the Germans or the Japanese would move in and colonize the islands. Finally, many ministers supported keeping the Philippines so missionaries could convert the people to Christianity, heedless of the fact that most Filipinos were already Catholic.

After wrestling with the issue himself, President McKinley decided that the United States had to rule the Philippines for practical and moral reasons. He believed that the Filipinos were "unfit for self-government." If left alone they would fall into civil war and some predatory imperial power would gobble them up. The Filipinos did not acquiesce to American control easily. The United States fought a war against Filipino rebels from 1899 to 1902. This war was much bloodier than the better-known Spanish-American War; around 4,500 Americans and 200,000 Filipinos were killed. The fighting in the Philippines was brutal, and both sides occasionally committed atrocities. The Americans eventually won the war because they employed the skills that they had learned fighting Native Americans against the Filipinos. They ensured their victory by combining military measures with an effort to win hearts and minds by building schools and encouraging local self-government.

One reason for American interest in the Philippines was a desire to trade in what they hoped would be a lucrative market in China. The weakness of the Chinese government made that nation vulnerable to partition by imperial powers. In 1899, to prevent this, Secretary of State John Hay promoted an **Open Door policy** that would allow all nations equal access to trade in China. The next year, the United States joined with the European powers and Japan to suppress the Boxer Rebellion in China. The Boxers resented foreign influence in China and attacked missionaries, merchants, and diplomats. An international army that included a contingent of American troops bloodily defeated the rebels.

The Panama Canal

The election of 1900 was a rematch of 1896. Once again McKinley defeated William Jennings Bryan, who this time unsuccessfully campaigned on a platform of anti-imperialism. McKinley's running mate was Theodore Roosevelt, who had parlayed his wartime heroism into the governorship of New York. When McKinley was assassinated in 1901, Roosevelt succeeded him. McKinley's friend Mark Hanna lamented, "Now that damned cowboy is president of the United States." Roosevelt was still determined to expand America's global influence. He strongly supported the construction of the **Panama Canal**, which would provide merchant ships and American warships an easier and more rapid connection between the Atlantic and Pacific Oceans. Control of this canal would help ensure American dominance of the Western Hemisphere.

A French company had attempted to construct a canal through Panama, but failed. The United States made arrangements to buy out the French and negotiated for rights to build a canal with Colombia, which owned the Panamanian isthmus. When the Colombian Senate rejected a treaty because it felt that the United States was not offering enough money, President Roosevelt lost patience with the Colombians. In 1903, agents of the French company organized a rebellion in Panama. The United States immediately recognized the new government and stationed warships off Panama to prevent the Colombians from sending troops to crush the rebellion. The 1904 Hay-Bunau-Varilla Treaty, signed with the new Panamanian regime, gave the United States permanent sovereignty over a 10-mile-wide strip of land across the country. For this, the Panamanians received $10 million.

Construction of the canal began immediately, and it was opened for business in 1914. The Panama Canal was a technological, economic, and strategic success. This sophisticated engineering project facilitated trade, and made it much easier to shift American naval vessels between the oceans. The United States did pay a diplomatic price for this success in Latin America. The American collusion in the dismemberment of Colombia convinced many Latin Americans that the United States was a bullying power. Further actions taken by Roosevelt reinforced this view.

The Roosevelt Corollary

President Roosevelt's belief that military power was the final arbiter of international affairs was reflected in his recommendation to "speak softly and carry a big stick." In 1904, the Dominican Republic defaulted on its debts to Europeans during an economic crisis. Angry European powers threatened to collect these debts through military force. This inspired Roosevelt to declare the **Roosevelt Corollary** to the Monroe Doctrine. This asserted the right of the American government to police any country in the Western Hemisphere that acted in ways "harmful to the United States" and risked the intervention of outside powers.

In the Dominican Republic, Roosevelt took over the Dominican customs service and arranged for the orderly payment of that nation's foreign debt. In the years to come, the United States intervened in other Central American and Caribbean countries. Though this promoted the political stability the American government desired, it also intensified anti-American feelings.

President Roosevelt played an important role on the world stage. In 1905, Roosevelt mediated a peace treaty that ended the Russo-Japanese War. For this, he received the Nobel Peace Prize in 1906. Also in 1906, the United States participated in the Algeciras Conference that addressed colonial disputes between France and Germany.

William Howard Taft, Roosevelt's hand-picked successor, shied away from the "big stick" and preferred "dollars over bullets." During his administration he pursued a policy of extending American influence abroad through investment and economic engagement. Taft's critics called this financial approach to foreign relations **"Dollar Diplomacy."**

Chapter Review

Rapid Review

To achieve a perfect 5, you should be able to explain the following:

- America became the economic and imperialistic equal of the major European powers by the beginning of the twentieth century.
- The United States acquired territory in the years immediately following the Civil War but then entered a period where little foreign expansion took place.
- Americans and natives friendly to America increased the economic and political control of Hawaii by the United States, signaling a new trend in foreign policy.
- America desired trade in China; these desires were represented in John Hay's Open Door policy.
- Economic, political, and strategic motives pushed America to pursue imperialist goals in the 1890s.
- Many in this era also opposed imperialism, often on moral or humanitarian grounds.
- The Spanish-American War allowed American imperialistic impulses to flourish; religious figures also supported imperialism in this era.
- Spanish incompetence and the strength of the American navy were important factors in the American victory in the Spanish-American War.
- America was deeply conflicted but finally decided to annex the Philippines, with three years of fighting between Americans and Filipino rebels to follow.
- The Panama Canal was built by the United States for military, strategic, and economic reasons; its construction began in 1904 and was completed in 1914.
- The Roosevelt Corollary to the Monroe Doctrine increased American control over Latin America.

Time Line

1867: United States purchases Alaska from Russia
United States annexes Midway Islands
1871: Beginning of European "Scramble for Africa"
1875: Trade agreement between United States and Hawaii signed

1885: Publication of *Our Country* by Josiah Strong; book discusses role of Anglo-Saxons in the world

1890: Captain Alfred T. Mahan's *The Influence of Sea Power upon History* published

1893: Pro-American sugar planters overthrow Queen Liliuokalani in Hawaii

1895: Revolt against Spanish in Cuba; harsh Spanish reaction angers many in United States

1898: Explosion of U.S.S. *Maine* in Havana harbor; beginning of Spanish-American War
       Annexation of Hawaii receives final approval from Congress
       Anti-Imperialist League formed

1899: Secretary of State John Hay asks European leaders for an Open Door policy in China
       First fighting between American army forces and Filipino rebels in Manila

1900: Naval Act of 1900 authorizes construction of offensive warships requested by navy

1901: Assassination of President McKinley; Theodore Roosevelt becomes president

1904: Roosevelt Corollary to Monroe Doctrine announced
       United States begins construction of Panama Canal

1905: In a Portsmouth, New Hampshire, conference, Roosevelt mediates conflict between Japan and Russia

1914: Completion of the Panama Canal

› Review Questions

Fact Check

Check your knowledge of the historical period covered in this chapter.

1. The intent of the Roosevelt Corollary to the Monroe Doctrine was
   A. to prevent European powers from becoming directly involved in affairs of the Western Hemisphere.
   B. to allow the United States to "assist" countries in the area that demonstrated economic or political instability.
   C. to allow the United States to remove "unfriendly governments" in the Western Hemisphere.
   D. all of the above.

2. Many humanitarians in the United States initially supported the Spanish-American War because
   A. they were appalled at the Spanish policy of reconcentration in Cuba.
   B. they were able to ignore editorial comments found in most American newspapers.
   C. they desired to assist the Filipino natives.
   D. of American economic interests in Cuba.

3. The major criticism that some Americans had concerning the construction of the Panama Canal was that
   A. the canal would force America to have a navy in both the Pacific and the Atlantic.
   B. the canal would be outlandishly expensive to build.
   C. the tactics that the Americans used to get the rights to build the canal were unsavory at best.
   D. American forces would have to be stationed indefinitely in Panama to guard the canal.

4. The United States was able to annex Hawaii because
   A. Queen Liliuokalani desired increased American investment in Hawaii.
   B. pro-American planters engineered a revolt in Hawaii.
   C. public opinion in Hawaii strongly favored annexation.
   D. Hawaii felt threatened by other Pacific powers.

5. American missionary leaders supported imperialism in this era because
   A. they thought their involvement would temper the excess zeal of other imperialists.
   B. they admired the "pureness of spirit" found in the Filipinos and other native groups.
   C. religious leaders in Europe favored imperialism.
   D. they saw imperialism as an opportunity to convert the "heathens" of newly acquired territories.

Multiple-Choice Questions

Here are multiple-choice questions like the ones on the AP U.S. History exam.

Questions 6–8 refer to the quotation below.

I left these shores . . . a red-hot imperialist. I wanted the American eagle to go screaming into the Pacific. It seemed tiresome and tame for it to content itself with the Rockies. Why not spread its wings over the Philippines, I asked myself. And I thought it would be a real good thing to do. . . .

But I have thought some more, since then, and I have read carefully the treaty of Paris, and I have seen that we do not intend to free, but to subjugate the people of the Philippines. We have gone there to conquer, not to redeem. . . .

It should, it seems to me, be our pleasure and duty to make these people free, and let them deal with their own domestic questions in their own way. And so I am an anti-imperialist. I am opposed to having the eagle put its talons on any other land.

—Mark Twain, quoted in the New York *World*, October 15, 1900

6. Which of the following led to the United States acquiring the Philippines?
   A. World War I
   B. The Boxer Rebellion
   C. The Spanish-American War
   D. The Roosevelt Corollary of the Monroe Doctrine

7. The American desire for imperial acquisitions in the late nineteenth and early twentieth centuries can best be compared to which of the following?
   A. Native American Removal
   B. Manifest Destiny
   C. Isolationism
   D. The Containment Policy

8. Which of the following would be most likely to share Mark Twain's views on foreign policy?
   A. Supporters of the Open Door policy
   B. Supporters of the Fourteen Points
   C. Opponents of Communist expansion in the cold war

   D. Opponents of the Vietnam War

Short-Answer Question

The short-answer question below is similar to the ones you'll encounter on the AP U.S. History exam.

9. Answer Parts A, B, and C.
   A. Briefly explain ONE example of the United States asserting itself as a world power in the period 1890 to 1913.
   B. Briefly explain a SECOND example of the United States asserting itself as a world power in the period 1890 to 1913.
   C. Briefly explain ONE example of Americans rejecting the assertion of the United States as a world power in the period 1890 to 1913.

› Answers and Explanations

1. D. The Roosevelt Corollary allowed the United States to intervene in affairs of Latin American countries under several circumstances, but it was also intended to keep the European powers out of Latin America.

2. A. The Spanish policy of placing civilians in camps horrified many Americans. Most American newspapers initially supported the war as well. Concern for the Filipinos only became an issue during the debate over whether or not the United States should annex the Philippines.

3. C. The United States acquired the rights to build the canal through the encouragement of a "revolt" by Panamanians against Colombia. The American navy wanted the canal.

4. B. The United States was able to annex Hawaii after pro-U.S. planters led a rebellion against Queen Liliuokalani, who had opposed U.S. influence.

5. D. Missionary leaders worked in conjunction with other imperialists in this era. Little admiration of the natives was demonstrated by missionary leaders; the possibility of conversions was the major reason for religious support for imperialism.

6. C. The United States acquired the Philippines as a result of the Spanish-American War of 1898. Commodore George Dewey's victory at the Battle of Manila Bay gave the United States a claim to the islands. At the conclusion of the conflict the United States bought the Philippines from Spain; the United States was subsequently forced to subdue the Filipinos in a war that lasted from 1899 to 1902.

7. B. The American desire for imperial acquisitions in the late nineteenth and early twentieth centuries can best be compared to Manifest Destiny. Just as many Americans in the era of Manifest Destiny during the 1840s believed that it was America's mission to carry its civilization across the West to the Pacific Ocean, many members of a later generation believed that the time had come to carry American ideals and commerce across the seas.

8. D. Opponents of the Vietnam War would be most likely to share Mark Twain's views on foreign policy. Twain believed that the Filipinos should not be subjected to American rule by force. Opponents to the Vietnam War believed that the United States should not contain the expansion of Communism in Southeast Asia by force.

9. Parts A and B: In 1893, American sugar planters with the help of local U.S. officials overthrew the queen of Hawaii and declared the islands a republic. The United States officially annexed Hawaii in 1898. After a rebellion against Spanish rule in Cuba broke out in 1895, the American public grew increasingly sympathetic to the Cubans because of an exaggerated press campaign by "yellow journalists." The unexplained explosion of the USS *Maine* in Havana harbor intensified calls for war. The United States declared war on Spain in April 1898. In the brief Spanish-American War that ensued, the United States drove Spain out of Cuba and annexed Puerto Rico, Guam, and the Philippines. From 1899 to 1902, the United States fought a successful war to suppress a Filipino insurrection against American rule. In 1899, the U.S. secretary of state, John Hay, circulated an Open Door Note amongst the great powers calling for all countries to have equal access to Chinese markets. In 1900, American forces joined an international army in crushing the Boxer Rebellion, an anti-foreigner uprising in China. President Theodore Roosevelt supported a revolution that separated Panama from Colombia in 1904. That same year the United States signed the Hay-Bunau-Varilla Treaty with Panama, making possible the construction of the Panama Canal. Also in 1904, Roosevelt issued his Roosevelt Corollary to the Monroe Doctrine, stating that the United States had the right to intervene in Latin American countries if their actions threatened to precipitate European interventions in the Western Hemisphere. President William Howard Taft promoted "Dollar Diplomacy," which advocated for American economic investment as a way of encouraging stability in foreign countries.

Part C: Following the overthrow of the queen of Hawaii in 1893, President Grover Cleveland refused to annex the Hawaiian Islands because he believed that most Hawaiians still supported the monarchy. Many Americans opposed the annexation of the Philippines as a colony following the Spanish-American War. An Anti-Imperialist League was formed in 1898. Andrew Carnegie and Mark Twain were prominent anti-imperialists. After being renominated as a candidate for the presidency by the Democratic Party in 1900, William Jennings Bryan made anti-imperialism a central part of his platform during the presidential campaign.

CHAPTER 20

Progressive Era (1895–1914)

IN THIS CHAPTER

Summary: Progressivism began in the 1890s as a movement that attacked the political, social, and political inequalities of the age. Many Progressives blamed capitalism for the evils of society. However, unlike the Socialists, who wanted to destroy the capitalist system, the Progressives wanted to fix that system. Many Progressives were tied to the Social Gospel movement of the Protestant church; others wanted to reform city governments, while still others desired to instill even more democracy in the electoral process (direct primaries, more use of the referendum, etc.). Many Progressives launched projects to aid the immigrant population that existed in America's cities. One example was Hull House, a settlement house that aided Chicago's poor. A high point of the Progressive movement was the "Square Deal" of the presidency of Theodore Roosevelt. Progressives did much to reform America's cities but were less effective in aiding America's farmers and minorities.

Keywords

Social Gospel movement: movement originating in the Protestant church that aimed to help the urban poor; many Progressives were influenced by this movement.

Muckrakers: writers who exposed unethical practices in both government and business during this era; newspaper editors discovered that these types of stories increased circulation.

Seventeenth Amendment (1913): U.S. Constitutional amendment that allowed voters instead of state legislatures to elect U.S. senators; this amendment had been championed by Progressives.

Initiative process: this Progressive-supported process allowed any citizen to propose a law. If enough supporters' signatures could be procured, the proposed law would appear on the next ballot.

Referendum process: this process allowed citizens (instead of legislatures) to vote on proposed laws.

Recall process: this process allowed voters to remove an elected official from office before his or her term expired.

Direct primary: this process allowed party members to vote for prospective candidates; previously most had been chosen by party conventions.

Hull House: settlement house in Chicago founded by Jane Addams; Hull House became a model for settlement houses around the country.

National American Woman Suffrage Association: created in 1890 by a merger of two women's suffrage organizations and led in its early years by Elizabeth Cady Stanton and Susan B. Anthony; was instrumental in demanding women's right to vote.

Triangle Shirtwaist Fire (1911): fire in New York City that killed 146 female factory workers. It was later found that the workers had been locked in the factory; as a result, many factory reforms were enacted.

The Jungle: novel written by Upton Sinclair that highlighted numerous problems of the meatpacking industry and inspired the Pure Food and Drug Act and the Meat Inspection Act.

Roots of Progressivism

Progressivism was a complicated social and political phenomenon. There never was a unified Progressive movement. Progressives could be found in both major parties, and in both urban and rural settings; they often disagreed on the role of government and on the ideal size of American businesses. What all Progressives shared was a desire for reform.

Progressivism was rooted in many late nineteenth-century ideas and social causes. Many Progressives were influenced by books such as Henry George's *Progress and Poverty* (1879) and Edward Bellamy's *Looking Backward* (1888). **Taylorism** and the ideal of a "scientific" approach to work and social organization inspired some Progressives.

Progressives joined with Socialists in criticizing the excesses of big business. This did not mean that all Progressives wanted to overthrow the capitalist system as the Socialists did. Most Progressives believed in the economic benefits of capitalism; they intended to reform and regulate business and the markets to prevent the wealthy from abusing their power. Some Socialists played important roles in the Progressive movement. Upton Sinclair, the author of *The Jungle* (1906), believed that Progressive reforms could lay the foundation for a democratic socialism.

Many Progressives were influenced by religious convictions. The **Social Gospel movement** reflected a growing desire amongst some liberal Protestants to apply Christian principles in the quest for social justice. These church-based reformers worked to improve conditions for the working class poor. Proponents of the Social Gospel sometimes came into conflict with their coreligionists because they emphasized political and economic reforms over efforts to achieve personal salvation. Jane Addams was a reformer whose Progressivism was driven by her religious beliefs.

Progressivism derived much of its energy from the emerging mass media. Newspapers and magazines published many investigative reports on political corruption and the iniquities of business monopolies. These articles proved very popular, boosting circulation for the publishers of these exposés and disseminating Progressive ideas to a wide public. Theodore Roosevelt thought the writers of these investigations went too far in their criticisms; he called them "**muckrakers**," and the term stuck. There were many well-known muckrakers. Upton Sinclair became famous for his indictment of the meatpacking industry. Ida Tarbell wrote a critical history of Standard Oil. Lincoln Steffens denounced machine politics in *The Shame of the Cities* (1904). Jacob Riis publicized the depth of urban poverty in *How the Other Half Lives* (1890). These muckraking works became calls to action for Progressives.

Progressive Objectives

Most Progressives came from the middle class. Many came from the upper class. Because of their social background, very few Progressives wanted revolutionary changes in the United States. They wanted to reform society, not blow it up. Some Progressives such as Theodore Roosevelt saw themselves as conservatives working to head off potential uprisings by correcting abuses and improving social and political efficiency. Progressives wanted to help the lower classes, but they wanted power to remain in the hands of the middle and upper classes. This would be achieved by creating a regulatory state, with power shifting into the hands of a highly educated and professional bureaucratic elite. Increasingly, Progressives saw a powerful government as the answer to many of the challenges facing Americans.

Not everyone embraced Progressive goals. Many poor people resented the paternalistic approach of Progressive reformers and new government agencies. In the name of democracy Progressives attacked political machines and worked to weaken the power of the political parties, yet these machines and the parties had fostered a vibrant political culture; ironically the robust voter participation rates of the Gilded Age began to decline during the Progressive Era.

Because of the multifaceted complexity of the Progressive movement, it has been difficult for historians to assign an overall goal to Progressivism. Some see Progressivism as an attempt to resist the social forces transforming American life. Others see Progressivism as a means of adapting Americans to conditions in the new urban and industrialized social system.

Urban Progressivism

Progressive reforms were launched at every level of American politics. In many American cities, Progressives challenged the power of the political machines. In some cases, reform politicians built their own machines. In a few instances, traditional machines sponsored reforms to protect their power. "Reform mayors" such as Tom Johnson in Cleveland received national attention for their efforts to clean up local government and improve city services. In Cleveland, the city took over municipal utilities, believing that this would make these services more efficient. Some reform mayors established relief programs for the poor. A number of cities dispensed with politics altogether in crucial areas, replacing elected mayors with city managers and making elected utility commissioners appointed positions. By taking these offices out of political contention, Progressives reduced the power of urban politicians, but also that of the working class voters who had elected them. Almost invariably, the "professionals" who filled these ostensibly depoliticized positions came from the same middle class background as the Progressive reformers.

State-Level Progressivism

Important Progressive initiatives were launched at the state level. Progressive governors such as Robert La Follette in Wisconsin and Hiram Johnson in California sponsored measures to constrain the power of political parties and their state legislatures. Progressive political measures that were adopted in many states included the following:

1. The **initiative process**. The initiative enabled a citizen to propose a law and get it on the ballot during the next election.
2. The **referendum process**. A referendum allowed citizens to vote for the adoption of a proposed law during an election.
3. The **recall process**. The recall made it possible for voters to remove an elected official from office.
4. The **direct primary**. Traditionally party nominees had been picked at political conventions dominated by the party leadership. The direct primary allowed rank and file party members to pick a nominee through a public vote.

A national measure that diminished the influence of state legislatures was the **Seventeenth Amendment**, which was adopted in 1913. The Seventeenth Amendment changed the method of electing U.S. senators from election by state legislatures to direct election by the voters.

Progressivism and Women

Women played important roles in the Progressive movement. Women enjoyed an influence in progressive organizations that they could not have in the political parties. Florence Kelley founded the **National Consumers League**, which promoted legislation protecting women and children in both the workplace and the home. Kelley's organization, run mostly by women, was a conspicuous voice calling for laws limiting child labor and establishing minimum wages for female workers. From 1911 on, such laws began to be passed in various states.

Women were leaders in starting **settlement houses** in the slums of American cities. In 1889, Jane Addams and Ellen Gates Starr began serving the poor at **Hull House** in Chicago. Hull House became a model that was imitated in other cities. Settlement houses helped immigrants acculturate to life in the United States. They provided space for classes aimed at both children and adults. Often settlement houses ran kindergartens to prepare children for school. Settlement houses also sponsored clubs and recreational activities. Assisting poor women was a special focus with programs on child care and family health.

Progressive women did not have a single approach to helping the poor. Some focused on improving conditions for working men and women so they could better support their families. Others tackled social problems such as prostitution and alcoholism. The **Anti-Saloon League** argued that alcoholism was a major contributor to poverty as working men spent their paychecks in bars. The prohibition movement became increasingly powerful during the Progressive Era. Many women believed that economic and social issues would be better addressed if women got the vote. Beginning with Idaho, western states began giving women the vote in local elections during the Gilded Age. Colorado and Utah did so in the 1890s. In 1890, two women's suffrage organizations merged to form the **National American Woman Suffrage Association**. At first, Elizabeth Cady Stanton and Susan B. Anthony led this influential women's group. In 1916, Alice Paul founded the **National Woman's Party**, a more aggressive organization that was influenced by the radical British suffragette movement. Both groups played important roles in winning the vote for women in the aftermath of World War I.

Some women went beyond advocating the vote and began discussing **feminism**, which envisioned far-reaching changes in women's lives. The term *feminism* was first used by a group of women who gathered in New York City in 1914. Feminists no longer wanted to live with the restraints society placed upon women. A reality few women could avoid in the early twentieth century was the possibility of pregnancy. Margaret Sanger, who had worked with the poor of New York City as a nurse, became a well-known advocate of birth control. She scandalized many people by attempting to make such information readily available. Sanger was an enthusiast of eugenics and believed in fewer but better babies. She also thought birth control offered women greater personal freedom.

Laws designed to protect working women were passed during the Progressive Era. The Supreme Court provided sanction for this effort in *Muller v. Oregon*. This decision ruled that it was constitutional for states to limit the number of hours women could work. This reflected contemporary ideas about women. It was thought that working too long would overtax women's limited strength. It was also believed that overlong shifts would interfere with women's most important duty as mothers.

Workplace Reform

Industrial accidents were commonplace in the early twentieth century, leading to the death or injury of many workers. The tragic **Triangle Shirtwaist Fire**, where 146 workers were killed when a fire swept through a badly maintained factory, convinced many Progressives that safety regulations were needed in the workplace. Progressives also sought accident insurance programs for workers. Between 1910 and 1917, many states passed legislation to provide relief to the families of people killed or injured in workplace or mining accidents.

Progressives and labor unions had a complicated relationship. Progressives were not wholehearted supporters of union activity; some union members worried about Progressive interference in the workplace. One Progressive initiative that the unions endorsed was restricting immigration. It is a measure of the complexity of Progressivism that many of these middle-class reformers distrusted Southern and Eastern European immigrants who were "unlike ourselves" and tended to vote for machine politicians. Union members wanted to reduce immigration because recent immigrants avoided unions; unionists also believed that the influx of large numbers of immigrants drove down wages. Progressives laid the groundwork for the immigration restrictions of the 1920s.

Theodore Roosevelt's Square Deal

Theodore Roosevelt became president because of the assassination of William McKinley in 1901. Despite his unexpected ascent to power, Roosevelt aggressively used the powers of his office. He also was a master of public relations. This, and his exuberant personality, made him a larger-than-life figure on the American scene. Unlike the chief executives of the Gilded Age, Roosevelt believed that government should take the lead in reforming society. Roosevelt's activist approach to the presidency set a new standard for the presidents who would follow him.

In 1902, Roosevelt played an unprecedented role in negotiating an agreement between mine operators and the striking United Mine Workers union. He declared that the resulting contract was a "**Square Deal**" for both management and the workers. This term was later used to describe Roosevelt's policy of using the government to protect the interests of all members of society.

Roosevelt was easily elected president in 1904, defeating the Democratic candidate Judge Alton B. Parker. He used his victory as a mandate to press for Progressive legislation in Congress. 1906 was an active legislative year for him. The Hepburn Act strengthened the **Interstate Commerce Act**, giving the Interstate Commerce Commission more authority to regulate railroads. The **Pure Food and Drug Act** and the **Meat Inspection Act** gave the government power to regulate food products and medicine and addressed concerns raised by Upton Sinclair's *The Jungle*.

President Roosevelt reinvigorated the **Sherman Antitrust Act**. Though passed in 1890, little had been done to use the law to break up illegal **trusts** or monopolistic **holding companies**. Concern about the burgeoning power of big business was a driving force in the Progressive movement. Roosevelt decided to demonstrate that the people, through their government, still wielded final authority in the land. He ordered the Justice Department to use the Sherman Antitrust Act to sue for the breakup of the Northern Securities Company, a holding company that controlled most of the railroads in the northwest. The Supreme Court eventually upheld the Justice Department's suit. Roosevelt had the Justice Department sue to break up 45 corporations, including Standard Oil and the American Tobacco Company. Roosevelt acquired the reputation of a "trustbuster," but, in fact, he was not anti-big business. Roosevelt applied the Sherman Antitrust Act to corporations that he believed had used their size and power to exploit consumers.

Roosevelt made conservation of the nation's resources a major Progressive cause. An avid hunter and outdoorsman, as well as a gifted naturalist, he set aside 200 million acres of land for national forests and he increased the national park system. In 1905, he established the **U.S. Forest Service** to protect the nation's woodlands.

Taft and Progressivism

William Howard Taft was Theodore Roosevelt's chosen successor. Originally a judge, he was Roosevelt's friend and a member of his cabinet. In 1908, Taft defeated William Jennings Bryan, running for the third time as the Democratic presidential candidate. Taft attempted to follow in Roosevelt's Progressive footsteps, in some ways even going beyond his mentor. Taft was a far more aggressive trustbuster than Roosevelt; in four years he brought suit against 95 corporations.

Unfortunately, Taft lacked Roosevelt's political and public relations skills. He also was much more deferential to Congress. This led him to support the Payne-Aldrich Tariff of 1909, which angered many Progressives because it kept tariffs unnecessarily high on many products, which hurt consumers. Taft found it impossible to reconcile the conservative and Progressive wings of the Republican Party. Taft also ran afoul of Progressives in the **Ballinger-Pinchot Affair**. Richard A. Ballinger was Taft's secretary of the interior. He allowed businesses to purchase a million acres of public land in Alaska. This enraged Gifford Pinchot, the head of the Forest Service. He publically accused Ballinger of corruption. Taft investigated and fired Pinchot. This episode began to alienate Taft from many Progressives who accepted Pinchot's allegations that Taft was undermining conservation. Pinchot, a good friend of Roosevelt's, complained about his treatment to the former president. Relations between Taft and Roosevelt began to cool.

By 1910, Taft was relying for support on the Republican "Old Guard." He opposed some of his Progressive critics in the 1910 primaries. Theodore Roosevelt was back in the United States after a much-publicized safari in Africa. He vigorously campaigned for some of the Progressives that Taft opposed. As he barnstormed across the country, Roosevelt proposed an ambitious series of reforms to protect workers and consumers that would be implemented by a bigger and stronger federal government. Roosevelt called his plan the "**New Nationalism**." Progressive candidates made gains in the 1910 elections, reflecting a reformist mood in the country. This paved the way for the passage of the **Sixteenth Amendment**, which gave the federal government the power to collect income taxes. President Taft and a broad cross-section of the public supported this as a way to collect revenue and balance the fiscal cost of lowering tariffs. Initially it was thought that only the wealthy would pay an income tax. This amendment proved consequential for the future because it gave Congress the means to pay for expanded government and more government programs.

The Election of 1912

Many factors contributed to the breakdown of relations between President Taft and Theodore Roosevelt. Taft's decision to launch an antitrust suit against U.S. Steel over an acquisition that Roosevelt had approved in 1907 deeply angered the former president because it made it look as if he had colluded in an illegal action. Roosevelt also was frustrated on the political sidelines and wanted to be president again. He threw his "hat into the ring" in 1912. In the race for the Republican presidential nomination, Roosevelt won most of the primaries in states where these were held, but Taft controlled the party machinery and was supported by most of the delegates from nonprimary states. This allowed Taft to edge Roosevelt out for the Republican nomination.

Roosevelt believed that he had been robbed; his delegates withdrew from the Republican convention. Roosevelt and his supporters formed the Progressive Party, popularly known as the **Bull Moose Party**. The Progressives nominated Roosevelt for president and California governor Hiram Johnson for vice president. The new party called for the eight-hour day, women's suffrage, and the end of child labor. Many women were Bull Moose activists. The Progressives shied away from championing the cause of African Americans because Roosevelt hoped to win Southern support for the party.

The split in the Republican Party was an electoral gift to the Democrats. Taking advantage of this opportunity, the Democrats turned to a fresh face and nominated Woodrow Wilson, a first-term governor of New Jersey. Wilson was a Progressive who had sponsored many reforms in his two years as governor. Wilson proposed the **New Freedom policy**, which reflected what had long been a traditional Democratic suspicion of a powerful federal government. Wilson was more hostile to the bigness of business than Roosevelt. Instead of government regulating business, he called for the dismantling of monopolistic corporations. With Taft and Roosevelt dividing the once-ascendant GOP, Wilson easily won the election, even though he won only 42 percent of the popular vote. Roosevelt came in second with 27 percent, and Taft received 23 percent. Eugene Debs, running as the head of the Socialist Party, won 6 percent of the popular vote. Given the records of the candidates, 1912 was the electoral high-water mark of the Progressive Era.

Wilson and Progressivism

President Wilson immediately set to work to enact the New Freedom into legislation. He was just as much an activist president as Roosevelt, and he devoted much effort to marshaling his allies in Congress. The Underwood Tariff Act of 1913 imposed the greatest tariff reductions since the Civil War; the resulting loss of revenue was compensated for by the new income tax. The **Clayton Antitrust Act** of 1914 extended the prohibitions of the Sherman Antitrust Act by outlawing price discrimination and a list of other corporate abuses. The Clayton Act was a great victory for organized labor because it legalized strikes. In office, Wilson began to move from the New Freedom toward the New Nationalism. He decided to pursue a regulatory approach to government dealings with big business. The legislative manifestation of this new perspective was the Federal Trade Commission Act of 1914, which created the **Federal Trade Commission (FTC)**. The FTC was a bipartisan agency that regulated business activity by working closely with companies to help them avoid illegal activities. This began a relationship between business and government that would grow closer during the twentieth and twenty-first centuries. Wilson also addressed the perpetual problem of currency supply and financial panics with the Federal Reserve Act of 1913, which created the **Federal Reserve System**. This set up a system of twelve regional banks that could lend money to commercial banks in their districts. A Federal Reserve Board in Washington oversaw the system and controlled the issuing of a new form of paper money, the Federal Reserve notes that we use today. The authors of the Federal Reserve Act hoped that it would strengthen the American economy by establishing a decentralized support system for banks and by providing the country with a stable, yet flexible, currency.

Assessing Progressivism

Progressives could point to many achievements. On all levels of government a flood of legislation attempted to improve the efficiency of government and improve conditions for the disadvantaged. In the name of democracy, the Progressives attacked political machines and weakened political parties, though at the cost of shifting a growing amount of power to unelected bureaucrats and administrators. The enforcement of antitrust laws against some corporations had the important symbolic effect of affirming the people's authority to regulate big business. Progressivism ended the unfettered laissez-faire of the Gilded Age.

Progressives were primarily interested in urban issues; they did little to address the problems of the rural poor. Predominantly members of the middle class, most Progressives were uninterested in aggressively championing social equality. Many distrusted recent immigrants. Few wanted to assist African Americans. Theodore Roosevelt invited Booker T. Washington to a meal at the White House, but he received so much criticism from Southerners over this that he never did so again. Woodrow Wilson was born in the South. When he and the Democrats took over the executive branch in 1913, Wilson allowed members of his cabinet to resegregate the workers in their departments. D. W. Griffith's 1915 film *Birth of a Nation* was an epic tale of the Civil War and Reconstruction. Technically and artistically a landmark in the history of film, Griffith's movie reflected a Southern view of Reconstruction that had become dominant among historians, and it celebrated the Ku Klux Klan's suppression of the freedmen. Woodrow Wilson had written a history that was referenced in the film, and he said that its portrayal of Reconstruction was "truthful." The Progressive movement did not promote progress for African Americans. As a result, African Americans organized to help themselves. In 1909, a group of African American and white reformers founded the **National Association for the Advancement of Colored People (NAACP)** to combat racism and advocate equal rights for all.

American intervention in World War I marked the beginning of the end of the Progressive Era. Supporters of reforms such as women's suffrage and prohibition would achieve important victories during the war. But the war would turn the attention of many leaders to foreign affairs. The way the government conducted the war would exhaust many people's patience for reform and government activism.

Chapter Review

Rapid Review

To achieve the perfect 5, you should be able to explain the following:

- Political, economic, and social inequities and problems existed in America in the late 1890s, and the Progressive movement developed to attempt to address some of those problems.
- The Progressive movement did not have a unifying set of goals or leaders.
- Progressives shared some of the same critiques of American society as the Socialists, but wished to reform and not attack the American system.
- Progressive reformers were closely tied to the Social Gospel movement of the Protestant church; progressivism and religious fervor often marched hand in hand.
- Muckraking magazines and newspapers of the era often created and published the Progressive agenda.
- Many Progressives were determined to reform city government and the services provided by city government.
- Progressive political reforms included the initiative, the referendum, and the recall processes, and the direct primary.
- Hull House was an example of a settlement house copied by reformers across the country.
- The presidency of Theodore Roosevelt was a high point of progressivism; Roosevelt's "Square Deal" included many progressive measures.
- Roosevelt's successor, William Howard Taft, was unable to keep the loyalty of ardent Progressives; the advent of World War I blunted the Progressive reform impulse for many.
- Progressivism succeeded in achieving some of its goals but fell short in aiding farmers and minorities in America.

Time Line

1879: *Progress and Poverty* by Henry George published
1888: *Looking Backward* by Edward Bellamy published
1889: Formation of National Consumers League
1890: National American Woman Suffrage Association founded
1901: Theodore Roosevelt becomes president after the assassination of William McKinley
     Progressive Robert La Follette elected as governor of Wisconsin
     Progressive Tom Johnson elected as mayor of Cleveland, Ohio
1903: Founding of Women's Trade Union League
1904: *The Shame of the Cities* by Lincoln Steffens published

1905: IWW (Industrial Workers of the World) established

Establishment of U.S. Forest Service

1906: *The Jungle* by Upton Sinclair published

Meat Inspection Act enacted

Pure Food and Drug Act enacted

1908: William Howard Taft elected president

1909: Foundation of the NAACP

1910: Ballinger-Pinchot controversy

1911: Triangle Shirtwaist Company fire

1912: Progressive Party (Bull Moose Party) founded by Theodore Roosevelt

Woodrow Wilson elected president

Establishment of Industrial Relations Committee

1913: Establishment of Federal Reserve System

Ratification of Sixteenth Amendment, authorizing federal income tax

Ratification of Seventeenth Amendment, authorizing direct election of senators

1914: Clayton Antitrust Act ratified

Outbreak of World War I in Europe

Federal Trade Commission Act ratified

1915: First showing of D. W. Griffith's film *Birth of a Nation*

› Review Questions

Fact Check

Check your knowledge of the historical period covered in this chapter.

1. Successful reforms initiated by the Progressives included all but which of the following:
   A. Governments became more efficient in American cities such as Cleveland.
   B. Health and safety conditions improved in some large factories.
   C. The conditions of migrant farmers improved to some degree.
   D. The federal government began to collect a national income tax.

2. Theodore Roosevelt ran for president in 1912 because
   A. the policies of William Howard Taft's administration were almost exclusively antiprogressive.
   B. he desired to split the Republican Party and give the election to the Democrats.
   C. he was appalled by the results of the Ballinger-Pinchot Affair.
   D. of the Taft administration's decision to apply the Sherman Antitrust Act to United States Steel.

3. American blacks were discouraged by their lack of racial progress during the Wilson administration. Which of the following is *not* true?
   A. The film *Birth of a Nation* presented a positive view of blacks in Reconstruction states after the Civil War.
   B. Black and Progressive leaders forged tight political bonds during the Wilson administration and battled for many of the same causes.
   C. Booker T. Washington and Theodore Roosevelt developed close political ties after their two meetings together.
   D. All of the above.

4. Many Progressives agreed with Socialists that
  A. capitalism had created massive inequality in America.
  B. the American factory system had to be fundamentally altered.
  C. labor unions were inherently evil.
  D. revolutionary tactics were needed to reform the economic and social systems.

5. Which of the following was *least* likely to be a Progressive in this era?
  A. A member of the Protestant Social Gospel movement
  B. A large stockholder in United States Steel
  C. A follower of Eugene Debs
  D. A member of the Bull Moose Party

Multiple-Choice Questions

Here are multiple-choice questions like the ones on the AP U.S. History exam.

Questions 6–8 refer to the quotation below.

For the purposes hereinbefore set forth the Secretary shall cause to be made, by inspectors appointed for that purpose, an examination and inspection of all meat food products prepared for commerce in any slaughtering, meat-canning, salting, packing, rendering, or similar establishment, and for the purposes of any examination and inspection and inspectors shall have access at all times, by day or night, whether the establishment be operated or not, to every part of said establishment; and said inspectors shall mark, stamp, tag, or label as "Inspected and passed" all such products found to be not adulterated. . . .

—Federal Meat Inspection Act of 1906

6. The Federal Meat Inspection Act of 1906 was passed by Congress in part because of concerns raised by
  A. Upton Sinclair's novel *The Jungle*.
  B. meat-packers worried about foreign competition.
  C. the growing popularity of vegetarianism.
  D. reformers worried about the power of urban political machines.

7. The supporters of the Federal Meat Inspection Act of 1906 had goals similar to those of which of the following?
  A. Supporters of Prohibition
  B. Supporters of the Federal Aid Highway Act of 1956
  C. Supporters of the Consumer Product Safety Act of 1972
  D. Supporters of the Airline Deregulation Act of 1978

8. The Federal Meat Inspection Act of 1906 reflected the ideals of which of the following?
  A. Mugwumps
  B. Populists
  C. Socialists
  D. Progressives

Short-Answer Question

The short-answer question below is similar to the ones you'll encounter on the AP U.S. History exam.

9. Answer Parts A, B, and C.
  A. Briefly explain ONE example of Progressive actions aimed at reforming the American economy.
  B. Briefly explain a SECOND example of Progressive actions aimed at reforming the American economy.
  C. Briefly explain ONE example of Progressive actions aimed at reforming American politics.

› Answers and Explanations

1. **C.** Progressives did much less for workers in the agricultural sector than they did for factory workers.

2. **D.** The Taft administration enacted many important progressive measures. Roosevelt considered the actions against United States Steel to be a personal affront to him.

3. **D.** D. W. Griffith's film presented a very negative view of blacks during Reconstruction. Progressives and black leaders never worked closely together. Theodore Roosevelt met twice with Booker T. Washington but did little to help the conditions of blacks.

4. **A.** Progressives and Socialists were both critical of the effects of capitalism in the United States. Progressives, however, were intent on reforming that system.

5. **B.** Progressives were insistent that corporations like United States Steel be made to reform. Members of the Social Gospel movement and Socialist followers of Eugene Debs shared goals with the Progressives.

6. **A.** The Federal Meat Inspection Act of 1906 was passed by Congress in part because of concerns raised by Upton Sinclair's novel *The Jungle*. Although he was chiefly interested in promoting Socialism, Sinclair described unhygienic practices in the meatpacking industry that disgusted readers. President Theodore Roosevelt commissioned an investigation that confirmed what Sinclair had written. Following this, Roosevelt supported the passage of the Federal Meat Inspection Act.

7. **C.** The supporters of the Federal Meat Inspection Act of 1906 had goals similar to those who supported the Consumer Product Safety Act of 1972. In both cases these laws were designed to protect Americans from products that could threaten the health of consumers. The Consumer Product Safety Act of 1972 created the Consumer Product Safety Commission to regulate products not already regulated by other government agencies.

8. **D.** The Federal Meat Inspection Act of 1906 reflected the ideals of the Progressives. Progressives wanted to control the excesses of big businesses that abused their power. During the Progressive Era presidencies of Theodore Roosevelt, William Howard Taft, and Woodrow Wilson, efforts were made to break up some business trusts, and laws were passed to exert greater federal control over business practices.

9. **Parts A and B:** Progressive mayors like Tom Johnson in Cleveland took over utilities in an attempt to provide better service to their constituents. Progressive governors like Robert La Follette in Wisconsin worked to regulate railroads and other businesses. President Theodore Roosevelt intervened to mediate the 1902 coal strike. That same year, Roosevelt also directed the Justice Department to launch an antitrust suit against the Northern Securities Company, a large railroad corporation. Roosevelt would follow this up with more "trust-busting" suits. The Elkins Act of 1903 and Hepburn Act of 1906 strengthened the Interstate Commerce Commission. The Pure Food and Drug and Meat Inspection Acts of 1906 provided for federal regulation of food and medicines. The Sixteenth Amendment, adopted in 1913, allowed Congress to levy income taxes. In 1913, President Woodrow Wilson signed into law the Federal Reserve System, which created the modern American central banking system. He also promoted the Clayton Antitrust Act of 1914, which was intended to strengthen antitrust laws. The Federal Trade Commission Act of 1914 created a new federal agency to regulate business and trade practices.

Part C: In an effort to combat political corruption and inefficiency, many cities replaced elected mayors with appointed city managers. Other Progressive reforms on the local and state level included the initiative, which allowed citizens to propose laws, the referendum, which allowed citizens to vote on proposed laws, the recall, which allowed citizens to remove elected officials, and the direct primary, which allowed party members rather than bosses to pick political candidate. The Seventeenth Amendment, adopted in 1913, provided for the direct election of U.S. senators.

CHAPTER 21

United States and World War I (1914–1921)

IN THIS CHAPTER

Summary: The United States was officially neutral in the first two years of World War I. In 1916, one of President Woodrow Wilson's campaign slogans was "He kept us out of war." However, America was soon drawn into this conflict on the side of the British and French against the Germans (and the Austro-Hungarians). The 1915 sinking of the British passenger ship the *Lusitania* infuriated many Americans, as did the publication of the Zimmerman Note, in which Germany tried to entice Mexico to go to war against the United States. In January 1917, Germany announced a policy of unrestricted submarine warfare, and several American ships were sunk. These events caused President Wilson to call for a declaration of war against Germany. American entry into the war was a tremendous psychological lift for the British and the French. On the American home front, the government imposed unprecedented controls on the economy and on the spreading of news. The war ended with an armistice in November 1918. At the subsequent Paris Peace Conference, Wilson attempted to convince the Allies to accept his peace plan, called the "Fourteen Points." Britain and France were generally not enthusiastic about Wilson's proposals, but they did support the creation of a League of Nations. However, the League was opposed by many members of the U.S. Senate, and the United States never became a member of the League.

Keywords

American Expeditionary Force: American military force that served in France in 1917 and 1918 under the command of General John J. Pershing. Both women and blacks served in the American army during the war, although black units were segregated and usually had white officers.

War Industries Board: board that regulated American industry during World War I; it attempted to stimulate war production by allocating raw materials to factories that aided the war effort.

Committee on Public Information: agency created during the war whose mission was to spread pro-Allied propaganda through the press and through newsreels; newspapers were asked to print only articles that were helpful to the war effort.

Fourteen Points: plan for the postwar world that Woodrow Wilson brought to the Paris Peace Conference; Wilson's plan proposed open peace treaties, freedom of the seas, arms reductions, and a League of Nations. Britain and France were openly suspicious of these plans, but they supported the creation of a League of Nations.

League of Nations: world body proposed by Woodrow Wilson as part of his 14-point peace plan. The League was created but without the participation of Germany, Bolshevik or Communist Russia, or the United States (opposition in the Senate ensured that the treaty creating the League was never signed). As a result, the League remained a relatively ineffective body throughout its existence.

War and American Neutrality

Although few expected war in Europe in the summer of 1914, conditions were ripe for an explosion of violence. The growth of aggressive nationalisms set various countries against each other and threatened the stability of multinational states like the Austro-Hungarian Empire. Competition over colonial possessions and conflicts over spheres of influence in places like the Balkans further complicated relations between the great European powers. Most dangerous of all, the most important European states were grouped into two alliance systems. This meant that a conflict between two countries would likely entangle their allies and lead to a European-wide war. The assassination of the Austrian Archduke Franz Ferdinand by Serbian terrorists on June 28, 1914, sparked a diplomatic chain reaction that in August resulted in a war involving most of the European powers. Great Britain, France, and Russia made up the Triple Entente, or **Allied Powers**, and Germany and Austria-Hungary made up the **Central Powers**. Turkey later joined the Central Powers, and Italy later became one of the Allied Powers.

Great numbers of Americans had emotional ties to the warring powers. In 1914, over one-third of the American population were first- or second-generation immigrants. Many Americans felt an affinity for Great Britain because of long-standing cultural connections. Most German Americans sympathized with their former fatherland.

President Wilson deeply admired the British and their political system, and he distrusted German militarism. Despite this, he officially proclaimed American neutrality on August 4, 1914. Whatever their individual sympathies, Americans overwhelmingly wanted to stay out of the war. Americans also wanted to maintain their trade relationships with both warring parties. The war consumed enormous amounts of resources, and the United States became a desirable source of raw materials and manufactured goods. European war orders helped pull the United States out of a recession that had begun in 1913. In the competition for American trade, Great Britain and France had the advantage, because their navies controlled the Atlantic. The British used their naval power to prevent American ships from carrying goods to Germany. The Germans retaliated by using a new weapon, the submarine, to sink Allied ships carrying American goods to Britain and France.

Growing Ties to the Allies

Increasing economic ties drew the United States closer to the Allies. By 1916, almost all trade with the Central Powers had ceased, while trade with the Allies had gone up 400 percent. When the Allies ran out of cash in 1915, the Wilson administration allowed Wall Street banks to lend the Allies the money they needed to continue purchasing American products. This meant that many in the United States were literally banking upon an Allied victory. Some interest groups called on the federal government to prepare for war with the Central Powers. Beginning in late 1914, the **National Security League** launched an information campaign to convince Americans that war was necessary. By 1915, Congress began to take steps to strengthen the army and navy. Countering this, organizations promoting peace sprang up across the United States. Many of these were headed by women.

What decisively turned the American people against the Central Powers was German submarine warfare. Given that Allied warships dominated the surface of the sea, the only way that the Germans could strike at ships carrying supplies to Britain and France was with undersea or U-boats. Initially U-boats followed international law and warned ships before sinking them. Then the Allies armed their merchant ships with guns that could sink the unarmored submarines. From that point on, U-boats torpedoed ships without warning; this inevitably led to loss of life among the crew and passengers. Unsympathetic to the difficulties facing submariners, Americans found this form of warfare barbarous, and many began referring to Germans as the **"Hun."**

American opposition to the German submarine campaign came to a head with the sinking of the **_Lusitania_** on May 7, 1915. The _Lusitania_ was a passenger liner that carried munitions as well as people. The Germans had printed notices warning passengers against traveling on the ship. None of this mattered to American public opinion; Americans were horrified by the shocking casualties, with almost 1,200 men, women, and children dead, including 128 Americans. President Wilson lodged a strong diplomatic condemnation of the sinking, but he resisted calls for war.

In August, the Germans struck again at a passenger liner, sinking the _Arabic_. President Wilson strongly protested this attack. Anxious to placate the Americans, the German government announced that their submariners would not sink passenger ships without warning if they were allowed to search these vessels for military contraband.

Relations between the United States and Germany continued to deteriorate. On March 24, 1916, a U-boat sank the _Sussex_, a French ship carrying passengers and supplies. Among the injured were seven Americans. President Wilson sent an ultimatum to the Germans declaring that the United States would sever diplomatic relations if they persisted in attacking nonmilitary ships. The German government was anxious to avoid a possible American entrance into the war. The Germans backed down and subscribed to the **Sussex Pledge**, declaring that they would not sink any more ships without warning. This was a perilous diplomatic victory for Wilson; if the Germans resumed full submarine warfare, he would have few options other than war.

The Breakdown of German-American Relations

For a time it looked as if President Wilson had secured peace. In the election of 1916, he ran as the peace candidate, and the Democrats popularized the slogan "He kept us out of war." This enabled Wilson to win a narrow reelection victory over the reunited Republicans and their candidate, former New York governor and Supreme Court Justice Charles Evans Hughes.

Ironically, Wilson would take the country to war soon after his second inauguration. The war in Europe was a bloody stalemate. In an effort to achieve victory, the Germans announced **unrestricted submarine warfare** on January 31, 1917. From that point on, they would sink any ship carrying supplies to the Allies. Neutral flags would be no protection. The Germans realized that this would likely lead to war with the United States. They calculated that they could starve Britain and France into submission before the Americans could intervene effectively. Wilson ended diplomatic relations with Germany on February 3. He urged Congress to legalize the arming of merchant ships. As war loomed between Germany and the United States, Arthur Zimmermann, the German foreign minister, foolishly sent an inflammatory diplomatic note to the Mexican government. In the event of a German-American war, he encouraged the Mexicans to attack the United States and promised German support for a Mexican reconquest of the American Southwest. British intelligence intercepted the **Zimmermann Telegram** and passed it on to the Americans. Publication of the Zimmermann Telegram infuriated Americans and helped prepare them for war.

As they had promised, the Germans began sinking American ships headed to Britain and France. This violated the traditional American conviction that neutrals should have the freedom of the seas to sail wherever they wanted. On April 2, President Wilson made the short trip to Capitol Hill and in person asked Congress to declare war against Germany. The following day, Congress acceded to Wilson's request and voted for war. Though the overwhelming majority in Congress supported the war, six senators and 50 representatives voted against intervening in the conflict. Wilson had tried to preserve American neutrality, though by the time the United States entered the war it was effectively a supply depot for the Allies. The German submarine campaign proved unacceptable to many Americans; given the German conviction that it was essential for victory, war was hard to avoid. Once the United States became a combatant, Wilson looked forward to playing a major role in shaping the eventual peace.

America in the War

The war was not going well for the Allies in early 1917. Russia had been unable to effectively wage modern war. After a long series of defeats and growing domestic chaos, the tsar was overthrown in March 1917. The liberal government that succeeded the tsar hoped to stay in the war and sustain a relationship with the western Allies. The crumbling of Russian armies as soldiers deserted and went home put this in doubt. It appeared that the Germans might be able to transfer large numbers of troops from the Russian front to the western front. The British and French were strained to their limits. After a disastrous offensive that ended in bloody failure, large numbers of disgusted French soldiers mutinied, decrying callous leadership and calling for better treatment.

President Wilson decided to send American troops to fight in Europe. Their commander would be General John J. Pershing. The first contingent of the **American Expe-**

ditionary Force (AEF) arrived in France in June. Though numbering only 14,500 men, a paltry figure by World War I standards, this first detachment of the AEF helped revive Allied morale. In this handful of "doughboys" lay the promise of many more American soldiers to come.

One reason Pershing initially led so few men to France was the small size of the American army. To fight a modern total war, the American armed services would have to be massively increased. The most efficient way to do this was through a draft. Congress passed a Selective Service Act in May. All men between the ages of 21 and 30 could be drafted; the age limits were later extended to 17 and 46. Eventually 400,000 African Americans served in the military, though in segregated units with mostly white officers. 11,500 women wore uniform; most served as nurses and office staff.

The U.S. Navy was better prepared to take immediate action than the army. In the Atlantic, German U-boats were sinking enough ships to cause the Allies real hardship. The American navy took a leading role in organizing a **convoy system** in May 1917. Ships traveling in convoys protected by the navy were much more secure from submarine attack. Only two American troop transports were sunk during the war. A combination of convoys and better patrolling greatly reduced shipping losses. By the end of the war, the German submarines had failed in their strategic mission.

The American Expeditionary Force in France

Thanks to volunteers and the draft, the size of the American army increased to 4 million men by the end of the war; 2 million of those men were in France. They were needed. The Bolshevik Revolution in November 1917 ended Russian participation in the war. The Germans were able to transfer large numbers of soldiers to France. Beginning in March 1918, they launched a series of offensives that battered the Allied lines; by June the Germans were 50 miles from Paris.

American troops played an important role in stopping the Germans. At the **Battle of Chateau-Thierry**, Americans blunted the German drive on Paris. The AEF launched a successful offensive of its own in September and erased a German salient at St. Mihiel. In late September, the Americans began the **Meuse-Argonne Offensive**, which lasted into November. This massive offensive involved a million American soldiers, cut a vital German supply line, and helped convince the enemy that they had lost the war.

The Germans signed an armistice that ended the fighting on November 11, 1918. Around 115,000 Americans died in the war; roughly half of these lost their lives in battle, and the rest perished of disease, including the great flu epidemic of 1918. These losses were light compared to the 8 million European dead. Americans who returned home as heroes included Eddie Rickenbacker, the leading American flying ace, and Alvin York, who during the Meuse-Argonne fighting killed 25 German soldiers and captured 132 more.

The Home Front

For Americans the war was a conflict fought far away "over there." The government looked for ways to give Americans a sense of personal involvement in the war. Ordinary citizens could help finance the war by buying **Liberty Bonds**. Celebrities like the movie star Charlie Chaplin demonstrated their patriotism by promoting the purchase of these bonds.

In a vast expansion of regulatory power, the federal government took over much of the economy. The **Lever Food and Fuel Control Act**, passed in August 1917, gave the government the power to regulate the production and consumption of food. Herbert Hoover, who had become famous for feeding European refugees, headed the Food Administration. Here he worked to increase food production, and he encouraged Americans to conserve food with voluntary "Wheatless Mondays" and "Meatless Tuesdays." Daylight saving time was an innovation designed to give farmers more time to bring in their crops. A Fuel Administration was charged with conserving fuel supplies. It encouraged Americans to help with this through "Fuelless Mondays" and "Gasless Sundays." The **War Industries Board (WIB)** was given the power to support war production by allocating industrial resources. Under the leadership of the Wall Street tycoon Bernard Baruch, the WIB was beginning to harness the industrial might of the nation by the end of the war. The government also controlled the railroads, allowing it to set priorities in transportation.

This unprecedented control of the economy has led some historians to see World War I as the high-water mark of **Progressivism**. The wartime emergency allowed the government to exercise powers that would have been unthinkable a few years before. Thanks to the skill of administrators like Baruch and Hoover, much of this was accomplished with the cooperation of business and farm leaders. The mobilization of the economy during World War I would become a model for the later New Deal and government agencies during World War II. But such an aggrandizement of government power also raised concerns about freedom. This triumph of Progressivism would lead to a reaction against it.

Regulating Thought

Nothing did more to eventually discredit the extension of government power than efforts to regulate what people could think and express publically. In 1917, the government established the **Committee on Public Information (CPI)**. Headed by the journalist George Creel, the CPI was tasked with providing information about the war to the American people. Explanation soon became propaganda. In lectures, books, posters, and films, the Germans were depicted as bestial barbarians. Creel encouraged newspapers to censor stories that did not follow the government's line on the war. Liberty Leagues were organized across the United States; their members were tasked with spying on their neighbors and reporting any suspicious activity or disloyal talk to the authorities.

The war led to a heightened distrust of immigrants and "hyphenated-Americans," especially German Americans. The **National Security League** persuaded Congress to impose a literacy test on immigrants. In various communities anti-German hysteria led to the banning of German music and foods and the teaching of the German language in high schools. Individual German Americans were often subject to harassment or worse. In a notorious incident that took place in April 1918, a German-American man was mobbed and lynched in St. Louis; the victim had just enlisted in the navy.

The federal government added legal muscle to the suppression of dissent. The 1917 **Espionage Act** outlawed interfering with the draft and gave postal authorities the power to seize any publications sent through the mail that they considered treasonous. The 1918 Sedition Act went further and outlawed criticism of the government, the Constitution, or the armed forces. Thousands of Americans were charged with violating these laws, and over 1,000 were convicted. The Socialist leader Eugene Debs was sent to prison for speaking against the war. Robert Goldstein, a movie producer, was sentenced to three years in prison for making a movie about the American Revolution in which the British were portrayed as the villains; this previously unexceptionable view of the struggle for American independence was deemed seditions because the British were currently allies in the war. The government used these laws to break up radical organizations such as the IWW.

Social Change

The war opened up economic possibilities for African Americans. With millions of men entering the military and wartime demands on their capacity, northern industries needed workers. African Americans living in the South moved north in the **Great Migration**. During the war, 600,000 African Americans made this journey. The war also made it possible for women to step into jobs that had not been open to them before the war. Although most would leave these positions once the soldiers began returning home, their efforts during the war would help make the case for women's suffrage.

Wilson and the Peace

President Wilson was determined to play a leading role in shaping the new postwar international order. While the war was still in progress, he published his **Fourteen Points**, an idealistic program to lay the foundations for a peaceful world, which included open diplomacy (no more secret military treaties), freedom of the seas, national self-determination, and a League of Nations. Defying presidential precedent, Wilson sailed to France to take part in the Paris Peace Conference, which began on January 12, 1919. The peacemaking would be driven by the leaders of the "Big Four" allies—Britain, France, Italy, and the United States. While the ordinary people of Europe greeted Wilson as a hero for his inspiring vision of a better future, the other allied leaders were less impressed by his ideas and were determined to press their national interests. Wilson wanted a peace based on the Fourteen Points, but the French in particular were set on punishing Germany.

During the hard negotiating that took place in Paris, Wilson had to make many concessions. Harsh terms were imposed on Germany, which had to accept guilt for starting the war and pay reparations to France and Britain. Germany also lost its colonies, 10 percent of its territory, and most of its military. German diplomats were not allowed to discuss the terms of the Treaty of Versailles; they had to sign the document or face an Allied invasion. German bitterness over this treatment planted the seeds of World War II. Though disappointed by aspects of the Treaty of Versailles, Wilson believed that its establishment of a **League of Nations** would make it possible to rectify the treaty's errors in the future.

Americans and the Middle East

Aside from Theodore Roosevelt's diplomatic involvement in the 1905–1906 Moroccan crisis, the United States had shown little interest in the Middle East. Great Power rivalries during and after World War I focused American attention on the region.

Prior to the war, much of the Middle East was controlled by Turkey, or the Ottoman Empire. The Turkish empire had been declining for over a century. The leaders of the empire hoped that they could arrest this decline by entering the war on the side of the Central Powers. This proved a grave mistake. Defeat in the war brought on the final collapse of the Ottoman Empire. Since the late nineteenth century, Jews inspired by the Zionist movement had been settling in Ottoman-ruled Palestine. In 1917, in an effort to weaken the Turks, the British issued the Balfour Declaration, which expressed support for an independent Jewish state in Mandatory Palestine. President Wilson also favored the creation of a Jewish state. Many American Jews provided financial assistance to the Zionists.

As the war turned against them, the Turkish authorities grew suspicious of the Armenian minority who lived within the empire. In 1915, the Turks launched a bloody progrom against the Christian Armenians, massacring thousands and killing many more by starvation and ill-treatment. American missionaries and diplomats helped get word of these atrocities to the outside world. In 1916 and 1917, thousands of Americans rallied to protest the slaughter of the Armenians and to support Armenian relief organizations. (To this day, the Turkish government refuses to acknowledge that the Armenian massacres took place.)

President Wilson made the breakup of the Ottoman Empire American policy. (He also wanted to dismantle the German and Austro-Hungarian empires.) He called for the peoples of all the territories ruled by the Central Powers to work toward "autonomous political development." At the Paris Peace Conference, the United States was authorized to form the **King-Crane Commission** to study the political aspirations of the people living in the Middle East.

What the King-Crane Commission found was that the Middle Easterners wanted to be free from foreign control. They deeply distrusted the intentions of the British and French who had defeated the Turks. If any of the Allies were to be given a mandate to control territory in the Middle East, the people there preferred it to be the Americans, who they believed had no long-term interests in the region. The findings of the King-Crane Commission ran counter to the imperial ambitions of Britain and France. These Allied powers saw to it that the commission's report was buried. The British and French divided up most of the Middle East. The British received mandates in Palestine, Transjordan, and Iraq, and the French accepted mandates in Lebanon and Syria. By the early 1920s, only Saudi Arabia was independent.

Woodrow Wilson's Defeat

According to the Constitution, all treaties must be ratified by a two-thirds vote of the Senate. President Wilson did not appoint a senator to the delegation that he brought with him to Paris. Compounding this error, he failed to bring with him a leading Republican politician, despite the fact that the Republicans had won control of both houses of Congress in 1918. Having given the Republicans no reason to rally to his support, Wilson faced predictable opposition to the Treaty of Versailles when he returned to the United States. The most controversial element of the treaty was the League of Nations; most Republican and some Democratic senators worried that the League's collective security provisions threatened to embroil the United States in more conflicts. Twelve senators declared themselves **"irreconcilables"** and refused outright to vote for the treaty and the League. Most of the Republicans followed the lead of Henry Cabot Lodge, the chairman of the Senate Foreign Relations Committee. Lodge wanted to incorporate a series of reservations about the League into the American ratification of the treaty. As a result of this, his supporters were known as **"reservationists."** Lodge wanted to ensure that the League of Nations would not invalidate the Monroe Doctrine; he also wanted assurance that only Congress would authorize American military actions on behalf of the League.

Lodge was willing to guarantee the Senate's ratification of the treaty with his reservations. Important European leaders made it clear that they preferred the passage of the treaty with reservations to the failure of the treaty in the Senate. Despite this, Woodrow Wilson refused to compromise. The president had invested too much of himself into the struggle for the League to concede anything to his critics. Wilson's health had been failing for some time. Disregarding this, in September 1919 he set off on a strenuous speaking tour, hoping to make his case about the League to the American people. On October 2, Wilson suffered an incapacitating stroke. The president eventually made a partial recovery, but the stroke left him less willing to compromise on anything, including the League. Wilson ordered loyal Democratic senators to vote against the League with reservations. Given the equally firm positions of the reservationists and the irreconcilables, the Treaty of Versailles and the League of Nations were rejected by the Senate in successive votes in 1919 and 1920. The United States never joined the League of Nations. This gravely weakened the League, which proved ineffectual in preventing a second world war. The rejection of the League did not mean an American turn to isolationism, and the United States would play an important role in world affairs during the 1920s.

In 1921, President Wilson left office a physically broken man. That year his successor, Warren G. Harding, officially ended America's participation in World War I by signing separate peace treaties with the former member countries of the Central Powers.

Chapter Review

Rapid Review

To achieve the perfect 5, you should be able to explain the following:

- World War I greatly impacted the American mind-set and America's role in world affairs; this was the first time that America became directly involved in affairs taking place on the European continent.
- Many Americans expressed support for the Allied Powers from the beginning of the war; German U-boat attacks solidified American support for Britain and France.
- The sinking of the *Lusitania* and the Zimmermann Telegram did much to intensify American anger against Germany.
- Germany's decision to utilize unrestricted submarine warfare caused President Wilson to call for war in 1917; Wilson claimed that this policy violated America's rights as a neutral power.
- The American Expeditionary Force did much to aid the Allied war effort, both militarily and psychologically.
- The federal government did much to mobilize the American population at home for the war effort; Liberty Bonds were sold, voluntary rationing took place, and propaganda was used to encourage Americans to oppose the "Hun" however possible.
- Many blacks moved to northern cities to work in factories during World War I; this migration would continue through the 1920s.
- Woodrow Wilson's Fourteen Points met with opposition from French and English leaders at the Paris Peace Conference; many of them had to be abandoned to secure the creation of the League of Nations.
- The Treaty of Versailles was opposed by U.S. senators who believed that it compromised American interests and the powers of Congress. As a result, the treaty was never ratified by the United States and the United States never entered the League of Nations.

Time Line

1914: Outbreak of World War I in Europe
  Woodrow Wilson officially proclaims American neutrality in World War I
  National Security League founded to prepare America for war

1915: Sinking of the *Lusitania* by German U-boat

1916: Germany torpedoes *Sussex*, then promises to warn merchants ships if they are to be attacked
  Woodrow Wilson reelected with campaign slogan of "He kept us out of war"

1917: Zimmermann Telegram
  Germany declares unrestricted submarine warfare
  United States enters World War I, stating that U.S. rights as a neutral had been violated
  Russian Revolution; Russian-German peace talks
  Conscription begins in United States
  War Industries Board formed to create a war economy
  Espionage Act passed
  American Expeditionary Force lands in France

1918: Military success by American Expeditionary Force at Chateau-Thierry
  Sedition Act passed; free speech limited (illegal to criticize government or American military forces)
  Wilson announces the Fourteen Points
  Armistice ends World War I (November 11)

1919: Paris Peace Conference creates Treaty of Versailles
  Race riots in Chicago
  Wilson suffers stroke during speaking tour promoting Treaty of Versailles
  Senate rejects Treaty of Versailles; United States does not join the League of Nations

› Review Questions

Fact Check

Check your knowledge of the historical period covered in this chapter.

1. All of the following events prepared America for war against Germany *except*
   A. the Sussex Pledge.
   B. German policy concerning use of U-boats in 1917.
   C. the sinking of the *Lusitania*.
   D. the Zimmermann Telegram.

2. The French were opposed to many of Wilson's Fourteen Points because
   A. they were fundamentally opposed to the creation of a world body such as the League of Nations.
   B. they were angry that Wilson had insisted that the Germans not take part in the creation of the treaty.
   C. French diplomats had little respect for Wilson and his American counterparts.
   D. the Fourteen Points disagreed fundamentally with what the French felt should be contained in the Treaty of Versailles.

3. After America declared war in 1917
   A. ration cards were issued to all families.
   B. camps were set up to detain "troublesome" Americans of German background.
   C. drills took place in American cities to prepare Americans for a possible attack.
   D. movie stars and other celebrities helped sell Liberty Bonds to the American public.

4. Some critics maintained that the United States had no right to be outraged over the sinking of the *Lusitania* because
   A. the *Lusitania* was carrying contraband, which meant that it could legally be sunk.
   B. the Germans had sunk passenger ships before.
   C. the Germans had placed advertisements in American newspapers warning Americans not to travel on the *Lusitania.*
   D. all of the above.

5. Many senators were opposed to American entry into the League of Nations because
   A. they feared that the United States would end up financing the organization.
   B. they feared the U.S. Army would be sent into action on "League of Nations business" without congressional authorization.
   C. American opinion polls demonstrated that the American public was almost unanimously opposed to American entry into the League.
   D. they feared that the Germans and Russians would dominate the League.

Multiple-Choice Questions

Here are multiple-choice questions like the ones on the AP U.S. History exam.

Questions 6–8 refer to the quotation below.

You may call me selfish if you will, conservative or reactionary, or use any other harsh adjective you see fit to apply, but an American I was born, an American I have remained all my life. I can never be anything else but an American, and I must think of the United States first, and when I think of the United States first in an arrangement like this I am thinking of what is best for the world, for if the United States fails, the best hopes of mankind fail with it.

I have never had but one allegiance—I cannot divide it now. I have loved but one flag and I cannot share that devotion and give affection to the mongrel banner invented for a league. Internationalism, illustrated by the Bolshevik and by the men to whom all countries are alike provided they can make money out of them, is to me repulsive.

—Senator Henry Cabot Lodge, Speech on the League of Nations, August 12, 1919

6. Which of the following was a significant result of World War I?
   A. An increase in the international influence of the United States
   B. A decrease in the international influence of the United States
   C. The conquest of new territories for the American empire
   D. The loss of American overseas possessions

7. Supporters of the League of Nations saw it as a means to
   A. rebuild territories devastated by the war.
   B. assist new nations released from colonial domination.
   C. provide stability and security to the postwar world.
   D. rebuild the prewar alliance systems.

8. Senator Lodge and his supporters opposed the League of Nations because they believed that the League would
   A. encourage the spread of Bolshevism from the Soviet Union.
   B. reduce American sovereignty.
   C. reduce the political influence of President Woodrow Wilson.
   D. prevent Americans from trading in China.

Short-Answer Question

The short-answer question below is similar to the ones you'll encounter on the AP U.S. History exam.

9. Answer Parts A, B, and C.
   A. Briefly explain ONE example of the steps the American government took to mobilize the American people during World War I.
   B. Briefly explain a SECOND example of the steps the American government took to mobilize the American people during World War I.
   C. Briefly explain ONE example of a military contribution that the United States made to Allied victory in World War I.

❯ Answers and Explanations

1. **A.** In the Sussex Pledge, the Germans actually promised not to sink American merchant ships without warning. All of the other choices deeply angered many in America.

2. **D.** While Wilson saw the treaty as a chance to create a democratic world free of old diplomatic entanglements, the French saw it as an opportunity to punish the Germans, as much of the fighting of the war had taken place on French territory.

3. **D.** Charlie Chaplin and others appeared at rallies and urged Americans to buy Liberty Bonds. Rationing during World War I was voluntary.

4. **D.** Many maintain that the advertisements the Germans put in American newspapers were strong enough warnings that the ship was going to be sunk.

5. **B.** A major fear was that U.S. entry into the League would cause Congress to lose its right to declare war and approve American military actions. Germany and the Soviet Union were not initially members of the League of Nations.

6. **A.** A significant result of World War I was an increase in the international influence of the United States. Unlike its other victorious allies, the United States emerged from the war economically stronger. Though only involved in the fighting for a brief time, the United States created a formidable military that played an important role in defeating Germany. Many across the world expected the United States to exert leadership in the postwar world.

7. **C.** Supporters of the League of Nations saw it as a means to provide stability and security to the postwar world. President Woodrow Wilson believed that the League would be able to rectify any mistakes or injustices incorporated in the Treaty of Versailles. Article X of the League Covenant provided for a collective security pact in which League members would unite against any state that launched a war against one of them. Wilson saw this as an essential guarantee for world peace.

8. **B.** Senator Lodge and his supporters opposed the League of Nations because they believed the League would reduce American sovereignty. They worried that the League would nullify such traditional centerpieces of American foreign policy as the Monroe Doctrine. They were especially concerned that the collective security provisions of the League would take away the constitutional right of Congress to declare war.

9. **Parts A and B:** The American government helped finance the war by encouraging citizens to purchase Liberty Bonds. The Lever Food and Fuel Control Act of 1917 gave the govern-

ment regulatory authority over the production and consumption of food and fuel. Herbert Hoover headed the Food Administration, which promoted "Wheatless Mondays" and "Meatless Tuesdays." A Fuel Administration instituted similar attempts at rationing coal and gasoline. The government took control of the nation's railroads during the war. The War Industries Board, headed by Wall Street financier Bernard Baruch, controlled the allocation of raw materials and set production goals in industry. The government also moved to control the flow of ideas. Newspaperman George Creel headed the Committee on Public Information (CPI), which disseminated information about the war and worked to build American support for the war effort. The CPI employed thousands of "Four Minute Men," who gave brief pro-war addresses while reels were being changed in movie theaters. The Espionage Act of 1917 prohibited interference with military recruitment or operations. The 1919 Supreme Court decision *Schenck v. United States* upheld the constitutionality of the Espionage Act. The Sedition Act of 1918 outlawed criticisms of the government, the military, and the Constitution. Hundreds of people were charged with and convicted of violations of the Espionage Act and the Sedition Act.

Part C: The U.S. Navy played an important role in defeating the German submarine campaign. In addition to providing reinforcements to the British Navy, the American began organizing a convoy system that offered better protection to merchant ships. The U.S. Navy also mined the routes the German submarines followed when leaving their home ports. Losses from submarine attacks dropped dramatically. The U.S. Army organized the American Expeditionary Force (AEF) of American troops that fought in France. General John J. Pershing was appointed the commander of the AEF. He and the first soldiers of the AEF landed in France in June 1917. The presence of the American troops bolstered Allied morale and provided important reinforcements at a time when the Allied armies were worn down from years of fighting. The AEF was eventually built up to a force of 2 million men. In June and July 1918, American troops help stop German offensives at the Battles of Belleau Wood and Chateau-Thierry. American forces erased the German salient at Saint-Mihiel in September. One million American soldiers participated in the Meuse-Argonne Offensive, which lasted from September 26 to November 11, 1918. This attack cut crucial German supply lines. American forces played a vital role in defeating Imperial Germany on the Western Front.

CHAPTER 22

Beginning of Modern America: The 1920s

IN THIS CHAPTER

Summary: During the 1920s, Americans created a consumer culture in which automobiles, home appliances, and other goods were purchased at an unprecedented rate. Advertising helped to fuel this desire to purchase, and the popularity of radio and motion pictures helped to create a more uniform national culture. However, many small-town and rural Americans never felt totally comfortable with the values of the consumer-oriented, more urban "modern" America that they saw threatening their way of life. The conflict between urban and small-town American values was manifested in numerous ways: many in small-town America supported the Prohibition amendment banning alcohol, while many in America's cities tried to get around it. Many in small-town America feared immigration, while many American cities contained immigrant enclaves. Many in small-town America still opposed the teaching of evolution, while many urban newspapers mocked their views. The flapper and a more relaxed sense of morality were symbols of the Jazz Age; generally, these symbols were harder to find in small-town America. All Americans did rally around the two heroes of the age: aviator Charles Lindbergh and home run hitter Babe Ruth.

Keywords

KEY IDEA

Teapot Dome Scandal: major scandal in the administration of President Warren Harding; Secretary of the Interior Albert Fall had two oil deposits put under the jurisdiction of the Department of the Interior and leased them to private companies in return for large sums of money.

Red Scare: after World War I, the fear of the spread of communism in the United States.

Palmer Raids: as part of the Red Scare, in these 1919 to 1920 raids thousands of Americans not born in the United States were arrested, and hundreds were sent back to their countries of origin. Today many view the raids as a gross violation of the constitutional rights of American citizens.

National Origins Act (1924): anti-immigration federal legislation that took the number of immigrants from each country in 1890 and stated that immigration from those countries could now be no more than 2 percent of that. In addition, immigration from Asia was halted. The act also severely limited further immigration from eastern and southern Europe.

Scopes Trial (1925): trial of teacher John Scopes of Dayton, Tennessee, for the teaching of evolution. During this trial, lawyers Clarence Darrow and William Jennings Bryan squared off on the teachings of Darwin versus the teachings of the Bible.

Jazz Age: image of the 1920s that emphasized the more relaxed social attitudes of the decade; F. Scott Fitzgerald's *The Great Gatsby* is seen by many as the novel that best depicts this view.

Flapper: "new woman" of the 1920s, who was pictured as having bobbed hair, a shorter skirt, makeup, a cigarette in her hand, and somewhat liberated sexual attitudes. Flappers would have been somewhat hard to find in small-town and rural America.

"Lost Generation": group of post–World War I writers who in their works expressed deep dissatisfaction with mainstream American culture. *A Farewell to Arms* by Ernest Hemingway is a novel that is representative of the works of these writers.

Harlem Renaissance: 1920s black literary and cultural movement that produced many works depicting the role of blacks in contemporary American society; Zora Neale Hurston and Langston Hughes were key members of this movement.

The Prosperous Twenties

Following the end of World War I, the American economy experienced some difficulties as it transitioned back from a wartime to a peacetime footing. It suffered a major downturn in 1920–1921. Then the economy took off. The 1920s was one of the most prosperous decades in American history. Not everyone shared equally in this prosperity. Many farmers did not do as well as some urban dwellers. The wealthy benefited more than the working class. Nevertheless, a remarkably broad swathe of Americans saw their living conditions improve. A 1924 study showed that industrial workers had almost doubled their 1914 wages. Good times reduced industrial strife, and the number of strikes declined. Though businessmen still generally opposed unions, many were increasingly open to heading off labor organization by providing their workers better pay and benefits.

Business, which had been demonized in the Progressive Era, was celebrated in the 1920s. American industry became an increasingly dominant force in the world economy. At the forefront of this phenomenon was the American automobile industry. Competition left Ford, General Motors, and Chrysler dominating the car-making business; between them, these three corporations controlled 85 percent of the American market. Improved assembly line techniques made affordable cars readily available. In 1925, a Ford **Model T** was rolling off the factory floor every 24 seconds.

American industrialists had embraced Frederick W. Taylor's program of "scientific management." Efficiencies in production were bringing down the costs of consumer goods. This made it possible for growing numbers of Americans to purchase radios, refrigerators, vacuum cleaners, and a range of new electric appliances. What had once been luxuries were now readily available on the "installment plan," a marketing innovation that enabled consumers to buy goods over the course of 36 to 48 monthly payments. By 1928, 65 percent of all cars were being bought this way. Eventually this marketing reliance on credit would cause problems, but these were difficult to anticipate in the boom years of the twenties.

This decade saw the exuberant dawning of the **advertising age**. The inventive promoters of Madison Avenue worked to convince consumers that the "good life" was only possible with a particular model of car or refrigerator. Advertising became a common cultural bond for all Americans, whether they lived in the city or the country. Everyone was being sold the same commercial dreams in print and radio ads.

The Republican "New Era"

The Republicans dominated the national government during the 1920s, controlling both houses of Congress and the presidency. Even the Supreme Court was headed by a Republican, Chief Justice William Howard Taft, who had served as president from 1909–1913. The Republicans of the "New Era" believed in limited government and supported free enterprise. In their hands the regulatory state became an exercise in government and business partnership. This was best exemplified by the creative statesmanship of Herbert Hoover, who as secretary of commerce under Presidents Warren G. Harding and Calvin Coolidge, helped organize a national radio system and encouraged industries to standardize parts and procedures.

Warren G. Harding as President

Warren G. Harding was not a frontrunner for the Republican presidential nomination in 1920. A U.S. senator from Ohio, he ran a clever dark horse campaign in which he attempted to make himself the second choice of most convention delegates. When the leading candidates deadlocked, he became an easy compromise choice as the nominee.

The Democrats nominated Governor James Cox as their presidential candidate. Cox's young running mate was Franklin D. Roosevelt, Woodrow Wilson's assistant secretary of the navy. Cox had to defend the Wilson administration and supported American entry into the League of Nations. Harding realized that Americans were tired of the stress and tumult associated with the war and Wilson. He waged an old-fashioned front-porch electoral campaign that evoked memories of the days of William McKinley. He promoted a traditional Republican platform of higher tariffs and lower taxes. Above all, Harding called for a "return to normalcy," a sentiment that resonated with millions of voters. On the first national election in which women could cast ballots, Harding won in a landslide, getting 61 percent of the popular vote. Harding saw his victory as a repudiation of Wilsonian idealism and the "social experiments" of Progressivism.

Harding's first order of business upon taking office was addressing the economy. He encouraged Congress to authorize a Bureau of the Budget to better manage the government's revenues and expenditures; he named Charles Dawes as the bureau's first head. Harding cut federal spending and persuaded Congress to cut taxes. Within a year, the

United States had recovered from the postwar depression. Unemployment fell from 12 percent in 1921 to a little over 3 percent for most of the decade. The economic boom economy of the twenties had been launched.

Harding wanted to surround himself with the "best minds" that he could find for his cabinet. Some of his cabinet appointees proved particularly distinguished. Former Supreme Court Justice and presidential candidate Charles Evans Hughes served as secretary of state. Hughes played a leading role in the 1921 **Washington Conference,** which was intended to head off a naval arms race. The United States invited diplomatic and military representatives from Great Britain, France, Japan, Italy, the Netherlands, Belgium, Portugal, and China to Washington. Here Hughes proposed the scrapping of many tons of battleships and a 10-year freeze on further construction of these expensive warships. The Five Power Agreement among the United States, Great Britain, Japan, France, and Italy acceded to this and set ratios for relative sizes of their navies. All the invited powers agreed to recognize Chinese sovereignty and uphold the Open Door in China. In the early 1920s, these agreements seemed to herald a period of peace and international cooperation. In the longer term, they failed to prevent the outbreak of World War II. Another notable American diplomatic success was the 1924 Dawes Plan. Charles Dawes persuaded the Allies to reduce the amount of German reparations. American banks provided loans to the Germans, which facilitated their reparations payments. This in turn gave the Allies funds to repay some of their war debts to the United States. This injection of American capital into the European economy helped spur an economic recovery there in the second half of the 1920s.

Harding chose Andrew Mellon as his secretary of the treasury. Mellon would serve in this position all through the rest of the 1920s. Mellon had headed the aluminum company Alcoa and was one of the richest men in America. Mellon believed in traditional Republican economics; he argued that limiting the size of government and cutting taxes would free up money for investment in business, which would then lead to more jobs. Over the course of the decade, Mellon worked to reduce tax rates. The immediate beneficiaries of his policies were the rich and corporations that paid the highest taxes. During the prosperous 1920s, Mellon's financial policies were regarded as successful, and he was hailed as a great secretary of the treasury.

Mellon also wanted to protect American industries and jobs with high tariffs. The 1922 **Fordney-McCumber Tariff** raised tariff rates on manufactured goods. Agricultural interests were still formidable in Congress, and a farm bloc composed of both Democrats and Republicans could not be ignored. To reconcile the farmers to the new tariff, rates also went up on imported agricultural products. The business-friendly Harding administration did not see a need to promote organized labor. The twenties were a period of doldrums for unions. The courts generally ruled in favor of employers and even sometimes ruled in favor of child labor.

President Harding struck some blows for civil liberties and civil rights. He freed Eugene Debs and other political dissidents imprisoned during World War I by the Wilson administration for violations of the Espionage and Sedition Acts. In October 1921, Harding made an unprecedented trip to Birmingham, Alabama, and gave a speech calling for political equality between the races.

Scandal and the Ruin of Harding's Reputation

Along with the "best minds," Harding also appointed to office men who betrayed his trust. Some of them were men that he had met during his rise in Ohio politics. Harding himself was not involved in their wrongdoing. The discovery of their corruption probably contributed to his death.

One of the worst of these malefactors was Charles Forbes, who as head of the Veterans' Bureau misappropriated $250 million. Harding fired Forbes when he learned what he had done, but he let him flee abroad for a time, before he returned home to a prison sentence. Attorney General Harry Daugherty, Harding's former campaign manager, was accused of taking bribes from bootleggers and others wanting government favors; a hung jury saved him from conviction and imprisonment.

The **Teapot Dome Scandal** became the best known malfeasance of the Harding administration. Prior to being appointed Harding's secretary of the interior, Albert Fall had been a well-regarded U.S. senator from New Mexico. Once in office, Fall experienced financial difficulties; in exchange for bribes, he leased the federal oil reserve in Teapot Dome, Wyoming, and other oil lands to private companies. Fall would become the first cabinet secretary to be convicted of a felony and was ordered to prison in 1929.

Harding was just beginning to become aware of the corruption in his administration in 1923. This knowledge greatly distressed him, and he was pondering what steps to take. He already suffered from bad health, and this stress aggravated his condition. On August 2, 1923, Harding died while on a political trip through the western states.

President Calvin Coolidge

Harding was succeeded by Vice President Calvin Coolidge. The new president had grown up in New England and was a man of simple tastes. He had come to national prominence in 1919, when as governor of Massachusetts he had quelled a strike by Boston policemen, declaring, "There can be no right to strike against the public safety by anybody, anywhere, anytime." At the time Coolidge assumed the presidency, little was known of the scandals afflicting the administration. Once they became public, Coolidge cleaned up the mess so thoroughly and efficiently that in 1924 he easily won the presidential election.

Coolidge was a more articulate advocate of limited government than Harding. He was an eloquent defender of free enterprise and became famous for the phrase "the business of the United States is business." As president, Coolidge worked with Treasury Secretary Mellon to reduce federal spending, the national debt, and taxes.

The Coolidge years were peaceful and prosperous. It ran against Coolidge's philosophy of government to launch major government programs or initiatives. During World War I, the federal government had built a dam on the Tennessee River at Muscle Shoals, Alabama; Coolidge proposed privatizing this public facility, but Congress rejected his plan. Coolidge and Mellon did convince Congress to pass the Revenue Act of 1926, which further reduced taxes. The president was willing to take unpopular stands in defense of his principles. Coolidge vetoed a bill providing a bonus to World War I veterans because he believed that it would cost too much; Congress overrode his veto.

The Election of 1928

Coolidge was popular enough to have run for another term as president. He chose not to and distributed a statement to the press saying, "I do not choose to run." This left the Republican field clear for Herbert Hoover. The Republican nominee was the embodiment of his party's economic philosophy. Orphaned and rendered penniless at an early age, Hoover worked his way through Stanford University and then made a fortune as a mining engineer. During World War I, he acquired an international reputation as an effective philanthropist for organizing relief for starving European civilians. He ran the Food Administration for President Wilson and was present at the peacemaking in Paris. He was a remarkably dynamic secretary of commerce for Harding and Coolidge, pioneering new levels of government cooperation with private industry. During the 1928 election campaign, Hoover defended the Republican economic record and extolled "American individualism."

During the 1920s, the Democrats had been divided between Northern urban politicians and Southerners, often heavily influenced by the Ku Klux Klan. In 1928, the Northerners were able to nominate New York Governor Al Smith. A product of New York City's Tammany Hall machine, Smith seemed to embody the spirit of America's bustling metropolis. This did not endear him to the many Americans who distrusted urban values. For these rural voters, his opposition to Prohibition and his Roman Catholicism disqualified him for the presidency. As a result, Smith lost to Hoover in a landslide; the popular vote margin was almost 60 to 40 percent, and Smith won only eight states in New England and the Deep South.

The City Versus the Country in the 1920s

Though Smith was heavily defeated in 1928, he did carry the 12 largest cities in the country. The rural and urban divide that brought him electoral disaster reflected a larger cultural divide of the 1920s. According to the Census, the United States became a predominantly urban country at the beginning of the decade. This did not mean that most Americans lived in big cities, but the momentum was moving in that direction. More important, with the rise of the modern mass media, urban values were being disseminated across the country. Many rural and small-town Americans resented this influx of unfamiliar and unpalatable manners and mores.

Race Relations

One manifestation of a resistance to social and cultural change came in race relations. During the war years, many African Americans had moved to the North looking for work; they took jobs in urban factories. Once the war ended, these African Americans were seen as an economic threat by many returning soldiers who feared that they would prevent them from returning to their prewar positions. Other Northern workers did not want to compete for jobs with these migrants. In 1919 bloody race riots erupted in Washington, D.C.; Tulsa, Oklahoma; Omaha, Nebraska; and other cities. In Chicago, the rioting went on for two weeks. Thousands of African Americans saw their homes go up in flames; 15 whites and 23 African Americans were killed.

Southern repression of African Americans intensified, perhaps in reaction to the return home of black veterans. In 1919, 70 African Americans were lynched. Against this backdrop of renewed racial violence, Marcus Garvey started the **Universal Negro Improvement Association** in 1920. Garvey wanted to lead African Americans back to Africa, where he would found a new state. Eventually a half million people joined his association. Garvey's dream eventually fell apart. He was convicted of mail fraud in 1925. Few African Americans were actually prepared to embrace racial separatism, and Garvey's projected migration to Africa never took place. Garvey himself was deported to Jamaica in 1927.

In part inspired by the cinematic heroics of *The Birth of a Nation*, in part the beneficiary of modern marketing techniques, the **Ku Klux Klan** became a political and cultural phenomenon in the early 1920s; by 1925, it boasted a membership of over 5 million. This modern Klan was not an exclusively Southern organization. It gained recruits from across the country and was especially popular in small-town America. The Klan briefly controlled the politics of Indiana in the mid-1920s. This latter-day Klan opposed any concessions to African Americans, but it was equally driven by an animus against immigrants and Catholics, who were associated with the big cities. For a time, the Klan was a political force to be reckoned with.

The decline of the Klan was almost as rapid as its rise. In the Hoosier state, the head of the Indiana Klan was convicted of rape and second-degree murder. Other Klan leaders were credibly accused of sexual and financial corruption. Amidst this atmosphere of scandal, support for the Klan ebbed away. The prejudices it had championed remained.

Immigration and the Red Scare

Since the 1886 Haymarket Square bombing, many Americans had associated immigrants with political radicalism. Following the Bolshevik Revolution that imposed communism on Russia, there were concerns that agitators would try to import communism to the United States. These fears were intensified by a series of anonymous terrorist bombings in 1919. These outrages convinced many people that a communist revolution was coming and led to the **Red Scare**.

One of the bombs went off at the house of Woodrow Wilson's attorney general, A. Mitchell Palmer, and destroyed his front porch. Palmer responded by launching a roundup of suspected radicals. The **Palmer Raids** led to the arrest of thousands of people, most of them immigrants. In what was still a wartime atmosphere, little attention was paid to the civil rights of the people Palmer incarcerated. Hundreds of the accused were summarily deported. Palmer genuinely believed that the nation was threatened by a communist conspiracy. He also hoped his vigorous actions would further his political career. The Red Scare began to recede after Palmer erroneously predicted a radical uprising on May 1, 1920. When a bombing on Wall Street killed 33 people and wounded over 200 in September, most Americans attributed the atrocity to deranged zealots rather than a widespread communist plot. The Red Scare was over.

Suspicions about foreigners and radicals remained. This played a part in the 1921 trial of Sacco and Vanzetti, two immigrant Italian anarchists who were convicted of robbing a shoe factory and murdering two employees. Although some observers questioned the fairness of their trial, the men were executed in 1927.

Following the war, the massive flow of immigrants into the United States resumed. Many Americans worried that this influx would lower wages. The Red Scare had left a sense that immigrants could bring with them subversive and dangerous political ideas. Eugenicists like Madison Grant published works that warned of the dangers of Americans mixing with "lesser breeds." Small-town Americans continued to associate immigrants with the urban culture that threatened their values. The result of all this was legislation restricting immigration.

In 1921, Congress passed the **Emergency Quota Act,** which restricted new immigration to 3 percent of the population of a given nationality living in the United States in 1910. The effect of these quotas was to reduce the number of immigrants coming from Southern and Eastern Europe. In 1922, this cut the number of immigrants by 60 percent. The **National Origins Act** of 1924 imposed even stricter limits on immigration. This law set the immigration quota for every nationality at 2 percent of the population from that country living in the United States in 1890. A cap of 150,000 was set on all immigrants coming from outside the Americas. Immigration from Asia was prohibited. This act achieved the goal of the lawmakers to end the flow of immigrants from places like Italy, the Balkans, Poland, and Russia. The National Origins Act created a pause in mass immigration to the United States that would last for over forty years.

Prohibition

Another major flashpoint in the confrontation between rural and urban America was Prohibition. Rural America largely supported Prohibition. In 1924 it was estimated that 95 percent of the people in Kansas were respecting Prohibition, as opposed to only 5 percent in New York State. Many rural Americans associated liquor consumption with the big cities, with their immigrants, political machines, and gangsters. They saw alcohol as the "instrument of the devil," and the cities were the devil's playground. Prohibition certainly did unleash monsters in urban America. The high-minded attempt to ban alcohol consumption was a gift to organized crime.

When the government passed Prohibition in 1919, it did very little to ensure enforcement of the law. In cities like New York where few people supported full compliance with the law, efforts to enforce Prohibition failed. Illegal bars known as **speakeasies** proliferated in the cities. Often speakeasies were covertly protected by the local authorities, who would collect a cut of the profits. Sometimes speakeasies would sell "bathtub gin," liquor so bad it tasted like what an enterprising individual might distill in a bathroom. A demand for better liquor was met by bootleggers, criminals who organized the production and distribution of alcohol. This became a very big and profitable business, and bootleggers like Al Capone in Chicago became notorious. Capone controlled hundreds of gunmen and fought bloody turf wars with other gangsters. This street warfare culminated with the St. Valentine's Day Massacre in 1929, when some of Capone's men executed rival gangsters in a garage.

Religion and the Theory of Evolution

Rural and urban sensibilities also clashed over religion and the theory of evolution. Many fundamentalist Christians rejected Darwinian evolution, which contradicted the Bible. Other Christians worried about the implications of the theory of evolution for the traditional understanding of human beings as a special creation of God. These predominantly small-town Americans found a leader in William Jennings Bryan, who three times had been the Democratic presidential candidate. Bryan helped Tennessee legislators pass a law outlawing the teaching of evolution in the state's schools. In 1925, the American Civil Liberties Union (ACLU) announced that it would support any teacher who defied the law. John Scopes, a high school teacher in Dayton, Tennessee, took them up on their offer. The resulting **Scopes Trial**, popularly known as the "Monkey Trial," attracted national attention.

Clarence Darrow, one of the nation's most famous defense attorneys represented Scopes. William Jennings Bryan assisted the prosecution. Scopes was found guilty, though his conviction was later overturned on a technicality. The real point of the trial was a debate over the conflicting claims of science and religion, and the ability of rural Americans to resist ideas they found objectionable. The dramatic highpoint of the trial came when Bryan took the stand as an "expert on the Bible" and was cross-examined by Darrow. To the dismay of his supporters, Bryan revealed that he was not a full adherent of **creationism** and the literal accuracy of everything in the Bible, when he admitted that the world was not created in six days. The ailing Bryan died shortly after the conclusion of the trial.

Popular Culture in the 1920s

The mass media came of age in the 1920s. Americans in both the city and country were exposed to a glittering roster of heroes whose exploits were vigorously publicized in newspapers and magazines. It took an effort for Americans in the new media environment to be ignorant of athletes like the baseball home run king Babe Ruth, college football star Red Grange, or boxing champion Jack Dempsey. The faces of movie stars like Charlie Chaplin, Mary Pickford, Clara Bow, and Rudolph Valentino became familiar to millions. Favored actors and actresses enjoyed large followings of devoted fans. The most dramatic media event of the decade was the reaction to Charles Lindbergh's 1927 solo flight across the Atlantic Ocean in his plane *The Spirit of St. Louis*. The undeniably brave, handsome, and modest aviator was lionized as the quintessential American hero, a modern exemplar of the pioneer spirit. To his great regret, Lindbergh became an international celebrity.

The mass media promoted ideas and attitudes as well as individuals. In the 1920s the media embraced the business culture at the center of the New Era. It affirmed the pursuit of wealth and spread the message that with smarts and hard work anyone could become a millionaire. The media even contributed to financial boondoggles, most notably in booming a Florida real estate bubble that burst with disastrous results for many investors. The popular culture of the day did nothing to put a damper on Wall Street speculations.

Jazz Age Experimentation and Rebellion

In the postwar years many Americans were ready to reject traditional attitudes toward personal expression and sexuality. They believed that the manners and morals of the previous generation had been discredited by the war and had become out of date in the faster-paced modern America. Younger Americans in particular enthusiastically danced to jazz music. Doing so was pleasingly rebellious because this form of music had originated among African Americans and lower class whites, and was associated with uninhibited sexuality. The more traditionalists denounced jazz as "the devil's music," the more popular it became, much like rock and roll three decades later. Jazz music became the soundtrack of the decade, giving it its nickname as the **Jazz Age**.

Young women placed themselves on the cutting edge of social change in the 1920s. They shed the long hair and voluminous skirts that had been associated with prewar femininity. The **flapper** emerged—a girl with bobbed hair, short dress, de-emphasized bustline, and a powder case, cigarette, or drink in hand, an emancipated companion for equally carefree young men. Having won the vote with the Nineteenth Amendment in 1919, most, young women pursued personal self-expression rather than political influence. Compared to later years, the sexual revolution of the 1920s was fairly tame, but it shocked defenders of tradition at the time. Thanks to the efforts of Margaret Sanger and other advocates, birth control was more readily available. Automobiles revolutionized dating and courtship, enabling young people to escape the supervision of their elders. Drinking and premarital sex increased in the 1920s, but most young people were far from the giddy "flaming youth" who fascinated and appalled contemporary social critics.

Although women did not move into politics en masse and failed to vote as a bloc, they did continue the gradual movement away from the cult of domesticity. More women entered the workforce, though most of these were single; married women were still expected to focus on the home. Though the numbers of working women rose, their labor was concentrated in traditionally female categories such as teachers, nurses, clerks, and, increasingly, secretaries.

Women's wages typically remained lower, and women rarely ascended to the managerial rank. A rise in the number of divorces was a measure of the growing personal freedom of women and the weakening of traditional social structures.

The Growth of the Mass Media

Undergirding the influence of the mass media in the 1920s was a massive growth in the number of people exposed to the press and popular entertainment. Newspaper reading was ubiquitous in this prosperous decade as most families could afford to subscribe to one or more newspapers. Movie attendance skyrocketed as the movie industry took shape and Hollywood became the center of American filmmaking. In 1922, 35 million people went to the movies every week; by 1929, the number had increased to 90 million. Films were silent for most of the 1920s. In 1927 moviemaking was altered forever by *The Jazz Singer*, a "talking" feature starring the popular entertainer Al Jolson. Silent movies, and along with them many famous silent stars, were quickly superseded by sound technology.

Possibly even more pervasive than movies in the 1920s was the new medium of radio. The commercial development of radio was explosive. In 1920, Station KDKA was the first radio station to get a license. Secretary of Commerce Herbert Hoover helped establish regulations for the new industry. In 1926, the National Broadcasting Company (NBC) organized the first radio network. By the end of the decade, listeners across the country had access to a wide range of news, entertainment, and sports programming.

A Lost Generation?

Many books celebrated the dominant business culture of the 1920s. One of the most popular, and to some egregious, was advertising executive Bruce Barton's *The Man Nobody Knows* (1925). Here Barton envisioned Jesus Christ as a dynamic businessman, whose leadership skills and gift for promotion enabled Him to build the most successful organization in history. Very different in spirit were the writers Gertrude Stein termed the **"Lost Generation."** Several of these writers had been heavily influenced by the disorienting experience of World War I. Most scorned the business, political, and cultural values of Republican "New Era" America. Some joined Stein in Paris, which became a rallying point for expatriate American writers. Others headed for the big cities, especially New York.

Sinclair Lewis achieved fame and financial success attacking what he perceived as the crass materialism and cultural philistinism of middle America. In *Main Street* (1920) and *Babbit* (1922) he produced devastating satires of small-town life and the people who lived by small-town values. Sherwood Anderson's *Winesburg, Ohio* (1919), was a similarly bleak portrayal of desperate people trapped in the social prison of a remote Midwestern community.

F. Scott Fitzgerald was critical of but also fascinated by Jazz Age materialism. In *The Great Gatsby* (1925) he brilliantly depicted the spiritual emptiness of upper-class characters living a life of decadent self-indulgence in the environs of New York City. Ernest Hemingway painted a similar picture of expatriate writers and artists journeying between France and Spain in *The Sun Also Rises* (1926). Hemingway was especially eloquent about the disillusioning impact of World War I. His *A Farewell to Arms* (1929) centers on a character who rejects the false idealism and brutal hypocrisy of the conflict and attempts to walk away from the war with the woman that he loves. At the time, the most influential critic of American society was the journalist H. L. Mencken. Gifted with a brilliant literary style and a taste for invective, Mencken heaped scorn on ordinary Americans, terming them the "ignorant mob" and the "booboisie." Mencken was a favorite with college students hoping to be fashionable in their opinions.

The 1920s saw a flowering of African American artistic expression in the **Harlem Renaissance**. Centered on, but not limited to, the Harlem neighborhood of New York City, African American intellectuals wrestled with the challenges of their American identity in a land where they were still second-class citizens. Many members of the Harlem Renaissance immersed themselves in African American folk art and Negro spirituals, looking for an authentic form of expression to convey the black experience. Leading writers of the Harlem Renaissance were the poet Langston Hughes and the novelist Zora Neale Hurston. The popularity of jazz music opened up opportunities for African American musicians. Amongst many others, musicians like Louis Armstrong and Duke Ellington achieved great success; through performances in clubs and in recordings they reached a mainstream audience.

As the decade of the 1920s neared its end, many believed the era of prosperity would continue indefinitely. Early in 1929, the stock market reached an all-time high. Herbert Hoover, inaugurated as president in March, spoke of ending poverty. Given his stellar record as a philanthropist and administrator, this did not seem to be empty posturing. For a moment, all the promise of the American dream seemed possible. The contrast between the hopes of early 1929 and what followed the events of October intensified the inexplicable cruelty of the ensuing Great Depression.

Chapter Review

Rapid Review

To achieve the perfect 5, you should be able to explain the following:

- A consumer economy was created in the 1920s on a level unprecedented in American history.
- Advertising, newspapers, radio, and motion pictures provided new forms of entertainment in the 1920s and helped create a uniform national culture.
- The changes of the 1920s were resisted by many in small-town/rural America, creating many of the cultural conflicts of the decade.
- Assembly line techniques and the ideas of scientific management of Frederick W. Taylor helped make industrial production in the 1920s quicker and more efficient, ultimately creating cheaper goods.
- Installment buying helped fuel consumer buying in the 1920s.
- The Republican Party controlled the White House, Congress, and the Supreme Court in the 1920s, and claimed credit for the decade's prosperity; the Republicans generally sponsored policies friendly to business.
- The scandals of the Harding administration tarnished Harding's long-term reputation.
- Resentment against blacks existed in both the American South and North in the years after World War I, resulting in race riots in the North and lynchings and the rebirth of the Ku Klux Klan.
- The Red Scare of 1919 and 1920 resulted in the suspension of civil liberties and deportation of hundreds of immigrants, the vast majority of whom had committed no crime.
- Nativist fears also resulted in restrictive quota legislation passed in the early 1920s.

- Cultural conflicts between urban and rural America also developed over the issues of Prohibition and the teaching of evolution in schools (resulting in the Scopes Trial).
- During the Jazz Age, many Americans rejected the prominent business values of the decade and turned to jazz, alcohol, and looser sexual mores for personal fulfillment.
- The flapper was the single most prominent image of the Jazz Age.
- Writers of the Lost Generation expressed extreme disillusionment with American society of the era; writers of the Harlem Renaissance expressed the opinions of American blacks concerning American culture.

Time Line

1917: Race riots in East St. Louis, Missouri
1918: Armistice ending World War I
1919: Race riots in Chicago
  Major strikes in Seattle and Boston
  Palmer Raids
1920: Warren Harding elected president
  First broadcast of radio station KDKA in Pittsburgh
  Publication of *Main Street* by Sinclair Lewis
  Arrest of Sacco and Vanzetti
  Prohibition takes effect
1921: Immigration Quota Law passed
  Disarmament conference held
1922: Fordney-McCumber Tariff enacted
  Publication of *Babbitt* by Sinclair Lewis
1923: Teapot Dome scandal
  Death of Harding; Calvin Coolidge becomes president
  Duke Ellington first performs in New York City
1924: Election of Calvin Coolidge
  Immigration Quota Law enacted
  Ku Klux Klan reaches highest membership in history
  Women governors elected in Wyoming and Texas
1925: Publication of *The Man Nobody Knows* by Bruce Barton
  Publication of *The Great Gatsby* by F. Scott Fitzgerald
  Scopes Trial held in Dayton, Tennessee
1926: Publication of *The Sun Also Rises* by Ernest Hemingway
1927: *The Jazz Singer*, first movie with sound, released
  Charles Lindbergh makes New York to Paris flight
  Execution of Sacco and Vanzetti
  15 millionth car produced by Ford Motor Company
  $1.5 billion spent on advertising in United States
  Babe Ruth hits 60 home runs
1928: Election of Herbert Hoover
1929: Nearly 30 million Americans have cars
  Stock market crash

› Review Questions

Fact Check

Check your knowledge of the historical period covered in this chapter.

1. Many in rural/small-town America would support legislation that
   A. increased immigration from Eastern Europe.
   B. mandated the teaching of creationism in schools.
   C. lessened the penalties for those who sold illegal alcohol.
   D. made it harder to deport immigrants who might have "Red" ties.

2. The novel that supported the business philosophy of the 1920s most definitively was
   A. *Main Street.*
   B. *The Great Gatsby.*
   C. *The Man Nobody Knows.*
   D. *Babbitt.*

3. In 1928, in most Eastern cities, one could find
   A. a speakeasy.
   B. a continual flow of immigrants from Northern, Southern, and Eastern Europe.
   C. large numbers of supporters of the Ku Klux Klan.
   D. the first bread lines.

4. Republican leaders of the 1920s believed all of the following *except*
   A. "the business of government is business."
   B. the government should do as little as possible.
   C. labor unions should be strengthened through legislation.
   D. immigration should continue to be restricted.

5. The election of Herbert Hoover in 1928 demonstrated all of the following *except*
   A. most Americans believed that Republican policies had been responsible for the prosperity of the 1920s.
   B. fewer divisions existed between the urban and rural populations than had existed at the beginning of the decade.
   C. Prohibition was still a "hot-button issue" for many Americans.
   D. America was not ready for a Catholic president.

Multiple-Choice Questions

Here are multiple-choice questions like the ones on the AP U.S. History exam.

Questions 6–8 refer to the quotation below.

Well, Aimee Semple McPherson has written a book. And were you to call it a little peach, you would not be so much as scratching its surface. It is the story of her life, and it is called "In the Service of the King," which title is perhaps a bit dangerously suggestive of a romantic novel. It may be that this autobiography is set down in sincerity, frankness and simple effort. It may be, too, that the Statue of Liberty is situated in Lake Ontario.

—Dorothy Parker, "Our Lady of the Loudspeaker," *The New Yorker*, February 25, 1928

6. The writer Dorothy Parker and the evangelist Aimee Semple McPherson both illustrate which of the following?
   A. The decline of religious feeling in the 1920s
   B. Increasing social repressiveness in the 1920s
   C. The decline of American literature in the 1920s
   D. The growing freedom of women in the 1920s

7. Which of the following would be most likely to read Dorothy Parker in *The New Yorker*?
   A. A religious fundamentalist
   B. A college student
   C. A farmer
   D. An immigrant

8. Many American writers in the 1920s produced powerful critiques of
   A. the materialism caused by American prosperity.
   B. the inability of the government to combat the Great Depression.
   C. the rise of totalitarian regimes overseas.
   D. the decline of traditional religious values in the United States.

Short-Answer Question

The short-answer question below is similar to the ones you'll encounter on the AP U.S. History exam.

9. Answer Parts A, B, and C.
   A. Briefly explain ONE example of social and cultural change in the 1920s.
   B. Briefly explain a SECOND example of social and cultural change in the 1920s.
   C. Briefly explain ONE example of resistance to social and cultural change in the 1920s.

› Answers and Explanations

1. **B.** All of the other "causes"—more immigration, the lessening of Prohibition, and the lessening of methods to deport potential Communists—were vehemently opposed by most in small-town America. They would, however, support the elimination of the teaching of evolution, and the continued teaching of creationism in American schools.

2. **C.** All of the other novels are unsympathetic to the world of business—both A and D are by Sinclair Lewis. In *The Man Nobody Knows*, Jesus Christ is portrayed as a businessman.

3. **A.** The influx of immigrants had been greatly reduced by immigration legislation passed in the first half of the decade. Supporters of the KKK were largely not city dwellers; the KKK had also lessened in importance by 1928. Bread lines were not found until the beginning of the Great Depression.

4. **C.** All of the other answers are solid beliefs of Republican leaders of the 1920s. Republicans did very little for labor unions in the decade.

5. **B.** Hoover's overwhelming election demonstrated the appeal of his business background and the fact that many Americans credited the Republicans for prosperity. The fact that Al Smith was defeated in this election demonstrated that his anti-Prohibition statements definitely hurt him. However, many in urban centers voted for him; this demonstrated that the divisions between urban and rural America were still wide at the end of the decade.

6. **D.** The writer Dorothy Parker and the evangelist Aimee Semple McPherson both illustrate the growing freedom of women in the 1920s. This was an era of widening horizons for women. Women had received the vote, and more were entering the workforce. Emblematic of the period was the young "flapper" who embraced the freedoms of the "Jazz Age."

7. **B.** A college student was most likely to read Dorothy Parker in *The New Yorker*. A divide arose in the 1920s between the consumerist "modern" urban culture that Parker represented and an attachment to more traditional values that appealed to many in rural and small-town America. Emblematic of this divide was the clash of ideas associated with the teaching of evolution and the 1925 Scopes Trial. A college student would be more likely to be exposed to current philosophies and identify with the new cultural ideas.

8. **A.** Many American writers in the 1920s produced powerful critiques of the materialism caused by American prosperity. The writers of the so-called Lost Generation rejected a complacent acceptance of the American status quo; some ended up living abroad as expatriates in places like Paris. Famous American writers who directly questioned the materialistic ethos of their day were Sinclair Lewis in *Main Street* (1920) and F. Scott Fitzgerald in *The Great Gatsby* (1925).

9. **Parts A and B**: The 1920s was a decade of prosperity for most Americans. Consumer goods such as refrigerators and radios became readily available; they could be purchased on installment plans. Sales were encouraged by a proliferation of the new advertising industry. Automobile ownership became widespread, with most Americans owning cars made by Ford, General Motors, and Chrysler. The United States experimented with Prohibition during the 1920s. The mass media helped drive a flourishing popular culture in the 1920s.

Sports and movie stars became widely known celebrities. Many people in the 1920s began to reject traditional values. They embraced the rebellious spirit of the Jazz Age, with a soundtrack of raucous jazz music often associated with African Americans. Many young women shed the inhibitions of the past, wearing short dresses, smoking and drinking with their male friends, and bobbing their hair. The "Lost Generation" of American writers wrote critically of American society in the postwar years.

Part C: Many American resisted social change. Concern about mass immigration and the possibility of imported political radicalism helped spur the Red Scare. The Emergency Quota Act of 1921 and the National Origins Act of 1924 greatly restricted immigration, especially from Southern and Eastern Europe. The Ku Klux Klan grew influential in the early 1920s by agitating against immigrants and Catholics, as well as maintaining hostility toward African Americans. Many rural people rejected ideas that they associated with the Jazz Age. A law in Tennessee outlawing the teaching of evolution in public schools led to the Scopes Trial in 1925, and a famous forensic duel between the well-known lawyer Clarence Darrow criticizing the law and William Jennings Bryan defending it. Many Americans refused to adhere to Prohibition. The illicit sale of liquor led to the rise of organized crime and famous gangsters like Al Capone in Chicago. People patronized "speakeasies," where illegal alcohol could be found in great supply.

CHAPTER 23

Great Depression and the New Deal (1929–1939)

IN THIS CHAPTER

Summary: The Great Depression had a monumental effect on American society, and its effects are still felt today. Franklin Roosevelt, the architect of the New Deal, is considered by many to be one of America's greatest presidents, and he was the model for activist presidents who desired to utilize the power of the federal government to assist those in need. The origins of the Great Depression can be found in economic problems in America in the late 1920s: "installment buying" and buying stocks "on the margin" would come back to haunt many homeowners and investors. The stock market crash of 1929 was followed by bank failures, factory closings, and widespread unemployment. President Herbert Hoover believed that voluntary action by business and labor interests could pull America out of its economic doldrums. Franklin Roosevelt was elected president in 1932 with the promise of a "New Deal" for the American people. During his first hundred days in office, Roosevelt acted forcefully to restore confidence in the banks, stabilize prices, and give many young people work through the establishment of the Civilian Conservation Corps. During the Second New Deal later in the 1930s, measures such as the Social Security Act were enacted to provide a safety net for Americans in need. Some critics of the New Deal branded it socialism; others said it didn't go far enough to fight poverty in America. New Deal policies never ended the Great Depression; America's entry into World War II did.

KEY IDEA

Keywords

Hoovervilles: settlements of shacks found on the outskirts of many American cities beginning in the early 1930s.

Dust Bowl: name given in the 1930s to regions of Oklahoma, Kansas, Nebraska, Colorado, and Texas, where severe drought and poor farming practices caused massive dust storms. By the end of the decade, nearly 60 percent of all farms there were either ruined or abandoned. Many from the Dust Bowl ended up moving westward in search of jobs.

Hawley-Smoot Tariff (1930): tariff act that imposed severe tariffs on all incoming goods; European countries responded with their own high tariffs. Most historians say this tariff did little to help the American economy and probably deepened the depression.

Federal Deposit Insurance Corporation (FDIC): federal agency established during the "First Hundred Days" of the New Deal in 1933 in an effort to halt panic over bank closings. The FDIC insures the bank deposits of individual citizens.

Civilian Conservation Corps (CCC): also established in 1933, the CCC eventually provided jobs for 2.5 million young Americans in forest and conservation programs.

National Industry Recovery Act: New Deal legislation requiring owners and labor unions in various industries to agree upon hours, wages, and prices; as a result, wages did go up for many workers but so did prices.

Tennessee Valley Authority: agency created in the New Deal to oversee the construction of dams, providing electricity and flood control for many in the Tennessee River Valley; for many in the region, this was the first time their homes had electricity.

Works Progress Administration (WPA): New Deal program that employed nearly 8 million Americans; WPA projects included the construction of schools and roads. Unemployed artists and musicians were also employed by the WPA.

Wagner Act: critical piece of New Deal legislation that protected the right of workers to form unions and utilize collective bargaining.

Social Security Act (1935): New Deal legislation providing pensions for workers reaching retirement age. Both workers and employers pay into the fund that provides this benefit. Initially, farm workers and domestic workers were not covered by Social Security.

New Deal Coalition: The political coalition created by Franklin Roosevelt that, by and large, kept the Democratic Party in power from the 1930s through the 1960s. This coalition consisted of workers in American cities, voters in the South, labor unions, and blacks.

Scottsboro Boys: nine black defendants in a famous 1931 case; they were accused of raping two white women on a train, and despite the lack of evidence, eight were sentenced to death. The American Communist Party organized their defense.

Harbingers of Crisis: Economic Weaknesses of the 1920s

In 1929, most Americans assumed that prosperity would continue. As he took office in March, President Herbert Hoover expressed his wish to end poverty in the United States. This did not seem an outlandish goal. By September, the value of the stocks being traded on the New York Stock Exchange had reached a new high. Many Americans assumed that the modern economy that had come of age in the 1920s had made sharp economic downturns a thing of the past.

Despite the general well-being, a number of observers doubted that the laws of economics had been overturned. They noted increasingly worrisome economic trends that could portend greater problems. These included the following:

1. **Agricultural prices:** World War I brought great prosperity to rural America, driving up the price of farm products to record highs. The end of the war brought a correction in prices that proved devastating to farmers who had invested in land and equipment to boost production. The collapse in the price of agricultural goods led to the failure and foreclosure of many farms. This in turn led to the closing of 6,200 rural banks. Congress passed legislation to provide support to farmers, but this was twice vetoed by President Coolidge.

2. **Buying on the installment plan:** The consumer buying spree of the 1920s was in large part made possible by the availability of easy credit. Most Americans could not afford to buy their automobiles, refrigerators, radios, and other products with a lump-sum cash payment. Instead, they purchased these goods in installments, making monthly payments. By 1928 and 1929, many people were tied up paying for products they already possessed. They did not have money to buy more things. Factories continued to produce consumer goods, but inventories of un-purchased goods grew. Some industries were cutting back on their workforces in 1928.

3. **The gap in the distribution of wealth:** Americans generally prospered in the 1920s, but wealthier Americans did much better than those lower on the income scale. By 1929, 0.02 of the American population possessed more than 40 percent of the nation's savings. At the same time, three-quarters of American families earned less than $3,000 a year. The consequence of this economic disparity was that by the end of the 1920s, most Americans were no longer in a position to sustain the decade's consumer binge. Affluent Americans could not sustain the economy on their own. As the economy began to falter, wealthy Americans prudently began to cut back on their spending, further exacerbating the consumption problem facing manufacturers and retailers.

4. **A stock market out of control:** As the economy boomed in the 1920s, many Americans bought stock in American companies. A few became rich because of their shrewdness or luck in purchasing stocks. Many investors lived more dangerously, engaging in **speculation,** acquiring stock in risky ventures like Florida real estate that held out the promise of high returns. The stock market of the 1920s operated with far fewer controls than exist today. Stockbrokers could sell shares of stock **on the margin.** This allowed buyers to purchase stock by putting down only a fraction of the price of the stock, sometimes as little as 10 percent. As long as stock prices rose, as they did for most of the 1920s, this posed no problems for buyers or their brokers; buyers could pay back their loans from brokers with the profits from their

appreciating stocks. A drop in prices, however, could be disastrous for both buyers and lenders. Once the market crashed and prices fell, brokers demanded that investors pay off the full price of their stock, something many could not do.

Black Tuesday and the End of the Bull Market

The high point of the bull market came in September 1929. Then, from September into early October, stock prices began a slow decline. Rumors spread on Wall Street that the market may have hit its peak and that a price correction was on its way. Shrewd investors noted that some factories were laying off workers because of unsold inventory.

On Wednesday, October 23, the value of stock shares fell around 20 points in the last hour of trading. This set in motion a panic. The next day, a wave of selling led to a dramatic drop in stock prices. Stockbrokers attempted to reassure investors. President Hoover declared that the stock market and the economy were "on a sound and prosperous basis."

Influential bankers and brokers formed a consortium to buy stock and halt the slide in share values. Their efforts could not stem the growing panic. Prices fell further on Monday, October 28. The next day would go down in history as Black Tuesday. The market collapsed, with prices falling by 40 points, costing investors more than $20 million. Here the folly of buying on the margin became obvious as banks and stockbrokers called in loans that market speculators could not repay. An urban legend quickly emerged that bankrupted investors began leaping from the windows of tall buildings. In fact, only two people killed themselves this way. The dramatic mythology of financially ruined suicides reflected the truth that many Americans invested in the stock market had suffered heavy financial losses.

The Stock Market Crash and the Great Depression

It was not at all obvious at first that the stock market crash would lead to a global depression. Many observers saw the events of October 1929 as an inevitable correction to an overheated stock market. President Hoover reiterated his conviction that the American economy remained fundamentally sound. He reminded his fellow citizens that the economy was much more than a volatile stock market that traditionally went up and down. He saw the heart of the economy as the production of goods and services, which could go on despite the upheaval on Wall Street. Unfortunately, the stock market crash did prove to be a direct and indirect catalyst of the Great Depression for the following reasons:

1. **An increase in bank failures:** Rural banks had already been closing at a high rate during the 1920s. Now urban banks began to fail. The stock market crash led to a crisis in credit. Lenders began calling in loans to protect themselves. When creditors could not repay their loans, more vulnerable banks failed. The Great Depression would see the phenomenon of "runs" on banks: rumors would circulate that a bank was failing, leading customers to rush to the bank to withdraw their savings. Banks that could not weather such panic withdrawals failed. When banks failed, their depositors lost the money in their accounts. By 1932, 5,000 banks had closed, costing over 5 million Americans their life savings.

2. **An industrial contraction:** The credit crunch hurt industry. Many big businesses suffered big losses in the market crash. Needing to make up losses, and with fewer people

purchasing their products, businesses began to retrench, shutting down factories and cutting the number of their employees. Facing unemployment or fewer hours and less pay, workers also reduced their spending. This cutback in consumption led to further belt-tightening by business, spurring a vicious circle of closures and layoffs that resulted in an unemployment rate of almost 25 percent by 1933.

3. **Global repercussions:** The contraction in credit following the stock market crash had an international impact. European countries such as Germany were dependent on American loans for their recovery from the economic effects of World War I. American loans dried up in the wake of the market collapse. This led to an economic downturn across Europe and political upheaval in Germany. The growing disorder in Germany following the stock market crash opened a path to power for Adolf Hitler and his Nazi Party.

The Great Depression and American Society

The Great Depression affected Americans in all walks of life. Both hourly workers and white-collar professionals lost their jobs. Many other Americans were underemployed. In an effort to protect the jobs of male family breadwinners, women workers were often the first to be fired. Minority workers also were easy targets for bosses forced to make hard choices. Large numbers of men suffered from mental depression because of their inability to support their families. Out of necessity, men took jobs that had previously been reserved for women, minorities, or teenagers. The 1930s were a disorienting time for many Americans, for whom it became a period of reduced expectations and withered hopes.

In the early 1930s, private and local groups attempted to meet the needs of the unemployed and homeless with shelters and soup kitchens. Their efforts often seemed to fall short of the need. Some people who lost their homes began living in encampments on the outskirts of cities, where they constructed ramshackle dwellings out of scraps of wood, metal, and cardboard; they named these settlements **Hoovervilles** after the man they blamed for their troubles. Large numbers of young men and women took to the road, drifting across the country by stowing away in empty railroad cars.

A natural disaster heightened economic suffering during the **Dust Bowl.** An extended drought aggravated erosion problems brought on by poor soil conservation practices in the states of Oklahoma, Kansas, Nebraska, Colorado, and Texas. Enormous dust storms ravaged the region during the 1930s. By the end of the decade, nearly 60 percent of the farms affected by the Dust Bowl had been devastated. Most of the affected families abandoned their farms. Many immigrated to California, hoping to rebuild their lives by finding work in that state's rich agricultural industry. Californians looked down upon these countrified "Okies," who often ended up laboring in the fields from dawn to dusk as migrant agricultural workers. The novelist John Steinbeck memorably described the travails of these people in *The Grapes of Wrath* (1939).

The people who lived through the Great Depression developed enduring habits of mind. Even when prosperity returned in the 1940s, many refused to buy on credit, preferring to purchase automobiles and other products with lump-sum cash payments. Others retained Depression era habits of frugality, and they became "savers" of commonplace items like paper, string, and bags. Young people who grew up in the straitened 1930s became determined that their children would not experience similar deprivations, which would have profound consequences for the children born during the baby boom.

President Hoover and the Depression

It is a myth that President Herbert Hoover did nothing to combat the suffering of people during the Great Depression. He took strenuous action to relieve the desperation of his fellow citizens. Conservative critics now argue that he did too much and that, along with Franklin Roosevelt's subsequent New Deal, his actions helped prolong the crisis through too much government action.

Hoover used the powers of his office to encourage business leaders to maintain current payrolls and wage levels. As the crisis intensified, he helped coordinate the work of charities and local relief organizations. Hoover believed that Americans should meet the challenge of the Great Depression through the spirit of **voluntarism,** with neighbors helping neighbors help themselves. He feared that a program of direct federal payments to the unemployed would foster dependence upon the government.

Hoover backed legislation intended to help combat the effects of the Depression. Hoover had been concerned about the problems of rural America before the stock market crash. In June 1929, he signed the **Agricultural Marketing Act** that established the federal Farm Board empowered to provide loans to farmers and to purchase crops as a way of supporting higher farm prices. This bill proved to be a precursor to New Deal efforts to bolster the agricultural economy. In 1930, despite misgivings, Hoover joined Congress in enacting the **Hawley-Smoot Tariff,** which raised tariffs to near record levels. The intent of the tariff was to protect American jobs by making foreign-made products more expensive. Other nations responded to this by raising their tariffs on American goods. The resulting decrease in international trade probably contributed to making the Great Depression a global phenomenon. While Americans making products for the domestic market may have been helped by the tariff, workers who made products for export were hurt. The tariff failed in its purpose of reviving the American economy.

In an effort to prime the American economy through government spending and to provide jobs for the unemployed, President Hoover authorized many public works projects, including the construction of the dam on the Colorado River that was eventually named after him. In 1932, he supported the establishment of the **Reconstruction Finance Corporation (RFC).** The RFC provided federal credit to banks, which could in turn loan this money to railroads and other businesses. A similar measure enabled the federal government to make loans to banks in danger of failing. Also in 1932, Hoover signed legislation that authorized federal loans to the states; the states could then use this capital to fund relief programs. Despite all this legislative activity to combat the Great Depression, Hoover resolutely refused to provide direct federal support to the poor and unemployed. He feared such activity by the central government would undermine federalism, and he still worried that federal "welfare" would undermine the American character. This left the president open to charges by his political opponents that he was interested only in protecting banks and big businesses and that he was indifferent to the woes of the "common man." Though famed as a philanthropist and problem solver before he became president, Hoover lacked the charismatic personality and oratorical skills that might have convinced many ordinary people that he was in their corner. Instead, as the Depression ground on, he became a reviled figure, blamed by many for a phenomenon beyond the power of any one individual to control.

The fate of the **Bonus Army** confirmed the popular impression of President Hoover as an out-of-touch and unfeeling leader. In the summer of 1932, thousands of unemployed veterans of World War I converged on Washington to lobby for an early payment of bonuses that were legally due them in 1945. Hoover and Congress rejected the demands of the veterans. Most then went home. However, several thousand of those veterans, many of them accompanied by their wives and children, set up an impromptu encampment along the Anacostia River. After clashes with police that left two veterans dead, Hoover ordered Army Chief of Staff Douglas MacArthur to use federal troops to clear protesters from downtown Washington. The zealous MacArthur exceeded his instructions and stormed the veterans' encampment with fixed bayonets and tear gas; dozens of people were injured and the shelters that the veterans had built were burned to the ground. The brutal dispersal of the Bonus Army haunted President Hoover as the country prepared for a presidential election.

The Election of 1932

The outcome of the election of 1932 was a foregone conclusion. President Hoover had failed to find a solution to the Great Depression, and he had become a living symbol of hard times. Lacking a viable alternative, the Republicans renominated Hoover in a listless convention. Hoover remained convinced that his policies relying on increased volunteerism would lead to renewed prosperity. Worried about the growing impatience of his fellow Americans, he cautioned them against "mindless experimentation" that would lead to a growth in an overpowerful government. Hoover's distrust of intensive government involvement in the economy reflected the orthodox economic theory of the time, as well as the formula for Republican success in the 1920s. Unfortunately for Hoover, articulating the economic equivalent of platitudes was unconvincing because he was the person giving voice to them.

The Democrats looked forward to the election with much more confidence. The Democratic presidential nominee was the governor of New York, Franklin Delano Roosevelt. A distant relation of former president Theodore Roosevelt, Franklin Roosevelt was a well-to-do gentleman who had entered politics and become a leader of the anti-Tammany Hall Democrats in New York State. He had served as assistant secretary of the Navy in Woodrow Wilson's administration, and he had been the Democratic candidate for the vice presidency in the election of 1920. Roosevelt's life was transformed when he contracted polio in the summer of 1921. He lost the ability to walk and would be confined to a wheelchair for the remainder of his life. Some observers believed that Roosevelt's long struggle with polio made him more sympathetic to the troubles of other people.

Before he entered politics, Roosevelt married Eleanor Roosevelt, a distant cousin and the niece of Theodore Roosevelt. Eleanor Roosevelt became an invaluable political partner for her husband. She helped keep his name visible in New York politics as he recovered from his initial attack of polio. When he became president, Eleanor Roosevelt acted as his eyes and ears, traveling around the country and investigating the challenges facing ordinary Americans. She also became a trusted advisor to the president, urging him to move faster and further in combating the effects of the Depression.

Franklin Roosevelt was much more open to providing direct government relief to the unemployed than Herbert Hoover had been. As governor of New York during the early stages of the Great Depression, Roosevelt had established an extensive relief program. Much of his effort was devoted to providing people employment on public works. He declared that this relief "must be extended by Government, not as a matter of charity, but as a matter of social duty." During the 1932 presidential campaign, Roosevelt largely promoted traditional economic bromides, and he called for a sound currency and reduction in the size of government. But most importantly, Roosevelt pledged to the American people that he would provide them with a **"New Deal."** This promise of change, along with his jaunty optimism proved enough. The majority of American voters were ready to embrace a man who seemed to care about their woes and offered an alternative to the care-worn incumbent.

Franklin Roosevelt carried the 1932 presidential election in a landslide, winning a plurality of 7 million votes. President Hoover won the electoral votes of only six Northeastern states. The Democratic Party also consolidated solid control of both houses of Congress. In voting for Roosevelt at the low point of the Great Depression, Americans emphatically rejected political radicalism. The Communist Party was electorally insignificant, and Norman Thomas, the candidate of the Socialist Party won fewer than a million votes.

The Hundred Days

President Roosevelt set the tone for his new administration in his inaugural address. He set out to rally his fellow citizens to the battle against the Depression, declaring, "So first of all let me assert my firm belief that the only thing we have to fear is fear itself." Within a week, he made brilliant use of the medium of the radio to reach out to the nation in the first of his **fireside chats**, explaining his policies and making himself a vivid and reassuring presence in the lives of millions.

Roosevelt prioritized action over ideological consistency. He gathered an able and often contentious body of men, and some women, to serve in his cabinet and in other top posts. He drew on the expertise of a group of scholars and reformers who were described as his "brain trust." Because Roosevelt called on his officials to "do something," there was a strong ad hoc and experimental quality to his early policies. Some policies conflicted with others. But with an emphasis on getting things done during the first **Hundred Days** of the new administration, many new programs were proposed by Roosevelt's team and authorized by a compliant Congress.

When Roosevelt took office in March 1933, banks were failing at an alarming rate as frightened depositors withdrew their money. Saving the banking system became the first priority. On March 5, the president closed all banks for four days, to allow the federal government to inspect their assets. Most banks were allowed to resume operations by March 15. The "Bank Holiday" reassured people that the reopened banks were secure. In an effort to prevent further "bank runs," the Banking Act of 1933 established the **Federal Deposit Insurance Corporation (FDIC)**, which provided insurance for savings accounts.

Beginning with the Hundred Days and continuing through the "First" New Deal, large amounts of federal money was channeled to relief agencies. The Federal Emergency Relief Administration headed by Harry Hopkins provided loans to states to provide jobs to the unemployed. Another agency, the Public Works Administration, run by Secretary of the Interior Harold Ickes, employed workers to build such public construction projects as highways, bridges, dams, and schools.

Another early New Deal program was the **Civilian Conservation Corps (CCC)**, which eventually employed 2.5 million young men on forest and conservation projects. The CCC provided much needed work opportunities for these youths at a difficult time, and, since most of their small salary was mailed to their homes, the work enabled them to help support their families. Most veterans of the CCC were grateful for their experiences in the program.

A major goal of the New Deal was to revive industrial production, which was essential for the renewal of the American economy. In addition, President Roosevelt and his New Dealers believed that deflation, or a fall in prices, had contributed to the closing of businesses and the laying off of workers. The **National Industrial Recovery Act (NIRA)** attempted to stabilize business conditions. In each industry, committees of businessmen and labor leaders established agreed-on prices, wage levels, and working hours. The NIRA protected unions and the principle of collective bargaining. The National Recovery Administration (NRA) was established to implement the new industrial policies. The display of a Blue Eagle poster advertised a business's compliance with the new regulations. The NIRA proved to be a political and economic failure. Wages for workers rose, but so did prices, negating any positive effect for workers. Many people in and out of business worried about its cartelization of industry. In its 1935 *Schecter v. United States* decision, the Supreme Court declared the NIRA unconstitutional. By then, few people mourned the passing of the Blue Eagle.

The Roosevelt administration also addressed the agricultural sector of the economy in its first Hundred Days. The **Agricultural Adjustment Administration (AAA)** aimed to help farmers by raising prices for agricultural goods. The government attempted to do this by encouraging farmers to reduce the amount of crops and livestock that they brought to market. The resulting slaughter of millions of pigs shocked people at a time when many were hungry. The **Tennessee Valley Authority (TVA)** was an innovative experiment in regional economic development by the federal government. The TVA built a series of dams that provided electricity and flood control to the Tennessee River Valley. This modernization helped bring greater prosperity to a region that had been an economic backwater.

The First New Deal that was launched during the Hundred Days helped revive the morale of the American people and provided some relief to millions. What these programs failed to do was end the Great Depression. Two years later, in 1935, 20 percent of American workers were still unemployed. Despite its limitations, Americans continued to support the New Deal, and in the 1934 midterm elections increased the Democratic majorities in Congress. A popular initiative unrelated to the New Deal was the ending of Prohibition. Congress approved a repeal amendment in February 1933, before Roosevelt took office. By December 1933, enough states had ratified the Twenty-First Amendment to conclude the ambitious but unsuccessful experiment with Prohibition.

The Second New Deal

By 1935 it was obvious that the first New Deal had run its course and that new initiatives were needed to deal with problems intensified by the Depression. Critics on both the left and the right were attacking Roosevelt's record. The president needed a strong program to support his reelection campaign in 1936. The result was a new wave of legislation and the **Second New Deal**.

The Agricultural Adjustment Act of 1933 had failed to solve the problems facing rural America. Many farmers were losing their land because they could not make mortgage payments. In May 1935, the **Resettlement Administration (RA)** was created to help resettle farmers who could no longer work their exhausted land. The RA also set up camps to house migrants forced off their farms by the Dust Bowl. The Farm Security Administration (FSA), established in 1937, helped arrange loans for farmers who needed credit.

A highly visible element of the Second New Deal was the **Works Progress Administration (WPA)**. The WPA provided jobs for the unemployed, offering them 30 to 35 hours of work a week. The WPA payroll averaged around 2 million people per month. WPA workers built schools, post offices, bridges, and roads, many still in use in the twenty-first century and bearing WPA dedication markers. Not all WPA employees worked on construction projects. The WPA also hired actors, musicians, and artists. The actors and musicians performed for audiences that normally could not pay to attend concerts and the theater, while the artists decorated public buildings with murals. The WPA hired a number of writers to produce a well-regarded series of state guidebooks.

The Second New Deal saw the Roosevelt administration side openly with the labor movement. The demise of the NIRA also saw the end of its protections for unions. However, the **Wagner Act** of 1935 guaranteed the right of workers to organize unions and engage in collective bargaining. The Wagner Act also prohibited unfair labor practices and established the **National Labor Relations Board (NLRB)** to enforce the new labor laws.

The most important and far-reaching legislative component of the Second New Deal was the 1935 **Social Security Act**. The heart of this act was the creation of a retirement pension for workers over the age of 65. This was funded by contributions from workers and employers. The first payments to retirees were scheduled for January 1942. Initially, the Social Security Act did not apply to agricultural and domestic laborers. The law would be extended to these categories of workers in later years.

The Social Security Act also inaugurated a program of unemployment insurance for workers that involuntarily lost their jobs. The money for this came from a payroll tax on employers with eight or more workers. The states managed this unemployment insurance with the funds coming from the federal government. The Social Security Act also set up programs to aid dependent children, the blind, and people with other physical challenges.

Although the Social Security Act did not initially cover all Americans, it was a landmark in changing the American understanding of the nature of government. Once most Americans had believed that "government is best which governs least." Now, under the stress of the Great Depression, many Americans came to believe that the role of government was to care for those who could not care for themselves. This revolutionized the relationship between American citizens and their government. The Social Security Act of 1935 was the beginning of the welfare state in the United States. This intensified the fears of critics of the New Deal who believed that it was taking America in the wrong direction.

The Election of 1936

Both President Roosevelt and his political opponents saw the 1936 election as a referendum on the New Deal. Roosevelt indulged in the rhetoric of class warfare, arguing that his critics from the business world opposed his policies because the New Deal cut into the profits of the rich. The Republicans attempted to counter Roosevelt's assertions by nominating Governor Alfred Landon of Kansas, a moderate who accepted some elements of the New Deal. During the presidential campaign, Landon focused on the importance of balancing the budget and trimming the size of government.

Roosevelt and the New Deal won a resounding endorsement. Roosevelt enjoyed one of the most commanding electoral victories in presidential history, winning the Electoral College with a vote of 523 to 8. Landon carried only the states of Maine and Vermont. Roosevelt was able to build an electoral coalition that would enable the Democrats to dominate national politics from the 1930s to the 1980s. This coalition included white people living in the cities who had been moving strongly into the Democratic column since Al Smith's presidential campaign in 1928, and whites in the Solid South who had been reliably Democratic since the Civil War and Reconstruction. Roosevelt added to this coalition members of labor unions grateful for New Deal support for organized labor. Also joining the new Rooseveltian Democratic Party were growing numbers of African Americans. It was a measure of Roosevelt's charisma and the appeal of New Deal antipoverty programs that African Americans, who had traditionally voted for the Republican Party of Abraham Lincoln, increasingly found themselves in the party that had long been the home for Southern segregationists and race baiters. Roosevelt's agricultural policies also helped the Democrats make some inroads into formerly Republican agricultural communities.

Critics of the New Deal

Although Franklin Roosevelt enjoyed a political triumph in 1936, many Americans strongly opposed the New Deal. Though a minority, critics of the New Deal made themselves heard in the 1930s. Upper-class opponents of the New Deal often saw the wealthy Roosevelt as a traitor to his class. They and businessmen appalled by his policies often vented their frustration by calling him a Socialist or Communist. On the other hand, critics of the left believed that Roosevelt and his New Deal were more concerned with propping up American capitalism and the current social system than addressing what they saw as the root causes of the suffering across the country. These leftists wished that Roosevelt really was a Socialist or a Communist.

One prominent organization that argued that the New Deal was attacking traditional values and virtues was the **American Liberty League**. This group appealed to wealthier citizens, most, but not all Republicans. Members of the Du Pont family and other leading businessmen served in its leadership, but its most prominent spokesman was former Democratic presidential candidate Al Smith. The American Liberty League was outraged by the **Revenue Act of 1935** that sharply increased taxes for people making over $50,000. The publications of the American Liberty League denounced the New Deal as an Americanized form of "bolshevism."

More opponents of the New Deal criticized it for not going even further in challenging American institutions. Dr. Francis Townsend believed that he had devised a plan that would simultaneously end the Great Depression and solve the social problem of indigent elderly people. His **Old Age Revolving Pension Plan** proposed that every American over the age of 60 be paid a monthly $200 pension. This would be paid for by a national sales tax. A condition of this pension was that the recipient had to spend the $200 every month. Townsend argued that his plan would end poverty amongst older Americans and also finish the Depression because their huge surge in consumer spending would revive the economy. Townsend's plan helped spur the Roosevelt administration to develop the Social Security Act. Upton Sinclair, the author of *The Jungle*, ran for the governorship of California on the Democratic ticket in 1934. He advanced his "End Poverty in California" (EPIC) plan, which called for factories and farms to be placed under state control. Sinclair's program was so radical that Roosevelt and other establishment Democrats joined with Republicans to undermine his campaign and defeat him at the polls that fall.

The most dangerous and popular enemies of the New Deal were two charismatic demagogues. Father Charles Coughlin was a Roman Catholic priest who had developed a radio ministry that had become increasingly political. At first a supporter of Roosevelt, Coughlin later publically derided him as a "liar" and "the great betrayer." Coughlin became a supporter of Hitler and Mussolini, and he made anti-Semitic statements in his radio speeches. As a result of government pressure, his church superiors ordered Coughlin to cease his broadcasting in 1942.

Huey Long served as governor and a U.S. senator from Louisiana. He built up a political machine in Louisiana that made him the virtual dictator of the state. He was an enormously popular political boss because he built schools and hospitals and offered free textbooks for schoolchildren. Clearly setting his sights on the presidency in 1936 or 1940, Long claimed that Roosevelt and the New Deal were not doing enough to help the people hurt by the Depression. He began publicizing his "Share Our Wealth" program, which would redistribute wealth in the United States by capping personal fortunes at $50 million and limiting the annual income of the rich to $1 million; the surplus taken as taxes would be used to give every household a grant of $5,000 and then assure families an annual income of $2,000. This controversial plan gained Long a large amount of support across the nation. His ambitions were cut short in 1935, when he was assassinated by a political opponent in Louisiana.

Twilight of the New Deal

Franklin Roosevelt's triumph in 1936 led him to an act of political overconfidence in 1937 that ended the legislative phase of the New Deal. The president was angered when the Supreme Court ruled elements of the first New Deal unconstitutional in 1935 and 1936. Soon after being sworn in for his second term, Roosevelt unveiled a plan that was entitled the **Justice Reorganization Bill**. The legislation suggested by the president gave him the power to nominate an additional Supreme Court justice every time a sitting justice reached the age of 70 years. Roosevelt improbably claimed that he was concerned about helping aged justices with their workload; critics observed that his plan would enable him to name six new justices, and they charged that he was attempting to "pack" the Supreme Court. The president's attack on the Supreme Court angered his opponents and alienated many of his supporters. Roosevelt was seen as arrogantly breaking down the separation of powers between the different branches of government for narrowly partisan reasons. Newspaper editorials and political cartoons likened the president to contemporary dictators like Mussolini and Hitler. Republicans and conservative (mostly Southern) Democrats killed Roosevelt's Supreme Court bill in Congress. An effort by the president to purge dissident Southern Democrats in the 1938 elections failed dismally. From this point on, an unofficial coalition of Republicans and Southern Democrats blocked the passage of more New Deal legislation. Ironically, the retirement of several Supreme Court justices allowed Roosevelt to appoint justices sympathetic to the New Deal, and the high court moved in a liberal direction despite the failure of his bill.

Another blow to the New Deal was a severe recession that began in mid-1937. While conditions had improved since 1933, the New Deal had not ended the Great Depression, and in early 1937 unemployment was still around 14 percent. As a result of the recession, industries cut back on production, and unemployment spiked even higher. Some blamed the recession on budget cuts by the Roosevelt administration, while others worried that payroll deductions for the Social Security fund cut into consumer spending. The economy began to recover in 1938, but employment did not reach 1937 levels until the outbreak of World War II in 1941.

Impact of the New Deal

The New Deal made organized labor an economic and political force. The Wagner Act's legal protection of unions and collective bargaining spurred a wave of union activity. The automobile industry resisted the unionization of its workers. Labor organizers in the late 1930s responded with **sit-down strikes,** where workers refused to leave manufacturing plants, essentially holding the expensive machinery there hostage. In December 1936, a major sit-down strike began at the General Motors plant in Flint, Michigan. After a two-month stand-off, General Motors accepted that its workers would be represented by the United Automobile Workers (UAW). Other strikes resulted in violence; in 1937, 10 strikers were killed by police at the Republic Steel plant in Chicago. Despite the fact that many people, including President Roosevelt, were sometimes disturbed by the tumultuous battles to organize labor, union membership grew steadily in the 1930s.

The creation of the **Congress of Industrial Organizations (CIO)** drove much of the decade's industrial unionization. The leading labor organization since the late nineteenth century had been the American Federation of Labor (AFL), a coalition of unions representing skilled workers such as cigar makers, miners, and construction workers. The goal of the CIO and its first president John L. Lewis was to organize unskilled workers on an industry-wide basis; this led to tensions with the leadership of the AFL, which still preferred to group workers according to their craft skills. The CIO made great strides in the automobile and steel industries, and it represented over 4 million workers by 1938.

Women faced many challenges during the Great Depression. Many lost their jobs as employers attempted to save remaining spots for male "breadwinners." Other women had to take whatever low-paying jobs they could find to help support their families. Some women attained great prominence during the New Deal. Frances Perkins, the Secretary of Labor, was the first female cabinet secretary, and she served through the whole of Franklin Roosevelt's presidency.

African Americans suffered greatly during the Depression years. African Americans, like women, were often amongst the first workers fired. In the South, they were often shortchanged on New Deal relief programs. Lynching remained a reality in the South during these years. Liberal Democrats and Republicans in Congress attempted to pass an anti-lynching law in 1935, but President Roosevelt refused to support it because he feared it would cost him the support of Southern Democrats in the 1936 election. A notorious case of Southern racial injustice captured national attention in the 1930s. In 1931, nine young African-American men, later termed the **Scottsboro Boys**, were accused of raping two white women on a train. On the basis of hurried and unfair trials, eight of the nine were convicted of rape and sentenced to death. The American Communist Party rallied to the defense of the Scottsboro Boys, and some of their convictions were overturned. Eventually, all the young men were exonerated.

Despite the persistence of Jim Crow laws in the Democratic South, African Americans valued Roosevelt's efforts to combat the Depression, and they generally believed that he was sympathetic to their dream of greater civil rights. Roosevelt did appoint some African Americans to government offices. One of his most prominent African-American advisors was Mary McLeod Bethune, the founder of the National Council of Negro Women, who in 1936 became the director of the Division of Negro Affairs in the National Youth Administration.

American Culture During the New Deal

The Great Depression focused the attention of many American authors upon the suffering of ordinary people. These writers captured the variegated texture of American life. Zora Neale Hurston's *Their Eyes Were Watching God* (1937) described the experience of African Americans living in a small Florida town. In *Studs Lonigan* (1932–1935), James T. Farrell exhaustively explored the fate of a middle-class Irish-American youth growing up on the South Side of Chicago. John Steinbeck recounted the challenges of a family fleeing the Dust Bowl in *The Grapes of Wrath* (1939). Erskine Caldwell shocked readers with his depiction of Georgia sharecroppers in *Tobacco Road* (1932). Not all American literature in the 1930s addressed current social problems. The first-time novelist Margaret Mitchell enjoyed an immense popular success with *Gone With the Wind* (1936), a sprawling tale about the life and loves of a feisty Southern belle during the Civil War and Reconstruction.

For most Americans, the radio was an inexpensive and readily available form of entertainment. Radio programming in the 1930s was remarkably varied. Radio networks like the National Broadcasting Company (NBC), the Columbia Broadcasting System (CBS), and the Mutual Broadcasting System (MBS) offered an array of dramas, comedies, and soap operas. Popular music was ubiquitous, and listeners were also exposed to "high culture" through the broadcast of symphonic music and operas. The sensational response to Orson Welles's 1938 adaption of *The War of the Worlds*, self-consciously modeled on journalistic dispatches on the recent Munich Crisis, demonstrated the power of radio and the modern mass media.

Regular attendance at the movies was a feature of American life in the 1930s. Nearly 70 percent of adults went to the movies at least once a week, and children were especially devoted fans of their cinematic heroes. Ticket prices were inexpensive, and the movies offered Americans an easy, if brief, escape from their daily cares. Audiences loved lavishly produced musicals like *42nd Street* (1933) and light comedies such as those featuring the glamorous dancing team of Fred Astaire and Ginger Rogers. The most popular film icon of the decade was the lovable child-star Shirley Temple. Popular dramas like Frank Capra's *Mr. Smith Goes to Washington* (1939) reaffirmed America's democratic values. Promoters attempted to make moviegoing an event in the 1930s. Theaters were air-conditioned, contests gave away dishes and other prizes, cartoons, newsreels, and double features added value to the price of a ticket, and sometimes live entertainment preceded the screening of the main attraction.

Chapter Review

Rapid Review

To achieve the perfect 5, you should be able to explain the following:

- The Great Depression had numerous long-lasting effects on American society.
- Franklin Roosevelt was the first activist president of the twentieth century who used the power of the federal government to help those who could not help themselves.
- The Great Depression's origins lay in economic problems of the late 1920s.
- The 1929 stock market crash was caused by, among other things, speculation on the part of investors and buying stocks "on the margin."
- The stock market crash began to affect the economy almost immediately, and its effects were felt by almost all by 1931.

- Herbert Hoover did act to end the Depression, but believed that voluntary actions by both business and labor would lead America out of its economic difficulties.
- Franklin Roosevelt won the 1932 election by promising the New Deal to the American people and by promising to act in a decisive manner.
- Suffering was felt across American society; many in the Dust Bowl were forced to leave their farms.
- During the first Hundred Days, Roosevelt restored confidence in the banks, established the Civilian Conservation Corps, stabilized farm prices, and attempted to stabilize industry through the National Industrial Recovery Act.
- During the Second New Deal, the WPA was created and the Social Security Act was enacted; this was the most long-lasting piece of legislation from the New Deal.
- Roosevelt was able to craft a political coalition of urban whites, Southerners, union members, and African Americans that kept the Democratic Party dominant in national politics through the 1980s.
- The New Deal had opponents from the left who said it didn't do enough to alleviate the effects of the Depression and opponents from the right who said that the New Deal was Socialist in nature.
- Roosevelt's 1937 plan to pack the Supreme Court and the recession of 1937 demonstrated that New Deal programs were not entirely successful in ending the Great Depression.
- Many Americans turned to radio and the movies for relief during the Depression.

Time Line

1929: Stock market crash
1930: Hawley-Smoot Tariff enacted
1931: Ford plants in Detroit shut down
      Initial trial of the Scottsboro Boys
1932: Glass-Steagall Banking Act enacted
      Bonus marchers routed from Washington
      Franklin D. Roosevelt elected president
      Huey Long announces "Share Our Wealth" movement
1933: Emergency Banking Relief Act enacted
      Prohibition ends
      Agricultural Adjustment Act enacted
      National Industrial Recovery Act enacted
      Civilian Conservation Corps established
      Tennessee Valley Authority formed
      Public Works Administration established
1935: Beginning of the Second New Deal
      Works Progress Administration established
      Social Security Act enacted
      Wagner Act enacted
      Formation of Committee for Industrial Organization (CIO)
1936: Franklin Roosevelt reelected
      Sit-down strike against GM begins
1937: Recession of 1937 begins
      Roosevelt's plan to expand the Supreme Court defeated
1939: *Gone with the Wind* published
      The Grapes of Wrath published

❯ Review Questions

Fact Check

Check your knowledge of the historical period covered in this chapter.

1. Which of the following was *not* a cause of the stock market crash?
   A. Excessive American loans to European countries
   B. Uneven division of wealth
   C. Installment buying
   D. Purchasing of stocks "on the margin"

2. Wealthy businessmen who objected to the New Deal programs of Franklin Roosevelt claimed that
   A. they unfairly aided the many who did not deserve it.
   B. New Deal programs smacked of "Bolshevism."
   C. New Deal programs unfairly regulated businesses.
   D. all of the above.

3. The purpose of the Federal Deposit Insurance Corporation (FDIC) was to
   A. ensure that poor Americans had something to fall back on when they retired.
   B. inspect the financial transactions of important businesses.
   C. insure bank deposits of individual citizens.
   D. increase government control over the economy.

4. One group of women who were able to keep their jobs during the Great Depression were
   A. schoolteachers.
   B. clerical workers.
   C. domestic workers.
   D. government employees.

5. The popularity of Huey Long and Father Coughlin in the mid-1930s demonstrated that
   A. most Americans felt that the New Deal had gone too far in undermining traditional American values.
   B. more Americans were turning to religion in the 1930s.
   C. most Americans favored truly radical solutions to America's problems.
   D. many Americans felt that the government should do more to end the problems associated with the Depression.

Multiple-Choice Questions

Here are multiple-choice questions like the ones on the AP U.S. History exam.

Questions 6–8 refer to the quotation below.

It has been very obvious to all of us that it would be quite impossible to start pensioning all of the old folks who have attained the age of 60 at one particular time, but it is also very obvious that it will take several years even to register them—a good many months. Now if we were to start at the age of 75, we will say, and register these old folks as rapidly as possible and place them upon a $200 per month basis of pensioning, by the time we get down to the 60-year-olds, all the way through, time enough would have elapsed and the new amount of money put into circulation would so stimulate the productive ability of America, that we could easily take care of these classes as they came along on a $200 a month basis.

> —Testimony of Dr. Francis E. Townsend before the House Ways and Means Committee,
> February 12, 1935

6. The Townsend Plan was intended to do which of the following?
   A. Relieve unemployment by retiring workers over the age of 60
   B. Provide benefits for veterans of World War I
   C. Reduce the role of government in people's lives
   D. Combat the Great Depression by putting more money into circulation

7. Which of the following was influenced by the Townsend Plan?
   A. The Works Progress Administration
   B. The Social Security Act
   C. The National Labor Relations Act (Wagner Act)
   D. The Glass-Steagall Banking Act

8. Supporters of the Townsend Plan would be most likely to support which of these later legislative acts?
   A. The GI Bill
   B. The Civil Rights Act of 1957
   C. Medicare
   D. The National Environmental Policy Act of 1969

Short-Answer Question

The short-answer question below is similar to the ones you'll encounter on the AP U.S. History exam.

9. Answer Parts A, B, and C.
   A. Briefly explain ONE example of a way that government was expanded to combat the effects of the Great Depression in the 1930s.
   B. Briefly explain a SECOND example of a way that government was expanded to combat the effects of the Great Depression in the 1930s.
   C. Briefly explain ONE example of resistance to the expansion of government in the 1930s.

› Answers and Explanations

1. **A.** All of the others were major underlying reasons for the crash. American loans to Europe benefited both European countries and American banking houses until the crash.

2. **D.** All of the criticisms listed were heard throughout the 1930s.

3. **C.** The FDIC was established after the bank holiday to insure individual accounts in certified banks and to increase confidence in the banking system. Americans began to put money back into banks after its institution.

4. **C.** In the other occupations, women were often fired before men, or had their hours drastically reduced. Those women who were employed as domestic workers were relatively safe, as this was one occupation that men, as a whole, rejected.

5. **D.** Many Americans wanted more New Deal–style programs and felt that Roosevelt should have gone even further in his proposed legislation. Many may have listened to Long and Coughlin, but when the time to vote came, cast their ballots for Roosevelt—thus negating answer C. The idea that the New Deal went too far in destroying American capitalism was popular in the business community, but it was not widely shared in mainstream America.

6. **D.** The Townshend Plan was intended to combat the Great Depression by putting more money into circulation. Dr. Francis E. Townsend called for the creation of a national sales tax that would fund monthly payments of $200 for all Americans over the age of 60; those receiving this pension would be required to spend all the $200 each month. Dr. Townsend believed that this scheme would simultaneously end the problem of elderly Americans living in poverty and revive the American economy by increasing the consumption of American goods and services by many millions of dollars.

7. B. The Social Security Act was influenced by the Townsend Plan. Worried about the popularity of the Townsend Plan, and other programs promoted by charismatic agitators such as Louisiana Senator Huey Long and Fr. Charles Coughlin, President Franklin D. Roosevelt launched the Second New Deal in 1935. A centerpiece of this new round of New Deal legislation was the Social Security Act that provided for pensions for many Americans over the age of 65, addressing in part the concerns of Dr. Francis Townsend.

8. C. Supporters of the Townsend Plan would be most likely to support the passage of Medicare. A key component of President Lyndon B. Johnson's Great Society, Medicare was created in 1965 to provide Americans over the age of 65 with health insurance.

9. Parts A and B: President Herbert Hoover took vigorous measures to combat the Great Depression. He urged business leaders to avoid wage reductions and employee layoffs. He organized charitable giving to help the unemployed. In 1932, he supported the establishment of the Reconstruction Finance Corporation (RFC) to lend money to banks and businesses. President Franklin Roosevelt launched his First New Deal to combat the Depression. Among the many programs authorized by Congress in 1933 were the Civilian Conservation Corps (CCC), which employed young men in conservation work, and the Tennessee Valley Authority (TVA), which constructed a series of dams to provide electricity to people living in the Tennessee River Valley. The National Industrial Recovery Act (NIRA) created the Public Works Administration (PWA), which provided jobs constructing public works, and the National Recovery Administration (NRA), which encouraged industries to set standards for prices and wages. The Agricultural Adjustment Administration (AAA) attempted to revive agricultural prices by compensating farmers for limiting production. Roosevelt's Second New Deal in 1935 created more government agencies. The Resettlement Administration helped farmers facing foreclosure. The Works Progress Administration (WPA) provided jobs to people who were on relief. The Wagner Act protected workers' right to organize unions and bargain collectively. It created the National Labor Relations Board (NLRB) to ensure that collective bargaining rights were enforced. The Social Security Act created a pension program for workers over 65 years old. It also set up a system to fund unemployment insurance. The Social Security Act is seen as a landmark in the development of the welfare state in the United States.

Part C: Herbert Hoover became a leading critic of the New Deal's expansion of the government. Former New York governor and Democratic presidential candidate Al Smith led the American Liberty League, which opposed the New Deal, especially its increases in taxation on people making more than $50,000. In 1937, following the Supreme Court's striking down of some parts of the First New Deal, President Roosevelt attempted to "pack" the Supreme Court with supporters through his proposed Justice Reorganization Bill. This effort to expand the Supreme Court generated much opposition from both Republicans and conservative Democrats. From this point on, a coalition of Republicans and conservative, mostly Southern, Democrats blocked further New Deal legislation.

CHAPTER 24

World War II (1933–1945)

IN THIS CHAPTER

Summary: Throughout the 1930s the United States followed a foreign policy based on isolationism, which emphasized noninvolvement in European and Asian affairs. After World War II began in Europe, President Roosevelt sensed that America would eventually be drawn into it and began Lend-Lease and other measures to help the British. The December 7, 1941, Japanese attack on Pearl Harbor mobilized American public opinion for war. Americans fought on two fronts during the war: against the Germans and the Italians in Europe and against the Japanese in the Pacific. In Europe, U.S. forces and their British and Soviet Allies eventually invaded Germany and crushed the Nazis. In the Pacific, superior American air and sea power led to the defeat of the Japanese. The decision to drop the atomic bomb on two Japanese cities is still considered controversial by some historians today. At the time, President Truman decided to drop the bomb based on calculations of the human cost of an American invasion of Japan. Americans contributed greatly to the war effort at home through rationing, working extra shifts, and the purchase of war bonds. As a result of World War II, the United States and the Soviet Union emerged as the two major world powers.

Keywords

Isolationism: American foreign policy of the 1920s and 1930s based on the belief that it was in the best interest of the United States not to become involved in foreign conflicts that did not directly threaten American interests.

Yalta Conference: meeting held at Yalta in the Soviet Union between President Roosevelt, British Prime Minister Winston Churchill, and Soviet leader Josef Stalin in February 1945; at this meeting critical decisions on the future of post-war Europe were made. At Yalta it was agreed that Germany would be divided into four zones, that free elections would take place after the war in Eastern Europe, and that the Soviet Union would join the war against Japan.

Bataan Death March: after the Japanese landed in the Philippines in May 1942, nearly 75,000 American and Filipino prisoners were forced to endure a 60-mile march; during this ordeal, 10,000 prisoners died or were killed.

Manhattan Project: secret project to build an atomic bomb that began in Los Alamos, New Mexico, in August 1942; the first successful test of a bomb took place on July 16, 1945.

Rosie the Riveter: figure that symbolized American working women during World War II. After the war, women were expected to return to more traditional roles.

Double V campaign: campaign popularized by American black leaders during World War II emphasizing the need for a double victory: over Germany and Japan and also over racial prejudice in the United States. Many blacks who fought in World War II were disappointed that the America they returned to still harbored racial hatreds.

Internment camps: mandatory resettlement camps for Japanese Americans from America's West Coast, created in February 1942 during World War II by executive order of President Franklin Roosevelt. In 1944, the Supreme Court ruled that the camps were legal.

American Isolationism in the 1930s

During the 1930s most Americans believed that the government of the United States should focus its energies on combating the Great Depression. This decade would be the period of greatest support for **isolationism**. Wary of involvement in another Great War, the American people showed no enthusiasm for interfering as Japan, Italy, and Germany began expanding their power.

In retrospect, many people believed that American participation in World War I had been a mistake. The world had not been made safe for democracy. The results of the conflict did not seem to justify its loss of life. Some fell back upon conspiracy theories to explain the American declaration of war in 1917. Senator Gerald Nye chaired a committee that investigated the popular belief that arms manufacturers and Wall Street bankers maneuvered the United States into war. The Nye Committee never found proof that the so-called Merchants of Death were responsible for American intervention in the war, but the committee did a lot to publicize such suspicions. The activities of the Nye Committee contributed to the climate of opinion that resulted in the **Neutrality Act of 1935**. This legislation outlawed any American trade in weapons or military supplies with warring powers. Subsequent neutrality acts in 1936 and 1937 strengthened isolationist America's defenses against involvement in another World War I; more questionable was their ability to insulate the United States against the threats posed by the increasingly aggressive totalitarian powers.

War clouds shadowed the 1930s. Japan conquered the province of Manchuria from China in 1931 and launched a full-scale war against the Chinese republic in 1937. Italy attacked and overran Ethiopia in 1935–1936. After Adolf Hitler became the head of the German government in 1933, Germany began expanding its power in Europe. President Roosevelt worried about the danger posed by Nazi Germany, and he moved away from isolationism. The Nazi-Soviet Non-Aggression Pact of August 1939, dividing up Eastern Europe between Germany and the Soviet Union, enabled Germany to attack Poland on September 1. Two days later Great Britain and France went to war against Germany. Roosevelt urged Congress to pass the **Neutrality Act of 1939**, which included a "cash and carry" provision that would allow warring countries to buy American arms if they paid cash and carried the goods away in their own ships. Roosevelt knew that this would give an advantage to the British and French because of their command of the sea. Congress acceded to Roosevelt's wishes in November.

Germany's dramatic victories in 1939 and 1940 led many Americans to question an isolationist foreign policy. The fall of France after only two months of fighting in May and June of 1940 shocked Americans. Germany seemed poised to dominate the continent of Europe. The United States began building up its military. In September 1940, President Roosevelt signed the Destroyers for Bases Agreement with Great Britain. Roosevelt exchanged 50 World War I–vintage American destroyers for leases on bases in British possessions in the Western Hemisphere. Great Britain needed the ships to fight German submarines, while the bases allowed the United States to strengthen its hemispheric defenses. Despite concerns about German aggression, many Americans remained isolationists. They were willing to support increasing the defensive military power of the United States, but they opposed any involvement in the European war. The isolationist **America First Committee** boasted 820,000 members in 1940.

The United States, the Middle East, and Anti-Semitism

The United States had very little involvement with the Middle East during the interwar years. The dominant western powers were Great Britain, which supervised Iraq, Transjordan, and Mandatory Palestine for the League of Nations, and France, which held the League mandates for Lebanon and Syria. As the American automobile industry boomed in the 1920s, oil companies in the United States began looking to the Middle East as an alternate source of petroleum. In 1928, American firms joined with British, French, and Dutch oil companies in the Red Line Agreement to cooperatively export oil from the region. In 1933, the king of Saudi Arabia gave Standard Oil of California permission to export oil from the desert kingdom. Standard Oil geologists were the first to recognize that Saudi Arabia possessed immense reserves of oil.

Aside from oilmen, few Americans were interested in the Middle East. In movies and other expressions of popular culture, the Middle East was a locale for exotic adventures, and little else. Economically underdeveloped and often difficult to visit, real conditions in the Arab lands received little attention. Most Americans were unaware of the region's widespread poverty, and a growing nationalistic resentment of the domination by outside powers. One powerful force in the Middle East that did resonate with Americans was religion. Devout American Christians recognized Mandatory Palestine as the birthplace of their faith. Attention to Zionism and the Jewish connection to the Holy Land waned for most Americans during the 1920s and 1930s.

Jews in the United States grew alarmed at the rise of European anti-Semitism in the 1930s. After Adolf Hitler and his Nazi Party came to power in Germany, the new government encouraged anti-Semitic hatred and discrimination. The increasingly virulent persecution of German Jews led them to seek refuge in other European countries and the United States. Unfortunately, few countries, including the United States, were interested in providing these people refuge.

During the Great Depression there was little sympathy for encouraging immigration to the United States. There was a consensus amongst politicians, editorial writers, and many ordinary citizens that immigrants would increase the competition for scarce jobs. The National Origins

Act of 1924 had already drastically limited the number of immigrants allowed into the country. Under the terms of the law, the German quota of immigrants was 25,000 a year. In addition, immigrants had to be able to prove that they would be able to support themselves once admitted to the United States, something difficult to do in the midst of a depression. As a result of this, during the 1930s the number of German Jews allowed into the country per year averaged fewer than 9,000. Widespread knowledge of German anti-Semitism and of the barbarity of the Nazi regime did not lead to an easing of restrictions on Jewish immigration. Unfortunately, anti-Semitic sentiments led many Americans to oppose the admission of more Jews into the country.

Zionists hoped that German Jews could immigrate to Mandatory Palestine. These hopes were dashed when tensions between the Jewish and the Arab inhabitants of the land led to conflict. The British government issued a White Paper in 1939 that severely restricted the number of Jews allowed into Mandatory Palestine. As war loomed in Europe, German Jews found themselves in a desperate plight, trapped between Nazi savagery and a world indifferent to their suffering.

The Election of 1940 and the End of Isolationism

The outbreak of war led Franklin Roosevelt to break with the tradition established by George Washington of presidents serving no more than two terms. Anxious to stay in office at this time of international crisis, Roosevelt let it be known that he would accept a nomination for a third term. Despite Roosevelt's political setbacks since 1936, he had no plausible challengers in the Democratic party and was easily nominated.

Although President Roosevelt remained personally popular, many Americans were bothered by his running for a third term. The Republicans attempted to capitalize on this sentiment by nominating Wendell Wilkie, a businessman and former Democrat who proved to be a talented newcomer to politics. In the election of 1940, Wilkie did better than Hoover and Landon had before him, but still he came up well short of defeating the incumbent president. The political coalition that Roosevelt had created held firm.

With the New Deal moribund, foreign affairs dominated Roosevelt's agenda as he began his third term. He regarded his reelection as a mandate for his policy of aiding the opponents of the totalitarian powers. In early 1941, Roosevelt proposed a plan to assist the British and their allies, who were running out of money to purchase weapons and war supplies in the United States. Under the terms of the **Lend-Lease Act,** the United States would send military equipment to the British, with payment deferred until the end of the war. After a spirited debate between the supporters of the president and isolationists, Congress passed the legislation. Roosevelt promptly approved billions of dollars of aid to Great Britain. In a 1940 speech, he had envisaged the United States as the "arsenal of democracy." By 1941 his vision was becoming a reality.

Anglo-American cooperation deepened in August 1941, when British Prime Minister Winston Churchill and President Roosevelt met aboard warships off the coast of New-foundland. Both leaders believed that the United States would eventually enter the war. They agreed that the war should be fought to preserve democracy from the challenge posed by totalitarianism. Churchill and Roosevelt jointly issued a document entitled the **Atlantic Charter,** which endorsed the principles of national self-determination and free trade and rejected territorial expansion by conquest. In the Atlantic Charter, Churchill and Roosevelt urged the creation of a world organization to replace the League of Nations that would have the power to police aggressor nations. At this meeting Roosevelt agreed that the U.S. Navy would convoy ships carrying lend-lease goods as far as Iceland, allowing the British to concentrate their forces to protect these vessels in the dangerous final stretch to the British Isles. Roosevelt's decision meant that the United States was in an undeclared naval war with German submarines by the fall of 1941.

The Japanese Attack on Pearl Harbor

The desire to create an economically self-sufficient empire drove Japanese foreign policy in the 1930s. China, divided by civil war, seemed an easy target, and the Japanese attacked and conquered the province of Manchuria in 1931. In 1937, the Japanese widened their attacks in China, committing appalling atrocities in places like Nanking, where they slaughtered tens of thousands of people. In 1941, the Japanese took advantage of Germany's successes in Europe to take control of French Indochina. Despite the U.S. government's disapproval of Japanese aggression in China, it had allowed American firms to sell Japan metals and oil vital to its war effort. The Japanese seizure of French Indochina proved to be the last straw for the Roosevelt administration. In the summer of 1941 the president ended the sale of oil to Japan, froze Japanese assets in the United States, and prohibited Japanese ships from using the Panama Canal.

This action by the U.S. government forced the Japanese leadership to make a decision. The Americans demanded that the Japanese abandon their Chinese conquests before trade relations could be resumed. This was unacceptable to the Japanese. As diplomatic talks dragged on inconclusively from July to December, Japan's rulers came to the conclusion that they had to acquire new sources of oil and other crucial resources in British and Dutch colonies in Southeast Asia. The only way to safely accomplish this would be to cripple American military power in the Pacific. Planning began for a surprise attack on Pearl Harbor that would destroy the U.S. Pacific Fleet.

Over the years, a few revisionist historians have argued that President Roosevelt was aware of the impending Japanese attack on Pearl Harbor, but he allowed it to happen as a way of overcoming opposition to American intervention in the war. However, the truth is that Naval intelligence was able to read some Japanese codes, but the information gathered from this fragmentary evidence did not provide a blueprint for the attack on Pearl Harbor. Some American officials were convinced that the Japanese were planning an offensive, but they assumed that it would be aimed at the Dutch or British. Conspiracy theories about Pearl Harbor don't hold up.

Early in December 1941 a Japanese aircraft carrier task force stealthily maneuvered into the vicinity of Hawaii. On Sunday morning, December 7, over 180 Japanese planes struck the American naval base at Pearl Harbor. Attacked without warning, the Americans were unable to prevent the Japanese from inflicting devastating damage. Six warships were sunk, and many others were seriously damaged. There were 188 American planes destroyed, most of them on the ground. Some 2,400 Americans were killed. Fortunately for the United States, the American aircraft carriers were away at sea, and the Japanese failed to destroy Pearl Harbor's maintenance facilities and fuel depots, enabling it to continue functioning as a working naval base.

The next day, President Roosevelt asked Congress for a declaration of war against the empire of Japan, asserting that the anniversary of the Japanese attack would be "a date which will live in infamy." Congress immediately complied. In 1940, Germany and Italy had joined with Japan in the Tripartite Pact (the Axis). On December 11, Germany and Italy foolishly declared war on the United States as a gesture of solidarity with their Axis ally. The United States now faced a global conflict.

The events of December 1941 made it clear to Americans that they were engaged in a life-or-death struggle against fascist totalitarianism. As a result, support for the war effort was remarkably widespread, and most Americans saw the conflict as a crusade to safeguard democracy.

The War Against Germany

The United States was better prepared for war in 1941 than it had been in 1917. In September 1940, Congress had agreed to Roosevelt's proposal for a peacetime draft to build up the military. A **conscription** system was established that continued to run effectively after Pearl Harbor. In addition to draftees, large numbers of men and women volunteered for service. American soldiers were nicknamed **"GIs,"** a reference to the "Government Issued" stamp on many articles of military equipment. Men in uniform served in combat and in a wide range of supporting roles. Women in the military performed noncombat tasks in auxiliary branches of the Army and the Navy. Many women helped care for the wounded as nurses.

The Council for National Defense had been established in 1940 to coordinate the growth of defense production; new agencies carried forward this reorganization of the economy to meet wartime production goals. As the United States went on a wartime footing in early 1942, the General Maximum Price Regulation Act attempted to freeze prices and set up a rationing system for products like gasoline, meat, and sugar. The **Revenue Act of 1942** helped pay for the war by increasing tax rates and expanding the number of people liable to pay the federal income tax.

The United States confronted two major theaters of combat in Europe and the Pacific. Believing Germany to be more dangerous than Japan, American strategists prioritized the European theater. Here the first task was for the U.S. Navy to help the British protect convoys carrying vital supplies to Great Britain. Initially Allied shipping suffered devastating losses to German submarines. Between January and August 1942, German submarines sank over 500 ships. Eventually a combination of effective antisubmarine tactics and increasingly effective technology, including sonar, enabled the allies to win the **Battle of the Atlantic**.

American infantrymen first saw combat in North Africa. The American and British invaded French North Africa in late 1942 in an effort to outflank General Erwin Rommel's Afrika Korps, which was threatening the Suez Canal in Egypt. After hard fighting, the remaining German and Italian forces in North Africa were forced to surrender in May 1943. The Americans and British next overran Sicily in July and August. They landed in Italy in September. The Italian government surrendered, but German forces tenaciously resisted the Allied advance. Though Rome fell in June 1944, the Germans kept on fighting in northern Italy until May 1945.

The Soviet Union cooperated with Nazi Germany in the early stages of World War II; it helped dismember Poland, attacked Finland, and overran the Baltic states. In June 1941, Hitler launched a massive invasion of the Soviet Union. This newly opened Eastern Front became a cauldron that eventually consumed the bulk of the German army. The Soviets paid a horrendous price, losing between 20 and 30 million people. Because of the enormous German pressure on his forces, the Soviet dictator Josef Stalin demanded that the Americans and British open a second front in Western Europe. Roosevelt and Churchill promised Stalin an invasion in 1944.

On June 6, 1944, Allied forces under the command of the American General Dwight D. Eisenhower carried out the D-Day landings in France. Casualties were heavy, but the success of the landing left Germany in a militarily untenable situation. By the end of July, over 2 million Allied troops were crowded into the beachhead; after a successful breakout attack, they swept across France. Paris was liberated in August. At the same time, Soviet offensives drove Hitler's weakening armies back toward the German frontier.

In December 1944, the Germans made one last desperate effort to stop the Allied advance in the West. The ensuing German offensive forced the American line back in places, but counterattacks by General George S. Patton halted and repulsed the German attackers. The **Battle of the Bulge** cost the United States over 85,000 troops killed, wounded, or captured. German commanders realized that defeat was inevitable. By this time the Allied strategic bombing campaign had wrecked the German Luftwaffe and severely weakened German industrial production.

As the German empire collapsed, advancing American, British, and Russian troops entered Nazi concentration camps and discovered horrifying evidence of the **Final Solution** Hitler had planned for what he perceived to be the "Jewish problem." Between 1941 and 1945, the Nazis murdered 6 million Jews in what is now called the **Holocaust**. As previously noted, the U.S. government had not been receptive to increased Jewish immigration before the war. President Roosevelt learned of the existence of the death camps in late 1943. He and his military commanders chose not to bomb these sites or the railroads leading to them, arguing that the best way to help the Jews was to devote military resources to winning the war as quickly as possible. American troops were outraged by what they saw in the camps, often shooting captured SS guards. Sympathy for the atrocities suffered by European Jewry would strengthen American support for the creation of the State of Israel after the war.

Allied troops crossed the Rhine River in March 1945. American soldiers met advancing Russians at the Elbe River on April 25. The Soviets stormed Berlin in a bloody battle. As the fighting raged nearby, Adolf Hitler committed suicide in his bunker on April 30. The remaining German government surrendered on May 8, which became known as V-E Day (Victory in Europe Day).

In February 1945, Roosevelt, Churchill, and Stalin gathered at the **Yalta Conference**. With the end of the war in Europe in sight, decisions had to be made about the postwar settlement. President Roosevelt had recently been reelected to a fourth term, but was in failing health. He would die in April. At Yalta, the Allied leaders agreed that Germany would be divided into four occupation zones, controlled by the Soviet Union, the United States, Great Britain, and France. The German capital of Berlin, located in the Soviet zone, would be split up the same way. Stalin, whose armies were overrunning Eastern Europe, promised to permit free elections in Poland and the other Eastern European countries. Roosevelt also secured Stalin's commitment to declare war on Japan once Germany was defeated.

The issues discussed at Yalta foreshadowed tensions that later emerged in the cold war. Ardent cold warriors would later criticize Roosevelt for territorial concessions that he made to Stalin in Eastern Europe, Mongolia, Manchuria, and Korea. At the time, Roosevelt believed that he had little choice but to work with the Soviet dictator. Stalin's armies were on the ground in Eastern Europe, a military fact that could not be denied. Roosevelt and his commanders thought that Soviet troops would be needed for the bloody battles expected in the Japanese home islands. Roosevelt also held out hope that he could persuade Stalin to moderate his demands after the war. Winston Churchill was much more skeptical of Soviet intentions. He was already maneuvering to limit Soviet influence in postwar Europe. He would later eloquently articulate his concerns about Soviet aggression in his March 1946 "Iron Curtain" speech.

The Middle East in World War II

Allied military planners recognized the strategic significance of the Middle East during World War II. The Americans and British were determined to prevent the Germans from seizing the region's oil reserves. They wanted this oil to fuel their own war effort. At one point in 1942, they were worried that the Germans driving across North Africa and the Japanese sailing into the Arabian Sea would link up in the Middle East. This nightmare scenario was avoided, and the Allies solidified their influence in the region.

The Americans cultivated good relations with Saudi Arabia, establishing a longstanding relationship between the U.S. government and the desert kingdom. The Americans also encouraged Turkey to stay neutral in the war, blocking another potential German point of entry into the Middle East. The Anglo-American landings in North Africa helped consolidate Allied dominance in the Mediterranean.

Growing Allied security in the region enabled the United States to channel Lend-Lease aid to the Soviet Union through the Middle East. The Americans built port facilities in Iran, where war supplies were assembled and then sent north by train to the Soviets. American aid played an important role in turning the tide against Germany on the Eastern Front. While the American presence in Iran was a military success, relations with the Iranians proved mixed, with Iranian laborers appreciating American largesse but resenting the cultural insensitivity of many American personnel.

The War Against Japan

For six months after the attack on Pearl Harbor, the Japanese enjoyed a string of victories. By March 1942, the Japanese had conquered Hong Kong and the great military base of Singapore from the British, and Indonesia from the Dutch. The Americans resisted a bit longer. The Japanese invaded the Philippines in December 1941. General Douglas MacArthur was in charge of the defense until he was ordered to escape and take command of forces gathering in Australia. American and Filipino troops held out on the Bataan Peninsula until April, and on Corregidor Island in Manila Bay until May 6, 1942. The 75,000 American and Filipino troops that surrendered at Bataan were worn down by disease and malnutrition. The Japanese forced these weakened prisoners to undertake the 60-mile **Bataan Death March** to a new concentration point. Along the way these men were treated with extreme brutality by their Japanese captors, and around 10,000 were murdered or died from disease or overexertion.

Just two days after the last stronghold surrendered in the Philippines, the tide began to turn against the Japanese. A Japanese fleet carrying troops to threaten Australia was turned back by a force of American aircraft carriers at the **Battle of the Coral Sea**. This was the first major naval battle in history where the combatant ships did not see each other; all the fighting was carried out by naval aircraft. The hard-pressed American aircraft carriers also played a central role in the decisive **Battle of Midway** in early June 1942. The American carriers ambushed a large Japanese fleet threatening the island of Midway. The Japanese lost four aircraft carriers and over 200 planes, the heart of the force that had attacked Pearl Harbor. The Americans lost one carrier. This battle was the turning point of the war in the Pacific. From Midway on, the Japanese would be on the defensive. They would not be able to replace their heavy losses. Soon the "arsenal of democracy" would be swelling the size of the American navy in the Pacific, more than replacing the ships lost at Pearl Harbor.

The United States went on the attack in August 1942, landing Marines on the Japanese-held island of Guadalcanal. Months of brutal jungle fighting followed; the Japanese did not withdraw the remnants of their forces on the island until February of the next year. This campaign set the pattern for the Pacific war of the Japanese fighting fanatically, often to the last man, and the Americans taking advantage of their growing technological and material advantage to overwhelm their opponents. In 1943, the Americans adopted the strategy of **island-hopping**, isolating and neutralizing major Japanese bases through air and naval strikes, and then landing Marine and Army troops at key points on the way to Japan. By late 1944, American submarines were sinking large numbers of Japanese merchantmen and tankers, cutting Japan off from outside resources, while the Air Force acquired bases from which its bombers could hit Japanese cities. In 1945, the United States would launch a devastating bombing campaign that would destroy much of urban Japan.

Despite the growing odds, the Japanese military insisted on continuing the fight. In late October 1944, General MacArthur returned to the Philippines, beginning a campaign of liberation that would last until the end of the war. Much of what was left of the Japanese Navy was sunk in the Battle of Leyte Gulf. The desperate Japanese, running out of gasoline and trained aviators, resorted to **kamikaze pilots** who set off on suicidal one-way flights, hoping to crash their planes into American ships. Casualties mounted as American forces drew closer to Japan. The Americans suffered 25,000 casualties at Iwo Jima in February to March 1945, and 50,000 casualties at Okinawa in fighting that lasted from April to June.

The Decision to Drop the Atomic Bomb

The crescendo of violence in the battles of early 1945 worried American military planners. The Japanese government refused to surrender, and the Japanese military began stockpiling troops, weapons, and kamikaze planes for the defense of the home islands. Estimates of American casualties in an invasion of Japan ran into the hundreds of thousands.

When Harry Truman became president following the death of Franklin Roosevelt in April 1945, he was for the first time informed about the effort to build an atomic bomb. The **Manhattan Project** was started in August 1942, driven largely by fears that Germany might be working on an atomic weapon. J. Robert Oppenheimer headed the scientific team that designed and built the atomic bomb at Los Alamos, New Mexico. An atomic bomb was successfully detonated at Alamogordo, New Mexico, on July 16, 1945.

In retrospect, controversy has swirled around the United States becoming the first power to use atomic weapons against cities. For President Harry Truman, the use of this new device was not a difficult decision. He shared the concern about heavy American casualties in an assault on the Japanese home islands. American bombers were already causing enormous death and destruction in Japanese cities with conventional bombs. Truman was aware of the Bataan Death March and other Japanese atrocities. He shared the general American disdain for the Japanese, which resulted in their being portrayed in popular culture with crude racial stereotypes. The president saw no reason not to use a weapon that might bring the war to a rapid conclusion.

On August 6, 1945, the B-29 **Enola Gay** dropped an atomic bomb on the city of Hiroshima, the location of a number of Japanese military headquarters. The number of people who died in the attack was 75,000. When the Japanese made no move to give up, on August 9 a second bomb was dropped on the city of Nagasaki, killing over 40,000 people. The Japanese government finally indicated its willingness to surrender. Also influencing its decision was the Soviet invasion of Manchuria on the same day as the Nagasaki bombing. Americans celebrated V-J Day on August 14. The formal Japanese surrender came on September 2, 1945.

The Home Front

The United States benefited from gearing up its war industries before Pearl Harbor. The New Deal faded away, and Franklin Roosevelt made peace with big business. Thousands of highly skilled businessmen took jobs in Washington helping to organize the war effort; since most continued to be paid by their employers rather than the government, they were known as "dollar-a-year" men.

Unemployment ceased to be a problem during the war with millions of men and women in the military and factories churning out military equipment and other goods. Unions thrived during the war, gaining membership. Early in the war unions for the most part respected "no-strike" agreements with the government. From 1943 on, labor unrest grew and strikes increased, especially in the coal industry.

To raise money to pay the enormous expenses of the war, the government increased taxes and widened the tax base. It also revived a practice from World War I and sold **war bonds**. Movie stars and other celebrities appealed to the public to buy these bonds, raising millions of dollars.

Although far better off than European civilians, average Americans sacrificed some luxuries during the war. Products such as gasoline, meat, sugar, and butter were rationed. Families were issued **ration cards** to regulate their purchases of these goods. Recycling was common during the war. Some products became unavailable; women who had grown used to wearing silk stockings drew a line up the back of their legs to simulate the fashionable appearance of prewar hosiery.

Life changed in other ways. People living in cities had to participate in "blackouts," where outside lights were turned off and shades pulled down over windows. This was a defense against hypothetical enemy air attacks, and along the coast it helped prevent ships from being silhouetted against bright city skylines, making them easy targets for predatory submarines. Citizens volunteered to serve as observers and air raid wardens, watching for and ready to react to bombing attacks. Many high schools ran year-round so that classes could end early, allowing students to do war work. Workers often worked extra shifts, called "victory shifts."

Popular culture reflected the wartime atmosphere. While many movies aimed to help audiences forget their troubles with comedy, song, dance, and alluringly costumed beauties, Hollywood also churned out many patriotic films justifying the war effort and celebrating the achievements of the military. One such film, the now-classic *Casablanca* (1942), brilliantly dramatized the self-sacrifice necessary to defeat Nazism. The song "White Christmas," written by Irving Berlin and sung by Bing Crosby, became a favorite with GIs because it captured their nostalgia for home. Major League Baseball remained the national pastime during the war, despite many players being drafted. Teams used players who were older or who had been rejected by the military for physical reasons. During the war, baseball fans could also follow the All-American Girls' Baseball League, founded in 1943.

With millions of men in the military, large numbers of women were needed to replace them in manufacturing jobs. **Rosie the Riveter** became the iconic symbol of these wartime working women. Taking a job in a war production plant was seen as a patriotic act. Despite this, most women with children remained at home during the war. Those women who did take jobs in defense industries were often paid less than their male counterparts. Once the war ended, these female workers were encouraged to patriotically give up their jobs and make way for the returning servicemen.

Civil Rights During the War

African Americans benefited from new job opportunities during the war. Many African Americans also volunteered for service against enemies that glorified racial distinctions. Unfortunately racial discrimination persisted in the United States. Military units were segregated by race, and African Americans were often regarded as being better suited for labor duties than combat. African-American newspapers promoted the **Double V campaign,** which called for the defeat of Nazism and Japanese imperialism abroad and racial discrimination at home. A group of African-American and white civil rights activists founded the Congress for Racial Equality (CORE) in 1942. CORE began coordinating protests that served as precursors for the civil rights movement of the 1950s and 1960s.

In the early days of the war, many Americans living on the West Coast were afraid that the Japanese living among them would act as spies and saboteurs for the enemy. Responding to these concerns, President Roosevelt signed Executive Order 9066, which forced all Japanese on the West Coast, even Japanese-American citizens, to move to **internment camps**. Because of the speed of the relocation, many of the internees lost all their property. Government officials told the Japanese Americans that they were being protected from widespread anti-Japanese sentiment, which was in fact virulent. This was little consolation to people who found themselves in relocation centers surrounded by fences and armed guards.

Japanese-American citizens deeply resented being treated as enemy nationals. A legal challenge went to the Supreme Court. In *Korematsu v. United States* the Supreme Court rejected the challenge, ruling that the internment was lawful because it was based "on military necessity." In 1988, the U.S. government belatedly apologized to the internees and paid survivors $20,000 in compensation. Despite this, Japanese-American soldiers served in their own units during the war. The 442nd Regiment, recruited mostly from Japanese Americans in Hawaii, was the most highly decorated American unit of the war.

Chapter Review

 **KEY IDEA**

Rapid Review

To achieve the perfect 5, you should be able to explain the following:

- War production for World War II pulled America out of the Great Depression.
- World War II turned America into one of the two major world powers.
- America continued to pursue a foreign policy of isolationism throughout the 1930s.
- Lend-Lease and other measures by Franklin Roosevelt brought America into the war on the side of England one year before America actually entered the war.
- The Pearl Harbor attack was part of an overall Japanese strategy, and it mobilized American public opinion for war.
- Battles fought by American GIs in Africa, Italy, and Western Europe were crucial in creating a "second front" and important in the eventual defeat of Hitler.
- Decisions made at the Yalta Conference did much to influence the postwar world.
- Superior American air and sea power ultimately led to the defeat of the Japanese in the Pacific.
- The decision to drop the atomic bomb was based on the calculations of the human cost of an American invasion of Japan and as retaliation for Japanese actions during the war.
- Americans sacrificed greatly during the war and contributed to the Allied victory through rationing, extra work, and the purchase of war bonds.
- American women contributed greatly to the war effort, especially by taking industrial jobs that had been held by departed soldiers.
- African Americans continued to meet with discrimination both in and out of the armed services, as did the Japanese. Japanese citizens from the West Coast were forced to move to internment camps. The American government in 1988 issued a formal apology for these actions.

Time Line

1933: Hitler comes to power in Germany
1935: Neutrality Act of 1935
1938: Hitler annexes Austria and Sudetenland

1939: Nazi-Soviet Pact
Germany invades Poland
Beginning of World War II
1940: Roosevelt reelected for third term
American Selective Service plan instituted
1941: Lend-Lease assistance begins for England
Japanese attack on Pearl Harbor
United States officially enters World War II
Germany declares war on United States
1942: American troops engage in combat in Africa
Japanese interment camps opened
Battle of Coral Sea, Battle of Midway
Casablanca released
1943: Allied armies invade Sicily
United Mine Workers strike
1944: D-Day Invasion
Roosevelt defeats Thomas Dewey, elected for fourth term
Beginning of Battle of the Bulge
1945: Yalta Conference
Concentration camps discovered by Allied forces
FDR dies in Warm Springs, Georgia; Harry Truman becomes president
Germany surrenders unconditionally
Atomic bombs dropped on Hiroshima and Nagasaki
Japan surrenders unconditionally

❯ Review Questions

Fact Check

Check your knowledge of the historical period covered in this chapter.

1. The internment of Japanese Americans began for all of the reasons listed *except*
   A. it was felt that Japanese living in California had divided loyalties when war began.
   B. newspapers on the West Coast reported incidents of Japanese Americans aiding the Japanese military effort.
   C. Japanese Americans needed protection, and the camps would provide it for them.
   D. the portrayal of the Japanese in American films and magazines.

2. Which was *not* a reason for the hatred many felt toward the Japanese during the war?
   A. The bombing of Pearl Harbor
   B. The fact that they were physically different in appearance from most Americans
   C. The outrage over the Bataan Death March as soon as Americans first learned of it in late 1941
   D. The portrayal of the Japanese in American films, magazines, and newspapers

3. Many observers would later be critical of the Yalta Conference for all of the following *except*
   A. at the conference the Soviet Union was given control over more of Germany than the other Allied powers.
   B. the Soviet Union did not promise to join the war against Japan immediately.
   C. Franklin Roosevelt was near death at the time of the conference.
   D. all of the countries liberated by the Soviet Union would remain at least temporarily under Soviet control.

4. The United States did little to stop the spread of Hitler and Nazi Germany in the 1930s because
   A. the United States was much more concerned with diplomatic and political affairs in the Pacific than in Europe in the 1930s.
   B. the United States was more interested in solving domestic problems in the 1930s.
   C. the findings of the Nye commission did much to sour Americans on future military involvement.
   D. B and C

5. Americans continued to crave diversions during World War II and went in large numbers to see all of the following *except*
   A. auto racing.
   B. professional baseball.
   C. movies.
   D. big band concerts.

Multiple-Choice Questions

Here are multiple-choice questions like the ones on the AP U.S. History exam.

Questions 6–8 refer to the quotation below.

Sixteen hours ago an American airplane dropped one bomb on Hiroshima and destroyed its usefulness to the enemy. That bomb had more power than 20,000 tons of T.N.T. It had more than two thousand times the blast power of the British "Grand Slam" which is the largest bomb ever yet used in the history of warfare.

The Japanese began the war from the air at Pearl Harbor. They have been repaid many fold. And the end is not yet. With this bomb we have now added a new and revolutionary increase in destruction to supplement the growing power of our armed forces. In their present form these bombs are now in production, and even more powerful forms are in development.

It is an atomic bomb. It is the harnessing of the basic power of the universe. The force from which the sun draws its power has been loosed against those who brought war to the Far East.

—Press Release from President Harry S. Truman on August 6, 1945

6. The atomic bomb was a product of a large and complex program that was code-named
   A. Plan Orange.
   B. the Manhattan Project.
   C. the Enigma Program.
   D. the Containment Program.

7. The American victory that turned the tide against the Japanese offensive surge in 1942 was
   A. the Battle of Midway.
   B. the Battle of the Bulge.
   C. the Battle of Bataan.
   D. the Battle of the Atlantic.

8. As the press release makes clear, which of the following made it easier to make the decision to drop the atomic bomb on Hiroshima?
   A. American anger at the Japanese
   B. American competitiveness with the British
   C. American concern about Japanese subversion in the United States
   D. American doubts about the effectiveness of the U.S. military

Short-Answer Question

The short-answer question below is similar to the ones you'll encounter on the AP U.S. History exam.

9. Answer Parts A, B, and C.
   A. Briefly explain ONE example of an American military contribution to Allied victory in World War II.
   B. Briefly explain a SECOND example of an American military contribution to Allied victory in World War II.
   C. Briefly explain ONE example of an effect of World War II on the American home front.

› Answers and Explanations

1. **C.** Although this was the official reason given at the time, the other reasons listed were the actual reasons. California newspapers reported fabricated stories of Japanese Americans assisting the Japanese war effort.

2. **C.** The Bataan Death March did not occur until 1942, and most Americans did not know about it until 1945.

3. **A.** At the conference, the Soviet Union, England, France, and the United States were all to administer parts of Germany; the Soviets did not get more than anyone else. Criticism existed because by the decisions made at Yalta, the Soviet Union joined the war against Japan only days before Japan was defeated. In addition, "temporary" Soviet control over Eastern Europe allowed Communist governments to be set up there. Other historians question the decisions Franklin Roosevelt made at Yalta; many wonder if his physical and mental condition were adequate for such a conference.

4. **D.** American policies in the 1930s were largely concerned with solving the problems of the Depression, and the Nye commission reported that arms manufacturers, looking for profits, were largely responsible for pushing America into World War I.

5. **A.** Because of shortages of gasoline and rubber for tires, auto racing was almost totally eliminated for much of the war.

6. **B.** The atomic bomb was a product of a large and complex program that was code-named the Manhattan Project. Work on constructing an atomic bomb began in 1942, and it eventually involved 130,000 people working at a number of sites in the United States and Canada. The first atomic bomb was successfully exploded during a test at Alamogordo, New Mexico, on July 16, 1945.

7. **A.** The American victory that turned the tide against the Japanese offensive surge in 1942 was the Battle of Midway. On June 4–7, 1942, the U.S. Navy successfully repulsed a Japanese attack on the American base at Midway that was intended to wipe out the remainder of the American fleet in the Pacific. Instead, the Americans inflicted a crushing defeat on the Japanese, sinking four enemy aircraft carriers while losing one of their own. Unable to replace their losses, the Japanese were forced on the defensive for the rest of the war.

8. **A.** As the press release makes clear, American anger at the Japanese made it easier to drop the atomic bomb on Hiroshima. The Japanese attack on Pearl Harbor convinced many Americans that the Japanese were a treacherous foe. The tendency of Japanese soldiers to fight to the death and the discovery of Japanese atrocities such as the Bataan Death March further embittered Americans against the Japanese. By 1945, American bombers were destroying Japa-

nese cities with fire-bombs and killing hundreds of thousands of Japanese. For many, dropping an atomic bomb on a Japanese city seemed a logical extension of this campaign against a hated enemy.

9. **Parts A and B**: Because of its industrial might, the United States became the "Arsenal of Democracy." The United States provided tanks, trucks, and other military supplies to its allies through the Lend-Lease program that began in 1941. American military forces played an important role in defeating the Axis powers. In the Battle of Midway, fought on June 4 to 7, 1942, the U.S. Navy turned the tide of the war in the Pacific, decisively defeating the Japanese fleet, sinking four Japanese aircraft carriers. In August, the American troops landed on the island of Guadalcanal, beginning a campaign of island-hopping toward Japan that culminated in the bloody battles of Iwo Jima and Okinawa in 1945. In the European theater of war, the U.S. Navy helped defeat the German submarine threat. Bombers of the Army Air Force weakened German industrial production. American and British forces landed in North Africa in 1942, and Sicily and Italy in 1943. On June 6, 1944, the Allies invaded France, landing at beaches in Normandy. In December, American forces turned back a desperate German counterattack in the Battle of the Bulge. American forces helped force Germany to surrender on May 8, 1945. The Japanese Empire was still fighting on. The United States had been working on an atomic bomb since August 1942, in a top-secret program code-named the Manhattan Project. An atomic bomb was successfully tested at Alamogordo, New Mexico, on July 16, 1945. On August 6 an atomic bomb was dropped on the Japanese city of Hiroshima. Another bomb was dropped on the city of Nagasaki three days later. The Japanese surrendered soon afterward.

Part C: The Revenue Act of 1942 greatly increased the number of Americans who paid income tax. The government raised more money selling Americans war bonds. Goods such as gasoline, meat, and sugar were rationed during the war. Families received ration cards that indicated what they could purchase at any given time. Many women replaced male workers who had joined the military. "Rosie the Riveter" symbolized the important contributions that women made to war industries. Most Americans supported the war effort following the Japanese attack on Pearl Harbor. Many songs and movies expressed patriotic themes.

CHAPTER 25

Origins of the Cold War (1945–1960)

IN THIS CHAPTER

Summary: Even before the end of World War II, strains began to develop in the wartime alliance between Great Britain, the United States, and the Soviet Union. At the Yalta Conference, Soviet leader Josef Stalin had promised free elections in Eastern European countries the Soviet Union had liberated from Nazism; in the months after the war it became obvious that these elections would not take place. British Prime Minister Winston Churchill warned that the Soviet Union was creating an "iron curtain" between Eastern and Western Europe; the United States began to follow a policy of containment to stop the spread of communism. Through the Marshall Plan, the United States spent millions to rebuild Western Europe after the war. Stalin tested Western will by enforcing a blockade of Berlin in 1948. Western anxieties increased in 1949 when the Soviets announced that they had an atomic bomb and when Communist forces led by Mao Zedong took power over mainland China. The cold war had a major impact at home; the House Un-American Activities Committee (HUAC) began to search for Communists in the entertainment industry, State Department official Alger Hiss was accused of being a Communist spy, and Julius and Ethel Rosenberg were executed for giving atomic secrets to the Soviet Union. During the Korean War, United Nations and American forces were severely tested as they attempted to "contain communism" in Korea. Senator Joseph McCarthy claimed knowledge of Communists in the State Department, the army, and in other branches of government. Both the United States and the Soviet Union built up their military arsenals in the 1950s; by the end of the decade, President Eisenhower warned of the spreading "military-industrial complex."

Keywords

Satellite countries: Eastern European countries that came under the control of the Soviet Union after World War II; the Soviets argued that they had liberated these countries from the Nazis and thus they had a right to continue to influence developments there.

Iron Curtain: Term coined by former British Prime Minister Winston Churchill in a March 1946 speech in Fulton, Missouri; Churchill forcefully proclaimed that the Soviet Union was establishing an "iron curtain" between the free countries of Western Europe and the Communist-controlled countries of Eastern Europe.

Containment Policy: policy devised by American diplomat George F. Kennan; Kennan believed that the United States needed to implement long-term military, economic, and diplomatic strategies in order to "contain" the spread of communism. Kennan's ideas became official U.S. government policy in the late 1940s.

Truman Doctrine: articulated in 1947, this policy stated that the United States would support any democratic nation that resisted communism.

Marshall Plan: American plan that spent $12 billion for the rebuilding of Western Europe after World War II; the plan helped produce an economic revival and helped stave off the growth of Communist influence.

Berlin Airlift: American effort that flew in supplies to West Berlin after the Soviet Union and the East German governments blocked the roads to that city beginning in June 1948; American airplanes flew in supplies for 15 months, causing the Soviet Union to call off the blockade.

NATO: North Atlantic Treaty Organization, a military alliance between the United States and Western European countries that was formed in April 1949.

Warsaw Pact: military pact formed in 1955 between the Soviet Union and its Eastern European satellite countries.

HUAC: House Un-American Activities Committee; in 1947 this committee began to investigate the entertainment industry for Communist influences.

Blacklist: list created by HUAC and various private agencies indicating individuals in the entertainment industry who might be Communists or who might have been influenced by Communists in the past; many individuals named in the blacklist could not find work in the industry until the 1960s.

McCarthyism: term used to describe the accusations by Wisconsin Senator Joseph McCarthy and his supporters in the early 1950s that certain people in government, academia, and the arts were secret Communists. McCarthy's charges were largely unsubstantiated.

Domino theory: theory that if one country in a region fell under Communist rule, then other countries in the region would follow; this theory would be used to justify American involvement in Vietnam.

Sputnik: first artificial satellite, launched in 1957 by the Soviet Union; the fact that the Soviets launched a satellite before the United States shocked many in the American scientific community.

The Beginnings of the Cold War

The **cold war** dominated American foreign policy from 1945 until 1991. American domestic politics was also heavily marked by the long struggle with the Soviet Union and its communist allies. The defense industry became a key component of the American economy. Politicians usually felt the need to demonstrate that they were not "soft on communism."

Historians have long debated the causes of the cold war. In the early years of the cold war, American historians blamed the Soviet Union for the conflict. In the 1960s, **"revisionist"** historians argued that actions taken by the United States forced the Soviet Union to assume a belligerent posture in the postwar years. Still later, a group of "post-revisionist" historians made the case that some sort of friction was inevitable between the United States and the Soviet Union and that neither side was fully at fault for the cold war.

Sources of Tension: 1945

The United States, Great Britain, and the Soviet Union had cooperated to defeat Nazi Germany in World War II, though relations were much closer between the United States and Great Britain than between either of these countries and the Soviet Union. This is not surprising, given that both the United States and Great Britain had strong democratic traditions while the Soviet Union was a totalitarian dictatorship. Tensions were growing between the wartime allies by the time of the **Yalta Conference.** Though he promised during the conference that he would allow free elections in Poland, the Soviet leader Josef Stalin was unwilling to give the Poles any real choice in their future; after the heavy losses of World War II, he intended to turn the Eastern European countries his armies had overrun into a cordon of Communist **satellite countries** blocking the invasion routes from the West.

President Franklin Roosevelt believed that he could "understand" Stalin and deal effectively with him. True or not, Roosevelt's death brought to power Harry Truman, a diplomatic novice whom Roosevelt had not briefed on Soviet relations. In July 1945, Truman met Stalin for the first time at the **Potsdam Conference**. Clement Atlee, who succeeded Winston Churchill following an election, represented Great Britain by the end of the conference. The three leaders discussed the future of Eastern Europe. They agreed to put the Nazi leadership on trial for war crimes. (The most famous of these trials would take place at Nuremburg.) At one point, Truman took Stalin aside and informed him of the successful test of an atomic bomb. He did not know that Soviet spies had kept Stalin up to date on atomic developments in the United States. During the Potsdam Conference the ideological differences between the Western powers and the Soviet Union became increasingly apparent.

Europe and the Cold War

The Emergence of the Iron Curtain

In 1946 and 1947, the Soviet Union tightened its grip on the Eastern European countries of Romania, Hungary, Bulgaria, Poland, East Germany, and Czechoslovakia. The free and fair elections that Stalin had promised did not materialize. Non-Communists in the governments of these countries were forced out by Communists loyal to Stalin. The new Stalinist regimes ruled through repression and terror.

In March 1946, Winston Churchill gave a speech at a small college in Fulton, Missouri, during which he announced that the Soviet Union had drawn an **iron curtain** across

Europe, separating the Communist East from the non-Communist West. Churchill's speech was one of the earliest acknowledgements of a new reality that a cold war was developing in Europe. The American diplomat George Kennan helped the Truman administration clarify its strategy regarding the emerging cold war. In a 1946 "long telegram" sent from the U.S. embassy in Moscow, and an anonymous article published in *Foreign Affairs* magazine in July 1947, Kennan argued that the Soviet leadership was driven by Marxist-Leninist ideology and traditional Russian insecurity to take a hostile approach to the West and attempt to expand its influence. He said that the best response to Soviet aggressiveness was a long-term **containment policy** to restrain Communist advances. Kennan believed that if Communism was contained, it would eventually collapse in the Soviet Union and elsewhere. Containment would be the foundation of American policy toward the Soviets for the remainder of the cold war.

The emerging containment policy first found active expression in the Eastern Mediterranean. The Soviets were putting increasing pressure on Turkey because of their desire to dominate the Dardanelles Strait near Istanbul; control of this strategic waterway would enable the Soviets to easily transfer warships from the Black Sea to the Mediterranean. In Greece, Communist rebels were waging a civil war against the government. Until 1947, Great Britain had provided support to the Turkish and Greek governments. In February, the British informed the Truman administration that they could no longer continue this role; exhausted by World War II, Great Britain needed to reduce its imperial presence around the world. In a dramatic break with traditional American foreign policy, the United States stepped forward to take a more active role in world affairs. In March, the president in an appearance before a joint session of Congress announced the **Truman Doctrine**, which committed the United States to support any country threatened by Communist aggression or internal subversion. Congress responded to Truman's address by authorizing $400 million in aid for Greece and Turkey.

The Marshall Plan

Most Americans supported the Truman Doctrine and containment. Believing that the unchecked rise of aggressive totalitarian powers in the 1930s had led to World War II, Americans saw the importance of the United States promoting postwar stability. Many experts believed that political and economic uncertainty in Germany had led to the rise of Hitler. As war-ravaged Europe struggled to revive its economy, it seemed wise policy to assist in the reconstruction effort. This would promote international prosperity and undermine growing Communist parties in Western Europe.

In June 1947, Secretary of State George Marshall proposed the **Marshall Plan**, which was authorized and funded by Congress and signed into law in 1948. Marshall Plan aid was nonmilitary. It was open to all European nations, but Stalin rejected this assistance and compelled the Soviet satellite states to do so as well. Seventeen Western European countries accepted Marshall Plan aid. Encouraged by the Americans to coordinate their efforts, the period of the Marshall Plan helped lay the foundations of greater economic integration amongst the Western Europeans. The Marshall Plan was a notable success, playing a significant role in reviving prosperity in Western Europe; this initiative also brought economic benefits to the United States as the Europeans became important trading partners.

The Berlin Airlift

In 1948, the Americans, British, and French decided to merge their occupation zones in Germany into the Federal Republic of Germany. West Berlin, the part of Berlin controlled by the Western allies, was slated to become a part of the new Federal Republic. West Berlin, located in the midst of the Soviet occupation zone, was already an irritant for Stalin because the enclave offered a convenient escape route for Easterners fleeing Communism.

In June, angry over these Western plans, Stalin ordered Soviet and East German troops to block the roads into West Berlin. Stalin hoped that the Western allies would back down in the face of this challenge and evacuate West Berlin. Instead, President Truman defied the blockade with the **Berlin Airlift**. For almost 15 months, American and British planes flew into West Berlin, transporting enough food and supplies to sustain the city. Stalin ended the blockade in May 1949. Shortly afterward, as scheduled, the Federal Republic of Germany became an independent country.

The Berlin blockade alarmed the Western allies. They also worried about the large number of Soviet troops stationed in Eastern Europe. To defend themselves against the perceived Soviet threat, the United States, Canada, and 10 western European countries joined together in the **North Atlantic Treaty Organization (NATO)**. This collective security pact obligated all the signatories to come to the defense of any member state that was attacked. The NATO treaty was a watershed in American diplomatic history. It marked the first time the United States had entered into an alliance since it had bought its way out of the Revolutionary War treaty with France in 1800. The United States committed itself to maintaining large military forces in Europe for decades. NATO began to expand in the 1950s. The Soviet Union responded by organizing the **Warsaw Pact** with its satellite states in 1955.

Communist Victories

The crowded year of 1949 saw two events that shook American confidence. In September, the Soviet Union announced the successful explosion of an atomic bomb. The brief American monopoly on atomic armaments had passed. The terrifying prospect of a nuclear war became a worrisome possibility that Americans would have to learn to live with during the 1950s. Upping the nuclear ante, President Truman approved the development of the **hydrogen bomb**, a weapon many times more destructive than the atomic bombs dropped on Hiroshima and Nagasaki.

Following the end of World War II, a civil war raged in China between the Nationalist forces of Chiang Kai-shek and the communists led by Mao Tse-tung. The United States provided large amounts of weapons and supplies to Chiang Kai-shek. Despite this assistance, the Nationalists steadily lost ground to the Communists. In 1949, Communist troops seized Peking, and on October 1 Mao proclaimed the establishment of the People's Republic of China. Chiang Kai-shek and the remnants of his Nationalist armies retreated to the island of Formosa (now Taiwan). The United States would recognize Chiang Kai-shek's regime on Formosa as the true government of China for many years. The question of "who lost China" would become politically potent issue in the United States. Republicans blamed President Truman and the Democrats for the fall of the most populous nation on earth to Communism.

The Middle East and the Cold War

The British had played a dominant role in the Middle East for many years. As British power declined, the United States grew more deeply involved in Middle Eastern affairs. A major American interest remained oil. The United States produced most of the oil that it consumed in the 1940s and 1950s, but American diplomats were aware that Western Europe and Japan depended on Middle Eastern oil.

The Truman administration deepened the American relationship with Saudi Arabia. The U.S. government encouraged American oil companies to invest in Saudi Arabia. President Truman promised to protect the Saudis from the Soviet Union.

The intensifying American involvement with the religiously conservative and thoroughly undemocratic Saudi monarchy was an important element in the United States' containment strategy in the Middle East. American policymakers were willing to work with a range of regional rulers in an effort to keep out the Soviets. In the late 1950s, the United States placed nuclear missiles in Turkey that would become an issue during the Cuban missile crisis.

The United States and the Creation of Israel

Pressure to establish a Jewish state in Mandatory Palestine intensified as a result of the Holocaust. Many surviving European Jews hoped for a new life in the ancient Jewish homeland. Great Britain, which had held Mandatory Palestine as a mandate since the end of World War I, was unable to broker a peaceful settlement between Jewish inhabitants and the Arab inhabitants of the land. Disgusted by Jewish and Arab attacks on its soldiers, Great Britain announced its withdrawal, and it turned the future disposition of Mandatory Palestine over to the United Nations.

Diplomats at the United Nations called for a division of Mandatory Palestine into Jewish and Arab states. The Palestinian Arabs and neighboring Arab states rejected this partition. They objected to a Jewish state in lands they believed should be controlled by the Arab majority. The U.S. State Department also opposed the United Nations plan, believing it was in the long-term American interest to support the Arabs. Despite the attitude of his diplomats, President Truman threw his support behind the creation of a Jewish state.

War broke out as the British left in 1948. The Jewish community in Mandatory Palestine declared the establishment of the State of Israel. President Truman immediately recognized the new nation. Many Arabs fled their homes, either hoping to avoid the fighting, were encouraged by their leaders to leave and return during a later period, or forced out by Israeli troops. The neighboring Arab states invaded, but their armies were defeated by the Israelis. Over 850,000 Jewish inhabitants, from surrounding Arab and Muslim states, would also ultimately flee their homes due to the conflict.

The State of Israel became a reality, but its legitimacy was not recognized by the Arab world. More wars would follow. American support for Israel was strong from the beginning, and the United States eventually became the greatest international defender of Israel. The United States provides crucial diplomatic backing to Israel and supplies it with millions of dollars of military hardware. The "special relationship" between the United States and Israel has led to much ill-will toward America in the Arab world.

The United States and Iran

Upon becoming president in 1953, Dwight D. Eisenhower faced new challenges in the Middle East. Arab nationalism had become a potent force. Populations were growing restive under the rule of corrupt monarchies. Eisenhower publically supported greater freedom for the people of the region. He cautioned against moving toward this "too quickly" because unrest and instability might enable the Soviets to spread their influence.

In 1951, Prime Minister Mohammed Mossadeq of Iran began to nationalize British oil assets in his country. This outraged the British who blockaded Iranian oil exports. Mossadeq gained popularity through his confrontation with the British, positioning himself as a champion of the Iranian people against the imperial powers. Washington grew increasingly disillusioned with Mossadeq as he moved to take powers away from the Shah, who was close to the Americans.

The American government initially opposed British proposals to overthrow Mossadeq. By the time President Eisenhower took office in 1953, the Americans were fed up with Mossadeq. Eisenhower approved a CIA operation to topple the Iranian prime minister. The CIA organized protests that forced Mossadeq out of office. The former prime minister was arrested and jailed. The Shah established a repressive regime that would last until his own overthrow in 1979. For Iranians, the United States was closely associated with the Shah, and the 1979 occupation of the American embassy was motivated in part by resentments that reached back to the events of 1953.

The Cold War at Home

As the cold war intensified and the U.S. government began to implement a containment strategy overseas, concerns grew about Communist subversion at home. Although never numerous, Communists had been conspicuous in the arts and the labor movement during the 1930s and early 1940s. As the wartime alliance with the Soviet Union soured into overt hostility, a series of espionage cases raised suspicions about widespread Communist infiltration of the government and other institutions.

The Second Red Scare

To respond to these concerns and refute Republican charges that his administration was "soft on communism," President Truman instituted a **Loyalty Review Board** that examined the loyalty of government employees. Three or four million federal workers were investigated, and over a hundred workers were discharged. Some of the removed workers were homosexuals, who were seen as security risks because of their vulnerability to being blackmailed because of their sexual orientation. The Truman administration also used the 1940 Smith Act to prosecute some leaders of the American Communist Party. The Smith Act outlawed organizations that advocated the overthrow of the American government by force.

Congress also investigated Communists in the federal bureaucracy, and it branched out into the entertainment industry. The **House Un-American Activities Committee (HUAC)** had been created in the 1930s to explore Nazi infiltration into the United States; in the 1940s it shifted its focus to the Communist threat. In 1947, HUAC held hearings on the movie industry. Investigators sought out actors, directors, and writers with Communist ties. The fear was that these left-wing activists were inserting Communist messages into otherwise inoffensive movies. Filmmakers who had made movies favorably depicting our Soviet allies during World War II were also hauled before the committee for questioning. The Hollywood Ten were a group of writers and directors with strong Communist ties. They refused to answer questions at a HUAC hearing. They were given one-year jail sentences for contempt of Congress.

The HUAC investigation of Hollywood proved to have major consequences for the film industry. Eager to demonstrate their patriotism, the heads of the major movie studios established a **blacklist** of politically suspect actors, writers, and directors. People named on the blacklist would no longer be hired to work on American movies. This ruined the careers of many people in the industry. Some found work overseas. A few blacklisted writers continued to work by using assumed names or employing "fronts" to turn in their work. A similar blacklist took effect for theatrical workers on Broadway. The Hollywood blacklist lasted until 1960.

The U.S. Senate also responded to the Second Red Scare. Senator Pat McCarran was a leader in sponsoring bills to "stop the spread of communism" in the United States. The **McCarran Internal Security Act** of 1950 required all Communist or Communist-front organizations to register with the government; it also prohibited members of these organizations from working in any position related to national defense. The **McCarran-Walter Act** of 1952 made revisions to immigration law and placed limits on immigrants from Asia and Eastern Europe in order to prevent an "influx of communism" into the United States. President Truman vetoed both these bills, but Congress overrode his vetoes and enacted them into law.

Soviet Espionage in the United States

In the late 1940s and early 1950s, a series of revelations about Soviet spying in the United States helped spur a Second Red Scare. In 1948, HUAC investigated Alger Hiss, a former State Department official and advisor to Franklin Roosevelt at the Yalta Conference. Whitaker Chambers, an editor at *Time* magazine and a former Communist, accused Hiss of being a Communist and of engaging in espionage for the Soviet Union. Hiss denied these charges, and Chambers dramatically produced some of the stolen documents. Hiss was later convicted of perjury and sentenced to four years in prison.

One of the greatest shocks of the postwar years was the discovery that Soviet agents had stolen American nuclear secrets, helping the Soviet Union to accelerate its own nuclear program. In 1950, Julius and Ethel Rosenberg were indicted for being part of a spy ring that passed information about the atomic bomb and other weapons systems to the Soviets. Although Julius was more deeply implicated in these activities than his wife, both were convicted of espionage in 1952 and sentenced to death. Despite pleas for clemency, they were executed. For years, defenders of Alger Hiss and the Rosenbergs argued that they were innocent victims of anti-Communist hysteria. Following the end of the cold war, however, declassified documents from both the United States and the Soviet Union indicated that Hiss and the Rosenbergs were indeed Soviet agents. For some American Communists, sympathy for Moscow led to acts of treason.

The Korean War

At the end of World War II, the United States and the Soviet Union liberated Korea from Japanese control, dividing their occupation zones along the **38th Parallel**. South Korea became pro-American and anti-Communist, while North Korea became a Communist dictatorship. In June 1950, North Korea sent armed forces across the 38th parallel in a bid to unify the peninsula by force. The United Nations Security Council condemned the attack and voted to send military assistance to South Korea. (The Soviet Union was boycotting the United Nations over its failure to recognize Communist China, preventing it from vetoing these Security Council resolutions.) The United States had already begun to deploy air and naval power in South Korea. General Douglas MacArthur was assigned command of UN forces in the **Korean War**.

At first South Korean and hastily deployed American units fell back before the North Korean onslaught. Then MacArthur organized a brilliant amphibious landing at the Port of Incheon behind the North Korean lines. The North Koreans were routed and MacArthur's victorious forces moved north of the 38th parallel. Communist China opposed the approach of UN forces to its border. In November, the Chinese launched a massive attack that drove MacArthur's troops back into the south. By March 1951,

UN forces were once again counterattacking and driving back to the old border along the 38th parallel. By this point, General MacArthur wanted to expand the war by attacking China with Chinese Nationalist forces and American bombers. This was too much for President Truman, who, aware of American military commitments elsewhere, wanted to limit the Korean War and avoid a World War III. In April 1951, Truman relieved MacArthur of his command. Armistice talks began in July 1951 and dragged on for two years. When an armistice was finally signed in July 1953, North and South Korea remained divided along roughly the same 38th parallel border that had existed before the war. This "forgotten war" cost around 40,000 American lives.

Joseph McCarthy and McCarthyism

The frustrations that Americans were feeling about the cold war in 1949–1950 sparked the meteoric career of Joseph McCarthy. The junior senator from Wisconsin captured the attention of the nation on February 9, 1950, when in a speech in Wheeling, West Virginia, he claimed that he had a list of 205 Communists who were working in the State Department. This list would expand and contract over time, and it was never fully revealed. Fogginess about the details did not hurt McCarthy. His list was rhetorically, rather than practically, important. With his charges, McCarthy was letting the American people know that he shared their concerns and was on their side against a political establishment that seemed complacent in the face of the Communist threat. The Wisconsin senator was so successful that **McCarthyism** became the term to describe the practice of accusing people of Communism in the overwrought atmosphere of the Second Red Scare.

McCarthy wielded great power for four years. Some fellow senators who criticized his methods were defeated for reelection. McCarthy's message that reverses in the cold war were due to the presence of Communists in the government was easy to understand and believe, and it resonated with many Americans. Despite the fact that many of his fellow Republicans were dubious about his "investigations," they recognized the political value of his popular anti-Communism. McCarthy was an attack dog who would go places more judicious politicians would not. McCarthy went so far as to charge President Truman and the former secretary of state George Marshall of being "unconscious" agents of Communism.

Reluctantly, President Eisenhower at first tolerated McCarthy. Then in March 1954, the senator gave a speech in which he claimed that the U.S. Army was harboring a number of Communists. With these charges, McCarthy went too far. He was attacking a revered institution. The president, a product of that institution, privately decided that McCarthy had to be stopped.

McCarthy's investigation of the Army proved a public relations disaster for the senator. The **Army-McCarthy Hearings** were carried live by two television networks, giving them a large daily audience. As the hearings progressed, it was revealed that McCarthy had asked the Army to provide favorable treatment to one of his aides who had been drafted. During the course of questioning, the senator behaved like a bully, prompting the Army's attorney Joseph Welch to ask McCarthy, "Have you no sense of decency, sir, at long last?" Welch's famous riposte garnered loud applause. Another sign of the changing tide was a hostile profile of Senator McCarthy on Edward R. Murrow's *CBS News* program *See It Now*. President Eisenhower worked behind the scenes to gather Senate support for a motion censuring McCarthy. In December 1954, the Senate formally censured McCarthy. Although he remained in the Senate, McCarthy lost his investigative committee and his political power.

He died three years later. Joseph McCarthy remains a controversial figure. Defenders have maintained that he was essentially correct about the presence of some Communists in the government; his many critics deplore his blackening of many people's reputations with unsubstantiated accusations, in the process helping to create a political climate of paranoia and suspicion.

President Eisenhower and the Cold War

President Eisenhower saw the world through the lens of the cold war. Although very much in charge of his administration, Eisenhower preferred to work behind the scenes. The public face of the administration's foreign policy was Secretary of State John Foster Dulles. Secretary Dulles often used aggressive rhetoric, arguing that the United States must go beyond containment and "make communism retreat." To cut back on the huge expense of the defense budget, the Eisenhower administration relied more heavily on its nuclear deterrent. Dulles then spoke of **"massive retaliation"** if a Communist power encroached on the free world.

Despite his subordinate's strong words, Eisenhower generally followed a cautious course of action, and he hoped for a "new understanding" between the United States and the Soviet Union when Joseph Stalin died in 1953. Nikita Khrushchev, the new Soviet leader, also seemed hopeful for a détente with the Unites States, talking of "peaceful coexistence." But in 1956, when the people of Hungary rose up against Soviet domination, Khrushchev crushed the rebellion with military force. Up to this point, Dulles had talked boldly of aiding Eastern Europeans who tried to "liberate" themselves. But when the Hungarians made their desperate bid for freedom, the United States held back; Eisenhower was unwilling to risk war with the Soviets.

Eisenhower demonstrated a similar unwillingness to employ military force in Southeast Asia. Since 1946, France had been battling a nationalist uprising in Vietnam, led by the Communist Ho Chi Minh. The French persuaded the Truman administration that they were helping to contain Communism, and they received large amounts of American military aid. In 1954, the French were decisively defeated at the **Battle of Dien Bien Phu**. As the situation at Dien Bien Phu deteriorated, the French asked the United States to intervene with military force, even atomic bombs. Many in the American government were sympathetic to the French position, but Eisenhower refused to involve the United States in the war.

The war in Indochina was ended with the **Geneva Accords**, which divided Vietnam into a North Vietnam run by Ho Chi Minh and a South Vietnam in the hands of anti-Communist Vietnamese. While President Eisenhower was unprepared to fight a war in Southeast Asia, he was not uninterested in the region. He believed in the **domino theory**, which held that if one country in Southeast Asia fell to Communism, others in the area would topple as well. The United States began providing substantial aid to the South Vietnamese.

Crises erupted in other parts of the world. The United States had provided assistance to the Egyptian leader Colonel Gamal Abdul Nasser, who was preparing to build the Aswan Dam. Nasser also wanted to purchase large amounts of American weaponry. Nasser's hostility to Israel led Congress to prevent an arms deal. Frustrated at this, Nasser bought arms from the Soviet bloc. This infuriated the Western powers, and the United States cut its financial support for Egypt. Nasser responded by nationalizing the British and French-owned Suez Canal. Determined to overthrow Nasser, the British and French joined with

Israel in an attack on Egypt in October 1956. The United States was not a party to these plans, and Eisenhower was disgusted with the actions of his allies, believing that they would stoke anti-Western feeling in the Middle East. The Suez Crisis intensified when the Soviet Union threatened to intervene on the side of Egypt. Eisenhower defused the situation when he persuaded the British and French to withdraw their forces from Egypt.

Eisenhower and Dulles were worried about the Communist threat in the Middle East. In January 1957, the president promulgated the **Eisenhower Doctrine**, which promised assistance to any Middle Eastern state being threatened by Communism; American military forces would be deployed to any country that asked for their assistance. The Eisenhower Doctrine was implemented in July 1958 when American troops were sent to Lebanon to bolster the pro-Western government.

The American government was especially sensitive to the spread of Communism in Latin America, a region in which the United States had long-standing economic and strategic ties. In 1947, most of the nations in the Western Hemisphere signed the **Rio Pact**, a collective security agreement in which the signatories agreed to mutual support in case of an attack. The United States continued to act as a policeman in the hemisphere when it believed that Soviet sympathizers challenged its interests. In 1954, President Eisenhower authorized a CIA coup to overthrow a president in Guatemala who had seized lands from the United Fruit Company.

In 1959, Fidel Castro overthrew Fulgencio Batista, the dictator of Cuba. Castro soon instituted his own dictatorship, and he announced his intention to create a Communist revolution in Cuba. Castro nationalized American-owned property, and he established cordial relations with the Soviet Union. In response, the United States severed diplomatic relations and imposed a trade embargo against Cuba.

Tensions with the Soviet Union

During the 1950s the United States and Soviet Union dramatically increased their nuclear arsenals. By August 1953, both had exploded hydrogen bombs, many times more destructive than the first atomic bombs. Each country carried out nuclear testing below and above ground. Concerns about nuclear fallout led to a 1958 agreement between Eisenhower and Khrushchev to stop atmospheric tests.

The Americans and Soviets began developing the capacity to place nuclear warheads on missiles. Worries grew in the United States that the Soviets might be gaining a technological or numerical edge in missiles, creating a "missile gap." These concerns were intensified in 1957 when Americans were shocked to learn that the Soviet Union had launched the *Sputnik* satellite into space. Fascinated American observers could actually see *Sputnik* orbiting the earth. In an effort to "keep up" with the Soviets, American schools placed a stronger emphasis on math and science. To push forward the American space program, President Eisenhower created the National Aeronautics and Space Administration (NASA) in 1958.

The U.S. government was embarrassed in May 1960, when the Soviets shot down an American **U-2** spy plane. Initially, the Americans denied that an American plane had been spying over the Soviet Union, saying that instead a NASA test plane in Turkey had gone missing. Then the Soviets produced Francis Gary Powers, the captured pilot. With the American cover story blown, President Eisenhower took full responsibility for the U-2 espionage program. The U-2 incident led to the failure of a peace summit in Paris between Eisenhower and Khrushchev.

Chapter Review

Rapid Review

To achieve the perfect 5, you should be able to explain the following:

- Winning the cold war was the central goal of American policy for 45 years.
- Economic impact of the cold war on American industry was enormous; many plants continued making military hardware throughout the cold war era.
- Debate over who "started" the cold war has occupied the minds of historians since 1945.
- Decisions made at the Yalta and Potsdam Conferences ushered in cold war tensions between the World War II victors.
- Concept of the "iron curtain" was first articulated by Winston Churchill in 1946.
- American strategy of containment motivated many foreign policy decisions in the cold war era.
- The Truman Doctrine, the Marshall Plan, and NATO united America and Western Europe both militarily and economically against the Soviet Union and its satellites.
- America's resolve to oppose communism was tested during the Berlin Crisis and the Korean War.
- 1949 was a critical year in the cold war, as the Soviet Union got the atomic bomb and mainland China turned Communist.
- Some Americans feared that Communists had infiltrated the American government and the entertainment industry; investigations by the House Un-American Activities Committee and Senator Joseph McCarthy were dedicated to "rooting out" Communists in America.
- Under President Dwight Eisenhower, Secretary of State John Foster Dulles formulated an aggressive foreign policy that would not just contain communism but also attempt to roll communism back whenever possible.
- During the Eisenhower administration, crises in Southeast Asia, the Middle East, and Latin America further tested American resolve.
- Both the Soviet Union and the United States built up their nuclear arsenals to dangerous levels in this era.

Time Line

1945: Yalta Conference
  Harry Truman becomes president
  Potsdam Conference
1946: Winston Churchill gives "iron curtain" speech
  Article by George Kennan on containment
1947: HUAC begins probe into movie industry
  Introduction of Federal Employee Loyalty program
  President Truman articulates Truman Doctrine
1948: Berlin Airlift
  Implementation of Marshall Plan
  Creation of nation of Israel
  Alger Hiss implicated as a Communist
1949: NATO established
  Soviet Union successfully tests atomic bomb
  Mainland China turns Communist

1950: Joseph McCarthy gives speech on Communists in the State Department
Alger Hiss convicted of perjury
McCarran Internal Security Act enacted
Beginning of Korean War
1952: Dwight Eisenhower elected president
1953: CIA orchestrates return of Shah of Iran to power
Death of Joseph Stalin
Execution of the Rosenbergs
1954: Army-McCarthy hearings
Government in Guatemala overthrown
French defeated at Dien Bien Phu
Geneva Conference
1955: Creation of the Warsaw Pact
1956: Hungarian Revolt suppressed by Soviet Union
Suez crisis
1957: *Sputnik* launched by Soviet Union
1959: Castro comes to power in Cuba; United States halts trade with Cuba
1960: U-2 incident
John Kennedy elected president

› Review Questions

Fact Check

Check your knowledge of the historical period covered in this chapter.

1. The Army-McCarthy hearings proved
   A. that Americans were largely uninterested in the issue of communism.
   B. that Eisenhower would support McCarthy at any cost.
   C. that McCarthy had little proof for his claims.
   D. the massive popularity of Joseph McCarthy.

2. The policy of containment stated that
   A. America should go out and attempt to dislodge Communist leaders wherever possible.
   B. America should hold firm against Communist encroachment in all parts of the world.
   C. America should not hesitate to use atomic weapons against the Soviet Union.
   D. the United States should depend on its Western European Allies for help against the Soviet Union.

3. America was especially interested in stopping Communist expansion in Latin America because
   A. the United States had many economic interests in the region.
   B. both presidents Truman and Eisenhower were close to many of the Latin American leaders.
   C. the Soviet Union expressed a special interest in expanding in this region.
   D. the CIA had repeatedly failed in operations in Latin America in the past.

4. When the HUAC began their investigation of the movie industry, they looked with suspicion at writers, actors, and directors who
   A. attended Communist Party meetings in the 1930s.
   B. wrote or appeared in World War II–era films that were sympathetic to the Soviet Union.
   C. invoked the Fifth Amendment when testifying before the HUAC.
   D. all of the above

5. Republicans claimed that the Democrats were "soft on communism" for all of the following reasons *except*
   A. during the Truman administration mainland China had gone Communist.
   B. Alger Hiss was an advisor to Franklin Roosevelt at Yalta.
   C. the Truman administration failed to establish a system to check on the possibility of Communists working for the federal government.
   D. decisions made by Roosevelt and Truman at the end of World War II made it easier for the Soviet Union to control Eastern Europe.

Multiple-Choice Questions

Here are multiple-choice questions like the ones on the AP U.S. History exam.

Questions 6–8 refer to the quotation below.

Mr. Stripling: Could you elaborate on the military information which you secured from the Silvermaster group?

Miss Bentley: Well, . . . as I said, it was information of the most varied things you could think of. We had complete data as to almost all of the aircraft production in the country, as to types, how many were being produced, where they were allocated, and so on. We had all sorts of inside information on policies of the Air Corps. As I said, we knew D-Day long before D-Day happened, and we were right. Practically all the inside policies that were going on inside the Air Corps.

—Elizabeth Bentley, testimony before the House Committee on Un-American Activities, July 31, 1948

6. Elizabeth Bentley's congressional testimony concerned espionage by which of the following countries?
   A. Great Britain
   B. Japan
   C. Germany
   D. Soviet Union

7. Postwar revelations of espionage contributed to which of the following?
   A. The Civil Rights Movement
   B. Japanese Internment
   C. The Red Scare
   D. Isolationism

8. The concerns addressed by the House Committee on Un-American Activities can be most directly compared to which of the following?
   A. American concerns about British legislation in the 1760s and 1770s
   B. Republican concerns about Copperheads during the Civil War
   C. Southern concerns about Northern attacks on slavery
   D. Settlers' concerns about Native American attacks

Short-Answer Question

The short-answer question below is similar to the ones you'll encounter on the AP U.S. History exam.

9. Answer Parts A, B, and C.
   A. Briefly explain ONE example of an American effort to contain communism overseas during the period 1945 to 1960.
   B. Briefly explain a SECOND example of an American effort to contain communism overseas during the period 1945 to 1960.
   C. Briefly explain ONE example of an effort to combat communism within the United States during the period 1945 to 1960.

› Answers and Explanations

1. **C.** The hearings did much to discredit McCarthy. By this point, Eisenhower had broken from McCarthy, and many Americans watched these hearings from beginning to end.

2. **B.** Containment emphasized stopping communism whenever it attempted to expand; containment did not emphasize attacking communism where it already existed.

3. **A.** The United States had factories in and active trade relationships with many Latin American countries, and feared that communism would destroy American economic interests in the region. The CIA had actually been quite successful in their operations in the region in the past—witness their role in Guatemala.

4. **D.** As a result of the HUAC hearings, the American movie industry changed dramatically.

5. **C.** All of the other three were used by Republicans to say that the Democrats were indeed "soft on communism." Truman instituted a Loyalty Review Board to verify that nearly 4 million federal workers were "true Americans."

6. **D.** Elizabeth Bentley's congressional testimony concerned espionage by the Soviet Union. In the years following the end of World War II evidence surfaced concerning Soviet espionage in the United States. Eventually it would be learned that the Soviet Union had even stolen secrets about the atomic bomb. Hearings like those conducted by the House Committee on Un-American Activities contributed to a growing fear of Communist subversion in the United States.

7. **C.** Postwar revelations of espionage contributed to the Red Scare. Concern grew that Soviet agents had infiltrated the U.S. government. The revelation that the former State Department official Alger Hiss had passed information on to the Soviets seemed to confirm this fear. Beginning in 1950, Senator Joseph McCarthy became politically powerful charging that there were Communists in the State Department and other government offices. Many feared that Communists loyal to the Soviet Union were also trying to subvert other American institutions. The House Committee on Un-American Activities investigated the entertainment industry. The Hollywood Ten were a group of writers and directors who spent time in jail for refusing to answer questions at their congressional hearing. Entertainers accused of Communist sympathies saw their careers derailed through a blacklist.

8. **B.** The concerns addressed by the House Committee on Un-American Activities can be most directly compared to Republican concerns about Copperheads during the Civil War. Copperheads were northern Democrats with southern sympathies who wanted an end to the war. Republican supporters of the war believed that the Copperheads, like the later American Communists, were subversives working to aid the enemy. Some Copperhead leaders, like Clement Vallandigham of Ohio, were arrested by federal authorities.

9. **Parts A and B**: Inspired by the writings of the American diplomat George Kennan, the U.S. government began to develop a containment

policy to limit the expansion of communism in 1947. President Harry Truman formulated the Truman Doctrine, which stated that the United States would assist any country threatened by Communist aggression or internal Communist subversion. In an effort to prevent the spread of communism in Europe, the United States launched the Marshall Plan, a program of economic assistance to Western Europe designed to help the European democracies recover economically from World War II. In 1948, when the Soviet Union cut off access to West Berlin, the United States and Great Britain supplied the city through the Berlin Airlift. In 1949, the United States, Canada, and 10 Western European countries formed the North Atlantic Treaty Organization (NATO); this military alliance confronted the Soviet Union and its allies for the next 40 years. In 1950, the United States came to the assistance of South Korea after it was invaded by Communist North Korea. The Korean War lasted until 1953. Following the defeat of French forces in Vietnam at the Battle of Dien Bien Phu in 1954, President Dwight D. Eisenhower provided support to the new country of South Vietnam. Eisenhower believed in the domino theory, arguing that if one country in Southeast Asia fell to communism, others would soon follow. In 1957, the president announced the Eisenhower Doctrine, which stated that the United States would provide support to any Middle Eastern country being threatened by other Middle Eastern countries associated with the Soviet Union. The United States engaged in an arms race with the Soviet Union, building atomic bombs, hydrogen bombs, and nuclear-armed guided missiles. The United States used U-2 spy planes to monitor nuclear missile sites in the Soviet Union; in 1960, the Soviets shot down a U-2 plane and captured its pilot, embarrassing the American government.

Part C: The revelation that Communist spies had penetrated the U.S. government and even acquired information about the atomic bomb contributed to the Second Red Scare. President Truman created a Loyalty Review Board to remove security risks from the federal workforce. The House Un-American Activities Committee (HUAC) launched investigations into the infiltration of communists into the government and the entertainment industry. This contributed to a growing hysteria about communist activities in the United States. Many Hollywood and Broadway actors, writers, and directors were blacklisted because of their supposed Communist sympathies. The McCarran Internal Security Act of 1950 compelled Communist and Communist associated organizations to register with the government; the act also provided for the investigation of people suspected of subversive activities. In 1950, Senator Joseph McCarthy of Wisconsin accused the State Department of harboring large numbers of Communists. Following this, McCarthy launched a number of investigations of supposed Communists in the U.S. government. McCarthy became very popular. He was finally censured by the Senate in 1954 after he was deemed to have gone too far in an investigation of the U.S. Army.

CHAPTER 26

Prosperity and Anxiety: The 1950s

IN THIS CHAPTER

Summary: In the 1950s, many middle-class, white American families experienced a prosperity they had never known before. Many young couples moved to the suburbs and purchased their first home (for veterans, this could be partially financed by the GI Bill). Observers noted that Dwight Eisenhower was the perfect president for the seemingly placid 1950s. Many commentators wrote on the conformity of American suburban life in the period. However, there were also many Americans pushing for change. Proponents of civil rights for black Americans were heartened by the 1954 *Brown v. Board of Education* Supreme Court decision outlawing segregation in public schools, yet found that their struggles would continue throughout this decade and all through the next. Some women felt frustrated in the role of housewife that they were expected to play in suburban America. Many teenagers rebelled in the decade as well, by emulating the "rebellious" movie star James Dean, by dabbling in Beat poetry, or by listening to the new rock 'n' roll music.

Keywords

***Brown v. Board of Education* (1954):** Supreme Court decision stating that "separate but equal" schools for white and black students were unconstitutional and that school districts across America must desegregate with "all deliberate speed"; controversy over enforcement of this decision was to last for more than a decade.

Montgomery bus boycott (1955): effort by blacks in Montgomery, Alabama, to have the local bus company end discriminatory seating and hiring policies. The movement started with the arrest of Rosa Parks for refusing to give up her bus seat to a white man; the boycott was later led by the Rev. Martin Luther King, Jr.

Baby boom: from 1947 to 1962 Americans married and had children at a record pace; the "high point" of the baby boom was 1957.

The Feminine Mystique: book written by Betty Friedan describing the frustration felt by suburban women in the 1950s; this book was a landmark for feminists of the 1960s and 1970s.

James Dean: young actor whose character in the film *Rebel Without a Cause* inspired many rebellious young people of the 1950s.

Beat Generation: literary movement of the 1950s; writers of this movement rejected the materialistic American culture of the decade. Jack Kerouac, Allen Ginsberg, and William Burroughs were key writers of this movement.

The Return of Prosperity

Many people, from ordinary citizens, to politicians, to economists, worried that the end of World War II would see a serious recession, if not a return to the Depression conditions of the 1930s. The feared economic downturn did not materialize. Instead, the American economy boomed between 1945 and 1960. The American gross national product (GNP) grew from $200 billion in 1945 to more than $500 billion in 1960.

A number of factors contributed to this economic growth. During World War II, workers earned lots of money, but because of wartime restrictions, there were fewer goods available for them to purchase. Automobile manufacturers and the makers of other consumer goods had switched to the production of military hardware. Once the war ended, manufacturers returned to civilian production, and consumers were ready to spend. The result was a consumption binge that lifted the American economy. In addition, credit cards became a popular and convenient way of facilitating purchases in the postwar years. Diner's Club cards appeared in 1950, providing a boost to the restaurant industry.

The American love affair with the automobile had been frustrated for many during the hard years of the Depression, and then the switch to war production after Pearl Harbor. Once the war ended, demand for new cars skyrocketed. A rejuvenated advertising industry helped stoke this demand and channel consumer tastes. By the 1950s, advertising had attained levels last seen in the prosperous 1920s. Consumers were tantalized in the 1950s by increasingly large and luxurious vehicles, sporting racy fins and growing amounts of glittering chrome. The centrality of cars to American life was reflected in legislation sponsored by the Eisenhower administration to create a massive interstate highway system. Initially designed to facilitate the movement of troops and urban populations in the event of the outbreak of a World War III, the interstate highways facilitated the expansion of America's car culture by enabling drivers to speedily travel to suburban enclaves. With interurban travel easier by car, motels and fast-food restaurants sprouted up across the country.

Defense spending as a result of the cold war also stimulated the economy. In addition to spending on the military and weapons systems, millions were lavished on technological research and development. What President Eisenhower termed the "military-industrial complex" accounted for billions of dollars of spending in the 1950s and ensuing decades.

Another industry that prospered in the postwar years was the housing construction business. At the end of the war, demand for housing far outstripped supply. In some cities, two families had to live in an apartment designed for one. A surge of building began to meet the pressing need for new homes. The **GI Bill** of 1944 helped spur the construction boom by authorizing low-interest mortgage loans for returning servicemen. The GI Bill also helped expand the middle class (and pool of potential home buyers) by providing educational subsidies to those who had served in the military.

The innovative builder William Levitt helped ease the housing shortage with his first development in Levittown, New York. Making use of prefabrication techniques learned during the war, he began erecting **Levittowns** in assembly line fashion. The homes in these rapidly constructed developments initially looked very much alike, but they were well made and reasonably priced. Levitt helped make possible a massive migration of middle-class families to the suburbs. This demographic shift of population from the cities to the suburbs was one of the most significant social trends of the postwar period.

Politics in the Postwar Era

Harry Truman faced a great challenge when he became president in 1945. The charismatic Franklin Roosevelt had held office for 12 years and led the American people through more than a decade of crisis. Truman seemed an obscure and ordinary figure compared to his predecessor. Nevertheless, the new president attempted to extend the liberal policies of the New Deal and establish his own political legacy. This was not easy given the increasingly conservative mood of the country. The Republicans recaptured control of Congress in 1946, the first time that they had had majorities in the House of Representatives and Senate since 1930. Following a wave of strikes, Congress passed the **Taft-Hartley Act** in 1947. This legislation placed restrictions on unions, forbidding the use of contributions of union members in federal elections, and compelling union leaders to publically declare that they were not Communists. In the case of strikes that might affect public safety or health, the president could enforce an 80-day cooling off period, during which workers would return to their jobs and negotiations would take place between labor and management. The unions opposed the Taft-Hartley Act and President Truman vetoed it, but Congress overrode his veto to make the bill law.

During the election of 1948, Truman proposed a series of initiatives that he would later term the **Fair Deal**. He called for national healthcare, increases in spending for education and public housing, and the repeal of the Taft-Hartley Act. More controversially for a Democrat whose roots were in the South, he proposed a civil rights bill.

Most political prognosticators believed that Truman would lose the presidential election of 1948 to Thomas Dewey, the Republican governor of New York who had run a creditable race against Franklin Roosevelt in 1944. Truman had never enjoyed Roosevelt's popularity. Splits in the Democratic Party seemed to doom his candidacy. Southern Democrats offended by Truman's civil rights bill ran South Carolina governor Strom Thurmond as the Dixiecrat candidate for president. Left-wing Democrats upset with Truman's cold war policies rallied behind former vice president Henry Wallace, the nominee of a newly organized Progressive Party. Unwilling to accept defeat, Truman campaigned vigorously, criticizing the Congress that rejected his proposed legislation as "do-nothing" and appealing to the different elements of the 1930s New Deal coalition. Truman's efforts paid off, and he won one of the great upset presidential election victories. The Democrats also recaptured control of Congress. Despite this historic success, in his second term Truman was unable to pass much of his Fair Deal program. The Republicans and conservative Democrats were still strong enough to foil his efforts. Charges of being "soft on communism," the drawn-out and inconclusive Korean War, and corruption scandals in his administration all undermined Truman's personal standing and political capital. He decided not to run for reelection in 1952.

With the Democrats being very unpopular after 20 years of almost unbroken power in Washington, in 1952 the Republican presidential candidate Dwight D. Eisenhower won an easy victory over Illinois governor Adlai Stevenson. As the commander of Allied forces in Europe during World War II, Eisenhower possessed great prestige and popularity. As president, he proved to be a moderate conservative who did not attempt to roll back the welfare state created by the New Deal. He attempted to limit the growth of government, and he worked to enhance the prestige of the courts and Congress. He worked well with legislators of both parties in passing legislation such as the Interstate Highways Act and two civil rights acts. Although he delegated lots of responsibilities to his cabinet, Eisenhower was a skilled executive who dominated his administration behind the scenes. Like the Republican presidents of the 1920s, Eisenhower believed that the fundamental business of America was business. He was very friendly with businessmen, and he appointed a number of business executives to his cabinet. Eisenhower's sympathy for private enterprise made him a fitting president for the prosperous 1950s.

Eisenhower's vice president was Richard Nixon, an able and ambitious politician who had represented California, first as a member of the House of Representatives and later as a senator in the Senate. Nixon first attained political prominence by pursuing the Alger Hiss case while serving on HUAC. He was best known for his vociferous anti-Communism. During the 1952 election campaign, Nixon was accused of benefiting from a slush fund set up by political supporters to cover some of his personal expenses. Eisenhower came under pressure to drop his running mate. Nixon responded to the criticism with a nationally televised address. In his emotional **Checkers Speech**, Nixon denied that he had done anything illegal or unethical. He pointed out that his wife Pat wore a "very respectable Republican cloth coat" rather than a fur and that the only gift that he had received was a dog named Checkers, now the beloved pet of his two daughters. The public reaction to this speech was overwhelmingly positive. Nixon stayed on the ticket, and over the next quarter century he would go on to one of the most dramatic careers in American political history.

The Rise of the Civil Rights Movement

The struggle against Nazi anti-Semitism during World War II stimulated African-American resistance to racism at home. African-American veterans were dismayed that progress against discrimination had moved so slowly and that Jim Crow laws remained entrenched in the South. President Truman had sought the political support of civil rights leaders in 1948. He signed orders outlawing discrimination in hiring federal workers and ending segregation in the military. However, Truman's initiative met resistance in the government, and the military was not fully integrated until the Eisenhower administration.

African-American athletes had occasionally broken out into wider national acclaim, and they had served as heroes and role models for African-American youth. In the 1930s, the boxer Joe Louis and the Olympic athlete Jesse Owens had become inspirational public figures. In 1947, Jackie Robinson became the first African American given a contract in Major League Baseball, playing for the Brooklyn Dodgers. Robinson faced constant racial harassment in his first season. Despite this, Robinson always maintained his dignity and played brilliantly. He was voted the National League Rookie of the Year in 1947.

Civil rights leaders set their sights on legally overturning the 1896 Supreme Court *Plessy v. Ferguson* decision, which had established the constitutionality of "separate but equal" facilities for African Americans. Schools were at the forefront of their concerns. In the early 1950s, the schools for whites and African Americans were separate but hardly equal. White schools often received 80 to 85 percent of the educational funding in Southern school districts. The NAACP challenged this status quo by supporting Oliver Brown, who sued the school district of Topeka, Kansas, because his daughter could not attend a nearby white school, but instead had to be bussed to an all-African-American school on the other side of town.

This case eventually reached the Supreme Court. The NAACP's lawyer Thurgood Marshall defended Brown's suit. He would later become the first African-American Supreme Court justice. The Supreme Court was ready to overturn *Plessy v. Ferguson*. The new chief justice, Earl Warren, recently appointed by President Eisenhower, was determined to strike a blow against racial inequality. He skillfully negotiated with his fellow justices and crafted a unanimous decision that ruled "separate but equal" unconstitutional. The landmark 1954 ***Brown v. Board of Education*** decision also announced that all school districts should desegregate with "all deliberate speed." Officials, parents, and students in many places in the South refused to comply with the court order, declaring "2, 4, 6, 8. We don't want to integrate." Earl Warren served as chief justice from 1953 to 1969. The "Warren Court" became known for its liberal orientation and its "judicial activism," making controversial decisions on issues such as school prayer and the rights of accused criminals.

In 1955, the town of Montgomery, Alabama, became a flashpoint in the struggle for civil rights. Under Montgomery's Jim Crow rules, African Americans literally had to sit at the back of the bus and give up their seats to white people if asked. Rosa Parks, who worked for the Montgomery NAACP, refused to surrender her seat to a white man, and she was arrested. This led civil rights leaders to launch the **Montgomery bus boycott.** African Americans walked or carpooled instead of patronizing city busses.

Despite this impressive show of solidarity in the African-American community, the bus company upheld its discriminatory seating policies. In 1956, the Supreme Court resolved the dispute by ruling that segregation in public transportation was unconstitutional. The civil rights movement had won a significant victory. Martin Luther King, Jr., a young African-American minister who had been the spokesman for the boycotters attained national prominence as a civil rights leader.

Many white Southerners continued to resist the implementation of *Brown v. Board of Education*. In 1957, a small group of African-American students were prepared to attend classes at Central High School in Little Rock, Arkansas. Orval Faubus, the governor of Arkansas, ordered the state's National Guard to block these students from entering the school. President Eisenhower refused to accept this challenge to the Supreme Court and federal law. He nationalized the Arkansas National Guard and sent federal troops to escort the African-American students into Central High School. Federal troops protected these students for the rest of the school year. The crisis in Little Rock prefigured the civil rights tumult of the 1960s.

Life in Suburbia

Many in the generation that grew up during the Great Depression and then experienced World War II made the choice to raise families in the suburbs. After years of deprivation, these people sought happiness in **domesticity**. This contributed to a **baby boom** during which the birth rate soared. The baby boom lasted from 1945 to 1962. At its height in 1957, 4.5 million babies were born.

The suburbs were a good place for parents to raise these children. At the time, the suburbs were criticized for their conformity because many of the houses in new developments looked alike, and their residents drove similar cars, used similar appliances, wore similar clothes, and watched the same shows on TV. William H. Whyte published an influential analysis of the conservative values of suburban life in *The Organization Man*, published in 1956. But such an environment provided a good deal of security for children. Life in the suburbs revolved around children, especially for their mothers who drove them to scout meetings and sports practices and attended meetings of the PTA. A number of social historians argue that the parents of the baby boomers were attempting to protect their children from the economic and social dislocations that had disrupted their own childhoods.

Some men who fought in World War II had difficulty adjusting to peacetime life. Others were dissatisfied with ordinary 9-to-5 work. The book and film ***The Man in the Gray Flannel Suit*** dramatized the plight of men caught up in unrewarding corporate jobs. Many men found hobbies like hunting and fishing more meaningful. Popular men's magazines of the 1950s ran the gamut from *Field and Stream* to Hugh Hefner's *Playboy*.

Some women also found the 1950s frustrating. The mass media promoted the role of women as homemakers. One of the most popular movie stars of the decade was Doris Day, who projected an appealing and unthreatening "girl-next-door" image. Large numbers of women attended college, though often with the pragmatic goal of finding an appropriate husband. Many women found their role as mothers and homemakers fulfilling, but an increasingly vocal minority did not. Ironically, given the cultural emphasis on feminine domesticity, more women were working in the late 1950s than had held jobs during World War II. Many of these women were working out of financial necessity, but some were doing so for personal satisfaction. Betty Friedan in ***The Feminine Mystique*** (1963) gave a voice to the women who felt frustrated with the role of housewife. In 1966, Friedan would found the National Organization for Women (NOW).

Teenagers in the 1950s enjoyed the benefits of prosperity, and they were the first generation of adolescents extensively targeted by advertisers. Thanks to the burgeoning mass media, they wore the same clothes and listened to the same music. Teenagers of the 1950s have been called the "silent generation" because they were generally more interested in school and socializing than politics. Parents and school officials discouraged rebellious behavior. Educational films shown in schools emphasized self-control and respect for authority. Popular television shows such as *Ozzie and Harriet* featured young people who followed these rules.

Despite the efforts of their elders, many young people in the 1950s showed varying degrees of rebelliousness. A few students adopted the antiestablishmentarian attitudes of the characters played by Marlon Brando in *The Wild One* (1953) and James Dean in ***Rebel Without a Cause*** (1955). In addition to signs of a youth rebellion, other forms of cultural iconoclasm demonstrated that the 1950s were not a period of monolithic conformity. Jackson Pollock and other artists pioneered the radically nonrepresentational "abstract expressionist" style of painting. The **Beat Generation** is a term describing a loosely connected group of writers, poets, and artists who rejected the rules and values of a materialistic America living in the shadow of the atomic bomb. Instead, the Beats valued freedom, spontaneity, and artistic improvisation. They experimented with drugs, enthused over jazz, and explored Eastern spirituality. The most influential Beat work was Jack Kerouac's novel *On the Road* (1957), which follows the journeys of two friends across America. Allen Ginsberg's poem *Howl* (1955) denounces the corrupting influence of modern society on people's lives. While few young people actively participated in the Beat movement, many adopted a "Beatnik" style, wearing black turtleneck sweaters, dark eyeglasses, and berets and listening to experimental poetry in coffeehouses. This spirit of alienation from middle-class American values was famously captured in J.D. Salinger's novel *Catcher in the Rye* (1951), in which a young Holden Caulfield tries to understand his place in the world.

The most widespread expression of youthful rebellion in the 1950s was the popularity of rock 'n' roll. Many adults were horrified by the unrestrained rhythms and beats of rock 'n' roll, and they regarded it as immoral and the "devil's music." Some overwrought adults charged that rock music led to juvenile delinquency and Communism. By listening to rock 'n' roll and dancing to it at "sock hops," young people could collectively defy the buttoned-down expectations of their elders. Music such as Little Richard's "Good Golly Miss Molly" did not encourage young people to "control their emotions."

Many concerned parents associated rock 'n' roll with "uninhibited" African-American music. In fact, rock was heavily influenced by jazz music, country music, gospel, the blues (R&B, boogie-woogie piano style), and many African-American performers became popular with white teens in the 1950s. White rock musicians were influenced by African-American music and performance styles, none more so than Elvis Presley, who delighted young audiences but shocked many older people with his sexually charged performances on TV. Elvis was quieted for a time when he was inducted into the Army in 1958. Gradually rock 'n' roll became tamer and more commercially oriented as the 1950s came to an end.

The cultural rebels of the 1950s profoundly influenced the much more radical social upheaval of the 1960s. The Beats prepared the way for the hippies. Young people in the 1960s would go much further in defying the values of their elders.

Chapter Review

Rapid Review

To achieve the perfect 5, you should be able to explain the following:

- The 1950s is viewed by some as a decade of complacency and by others as a decade of growing ferment.
- Large-scale economic growth continued throughout the 1950s, spurred by cold war defense needs, automobile sales, housing sales, and the sale of appliances.
- The advertising industry did much to shape consumer desires in the 1950s.
- The GI Bill gave many veterans low-income mortgages and the possibility of a college education after World War II.
- Many families moved to suburbia in the 1950s; critics maintain that this increased the conformity of American society.
- During the baby boom, the birthrate drastically increased; the baby boom lasted from 1945 to 1962.
- Presidents Truman and Eisenhower were both dwarfed by the memory of the personality and the policies of Franklin Roosevelt.
- Jackie Robinson did much to advance the cause of rights in the postwar era.
- *Brown v. Board of Education* was a tremendous victory for those pushing for school integration in the 1950s.
- The Montgomery bus boycott and the events at Central High School in Little Rock, Arkansas, demonstrated the techniques that would prove to be successful in defeating segregation.
- Many men and many women felt great frustration with suburban family life of the 1950s.
- 1950s teenagers are often called the "silent generation," although James Dean, the Beat Generation writers, and Elvis Presley attracted followers among young people who did rebel in the 1950s.

Time Line

1944: GI Bill enacted
1947: Taft-Hartley Act enacted
      Jackie Robinson first plays for Brooklyn Dodgers
1948: Truman elected president in stunning upset
      Truman orders desegregation of armed forces

1950: Diner's Club credit card offered
1951: Publication of *The Catcher in the Rye* by J. D. Salinger
1952: Dwight D. Eisenhower elected president
1953: Defense budget at $47 billion
Alan Freed begins to play rock 'n' roll on the radio in Cleveland, Ohio
1954: *Brown v. Board of Education* Supreme Court decision
1955: First McDonald's opens
Rebel Without a Cause released
Bus boycott in Montgomery, Alabama
1956: Interstate Highway Act enacted
Majority of U.S. workers hold white-collar jobs
Howl by Allen Ginsberg first read
1957: Baby boom peaks
Publication of *On the Road* by Jack Kerouac
Resistance to school integration in Little Rock, Arkansas
1960: Three-quarters of all American homes have a TV set

› Review Questions

Fact Check

Check your knowledge of the historical period covered in this chapter.

1. Consumer spending increased in the 1950s because of all of the following *except*
   A. many Americans were once again purchasing stock.
   B. many families were buying automobiles.
   C. many Americans were buying homes.
   D. advertising had a major impact on the American consumer.

2. The policies of the presidency of Dwight D. Eisenhower are most similar to the policies of the presidency of
   A. Franklin Roosevelt.
   B. William Howard Taft.
   C. Calvin Coolidge.
   D. Theodore Roosevelt.

3. How did their experiences in the Great Depression and World War II affect the generation who began to raise families in the postwar era?
   A. They turned inward to family for comfort.
   B. They were likely to want to give their children many of the things they had not been able to have.
   C. Interested in consumer goods, they would be likely to buy many things on credit.

D. A and B above.

4. The most important impact of television on viewers of the early 1950s was that
   A. it provided them with comedies that allowed them to forget the difficult years of the 1950s.
   B. it allowed them to receive the latest news of the day.
   C. it imposed a sense of conformity on American society.
   D. it fostered a growing youth culture.

5. Many Americans were especially fearful of rock 'n' roll in the 1950s because
   A. many of the musicians who played it were black.
   B. Elvis Presley and many of the early performers of rock 'n' roll came from a decidedly lower-class background.
   C. Elvis Presley and many other early rock 'n' roll performers came from the American South.
   D. the messages found in early rock 'n' roll supported communism.

Multiple-Choice Questions

Here are multiple-choice questions like the ones on the AP U.S. History exam.

Questions 6–8 refer to the quotation below.

The more people have studied different methods of bringing up children, the more they have come to the conclusion that what good mothers and fathers instinctively feel like doing for their babies is usually best after all. All parents do their best job when they have a natural, easy confidence in themselves. Better to make a few mistakes from being natural than to try to do everything letter-perfect out of a feeling of worry.

—Dr. Benjamin Spock, *The Common Sense Book of Baby and Child Care*, 1946

6. Dr. Spock's book on baby care became very popular in part because it coincided with
  A. the baby boom.
  B. the Great Depression.
  C. the women's movement.
  D. the youth counterculture.

7. Where did many of Dr. Spock's readers live?
  A. The frontier
  B. Dumbbell tenement houses
  C. On farms
  D. In suburbs

8. Dr. Spock's book on baby care can best be compared to which of the following?
  A. *The Old Man and the Sea* by Ernest Hemingway
  B. *How to Win Friends and Influence People* by Dale Carnegie
  C. *Common Sense* by Thomas Paine
  D. *The Federalist* by James Madison, Alexander Hamilton, and John Jay

Short-Answer Question

The short-answer question below is similar to the ones you'll encounter on the AP U.S. History exam.

9. Answer Parts A, B, and C.
  A. Briefly explain ONE example of a social phenomenon reflecting American prosperity in the 1950s.
  B. Briefly explain a SECOND example of a social phenomenon reflecting American prosperity in the 1950s.
  C. Briefly explain ONE example of a critique of the prosperous American society of the 1950s.

› Answers and Explanations

1. A. Americans were buying consumer goods in the postwar era. Many had money but not goods to buy in World War II. The purchase of stock would become pronounced only after this post–World War II buying spree ended.

2. C. Although each was somewhat different in style, Coolidge and Eisenhower were both friends of big business, believed in a balanced budget, and believed in a smaller role for the federal government and the presidency.

3. D. Many of those who lived through the Depression were never comfortable with the idea of buying on credit; some never got credit cards at any point in their lives. Some historians say that this generation of parents spoiled their children, forming the expectations that some of these children would have as young adults in the 1960s.

4. C. TV viewers could get comedies and news on the radio. There was little on television in the early 1950s that specifically appealed to youth.

5. A. Elvis, Carl Perkins, Jerry Lee Lewis, and others were of lower-class backgrounds and were from the South, but the main objection to rock 'n' roll was its connection to black culture—for instance, Fats Domino, Chuck Berry, and Little Richard. No known early rock 'n' roll song supported communism.

6. A. Dr. Spock's book on baby care became very popular in part because it coincided with the baby boom. Beginning in the early 1940s there was a sharp spike in births, cresting in 1957, with 4.3 million babies being born in one year. The baby boom was in part a reaction to the birth dearth of the 1930s, when couples had fewer children or postponed parenthood for economic reasons. The prosperity that began during World War II and then accelerated after the war made it possible for couples to have more children. The cultural ideal of a working father and stay-at-home mother also favored larger families.

7. D. Many of Dr. Spock's readers lived in the suburbs. There was an explosion of suburban development in the postwar years. Builders like Abraham and William Levitt created Levittowns in New York and elsewhere, providing buyers with inexpensive single-family homes. Many Americans saw the new suburban developments as ideal places to raise families.

8. B. Dr. Spock's book on baby care can best be compared to Dale Carnegie's *How to Win Friends and Influence People*. Like Dr. Spock, Dale Carnegie wrote a self-help book that emphasized the power of people to shape their own lives. Dr. Spock told women and men to trust themselves as parents. Dale Carnegie encouraged people to improve their lives by developing their self-confidence. Both books were long-term bestsellers.

9. Parts A and B: The postwar prosperity increased demand for American-made consumer goods. The economist John Kenneth Galbraith wrote that America had become an "affluent society." The American automobile industry boomed. The American love affair with cars encouraged the launching of the interstate highway system in 1956. The mobility provided by automobiles also contributed to the growth of suburbs. Many Americans in the postwar years wanted to own their own homes. Veterans could use the GI Bill of 1944 to get low-interest mortgage loans. The homebuilder William Levitt used assembly line techniques to construct several Levittowns filled with affordable, but nearly identical suburban homes. Also helping fuel the rush to the suburbs was the postwar baby boom. Many Americans wanted to raise their growing families in a safe and comfortable suburban environment.

Part C: African Americans wanted to share fully in the prosperity of the 1950s, but they were held back by racial segregation. The 1954 Supreme Court decision *Brown v. Board of Education* ruled that "separate but equal" was unconstitutional, and ordered the desegregation of public schools. In 1955, Rosa Parks refused to surrender her seat to a white man on a Montgomery, Alabama, bus. Her arrest led to the Montgomery bus boycott. Victory in this struggle to desegregate public transportation in Montgomery brought Rev. Martin Luther King, Jr., to national prominence. In 1957, President Dwight D. Eisenhower used federal troops to protect African American students desegregating Central High School in Little Rock, Arkansas. Feminists rejected the role of housewife for women. Betty Friedan began collecting material for her book *The Feminine Mystique* (1963). A variety of writers criticized what they perceived as the conformity of the 1950s. William H. Whyte's *The Organization Man* (1956) condemned the conformity of modern corporate culture. The countercultural writer Jack Kerouac, a leader of the Beat Generation, described a free and highly individualistic lifestyle in *On the Road* (1957). For some young people, rock 'n' roll music became a way of expressing rebellion against the values of their parents.

CHAPTER 27

America in an Era of Turmoil (1960–1975)

IN THIS CHAPTER

Summary: The events and consequences of the 1960s still have the ability to provoke contentious debate. Many claim the changes that came out of the decade have had a positive long-term effect on American society; for example, women's rights and protection of the environment became popular causes during this period. Others point to destructive consequences of the decade, including the loosening of morality and excessive drug use, as more emblematic of the 1960s. The election of John Kennedy as president in 1960 caused many in America to feel optimistic about the future. But for some, Kennedy's assassination in 1963 was a sign of the violence that would consume America later in the decade. The construction of the Berlin Wall, the Cuban Missile Crisis, and the Vietnam War were the major foreign policy issues of the decade; opposition to the Vietnam War eventually drove President Lyndon Johnson from the White House. Blacks made many civil rights gains during the decade, but a number of younger blacks now called for "black power" rather than integration into white society. Many college and high school students became increasingly empowered in the decade; hundreds of thousands protested against the Vietnam War. While a number of students were increasingly involved in political affairs, other young people supported cultural instead of political revolution and became members of a widespread counterculture.

Keywords

New Frontier: group of domestic policies proposed by John Kennedy that included Medicare and aid to education and urban renewal; many of these policies were not enacted until the presidency of Lyndon Johnson.

Great Society: overarching plan by President Lyndon Johnson to assist the underprivileged in American society; it included the creation of the Department of Housing and Urban Affairs and the Head Start and Medicare programs. Some Great Society programs were later reduced because of the cost of the Vietnam War.

Civil Rights Act of 1964: major civil rights legislation that outlawed racial discrimination in public facilities, in employment, and in voter registration.

Black power: philosophy of some younger blacks in the 1960s who were impatient with the slow pace of desegregation; its advocates believed that blacks should create and control their own political and cultural institutions rather than seeking integration into white-dominated society.

Roe v. Wade (1973): Supreme Court decision that made abortion legal (with some restrictions).

Gulf of Tonkin Resolution: congressional resolution passed in August 1964 following reports that U.S. Navy ships had been fired on by North Vietnamese gunboats off the Vietnam coast; in essence it gave the president the power to fight the Vietnam War without approval from Congress.

Students for a Democratic Society (SDS): radical, activist student organization created in 1960 that advocated a more democratic, participatory society. SDS was one of the major student organizations opposing the Vietnam War.

Counterculture: movement by young people in the 1960s who rejected political involvement and emphasized the need for personal instead of political revolution. Many members of the counterculture wore long hair and experimented with various drugs, with sex, and with unconventional living arrangements.

Kent State University: campus in Ohio where four students who were part of a 1970 protest against U.S. involvement in Cambodia were shot and killed by National Guardsmen.

The 1960 Election

The election of 1960 marked a political watershed—though this may not have been obvious at the time. The electoral victory of John F. Kennedy ushered in a period of dynamic and often tumultuous change. At age 43, Kennedy made a stark contrast to the septuagenarian Dwight Eisenhower. Charismatic and well spoken, Kennedy appeared to exemplify youth and vigor. He had served in the House of Representatives and as a senator from Massachusetts. Roman Catholic in religion, and the first president born in the twentieth century, Kennedy made it clear that he would take the country in new directions. At his inaugural, he challenged his fellow Americans, saying, "Ask not what your country can do for you—ask what you can do for your country."

The Republican presidential nominee in the election, Vice President Richard Nixon, was only four years older than Kennedy, but he was perceived by some voters to be "too tied to the past" because of his association with the Eisenhower administration. Nixon was also the victim of technological change. The 1960 election was the first in which the presidential candidates debated on television. In the four debates Kennedy, whose father had once run a Hollywood movie studio, was well made up and appeared relaxed and vigorous, while Nixon's appearance suffered from having a five o'clock shadow, and he looked ill at ease. People who watched the debates on television believed Kennedy the winner, while those who listened on the radio thought Nixon had come out ahead. Unfortunately for Nixon, more people now watched television than listened to the radio. In an extremely close election, Kennedy won by only 120,000 votes out of 34 million votes cast.

The Liberal Hour of the 1960s

Hearkening to America's pioneer past, President Kennedy declared that the United States was on the verge of a **New Frontier**. Journalists used this term to describe Kennedy's ambitious legislative agenda. A fervent cold warrior, the president launched a massive military build-up. He also hoped to stimulate the economy and eradicate poverty in the United States. Kennedy was deeply moved by Michael Harrington's book *The Other America* (1962), which reminded Americans that many people remained impoverished despite the nation's general prosperity. Kennedy wanted to devote more federal resources to healthcare, education, and urban renewal. Liberals like Kennedy and his vice president, Lyndon Johnson, firmly believed that a more activist federal government could effectively contain Communism abroad and reform American society at home.

Despite his popularity, President Kennedy was unable to persuade Congress to pass much of his ambitious legislative agenda. Congress did increase the minimum wage from $1.00 an hour to $1.25, and it authorized the president's Peace Corps program, which sent young volunteers to assist people in the developing world.

The space program, like the Defense Department, benefited from cold war tensions. Early in 1961, the Soviets humiliated the United States by making cosmonaut Yuri Gagarin the first human being to travel into space and orbit the earth. In May, Alan Shepard became the first American in space, and in February 1962, John Glenn became the first American to orbit the earth. Stung by Soviet success, Kennedy promised that the United States would land a man on the moon by the end of the decade. To make this a reality, he and Congress began pouring money into the National Aeronautics and Space Administration (NASA).

President Kennedy was on a trip to build up political support in Texas on November 22, 1963. While riding in a motorcade in Dallas, Kennedy was shot and killed by Lee Harvey Oswald, an ex-marine and Communist sympathizer. Oswald was apprehended, but two days later a Dallas nightclub owner named Jack Ruby murdered him. The shocking circumstances of President Kennedy's death led to the formation of the **Warren Commission** to investigate his assassination. The Warren Commission concluded that Oswald had acted alone. Despite the commission's exhaustive research, many people persisted in believing that Kennedy had been the victim of a conspiracy.

Vice President Lyndon Johnson was sworn into office on the plane taking the presidential party home from Dallas. A former Senate majority leader, Johnson was a skilled legislator, and in 1964 he was able to guide much of Kennedy's stalled legislation through Congress, including a hefty tax cut intended to spur economic growth.

That year Johnson hoped to win the presidency in his own right. His Republican opponent was Senator Barry Goldwater of Arizona, a principled conservative who wanted to roll back much of the welfare state created since the 1930s. He was prone to robust rhetoric, talking about the possibility of using nuclear weapons in Vietnam and declaring that "extremism in the defense of liberty is no vice." Goldwater proved a polarizing figure in 1964, and Johnson easily defeated him, winning 62 percent of the vote. Johnson used his landslide victory, and the large majorities of Democrats elected to Congress alongside him, to push for one of the most ambitious legislative programs in American history. In early 1965, Johnson told the American people in an address that his goal was to launch a **Great Society**.

Years of American economic, technological, and social achievements led President Johnson to believe that the government could eliminate poverty in America. This same faith in the ability of Americans to accomplish anything they set their minds to underlay the hubris that would lead Johnson to disaster in Vietnam. The president began laying the foundations of his Great Society in 1964, creating the **Volunteer in Service to America (VISTA)** program, which acted as a Peace Corps for the United States, sending volunteers to help poor communities. In 1965, Congress passed the Housing and Urban Development Act that established the Department of Housing and Urban Development to supervise the construction of affordable housing and $3 billion in improvements for American cities. Congress also authorized legislation providing grants to assist schools in poor areas of the United States and creating **Head Start**, a program focused on helping disadvantaged pre-school children. The Immigration and Nationality Act of 1965 repealed the immigration quota system set up in the 1920s. This legislation would eventually have a profound demographic effect on the United States as increasing numbers of immigrants arrived from Asia, Africa, and Latin America. Another key piece of Great Society legislation was **Medicare**, which provided health insurance to American citizens 65 years of age and older. Medicaid offered medical coverage to Americans who could not afford their own medical insurance.

Lyndon Johnson's Great Society programs led to a massive extension of the American welfare state. Programs like Medicare and Medicaid helped many people, and the poverty rate in the United States was cut by 40 percent. But despite Johnson's ambitious prediction, the Great Society did not end poverty. This sparked frustration and anger in communities where people continued to fall between the cracks of American prosperity. The financial cost of the Great Society was high, leading to resentment from increasingly burdened tax-payers. Some critics argued that the Great Society programs fostered a culture of dependency amongst the people they were trying to help. The fiscal strains of the Vietnam War spurred Congress to reduce or eliminate some of these initiatives. But much of Johnson's Great Society remained, a legacy that would endure into the twenty-first century.

The Civil Rights Movement in the 1960s: From Integration to Black Power

At the beginning of the 1960s, Martin Luther King, Jr., was the most prominent leader in the civil rights movement. After coming to prominence during the Montgomery Bus Boycott, King and other clergymen founded the Southern Christian Leadership Conference (SCLC). King and the other leaders of the SCLC believed that greater civil rights for African Americans had to be achieved by peaceful means. They preached nonviolence as the pace of civil rights agitation increased.

Younger African Americans wanted to push harder and faster for their rights. In 1960, a group of these young people organized the Student Nonviolent Coordinating Committee (SNCC). The leaders of SNCC demanded immediate changes in the country. When it was formed, the SNCC included both African-American and white students, many of whom attended schools in the North.

One of the most effective tactics of civil rights protesters in the early 1960s was the **sit-in**. Protesters would sit at lunch counters where African Americans were denied service, and they would refuse to leave until they were served. Despite being jeered at and sometimes attacked by angry whites, the sit-in tactics proved quite effective. The targeted businesses lost money and eventually integrated their lunch counters.

In 1961, the dramatic **Freedom Rides** captured the attention of the nation. In an effort to enforce a Supreme Court ruling that bus stations and their waiting rooms should be integrated, the Congress for Racial Equality organized groups of African-American and white volunteers to ride busses through the South. At Anniston, Alabama, the Freedom Riders were met by a white mob that beat them up and burned their bus. More Freedom Riders headed into the South. Many were attacked by mobs or arrested by Southern authorities.

Much of this was captured on television. Many Americans were disturbed by images of shattered busses and bruised and bloodied Freedom Riders. They put pressure on the federal government to protect these civil rights activists. The Kennedy administration ordered federal marshals from the Justice Department put an end to attacks on Freedom Riding buses. With the Freedom Rides, public opinion began to shift in favor of the civil rights movement.

Attorney General Robert Kennedy saw to it that the federal government took a larger role in enforcing civil rights laws. In September 1962, the attorney general sent 500 U.S. marshals to escort James Meredith as he enrolled at the University of Mississippi, defying both protesters and the governor of the state. Public opinion was once again roused when officials in Birmingham, Alabama, unleashed police dogs and fire hoses on people marching for civil rights. These ugly scenes embarrassed many Americans and fed a growing distaste for the attitudes and tactics of Southern segregationists.

Concerned about winning reelection, and anxious to not alienate the Southern wing of the Democratic party, President Kennedy moved slowly and cautiously on civil rights issues. In the summer of 1963, he finally sent an ambitious civil rights bill to Congress that would have cut federal funding to states that persisted in promoting racial segregation. On August 28, 1963, civil rights leaders led the **March on Washington**. Over 200,000 people walked from the Washington Monument to the Lincoln Memorial. There Martin Luther King, Jr., inspired the gathering with his "I Have a Dream" speech.

Following the assassination of President Kennedy, Lyndon Johnson was determined to vigorously push forward the civil rights agenda. He sent Congress the most ambitious civil rights legislation since Reconstruction. The **Civil Rights Act of 1964** outlawed discrimination based on race, sex, religion, or country of national origin. This comprehensively barred discrimination in public venues. The bill also created the Equal Employment Opportunity Commission (EEOC) to protect employees against workplace bias. Johnson followed this up with the Voting Rights Act of 1965, which outlawed practices such as literacy tests that had been used to keep African Americans from voting. Political momentum for the Voting Rights Act solidified after three civil rights activists were murdered in the summer of 1964 because they were helping to register African-American voters in Mississippi. Televised footage of violence directed against civil rights protesters continued to undermine the case for segregation. Attacks on the participants of Martin Luther King Jr.'s march on Selma, Alabama, persuaded many Americans to support Johnson's civil rights legislation.

The Civil Rights Act of 1964 and the Voting Rights Act of 1965 overcame most of the remaining legal barriers to African-American equality in the United States. Despite this, many African Americans still living in poverty, especially those living in Northern cities, became angry because the successes of the civil rights movement seemed to be having little effect on their lives. Bloody rioting erupted in the Watts neighborhood of Los Angeles in August 1965. Over the next few years devastating riots wracked cities such as Chicago, Newark, and Detroit. President Johnson appointed the **Kerner Commission** to determine the causes of this urban upheaval. The Kerner Commission attributed the rioting to poverty and hopelessness in African-American neighborhoods. The commission declared that there were two Americas, one well off and white, the other poor and black.

One response to the seemingly slow pace of social change was **black nationalism**. Black nationalists disdained the integrationist goals of the early civil rights movement. The **Nation of Islam**, also known as the Black Muslims, promulgated a doctrine of racial separation; because whites were regarded as racial antagonists, African Americans were encouraged to rely on their own efforts to better themselves. Malcom X became the most charismatic spokesman for the Nation of Islam and black nationalism. After Malcolm X began to question some of the racial tenets of the Nation of Islam, he was shot down by Black Muslim assassins in February 1965.

Black nationalism appealed to many younger African-American members of the SNCC. Stokely Carmichael expelled whites from the SNCC and urged African Americans to arm themselves. Carmichael became a prominent exponent of **black power,** which promoted pride in African-American history and culture. Many black power advocates argued that African Americans should create their own economic and social institutions, separating themselves from the white majority.

The **Black Panthers** became a visible symbol of black power. Established in San Francisco by Bobby Seale and Huey Newton, the Black Panthers deliberately cultivated a militant image, often prominently displaying their firearms. The Black Panthers set up food programs and black nationalist schools in San Francisco. They also engaged in criminal activity, and several members were killed by the police. The violence associated with the Black Panthers eventually ended their social and political effectiveness.

The Expansion of Rights Movements

Many women were inspired by the civil rights movement to push for more freedoms and opportunities. Some women were frustrated by the homemaker role extolled in the 1950s. A number of women had been active in the civil rights movement, and they resented being passed over for leadership positions. Betty Friedan's *The Feminine Mystique* and the spread of women's support groups on college campuses and in the suburbs helped focus this discontent and encouraged the growth of the **feminist movement**.

Friedan founded the **National Organization for Women (NOW)** in 1966. NOW represented the aspirations of educated, upwardly mobile women, and it focused on securing equal pay in the workplace and combating stereotypical images that feminists believed objectified women. Resistance to feminist goals in the workplace crumbled relatively easily. In 1972, Gloria Steinem began publishing *Ms.* Magazine, which helped popularize a new term of address for women that did not reflect their marital status. The 1973 *Roe v. Wade* Supreme Court decision recognized a right for women to have an abortion in the first trimester of pregnancy and, with some restrictions, in the second trimester. An unusual defeat for the feminist movement came with the failure to enact an Equal Rights Amendment (ERA). Despite political encouragement from Congress and a good deal of momentum, grassroots activists led by Phyllis Schlafly defeated the ERA by claiming that passage would lead to such undesirable consequences as the drafting of women and coed bathrooms.

Other groups agitated for rights and recognition during these years. The **American Indian Movement (AIM)** promoted Native American pride and protested the policies of the U.S. government on reservations. AIM called for the return of lands taken from Native

Americans. In 1973, a confrontation between members of AIM and government authorities led to a 71-day siege at Wounded Knee, South Dakota. Congress responded to this unrest by giving Native Americans more authority to govern their tribes.

Latino groups became increasingly self-conscious and assertive in the 1960s and 1970s. Cesar Chavez began organizing Latinos who worked as migrant farm workers in California. His **United Farm Workers** garnered a great deal of publicity and support protesting working conditions in the Californian grape fields. Environmentalists also made their voices heard. In 1962, Rachel Carson's *Silent Spring* argued that the use of the pesticide DDT was dangerous. Opposition to nuclear power intensified in this period. In June 1969, the Stonewall Riots erupted after a police raid of a gay bar in New York City. This led to growth in a gay pride movement.

Cold War Crisis

The cold war intensified in the early 1960s. President Kennedy was a determined cold warrior, and he was committed to stopping the spread of Communism. The United States and the Soviet Union continued to openly test nuclear weapons. Fear of a nuclear war remained widespread. Popular movies such as *Fail-Safe* (1964) and *Dr. Strangelove* (1964) addressed the danger of a nuclear war being triggered by an "accident."

President Kennedy inherited from the Eisenhower administration a CIA plan to overthrow Fidel Castro, the Communist dictator of Cuba. The CIA had intended to invade Cuba with a small army of anti-Communist Cubans supported by American warplanes. Lacking Eisenhower's military experience and expertise, Kennedy allowed the ill-conceived operation to go ahead. The landing of the anti-Communist Cubans at the **Bay of Pigs** in April 1961 turned into a military disaster; Castro's army killed or captured most of the invaders. This debacle severely embarrassed the fledgling Kennedy administration.

The Soviet and East German authorities had long resented the fact that West Berlin offered refugees from Communism an easy escape route to the West. In August 1961, the Communists began building a concrete **Berlin Wall** to separate the two halves of the city. The Berlin Wall soon became a symbol of Communist tyranny.

Another crisis concerning Cuba almost led to a third world war. In October 1962, American U-2 reconnaissance flights discovered Soviet missile sites under construction in Cuba. The Soviets saw the emplacement of missiles in Cuba as a way of protecting the Castro regime and exerting pressure on the United States; the American government saw the presence of Soviet short-range missiles on the nearby island as an unacceptable threat. President Kennedy ordered a naval blockade of Cuba and demanded that the Soviet Union withdraw the missiles from Cuba. For a time, the world balanced on the brink of war. The Americans debated landing troops in Cuba, while the Soviets considered using their missiles if American troops invaded. After almost two weeks of tension, the Soviet leader Nikita Khrushchev decided to remove the missiles from Cuba. In turn, the United States dismantled some missile sites in Turkey. Diplomacy had averted catastrophe. Chastened by the crisis, the United States and the Soviet Union soon signed a Limited Test Ban Treaty. A "hotline" was set up between the White House and the Kremlin to speed up communications between the American and Soviet leaders and avert future crises.

The Vietnam War

Ever since France had withdrawn from Indochina in the 1950s, the United States had provided aid to the anti-Communist regime in South Vietnam. When the **Vietcong**, guerilla fighters supported by Communist North Vietnam, began an insurgency against the government, the United States sent military advisors to train the South Vietnamese army. President Kennedy greatly increased the number of American military advisors in Vietnam and expanded their role. When American officials became doubtful about the effectiveness of the South Vietnamese president Ngo Dinh Diem, they did nothing to discourage a cabal of military officers who overthrew and assassinated Diem a few weeks before President Kennedy was murdered in 1963.

President Lyndon Johnson attempted to carry on the policies of his predecessor in Vietnam. In time, he became convinced that the American role would have to be increased to achieve victory. In August 1964, Johnson reported that North Vietnamese gunboats had attacked American destroyers in the Gulf of Tonkin, leaving out of his account such crucial details as that the American warships were gathering intelligence on North Vietnam and that South Vietnamese gunboats had been operating nearby. Outraged by what seemed to be an unprovoked attack, Congress passed the **Gulf of Tonkin Resolution**, which authorized the president to "prevent further aggression" in Southeast Asia. This resolution enabled the president to expand the war in Vietnam without consulting Congress.

With the war turning against the South Vietnamese, Johnson intervened with ground combat troops in 1965. For the next three years, Johnson increased this military commitment, until in 1968 there were some 540,000 American troops in Vietnam. In 1965, the United States also launched a bombing campaign against the North Vietnamese. The war in Vietnam often proved very frustrating to American GIs. It was an unconventional war fought against an often invisible enemy. There were no traditional measures of victory, such as the taking of territory or the occupation of enemy cities. The Vietcong and North Vietnamese troops had to be sought out in jungles and rice paddies, where it was difficult to distinguish enemy guerillas from civilians.

The most significant military engagement of the war was the **Tet Offensive**, launched by the Communists on January 30, 1968. Hoping to overthrow the South Vietnamese government and undermine the American position in the country, the Communists used the holiday truce to attack all across South Vietnam. In Saigon, infiltrators briefly held parts of the American embassy, and the Communists took control of the city of Hue, massacring thousands of government supporters. But the Americans and South Vietnamese quickly regrouped and inflicted devastating losses on the Vietcong and North Vietnamese. Militarily, Tet was an overwhelming American and South Vietnamese victory. Politically, however, the Tet Offensive weakened American support for the war. After being assured by government officials that "victory was just around the corner," many Americans wondered how the enemy could initiate such a massive attack. Rattled by hostile news coverage, members of the Johnson administration began to wonder if the war could be won.

The Vietnam War ended Lyndon Johnson's political career. Administration insiders noted that he was increasingly preoccupied by the war. Everywhere he went, he was trailed by antiwar protesters denouncing him. In early 1968, Johnson hoped to run for a second term. He was challenged in the New Hampshire primary by Senator Eugene McCarthy of Minnesota, who was campaigning as a peace candidate. Johnson won the primary, but not by much for a sitting president—just 48 percent to McCarthy's 42 percent. Disheartened by this political embarrassment and the media storm surrounding the Tet Offensive, Johnson announced that he would not seek reelection. Vice President Hubert Humphrey became the administration candidate for the presidency. Senator Robert Kennedy, brother of John Kennedy, also entered the race.

The Vietnam War grew more and more unpopular in 1968. Television brought brutal images of combat into America's living rooms; many Americans were troubled by the military use of **napalm**, a combustible that could inflict horrible burns, in and around civilian villages. Although it would take more than a year for the story to be publicized, in March 1968, a group of American soldiers slaughtered around 400 Vietnamese civilians, including children and infants, in the **My Lai Massacre**. News of this atrocity led some people in the United States to question any continuing involvement in the war. The Republican candidate for president, Richard Nixon, sought votes by claiming to have a "secret plan" to end the conflict.

A student antiwar movement received a lot of attention. Many students had become more politically active working in the civil rights movement of the early 1960s. The leftist **Students for a Democratic Society (SDS)** was founded in 1960. The **Port Huron Statement** became the manifesto of the SDS, challenging American consumerism and calling for "participatory democracy." The SDS became a vocal opponent of the Vietnam War.

In 1964, the **Free Speech Movement** was born at the University of California at Berkeley when school officials prohibited political advocacy on campus. This sparked student demonstrations that forced the university administration to back down. Some students began demanding changes in the curriculum and other student policies. The protests at Berkeley were imitated by students at other schools.

The Vietnam War intensified political activism amongst students. Many students believed that the American intervention in Southeast Asia was morally wrong; others admitted that they opposed the war because they feared being drafted. Antiwar demonstrations became a form of political theater that attracted television cameras. The size of these student gatherings grew dramatically; in 1967, an antiwar rally in New York's Central Park involved 500,000 participants. Despite this, it should be remembered that in the 1960s most students were not antiwar protesters; more students belonged to conservative political organizations than groups like the SDS.

The year 1968 was politically tumultuous. Dr. Martin Luther King was assassinated by a white supremacist, setting off riots in 100 cities. Senator Robert Kennedy was assassinated by a Palestinian angry at Kennedy's support for Israel. Americans were dismayed that another member of the Kennedy family had been murdered. Richard Nixon and Hubert Humphrey became the favorites for their parties' presidential nominations. Student radicals regarded both men as pillars of a discredited establishment. The political divisions in the country were shockingly displayed in August, when Chicago police initiated a battle with demonstrators at the Democratic National Convention. The SDS reached its peak in 1968, helping organize major protests at Columbia University and on other campuses. As some SDS members became increasingly militant, the organization began to split up; one splinter group formed the Weather Underground and engaged in terrorist activities.

Other young people spurned politics and sought to change American society through a cultural revolution. These advocates of the **counterculture** disdained the middle class values of their parents and argued for an ethic of open and uninhibited expression and personal freedom. The "hippies" had little in common with political activists from the SDS; their revolution focused on private acts such as growing long hair, listening to the latest rock music, and experimenting with various types of drugs. Timothy Leary, a former professor and proponent of the psychedelic drug LSD, urged America's youth to "tune in, turn on, and drop out." The development of the birth control pill helped foster a more permissive attitude toward premarital sexual activity. A popular button in the 1960s declared, "If It Feels Good, Do It!" In 1967, the Haight-Ashbury neighborhood of San Francisco became for a time a gathering place for hippies; here rock groups like the Grateful Dead and Jefferson Airplane produced "acid" rock that briefly was the soundtrack for what some hoped would be a new "Age of Aquarius." The climactic moment for the "peace and love" counterculture came with the **Woodstock Music Festival** in the summer of 1969. Over 400,000 young people gathered on the grounds of a dairy farm in New York to hear a stellar lineup of musicians perform. Such was the ascendency of the personal over the political at Woodstock that when radical activist Abbie Hoffman attempted to grab a microphone during a performance by The Who, guitarist Pete Townshend chased him off the stage.

Richard Nixon won the 1968 election. As president, he introduced a policy of **Vietnamization** of the war, ramping up the training and arming of South Vietnamese forces so that growing numbers of American troops could be withdrawn from combat. By 1972, the number of American military personnel in Vietnam had been reduced to 24,000. Nixon did not intend to allow the Communists to conquer South Vietnam; while reducing American ground forces, he intensified the bombing campaign against the North. In 1970, Nixon authorized an incursion into Cambodia to destroy Communist bases along the border. This led to the last great wave of student protests. At **Kent State University,** Ohio National Guardsmen shot and killed four students during a demonstration. Police killed two students at Jackson State University in Mississippi. Despite these outrages, student activism declined precipitously in the early 1970s as troop numbers fell in Vietnam and the draft was ended. Student protesters evoked hostility as well as support, as the Chicago police demonstrated in 1968. In 1970, 100,000 New York construction workers, or "hardhats," marched to show their support for President Nixon's policies.

In 1971, a former Defense Department official named Daniel Ellsberg leaked the **Pentagon Papers** to the *New York Times*. These documents, dating from the Kennedy and Johnson administrations, revealed that the government had lied to Congress and the American people about the situation in Vietnam. These disclosures further disillusioned the public about the war. Though none of the leaked documents dated to his time in office, President Nixon was outraged by Ellsberg's action.

Since 1968, the United States had been engaged in peace negotiations with the North Vietnamese in Paris. A peace agreement seemed in sight in late 1972. When the negotiations stalled, President Nixon launched an intensive bombing campaign in North Vietnam. A peace accord was finally signed in January 1973. The United States agreed to withdraw its remaining forces from South Vietnam within 60 days. The North Vietnamese promised to repatriate all American prisoners. The Vietnam War cost 60,000 American lives. Once the Americans departed, war resumed between North and South Vietnam. Amply supplied by the Soviets and Chinese, the North Vietnamese overwhelmed the South with a military offensive that began in late 1974. Congress refused President Gerald Ford's pleas to provide a promised military aid package to the South Vietnamese. The United States was forced to hastily evacuate its diplomats and other Americans in Vietnam, a process completed just a day before North Vietnamese tanks rolled into Saigon on April 30, 1975.

Chapter Review

Rapid Review

To achieve the perfect 5, you should be able to explain the following:

- The events that dramatically altered America including protests and cultural rebellion in the 1960s are seen by some in a positive light and others in a negative light.
- John Kennedy projected a new image of presidential leadership, although few of his domestic programs were actually passed by Congress.
- The Cuban Missile Crisis was the critical foreign policy crisis of the Kennedy administration, and may have brought the world close to world war.
- After Kennedy's death, Lyndon Johnson was able to get Congress to pass his Great Society domestic programs, which included Head Start and Medicare.
- Nonviolence remained the major tactic of the civil rights movement throughout the 1960s, although some black leaders began to advocate "black power."
- Women strove to achieve equal rights in the 1960s through the National Organization for Women (NOW) and consciousness-raising groups.
- Lyndon Johnson determined early in his presidency that an escalation of the war in Vietnam would be necessary, and more materials and men went to Vietnam from 1965 to 1968.
- The military in Vietnam was frustrated by the military tactics of the enemy and by faltering support at home.
- The media portrayal of the Tet Offensive did much to turn American public opinion against the war.
- Student protesters held increasingly large demonstrations against the war; SDS was the main organization of student activists.
- Members of the counterculture advocated a personal and not a political rebellion in this era.
- Richard Nixon removed American troops from Vietnam through the policy of Vietnamization; the South Vietnamese government fell two years after American troops departed.

Time Line

1960: John Kennedy elected president
    Sit-ins began
    Students for a Democratic Society (SDS) formed
    Student Nonviolent Coordinating Committee (SNCC) formed

1961: Freedom Rides
    Bay of Pigs invasion
    Construction of Berlin Wall
    First American travels in space

1962: James Meredith enters University of Mississippi
    SDS issues *Port Huron Statement*
    Silent Spring by Rachel Carson published
    Cuban Missile Crisis
    The Other America by Michael Harrington published

1963: John Kennedy assassinated; Lyndon Johnson becomes president
    Civil rights march on Washington
    The Feminine Mystique by Betty Friedan published
    President Diem assassinated in South Vietnam

1964: Beginning of Johnson's War on Poverty programs
Civil Rights Act enacted
Free Speech Movement at Berkeley begins
Tonkin Gulf Resolution
Johnson reelected
1965: Elementary and Secondary Education Act passed
Johnson sends more troops to Vietnam
Voting Rights Act passed
Murder of Malcolm X
Watts riots burn sections of Los Angeles
Medicare passed
1966: Stokely Carmichael calls for "black power"
Formation of Black Panther party
Formation of National Organization for Women (NOW)
1967: Riots in many American cities
Antiwar demonstrations intensify
1968: Martin Luther King assassinated
Robert Kennedy assassinated
Student protests at Columbia University
Battle between police and protesters at Democratic National Convention
Richard Nixon elected president
American Indian Movement (AIM) founded
Tet Offensive
My Lai Massacre
1969: Woodstock Music Festival
1970: United States invades Cambodia
Killings at Kent State, Jackson State
1971: *Pentagon Papers* published by the *New York Times*
1972: Nixon reelected
1973: Vietnam cease-fire announced; American troops leave Vietnam
Roe v. Wade decision
1975: South Vietnam falls to North Vietnam, ending the Vietnam War

› Review Questions

Fact Check

Check your knowledge of the historical period covered in this chapter.

1. The initial fate of the Freedom Riders demonstrated that
   A. Southerners had largely accepted Northern orders to integrate bus stations and other public facilities.
   B. state governments were at the forefront in the enforcement of civil rights laws.
   C. television news broadcasts had a powerful hold on the American public.
   D. by 1961 the federal government was committed to vigorously protecting the civil rights of all citizens.

2. The Tet Offensive demonstrated that
   A. American forces were fairly close to a decisive victory in Vietnam.
   B. military and civilian officials had been less than candid with the American people on the progress of the war.
   C. the Vietcong could defeat American soldiers in the battlefield.
   D. cooperation between Americans and the South Vietnamese army was improving.

3. The membership rolls of Students for a Democratic Society were at an all-time high when
   A. the struggles of the civil rights movement in the South were shown on national television.
   B. Nixon invaded Cambodia.
   C. Nixon intensified the bombing to its highest levels of the war in 1972.
   D. more young men were being sent to Vietnam between 1965 and 1967.

4. Some Northern blacks were attracted to the call for "black power" for all of the following reasons *except*
   A. Martin Luther King and others in the civil rights movement seemed more interested in improving the position of Southern blacks.
   B. ghetto sections of Northern cities remained poor, and many residents there felt little hope.
   C. Malcolm X and Stokely Carmichael evoked powerful images of black pride.
   D. vast numbers of Northern blacks had joined the Nation of Islam.

5. Highlights for feminist leaders of this era included all of the following *except*
   A. the founding of *Ms.*
   B. the formation of NOW
   C. the drive for passage of the Equal Rights Amendment
   D. the increased awareness of "women's issues" in society

Multiple-Choice Questions

Here are multiple-choice questions like the ones on the AP U.S. History exam.

Questions 6–8 refer to the quotation below.

Now we are engaged in a psychological struggle in this country. And that is whether or not black people have the right to use the words they want to use without white people giving their sanction to it. (applause) And that we maintain whether they like it or not we gonna use the word "Black Power" and let them address themselves to that. (applause) But that we are not going to wait for white people to sanction Black Power. We're tired of waiting; every time black people move in this country, they're forced to defend their position before they move. It's time that the people who are supposed to be defending their position do that, that's white people. They ought to start defending themselves as to why they have oppressed and exploited us.

—Stokely Carmichael, Speech at the University of California, Berkeley, October 29, 1966

6. The Black Power movement emerged at a time of
   A. government repression of free speech.
   B. declining legal rights for African Americans.
   C. expanded legal rights for African Americans.
   D. a period of economic depression in the United States.

7. Which of the following was the African-American leader who most directly inspired the Black Power movement?
   A. Booker T. Washington
   B. A. Philip Randolph
   C. Martin Luther King
   D. Malcolm X

8. The struggle for African-American civil rights in the 1960s most directly served as a model for which of the following?
   A. The Know-Nothing movement
   B. Hippies
   C. The women's liberation movement
   D. The New Right

Short-Answer Question

The short-answer question below is similar to the ones you'll encounter on the AP U.S. History exam.

9. Answer Parts A, B, and C.
   A. Briefly explain ONE example of a movement calling for more rights in the 1960s.
   B. Briefly explain a SECOND example of a movement calling for more rights in the 1960s.
   C. Briefly explain ONE example of a response by the government to these movements.

› Answers and Explanations

1. C. The images of burned buses and beaten Freedom Riders horrified many Americans. At this point, neither the federal nor state governments protected the rights of Freedom Riders.

2. B. The Tet Offensive was a military defeat for the Vietcong. However, it did prove that victory was not "around the corner," which is what many military officials were publicly claiming.

3. D. By the time of the invasion of Cambodia and the massive bombing at the end of the war, SDS had split into factions. The civil rights movement attracted a relatively small number of new members to SDS.

4. D. All of the other reasons caused some Northern blacks to abandon Martin Luther King's call for integration. Only a small proportion of blacks ever joined the Nation of Islam.

5. C. After a long struggle, the drive to get the ERA into the Constitution was finally abandoned when it became obvious that not enough state legislatures would ever pass it.

6. C. The Black Power Movement emerged at a time of expanding legal rights for African Americans. The Civil Rights Movement of the 1950s and 1960s had culminated in the passage of the Civil Rights Act of 1964 that prohibited racial discrimination, and the Voting Rights Act of 1965 that overturned practices designed to prevent African Americans from voting.

7. D. The African-American leader who most directly inspired the Black Power movement was Malcolm X. A member of the Nation of Islam, Malcolm X promoted black separatism. Following a pilgrimage to Mecca, he began to moderate his views about race and left the Nation of Islam, but he was assassinated by a team of Black Muslims on February 21, 1965.

8. C. The struggle for African-American civil rights in the 1960s most directly served as a model for the women's liberation movement. The National Organization for Women (NOW) was founded in 1966. Like civil rights activists, feminists marched and engaged in demonstrations to publicize their cause.

9. Parts A and B: African Americans continued to work for full civil rights in the 1960s. African American students staged sit-ins at Southern lunch counters that refused them service. Black and white civil rights workers took Freedom Rides on buses to desegregate interstate transportation. Dr. Martin Luther King, Jr., and other civil rights leaders led marches the South, including the August 28, 1963, March on Washington. The later 1960s saw a growing movement of black nationalism, inspired by leaders like Malcolm X. This led to calls for black power, and a celebration of the African heritage of African Americans. Feminists agitated for more opportunities for women and specific objectives like equal pay for equal work. In 1966, Betty Friedan founded the National Organization for Women

(NOW). In 1972, Gloria Steinem launched *Ms.* Magazine. The American Indian Movement (AIM) protested the treatment of Native Americans. In 1973, AIM activists occupied Wounded Knee, South Dakota, and for a time defied federal authorities. Cesar Chavez started the United Farm Workers to organize Latino farm workers. In 1960, leftist students established the Students for a Democratic Society (SDS). The *Port Huron Statement* (1962), with its demand for "participatory democracy," launched the "New Left." In 1964, students at the University of California at Berkeley began the Free Speech Movement as a protest against the efforts of school administrators to limit the distribution of political materials on campus. Many students took the lead in organizing protests against the Vietnam War. Other students joined the counterculture, preferring to "tune in, turn on, and drop out."

Part C: Presidents John F. Kennedy and Lyndon B. Johnson expressed support for the civil rights movement. Johnson played a key role in passing the Civil Rights Act of 1964, which outlawed discrimination in public places, and the Voting Rights Act of 1965 that abolished practices such as literacy tests, which had been used to prevent African Americans from voting. The Supreme Court gave feminists a controversial victory with its 1972 *Roe v. Wade* decision legalizing abortion in the first two trimesters of a pregnancy. Following the Wounded Knee incident, the federal government passed laws giving Native American tribes more autonomy. In 1971, in response to student protests and the dispatch of many young men to the Vietnam War before they could vote, Congress and the states passed the Twenty-Sixth Amendment giving the vote to citizens 18 years of age.

CHAPTER 28

Decline and Rebirth (1968–1988)

IN THIS CHAPTER

Summary: Some historians claim that the accomplishments of the presidency of Richard Nixon are often overlooked. Nixon opened diplomatic relations with China, improved relations with the Soviet Union, and began to break the Democratic stranglehold on politics in the South that had existed since the New Deal. Despite these developments, Richard Nixon will always be associated with the Watergate scandal. Watergate began a period when faith in the national government sharply declined; this lasted through the presidencies of Gerald Ford and Jimmy Carter. With the election of Ronald Reagan, many Americans began to "have faith in America again." Just as Nixon began a new relationship with China, under Reagan, America entered into a more positive relationship with its formal rival, the Soviet Union.

Keywords

Southern Strategy: political strategy implemented by President Richard Nixon to win over Southern whites to the Republican party; the strategy succeeded through administration policies such as delaying school desegregation plans.

Détente: foreign policy of decreasing tensions with the Soviet Union; this began in the first term of the Nixon administration.

Watergate: series of events beginning with the break-in at the Democratic party headquarters in the Watergate complex in Washington, DC, that led to the downfall of President Richard Nixon; Nixon resigned as the House of Representatives was preparing for an impeachment hearing.

OPEC: Organization of Petroleum Exporting Countries; the group of 14 countries that produce most of the world's oil and, by determining production quantities, influence worldwide oil prices.

Camp David Accords (1978): peace agreement between Israel and Egypt that was mediated by President Jimmy Carter; many consider this the highlight of the Carter presidency.

Iranian Hostage Crisis: diplomatic crisis triggered on November 4, 1979, when Iranian protesters seized the U.S. embassy in Tehran and held 66 American diplomats hostage for 444 days. President Carter was unable to free the hostages despite several attempts; to many this event symbolized the paralysis of American power in the late 1970s.

Religious right: right-leaning evangelical Christians who increasingly supported Republican candidates beginning with Ronald Reagan.

Iran-Contra Affair: scandal that erupted during the Reagan administration when it was revealed that U.S. government agents had secretly sold arms to Iran in order to raise money to fund anti-Communist "Contra" forces in Nicaragua. Those acts directly contravened an ongoing U.S. trade embargo with Iran as well as federal legislation limiting aid to the Contras. Several Reagan administration officials were convicted of federal crimes as a result.

The Presidency of Richard Nixon

In 1968, Richard Nixon achieved one of the greatest comebacks in American political history. Nixon's political career had been written off after successive defeats in the presidential election of 1960 and a campaign for governor of California in 1962. Following the second of these losses, he told assembled newsmen that "you won't have Nixon to kick around anymore."

Nixon was a gifted but complicated man. He was not a "people person," and he was uncomfortable mixing with large groups of voters. After a tumultuous political career, he believed that powerful interests in the media and government were hostile to him. Suspicious of the government bureaucracy, he relied on a small group of trusted advisors that included H.R. Haldeman, his chief of staff, John Ehrlichman, his domestic affairs advisor, and Henry Kissinger, his national security advisor.

Domestic Policy

When Nixon entered office in 1969, the quarter-century economic boom that had followed World War II was drawing to a close. Inflation and unemployment were both rising. The gross national product was starting to stagnate, and a trade deficit was increasing. Some of these problems reflected long-term problems with the American economy, including an aging industrial infrastructure. Some were aggravated by Lyndon Johnson's reluctance to force voters to pay the full price for the Vietnam War and his expensive Great Society programs, creating a large federal budget deficit.

At first Nixon tried traditional means to balance the budget; he raised taxes and cut spending. This did not help the ailing economy. The president then resorted to more drastic measures. He ordered a 90-day freeze on prices and wages, and then imposed mandatory guidelines for increasing wages and prices. Nixon also pursued a policy of **deficit spending,** similar to the approach Franklin Roosevelt used during the Great Depression.

Nixon did not attempt to roll back the Great Society and even expanded upon it in places. He did try to turn the administration of many programs over to the states by giving them block grants to fund this, but Congress rejected this plan. Nixon agreed to increases in various entitlement programs, including food stamps, Medicaid, and Aid to Families with Dependent Children (AFDC). The Johnson administration had sponsored a number of laws to fight pollution and preserve the environment. Nixon continued this effort with the creation of the Environmental Protection Agency (EPA) and the Occupational Health and Safety Administration (OSHA) in 1970. The creation of these agencies along with the passage of the Clean Air Act of 1970 and the Endangered Species Act of 1973 ensured that ecological concerns would be a growing priority in the coming years.

Nixon's Southern Strategy

By 1968, the "Solid South," which had been reliably voting Democratic since Reconstruction, was finally beginning to crack. Eisenhower had won some Southern states in the 1950s. In 1968, George Wallace, the combative former governor of Alabama, ran a third-party campaign for president as the candidate of the American Independence Party. He received 13.5 percent of the popular vote and won the electoral votes of five Southern states.

Although he had supported the civil rights movement, and his administration encouraged the implementation of affirmative action in hiring and education, Richard Nixon hoped to exploit a reaction to 1960s liberalism to permanently weaken the hold of the Democrat party on the South. His **"Southern Strategy"** aimed at wooing conservative Southerners into the Republican party. Nixon sought to find ways to ease the transition to desegregation in the South. He also criticized enforced school busing after courts had mandated its use to further desegregate Northern cities like Boston. Nixon attempted to appoint two Southerners to the Supreme Court, but their nominations were rejected by the Senate. Despite these setbacks, Nixon appointed four judges to the Supreme Court, including Chief Justice Warren Burger. The court became generally more conservative, though in 1973 it endorsed a right to abortion in *Roe v. Wade*.

Foreign Policy

President Nixon's interests and expertise centered on foreign policy. It was in foreign affairs that his administration enjoyed its greatest successes. Distrusting the professional diplomats at the State Department, Nixon managed the most sensitive foreign negotiations from the White House, assisted by Henry Kissinger, his national security advisor, and from 1973, the secretary of state. Nixon used Kissinger as his representative in some of his most important diplomatic initiatives. Kissinger carried out secret talks with the Communist Chinese, and he played an important role in negotiating the Paris Peace Accords with the North Vietnamese.

Nixon's greatest achievement in foreign affairs was in improving relations with the Soviet Union and the People's Republic of China. Nixon had long been known for his vehement anti-Communist opinions. His record as a cold war hawk gave him the credibility to pursue a different policy with the great Communist powers. Nixon ushered in an era of **"détente"** with the Soviet Union. Nixon believed that reduced cold war tensions would both minimize the risk of world war and give the United States more diplomatic leverage in addressing conflicts like that in Vietnam.

Nixon was determined to diminish the dangers of nuclear war. He wanted to limit **nuclear proliferation**. During a visit to the Soviet Union in 1972, Nixon and the Soviet Premier Leonid Brezhnev agreed to place caps on their nuclear arsenals. The resulting **SALT I** treaty was a historic moment in the cold war, as the two superpowers took a momentous step toward easing the arms race.

Perhaps even more consequential was a trip Nixon took earlier in 1972. Since the 1950s, Nixon had been a vocal supporter of Nationalist China (the non-Communist territory established by refugees from the Chinese civil war on the island of Taiwan). He had urged vigilance against the ambitions of "Red" China. But Nixon's ideas changed over time. By the time he became president, Nixon, along with Henry Kissinger, had become a proponent of **realpolitik**. Looking at the world through the prism of power politics, Nixon and Kissinger realized that the United States had to acknowledge the growing strength of Communist China. They also believed that a diplomatic overture to China provided an opportunity to pressure the Soviet leadership, who now regarded the Chinese as rivals.

Nixon and Kissinger traveled to China in February 1972. They met with the Chinese dictator Mao Zedong and other government officials. The two sides agreed to cultural exchanges and trade talks. Nixon's trip paved the way for the eventual establishment of full diplomatic relations between the United States and Communist China.

The Watergate Scandal

President Nixon's foreign policy achievements put him in a strong position as he ran for reelection in 1972. High poll ratings demonstrated that he had effectively captured the political center as the election neared. The Democrats ran South Dakota Senator George McGovern, whose antiwar sentiments and liberal progressivism excited idealistic students but few others. Nixon won a landslide victory in 1972, capturing almost 61 percent of the popular vote and the electoral votes of every state but Massachusetts and the District of Columbia. Nixon's political triumph would prove to be short-lived. He soon found himself mired in a scandal that would ultimately end his presidency.

The obvious inevitability of Nixon's reelection in 1972 makes the decisions that led to the **Watergate Affair** seem inexplicable. In part, they reflect President Nixon's political paranoia. Convinced, with some justification, that members of the media establishment, the government bureaucracy, and the Democratic party were implacably hostile, Nixon responded by compiling an "enemies list," and he targeted some of the people on the list for wiretaps and harassment by the Internal Revenue Service.

In 1971, following the leak of the Pentagon Papers by Daniel Ellsberg, a former State Department employee, a group termed the **Plumbers** was established in the White House to "plug" leaks. Members of this group included former CIA operatives and FBI agents. The Plumbers vandalized the office of Daniel Ellsberg's psychiatrist looking for damaging information. The Committee to Reelect the President (CREEP) employed unsavory characters to play "dirty tricks" on the Democrats. These operatives spread malicious lies about Democratic candidates and engaged in childish antics like ordering 200 pizzas delivered unannounced to a Democratic campaign office.

On the evening of June 16, 1972, a group of five men associated with CREEP broke into the headquarters of the Democratic National Committee at the Watergate building in Washington, DC. They were hoping to gather intelligence on the Democrats by copying documents and planting electronic "bugs" in offices. The political burglars were discovered and arrested. They were quickly linked to CREEP. This set in motion the Watergate scandal.

There is no reason to believe that President Nixon had foreknowledge of the Watergate break-in. Instead of disavowing the actions of CREEP and cooperating with the police investigation, Nixon's worst political instincts kicked in and he began to participate in an illegal cover-up. The president declared that the White House had no connection to the burglars. He also urged CIA officials to encourage the FBI to call off its investigation of the break-in. As the case proceeded, officials from CREEP lied about their roles in the Watergate affair. "Hush money" was paid to the burglars to keep them quiet.

The Watergate story was pursued vigorously by reporters Bob Woodward and Carl Bernstein of the *Washington Post*. They were given scoops by a mysterious source they named "Deep Throat." In 2005, their informant was revealed as Mark Felt, who at the time of the Watergate break-in was serving as the associate director of the FBI.

The burglars were convicted and sentenced to prison terms in January 1973. By this point enough questions had been raised for Congress to investigate the case. The Senate

Select Committee on Presidential Campaign Activities began its work in February. During the committee's hearings, the White House counsel John Dean admitted that President Nixon had been a party to a cover-up concerning Watergate. An assistant to the president testified that a taping system recorded Oval Office conversations. As a result of the ensuing political firestorm, Attorney General Richard Kleindienst and presidential aides H.R. Haldeman and John Ehrlichman resigned.

Hoping to save his presidency, Nixon appointed a **special prosecutor** to investigate Watergate. Nixon then resisted Special Counsel Archibald Cox's efforts to secure the White House tapes. When Cox persisted, Nixon ordered Attorney General Elliot Richardson to fire him. Richardson refused to do this, and he and his deputy attorney general resigned. These resignations and the eventual firing of Cox took place on October 20, 1973, and became known as the **"Saturday Night Massacre."**

By this point the president's public approval ratings were plummeting. The Judiciary Committee in the House of Representatives began to investigate impeachment procedures. When President Nixon released edited transcripts of his Oval Office tape to the new special prosecutor, Leon Jaworski, many people were shocked by the crude language used by the president and his associates. Adding to Nixon's troubles, Vice President Spiro Agnew was forced to resign in October 1973 because of corruption charges regarding his earlier political career in Maryland. Nixon chose Congressman Gerald Ford of Michigan to replace Agnew, and under the terms of the 25th Amendment, Congress confirmed his nomination.

His credibility shattered, Nixon could do nothing to silence increasing calls for his resignation. He released more tapes in April 1974, but this did nothing to dispel the cloud hanging over him. In July, the House Judiciary Committee approved three articles of impeachment. These charged Nixon with ignoring House subpoenas, abusing presidential power, and obstructing justice.

At this point, the Supreme Court ordered the president to surrender the remaining tapes. One had a mysterious 18½ minute gap on it; another proved that Nixon was involved in the Watergate cover-up a week after the break-in. This was the "smoking gun" that decided President Nixon's political fate. Republican party leaders told Nixon that if he did not leave office, he would be impeached. Nixon resigned on August 9, 1974. Gerald Ford was sworn in as president, and in a public address he declared that "our long national nightmare is over."

The Ford Administration

Gerald Ford became president after one of the most devastating political crises in American history. Ford was a popular and respected legislator who had served as the Republican minority leader in the House of Representatives. He had never expected to become president, and he remains the only man to fill the offices of vice president and president without being elected. Ford lost much of the goodwill that he had initially enjoyed on September 8, 1974, when he pardoned Richard Nixon for any crimes that he might have committed as president. Ford believed that a protracted trial of the former president would needlessly prolong the national trauma over Watergate. At the time, many people disagreed with this decision. Ford was widely criticized, and the Democrats won large congressional majorities in the 1974 elections. In later years, opinions changed, and Ford's pardon was regarded by even some of his critics as a wise and courageous act.

Ford was not in office long when the North Vietnamese launched their decisive offensive against South Vietnam. Ford wanted to help the South Vietnamese, but he could not persuade Congress to provide more aid to Saigon. Most Americans supported the hands-off attitude of Congress; the Vietnam War was already a bad memory that they wanted to forget. In other respects, Ford carried on the foreign policy of the Nixon administration, and he retained Henry Kissinger in office as secretary of state. Ford visited China, and he was the first American president to visit Japan.

The economy dominated Ford's presidency. The American economy continued to sputter. It suffered problems that rarely went together, inflation and unemployment. This economic malady of the 1970s was called "**stagflation**." The president attempted to combat this with the traditional conservative economic remedies of tax cuts and reduced government spending. Despite this, inflation continued and unemployment rose to 10 percent. Ford's initiative to raise morale and boost confidence in the economy by encouraging people to wear "WIN" ("Whip Inflation Now") buttons was a dismal failure. The president contended with other problems as well. Ford, a physically fit man who had been a star athlete in college, tripped in public a few times, and he was soon portrayed by comedians as a bumbling klutz.

Determined to seek election to the presidency in his own right, Ford fended off a determined challenge to the Republican nomination by Ronald Reagan, the former governor of California. The Democrats nominated Jimmy Carter, who had served a term as the governor of Georgia. Carter stressed that he was an outsider to Washington, and he appealed to the post-Watergate mood of the electorate by promising "I'll never lie to you." Ford hurt himself in a televised debate by inexplicably seeming to assert that Eastern Europe was not controlled by the Soviet Union. In the end, Carter won a narrow electoral victory by appealing to traditional Democratic constituencies and winning back Southern Democrats who had supported Richard Nixon in 1968 and 1972.

The Carter Administration

Jimmy Carter's outsider status had helped him win the presidency, but it hurt him as he attempted to govern. Even some congressional Democrats resented the president's condemnations of traditional Beltway politics. Carter was a devout evangelical Christian who claimed to have been "born again." His overt religiosity was off-putting to some of the legislators with whom he had to work. Carter attempted to bring a more informal style to the presidency; he sometimes made televised public addresses wearing a sweater, and he famously carried his own suitcase when traveling. He also made an effort to appoint more women and minorities to positions on his staff.

Like Nixon and Ford, Carter wrestled unsuccessfully with an ailing economy. Stagflation continued. Carter also attempted to curb inflation by cutting government spending, a policy that alienated many liberal Democrats. The president encouraged the Federal Reserve Board to combat inflation by restricting the money supply; this produced high interest rates, and it depressed the economy without fully reigning in inflation. When Carter left office, inflation was still high at 12 percent, and unemployment stood at 8 percent.

Adding to America's economic woes in the 1970s was the effort of **OPEC,** a cartel of mostly Middle Eastern oil producing nations, to drive up the price of crude oil. This resulted in much higher prices for gas and other petroleum products, helping to "fuel" inflation. President Carter made energy a priority of his administration, and he pushed for the establishment of the Department of Energy in 1977. Congress passed the National Energy Act in 1978, which deregulated the oil and gasoline markets and encouraged energy conservation.

Carter encouraged deregulation in other industries as a way of stimulating the economy. During his presidency, the airline and brewing industries were deregulated. His successor Ronald Reagan would carry this program of economic deregulation further in the 1980s.

President Carter made the promotion of human rights the centerpiece of his foreign policy. This idealistic approach marked a distinct contrast to the realpolitik of the Nixon and Kissinger era. Carter decided to sign a treaty with Panama, which would return the Canal Zone to Panamanian sovereignty in 1999. Critics like Ronald Reagan decried this treaty as a sacrifice of American interests. The president extended formal diplomatic recognition to the People's Republic of China. In 1979, building on diplomacy begun during the Ford administration, Carter signed a SALT II agreement with the Soviet leader Leonid Brezhnev that placed further limitations on the nuclear arsenals of the two superpowers. This treaty was never ratified by the U.S. Senate. In December of that year, the Soviet Union invaded Afghanistan. Alarmed by this aggression and what seemed like a Soviet drive toward the oil-rich Middle East, Carter canceled American participation in the 1980 Moscow Summer Olympics. He significantly increased the military budget. The period of détente with the Soviet Union was over.

President Carter's greatest diplomatic achievement was his mediation of talks between Menachem Begin of Israel and Anwar Sadat of Egypt that resulted in the **Camp David Accords.** This agreement provided the foundation for a longstanding peace between these two countries. Israel returned the Sinai Peninsula, which it had captured from Egypt in the Six Day War of 1967, and Egypt officially recognized Israel's right to exist.

In 1979, a revolution overthrew the Shah of Iran, and forced him to leave the country. The revolutionary government was increasingly dominated by fundamentalist Muslim clerics. One of these, the Ayatollah Khomeini, became the ruling force in Iran. In October 1979, President Carter allowed the ailing Shah into the United States to receive treatments for cancer. What Carter saw as a humanitarian gesture infuriated the Khomeini regime. On November 4, protestors instigated by the government overran the American embassy in Tehran, Iran. The 66 Americans working there were taken hostage.

The Iranians held the hostages for 444 days. After the initial assault on the embassy, President Carter cut off American trade with Iran and froze Iranian assets in the United States. Working with third parties, he tried to negotiate the release of the hostages. When the Iranians proved intransigent, Carter authorized a military operation to liberate the hostages. This proved to be a fiasco when sandstorms forced some of the mission's helicopters to land too soon or turn back. At the rendezvous point in Iran, two of the aircraft involved collided and exploded, killing eight men and forcing the immediate abandonment of the rescue attempt. Carter was forced to publically accept responsibility for this ignominious failure. The Iranians began guarding the hostages even more closely, and the Carter administration appeared ineffectual and weak because it could not secure their freedom. The hostages were not released until January 1981, shortly after the inauguration of Ronald Reagan as president.

The Election of 1980

President Carter waged his campaign for reelection in 1980 weighed down by a poor economy and the Iran crisis. Despite this, he was able to turn back a challenge for the Democratic nomination by Senator Edward Kennedy, brother of John F. Kennedy and Robert Kennedy. The veteran conservative champion Ronald Reagan easily captured the Republican nomination. Reagan hammered Carter's record and vowed to restore American military strength while at the same time cutting taxes. Reagan also promised to devolve power from the federal government back to the states. He openly appealed to traditional conservative values such as patriotism and support for the nuclear family, which seemed to be underappreciated in the post-Watergate years. Reagan's message resonated with many voters, and he won a decisive victory, both with the popular vote and in the Electoral College.

The election of 1980 was a turning point. The New Deal Democratic coalition that had dominated electoral politics on the national level for almost a half century began to fall apart. Ronald Reagan won the votes of many traditionally Democratic blue-collar workers who had been alienated from their party because of its liberal positions on abortion, sexual freedom, and **affirmative action.** Reagan successfully associated liberalism with the cultural upheaval, economic malaise, and international embarrassments of the 1970s. Members of the **religious right,** offended by challenges to traditional morality, started to vote overwhelmingly for the Republican party. Often politically and culturally more conservative than voters in other parts of the country, white Southerners continued a historic shift from the Democratic to Republican parties. Thanks to these broad political trends, the **New Right** heavily influenced American politics in the ensuing decades, beginning with helping to elect a Republican majority in the Senate along with Ronald Reagan in 1980.

The Reagan Administration

Ronald Reagan was a masterful communicator who helped transform American politics. He used skills developed as an actor in Hollywood during the 1930s and 1940s to effectively shape and deliver his message to many different audiences. As president, Reagan set general policy and left the details of implementing this to capable subordinates.

Reagan implemented a bold economic agenda. He persuaded Congress to cut federal taxes by 5 percent in 1981 and another 10 percent in the two following years. The president was an adherent of the theory of **"supply-side economics."** He believed that tax cuts would enable wealthier Americans to put more money back into the economy, spurring economic growth and job creation. This prosperity in turn would lead to higher tax revenue, because, even at lower rates, there would be more money to tax. To stimulate investment, capital gains taxes were lowered. The Reagan administration also continued the process of deregulation begun in the Carter years, easing regulations in such industries as banking, cable television, and long-distance phone service.

Liberals denounced President Reagan's economic priorities. Anticipating lower initial tax revenues, the Reagan administration cut funds for such domestic programs as urban housing and aid to education and the arts. At the same time, Reagan poured an additional $13 billion into the defense budget. The president also received a great deal of criticism for his expensive Strategic Defense Initiative (SDI), which was derisively nicknamed "Star Wars." The goal of this program was to develop defenses that could shoot down enemy missiles before they struck the American homeland. While technologically overambitious in Reagan's day, this program eventually led to significant breakthroughs in missile defense. Another contentious Reagan policy was his **New Federalism.** His administration gave states greater control over how federal money was spent within their borders. Environmentalists were incensed when he cut funding for the Environmental Protection Agency. Labor activists were angered when Reagan fired air traffic controllers who defied a federal statute by engaging in a strike.

Reagan was determined to reverse what he believed was the weakness of American foreign policy in the 1970s. He believed that the United States could win the cold war. His military build-up was intended to restore American military superiority over the Soviet Union. Despite much opposition, he responded to the emplacement of Soviet short-range nuclear missiles in Eastern Europe by stationing American cruise missiles in Western Europe. He outraged newspaper editorialists by calling the Soviet Union an "Evil Empire," but his rhetorical frankness pleased many voters. When the Marxist government of the Caribbean island of Grenada collapsed into civil war in 1983, Reagan sent in American troops. Grenada was an easy American victory. A peace-keeping mission in Lebanon ended less happily when a suicide truck attack killed 241 American servicemen.

President Reagan was in a strong position when he ran for reelection in 1984. After a deep recession in 1981–1982, the economy bounced back and was booming. Reagan's personal popularity remained high. He had won the hearts of many with his gutsy behavior after being shot by a deranged assassin in 1981. Reagan's Democratic opponent was Walter Mondale, who had served as Jimmy Carter's vice president. Mondale picked Congress-woman Geraldine Ferraro as his running mate, the first woman to be nominated to run on a major party's presidential ticket. Mondale criticized Reagan's supply-side economics and conceded that he would raise taxes. Reagan campaigned on the theme that it was "morning again in America." Prosperity and Reagan's nationalistic revival of American pride at home and abroad made him politically irresistible; he crushed Mondale in the election, claiming almost 60 percent of the popular vote and winning all the electoral votes except those of Minnesota and the District of Columbia.

In his second term, Reagan pursued deeper tax cuts. The **Tax Revenue Act of 1986** further reduced federal tax rates; that of the wealthiest Americans fell from 50 percent to 28 percent. In this period economic good times continued, with both unemployment and inflation falling. Reagan wanted to appoint conservative justices to the Supreme Court. He nominated William Rehnquist to serve as chief justice. He nominated Sandra Day O'Connor, the first woman appointee to the high court, as well as justices Antonin Scalia and Anthony Kennedy.

Reagan also faced challenges in his second term. On "Black Monday," October 19, 1987, the stock market saw a sudden and dramatic 20-percent drop in stock prices. Although it did not stop economic growth, this was a troubling event. Also worrisome was the rise in the federal deficit as a result of tax cuts and heavy defense spending. In another disturbing development, for the first time since World War I, the United States began importing more goods than it exported.

The Reagan administration was badly shaken by the **Iran-Contra Affair** in 1986 and 1987. Shiite Muslims aligned with Iran had been taking Americans hostage in Lebanon. In order to gain Iranian assistance in securing the release of these hostages, the Reagan administration violated an official trade embargo and sold weapons to Iran. National Security Advisor John Poindexter, Lieutenant Colonel Oliver North, and other administration officials then used the money from this "arms for hostages" scheme to assist the "Contras," rebels against the Communist-leaning government in Nicaragua. This covert funding of the Contras defied congressional limits on support for the Nicaraguan rebels. When these activities were discovered, Congress held nationally televised hearings. Several figures in the administration lost their jobs and faced legal penalties for their actions. President Reagan took responsibility for the Iran-Contra dealing, but he claimed that he did not know what his subordinates were up to. This made Reagan look like a detached figurehead in his own administration, and his poll numbers dropped precipitously.

But Reagan bounced back. Relations with the Libyan dictator Muammar al-Gadhafi had been poor since the 1981 Gulf of Sidra incident when American naval jets shot down two Libyan jets that challenged them. In April 1986, The U.S. government blamed Gadhafi for the terrorist bombing of a discotheque in Berlin that killed an American serviceman and wounded many more. Reagan ordered the bombing of military targets in

Libya. By Reagan's second term, the Soviets were finding it increasingly difficult to maintain their cold war competition with the United States; the Soviet economy was beginning to collapse. Mikhail Gorbachev, a new and younger leader of the Soviet Union, worked to establish better relations with the United States. President Reagan proved receptive to his overtures. In 1987, Reagan and Gorbachev signed the Intermediate-Range Nuclear Forces (INF) Treaty, which called for both states to eliminate an entire class of missiles. That same year Reagan traveled to Berlin, and speaking near the Berlin Wall, he demanded, "Mr. Gorbachev, tear down this wall!" By the time Reagan left office in January 1989, the Communist dictatorships of Eastern Europe were crumbling.

Ronald Reagan was one of the most successful presidents of the modern era. Many Americans saw him as a great leader who revived American pride, defended "traditional" American values, revitalized the economy, and won the cold war. Critics charged that Reagan's economic policies disproportionally benefited the wealthy and increased the gap between the rich and the poor. In 1988, this argument failed to resonate with the American public. Vice President George H. W. Bush's most compelling advantage in that year's election was that he represented a continuation of the policies of Ronald Reagan.

Chapter Review

Rapid Review

To achieve the perfect 5, you should be able to explain the following:

- One of the low points of American political life in the twentieth century was the Watergate Affair.
- Richard Nixon's greatest accomplishments were in the field of foreign policy, as he crafted new relationships with both China and the Soviet Union.
- The Watergate Affair developed from the paranoid view of American politics held by Richard Nixon and several of his top aides.
- Gerald Ford's presidency was hurt from the beginning by his pardoning of Richard Nixon.
- Ford faced huge economic problems as president; during his presidency, America suffered from both inflation and unemployment.
- Jimmy Carter and many politicians of the post-Watergate era emerged victorious by campaigning as outsiders.
- President Carter's outsider status hurt him, especially in terms of getting legislation passed in Congress.
- Carter demonstrated his diplomatic skills by helping Egypt and Israel bridge their differences through the Camp David Accords; he was unable to negotiate a release of the American hostages in Iran, and this may have cost him the presidency.
- Ronald Reagan was elected as a conservative and restored the pride of many Americans in America.
- Reagan practiced "supply-side" economics, which benefited the American economy but which also helped create large deficits.
- Under Reagan, the gap between the wealthiest Americans and the poorest Americans increased.
- Reagan reinstituted cold war rhetoric, but he later created cordial relations with leaders of the Soviet Union.
- Reagan's lack of direct control over the implementation of some presidential policies was demonstrated by the Iran-Contra Affair.

Time Line

1968: Richard Nixon elected president

1971: Nixon imposes wage and price controls
Pentagon Papers released

1972: Nixon visits China and Soviet Union
Nixon reelected
SALT I signed
Watergate break-in

1973: Watergate hearings in Congress
Spiro Agnew resigns as vice president
"Saturday Night Massacre"

1974: Inflation peaks at 11 percent
Nixon resigns; Gerald Ford becomes president
Ford pardons Richard Nixon
WIN economic program introduced

1975: South Vietnam falls to North Vietnam, ending Vietnam War

1976: Jimmy Carter elected president

1977: Carter signs Panama Canal treaty
Carter issues Vietnam-era draft amnesty

1978: Camp David Accords

1979: Americans taken hostage in Iran

1980: Ronald Reagan elected president

1981–1982: Major recession
Assassination attempt on Reagan

1981–1983: Major tax cuts instituted

1983: Reagan proposes "Star Wars"
Americans victorious in Grenada

1984: Reagan reelected

1985: Gorbachev assumes power in Soviet Union

1986: Additional tax reform measures passed
Iran-Contra Affair

1987: "Black Monday"

1988: George H. W. Bush elected president

› Review Questions

Fact Check

Check your knowledge of the historical period covered in this chapter.

1. What tactic was *not* used by supporters of Richard Nixon in the 1972 presidential campaign?
   A. Breaking into private offices
   B. Reviewing income tax records of suspected "enemies"
   C. Falsifying war records of opposing presidential candidates
   D. Attempting to halt official investigations of actions of campaign officials

2. According to supply-side economics, when wealthy Americans received tax cuts, they would proceed to do all but which of the following?
   A. Invest heavily in the economy
   B. Open new factories
   C. Purchase stocks
   D. Increase their savings dramatically

3. Which of the following did *not* help create the deficits of the second term of the Reagan years?
  A. Reduction of federal tax rates
  B. Desperately needed increases in funding for education
  C. Increases in military spending
  D. Changes in the tax code that favored wealthier Americans

4. Critics of Ronald Reagan would most emphasize
  A. the effects of the 1981–1983 tax cuts.
  B. the U.S. response to threats from Libya.
  C. the effects of Reagan's economic policies on the middle and lower classes.
  D. his public image and political skills.

5. Gerald Ford's WIN program demonstrated to many Americans that Ford
  A. had no real grasp of economic issues.
  B. had the uncanny knack of knowing how to inspire the American public.
  C. was still under the shadow of Richard Nixon.
  D. understood sophisticated foreign policy issues.

Multiple-Choice Questions

Here are multiple-choice questions like the ones on the AP U.S. History exam.

Questions 6–8 refer to the quotation below.

Higher taxes would not mean lower deficits. . . . In 1980 tax revenues increased by $54 billion, and in 1980 we had one of our all-time biggest deficits. Raising taxes won't balance the budget; it will encourage more government spending and less private investment. Raising taxes will slow economic growth, reduce production, and destroy future jobs, making it more difficult for those without jobs to find them and more likely that those who now have jobs could lose them. So, I will not ask you to try and balance the budget on the backs of the American taxpayers.

—President Ronald Reagan, Address Before a Joint Session of the Congress Reporting on the State of the Union, January 26, 1982

6. President Ronald Reagan believed that the economic problems of the late 1970s and early 1980s could be best addressed by
  A. reducing the size of government.
  B. increasing the size of government.
  C. providing free healthcare to all Americans.
  D. increasing government regulation of businesses.

7. Which of the following was a term used to describe President Reagan's tax policies?
  A. Keynesian economics
  B. Supply-side economics
  C. The Great Society
  D. Globalization

8. Which of the following was an important element of President Reagan's foreign policy?
  A. Confronting the Soviet Union in the cold war
  B. Limiting American engagement abroad to reduce military expenses
  C. Promoting a policy of détente with China and the Soviet Union
  D. Making the spread of human rights the focus of American diplomacy

Short-Answer Question

The short-answer question below is similar to the ones you'll encounter on the AP U.S. History exam.

9. Answer Parts A, B, and C.
   A. Briefly explain ONE example illustrating the conservative direction of the nation in the 1970s and 1980s.
   B. Briefly explain a SECOND example illustrating the conservative direction of the nation in the 1970s and 1980s.
   C. Briefly explain ONE example of an approach taken to the cold war by a president of the 1970s and 1980s.

› Answers and Explanations

1. **C**. Of all of the "dirty tricks" practiced by the Republicans in 1972, this was not one of them.

2. **D**. The key to supply-side economics is that when tax cuts give individuals large amounts of money, they will reinvest that money in the economy.

3. **B**. Even though education advocates were saying that funding had to be drastically increased in many urban school districts, funding for education declined during the Reagan era.

4. **C**. The 1981 to 1983 tax cuts did help bring down inflation; at this same time, employment possibilities increased. Compared to the wealthiest Americans, the middle and lower classes experienced little benefit from Reagan's economic policies, especially from the tax cuts of the second term.

5. **A**. Many Americans saw the WIN program as a public relations gimmick, demonstrating that Ford did not truly understand the economic problems of America; many equated WIN to some of the public pronouncements of Herbert Hoover in 1930 and 1931.

6. **A**. President Ronald Reagan believed that the economic problems of the late 1970s and early 1980s could be best addressed by reducing the size of government. Reagan argued that a growing government was wasting resources and impinging on American freedoms. He advocated tax cuts, deregulation of many industries, and a New Federalism plan to strengthen the power of the states.

7. **B**. A term used to describe President Reagan's tax policies was supply-side economics. Reagan and his supporters believed that reducing the tax burden of Americans would stimulate investment in the economy. This would result in more prosperity, jobs, and seemingly paradoxically, higher tax revenues. Reagan persuaded Congress to cut federal income taxes and capital gains taxes.

8. **A**. Confronting the Soviet Union in the cold war was an important element of President Reagan's foreign policy. Responding to what he thought had been weakness in American policy towards the Soviet Union, Reagan called the Soviet Union an "evil empire." He bolstered the NATO alliance by putting cruise missiles in Europe, launching a massive military buildup, and beginning work on a Strategic Defense Initiative (SDI) designed to protect the United States against Soviet missiles.

9. **Parts A and B**: During the 1970s and 1980s there was only one Democratic president, who served for one term. In 1968, the victorious Republican presidential candidate Richard Nixon campaigned on a platform calling for

"law and order," appealing to voters disturbed by the rioting and social upheaval caused by racial unrest and the Vietnam War. In office, Nixon advocated a "New Federalism," hoping to transfer some government functions back to state and local governments. In 1972, he signed into law a revenue sharing bill that sent some federal income tax money to local governments. Nixon also worked to build his political base by taking a conservative stance on cultural and social issues like abortion and busing. He claimed to speak for the "silent majority" of Americans. Nixon's successor, Gerald Ford, attempted to combat the economic stagflation of the 1970s through the conservative remedies of tax cuts and lower government spending. President Jimmy Carter, though a liberal Democrat, also wrestled unsuccessfully with stagflation. He encouraged the deregulation of the transportation industry. During the Carter years, voter dissatisfaction with high taxes became a political issue. In 1978, businessman Howard Jarvis successfully lobbied for Proposition 13, which slashed property taxes in California. Also during the late 1970s, the religious right emerged as a political force, with ministers like Jerry

Falwell, head of the Moral Majority, becoming prominent figures. President Ronald Reagan came into office in 1981 advocating "supply-side economics," which argued that tax cuts would lead to greater consumer spending, a revitalized economy, and ultimately, because of renewed prosperity, greater tax revenues. Reagan secured significant tax cuts during his presidency. He also called for a New Federalism, sending more powers and money back to the states. Under Reagan, deregulation intensified, spreading from transportation to energy and other industries.

Part C: Richard Nixon and his National Security Advisor Henry Kissinger believed in realpolitik, or power politics in foreign policy. They also recognized that the world was becoming multipolar with more nations than just the United States and the Soviet Union exercising power. Nixon and Kissinger orchestrated a diplomatic opening to Communist China, while simultaneously pursuing a policy of détente, or improved relations, with the Soviet Union; they hoped to be able to play the two communist powers against each other. Presidents Gerald Ford and Jimmy Carter continued détente with both the Soviet Union and China for most of the 1970s. The Soviet invasion of Afghanistan in 1979 led Carter to cool relations with Moscow and to begin a rebuilding of the American military. President Reagan was a committed anti-communist who believed that the United States could win the cold war. He responded vigorously to the Soviet placement of short-range nuclear missiles in Eastern Europe, placing equivalent American missiles in Western Europe. He denounced the Soviet Union as an "evil empire." He increased the defense budget by $13 billion, putting enormous strain on the ailing Soviet Union. Late in Reagan's second term, as the Soviets attempted to improve relations with the United States, cold war tensions began to recede. In 1987, Reagan signed the INF Treaty with the Soviet Union, eliminating intermediate range nuclear missiles.

CHAPTER 29

Prosperity and a New World Order (1988–2000)

IN THIS CHAPTER

Summary: For much of the post–World War II era, the popularity of a president was largely determined by his success in foreign policy and in handling foreign crises. With the ending of the cold war at the end of the 1980s, skills in handling domestic issues became equally important for presidents and their staffs. Presidents George H. W. Bush and Clinton are perfect examples of this: Bush's popularity was sky-high after his Desert Storm victory, yet he ended up being defeated by Bill Clinton largely because of economic problems that developed in the closing years of his term. Despite a mountain of personal and ethical issues that surrounded him, President Clinton was able to keep high approval ratings because of a continuing successful economy.

Keywords

New Right: conservative movement that began in the 1960s and supported Republican candidates into the twenty-first century; many voters from the South and from the middle class were attracted by the New Right's emphasis on patriotism and strict moral values.

Operation Desert Storm (1991): military action by the United States and a coalition of Allied nations against Iraq and its leader Saddam Hussein after Iraq had invaded Kuwait; this operation was a resounding success, although the decision was made not to force Saddam Hussein from power.

Whitewater: series of real estate dealings in Arkansas involving Bill Clinton long before he became president. Republicans accused Clinton of financial improprieties in the Whitewater affair; a number of his former associates went to jail, but no charges against the president were ever proven. The Whitewater affair was one of several accusations that eventually led to Clinton being impeached by the House of Representatives but acquitted by the Senate.

Contract with America: list of conservative measures proposed by Republicans after winning control of the House of Representatives in 1994; it included term limits and promises to balance the federal budget and to reduce the size of the federal government. Republican supporters of the Contract were led by Speaker of the House Newt Gingrich.

The Election of 1988

George H. W. Bush had an impressive résumé. Before becoming Ronald Reagan's vice president, he had served in Congress, as the U.S. ambassador to the United Nations, as chairman of the Republican party, as a diplomat in China, and as the director of the CIA. Republican ads in 1988 praised him as "the most qualified man of our times" to run for president. Because Senator Dan Quayle of Indiana, a vocal Reaganite, had never been identified with the **New Right,** Bush shored up his support with conservatives by choosing him to be his running mate.

Massachusetts Governor Michael Dukakis won the Democratic nomination. Dukakis stressed his competency as a governor and took credit for reviving his state's economy in a "Massachusetts miracle." Both candidates relied on negative television advertising. Bush connected his opponent with Willie Horton, an African-American convict who raped a woman after being furloughed from prison through a program established by Dukakis. Despite some attempts by members of the media to portray him as a "wimp," and an early lead by Dukakis in the polls, Bush won a solid victory on election night.

The Presidency of George H. W. Bush

Bush called for a "kinder, gentler America" when he accepted the Republican nomination for president in 1988. Once in office, he found himself stymied by political **gridlock;** little domestic legislation resulted with a Republican president and Democratic congress checkmating each other. One notable exception was the passage of the Americans with Disabilities Act of 1990. The ballooning federal budget deficit became a major problem during the Bush presidency. To reduce the deficit, Bush agreed to a deal with congressional Democrats, which increased taxes. This violated a "no new taxes" pledge that Bush had made during the presidential campaign, and it cost him the support of many conservatives.

President Bush had much more success with his foreign policy. When Bush took office, the cold war was winding down. The Soviet economy could no longer bear the strains of competing with the United States. In late 1988, the Soviet leader Mikhail Gorbachev acknowledged to Communist party leaders that military spending and "protecting" the satellite states was suffocating the economy. In 1989, the Soviets began reducing their aid to the Communist regimes in Eastern Europe. Without Soviet support, these Communist governments proved too fragile and unpopular to survive. In Poland, the Solidarity labor movement forced the Communists from power. By the end of 1989, the Communist rulers had been overthrown in all the Eastern European states. The Soviet Union itself grew increasingly unstable as Gorbachev's efforts to open its society and modernize the economy failed. Independence movements emerged in several Soviet republics. After a failed coup attempt by Communist hardliners weakened Gorbachev, Boris Yeltsin, the president of the Russian Republic, proclaimed the dissolution of the Soviet Union in December 1991.

President Bush skillfully managed the end of the cold war. His diplomacy helped ease the breakup of the Soviet empire. He encouraged German reunification and ensured that the new Germany would remain in NATO. Bush worked with both Gorbachev and Yeltsin to reduce stockpiles of nuclear weapons in both countries. The United States provided financial assistance to help former Soviet republics dispose of nuclear weapons stored in their territories. American experts traveled to Moscow and Eastern European countries to provide advice on transitioning to a market economy; they met with limited success.

Bush used the military that Ronald Reagan had built up. In December 1989, after an American officer was murdered by Panamanian troops, Bush ordered an invasion of Panama that overthrew its dictator Manuel Noriega. On August 2, 1990, The Iraqi strongman Saddam Hussein occupied the small neighboring state of Kuwait. Iraqi tanks were poised on the border of Saudi Arabia, raising the prospect that Saddam Hussein might seize control of a great chunk of the world's oil reserves. President Bush condemned the attack on Kuwait and quickly organized an international force to defend Saudi Arabia. He then diplomatically orchestrated a large multinational military coalition to drive the Iraqis from Kuwait. An air offensive against Iraq began on January 17, 1991. For a month Iraqi defenses were weakened by this aerial pounding. On February 24, in **Operation Desert Storm,** American and allied ground forces rolled into Kuwait, routing the Iraqi occupiers. In this swift and decisive victory, the Iraqis suffered over 40,000 casualties. The number of Americans killed was 150. Because his coalition was unified around ejecting Iraq from Kuwait, but not overthrowing Saddam Hussein, Bush ordered his forces to stop at the Iraqi border. The United Nations supported this limited mandate. As a consequence, the UN would be forced to deal with an uncooperative Saddam Hussein for many more years.

The Gulf War brought Bush's popularity to the highest levels of his presidency. This did not last. Economic troubles, including a recession, caused concern in 1992. Instability in the successor states to the former Soviet Union proved worrisome. Following the breakup of Yugoslavia, a brutal civil war in which Serbs launched a campaign of "ethnic cleansing" against Bosnian Muslims horrified the world. A master of great power diplomacy, President Bush had little interest in and no solutions for these conflicts.

The Election of 1992

Americans in 1992 were looking for "change." Ironically, President Bush's foreign policy successes weakened his case for a second term. With the cold war over and a "New World Order" of international cooperation inaugurated by the Gulf War, Americans hoped for a "peace dividend" and focused on domestic affairs. A World War II veteran and long-term public servant, Bush seemed increasingly out of touch with the concerns of everyday Americans.

Arkansas Governor Bill Clinton won the Democratic nomination for president. A younger man than Bush, he was a member of the baby boom generation. Clinton had a better feel for the mood of the American people. The unofficial slogan of his campaign was, "It's the economy, stupid." After the Democrats had lost in the preceding three presidential races, Clinton ran as a centrist **"New Democrat."** He distanced himself from the traditional liberal faith in big government, and he claimed to be open to good ideas from the Republicans. This frustrated conservative commentators like Rush Limbaugh, who believed that Clinton was insincere and would say anything to get elected.

The Texas multibillionaire Ross Perot ran as an independent candidate for the presidency. He called for a balanced budget and promised to bring "common sense" to the White House. Perot's message resonated with voters alienated from the major parties, and his willingness to spend lots of money on advertising enabled him to remain competitive.

Clinton won a solid victory in the three-man race. He was able to recapture the votes of many Democrats who had deserted the party for Ronald Reagan and Bush in 1988. Perot won 19 million votes, 19 percent of the popular vote, the best tally for a third-party candidate since Theodore Roosevelt's Bull Moose run in 1912.

The Presidency of Bill Clinton

Once in office, President Clinton attempted to assemble a dynamic cabinet that was representative of the nation at large, and he appointed to it more women and minorities. In his first term he enjoyed some legislative successes. In an effort to balance the budget, he signed a bill increasing taxes on higher-income Americans. The Brady Bill instituted federal background checks and five-day waiting periods for people purchasing guns. Clinton persuaded the Senate to ratify the **North American Free Trade Agreement (NAFTA)**, which had been negotiated by President George H. W. Bush. This treaty removed tariffs and other trade barriers between the United States, Mexico, and Canada. NAFTA was opposed by many unions, fearful of losing jobs. The president pressed ahead anyway because he supported lowering tariffs around the world to facilitate the growing **globalization** of the American economy. Clinton also suffered some defeats. An effort to protect gays in the military with a "Don't Ask, Don't Tell" directive to the Defense Department angered advocates for both sides of the issue. First Lady Hillary Clinton led an ambitious attempt to revamp healthcare in the United States. Intense lobbying and advertising by the American Medical Association and the healthcare industry led to the plan's failure in Congress.

Clinton faced other problems as well. Reports of sexual infidelities had surfaced during his presidential campaign. Questions were also raised about the financial activities of the Clintons while they were still in Arkansas. Their involvement with a failed savings and loan and their investment in the **"Whitewater"** land development deal caused the most controversy. In August 1994, Kenneth Starr was appointed independent counsel to investigate the Whitewater scandal. Fifteen people were convicted of crimes connected to Whitewater, but the Clintons were never charged with wrongdoing in this affair.

In a dramatic political upset, the Republicans won control of Congress in the election of 1994. This was the first time that the Republicans had won control of the House of Representatives since 1952. The results of the election were widely seen as a rejection of President Clinton's policies. The new Speaker of the House Newt Gingrich promoted the **Contract with America,** an ambitious conservative legislative agenda. Their efforts to cut taxes and reduce government led the Republican congressional majority into conflict with the president. Clinton proved a capable political tactician. When the Republicans briefly shut down the federal government in 1995 and 1996, Clinton gained stature by opposing this unpopular measure.

Clinton quickly adjusted to the new political climate, declaring that "the era of big government is over." He returned to his centrist "New Democrat" roots, and on some issues he proved willing to compromise with the Republicans. The Personal Responsibility and Work Opportunity Reconciliation Act of 1996 reformed the welfare system. This legislation placed time limits on welfare assistance, imposed stricter requirements for programs like food stamps, and empowered states to develop "welfare-to-work" programs. Supporters hailed the end of "welfare as we know it."

Following the end of the cold war, American foreign policy needed to be reoriented. President Clinton, like President Bush in 1992, was accused of a lack of "focus" in his diplomacy. Clinton inherited a humanitarian mission in Somalia from Bush. He allowed the American troops in Somalia to attack local warlords, and in 1993, 18 American servicemen were killed in an ambush in the city of Mogadishu. Clinton pulled American troops out of Somalia, and he became reluctant to commit American troops to peacekeeping operations. He did nothing during the Rwandan genocide of 1994. He did send American troops to restore the deposed president of the Caribbean nation of Haiti. Clinton eventually joined with NATO to stop the Serbian "ethnic cleansing" of Muslims in Bosnia. In 1995, American diplomats brokered a peace in Bosnia. American troops are part of the NATO force that continues to enforce this settlement.

Clinton's move to the center paid political dividends in the election of 1998. His embrace of welfare reform and other conservative initiatives gave his opponents little to run on. He easily defeated the Republican candidate, Kansas Senator Robert Dole, and the Reform party candidate, Ross Perot, who campaigned for the presidency a second time. Clinton's second term got off to a start that seemed to promise a period of constructive compromise between the parties when he signed a bill designed to lower the federal budget.

Then Kenneth Starr's Whitewater investigation suddenly veered in an unexpected direction. Starr discovered that Clinton had carried on an affair with a White House intern named Monica Lewinsky. Both Clinton and Lewinsky had denied a relationship in depositions made because of a lawsuit lodged against the president by an Arkansas state employee named Paula Jones, who accused him of sexually harassing her. Clinton went before the cameras and claimed that he never had sexual relations with Monica Lewinsky, but she possessed physical evidence that indicated otherwise.

Clinton's lies led to the Republican House of Representatives impeaching him for perjury and obstruction of justice on December 19, 1998. After a trial in the Senate, on February 12, 1999, votes were held on the two articles of impeachment. Neither received enough votes to remove the president from office. The Lewinsky scandal and the impeachment crisis embarrassed Clinton and preoccupied him for much of his second term. He remained personally popular through this period, in large part because the nation was prospering economically. In the short run, the Republicans were damaged by their anti-Clinton zeal, losing five House seats in the 1996 election. Public fatigue with the scandals may have hurt the Democrats in 2000.

Though little understood by most Americans, some deadly foreign policy challenges grew during President Clinton's second term. Islamic extremists had set off a bomb at the World Trade Center in New York City in 1993. In 1998, Osama bin Laden, the head of the Islamist Al Qaeda network, organized terrorist bombings of the American embassies in Tanzania and Kenya that killed hundreds of people. In response, Clinton ordered cruise missile strikes against Al Qaeda sites in Afghanistan and Sudan, but the strikes failed to kill bin Laden. That same year, Clinton launched a brief bombing campaign against Iraq because Saddam Hussein was violating UN mandates and pursuing weapons of mass destruction. Clinton signed the Iraq Liberation Act of 1998, which called for "regime change" in Iraq. In 1999, the United States and NATO allies waged an air war against Serbia to prevent another campaign of "ethnic cleansing" against the Albanian population of Kosovo. In 2000, Clinton was unsuccessful in brokering a peace deal between Israel and the Palestinians.

The Election of 2000

After eight years of prosperity and scandal, few knew what to expect as the election of 2000 approached. Aiming for continuity, the Democrats nominated Vice President Al Gore, who had a reputation as a policy wonk but lacked the popular touch of Bill Clinton. The Republicans turned to a familiar name, Texas Governor George W. Bush, the son of former president George H. W. Bush. The consumer and environmental activist Ralph Nader ran as the candidate of the Green Party.

A lack of excitement during the campaign was more than made up for on election night; the election proved to be one of the closest in history. Gore lost his home state of Tennessee, but he ended up with 500,000 more popular votes. Victory in the Electoral College hinged on winning Florida, where Bush held a lead of several hundred votes. The closeness of the outcome in Florida, where many ballots had been incompletely or incorrectly filled out, led to a prolonged and confusing series of legal disputes between the Gore and Bush campaigns, as several Florida counties began recounting the ballots using different standards. This process came to an end on December 9, 2000, when the U.S. Supreme Court in a 5-to-4 decision ordered a halt to the recounts. Three days later, on December 12, the Supreme Court by the same margin ruled that recounts in selected counties violated equal protection standards; this decision assured Bush's victory. Bush was certified the winner in Florida by 537 votes, giving him a narrow presidential victory in the Electoral College. Early in 2001, news organizations did their own recount of the Florida ballots, and they determined that by using the standard for evaluating ballots pushed by the Gore campaign, Bush would still have won the election.

Chapter Review

Rapid Review

To achieve the perfect 5, you should be able to explain the following:

- The ability to manage domestic issues were critical for a president's political success in the post-cold war era.
- George H. W. Bush alienated many conservatives, especially when he broke his "no new taxes" pledge.
- The end of the cold war can be attributed to American policy decisions and to weaknesses in the infrastructure of the Soviet Union.
- George H. W. Bush skillfully managed the Desert Storm operation against Iraq.
- Bill Clinton presented himself as a "New Democrat" and focused on economic issues in the 1992 presidential campaign; these were important factors in his victory.
- Clinton's failure on national health insurance helped pave the way for large Republican gains in the 1994 congressional elections.
- Clinton and Newt Gingrich were formidable opponents in the budget battles of the mid-1990s.
- The Whitewater scandal and investigations of the personal life of Bill Clinton were the defining political events of the second term of Clinton's presidency.
- George W. Bush's election demonstrated the difficulties of arriving at a "final tally" in any election and was finally secured by the intervention of the U.S. Supreme Court.

Time Line

1988: George H. W. Bush elected president
Solidarity replaces Communist government in Poland
1989: Berlin Wall opened, Communist governments fall in Eastern Europe
1991: Persian Gulf War
Breakup of the Soviet Union
Beginnings of economic recession
1992: Election of Bill Clinton
1993: NAFTA ratified by Senate
Terrorist bombings at World Trade Center
American troops killed in Somalia
1994: Republicans sweep congressional elections
U.S. military enters Haiti
Kenneth Starr becomes Whitewater independent counsel
1996: Clinton reelected
1998: Federal budget surplus announced
Articles of impeachment passed in House of Representatives
1999: Clinton acquitted in impeachment trial in U.S. Senate
2000: George W. Bush elected president

〉 Review Questions

Fact Check

Check your knowledge of the historical period covered in this chapter.

1. A defining characteristic of the Clinton presidency was his
   A. strict adherence to traditional Democratic values.
   B. pragmatic policy making.
   C. close alliance with liberals in the Democratic party.
   D. unprecedented alliance with labor unions.

2. George H. W. Bush alienated many conservative Republicans by
   A. appointing the relatively inexperienced Dan Quayle as vice president.
   B. continuing to urge the tearing down of the Berlin Wall.
   C. signing the 1990 agreement with the Democrats to reduce the deficit.
   D. pursuing policies against Iraq.

3. Critics accused George H. W. Bush of lacking "vision" because
   A. he failed to articulate a successful policy to end the economic deficit.
   B. he failed to remove Saddam Hussein from power.
   C. he failed to sign an arms treaty with Mikhail Gorbachev.
   D. he failed to explain his perception of America's role in the post-cold war world.

4. All of the following were reasons for the end of the cold war *except*
  A. the U.S. military buildup under Ronald Reagan.
  B. the fact that many producers of military weaponry in the United States did not want to continue to produce this weaponry.
  C. the weaknesses of the Soviet economy.
  D. the cold war rhetoric of both Ronald Reagan and George H. W. Bush.

5. Bill Clinton was a formidable political opponent for the Republicans for all of the following reasons *except*
  A. his ability to eventually win over former Republicans of the New Right.
  B. his support in the black community.
  C. his ability to take Republican positions and make them appear to be his own.
  D. his ability to withstand political scandal.

Multiple-Choice Questions

Here are multiple-choice questions like the ones on the AP U.S. History exam.

Questions 6–8 refer to the quotation below.

But where do we draw the line on what prices matter? . . . Clearly, sustained low inflation implies less uncertainty about the future, and lower risk premiums imply higher prices of stocks and other earning assets. We can see that in the inverse relationship exhibited by price/earnings ratios and the rate of inflation in the past. But how do we know when irrational exuberance has unduly escalated asset values, which then become subject to unexpected and prolonged contractions . . . ? We as central bankers need not be concerned if a collapsing financial asset bubble does not threaten to impair the real economy, its production, jobs, and price stability.

> —Chairman of the Federal Reserve Alan Greenspan, Remarks at the Annual Dinner and Francis Boyer Lecture of the American Enterprise Institute for Public Policy Research, December 5, 1996

6. Chairman Alan Greenspan's "irrational exuberance" speech refers to which of the following?
  A. The practice of purchasing stocks on "margin"
  B. The Florida real estate bubble
  C. The practice of selling people homes they could not afford
  D. The dot-com bubble

7. Which president benefited politically from the economic effects of the "irrational exuberance" described by Greenspan?
  A. Ronald Reagan
  B. George H. W. Bush
  C. Bill Clinton
  D. George W. Bush

8. The economy of the 1990s can best be compared to that of which of the following decades?
  A. 1900s
  B. 1910s
  C. 1920s
  D. 1930s

Short-Answer Question

The short-answer question below is similar to the ones you'll encounter on the AP U.S. History exam.

9. Answer Parts A, B, and C.
  A. Briefly explain ONE example of an effect of the end of the cold war on American foreign policy or domestic politics.
  B. Briefly explain a SECOND example of an effect of the end of the cold war on American foreign policy or domestic politics.
  C. Briefly explain ONE example of the "centrist" political policies pursued by President Bill Clinton during the 1990s.

› Answers and Explanations

1. B. In claiming to be a "New Democrat," Clinton sometimes adopted traditional Republican ideas as his own. To many critics, the pragmatism of the Clinton White House masked the fact that President Clinton had few principles that he actually believed in.

2. C. This was the agreement where Bush broke his "no new taxes" pledge and broke with traditional Republican policy.

3. D. Several historians state that a weakness of both Bush and Clinton was that they were unable to articulate a coherent post-cold war foreign policy.

4. B. Most manufacturers had no desire to stop producing weaponry for the cold war. When the cold war finally ended, many of these companies were forced to lay off workers, and some that could not diversify were forced to close.

5. A. The New Right was the group that came to despise Bill Clinton the most. Members of the New Right interested in social issues were among Clinton's most passionate detractors during the Whitewater scandal.

6. D. Chairman Alan Greenspan's "irrational exuberance" speech refers to the dot-com bubble. During the 1990s Internet companies proliferated, benefiting from a burst of technological innovation. Internet companies that went public and sold stock often saw the value of their stock rise dramatically. The crash that ended the booming dot-com bubble came in 2000–2001 when a number of Internet companies failed and others lost much of their stock value.

7. C. The president who benefited politically from the economic effects of the "irrational exuberance" described by Greenspan was Bill Clinton. President Clinton used the prosperity that began in the middle 1990s as an argument for his reelection. The goodwill generated by this prosperity helped Clinton survive the Monica Lewinsky scandal.

8. C. The economy of the 1990s can best be compared to that of the 1920s. Both decades began with a recession. Then came a time of general prosperity. Both decades ended with an economic downturn.

9. Parts A and B: President George H. W. Bush skillfully handled the diplomacy of ending the cold war. The Berlin Wall fell in 1989, and Bush helped with the reunification of Germany the following year. At the same time, the Communist regimes in Eastern Europe were replaced by non-communist governments. Good relations with the Soviet Union enabled Bush to build an international coalition to respond to Iraqi dictator Saddam Hussein's 1990 invasion of Kuwait. In February 1991, Kuwait was liberated in Operation Desert Storm. Once the Soviet Union collapsed in late 1991, Bush began talking about a "peace dividend," arguing that with the end of the cold war the United States and other Western powers could reduce defense spending. With the world seemingly peaceful after the end of the cold war and the successful resolution of the Gulf War, Americans began to focus on domestic economic problems. President Bush, an old cold warrior, seemed increasingly out of touch. In the 1992 presidential election, Americans turned to Bill Clinton, the first baby boomer president. President Clinton was primarily interested in domestic policy. Clinton favored the growth of economic globalization. In 1993, he secured ratification of the North American Free Trade Agreement (NAFTA), which had been negotiated by President Bush. Clinton also addressed some of the aftershocks in the Balkans that followed the end of the cold war, launching brief bombing campaigns in Bosnia in 1995 and Kosovo in 1999. In each case, these bombing campaigns led to peace agreements.

Part C: Bill Clinton campaigned for the presidency as a "New Democrat," claiming to be a more centrist and economically conservative Democratic leader. In his first term, Clinton pushed some liberal policies such as health-care reform and higher taxes, but he also took some more conservative positions. He supported NAFTA despite the opposition of many Democrats who worried about the treaty's effects on organized labor. He also signed the 1994 Omnibus Crime Bill, which increased the number of federal crimes for which the death penalty could be imposed. After the Republicans won control of Congress in the 1994 elections, Clinton signed a number of laws that reflected political compromises with the new Congressional majority. These included the 1996 Defense of Marriage Act (DOMA), which recognized only marriages between one man and one woman; the 1996 Personal Responsibility and Work Opportunity Act, which put some limits on welfare and imposed some work requirements on recipients; and the 1997 Balanced Budget Act, designed to cut federal spending and balance the federal budget by 2002.

CHAPTER 30

Threat of Terrorism, Increase of Presidential Power, and Economic Crisis (2001–2016)

IN THIS CHAPTER

Summary: The threat of terrorism following the September 11, 2001, attacks on the World Trade Center in New York City and the Pentagon in Washington, DC, revived the historic conflict between the need for a strong central authority during wartime and the need to protect civil liberties. President George W. Bush and Congress enacted the Patriot Act, giving the federal government wide powers to investigate terrorists in the United States. Civil libertarians opposed this extension of federal authority.

U.S. forces attacked terrorist strongholds in Afghanistan in late 2001. In 2003, U.S. and Allied forces invaded Iraq and toppled the regime of Saddam Hussein. The Bush administration regarded Iraq as a military threat and potential terrorist ally. Critics disputed this view of Iraq.

At home, America remained politically divided. When sectarian violence broke out in Iraq, public opinion questioned the rationale for the invasion and the continued American military presence there. Social issues such as abortion and gay marriage also caused huge divides in American society.

The presidential election of 2008 took place just as the U.S. economy entered a severe downturn. In the voting, Democratic Senator Barack Obama defeated Senator John McCain for the presidency, and the Democrats increased their majorities in Congress.

Under President Obama, efforts to revive the economy and to lower the unemployment rate had only mixed results. President Obama oversaw the passage of the Affordable Care Act in 2010, which restructured the American healthcare system. The Obama administration continued the war in Afghanistan but withdrew combat troops from Iraq. There was a rise in antigovernment sentiment led by the so-called Tea Party movement. This led to major Democratic losses in the 2010 election.

In the 2012 presidential election, President Obama won a second term, defeating the Republican candidate, former governor Mitt Romney. Problems implementing the Affordable Care Act contributed to further Democratic losses in the 2014 elections. The rise of the terrorist organization ISIL in Syria and Iraq forced President Obama to send limited numbers of American troops back into combat in the Middle East.

In 2016, an American electorate looking for change gave real estate mogul and reality TV star Donald Trump a narrow victory over former secretary of state Hillary Clinton.

Keyword

Neoconservatism: modern American political philosophy that opposes big-government approaches to domestic issues yet favors an interventionist and aggressive foreign policy; most neoconservatives advocated American intervention in Iraq in 2003.

The Presidency of George W. Bush

The 9/11 Attacks

When he became president, George W. Bush hoped to focus on domestic policy. He spent much of the spring and summer of 2001 working on the No Child Left Behind Act, which required states to set and assess standards for public education. Bush hoped to combat a recession that had begun as he took office by stimulating the economy through tax cuts.

On September 11, hijackers associated with the Al Qaeda terrorist organization seized control of four American airliners. They crashed two airliners into the World Trade Center and one airliner into the Pentagon. Passengers on the fourth plane, realizing the hijackers' intentions, resisted, causing the terrorists on their plane to dive it into a field near Shanksville, Pennsylvania. These attacks cost almost 3,000 lives. The attacks had been organized by the Al Qaeda leader Osama bin Laden, who lived under the protection of the Taliban government in Afghanistan. On September 20, President Bush appeared before a joint session of Congress and declared that Osama bin Laden would be brought to justice. The "War on Terror" had begun.

The Bush administration responded rapidly to the 9/11 attacks. On October 7, the United States and a coalition of allies unleashed "Operation Enduring Freedom" in Afghanistan. Within weeks, the Taliban government collapsed. Many Taliban and Al Qaeda leaders fled to remote mountains along the border with Pakistan. A fragile pro-western government was installed in the Afghan capital of Kabul. The Bush administration was influenced by the ideas of the **neoconservatives**, who believed that the problems of the Middle East would be solved by introducing democracy.

Institutionalizing Homeland Security

In the aftermath of the 9/11 attacks, investigators discovered that the Central Intelligence Agency (CIA) and the Federal Bureau of Investigation (FBI) had possessed information on the activities of the hijackers, but legal obstacles and bureaucratic inertia had kept these agencies from sharing the knowledge that might have enabled them to recognize and forestall this terrorist plot. In October 2001, President Bush created the Office of Homeland Security to coordinate efforts to protect the United States from terrorist threats. The **Homeland Security Act of 2002** established the Office of Homeland Security as a cabinet department. In October 2001, Congress passed the USA Patriot Act, which gave American intelligence agencies more powers to investigate people suspected of plotting terrorism.

The Iraq War

Following the Gulf War, Saddam Hussein frustrated attempts by United Nations (UN) arms inspectors to locate and destroy chemical and biological weapons in Iraq. This led to a brief American and British bombing campaign in 1998. Confrontations frequently occurred between Iraqi forces and American planes, enforcing no-fly zones established at the end of the Gulf War. Saddam Hussein's regime celebrated the 9/11 attacks.

In his January 2002 State of the Union Address, President Bush declared that Iraq, along with Iran and North Korea, was part of an "Axis of Evil." The CIA and allied intelligence agencies assured President Bush that Iraq possessed weapons of mass destruction. In the post-9/11 period, the president and many policymakers believed that this was a danger that could not be ignored. Planning for a war continued while the Bush administration worked with the UN Security Council to resume weapons inspections in Iraq. In October 2002, Congress passed the "Iraq Resolution," which authorized the use of force against Iraq. In early 2003, President Bush and his advisors decided that Saddam Hussein was not cooperating with the UN. On March 20, the United States, Great Britain, and other coalition partners invaded Iraq. The coalition forces swiftly overwhelmed the Iraqi army and occupied the country. Eventually Saddam Hussein and most of his associates would be captured.

Unfortunately, Iraq proved to be a much more fragile society than the Americans had expected. Repairs to basic water and electrical infrastructure went slowly. Efforts to promote democracy also faltered. Although some power was turned over to an interim Iraqi government in June 2004, and elections for a national assembly were held in January 2005, Iraqis were divided religiously between Shia and Sunni Muslims, and ethnically between Kurds and Arabs. These groups soon began to fight amongst each other. This was aggravated by an insurgency that was begun by Saddam loyalists, but which soon became dominated by Al Qaeda-affiliated Islamic extremists. The brutal insurgency, which specialized in terrorist bombings, killed many thousands of Iraqis and began inflicting heavy casualties on coalition troops. As time went on and casualties mounted, the war grew increasingly unpopular in the United States.

Politics in the Bush Era

Coming into office, President Bush promoted "compassionate conservatism," hoping to advance the welfare of the American people through conservative means. This underlay his approach to education reform and his support of the Medicare Act of 2003, which provided retirees with assistance in purchasing prescription drugs. President Bush was also able to secure tax cuts in 2001 and 2003.

In the presidential election of 2004, the Democrats nominated Massachusetts Senator John Kerry. A decorated Vietnam veteran, Kerry attacked the war in Iraq. He was, in turn, criticized by Republicans as a "flip-flopper" because of his earlier support for the war. Kerry gained votes from citizens disillusioned by what seemed a quagmire in Iraq, and from those who believed that President Bush's election in 2000 had been illegitimate. Bush rallied voters who wanted victory in Iraq and cultivated the allegiance of the **"religious right,"** which was worried about threats to moral values in the United States. At the end of a contentious election campaign, President Bush defeated John Kerry by a narrow margin. The Republicans also increased their majorities in the U.S. House and Senate.

President Bush hoped to capitalize on his victory by reforming the Social Security system, which was facing challenges to its long-term fiscal stability. He proposed a plan that would partially privatize Social Security. Despite his efforts, the public and Congress refused to embrace his reform program. President Bush also hoped to address the energy issues facing the United States. He declared that "America is addicted to oil" and called for the development of alternative sources of energy. **Environmentalists** remained suspicious of the president because of his willingness, in the interim, to drill for oil in Alaska and offshore. President Bush did enjoy one area of solid success in furthering his conservative agenda. In 2005, he was able to nominate two conservative justices to the Supreme Court, John Roberts, who became Chief Justice, and Samuel Alito.

As his second term progressed, troubles piled up for President Bush. In August 2005, Hurricane Katrina devastated New Orleans and much of Louisiana and Mississippi. Though the governments of New Orleans and Louisiana proved notably incompetent, the federal government and the Bush administration received most of the blame for the problems caused by the storm. A series of scandals tarnished some important Republicans in Congress. In the election of 2006, the Democrats regained control of both houses of Congress for the first time since 2006.

The war in Iraq dragged on. By 2007, many Democrats regarded the war as a failure, and the Democratic Senate Majority Leader Harry Reid declared publically that "this war is lost." President Bush responded by ordering a controversial "surge" of 20,000 more troops to Iraq. The president's dramatic military offensive proved to be a success. By 2009, the insurgency had been crippled and the number of American casualties had been significantly reduced.

In 2007, President Bush proposed a comprehensive immigration bill that would have enabled millions of undocumented immigrants to legally remain in the United States, and if they paid a modest fine and some back-taxes, they would be given a path to citizenship. Immigration was a highly contentious issue. An influx of newcomers from Latin America and Asia who disregarded the regular immigration system inflamed political passions. Critics argued that this wave of migration encouraged lawlessness and burdened educational and welfare services. Some Democrat politicians saw undocumented immigrants as the vanguard of an emerging Democratic majority, while many businessmen saw them as a welcome source of cheap labor. A political resolution of this debate proved elusive. Bush's bill died in Congress. Immigration would remain a divisive issue. In the meantime, immigration transformed the demographic makeup of the United States. By 2020, 26 percent of the American population were immigrants or the children of immigrants. The large numbers of immigrants in the South and West contributed to these regions becoming the fastest-growing areas in the United States, and increasing their political, economic, and cultural influence.

Late in his presidency, President Bush was beset with economic troubles. The federal deficit had grown rapidly because of tax cuts and increases in entitlement and defense spending. In December 2007, the United States fell into a "recession," the beginning of a protracted period of economic stagnation and high unemployment. This was aggravated by the bursting of the subprime mortgage bubble, which had been caused, in part, by the federal government encouraging lending institutions to give mortgage loans to homebuyers with questionable ability to repay their debts. A banking crisis followed in September 2008, when the powerful firm of Lehman Brothers filed for bankruptcy, and many banks seemed near collapse. President Bush organized a federal bailout program for financial institutions that saved them from failure and may have averted a major depression. Though the banking system was saved, the stock market suffered heavy losses, causing great hardship for many Americans.

The Election of 2008

A presidential election played out against this backdrop of economic upheaval. Arizona Senator John McCain won the Republican nomination in what looked like a bad year for President Bush's party. He chose Alaska Governor Sarah Palin as his running mate. New York Senator Hillary Clinton and Illinois Senator Barack Obama engaged in a closely contested race for the Democratic nomination. In a year in which voters were looking for change, the relative newcomer Obama upset the heavily favored Clinton and won the nomination. He became the first African American to be nominated for president by a major party. Obama picked Delaware Senator Joseph Biden to run as the Democratic candidate for vice president. During the campaign, McCain capitalized on his status as a hero of the Vietnam War, while Obama emphasized a message of "hope and change." Obama won the election decisively. The Democrats increased their numbers in the House of Representatives and the Senate, giving the new president a strong governing majority in Congress.

The Obama Presidency

Domestic Policy

President Barack Obama faced many challenges when he assumed his office in January 2009. The economy was in trouble, and wars continued in Iraq and Afghanistan. Though the new administration addressed the economic situation with bailout legislation for banks and the auto industry, it focused its energies on enacting an ambitious reworking of the American healthcare system. The Patient Protection and Affordable Care Act of 2010, popularly known as "Obamacare," was passed with only Democratic votes in Congress. This legislation ensured that more Americans had access to health insurance. It also disrupted established insurance markets, led to higher costs for many, and outraged those opposed to an extension of government power over healthcare.

The battle for healthcare reform used up most of President Obama's political capital. His political troubles began to proliferate. The government's reaction to a massive oil spill from a British Petroleum (BP) well in the Gulf of Mexico was compared to the Bush government's official response to Hurricane Katrina. President Obama's perceived indifference to illegal immigration angered citizens concerned about the rapidly growing number of immigrants in the country. Above all, unemployment remained high (around 10 percent) and the economic recovery from the recession proved sluggish.

President Obama's policies spurred the growth of the "Tea Party" Movement. Tea Party activists called for smaller government and lower taxes. For Tea Partiers "Washington," with its concentration of lobbyists and politicians, symbolized a rogue government that had abandoned the interests of ordinary citizens. While President Obama was a special focus of the Tea Partiers' ire, they also distrusted "establishment" members of the Republican party. The energy of the Tea Party movement proved to be a bellwether of the shifting political mood in the nation. In the 2010 elections, the Republicans retook control of the House of Representatives and increased their numbers in the Senate. For the next two years, President Obama and congressional Republicans feuded over issues, such as the budget, and the resulting political deadlock precluded the passage of significant legislation. In the spring of 2012, President Obama enjoyed an unexpected victory when the Supreme Court upheld the constitutionality of most of the Affordable Healthcare Act in a 5-to-4 vote.

Changes in Foreign Policy

President Obama entered office determined to move away from the foreign policy of former President George W. Bush, which President Obama believed was too unilateral and interventionist. He and Secretary of State Hillary Clinton attempted to "reset" and improve relations with Russia. President Obama called for "a new beginning" in American relations with the Islamic world. Taking advantage of the military results of the "surge," the president began drawing down the number of troops in Iraq. In 2011, against the advice of many of his advisors, President Obama ordered all the remaining troops out of Iraq; this fulfilled a campaign promise to end that war. Conditions in Afghanistan remained unsettled. In December 2009, President Obama reluctantly sent 30,000 more troops to Afghanistan, though he announced that the number of Americans in that country would be reduced by 2014.

In 2011, President Obama joined North Atlantic Treaty Organization (NATO) allies in using airpower to help Libyan rebels overthrow the dictatorship of Muammar Gaddafi. A new Libyan government proved unable to control the country, and it became a haven for terrorists. On September 11, 2012, terrorists attacked a U.S. consulate in Benghazi, killing the American ambassador and three other Americans. This attack and the changing Obama administration explanations of it became a long-standing source of controversy.

President Obama authorized a daring mission that resulted in the death of Osama bin Laden on May 1, 2011. After years of hunting for the Al Qaeda leader, the CIA tracked him to a compound in Abbottabad, Pakistan. In a nighttime raid, Navy SEALs shot Osama bin Laden and seized valuable papers and computer files.

The Election of 2012

In 2012, Mitt Romney, a former governor of Massachusetts, won the Republican presidential nomination. Romney picked Congressman Paul Ryan as the vice presidential nominee. Both President Obama and Romney made the economy the leading issue in the election. President Obama called for higher taxes on the wealthy, while Romney emphasized the need to cut government spending. Once again, President Obama won a solid victory in a presidential election, and his coattails helped the Democrats increase their numbers in Congress. Exit polling showed that while Romney won more votes from whites and senior citizens, he was perceived as a candidate of the well-to-do "one percent." President Obama consolidated an electoral coalition of the young and minorities.

President Obama's Second Term

Domestic Policy

In domestic policy, President Obama would find most of his legislative initiatives frustrated by Republicans in Congress. An attempt to strengthen gun control legislation after the shocking massacre of 26 schoolchildren and teachers at Sandy Hook Elementary School in Connecticut by a deranged gunman went nowhere. President Obama continued to spar with Congressional Republicans over the budget and economic policy.

The Obama administration was embarrassed by the disastrous rollout of the Healthcare .gov website through which citizens were supposed to enroll in new insurance plans under the Affordable Care Act. Numerous glitches caused consumers many problems. The failure to create a fully functioning website fed into popular perceptions of government incompetence. Although the problems with the website were eventually worked out, the Affordable Care Act remained unpopular with many Americans. This contributed to the sweeping Republican victory in the elections of 2014. The Republicans won control of the Senate, gaining nine seats, and increased their majority in the House of Representatives. With victories in gubernatorial and state legislative elections, the Republicans were in their strongest national position since 1928.

President Obama turned to pursuing his goals on immigration and the environment through executive orders and administrative regulations issued by government departments. The President still had the power of the veto, vetoing Republican bills to repeal the Affordable Healthcare Act and authorize the Keystone XL pipeline.

President Obama exercised the "bully pulpit" on social issues. He became a vocal supporter of gay marriage. In 2015, the Supreme Court's *Obergefell v. Hodges* decision legalized gay marriages across the country. In 2014, a young African American man named Michael Brown was fatally shot by a white police officer in Ferguson, Missouri. Although the Justice Department later ruled that the shooting was justifiable, this incident revealed pent-up African American frustration with policing methods. Protests spread from Ferguson across the country. The "Black Lives Matter" movement attained national prominence. Police shootings of African American men received greater scrutiny. A number of police officers were assassinated by gunmen. President Obama acknowledged the difficult job facing police, but he expressed sympathy for African American anger.

Domestic security became an issue in President Obama's second term. In 2013, Edward Snowden, a former National Security Agency (NSA) contractor, leaked important information about American surveillance programs. His revelations dealt a severe blow to American intelligence operations. Concern also rose about foreign cyber attacks on the United States, including a 2014 data breach at the U.S. Office of Personnel Management that resulted in the compromising of the records of millions of government employees. In 2013, two Chechen brothers, motivated by radical Islamist ideology, bombed the Boston Marathon. Other Islamic terror attacks followed in Chattanooga, Tennessee, and San Bernardino, California, in 2015 and in Orlando, Florida, in 2016. These incidents led to a growing debate about immigration and domestic terrorism.

Foreign Policy

The Syrian civil war that began in 2011 continued throughout President Obama's second term, destabilizing its neighbors and sending waves of refugees into Europe and elsewhere. President Obama condemned the government of Syrian President Bashar al-Assad, and declared that the Syrian dictator had to leave office. President Obama eventually authorized some ineffective programs to train pro-Western rebel forces, but resolutely opposed military intervention. He declared that President Assad's use of chemical weapons would cross a "red line" inviting American retaliation. In August 2013, Syrian government forces used chemical weapons, killing nearly 300 people. President Obama declined to attack the Syrian government, instead agreeing to a Russian proposal to have President Assad surrender his chemical weapons to them. This began a strong revival of Russian influence in the Middle East, and especially Syria. In 2015, Russian President Vladimir Putin intervened militarily in Syria. Russian air support helped turn the war in President Assad's favor.

The collapse of Syria into civil war offered an opportunity for formerly al-Qaeda-linked Islamic extremists in Iraq to expand their influence. They began to carve out a territory for themselves in Syria and styled themselves as the Islamic State of Iraq and the Levant (ISIL).

Initially, President Obama was dismissive of ISIL. Following the withdrawal of American troops from Iraq in 2011, the Iraqi government fell into sectarian dissension between the majority Shiite Muslims and the minority Sunni Muslims. In 2014, ISIL took advantage of this government disarray to launch a devastating military offensive into Iraq, which captured a great swathe of territory and the large city of Mosul. President Obama was forced to send several thousand troops back to Iraq to help the Iraqi army push back against ISIL. American Air Force and Navy pilots flew thousands of bombing sorties against the terrorists. American forces began bombing ISIL in Syria as well.

A centerpiece of President Obama's Middle Eastern policy was an effort to work out a deal with Iran to contain its nuclear weapons program. In 2015, the Obama administration and diplomats from the other permanent member states of the UN Security Council negotiated an agreement with the Iranians, which ended economic sanctions against Iran, and returned funds that had been sequestered since the 1970s, in exchange for concessions that would likely delay the development of an Iranian nuclear bomb for a decade or more. President Obama believed that the agreement would help preserve peace and begin a process of integrating the Iranian regime into the international community. Republican critics of the deal believed that the agreement would strengthen an enemy of the United States while failing to ensure that the Iranians would not acquire nuclear weapons. Because of opposition in the Senate, President Obama did not put forward the deal as a treaty, and it remained an executive agreement.

The Russians posed challenges to the United States in other places than in Syria. In 2014, President Putin seized Crimea from the Ukraine and sponsored a bloody rebellion in the eastern part of that country. Russian forces made threatening gestures towards the Baltic states, and the United States and its NATO allies were compelled to bolster the region's defenses. In late 2016, the Obama administration accused the Russian government of attempting to influence the American presidential election by hacking into, and leaking documents from, the Democratic National Committee; it responded to this by expelling a number of Russian diplomats.

The Election of 2016

Sixteen Republican candidates ran for the Republican presidential nomination in what looked to be a good year for the opposition party. Unexpectedly, well-known candidates including former Florida governor Jeb Bush, Senator Marco Rubio, and Senator Ted Cruz were defeated by the New York real estate developer and reality TV show host Donald Trump. Confounding the assumptions of most political prognosticators, Trump won the Republican nomination by positioning himself as an opponent of the Republican establishment, and championing such populist causes as building a wall along the border with Mexico to halt illegal immigration.

Former secretary of state Hillary Clinton was the clear Democratic front-runner. Before clinching the Democratic nomination she had to fend off a challenge from Bernie Sanders, the socialist senator from Vermont. This pulled Clinton to the left. The 2016 Democratic party platform would be one of the most liberal in history.

Both presidential candidates had high unfavorability ratings. Donald Trump had been a celebrity for decades. He was prone to making outrageous comments. A tape surfaced of him making lewd comments about women. Many questioned whether he had the temperament to be a president. Hillary Clinton had also been in the public eye for years. Many believed that she and her husband, former president Bill Clinton, were ethically challenged and had used their Clinton Foundation to enrich themselves. As secretary of state, Clinton had avoided using secure government computer systems and instead had set up an insecure private computer server, which raised a real possibility that foreign intelligence services had read classified e-mails. Clinton compounded her fault by initially lying about the contents of the server. FBI director James Comey eventually criticized her handling of her communications, but concluded that she had not intentionally broken government security regulations. A late and brief revival of Comey's investigation because of the discovery of more Clinton e-mails on another computer helped weaken the momentum of her campaign.

Donald Trump chose Indiana governor Mike Pence as his running mate. Pence had solid conservative credentials and appealed to traditional Republican voters. Clinton chose Virginia Senator Tim Kaine as her vice presidential candidate. Kaine had served as governor of Virginia before entering the Senate, and was seen as an experienced and reliable choice.

During the presidential campaign, Clinton spent much of her time questioning the fitness of Donald Trump to be president. She also touted the historic nature of her candidacy and the very real possibility that she would become the first woman to become the president of the United States. Trump continued to promote himself as an outsider who would clean up Washington. He defied political correctness, claimed that he would bring back American jobs from overseas, and called on his supporters to "make America great again."

In a historic political upset, Trump defeated Clinton by demolishing the Democratic "Blue Wall" of midwestern industrial states, capturing the electoral votes of Pennsylvania, Ohio, Michigan, and Wisconsin. Trump ended up winning the electoral vote, 306 to 232. Clinton carried the popular vote by almost 3 million votes, most of which came from California. Trump won the election by gaining the votes of white working-class voters who had fallen behind economically during the years of slow economic growth under President Obama. These voters also resented the politically correct attitudes of those they termed "the elites" and associated with the Democratic party. Trump also did better with African American and Hispanic voters than Mitt Romney had done in 2012. Following his victory, Trump set about selecting a cabinet that appeared notable for its conservatism.

Chapter Review

Rapid Review

To achieve the perfect 5, you should be able to explain the following:

- The 9/11 attack on the World Trade Center had a huge impact on America and its perceived role in the world, and it affected policy decisions.
- "Winning" the war in Iraq proved to be much more difficult than many of the supporters of the war initially imagined.
- The failure to find many weapons of mass destruction led many to question the overall purpose of American efforts in Iraq.
- Several conservative policy positions concerning social issues and taxation were enacted during the presidency of George W. Bush.
- Criticisms of the federal response to Hurricane Katrina weakened political support for the Bush administration.
- Continued dissatisfaction with Republican policies and a desire for new leadership helped lead to the election of Barack Obama in 2008.
- President Obama worked to promote a liberal legislative agenda, most notably the Affordable Care Act that reformed American healthcare.

- The Obama administration intervened militarily in Syria and Iraq to counter the expansion of the terrorist Islamic State.
- The Black Lives Matter movement emerged in 2014 after a police shooting of an African-American youth in Ferguson, Missouri.
- In the 2015 *Obergefell v. Hodges* decision, the U.S. Supreme Court legalized gay marriage.
- In 2016, Donald Trump won the presidency by promising to take the country in a new direction.

Time Line

2001: Terrorist attack on World Trade Center and the Pentagon
American and British troops invade Afghanistan
Planning for military operations against Iraq begins

2002: President George W. Bush terms Iran, Iraq, and North Korea the "Axis of Evil"
Creation of Department of Homeland Security
Homeland Security Act signed into law

2003: President George W. Bush warns of possible war with Iraq in State of the Union address
Operation Iraqi Freedom: U.S. and British invasion of Iraq
"Outing" of CIA agent Valerie Plame
Violence in Iraq between Kurdish, Shiite, and Sunni factions
Controversy develops as weapons of mass destruction are not found in Iraq

2004: President George W. Bush proposes budget with $521 billion deficit
Photographs show American soldiers torturing Iraqi prisoners at the Abu Ghraib prison
Provisional government with limited authority comes into power in Iraq
George W. Bush defeats John Kerry in presidential elections; Republicans increase their control of the House and the Senate

2005: Violence between Sunnis and Shiites in Iraq increases dramatically
John Roberts becomes Supreme Court chief justice
Hurricane Katrina devastates New Orleans
I. Lewis "Scooter" Libby, Vice President Cheney's chief of staff, indicted on obstruction of justice concerning the Valerie Plame case
Samuel Alito becomes Supreme Court justice

2006: Controversy develops over secret wiretapping program by the federal government
Under investigation regarding his connections with a lobbyist, Tom DeLay, Republican majority leader of the House of Representatives, resigns

2007: Nancy Pelosi of California becomes first female Speaker of the House
President George W. Bush orders a surge of 20,000 more troops to Iraq

2008: Barack Obama becomes first African American elected to the U.S. presidency
Severe economic downturn affects U.S. financial institutions

2009: Unemployment in the United States remains near 10 percent
President Obama announces "troop surge" in Afghanistan

2010: BP oil spill clogs Gulf of Mexico
Healthcare legislation passes
Tea Party candidates win some seats in midterm elections

2012: President Obama elected to a second term
Gunman murders 20 children and 6 staff members at Sandy Hook Elementary School in Connecticut
Supreme Court upholds the legality of most provisions of the Affordable Care Act

2013: Former National Security Agency contractor Edward Snowden leaks information about NSA surveillance practices

Supreme Court strikes down the Defense of Marriage Act, which limited federal benefits to marriages between a man and a woman

Two Islamic terrorist brothers bomb the Boston Marathon

Budget dispute between Congressional Republicans and President Obama leads to a partial shutdown of government for 16 days

Healthcare.gov website for purchasing Affordable Care Act health plans starts up but suffers many glitches

2014: U.S.-Russia relations deteriorate because of Russian takeover of Crimea

Supreme Court strikes down limits on biennial donations to politicians by individuals

Islamic State of Iraq and Syria (ISIS) makes great gains in the Middle East

Riots take place in Ferguson, Missouri, after a white police officer shoots and kills an African-American teen during a confrontation on a street

Republicans take control of the Senate in the 2014 elections

2015: The Obama administration negotiates a controversial nuclear deal with Iran

Supreme Court upholds Affordable Care Act subsidies

Islamic terror attacks take place in Chattanooga, Tennessee, and San Bernardino, California

The Supreme Court upholds the constitutionality of gay marriage

The United States resumes diplomatic relations with Cuba

2016: Islamic terrorist attack at a gay nightclub in Orlando, Florida

Hillary Clinton becomes the first female presidential nominee of a major political party

Donald Trump wins the presidential election

› Review Questions

Fact Check

Check your knowledge of the historical period covered in this chapter.

1. Major reasons stated by President George W. Bush for the war in Iraq included all but which of the following?
   A. Iraq possessed weapons of mass destruction.
   B. Saddam Hussein had tried to assassinate the president's father.
   C. Iraq had links to terrorism.
   D. Saddam Hussein had killed his own people in the past.

2. Which of the following was not a major policy goal of the religious right?
   A. Have a constitutional amendment banning gay marriage
   B. Limit abortions in the United States
   C. Cut the income tax of wealthy Americans
   D. Take steps to save the life of Terri Schiavo

3. Which of the following was President Barack Obama's most significant legislative achievement?
   A. The USA Patriot Act
   B. The No Child Left Behind Act
   C. The Emergency Economic Stabilization Act of 2008
   D. The Affordable Care Act (ACA)

4. All of the following hurt John Kerry in his bid for the presidency in 2004 *except*
   A. his statements on the Vietnam War when he returned home after the war.
   B. his voting record on the Iraqi war.
   C. his performance in the 2004 debates.
   D. the fact that questions on social issues (gay marriage, etc.) appeared on the ballots in many states.

5. In his expressed desire to expand democracy to the Middle East, President George W. Bush can be equated with which twentieth century president who wanted to expand American concepts of freedom and democracy to Europe and other parts of the world?
   A. Woodrow Wilson
   B. Franklin Roosevelt
   C. Dwight Eisenhower
   D. Lyndon Johnson

Multiple-Choice Questions

Here are multiple-choice questions like the ones on the AP U.S. History exam.

Questions 6–8 refer to the quotation below.

There's no excuse for mass murder, just as there is no excuse for genocide. Those who practice terrorism, murdering or victimizing innocent civilians, lose any right to have their cause understood by decent people and lawful nations. On this issue, terrorism, the United Nations must draw a line. The era of moral relativism between those who practice or condone terrorism and those nations who stand up against it must end. Moral relativism doesn't have a place in this discussion and debate. There's no moral way to sympathize with grossly immoral actions. And by so doing and trying to do that, unfortunately, a fertile field has been created in which terrorism has grown.

—New York City Mayor Rudy Giuliani, Opening Remarks to the United Nations General Assembly, Special Session on Terrorism, October 1, 2001

6. Which of the following was the mastermind behind the September 11, 2001, terrorist attacks against the United States?
   A. Vladimir Putin
   B. Saddam Hussein
   C. Muammar Khadafy
   D. Osama bin Laden

7. The attitude toward terrorism and sponsors of terrorism displayed by Mayor Giuliani most directly contributed to which of the following?
   A. The policy of Containment
   B. The invasion of Iraq
   C. The diplomacy that ended the war in Bosnia
   D. An American strategic shift to the Far East

8. The legislative response of President George W. Bush and Congress to the 9/11 attacks was the passage of
   A. the USA Patriot Act.
   B. the No Child Left Behind Act.
   C. the Affordable Care Act.
   D. the GI Bill.

Short-Answer Question

The short-answer question below is similar to the ones you'll encounter on the AP U.S. History exam.

9. Answer Parts A, B, and C.
   A. Briefly explain ONE example of a response of the American government to the 9/11 attacks.
   B. Briefly explain a SECOND example of a response of the American government to the 9/11 attacks.
   C. Briefly explain ONE example of a way that President Barack Obama attempted to move the country in a new direction following his election in 2008.

› Answers and Explanations

1. B. All of the other three were given by administration officials as reasons for war. The president noted in several speeches that Saddam Hussein had tried to kill his father, but this was not used by the administration as a major reason for war.

2. C. Many fiscal conservatives supported the reduction of income taxes in the United States. This was not an issue that was important to the socially conservative members of the religious right.

3. D. President Barack Obama's most significant legislative achievement was the 2010 Affordable Care Act (ACA), which dramatically changed the American healthcare system.

4. C. Many Vietnam War veterans were deeply offended by Senator Kerry's statements when he returned home after the war. Many voters were never sure where Kerry actually stood on the issue of the Iraqi war. President George W. Bush portrayed himself as the "moral" candidate; questions on any ballot dealing with morality served to help him. In reality, Senator Kerry did quite well in the 2004 debates.

5. A. Several observers have noted the similarity between President George W. Bush's desire to spread democracy in the Middle East with Woodrow Wilson's Fourteen Points, which proposed the creation of a more democratic and freer Europe, and world, after World War I.

6. D. Osama bin Laden was the mastermind behind the September 11, 2001, terrorist attacks against the United States. Bin Laden was the founder of al-Qaeda, an Islamist terrorist organization. He believed that the United States stood in the way of the spread of his version of Islam throughout the Middle East.

7. B. The attitude toward terrorism and the sponsors of terrorism displayed by Mayor Giuliani most directly contributed to the invasion of Iraq. President George W. Bush and his advisors believed that after 9/11, the United States could no longer tolerate a regime like that of Iraqi dictator Saddam Hussein, which had invaded its neighbors, supported terrorists, and plotted the assassination of President George H. W. Bush and which they believed had weapons of mass destruction. After getting bipartisan support from Congress in October 2002, President Bush launched the invasion of Iraq on March 18, 2003.

8. A. The legislative response of President George W. Bush and Congress to the 9/11 attacks was the passage of the USA Patriot Act. This legislation gave the federal government broader powers to protect American security. Among the many provisions of the USA Patriot Act, the federal government was given more authority to monitor American communications, and it was made easier for law enforcement agencies to cooperate in fighting terrorism.

9. Parts A and B: The government of the United States quickly mobilized to defeat the al-Qaeda sponsors of the 9/11 attacks. President George W. Bush spoke of a "War on Terror" in a speech on September 20, 2001. In November, the United States launched an attack on the Taliban government of Afghanistan, which provided refuge and support for Osama bin Laden, the founder of al-Qaeda. The Taliban government was quickly overthrown, but the United States would become embroiled in a long and difficult struggle to pacify Afghanistan. In 2002, the Bush administration established a detention center for captured terrorism suspects at Guantanamo Bay Naval Base in Cuba. The detainees at Guantanamo were extensively interrogated for intelligence information. The CIA admitted waterboarding three prisoners, including Khalid Sheikh Mohammed, the mastermind of the 9/11 attacks. In October 2001, Congress passed the USA Patriot Act, which gave the government more powers to investigate and surveil suspected terrorists. President Bush created an Office of Homeland Security in October 2001. In November 2002, Congress created the Department of Homeland Security, which controls a number of agencies charged with protecting the United States from domestic threats. A new agency in the department was the Transportation Security Administration (TSA), which handles security at airports.

The Iraqi dictator Saddam Hussein expressed support for the 9/11 attacks. President Bush charged that Iraq, along with Iran and North Korea, was part of an "Axis of Evil" because of their support for terrorism and efforts to acquire nuclear weapons. The CIA and other Western intelligence agencies believed that Saddam Hussein was working to build up Iraq's supply of weapons of mass destruction. Saddam Hussein had used poison gas against his own people in the past. The Iraqi regime was also evading full compliance with United Nations Security Council Resolutions. Bush and his advisors decided that post-9/11 the United States could take no chances with Saddam Hussein. On March 20, 2003, the United States and its allies invaded Iraq. The Iraqi government was soon overthrown and Saddam Hussein captured, but the United States found itself fighting a long and controversial war against Iraqi and al-Qaeda insurgents. In 2007, Bush ordered a "surge" of 20,000 more troops into Iraq; in conjunction with effective anti-insurgency techniques and cooperation with local militias, this initiative dramatically lowered the level of violence in Iraq, and for a time crippled al-Qaeda cadres in the country. Following years of patient intelligence work, President Barack Obama was able to order a commando raid that killed Osama bin Laden in Abbottabad, Pakistan, on May 2, 2011.

Part C: President Barack Obama came into office in 2009 promising "hope and change" to a nation unsettled by the frustrating war in Iraq and a recent banking crisis. Although he increased American forces for a time in Afghanistan, President Obama attempted to reduce the American military footprint in the Middle East. He withdrew American forces from Iraq in 2011, though he had to return some troops to that country in 2014 following the capture of Mosul by fighters of the Islamic State of Iraq and Syria (ISIS). Obama preferred to kill terrorists through drone strikes rather than through conventional military operations. His support for the overthrow of the Libyan dictator Muammar Gaddafi had equivocal results, with Libya descending into civil war and becoming a haven for terrorists. The Obama administration exerted little influence over the disastrous civil war in Syria. President Obama focused most of his attention on domestic policy. In 2009, he signed a $800 billion stimulus bill, which he hoped would spur economic recovery. His most important legislative achievement was the 2010 Affordable Care Act (ACA), which was intended to provide reasonably priced healthcare to most Americans. This highly ambitious reworking of the American healthcare system was controversial and passed with no Republican votes. Following the election of a Republican majority in the House of Representatives in 2010, President Obama was unable to pass any more major bills through Congress. He used his "bully pulpit" to encourage liberal causes such as gun control and gay marriage.

CHAPTER 31

Tumultuous Years: The Trump and Biden Presidencies (2017–2022)

IN THIS CHAPTER

Summary: As president, Donald Trump promised to "make America great again." He reversed many of President Obama's policies. He ended the JCPOA Agreement with Iran and forged an anti-Iranian coalition with Israel and a number of Arab states. President Trump intensified the war against ISIL, resulting in the overrunning of its territories in Syria and Iraq. His administration cut regulations and a tax cut passed by Congress seemed to spur growth. The United States became energy independent for the first time since the 1950s. For the first two years of his presidency, Trump faced accusations that he had colluded with the Russians in the 2016 election. The Democrats recaptured control of the House of Representatives in the 2018 midterm elections. In 2019, the House Democrats voted to impeach President Trump, though the Republican Senate acquitted him. The USMCA Agreement replaced NAFTA in 2020. A trade agreement was signed with China. President Trump appointed over 230 judges to the federal courts, including three Supreme Court justices. The Trump administration negotiated an agreement to begin a process of ending the war in Afghanistan. The COVID-19 pandemic had devastating social and economic effects. Accusations of police brutality led to widespread riots in the summer of 2020. Former vice president Joe Biden defeated President Trump in the 2020 presidential election. President Biden contended with a rocky recovery from COVID-19 at home and crises in Afghanistan and Ukraine abroad.

Domestic Affairs

Donald J. Trump arrived at the White House with few friends in government or the mainstream media. Although he was a wealthy businessman and entrepreneur who had been a celebrity for three decades, Trump had run for office as an outsider, promising to shake up the establishment. His unexpected victory was a shock that many could not accept. The resistance was born of people in and out of government who refused to accept a man they regarded as an illegitimate chief executive.

The new president enjoyed no honeymoon in office. Democrats slowed the confirmation of nominees to the executive departments; at the same time, there were protests on the streets. An academic study showed that more than 90 percent of news stories in the mainstream media were hostile to the president and his administration.

President Trump did little to reconcile his opponents to his leadership. His style, born of years in the limelight, was self-congratulatory and often confrontational. He communicated directly with his followers on the social media platform Twitter, bypassing his own press office and the traditional news outlets. His flamboyant and vituperative way of expressing himself often caused consternation and outrage. These tweets allowed him instant communication with his millions of followers, but even some of his most loyal supporters wished that he would show more verbal restraint.

Democratic charges that his campaign had colluded with Russian attempts to influence the election followed President Trump into the White House. Trump, in turn, was convinced that his campaign had been spied on by the Obama administration. In May 2017, Trump dismissed FBI director James Comey because of his dissatisfaction with the way the investigation into Russian collusion was being managed. The outcry over this led the Justice Department to appoint former FBI director Robert Mueller as a special counsel to handle the Russia inquiry.

President Trump busied himself signing executive orders that repealed executive orders signed by President Obama. He worked to eliminate regulations that he believed hampered economic growth.

During his campaign, Trump had promised to build a wall across the U.S. southern border to keep out illegal immigrants. Although funding for Trump's promised wall did not immediately materialize, levels of illegal immigration fell dramatically in 2017. The new president inherited a Supreme Court vacancy. Neil Gorsuch, Trump's first appointment to the Supreme Court, was confirmed by the Senate in April.

During the election campaign, Trump pledged to repeal and replace the Affordable Care Act (also known as Obamacare). Though the Republican House passed a healthcare bill on a party-line vote, repealing large elements of the ACA, divisions among Republicans in the Senate prevented the passage of a new law. The president next turned to promoting tax cuts. In December, Congress passed the Tax Cuts and Jobs Act of 2017. This far-reaching legislation reduced the corporate tax rate to 21 percent, lowered tax rates for individuals, and cut estate taxes. These tax reductions along with Trump's deregulatory efforts increased business confidence and spurred economic activity. In President Trump's first year in office the stock market boomed. By the middle of 2018, unemployment had fallen below 4 percent. The unemployment rates for African Americans, Hispanics, and women reached record lows. In 2019 American oil and gas production made the United States energy independent for the first time since 1957.

A major factor in Donald Trump's ability to unite Republicans behind him in the 2016 election was his promise to appoint conservative jurists to the courts. His nomination of Neil Gorsuch to the Supreme Court early in his presidency was a down payment on that promise. President Trump sent a steady stream of nominations to fill judicial vacancies to Capitol Hill. Senate Republicans confirmed more than 230 circuit and district court judges by early 2021. Politically this was very important, but Trump's supporters regarded the Supreme Court as the major prize. In June 2018, Supreme Court Justice Anthony Kennedy announced his retirement. Although generally conservative in his views, Kennedy was seen as a "swing" vote on the high court. The prospect of replacing him with a more conservative justice increased the political stakes when Trump nominated Brett Kavanaugh, who as a federal judge had compiled an impressive record as a constitutional "originalist." Judge Kavanaugh's confirmation hearings were contentious, with most Senate Democrats opposed to his nomination. After the public hearings had concluded, Democrats on the Senate Judiciary Committee revealed that Professor Christine Blasey Ford had come forward months earlier with an accusation that Kavanaugh had sexually assaulted her when they were in high school. Judge Kavanaugh firmly denied that he had done this and noted that Professor Ford could produce no witnesses to corroborate her story. Ford's allegations led to political uproar, a highly emotional Senate hearing, and an FBI investigation into the charges. In the end, Judge Kavanaugh was confirmed by a Senate vote of 50-48.

The 2018 elections ensured governmental gridlock. The Democrats recaptured control of the House of Representatives by gaining 41 seats in that chamber. The Republicans increased their majority in the Senate by 2 seats. President Trump's relations with the newly emboldened congressional Democrats quickly deteriorated into a budgetary confrontation over funding a wall on the Mexican border. This led to a government shutdown in December 2018 that lasted until January 2019, a total of 35 days. The president did not get his funding. He would work to divert funds from other sources such as the military budget to construct portions of his wall.

Debate over President Trump's purported collusion with the Russians remained a contentious issue. While many Democrats claimed that there had been ties between Trump and the Russians, Republican Representative Devin Nunes, then chair of the House Intelligence Committee, released a report charging that Crossfire Hurricane, the FBI investigation of this that began in 2016, relied on questionable information from Christopher Steele, a British operative working for the Clinton campaign. In March 2019, Robert Mueller submitted his report on Russian interference in the 2016 election. The report concluded that there was insufficient evidence that the Trump campaign cooperated with the Russians. Mueller and his team declined to exonerate the president from accusations that he had attempted to obstruct their investigation. Based on the evidence in the report, Attorney General William Barr decided that there were no grounds to charge the president with obstruction of justice. In July, Mueller testified in public congressional hearings. When no bombshells appeared, the long drama over alleged connections between the Trump campaign and Russia appeared to be over. Attorney General Barr ensured that the matter would not be quickly forgotten when he announced that he was appointing a federal prosecutor named John Durham to investigate the origins of the U.S. government's surveillance of the Trump campaign in 2016. In December, more questions were raised about this surveillance when Michael Horowitz, the Department of Justice Inspector General, issued a report that criticized the Justice Department and the FBI for submitting false information to justify their investigation to the Foreign Intelligence Surveillance Act (FISA) court. Documents surrendered during the discovery process in a case involving General Michael Flynn, President Trump's former National Security Advisor, added to doubts about the justification of the FBI investigation of the Trump campaign.

A new crisis between President Trump and congressional Democrats erupted in September, when the public learned of a whistleblower complaint about the contents of a phone call between the president and Ukrainian President Volodymyr Zelensky. The whistleblower alleged that President Trump conditioned American military aid to the Ukraine on Zelensky agreeing to launch an investigation into former Vice President Joe Biden and his son Hunter Biden, who during his father's tenure in office had taken a lucrative position on the board of an Ukrainian oil company that had been investigated for corruption. This looked like the president using his influence with a foreign government to seek dirt on a potential political rival. Trump denied any quid pro quo. He denounced this accusation as a political hit job. House Speaker Nancy Pelosi announced that the charges against the president were sufficiently grave to warrant an impeachment inquiry by several House committees. These committees began holding closed door hearings with various witnesses. Congressional Republicans complained about the secrecy of these proceedings and declared that the president was being denied due process. In October, on a party-line vote, the House adopted guidelines for the ongoing impeachment inquiry.

Foreign Policy

President Trump distinguished his approach to foreign affairs from that of his predecessors by declaring that he was pursuing a nationalist "America First" policy. An early example of this was the announcement that the United States would no longer observe the 2015 Paris Agreement on Climate Change, since the president believed that this agreement was economically unfair to the United States.

Hoping to bolster American credibility overseas, Trump demonstrated that he would act decisively when a "red line" was crossed, by ordering a missile strike against a Syrian air base after the Syrians used chemical weapons against civilians. He acted aggressively against ISIL, increasing the tempo of the war and giving his commanders more leeway in targeting airstrikes against the enemy. By late 2017, ISIL had lost most of its territory in Syria and Iraq. The last ISIL pockets of territory were mopped up in 2019, and in October of that year American special forces killed Abu Bakr al-Baghdadi, the head of the ISIL caliphate. Initially the new administration continued the war against the Taliban in Afghanistan. Hoping for an end to a seemingly endless conflict, President Trump authorized secret negotiations with the Taliban. These negotiations culminated in December 2019, leading to a peace agreement in February 2020 that called for a withdrawal of American and NATO troops in return for talks between the Taliban and the Afghan government, and a ban on Taliban support for al-Qaeda activity in Afghanistan.

President Trump reversed the Obama administration's policy of seeking an agreement with Iran on nuclear weapons. Trump and his advisors did not trust the leaders of Iran, and believed that their support of the Syrian regime, Houthi rebels in Yemen, and terrorist organizations like Hezbollah and Hamas demonstrated that they were seeking an Iranian strategic hegemony in the Middle East. In May 2018, President Trump withdrew the United States from the Joint Comprehensive Plan of Action (JCPOA) on the Iranian nuclear program that President Obama had negotiated with Iran. The Trump administration also provided support to the government of Saudi Arabia, which waged a war in Yemen against Houthi militias backed by Iran. In 2019, President Trump resisted calls for military retaliation after a series of provocative actions by the Iranian regime. Instead, he increased sanctions against the Iranians. When Turkey notified the United States that it was going to invade an area along the Turkish-Syrian border controlled by Kurdish forces, Trump pulled the few American troops in the area out of the way. Critics decried this as a betrayal of Kurdish allies who had helped the United States defeat ISIL. Defenders of the president saw this as another example of his unwillingness to defy a putative NATO ally and risk unnecessary military commitments overseas. In January 2020, after Iranian-backed Iraqi militias assaulted the American embassy in Baghdad, President Trump authorized a drone strike in that city, a precise attack that killed Qasem Soleimani, a major general in the Iranian Islamic Revolutionary Guards Corps (IRGC). As the head of the elite Iranian Quds Force, Soleimani had for years commanded Iranian special operations throughout the Middle East.

President Trump signaled his strong support for Israel in December 2017 by defying opposition from the Palestinians and recognizing Jerusalem as the Israeli capital. A new U.S. Embassy at Jerusalem officially opened in the spring of 2018. In March 2019, Trump recognized Israeli sovereignty over the strategic Golan Heights, taken from Syria in the Six-Day War of 1967. A shared antipathy to Iran and its actions in Syria, Yemen, and elsewhere drew Israel closer to some of its Arab neighbors. Patient diplomacy by the Trump administration led to an official recognition of this new reality. In September 2020, the Abraham Accords normalized relations between Israel and two Arab states, the United Arab Emirates and Bahrain. Later in the year, two more Arab countries, Sudan and Morocco, normalized ties with Israel. President Trump hailed these treaties as a major step toward peace in the Middle East.

Early in the administration, tensions rose with North Korea because of the North Korean regime's tests of intercontinental ballistic missiles and threats to launch nuclear attacks on the United States. President Trump engaged in a war of words with the North Korean dictator Kim Jong-un. Harsh public rhetoric led to quiet diplomacy. After preliminary talks between American and North Korean officials, President Trump and Kim Jung-un held a summit meeting in Singapore in June 2018. Another inconclusive face-to-face meeting between the two leaders followed in 2019. The North Koreans continued to occasionally test-fire missiles, but the threat of war receded.

At the same time tensions with China increased. Beginning in the Obama administration, the Chinese asserted expansive territorial claims in the South China Sea by building artificial islands to establish control over these waters. The Chinese also increased their forces across from Taiwan and pressed ahead with a major arms buildup. Concern also grew over Chinese economic initiatives around the world. Some commentators began talking about the possibility of a new cold war between the United States and China that could flare into an armed conflict. To prepare for this eventuality, the Trump administration increased defense spending. In December 2019, President Trump established the U.S. Space Force as a separate branch of the American military.

Strategic concerns about China merged into complaints about the large trade deficit with that nation. Trade was an issue that bound President Trump to his working-class voter base. Like the president, they believed that the United States was being treated unfairly by its trading partners. President Trump vowed to end or renegotiate American trade pacts with other nations. Close to home, one target of his ire was the North American Free Trade Agreement (NAFTA) with Mexico and Canada. The Trump administration worked out new trade arrangements with these countries that resulted in the United States-Mexico-Canada Agreement (USMCA). This replacement for NAFTA was ratified and went into effect in 2020. At the same time, President Trump also took aim at the chronic American trade imbalance with China. He criticized Chinese trade practices and China's lack of respect for American intellectual property rights. The Trump administration began imposing tariffs on Chinese goods, and the Chinese responded in kind. Trade talks continued into 2019. In December, an agreement was reached that was signed in January 2020. The "Phase One" trade deal cut American tariffs on Chinese goods in exchange for a Chinese promise to purchase more American products and to address property rights issues.

2020

As 2020 opened, the economy was strong, but the political class was obsessed with the impending impeachment of President Trump. On December 18, 2019, the House of Representatives voted to impeach the president for abuse of power and obstruction of Congress over his conversation about the Bidens with the Ukrainian president. All the Republicans and three Democrats voted against impeachment. House Speaker Nancy Pelosi delayed submitting the articles of impeachment until January 16. The Republican-controlled Senate held a trial limited to arguments by the prosecutors from the House and President Trump's defense lawyers. On February 5, the president was acquitted on both counts. Aside from Republican Senator Mitt Romney, who voted against Trump on the abuse of power charge, the votes were predictably partisan and came nowhere near the two-thirds majority needed to convict.

While Congress and the president were busy with the battle over impeachment, a dangerous virus was metastasizing in Wuhan, China. By January 2020 health officials in the United States began to grow increasingly concerned that the virus, called COVID-19, would reach the United States. On January 29 President Trump established a White House Coronavirus Task Force and on January 31 imposed controversial restrictions on travel to and from China. He later extended these bans to other countries. Despite this, the virus spread in the United States. It was especially threatening to older adults or people with weakened immune systems. In March, in an effort to avoid overwhelming hospitals with COVID-19 cases, the president urged people to avoid unnecessary travel and large gatherings. State governors began closing schools and businesses. Churches, sports venues, restaurants, specialty shops, and other public places were shut down or severely limited in the number of people allowed on their premises. Americans grew used to wearing masks and social distancing. As a result of the first shutdowns, around 20 million people lost their jobs, leading to an unemployment rate near 15 percent. This was the worst job loss since the Great Depression. Many small businesses were forced to close permanently. The government spent over 2.5 trillion dollars in COVID-19 relief. The economy began to recover later in the year. Some shutdowns began to be lifted in the summer, but a surge of infections in the fall led to some tightening of restrictions. The extent of COVID-19 shutdowns varied, with states like New York, California, Illinois, and Michigan more heavily regulated than states like Florida and South Dakota. By the end of 2020, the Centers for Disease Control and Prevention (CDC) reported over 300,000 deaths in the United States involving COVID-19. In May, President Trump launched Operation Warp Speed, a partnership of the government and private industry to develop medicines to combat COVID-19. Two COVID-19 vaccines were authorized by December, and the first vaccinations took place on the fourteenth of that month.

As the United States struggled with the COVID-19 pandemic, a series of killings involving the police heightened racial and social tensions. In March, Breonna Taylor was killed by Louisville, Kentucky, police in an exchange of gunfire between her boyfriend and officers executing a search warrant in the middle of the night. In late May, video footage showed George Floyd being choked to death by a Minneapolis, Minnesota, police officer. The deaths of Taylor, Floyd, and others set off a wave of unrest across the United States during the summer months, and in some places like Portland, Oregon, into the fall. At least 19 people were killed in the violence. Property damage was enormous, around $200 million in Minneapolis alone. Groups like Black Lives Matter (BLM) and Antifa were often on the cutting edge of protests. Many activists called for defunding the police and reallocating funding to other social services. In response, many police assumed a lower profile, contributing to a spike in crime in many areas. In Chicago, murders neared 800 by the end of the year.

On September 18, 2020, Justice Ruth Bader Ginsburg died. Despite protests from Democrats that it was too close to an election, President Trump and Senate Republicans pressed forward with naming a replacement. The president nominated Judge Amy Coney Barrett. On October 26, she was confirmed on a largely party-line vote, with pro-choice Republican Susan Collins joining with Democrats in voting against her. Barrett was President Trump's third successful Supreme Court nomination.

2020 was also an election year. Donald Trump faced no challenges in securing the Republican presidential nomination. He kept Vice President Mike Pence as his running mate. Former Vice President Joe Biden emerged from a crowded field of Democratic presidential candidates thanks to the support of party leaders who saw him as the most electable. He chose Senator Kamala Harris as his candidate for vice president. Harris was the first woman of Jamaican and Indian heritage to be nominated for this high office. The COVID-19 pandemic upended traditional campaigning. At 77 years old, Biden was particularly vulnerable to the virus. He did a variation of an old-fashioned front porch campaign, addressing people from his home and making occasional appearances elsewhere. In contrast, Trump gave speeches to large crowds of enthusiastic supporters. At one point he was diagnosed with the virus but bounced back quickly. Biden blamed the hardships of the pandemic on Trump. The president derided Biden as over the hill and a corrupt politician.

The pandemic had a powerful and controversial effect on the 2020 election. Concerns that traditional voting might be unsafe led to a heavy reliance on mail-in voting, which raised new challenges in counting and verifying ballots. The election proved to be close in crucial battleground states. President Trump gained more votes than he won in 2016. He made deeper inroads into the African American and Hispanic vote than any previous Republican presidential candidate. Down-ticket, the Republicans did well, gaining several House seats and adding seats in state legislatures. It seemed at first as if the Republicans had held on to control of the Senate, though a run-off election in Georgia in January later shifted power to the Democrats. But early Trump leads evaporated, and after some delays in counting Joe Biden emerged as the winner. Biden received 306 electoral votes to Trump's 232. President Trump and millions of his supporters became convinced that he had lost because of fraud. Seemingly mysterious late-night vote dumps, suspicious behavior by some Democratic election workers, and very impressive Biden vote totals in Democratic strongholds in key battleground states fed this unverified conviction. Democrats responded to this by noting that Trump had unusually high unfavorable ratings with certain demographics and that they had done a better job in turning out their voters. The courts proved unwilling to intervene in the election, turning down numerous Trump legal challenges, mostly on procedural grounds. As late as the January 6, 2021, certification of the electoral vote, President Trump showed no signs of acknowledging defeat. That day, he addressed a gathering of tens of thousands of his adherents in Washington, D.C., telling them that he would never concede. Following this, hundreds of people stormed the Capitol, disrupting the certification process. The building was later cleared and secured. President Trump urged his followers to go home peacefully, but many blamed him for the attack on the Capitol. Despite some Republican objections, Congress certified Joe Biden's election early on January 7. Trump was impeached a second time by Democrats outraged by the January 6 riot, but he was acquitted in the Senate after he had left office.

Biden: Domestic Affairs

The nation was deeply divided politically when Joe Biden was inaugurated on January 20, 2021. The Democrats controlled both houses of Congress for the first time since 2011, but their majority in the House of Representatives had narrowed and the Senate was split 50–50, giving Vice President Kamala Harris the deciding vote in the event of a tie. President Biden and congressional Democrats nevertheless attempted to enact an ambitious legislative agenda that would appeal to the party's dominant progressive base. Biden and the House and Senate leadership failed to achieve their goal of passing the massive Build Back Better Act, which addressed a variety of Democrat priorities ranging from climate change to universal preschool for three- and four-year-old children. The bill foundered on Republican objections and the public dissent of Democrat Senators Joe Manchin of West Virginia and Kyrsten Sinema of Arizona, who refused to change filibuster rules in the Senate and worried about the expense of the legislation.

Biden did have some legislative successes. In March, he signed a $1.9 trillion stimulus bill to address the lingering economic effects of the COVID-19 pandemic. This was passed over unanimous Republican opposition. In November, he signed a bipartisan $1.2 trillion infrastructure bill to improve the nation's transportation and electric power systems. He also signed legislation making Juneteenth a national holiday.

Upon entering office President Biden quickly issued 17 executive orders, an unprecedented number. Some of the most significant of these were aimed at reversing President Trump's energy policies. Biden rejoined the Paris Climate Agreement, and he stopped construction of the Keystone XL pipeline, which would have brought large amounts of oil into the United States from Canada. In addition to this, he cut back on oil and gas leases on federal land. Biden's energy policies grew controversial as gasoline prices rose rapidly.

Biden also relaxed Trump's immigration policies at the southern border, halting construction of the wall. This led to a massive surge in illegal immigration as migrants hoped to take advantage of the change in presidents. Televised scenes of overwhelmed Border Patrol officers and squalid encampments near the border spurred Republican criticism of the Biden administration's policies. By August 2022, over 3.2 million migrants had entered the United States.

COVID-19 proved a frustrating problem during President Biden's initial year in office. One of his first acts was an executive order mandating the use of masks in all federal buildings and lands. A short time later he required the use of face masks on public transportation. Biden had inherited two vaccines and began encouraging their production and distribution. Though many Americans had been vaccinated by the spring of 2021, the vaccination rate was declining when a new Delta variant of the disease swept through the country. Though the vaccines lowered the risk of death from Delta, they did not prevent infection. Booster shots were recommended. None of this was persuasive to many people who worried about side-effects from the vaccines or who believed that they had already developed a natural immunity to COVID-19. On September 9, President Biden issued an executive order calling for all businesses with 100 or more employees to demand that their employees be vaccinated or submit to weekly testing. This became a contentious political issue as many workers refused to get the shots and lost their jobs. In December, the highly infectious but less virulent Omicron variant spread rapidly through the population. Omicron raised the possibility of herd immunity finally taking hold and reducing the threat from COVID-19. This, in conjunction with the increasing political unpopularity of mask mandates, led to a loosening of COVID-19 regulations in early 2022.

In 2021 the economy continued to show signs of recovery from the previous year's COVID-19 shut-downs. Unemployment fell as people returned to jobs that they had lost in 2020. Wages increased as employers scrambled to find workers. Supply chain problems persisted, and Americans grew used to having difficulties finding certain products at retailers. All this, along with the enormous spending of the government and the higher cost of energy resulting from President Biden's cutbacks on oil production, contributed to an inflation rate of over 7 percent, the worst in 40 years. The economy slowed, and according to the traditional definition of two successive quarters of decline in the gross domestic product (GDP), the United States entered a recession in the summer of 2022. The Biden administration argued that because of economic indicators like a strong labor market, the country was not in a recession.

Supreme Court Justice Stephen Breyer announced his retirement in January 2022. President Biden nominated Judge Ketanji Brown Jackson to be the first African American woman on the Supreme Court. Jackson's nomination was confirmed by the Senate in April. The Supreme Court made history in June by overturning the 1973 *Roe v. Wade* decision in *Dobbs v. Jackson Women's Health Organization*, which sent the regulation of abortion back to the states. President Biden condemned this ruling. He had a major legislative success with the passage of the Inflation Reduction Act on a party-line vote. This authorized large expenditures on addressing energy and climate change, Affordable Care Act subsidies, and an expansion of the Internal Revenue Service.

In the midterm elections of 2022, the Republicans hoped to benefit from voter dissatisfaction with the economy, while the Democrats argued that abortion rights were in danger and denounced what they called GOP extremism. The result was something of a draw, with the Republicans gaining a narrow majority in the House of Representatives, while the Democrats retained control of the Senate.

Biden: Foreign Policy

As with domestic affairs, President Biden energetically distanced himself from the policies of his predecessor. His administration expressed interest in negotiating with Iran for a revival in some form of the JCPOA agreement regarding the Iranian nuclear program. Biden withdrew support for Saudi Arabia's war against the Iranian-backed Houthis in Yemen. One area where Biden maintained continuity with the Trump administration was in its concern about the threat posed by China. In September 2021, the United States joined in AUKUS, a security arrangement with Australia and the United Kingdom that will provide Australia with nuclear-powered submarines and deepen ties between the three signatories. This agreement was seen as a response to the growing military assertiveness of the Chinese.

President Biden long wanted to withdraw American troops from Afghanistan. President Trump had reached an agreement with the Taliban to pull American forces out of the country conditioned on their good behavior in suppressing terrorism and refraining from attacking Americans. Biden pressed ahead with the troop withdrawal from Afghanistan despite the qualms of some of his military advisors. The bulk of American forces were gone by July 2021. The rapid departure of the American troops demoralized the Afghan government's army. A series of military defeats escalated into a debacle, and on August 15 the Afghan government fell apart. The Taliban took control of the country and proudly displayed the American weapons that they had captured from the Afghan army. President Biden sent 6,000 Marines and airborne troops to the Kabul airport to help evacuate

Americans and Afghans who had assisted the United States during the war. Large crowds of desperate people surrounded the airport. A suicide bomber reached the airport perimeter and killed 13 American service members and 169 Afghans. The American rescue operation ended on August 30. Some Americans, green card holders, and Afghan allies had to be left behind. The chaotic withdrawal from Afghanistan was widely seen as a heavy blow to American international prestige.

President Biden hoped for good relations with Russia. He removed sanctions imposed by President Trump on the Nord Stream 2 oil pipeline that would bring Russian natural gas to Germany. With the reduction of American oil production, the United States began importing large amounts of Russian oil. President Biden and the Russian President Vladimir Putin agreed to talks on extending the 2010 START Treaty on nuclear weapons and held a brief summit in June 2021. In November, President Putin began expressing concerns that the neighboring country of Ukraine might join NATO. He asked for guarantees that NATO would not expand into Ukraine. The United States, its allies, and the Ukrainians declined to do this. The Ukrainians had lost the Crimea and the Donbass region to Russia in 2014 and feared further territorial encroachments. As tensions rose, the Biden administration warned of a possible Russian attack. Diplomatic efforts to prevent war failed, and on February 24, 2022, Putin launched a devastating assault on Ukraine, attacking from multiple directions. The Ukrainians resisted fiercely and casualties on both sides were heavy. The United States and its European allies imposed sanctions on Russia, including placing limits on Russian oil purchases, which helped push up gas prices. The Biden administration and NATO allies also provided Ukraine with billions of dollars of military assistance.

President Biden's political standing was improved by the Democrat showing in the midterm elections. He kept open the possibility that he would run for reelection in 2024. His old rival was also thinking of returning to presidential politics. Donald Trump announced on November 15 that he would seek the Republican nomination for president in 2024.

Chapter Review

To achieve the perfect 5, you should be able to explain the following:

- President Trump found himself embroiled in contentious political wrangling with Democrats who questioned the legitimacy of his presidency.
- In foreign affairs, President Trump pursued a nationalistic approach that he believed put American interests first.
- President Trump reversed many policies of President Obama, including the JCPOA Agreement with Iran.
- President Trump worked to diplomatically isolate Iran, successfully encouraging better relations between Israel and several Arab states.
- The Trump administration cut many regulations and worked with Congress to cut taxes.
- The economy prospered until the COVID-19 pandemic.
- President Trump negotiated what he believed were better and fairer trade deals, replacing NAFTA with the USMCA Agreement and signing a new trade deal with China.
- President Trump survived a Democratic attempt to impeach him for abuse of power.
- President Trump profoundly affected the American judiciary, appointing over 230 federal judges, including three Supreme Court Justices.
- The Trump administration began a diplomatic process to end American involvement in the war in Afghanistan.

- The COVID-19 pandemic contributed to the deaths of over 300,000 Americans and had profound social, economic, and political effects.
- The death of George Floyd in police custody led to unrest in many cities during the summer of 2020.
- Former Vice President Joe Biden defeated President Trump in the 2020 election.
- President Trump blamed his loss on electoral fraud.
- Inflation surged in 2021.
- President Biden withdrew all American forces from Afghanistan.
- Russia invaded Ukraine in February 2022, precipitating an international crisis.
- The Supreme Court overturned *Roe v. Wade* in *Dobbs v. Jackson Women's Health Organization*.

Time Line

2017: Neil Gorsuch appointed to the Supreme Court
      Hurricanes cause devastation to the Gulf Coast and Puerto Rico
2018: President Trump withdraws from the JCPOA nuclear deal with Iran
      The United States, Mexico, and Canada lay the foundation for the USMCA trade
          agreement to replace NAFTA
      Hurricanes cause severe damage in the Carolinas and the Florida Panhandle
      The Democrats recapture control of the House of Representatives
2019: Robert Mueller releases a report that finds no conclusive evidence that the 2016
          Trump campaign colluded with the Russians
      House Democrats launch an impeachment inquiry over President Trump's
          dealings with the Ukraine
2020: President Trump is acquitted by a Senate impeachment trial
      The COVID-19 pandemic spreads to the United States
      The death of George Floyd leads to antipolice riots
      Amy Coney Barrett appointed to the Supreme Court
      Joe Biden wins the 2020 presidential election
2021: A mob of Trump supporters storms the Capitol building to protest the certification
          of Joe Biden's electoral victory
2021: President Biden withdraws American forces from Afghanistan
2022: President Putin of Russia orders an invasion of Ukraine
      The Supreme Court sends abortion regulation back to the states in *Dobbs v. Jackson Women's Health Organization*

› Review Questions

Fact Check

Check your knowledge of the historical period covered in this chapter.

1. The Obama administration foreign policy initiative that Donald Trump vowed to overturn was which of the following?
   A. The Affordable Care Act
   B. Wall construction on the Mexican border
   C. The Joint Comprehensive Plan of Action (JCPOA) with Iran
   D. The USA Patriot Act

2. Donald Trump and his presidential campaign were accused of colluding with which of the following countries?
   A. Russia
   B. China
   C. France
   D. North Korea

3. President Joe Biden provided military and diplomatic support to which of these countries?
   A. Iraq
   B. Ukraine
   C. Afghanistan
   D. Russia

4. President Trump's populism and criticisms of the political status quo made him most like which of the following presidents?
   A. George Washington
   B. Abraham Lincoln
   C. Thomas Jefferson
   D. Andrew Jackson

5. The COVID-19 pandemic most closely resembles which of the following?
   A. The Great Depression
   B. The Spanish Flu of 1918
   C. The Red Scare
   D. The First Great Awakening

Multiple-Choice Questions

Here are multiple-choice questions like the ones on the AP U.S. History exam.

Questions 6–8 refer to the quotation below.

"In my inaugural address to the American People, I pledged to strengthen America's oldest friendships, and to build new partnerships in pursuit of peace. I also promised that America will not seek to impose our way of life on others, but to outstretch our hands in the spirit of cooperation and trust.

Our goal is a coalition of nations who share the aim of stamping out extremism and providing our children a hopeful future that does honor to God.

Our vision is one of peace, security, and prosperity—in this region, and in the world.

And so this historic and unprecedented gathering of leaders—unique in the history of nations—is a symbol to the world of our shared resolve and our mutual respect. To the leaders and citizens of every country assembled here today, I want you to know that the United States is eager to form closer bonds of friendship, security, culture, and commerce."

—President Donald Trump, Speech to the Arab Islamic American Summit in Saudi Arabia, May 21, 2017

6. In this speech President Donald Trump was attempting to gain the support of Arab governments against which of the following?
   A. Chinese economic expansion
   B. The growing power of Israel
   C. The Iraqi dictator Saddam Hussein
   D. Islamic terrorism

7. The Trump administration would take military action against terrorists in which of the following places?
   A. Syria
   B. Armenia
   C. Cuba
   D. Kuwait

8. The Trump administration's outreach to Arab governments eventually contributed to which of the following?
   A. NATO expansion
   B. The USMCA Agreement
   C. The Abraham Accords
   D. Peace with China

Short-Answer Question

The short-answer question below is similar to the ones you'll encounter on the AP U.S. History exam.

9. Answer Parts A, B, and C.
   A. Briefly explain ONE example of a political promise Donald Trump made to his supporters.
   B. Briefly explain a SECOND example of a political promise Donald Trump made to his supporters.
   C. Briefly explain ONE example of a political promise Donald Trump was unable to fulfill for his supporters.

› Answers and Explanations

1. **C.** President Trump ended President Obama's JCPOA agreement with Iran because he did not believe that it did enough to prevent the Iranians from getting an atomic bomb.

2. **A.** Democrats accused Donald Trump and his campaign of colluding with the Russians. The FBI Crossfire Hurricane and Mueller investigations carried this well into Trump's presidency, never proving such collusion existed.

3. **B.** President Biden provided military and diplomatic support to Ukraine after it was invaded by Russia.

4. **D.** President Trump's populism and criticism of the political status quo made him most like Andrew Jackson, who also saw himself as a representative of the people struggling against powerful establishment institutions like the Bank of the United States.

5. **B.** The COVID-19 pandemic most closely resembles the Spanish Flu of 1918, which killed over 600,000 people in the United States and around 50 million worldwide.

6. **D.** President Trump was attempting to rally the support of Arab governments against Islamic terrorism. In the speech he pointed out that these terrorists threatened Arab governments as well as the United States. He also identified non-Arab Iran as a state sponsor of terrorism.

7. **A.** The Trump administration would take vigorous military action against ISIL in Syria, destroying the Islamic State and killing its leader Abu Bakr al-Baghdadi.

8. **C.** The Trump administration's outreach to Arab governments eventually contributed to the Abraham Accords. In 2020, four Arab governments—the United Arab Emirates, Bahrain, Sudan, and Morocco—normalized relations with Israel. This reflected a growing recognition of common interests between the United States, Israel, and many Arab states as they opposed the growth of Iranian power in the Middle East.

9. **Parts A and B**: Donald Trump promised his supporters a number of things, including building a wall along the border with Mexico to curtail illegal immigration, cutting taxes, repealing the Affordable Care Act or Obamacare, pulling out of the JCPOA with Iran, revising NAFTA, moving the U.S. embassy in Israel to Jerusalem, and ending wars overseas. He did cut taxes, end the JCPOA, replace NAFTA with the USMCA trade deal, recognize Jerusalem as the capital of Israel, and in 2020 was on the way to ending the war in Afghanistan.

   Part C: President Trump was unable to build a wall all along the Mexican border, though he was able to refurbish about 420 miles of wall and build around 30 miles of new wall. He was unable to completely repeal the Affordable Care Act. He did end the individual mandate that required people not eligible for Medicare or Medicaid and who did not have insurance through their employer to pay a fine if they did not purchase health coverage through the Affordable Care Act exchanges.

STEP 5

Build Your
Test-Taking Confidence

AP U.S. History Practice Exam 1
AP U.S. History Practice Exam 2

PRACTICE EXAM 1

Answer Sheet for Multiple-Choice Questions

1 (A) (B) (C) (D)	16 (A) (B) (C) (D)	31 (A) (B) (C) (D)	46 (A) (B) (C) (D)
2 (A) (B) (C) (D)	17 (A) (B) (C) (D)	32 (A) (B) (C) (D)	47 (A) (B) (C) (D)
3 (A) (B) (C) (D)	18 (A) (B) (C) (D)	33 (A) (B) (C) (D)	48 (A) (B) (C) (D)
4 (A) (B) (C) (D)	19 (A) (B) (C) (D)	34 (A) (B) (C) (D)	49 (A) (B) (C) (D)
5 (A) (B) (C) (D)	20 (A) (B) (C) (D)	35 (A) (B) (C) (D)	50 (A) (B) (C) (D)
6 (A) (B) (C) (D)	21 (A) (B) (C) (D)	36 (A) (B) (C) (D)	51 (A) (B) (C) (D)
7 (A) (B) (C) (D)	22 (A) (B) (C) (D)	37 (A) (B) (C) (D)	52 (A) (B) (C) (D)
8 (A) (B) (C) (D)	23 (A) (B) (C) (D)	38 (A) (B) (C) (D)	53 (A) (B) (C) (D)
9 (A) (B) (C) (D)	24 (A) (B) (C) (D)	39 (A) (B) (C) (D)	54 (A) (B) (C) (D)
10 (A) (B) (C) (D)	25 (A) (B) (C) (D)	40 (A) (B) (C) (D)	55 (A) (B) (C) (D)
11 (A) (B) (C) (D)	26 (A) (B) (C) (D)	41 (A) (B) (C) (D)	
12 (A) (B) (C) (D)	27 (A) (B) (C) (D)	42 (A) (B) (C) (D)	
13 (A) (B) (C) (D)	28 (A) (B) (C) (D)	43 (A) (B) (C) (D)	
14 (A) (B) (C) (D)	29 (A) (B) (C) (D)	44 (A) (B) (C) (D)	
15 (A) (B) (C) (D)	30 (A) (B) (C) (D)	45 (A) (B) (C) (D)	

AP U.S. HISTORY
PRACTICE EXAM 1

Section I

Time: 95 minutes

Part A (Multiple Choice)

Part A recommended time: 55 minutes

Directions: Each of the following questions refers to a historical source. These questions will test your knowledge about the historical source and require you to make use of your historical analytical skills and your familiarity with historical themes. For each question select the *best* response and fill in the corresponding oval on your answer sheet.

Questions 1–4 refer to the following quotation.

At a meeting of working girls held at Hull House during a strike in a large shoe factory, the discussions made it clear that the strikers who had been most easily frightened, and therefore the first to capitulate, were naturally those girls who were paying board and were afraid of being put out if they fell too far behind. After a recital of a case of peculiar hardship one of them exclaimed: "Wouldn't it be fine if we had a boarding club of our own, and then we could stand behind each other in a time like this?" After that events moved quickly. We … discussed all the difficulties and fascinations of such an undertaking, and on the first of May, 1891, two comfortable apartments near Hull House were rented and furnished. The Settlement was responsible for the furniture and paid the first month's rent, but beyond that the members managed the club themselves. … At the end of the third year the club occupied all of the six apartments which the original building contained, and numbered fifty members.

—Jane Addams, *Twenty Years at Hull House*, 1912

1. Which of the following *best* reflects the perspective of Jane Addams in the passage above?
   A. Poor people need the leadership of reformers like herself.
   B. Poor people need support in helping themselves.
   C. Poor people don't need outside help.
   D. Poor people don't deserve help.

2. Settlement houses like Hull House expressed a desire of reformers to do which of the following?
   A. Convert immigrants to Christianity
   B. Prevent political radicalism
   C. Provide cheap labor for industry
   D. Improve conditions in urban neighborhoods

3. A settlement house worker was most likely to be motivated by which of the following?
   A. The Social Gospel
   B. Social Darwinism
   C. Communism
   D. The support of an urban political machine

4. The perspective of the passage above would most directly support which of the following political goals?
   A. Women's suffrage
   B. Trust-busting
   C. Greater rights for unions
   D. Weakening political machines

Questions 5–8 refer to the following image.

Advertisement, Charleston, South Carolina, 1780s

5. Which of the following *best* reflects the perspective of the above image?
   A. Slaves represent a public health threat.
   B. The importation of slaves is a legitimate enterprise.
   C. The importation of slaves needs to be halted.
   D. Smallpox is a major danger to Charleston.

6. During the 1780s, which of the following was the most widespread crop cultivated by slaves in North America?
   A. Wheat
   B. Sugar
   C. Tobacco
   D. Cotton

7. Following the American Revolution, many Founding Fathers believed which of the following?
   A. Slavery would gradually disappear in the United States.
   B. The freeing of slaves should be outlawed.
   C. Slavery would be the foundation of the American economy.
   D. Freed slaves deserved government reparations for their suffering.

8. Which of the following was a reference to slavery in the Constitution?
   A. The banning of slavery in the Northwest Territory.
   B. Slavery was outlawed above the Mason-Dixon Line.
   C. Slavery could not be outlawed.
   D. No federal law could ban the importation of slaves for 20 years.

Questions 9–12 refer to the following quotation.

Those who came before us made certain that this country rode the first waves of the industrial revolutions, the first waves of modern invention, and the first wave of nuclear power, and this generation does not intend to flounder in the backwash of the coming age of space. We mean to be a part of it—we mean to lead it. For the eyes of the world now look into space, to the moon, and the planets beyond, and we have vowed that we shall not see it governed by a hostile flag of conquest, but by a banner of freedom and peace. We have vowed that we shall not see space filled with weapons of mass destruction, but with instruments of knowledge and understanding. ... We choose to go to the moon. We choose to go to the moon in this decade and do the other things, not because they are easy, but because they are hard, because that goal will serve to organize and measure the best of our energies and skills, because that challenge is one that we are willing to accept, one we are unwilling to postpone, and one which we intend to win, and the others, too.

—John F. Kennedy, September 12, 1962

9. John F. Kennedy in this passage is urging his fellow Americans to emulate which of the following?
   A. The pioneers
   B. Progressive reformers
   C. Captains of industry
   D. The Green Berets

10. Kennedy's statement *best* reflects which of the following?
    A. American unease in a time of troubles
    B. American confidence in a time of prosperity
    C. A liberal concern for social justice
    D. A conservative fear of big government

11. Kennedy's speech can *best* be compared to which of the following?
    A. Dwight Eisenhower's speech on the "military-industrial complex"
    B. George Washington's Farewell Address
    C. Abraham Lincoln's Gettysburg Address
    D. Franklin D. Roosevelt's "Arsenal of Democracy" speech

12. Kennedy's speech most directly led to which of the following?
    A. The Vietnam War
    B. The Mutually Assured Destruction (MAD) nuclear strategy
    C. The Apollo space program
    D. The Great Society social programs

Questions 13–16 refer to the following quotation.

I appeal to any white man to say, if ever he entered Logan's cabin hungry, and he gave him not meat: if ever he came cold and naked, and he clothed him not? During the course of the last long and bloody war, Logan remained idle in his cabin, an advocate for peace. Such was my love for the whites, that my countrymen pointed as they passed, and said, "Logan is the friend of the white man." I had even thought to have lived with you but for the injuries of one man. Colonel Cresap, the last spring, in cold blood and unprovoked; murdered all the relations of Logan, not even sparing my women and children. There runs not a drop of my blood in the veins of any living creature. This called on me for revenge. I have sought it: I have killed many; I have fully glutted my vengeance. For my country, I rejoice at the beams of peace. But do not harbor a thought that mine is the joy of fear. Logan never felt fear. He will not turn on his heel to save his life. Who is there to mourn for Logan? Not one.

—Address attributed to Logan, a Native American leader, 1774

13. Which of the following *best* expresses the perspective of Logan in the passage above?
    A. Logan believes the expansion of British settlements must be stopped.
    B. Logan laments the loss of his family.
    C. Logan opposes a new peace treaty.
    D. Logan believes that Native Americans need to find strength in unity.

14. Which of the following most directly expresses why Logan's Address became very popular in the early United States?
    A. Many Americans believed that the Native Americans had been treated badly.
    B. Many Americans believed that the only good Indian was a dead Indian.
    C. Many Americans believed that Native Americans were a noble people who were disappearing.
    D. Many Americans believed that Native Americans should abandon their way of life.

15. Which of the following in later years would be most likely to see themselves in Logan's position?
    A. An opponent of big government in the 1930s
    B. An opponent of consumerism in the 1950s
    C. A supporter of liberalism in the 1960s
    D. A supporter of feminism in the 1970s

16. A sympathetic reader of Logan's Address in the early years of the United States would be most likely to support which of the following Native American policies?
    A. Exterminating all Native Americans
    B. Respecting Native American territory and sovereignty
    C. Encouraging Native Americans to migrate to Canada and Mexico
    D. Building reservations and encouraging Native Americans to change their ways

Questions 17–20 refer to the following cartoon.

Political cartoon, 1832

17. Which of the following groups would be most likely to support the perspective of the cartoon?
    A. Democrat supporters of Andrew Jackson
    B. Whig opponents of Andrew Jackson
    C. Know-Nothing opponents of immigration
    D. Anti-Masonic opponents of special privilege

18. The cartoon most likely refers to which of the following policies of Andrew Jackson?
    A. The "war" against the Bank of the United States
    B. Opposition to nullification threats in South Carolina
    C. Native American removal
    D. Support for the spoils system

19. Though a supporter of "strict construction" of the Constitution, Jackson was notable for which of the following?
    A. Weakening the presidency
    B. Spending on internal improvements
    C. Strengthening the presidency
    D. Weakening the party system

20. Andrew Jackson saw himself as a champion of which of the following continuities in United States history?
    A. The struggle for civil rights for all
    B. Government assistance for the underprivileged
    C. The cooperation of government and big business
    D. The democratization of American life

Questions 21–24 refer to the following quotation.

The 1980s have been born in turmoil, strife, and change. This is a time of challenge to our interests and our values and it's a time that tests our wisdom and skills.

At this time in Iran, 50 Americans are still held captive, innocent victims of terrorism and anarchy. Also at this moment, massive Soviet troops are attempting to subjugate the fiercely independent and deeply religious people of Afghanistan. These two acts—one of international terrorism and one of military aggression—present a serious challenge to the United States of America and indeed to all the nations of the world. Together we will meet these threats to peace. ...

Three basic developments have helped to shape our challenges: the steady growth and increased projection of Soviet military power beyond its own borders; the overwhelming dependence of the Western democracies on oil supplies from the Middle East; and the press of social and religious and economic and political change in the many nations of the developing world, exemplified by the revolution in Iran.

Each of these factors is important in its own right. Each interacts with the others. All must be faced together, squarely and courageously. We will face these challenges, and we will meet them with the best that is in us. And we will not fail.

—Jimmy Carter, State of the Union Address, January 23, 1980

21. Which of the following has some of its roots in the conditions discussed by Jimmy Carter in this passage?
    A. The War on Terror
    B. High unemployment
    C. Tensions with China
    D. High budget deficits

22. The problems that Carter faced in 1980 can *best* be compared to those of which of the following?
    A. Abraham Lincoln in the 1860s
    B. Theodore Roosevelt in the 1900s
    C. Warren Harding in the 1920s
    D. Franklin D. Roosevelt in the 1930s

23. The situation Carter described led most directly to which of the following?
    A. The creation of the North Atlantic Treaty Organization (NATO)
    B. Carter's defeat in the next presidential election
    C. An American invasion in the Middle East
    D. Carter's victory in the next presidential election

24. Which of the following *best* expresses Carter's approach to foreign policy in the passage above?
    A. Isolationism
    B. Appeasement
    C. Containment
    D. A call for war

Questions 25–28 refer to the following advertisement.

Ford advertisement, 1952
Used with permission of Ford Motor Company.

25. Which of the following *best* expresses the message of the advertisement?
    A. Ford cars are for the well-off.
    B. Ford cars are great work vehicles.
    C. Ford cars are for the whole family.
    D. Ford cars are for the lower classes.

26. The advertisement most directly reflects which of the following?
    A. The growing prosperity and leisure of Americans in the 1950s
    B. The materialistic excesses of the rich in the 1950s
    C. A push for social conformity in the 1950s
    D. The recreational limits imposed by a poor economy in the 1950s

27. The American embrace of the automobile in the twentieth century most directly reflects which continuity in U.S. history?

A. A desire for social justice

B. A desire for economic equality

C. A desire for higher social status

D. A desire for more personal freedom

28. In the 1950s the widespread availability of the automobile most directly helped make possible which of the following?

A. The rise of international corporations

B. The rapid growth of suburbs

C. The prevalence of stay-at-home moms

D. The baby boom generation

Questions 29–32 refer to the following quotation.

Let us not, I beseech you sir, deceive ourselves. Sir, we have done everything that could be done, to avert the storm which is now coming on. We have petitioned; we have remonstrated; we have supplicated; we have prostrated ourselves before the throne, and have implored its interposition to arrest the tyrannical hands of the ministry and Parliament. Our petitions have been slighted; our remonstrances have produced additional violence and insult; our supplications have been disregarded; and we have been spurned, with contempt, from the foot of the throne. In vain, after these things, may we indulge the fond hope of peace and reconciliation. There is no longer any room for hope. . . . It is in vain, sir, to extenuate the matter. Gentlemen may cry, Peace, Peace, but there is no peace. The war is actually begun! The next gale that sweeps from the north will bring to our ears the clash of resounding arms! Our brethren are already in the field! Why stand we here idle? What is it that gentlemen wish? What would they have? Is life so dear, or peace so sweet, as to be purchased at the price of chains and slavery? Forbid it, Almighty God! I know not what course others may take; but as for me, give me liberty or give me death!

—Patrick Henry, March 23, 1775

29. The sentiments expressed by Patrick Henry led most directly to which of the following?

A. The Declaration of Independence

B. The Albany Plan

C. The Boston Tea Party

D. The Constitution of the United States

30. In this passage, Henry expresses an abiding American concern about which of the following?

A. No entangling alliances with foreign countries

B. The dangers of standing armies

C. Self-government

D. The separation of church and state

31. Which of the following nineteenth-century groups most directly saw themselves as following in the tradition of Patrick Henry?

A. Supporters of Manifest Destiny

B. Members of the Republican Party

C. Abolitionists

D. Southern secessionists

32. The "storm" that Henry refers to was most directly the result of which of the following?

A. American efforts to trade with Spain and France

B. British efforts to shrink a budget deficit after the French and Indian War

C. British unwillingness to fight Native American tribes on the frontier

D. British impressments of American sailors and interference with American trade

Questions 33–36 refer to the following quotation.

Of all the band of adventurous cavaliers, whom Spain, in the sixteenth century, sent forth on the career of discovery and conquest, there was none more deeply filled with the spirit of romantic enterprise than Hernando Cortes. Dangers and difficulties, instead of deterring, seemed to have a charm in his eyes. ... He conceived, at the first moment of his landing in Mexico, the design of its conquest. When he saw the strength of its civilization, he was not turned from his purpose. ... This spirit of knight-errantry might lead us to undervalue his talents as a general, and to regard him merely in the light of a lucky adventurer. But this would be doing him injustice; for Cortes was certainly a great general, if that man be one, who performs great achievements with the resources which his own genius has created. There is probably no instance in history, where so vast an enterprise has been achieved by means apparently so inadequate. ... He brought together the most miscellaneous collection of mercenaries who ever fought under one standard: adventurers from Cuba and the Isles, craving for gold; hidalgos, who came from the old country to win laurels; ... wild tribes of the natives from all parts of the country, who had been sworn enemies from their cradles, and who had met only to cut one another's throats, and to procure victims for sacrifice; men, in short, differing in race, in language, and in interests, with scarcely anything in common among them. Yet this motley congregation was assembled in one camp, compelled to bend to the will of one man, to consort together in harmony, to breathe, as it were, one spirit, and to move on a common principle of action!

—William Hickling Prescott, *History of the Conquest of Mexico*, 1843

33. Given the perspective of the passage above, William Hickling Prescott believed which of the following about the conquest of the Aztec Empire?
  A. The actions of Hernando Cortes were irrational.
  B. The conquest of Mexico was a racist atrocity.
  C. Cortes was chiefly motivated by a desire for wealth.
  D. The Aztec Empire had to give way to the superior civilization of Spain.

34. As Prescott makes clear in the passage above, an important reason for Cortes's military success was which of the following?
  A. The advantage of superior numbers
  B. The superior military skill of mercenaries
  C. Taking advantage of divisions among the Indians
  D. Effective use of European artillery

35. The Spanish in America were interested in which of the following?
  A. Escaping oppression at home
  B. Expanding territories under Spanish control
  C. Seeking religious freedom for themselves
  D. Creating independent principalities for themselves

36. Prescott's interpretation of the conquest of Mexico resembles which contemporary nineteenth-century American political movement?
  A. Support for Manifest Destiny
  B. Support for Southern secessionism
  C. Support for abolitionism
  D. Support for Know-Nothingism

Questions 37–40 refer to the following quotation.

I come not to urge personal claims, nor to seek individual benefits; I appear as the advocate of those who cannot plead their own cause; I come as the friend of those who are deserted, oppressed, and desolate. In the Providence of God, I am the voice of the maniac whose piercing cries from the dreary dungeons of your jails penetrate not your Halls of Legislation. I am the Hope of the poor crazed beings who pine in the cells, and stalls, and cages, and waste rooms of your poor-houses. I am the Revelation of hundreds of wailing, suffering creatures, hidden in your private dwellings, and in pens and cabins—shut out, cut off from all healing influences, from all mind-restoring cares. . . . Could their melancholy histories be spread before you as revealed to my grieved spirit during the last three months, how promptly, how earnestly would you search out the most approved means of relief; how trifling, how insignificant, by comparison, would appear the sacrifices you are asked to make; how would a few dimes and dollars, gathered from each citizen, diminish in value as a possession, compared with the certain benefits and vast good to be secured for the suffering insane . . . by the consecration and application of a sufficient fund to the construction of a suitable hospital. . . .

> —Dorothea Dix, Memorial Soliciting a State Hospital for the Protection and Cure of the Insane,
> Submitted to the General Assembly of North Carolina, November 1848

37. Which of the following best reflects the perspective of Dorothea Dix in the passage above?
   A. The care of the mentally ill is a state concern.
   B. The mentally ill are best left to the care of their families.
   C. The federal government should regulate the treatment of the mentally ill.
   D. More democracy will help the mentally ill.

38. Which of the following was a popular reform movement of the 1840s?
   A. The free coinage of silver
   B. Regulation of big business
   C. The gay rights movement
   D. The temperance movement

39. A key motivating factor for many reformers of the 1840s was
   A. Marxism.
   B. Evangelical Christianity.
   C. distrust of big government.
   D. laissez-faire economics.

40. Dorothea Dix can best be compared to whom?
   A. Abigail Adams
   B. Clara Barton
   C. Shirley Temple
   D. Hillary Clinton

Questions 41–44 refer to the following quotation.

Now, we have organized a society, and we call it "Share Our Wealth Society," a society with the motto "Every Man a King." . . .

We propose to limit the wealth of big men in the country. There is an average of $15,000 in wealth to every family in America. That is right here today.

We do not propose to divide it up equally. We do not propose a division of wealth, but we do propose to limit poverty that we will allow to be inflicted on any man's family. We will not say we are going to try to guarantee any equality . . . but we do say that one third of the average is low enough for any one family to hold, that there should be a guarantee of a family wealth of around $5,000; enough for a home, an automobile, a radio, and the ordinary conveniences, and the opportunity to educate their children. . . .

We will have to limit fortunes. Our present plan is that we will allow no man to own more than $50,000,000. We think that with that limit we will be able to carry out the balance of the program.

> —Senator Huey P. Long of Louisiana, Radio Address, February 23, 1934

41. Senator Huey P. Long's "Share the Wealth Society" was a political program intended to
   A. demonstrate Senator Long's commitment to fighting communism.
   B. return the United States to the economic ideas of the late nineteenth century.
   C. persuade voters that Senator Long had a plan to combat the Great Depression.
   D. showcase Senator Long's understanding of the constitutional ideas of the Founding Fathers.

42. Senator Long ran a political machine that made him the virtual dictator of Louisiana. As a political boss, he can best be compared to whom?
   A. George Washington
   B. Theodore Roosevelt
   C. William M. Tweed
   D. Barack Obama

43. Senator Long's "Share the Wealth Society" attracted many followers in 1934 because
   A. the New Deal had not ended the Great Depression.
   B. a flourishing economy and a baby boom had led people to desire greater incomes.
   C. World War II encouraged an egalitarian ethos.
   D. Socialistic ideas were becoming popular in the United States.

44. President Franklin D. Roosevelt responded to political challenges like that of Senator Long by doing which of the following?
   A. Announcing that he would not run for reelection
   B. Launching the Second New Deal, a series of legislative acts including Social Security
   C. Diverting people's attention by allowing the Japanese to bomb Pearl Harbor
   D. Urging Congress to cut taxes and deregulate the economy

Questions 45–48 refer to the following quotation.

All this while the Indians came skulking about them, and would sometimes show themselves aloof off, but when any approached near them, they would run away; and once they stole away their tools where they had been at work and were gone to dinner. But about the 16th of March, a certain Indian came boldly amongst them and spoke to them in broken English, which they could well understand but marveled at it. At length they understood by discourse with him, that he was not of these parts, but belonged to the eastern parts where some English ships came to fish, with whom he was acquainted and could name sundry of them by their names, amongst whom he had got his language. He became profitable to them in acquainting them with many things concerning the state of the country in the east parts where he lived, which was afterwards profitable unto them; as also of the people here, of their names, number and strength, of their situation and distance from the place, and who was chief amongst them. His name was Samoset. He told them also of another Indian whose name was Squanto, a native of this place, who had been in England and could speak better English than himself.

—William Bradford, *History of Plymouth Plantation*

45. Which of the following best expresses the perspective of William Bradford in the passage above?
   A. The only good Indian is a dead Indian.
   B. The native peoples of America need to be converted to Christianity.
   C. Native Americans need to be incorporated into their new colony.
   D. Surprise that Native Americans could learn English and serve as cultural intermediaries.

46. The Pilgrims traveled to America and settled at Plymouth because
   A. they were hoping to escape crushing debts in England.
   B. they hoped to find gold or establish a lucrative trade in furs.
   C. they were religious Separatists looking for a place to freely practice their faith.
   D. they were ordered to establish an outpost to watch the French in Canada.

47. As the passage above makes clear, the Pilgrims were not the only Europeans in what would become Massachusetts during the 1620s. The area was already becoming important because of its
   A. fishing.
   B. farming.
   C. mining.
   D. shipbuilding.

48. Samoset and Squanto can most directly be compared to whom?
   A. Tecumseh
   B. Crazy Horse
   C. Sacagawea
   D. Geronimo

Questions 49–52 refer to the following poster.

Poster advertising Buffalo Bill Cody's Wild West Show

49. William "Buffalo Bill" Cody won his nickname because of his skills as a frontier scout and buffalo hunter. The disappearance of the great buffalo herds led to which of the following?
   A. The Dust Bowl
   B. Global warming
   C. Dietary changes in American cities
   D. The destruction of the Plains Native Americans' way of life

50. The economic significance of the cowboys that Cody celebrated in his show was
   A. driving herds of cattle to railroad depots where they were shipped to meatpackers in the east.
   B. clearing land for farmers by driving Native American tribes onto reservations.
   C. founding new towns in the west.
   D. opening up rich minefields to fuel growing industries.

51. Buffalo Bill's Wild West Show celebrated a growing nostalgia for which of the following?
   A. The horses that were being replaced by automobiles
   B. The rapidly disappearing frontier
   C. America's wilderness uncorrupted by development
   D. The loss of America's role as a great power in the world

52. Buffalo Bill's Wild West Show was a popular example of which of the following?
   A. The populist critique of Wall Street and big business
   B. New forms of entertainment for the urban masses
   C. The concern about Native Americans that led to the Dawes Severalty Act in 1887
   D. A growing demand for classical drama and the fine arts

Questions 53–55 refer to the following quotation.

Clearly, no longer can a dictator count on East-West confrontation to stymie concerted United Nations action against aggression. A new partnership of nations has begun. And we stand today at a unique and extraordinary moment. The crisis in the Persian Gulf, as grave as it is, also offers a rare opportunity to move toward an historic period of cooperation. Out of these troubled times, our fifth objective—a new world order—can emerge; a new era, freer from the threat of terror, stronger in the pursuit of justice, and more secure in the quest for peace. An era in which the nations of the world, east and west, north and south, can prosper and live in harmony.

   —President George Herbert Walker Bush, Speech to a Joint Session of Congress, September 11, 1990

53. President George Herbert Walker Bush's vision of a "new world order" was most directly made possible by
   A. American economic prosperity.
   B. President Ronald Reagan's Strategic Defense Initiative.
   C. the Iranian Hostage Crisis.
   D. the end of the cold war.

54. President Bush was responding to which of the following?
   A. Iraqi dictator Saddam Hussein's conquest of Kuwait
   B. The fall of the Berlin Wall
   C. Terror attacks by Al-Qaeda
   D. The breakup of Yugoslavia and the start of the Bosnian War

55. President Bush's "new world order" most directly resembles which of the following?
   A. The Monroe Doctrine
   B. Theodore Roosevelt's "Big Stick"
   C. Woodrow Wilson's Fourteen Points
   D. Containment policy toward the Soviet Union

Go on to Part B. ➔

Part B (Short Answer)

Part B recommended time: 40 minutes

Directions: Answer three questions. You must answer questions 1 and 2, and you can choose to answer either 3 or 4. Carefully read and follow the directions for each question. Some will refer to historical sources. These questions will require you to make use of your historical analytical skills and your familiarity with historical themes. These questions do *not* require you to develop a thesis in your responses.

Question 1 is based on the following passage:

Each side had advantages. But neither section understood the other. If the South had known that secession must result in war and that the foe would be a united North, it is doubtful if she would have proceeded to the last extremity. It is still more doubtful if the North would have fought, had she known that she must contend with a united Southern people. ... But now the North confronted five and a half million earnest and brave people, supported by three and a half million servants, who grew the food and took care of the women and children at home while the men fought in the field. The North was contending for the Union on the theory that a strong and unscrupulous minority had overridden the majority of Southerners who had no desire for secession, loathed the idea of civil war, and if protected and encouraged, would make themselves felt in a movement looking towards allegiance to the national government. Lincoln comprehended the sentiment of the North and he never gave public expression to any opinion that he did not sincerely hold. In his Fourth of July message to the special session of Congress he said: "It may well be questioned whether there is today a majority of the legally qualified voters of any State, except perhaps South Carolina, in favor of disunion. There is much reason to believe that the Union men are the majority in many, if not every other one, of the so-called seceded states."

—James Ford Rhodes, *History of the Civil War*, 1917

1. Using the excerpt, answer A, B, and C.
   A. Briefly explain Rhodes's perspective on Southern and Northern attitudes at the beginning of the Civil War.
   B. Briefly explain ONE historical event or development that supports Rhodes's argument.
   C. Briefly explain ONE historical event or development that illustrates an unwillingness on the part of many Americans to embrace war in 1861.

Question 2 is based on the following passages:

The problem lay buried, unspoken for many years in the minds of American women. It was a strange stirring, a sense of dissatisfaction, a yearning that women suffered in the middle of the twentieth century in the United States. Each suburban wife struggled with it alone. As she made the beds, shopped for groceries, matched slipcover material, ate peanut butter sandwiches with her children, chauffeured Cub Scouts and Brownies, lay beside her husband at night—she was afraid to ask even of herself the silent question—"Is this all?"

—Betty Friedan

It is my belief, based on working with this movement for quite a number of years, that the movement is having an adverse effect on family life, that it is a major cause of divorce today, and that it is highly detrimental to our country and to our families. … Motherhood must be a self-sacrificing role. The mother must be able to subordinate her self-fulfillment and her desire for a career to the well being of her children so she can answer her child's call any hour of the day or night. This is what marriage and motherhood are all about.

—Phyllis Schlafly

2. Using the excerpts, answer A, B, and C.
  A. Briefly explain ONE example of a political or social position supported by Betty Friedan.
  B. Briefly explain ONE example of a political or social position supported by Phyllis Schlafly.
  C. Briefly explain ONE example of a way one of these perspectives influenced American politics in the 1960s and 1970s.

Answer EITHER Question 3 OR Question 4.

3. Answer A, B, and C.
  A. Briefly explain how ONE of the following reflected American expansionism.
      The French and Indian War
      The Louisiana Purchase
      The Mexican War
  B. Briefly explain how a SECOND of these options reflected American expansionism.
  C. Briefly explain the perspective of someone opposed to ONE of the examples that you chose.

4. Answer A, B, and C.
  A. Briefly explain how ONE of the following reflected American concerns about internal subversion.
      Haymarket Square Riot
      First Red Scare
      Second Red Scare
  B. Briefly explain how a SECOND of these options reflected American concerns about internal subversion.
  C. Briefly explain ONE example of a way one of these events affected American politics.

STOP. End of Section I.

Section II

Time: 100 minutes

Part A (Document-Based Question)

Part A recommended time: 60 minutes

Directions: Use the documents to answer the question. You may want to spend up to 15 minutes outlining your response and 45 minutes writing the essay that answers the question.

Provide a thesis that responds to all elements of the question with a historically plausible argument. This thesis of one or more sentences must be in the introduction or conclusion.

Connect historical evidence supporting your argument to a broader historical context that reaches beyond the time frame of the question.

Use at least three of the documents to address the topic of the question.

Support your argument with evidence from at least six of the seven documents.

Support your argument by analyzing historical evidence that comes from outside the documents.

Base your analysis of no less than three documents on at least one of the following: the point of view of the author, the purpose of the author, the intended audience of the document, the historical context of the document.

Demonstrate a complex understanding of the subject of the question, using historical evidence to modify, qualify, or confirm your argument.

1. Analyze the effects of American foreign policy in Latin America during the period 1899 to 1917.

Document A
Source: Platt Amendment, May 22, 1903

> *Article III. The Government of Cuba consents that the United States may exercise the right to intervene for the preservation of Cuban independence, the maintenance of a government adequate for the protection of life property, and individual liberty, and for discharging the obligations with respect to Cuba imposed by the Treaty of Paris on the United States, now to be assumed and undertaken by the Government of Cuba.*

Document B
Source: Hay-Bunau-Varilla Treaty, November 18, 1903

> *The Republic of Panama grants to the United States in perpetuity, the use, occupation and control of a zone of land and land under water for the construction . . . of said canal. . . . The Republic of Panama further grants to the United States in perpetuity, the use, occupation and control of any other lands and waters outside the zone . . . which may be necessary and convenient for the construction . . . and protection of the said Canal.*

Document C
Source: Theodore Roosevelt, Annual Message to Congress, December 6, 1904

> *If a nation shows that it knows how to act with reasonable efficiency and decency in social and political matters, if it keeps order and pays its obligations, it need fear no interference from the United States. Chronic wrongdoing, or an impotence which results in a general loosening of the ties of civilized society, may . . . ultimately require intervention by some civilized nation, and in the Western Hemisphere the adherence of the United States to the Monroe Doctrine may lead the United States, . . . in flagrant cases of such wrongdoing or impotence, to exercise an international police power.*

Document D

Source: W. A. Rogers, "The Full Dinner Pail," *Harper's Weekly,* April 13, 1907; courtesy of Theodore-Roosevelt.com.

Document E

Source: William Howard Taft, Fourth Annual Message to Congress, December 3, 1912

> *The diplomacy of the present administration has sought to respond to modern ideas of commercial intercourse. This policy has been characterized by substituting dollars for bullets. . . . It is an effort frankly directed to the increase of American trade upon the axiomatic principle that the government of the United States shall extend all proper support to every legitimate and beneficial American enterprise abroad.*

Document F

Source: Erving Winslow, "Aggression in South America," excerpt from Report of the Thirteenth Annual Meeting of the Anti-Imperialist League, 1912

> *It is proposed that in the Honduras and Nicaragua . . . the United States government should be authorized to secure the collection and disbursement of the revenue in the interest of American capitalists who contemplate making loans to those countries. This involves serious risk of complications which may lead to further interferences and ultimate control.*

> *The delicacy of these and other foreign relations of the United States is such as should put our citizens upon their guard and confirm their determination to treat with justice all their neighbors and to recognize generally their independent right to govern (or misgovern) their own countries.*

Document G

Source: Woodrow Wilson, Address to Congress, April 20, 1914

A series of incidents have recently occurred which cannot but create the impression that the representatives of General Huerta were willing to go out of their way to show disregard for the dignity and rights of this government, . . . making free to show in many ways their irritation and contempt.

I, therefore, come to ask your approval that I should use the armed forces of the United States in such ways . . . as may be necessary to obtain from General Huerta and his adherents the fullest recognition of the rights and dignity of the United States, even amidst the distressing conditions now unhappily obtaining in Mexico.

Go on to Part B. ➜

Part B (Long Essay)

Part B recommended time: 40 minutes

Directions: Answer *one* of the following questions.

Provide a thesis that responds to all elements of the question with a historically plausible argument. This thesis of one or more sentences must be in the introduction or conclusion.

Connect historical evidence supporting your argument to a broader historical context that reaches beyond the time frame of the question.

Provide examples of historical information that are relevant to the question.

Use well-chosen examples of historical information that support your argument.

Use historical reasoning to construct an argument that answers the question.

Demonstrate a complex understanding of the subject of the question, using historical evidence to modify, qualify, or confirm your argument.

2. Evaluate the extent to which differing economies shaped differing social structures in the English colonies in North America.

3. Evaluate the extent to which late nineteenth century urbanization affected politics, immigration, and popular culture.

4. Evaluate the extent to which mobilization for total war during World War I and World War II influenced American political and social development in the twentieth century.

STOP. End of Section II.

ANSWERS TO PRACTICE EXAM 1

Multiple Choice

1. B	15. A	29. A	43. A
2. D	16. D	30. C	44. B
3. A	17. B	31. D	45. D
4. C	18. A	32. B	46. C
5. B	19. C	33. D	47. A
6. C	20. D	34. C	48. C
7. A	21. A	35. B	49. D
8. D	22. D	36. A	50. A
9. A	23. B	37. A	51. B
10. B	24. C	38. D	52. B
11. D	25. C	39. B	53. D
12. C	26. A	40. B	54. A
13. B	27. D	41. C	55. C
14. C	28. B	42. C	

Count the number you got correct and enter this number on the scoring worksheet on page 435.

Explanations for the Multiple-Choice Questions

1. **B.** Poor people need support in helping themselves *best* reflects the perspective of Jane Addams in the passage. Jane Addams was a pioneering social worker who became famous for her work with the poor. She was a leader in the settlement house movement, which established social centers in disadvantaged urban neighborhoods. Addams founded Hull House in Chicago.

2. **D.** Settlement houses like Hull House expressed a desire of reformers to improve conditions in urban neighborhoods. Settlement houses provided a variety of social services such as childcare for working mothers and English language classes. Settlement house workers also helped the people in their neighborhoods lobby government for better living conditions and city services.

3. **A.** A settlement house worker was most likely to be motivated by the Social Gospel. The Social Gospel was a liberal strain of American Protestantism that called on the church to battle injustices in society and to work for social betterment as a way of saving souls.

4. **C.** The perspective of the passage would most directly support greater rights for unions. In the passage, Jane Addams helps young women workers find secure communal housing so they can safely strike for better working conditions. Settlement house workers often helped immigrants and the poor organize to protect their rights in their working places and elsewhere.

5. **B.** The image reflects the perspective that the importation of slaves is a legitimate enterprise. The image is a notice for a slave auction in Charleston, South Carolina, in the 1780s. Slavery was believed to be crucial to South Carolina's plantation economy.

6. **C.** During the 1780s, the most widespread crop cultivated by slaves in North America was tobacco. Cotton did not become the chief cash crop in the South until after Eli Whitney's invention of the cotton gin in the 1790s.

7. **A.** Following the American Revolution, many Founding Fathers believed that slavery would gradually disappear in the United States. Economically, tobacco was losing some of its importance as new sources appeared elsewhere in the world. Also the human rights ideals of the Revolution seemed to be at odds with the institution of slavery. The 1787 Northwest Ordinance banned slavery in the Northwest Territory. The Constitution, while recognizing the existence of slavery for representation purposes, ended the importation of slaves from Africa after 1807. What the Founding Fathers did not anticipate was the cotton gin, the cotton boom, and the renewed economic importance of slavery.

8. **D.** The Federal government could not ban the importation of slaves for 20 years, or until 1808. In 1807, Congress passed legislation that made the importation of slaves illegal from January 1, 1808. This was part of the growing consensus in the years after the Revolution that slavery was a weakening institution, for both economic and ideological reasons. Slavery was gradually outlawed in the Northern states. George Washington and others freed their slaves upon their deaths. Then the invention of the cotton gin made slavery highly profitable again in the South.

9. **A.** President John F. Kennedy in this passage is urging his fellow Americans to emulate the pioneers. Kennedy ran for the presidency on a program that he termed the New Frontier. He wanted Americans to emulate their pioneer forebears and surmount a number of challenges, from domestic problems to the cold war. Taking the lead in the space race with the Soviets and landing the first men on the moon would be a dramatic way of demonstrating this pioneering spirit.

10. **B.** Kennedy's statement best reflects American confidence in a time of prosperity. The early 1960s were a time of prosperity that had endured since the end of World War II. Kennedy and his successor, Lyndon B. Johnson, believed that the United States could achieve any task it set out to accomplish, whether it was landing a man on the moon, ending poverty in the United States, or winning a war in Vietnam.

11. **D.** Kennedy's speech can *best* be compared to Franklin D. Roosevelt's "Arsenal of Democracy" speech. In the "Arsenal of Democracy" speech, Roosevelt also set a challenge for the American people, producing weapons and supplies for the nations resisting Axis aggression during World War II.

12. **C.** Kennedy's speech most directly led to the Apollo space program. The Apollo space missions focused on landing men on the moon. *Apollo 8* circled the moon in December 1968. The *Apollo 11* mission set a lunar module down on the moon. Neil Armstrong and Edwin "Buzz" Aldrin became the first and second men to walk on the moon.

13. **B.** In the passage, Logan laments the loss of his family. Logan was a Native American war chief. After members of his family were murdered by settlers, Logan led a series of retaliatory raids. This began Lord Dunmore's War in 1774, named after the Governor of Virginia. Logan refused to attend the talks that led to a peace treaty but sent the message in the passage instead.

14. **C.** Logan's Address became very popular in the early United States because many Americans believed that Native Americans were a noble people that were disappearing. As Native Americans became perceived as a minor and fading threat, many Americans expressed sympathy for their plight. They were sometimes portrayed as "noble savages" free of the corruptions of society. A good example of this is the character of Uncas in James Fenimore Cooper's novel *The Last of the Mohicans* (1825).

15. **A.** In later years, an opponent of big government in the 1930s would be most likely to sympathize with Logan. Like Logan, an opponent of big government during the years of the New Deal and the rapid expansion of the welfare state would feel as if events were moving in the wrong direction.

16. **D.** A reader of Logan's Address in the early years of the United States would most likely support building reservations and encouraging Native Americans to change their ways. Thomas Jefferson believed that the only hope for Native Americans was for them to adopt American culture. Until they did so, he thought that they should be moved away from the settlements, giving them time to "civilize" themselves. The consensus of American policymakers during the nineteenth century was that the key to Native American survival was a combination of reservations and eventual assimilation into American society.

17. **B.** Whig opponents of Andrew Jackson would be most likely to support the perspective of the cartoon. The Whigs saw Jackson as an overbearing and tyrannical chief executive, most notably for his veto of the rechartering of the Bank of the United States. Hence, the portrayal of Jackson in the cartoon as "King Andrew."

18. **A.** The cartoon most likely refers to the "war" against the Bank of the United States. President Jackson believed that the privately run Bank of the United States had too much power over the nation's finances. He thought its power was undemocratic. When Henry Clay and Bank supporters passed a rechartering bill through Congress, Jackson vetoed it. He also pulled federal funds from the Bank of the United States, depositing the money in state banks that came to be known as "pet banks." These banks soon began issuing large amounts of paper money. Hoping to rein in inflation, Jackson issued the Specie Circular, requiring gold or silver coins in payment for public lands. This spurred a financial panic and depression in 1837.

19. **C.** Though a supporter of "strict construction" of the Constitution, Jackson was notable for strengthening the presidency. While philosophically a believer in limited government, temperamentally, Jackson could not resist vigorously using the powers of his office in instances as varied as his defiance of the Supreme Court over Native American removal or taking a strong stand against advocates of nullification in South Carolina. Jackson's veto of the recharter of the Bank of the United States because he thought this would be bad policy was unprecedented. Previous presidential vetoes had been based on the perceived unconstitutionality of bills. Jackson here expanded the range of presidential prerogative.

20. **D.** Andrew Jackson saw himself as the champion of the democratization of American life. Jackson portrayed himself as the representative of the common man. During the period of his political ascendency in the 1820s and 1830s most property qualifications for voting disappeared. The emergence of a vigorous two-party political system encouraged politicians to court and celebrate

ordinary Americans. Historians use the term "Jacksonian Democracy" to describe this new era.

21. **A.** The War on Terror has some of its roots in the conditions discussed by President Jimmy Carter in this passage. The difficulties with revolutionary Iran and the Iranian hostage crisis, as well as concerns about the free flow of Middle Eastern oil, spurred increased American involvement in the region. Resentment of this American role played a part in motivating the Al Qaeda attacks on September 11, 2001.

22. **D.** The problems that Carter faced in 1980 can *best* be compared to Franklin D. Roosevelt in the 1930s. Roosevelt also had to deal with great powers, such as Japan, Italy, and Germany launching wars of aggression, and the resulting international instability. Carter was responding to the Soviet Union's invasion of Afghanistan and the problems caused by the new revolutionary regime in Iran. Within a few months, Saddam Hussein's Iraq would start a long and bloody war with Iran.

23. **B.** The situation Carter described led most directly to his defeat in the next presidential election. Carter's inability to secure the release of the Americans held hostage in Iran and the perception that American foreign policy was ineffective contributed to his defeat by Ronald Reagan in the 1980 election.

24. **C.** Containment *best* expresses Carter's approach to foreign policy in the passage. The containment of the Soviet Union and the spread of communism had been a centerpiece of American foreign policy since the late 1940s. Carter's determination to confront the Soviet Union over the invasion of Afghanistan was consistent with the policy of containment.

25. **C.** Ford cars are for the whole family *best* expresses the message of the advertisement. The 1950s were a time of general prosperity. The baby boom was underway, and popular culture celebrated family togetherness. The Ford ad addresses this by showing a family vacationing in their new Ford convertible.

26. **A.** The advertisement most directly reflects the growing prosperity and leisure of Americans in the 1950s. The United States was enjoying a postwar economic boom. This prosperity and government programs such as the GI Bill facil-

itated the movement of many Americans to new levels of affluence. Family vacations such as that pictured in the advertisement became an attainable reality for millions of Americans.

27. **D.** The American embrace of the automobile in the twentieth century most directly reflects a desire for more personal freedom. From the beginning, Americans desired the easy and affordable mobility provided by automobiles. As early as 1929, there was one automobile for every five Americans, more cars than in all the rest of the world. By the 1950s, cars symbolized the prosperity and openness of American society.

28. **B.** In the 1950s, the widespread availability of the automobile most directly helped make possible the rapid growth of suburbs. The rapid spread of new roads, facilitated in part by the 1956 Interstate Highway Act, encouraged developers like the Levitt brothers to create extensive suburban housing developments outside cities. Suburbanites could enjoy the amenities of single family dwellings in attractive surroundings while using their automobiles to commute to work in the cities.

29. **A.** The sentiments expressed by Patrick Henry led most directly to the Declaration of Independence. Speaking in March 1775, shortly before the outbreak of the Revolutionary War in April, Henry pointed out the unwillingness of the British authorities to compromise with the American colonists. Once fighting began, the British continued to show little inclination to address American concerns. This led more and more Americans to contemplate independence. On June 7, 1776, Richard Henry Lee of Virginia submitted a resolution to the Second Continental Congress calling for independence.

30. **C.** In this passage, Henry expresses an abiding American concern for self-government. Unlike the Spanish and French colonies, the English colonies had been largely self-governing from the time of their founding. The Virginia House of Burgesses dated back to 1619. That meant that by the 1770s some of the American colonies had been governing themselves for close to 150 years. This tradition of self-governance led the American colonists to resent new British taxation after 1763

and to stand up for what they believed were their rights as Englishmen.

31. **D.** The nineteenth-century group of Americans that most directly saw themselves in the tradition of Patrick Henry were Southern secessionists. The secessionists of 1860–1861 saw themselves as people whose states' rights were being threatened by a federal government headed by a man that they regarded as a "radical" Republican. They saw their secession from the Union as equivalent to the American colonies withdrawing from the British Empire.

32. **B.** The "storm" that Henry refers to was most directly the result of British efforts to shrink a budget deficit after the French and Indian War. Faced with enormous debts after the expensive war with the French, the British government looked to the American colonies as a new revenue source, leading Parliament to pass a series of taxes on the Americans. The American colonists resented this "taxation without representation," provoking a series of political crises that ended with a war.

33. **D.** Given the perspective of the passage, William Hickling Prescott believed that the Aztec Empire had to give way to the superior civilization of Spain. Prescott, like most nineteenth-century Americans, was convinced that the European conquest of America was part of the upward march of human progress. He saw Hernando Cortes as a hero whose actions were justified by history.

34. **C.** As Prescott makes clear in the passage, an important reason for Cortes's military success was taking advantage of divisions among the Native Americans. Cortes never had enough Spanish troops to overthrow the Aztec Empire. He built a coalition with other Native American peoples who resented the rule of the Aztecs. This provided him with the manpower to achieve victory.

35. **B.** The Spanish in America were interested in expanding territories under Spanish control. This was a major goal of Cortes and other conquistadors. They were also anxious to spread the Christian religion and win riches for themselves. But whatever they conquered became part of the Spanish Empire, under the rule of the Spanish king.

36. **A.** Prescott's interpretation of the conquest of Mexico resembles the contemporary nineteenth-century support for Manifest Destiny. Just as Prescott believed that the Spanish conquest of Mexico represented human progress and demonstrated the superiority of European civilization, the supporters of Manifest Destiny argued that the inevitable spreading of American settlement to the Pacific Ocean and beyond was a measure of the glorious role that the United States would play in the future.

37. **A.** "The care of the mentally ill is a state concern" best reflects the perspective of Dorothea Dix. Before the early nineteenth century, the mentally ill were often treated with great cruelty by people who did not understand their affliction. Dorothea Dix argued persuasively for the humane treatment of the mentally ill. She convinced the legislators of several states to create new hospitals for the mentally ill.

38. **D.** The temperance movement was a popular reform movement of the 1840s. Heavy drinking was a serious problem in early nineteenth-century America, sometimes aggravated by a lack of safe drinking water. The American Temperance Society was founded in 1826. Soon the push for temperance and the prohibition of the manufacture and sale of intoxicating liquor became widespread. Neal S. Dow became one of the most prominent leaders of the temperance movement. As the mayor of Portland, Maine, Dow sponsored the Maine Law of 1851, which established prohibition in the state.

39. **B.** A key motivating factor for many reformers of the 1840s was Evangelical Christianity. In the early nineteenth century, the Second Great Awakening stimulated a wave of religious enthusiasm in the United States. A "Benevolent Empire" of missionary and reform organizations was established by various Protestant denominations. Fueled by religious fervor, many reformers worked to create what they felt was a more godly and perfect society.

40. **B.** Dorothea Dix can best be compared to Clara Barton. Like Dix, Barton was a reformer who worked to help the suffering. After seeing the travails of wounded Union soldiers during the Civil War, Barton became a nurse. She later ran military hospitals and became famous as the "Angel of the Battlefields." After the war, Barton founded the American branch of the Red Cross.

41. **C.** Senator Huey P. Long's "Share the Wealth Society" was a political program intended to persuade voters that Senator Long had a plan to combat the Great Depression. Although initially a supporter of President Franklin D. Roosevelt, the ambitious Long broke with him and was laying the foundations of a presidential run of his own. He allied with other populist critics of Roosevelt such as Gerald
L. K. Smith and Father Charles Coughlin. Long was assassinated by a Louisiana physician outraged by Long's policies in September 1935, a month after announcing that he was planning to run for the presidency.

42. **C.** As a political boss, Long can best be compared to William M. Tweed. Tweed was the leader of Tammany Hall, the Democratic political machine of New York City during the 1860s. While Tweed was the dominant figure in city politics, many millions of dollars were appropriated by his political cronies in bribes and graft.

43. **A.** Senator Long's "Share the Wealth Society" attracted many followers in 1934 because the New Deal had not ended the Great Depression. Although conditions had improved since the worst of the Depression in 1932 and 1933, unemployment remained high, and many families continued to suffer.

44. **B.** President Franklin D. Roosevelt responded to political challenges like that of Senator Long by launching the Second New Deal, a series of legislative acts including Social Security. The Second New Deal of 1935–1936 provided more support and benefits for ordinary Americans, while increasing taxes on the wealthy and heightening rhetorical attacks on big business. In addition to the Social Security Act of 1935, other important pieces of legislation enacted during this period included the National Labor Relations Act (the Wagner Act), which provided support to unions, and the Emergency Relief Appropriation Act of 1935, which created the Works Progress Administration (WPA), which provided work to unemployed people.

45. **D.** "Surprise that Native Americans could learn English and serve as cultural intermediaries" best expresses the perspective of William Bradford in the passage. Bradford and the Pilgrims did not have a lot of experience dealing with Native Americans. As the passage makes clear, most of their prior experience with the locals had highlighted incomprehension and distrust between the two peoples. Samoset and Squanto were very important in helping the Pilgrims adjust to the new land and get to know their neighbors.

46. **C.** The Pilgrims traveled to America and settled at Plymouth because they were religious Separatists looking for a place to freely practice their faith. As Separatists, the Pilgrims rejected the practices of the Church of England. They moved to Holland in 1608 hoping to find religious sanctuary. They were not persecuted there but feared that their children were "becoming Dutch." So, in 1620, the Pilgrims sailed to America on the *Mayflower*, hoping for a new beginning and a place where they could live the lives they desired.

47. **A.** The area where the Pilgrims settled was already growing important because of its fishing. European fishing off North America was a very big business by the seventeenth century. Fishermen caught and salted cod, which they sold to Catholic countries in Europe where people did not eat meat on Fridays. As the passage makes clear, fishermen were already engaged in many interactions with the Native Americans of New England. Samoset was introduced to English by fishermen.

48. **C.** Samoset and Squanto can most directly be compared to Sacagawea. A young Shoshone woman married to a French fur trader, Sacagawea also served as a cultural intermediary. She acted as a translator for the Lewis and Clark Expedition of 1804 to 1806.

49. **D.** The disappearance of the great buffalo herds led to the destruction of the Plains

Indians' way of life. The Plains Indians were dependent on the buffalo, using them for food and their skins for clothes and shelter. American expansion west put great pressure on the buffalo. Working for a railroad, William "Buffalo Bill" Cody killed over 4,000 buffalo to feed construction crews. Military leaders like General Philip Sheridan also encouraged the killing of the buffalo as a means of weakening the Indians. In 1868, some 15 million buffalo were roaming the western plains; by 1885, this immense herd had been reduced to a few thousand. The Plains Indians were forced onto reservations and into economic dependence on the government.

50. **A.** The economic significance of the cowboys that Cody celebrated in his show was driving herds of cattle to depots where they were shipped to meatpackers in the east. The growing cities of the east needed new sources of meat. Western ranchers stepped up to satisfy this demand. In 1866, Texas cattlemen drove a herd of cattle to the railhead at Sedalia, Missouri. Over the next 20 years, the heyday of the "Long Drive," cowboys drove millions of cattle to places like Abilene, Kansas; Dodge City, Kansas; and Cheyenne, Wyoming.

51. **B.** Buffalo Bill's Wild West Show celebrated a growing nostalgia for the rapidly disappearing frontier. Following the 1890 census, the Census Bureau announced that the frontier had come to an end. In 1893, the historian Frederick Jackson Turner promulgated his "Frontier Thesis" of American history, arguing that the frontier experience had shaped the American character and American institutions. Influential writers like Owen Wister and Theodore Roosevelt and artists like Frederic Remington favorably evoked the disappearing world of the cowboy. Roosevelt saw imperialism in the Philippines and elsewhere as a new frontier in which Americans could test themselves.

52. **B.** Buffalo Bill's Wild West Show was a popular example of new forms of entertainment for the urban masses. New forms of entertainment arose for the inhabitants of America's burgeoning cities. In addition to Buffalo Bill's show, which brought the West to city dwellers, the late nineteenth century saw the development of circuses like that of Barnum and Bailey, professional baseball, college football, and by the very end of the period, the early beginnings of the motion picture.

53. **D.** President George Herbert Walker Bush's vision of a "new world order" was most directly made possible by the end of the cold war. With the end of four decades of dangerous confrontation between the United States and its allies and the communist bloc, many people looked forward to a peaceful future. Some commentators talked of "the end of history." Bush's skillful organization of a broad international coalition to expel Saddam Hussein from Kuwait seemed to some to be an example of this new and better path to the future. Even the Soviet Union provided some assistance to the coalition. The triumphant defeat of Saddam Hussein's forces in Kuwait appeared to confirm the "new world order."

54. **A.** President Bush was responding to Iraqi dictator Saddam Hussein's conquest of Kuwait. Following Saddam Hussein's August 2, 1990, invasion of neighboring and oil-rich Kuwait, Bush launched Operation Desert Shield, placing American forces on the border of Kuwait and Saudi Arabia to ensure that Saddam Hussein did not attack that important oil-producing country. After securing United Nations Security Council resolutions denouncing the invasion and demanding Iraqi withdrawal, Bush organized a broad international coalition of forces to liberate Kuwait. On January 16, 1991, the coalition unleashed Operation Desert Storm with an air campaign to soften Iraqi defenses. On February 23, ground forces attacked Kuwait, and by February 27, when combat operations ended, Kuwait had been liberated.

55. **C.** President Bush's "new world order" most directly resembles Woodrow Wilson's Fourteen Points. The Fourteen Points were President Woodrow Wilson's plan for a new liberal world order following the end of World War I and included a League of Nations. Wilson believed that in a world where national self-determination existed in Europe, there would be no secret treaties, freedom of trade would prevail, international disputes would be regulated by the League of Nations, and the world would enter a period of unprecedented peace and prosperity.

Explanations for the Short-Answer Questions

Each short-answer question is worth three points. Give yourself one point for each part of the question (A, B, and C) that you get right. Then enter your score on the scoring worksheet on page 435.

1. **A.** James Ford Rhodes is arguing that both sides underestimated and misunderstood the other at the beginning of the Civil War. He believes that if the North and South had been better informed, they would have avoided war. He says that the South did not realize that the North would unite to suppress the rebellion. He also makes the case that the North dramatically overestimated the number of pro-government loyalists in the South. Most Northerners, including President Abraham Lincoln, at first thought that most Southerners at heart remained loyal to the Union.

B. Both sides believed at first that the war would be short, perhaps decided by a single battle. At the start, President Lincoln only called up 75,000 volunteers to serve for three months. The Confederates were a bit more realistic, setting enlistments at one year or the duration of the war. The Federal general Winfield Scott was ridiculed in the press because he believed that the war would be a long struggle. His plan to gradually build up federal forces and stifle the Southern economy with a blockade was derided as the "anaconda plan."

C. In late 1860 and early 1861, legislators in Congress attempted to find a political compromise to the secession crisis. Senator John Crittenden of Kentucky proposed his "Crittenden Plan," which would have guaranteed the institution of slavery in states where it already existed, and which would have revived the Missouri Compromise line and extended it to the Pacific Ocean. Virginia, Tennessee, Arkansas, and North Carolina did not secede from the Union until after the surrender of Fort Sumter, and they faced the prospect of being called upon to fight fellow Southern slave-owning states. Kentucky attempted to remain neutral in the war, and did not declare for the Union until Confederate forces crossed its border in September 1861.

2. **A.** This is a passage from Betty Friedan's *The Feminine Mystique* (1963), a major work of the "Second Wave" feminism that emerged in the 1960s. Friedan argued that women were facing an existential crisis in the "comfortable concentration camp" of their homes, and could not find personal fulfillment in their role as housewives. She believed women needed to express themselves outside the home. Inspired by the African-American civil rights movement of the 1960s, "Second Wave" feminists (to distinguish them from the "First Wave" feminists who fought for the vote) worked to ensure equality for women in all fields of life, from the workplace to politics. Inspired by these ideas and changing economic circumstances, millions of women entered the workforce in the 1960s and 1970s.

B. Phyllis Schlafly was a woman who headed the conservative Eagle Forum. She defended the importance of the traditional role of women as mothers and housewives. She argued that modern feminists were "bitter women" who were inflicting their personal maladjustment on everyone else. She believed that feminism was hurting children and weakening the family. Schlafly led the successful opposition to the Equal Rights Amendment.

C. Betty Friedan helped found the National Organization for Women (NOW) in 1966. NOW became a major political force lobbying for feminist issues. In 1972, Title IX of the Educational Amendments prohibited discrimination by sex in any educational institution that received federal funding. This revolutionized women's athletics, opening up unprecedented options for female athletes. The 1973 Supreme Court decision *Roe v. Wade* guaranteed women the right to an abortion. Abortion became a polarizing political issue for decades to come. Congress passed an Equal Rights Amendment (ERA) to the Constitution in 1972. This amendment would have mandated that equality of rights could not be limited by sex. Within a short time, 28 states ratified the ERA. At the same time, opposition to the ERA grew in strength. Conservative critics of the ERA argued that such a sweeping amendment would lead to such things as the drafting of women into the military and same-sex bathrooms. As the momentum of the ERA stalled, Congress in 1979 extended the deadline for ratification. The opponents of the ERA, led by Phyllis Schlafly, redoubled their efforts, and by 1982 the campaign to ratify the ERA had failed.

3. A, B. The French and Indian War began because of British and colonial concerns about French activity in the Ohio Valley, and in particular, the construction of Fort Duquense on the site of what is now Pittsburgh, Pennsylvania. The British claimed this territory, and many American colonists wanted to develop lands there. Once the French and Indian War was underway, the British leader William Pitt decided to commit resources to the eradication once and for all of French claims in North America. The French in Canada were decisively defeated outside Quebec at the Battle of the Plains of Abraham, on September 13, 1759. At the 1763 Treaty of Paris, France signed away all its North American lands. The British took control of Canada and all the lands east of the Mississippi River. The British also acquired Florida from Spain. The French and Indian War opened up vast lands for possible American settlement, and removed the major military obstacle to moving westward. The Louisiana Purchase of 1803 greatly expanded the United States. President Thomas Jefferson was very interested in western lands. He envisioned a great republic of independent yeoman farmers. To make this possible, he needed land. When Jefferson learned that the weak government of Spain had transferred the Louisiana Territory to the control of Napoleon's France, Jefferson grew concerned that the French might try to reconstitute a strong empire in America. This disquietude was intensified when Spanish officials closed New Orleans to American trade, threatening the economic well-being of Americans living in the west. Jefferson sent James Monroe to join the American minister in France, Robert Livingston. They were to negotiate the purchase of New Orleans. By this time, Napoleon had decided that Louisiana was a liability. He had lost an army to disease trying to reconquer Haiti, and he assumed that he would be cut off from Louisiana by the British navy once war resumed with Great Britain. Napoleon offered to sell the whole Louisiana Territory to the startled American diplomats. For a purchase price of $15 million, the size of the United States was doubled. Jefferson had some constitutional scruples about the purchase because there was nothing in the Constitution about acquiring territory. He swallowed his scruples, and the Senate quickly ratified the purchase. The Mexican War took place at a time when many Americans were embracing the ideology of Manifest Destiny, and arguing that it was inevitable that American settlements and free institutions would spread throughout North America. President James Polk was elected in 1844 on a platform of American expansionism in Texas and Oregon.

Polk negotiated with the British on the Oregon border. Texas was annexed to the United States just before he became president. Mexico broke off diplomatic relations in protest. Polk sent the diplomat John Slidell to Mexico to resolve issues with the Mexicans. He also sent troops under General Zachary Taylor to the disputed border between Texas and Mexico along the Rio Grande. On April 24, 1846, Mexican forces attacked a troop of American soldiers. This began fighting between the United States and Mexico. Congress declared war on May 13. During the Mexican War, the United States won a series of victories that culminated in General Winfield Scott's occupation of Mexico City. In the 1848 Treaty of Guadalupe Hidalgo, Mexico ceded over 500,000 square miles of territory to the United States in return for a payment of $15 million. This included California, Utah, Nevada, New Mexico and Arizona, and set the border of Texas at the Rio Grande.

C. In the French and Indian War, the expansionism of American colonists was obviously opposed by the French. Many Native Americans also opposed this expansionism, which came at their expense. Many Native Americans allied with the French realized that the defeat of the French would eliminate one of the great restraints on western settlement by the Americans. Following the conclusion of the French and Indian War, the Ottawa leader Pontiac led a brief war against the British, driving them from a number of western outposts. Some opposition to the Louisiana Purchase came from Federalist politicians, unenthusiastic about acquiring more western lands likely disposed to return Democratic Republicans to Congress. Some people, including for a time Jefferson himself, had doubts about the Louisiana Purchase for constitutional reasons, seeing it as an example of federal overreach. The American acquisition of Mexican territory was opposed by the Mexicans, including many settlers in places like California, who did not like seeing their lands overrun by American invaders. There was strong opposition to the Mexican War in the United States. Many Americans believed that the war was unjust and was an excuse to acquire territories for the expansion of slavery. Among the opponents of the war were Congressman Abraham Lincoln and the writer Henry David Thoreau, who refused to pay his poll tax, was briefly arrested and then wrote the essay "Civil Disobedience."

4. **A, B.** In early May 1886, labor disturbances rocked Chicago, Illinois. Two strikers were killed by police at the McCormick Harvester Company. On May 4, a meeting was called at Haymarket Square to protest police brutality. When a phalanx of police arrived to disperse the gathering, someone threw a bomb into their ranks. The police responded by shooting into the crowd. Members of the crowd fired back. In this violent episode seven policemen were killed and 70 others were wounded. Four other people died, and many more injured. The Haymarket Square bombing was blamed on anarchists. These anarchists were radicals who called for the violent overthrow of government. Many were foreign-born. Eight anarchists were arrested and charged with the crime. All were convicted. Five were sentenced to death; one of these committed suicide in prison, and the other four were hanged. The Haymarket Square Riot and its legal aftermath convinced many people that bloody-minded anarchists threatened American institutions. During World War I, the federal government took action to stifle dissent with the Espionage Act of 1917 and the Sedition Act of 1918. The government also worked to suppress political radicalism, with federal agents rounding up activists of the International Workers of the World (IWW). Eugene Debs, the head of the Socialist Party, was sent to prison for criticizing the war. Concerns about radical subversion intensified after the Bolshevik Revolution in Russia late in 1917. In 1919, rapid demobilization led to labor unrest and fears of "Bolshevik" uprisings. A series of terrorist bombings in the spring and early summer, including the explosion of a bomb at the home of Attorney General A. Mitchell Palmer, heightened fears of radicals unleashing a systematic campaign of revolutionary violence. Attorney General Palmer launched a series of raids in November 1919 that arrested hundreds of political radicals. In December, 249 detained aliens, including the famous anarchist writer Emma Goldman, were put on a ship bound for the Soviet Union. More raids followed in 1920. Altogether, around 6,000 people were arrested. The First Red Scare began to die down after a predicted May 1, 1920, Communist outbreak failed to materialize. A terrorist bomb exploded on

September 16 on Wall Street, killing 33 people and wounding over a hundred. Hostility towards political radicals, especially if they were foreign-born continued into the 1920s, playing a role in the *Sacco and Vanzetti* case. The Second Red Scare emerged with the cold war following World War II. Former Communists like Elizabeth Bentley declared that Soviet spy-rings were operating in the U.S. government. The writer Whitaker Chambers accused Alger Hiss, a distinguished former government official, of having spied for the Soviet Union. Congressman Richard Nixon of the House Committee on Un-American Activities (HUAC) pursued the case, and Hiss was eventually convicted of perjury. It was learned that Soviet agents had stolen atomic bomb secrets. For participating in this, Julius and Ethel Rosenberg were convicted of espionage in 1951, and executed in 1953. To address the security issue in the federal government, President Harry Truman created the Loyalty

Review Board to screen federal employees. Anyone who belonged to a politically suspect organization, or who was thought to be a security risk because of behaviors such as alcoholism or homosexuality was removed from public service. Altogether about 3,000 federal employees were fired or resigned.

C. The Haymarket Square Riot decisively weakened the Knights of Labor, the leading labor union in the United States, and the group that had sponsored the strikes in Chicago. Many people assumed that the Knights of Labor were associated with the anarchists. Unfairly labeled a radical organization, the Knights of Labor rapidly lost members. John P. Altgeld, the Democratic Governor of Illinois, investigated the Haymarket bombing, and was troubled enough by the way the trial of the anarchists was conducted to pardon the three remaining defendants. Public opinion was outraged by this decision and Altgeld's political career was ruined. The First Red Scare led to a deep and long-standing hostility to political radicalism in the United States during the 1920s. Attorney General A. Mitchell Palmer hoped to use his crusade against radicalism as a platform to launch a presidential campaign. His overselling the threat led to the frustration of his political hopes. Weariness with the upheaval associated with the First Red Scare played a role in the election of Republican Warren G. Harding in the 1920 presidential election, with his promise of a "return to normalcy." The popular identification of political radicalism with immigrants contributed to the postwar restriction of immigration. In 1921, immigration was limited to 350,000 a year. The 1924 National Origins Act cut this number to 150,000, and set national quotas based on the 1890 Census, which reduced the number of people who could enter the United States from southern and eastern Europe. The Second Red Scare became a major political issue as fears grew of Communist infiltration of the federal government and other American institutions. Both parties worked to burnish their anti-communist credentials. HUAC not only worried about Communists in the government, but conducted investigations of Hollywood because of concerns that Communist messages might be inserted into movies and other forms of entertainment. Ten Hollywood writers and directors with Communist ties refused to cooperate in the investigation and went to jail. Leftists in Hollywood and the entertainment industry were blackballed, and saw their careers derailed. In 1950, Congress passed the McCarran Act, which forced Communists to register with the government, and gave authorities new powers to detain suspect aliens. In 1950, Senator Joseph McCarthy of Wisconsin claimed to have a list of Communists in the federal government. For the next four years, McCarthy launched a series of high-profile investigations in the Senate that made him a popular anti-Communist hero. He rarely could substantiate his accusations, but that did not matter to his supporters, and Senators who publically criticized him suffered politically. Finally, in 1954, after holding televised hearings on Communism in the Army, during which he appeared to be a bully, McCarthy was censured by the Senate. Though McCarthy's power waned, anti-Communism continued to be a force in the United States.

Explanation for the Document-Based Question

To do well on this question, be sure to follow all the directions! Provide a historically plausible thesis that addresses all aspects of the prompt. Your thesis should respond to and go beyond the prompt. Restating or paraphrasing the prompt is not an acceptable thesis. Your thesis can be at the beginning or the end of your essay; it will not be counted if it is anywhere else. Put your response in a broader context, referring to historical factors preceding, following, or taking place at the same time as the subject of the prompt. Be sure to use at least six of the documents. You need to explain the historical significance of the documents; simply referring to or quoting them will not count for points. For at least three of the documents, explain how the point of view of the author, the intended audience, or the document's historical context is relevant to your larger argument. Bring in as much evidence beyond the documents as you can. Evidence that you use to provide context or to deepen discussion of at least three of the documents will not be applied to the overall outside evidence point; you can't double-dip on these evidence points! The more historical information outside the documents that you can provide, the better. Finally, show a complex understanding of the subject matter of the prompt. You can do this in a variety of ways. For instance, you can connect this subject matter to similar historical events in another period. Other possibilities include highlighting differing perspectives on the subject matter, or exploring differing interpretations of the causes of the historical event that you are discussing. Relate this to your larger argument; an off-hand reference will not be counted.

Here is some information to help with this.

1. You might begin with a brief discussion of American foreign policy before the Spanish American War. That war was concluded by the Treaty of Paris (1898). An American military occupation of Cuba under General Leonard Wood followed ratification of the treaty. Wood oversaw the construction of infrastructure, revamped Cuba's political administration, and pioneered health reforms. However, the United States violated the Teller Amendment by not affording Cuba complete independence. Congress retained the right to intervene in Cuban affairs and curbed Cuban autonomy in the Platt Amendment (Document A). You could note that the United States sent troops into Cuba in 1906 and 1912 to quell rebellions and maintained a naval base at Guantanamo. You could also refer to "dollar diplomacy" by discussing how American corporations came to dominate the oil, railroad, and, most importantly, sugar industries. Some might compare American involvement in Cuba to a different policy toward Puerto Rico (Foraker Act of 1900, Jones Act of 1917). You should identify the policies of Theodore Roosevelt, William H. Taft, and Woodrow Wilson. You should examine how the Venezuela crisis (1902) precipitated the announcement of the "Roosevelt Corollary" to the Monroe Doctrine (Document C). You should apply your knowledge of this policy to American intervention in the Dominican Republic in 1905. Some might note that U.S. control of Dominican customs undermined the nation's independence. You might speculate on the results of involvement in the internal affairs of nations. A discussion of American interests in constructing an isthmian canal should include Secretary of State John Hay and overtures to Colombia. You could discuss Philippe Bunau-Varilla, the USS *Nashville,* and Panamanian Revolution. You should note how Panama reacted to the Hay-Bunau-Varilla Treaty (Document B). You could argue that the Hay-Bunau-Varilla Treaty enabled the United States to direct Panamanian affairs. An examination of "dollar diplomacy" under Taft (Document E) may touch upon his Secretary of State Philander C. Knox. You should note how the growing influence

of American mining companies in Nicaragua resulted in military intervention in 1909. You could also note that American banks financed and owned Nicaraguan railroads. American troops returned in 1912 to help maintain the government of Adolfo Diaz. You could state that Document D reflects the belief that the United States used its military to open or preserve economic opportunities. You could point to future problems with the Sandinistas or Contras. You may use Document F to indicate that American imperialism did not enjoy universal support in the United States. You could observe how the United States continued its involvement in the Dominican Republic and Nicaragua (Bryan-Chamorro Treaty, 1914) under Wilson. You could also touch upon how intervention in Haiti in 1915 paralleled involvement with its neighbor. You could discuss Wilson's relationship with Mexico. Alternatively, you could begin with the transfer of power from Porfirio Diaz to Francisco Madero to General Victoriano Huerta and Wilson's refusal to recognize the Huerta regime. You could observe that American businesses wanted to promote stability in Mexico in order to establish favorable trade. You should examine the instability related to conflicts between Huerta and Venustiano Carranza. You should discuss the effects of the Tampico affair (Document G) and seizure of Veracruz. You should also refer to the tenuous relationship between Wilson and Carranza and the issue of recognition. You could touch upon Pancho Villa and raids in the American Southwest that caused Wilson to send General John Pershing and an expeditionary force across the border. You should note that the United States and Mexico approached war and should speculate about the long-term effects of American policy.

Scoring for the Document-Based Question

TASKS	POINTS
Give yourself 1 point if you wrote a thesis that responds to the question with a historically plausible argument. You can't just restate or repeat the question. Your thesis can be expressed in one or more sentences in the introduction or conclusion of your essay.	
Give yourself 1 point if you put the question into a wider historical context. To do this, you should connect the topic of the question to events, developments, or processes that take place before, during, or after the period immediately covered in the question. A brief reference or phrase will not earn you this point.	
There are 2 points possible here. Give yourself 1 point for providing the historical content of at least three of the documents to address the question. Give yourself another point if you supported your argument by using the historical content of at least six of the documents. You must explain the historical significance of these documents. Simply quoting documents does not count. To get the second point, you must relate the six documents to your argument.	
Give yourself 1 point if you used at least one piece of historical information that goes beyond the evidence in the documents. A brief reference to a piece of information will not earn a point. You must describe the how this historical information relates to the question. The historical information for this point must be different from information that you use to earn the point for placing the question in a wider historical context.	
Give yourself 1 point if you explained the point of view of the author, the purpose of the author, or a document's intended audience or historical context for at least three documents. You must explain how or why these are relevant for your argument	
Give yourself 1 point if you demonstrated a complex understanding of the subject of the question, using historical evidence to modify, qualify, or confirm your argument. This understanding must be used to develop your argument, and it can't be merely a brief reference or phrase.	
TOTAL (7 points possible)	

Explanations for the Long Essay Questions

To do well on this question, be sure to follow all the directions! Provide a historically plausible thesis that addresses all aspects of the prompt. Your thesis should respond to and go beyond the prompt. Restating or paraphrasing the prompt is not an acceptable thesis. Use your historical analytical skills to construct your argument, emphasizing such aspects of the subject matter as cause and effect or change and continuity. Your thesis can be at the beginning or the end of your essay; it will not be counted if it is anywhere else. Put your response in a broader context, referring to historical factors preceding, following, or taking place at the same time as the subject of the prompt. Provide as much historical evidence as you can. You want to do this both to provide information that is relevant to the subject matter and also to support your argument. Finally, show a complex understanding of the subject matter of the prompt. You can do this in a variety of ways. For instance, you can connect this subject matter to similar historical events in another period. Other possibilities include highlighting differing perspectives on the subject matter, or exploring differing interpretations of the causes of the historical event that you are discussing. Relate this to your larger argument; an off-hand reference will not be counted.

Here is some information to help with this.

2. You can construct an argument making use of information that can include the following. The English colonies in the south were dominated by a plantation economy sustained through the production of staple crops for the market. In the Chesapeake Bay colonies of Virginia and Maryland, the chief cash crop was tobacco. In South Carolina, it was rice. These crops were labor intensive, and early on, plantations required more labor than could be supplied by the planter and his family. Virginia and Maryland encouraged the importation of indentured servants from Britain through the "headright" system. Planters received 50 acres of land for every laborer they brought into the colony. By 1700, over 100,000 indentured servants were brought into the Chesapeake Bay colonies. Indentured servants worked for their masters for a given term of years, then were released from service and provided with supplies, and possibly a piece of land. Indentured servants could not meet the labor needs in the southern colonies, where the hot and humid climate took a high toll on the new arrivals. Planters looked for other sources of workers. There were efforts to enslave Native Americans, but the susceptibility of Native Americans to European diseases and the relative ease of escape to the frontier made them an unreliable labor source. The first African slaves arrived in Virginia aboard a Dutch ship in 1619. At first, African slaves were too expensive to be bought in large numbers. Over time, their numbers grew. Coming from a tropical climate, Africans were believed to be more adaptable to the southern climate. At the end of the seventeenth century, greater competition in the slave trade led to a larger supply of slaves. At the same time, improving economic conditions in Britain limited the number of potential indentured servants. By the early eighteenth century, African slaves were becoming the major source of labor on southern plantations. Within 50 years, African slaves outnumbered white settlers in South Carolina, and they made up almost half the population of Virginia. At the same time that African slavery was establishing itself, a small number of large landowners were coming to dominate an increasingly hierarchical Southern society. These planters played a disproportionate role in politics and the economy. In Virginia, leading families like the Lees and Fitzhughs formed an informal landed aristocracy. Most white settlers were small farmers who owned few if any slaves. The plantation economy precluded the settlement and growth of many towns. The South was rapidly developing the agrarian model centered on slave-worked plantations that it would carry into the nineteenth century. In the northern colonies, the climate discouraged the growth of a plantation economy. Instead, the North was dominated by

small farms and a more mixed economy. Although indentured servants and slaves were found in the North, farms were more likely to be worked by the members of a family. The temperate climate in New England and elsewhere proved healthier for immigrants from Britain, and the population grew rapidly. Towns and cities played an important role in the more densely populated North. A thriving commercial economy developed, with merchants in Boston, New York, Philadelphia, and elsewhere trading with Europe and the other colonies. American merchants played a key role in the triangular trade between the American colonies, Africa, and the West Indies. The wealth of American seaports supported prosperous artisans and businessmen. Benjamin Franklin's print shop in Philadelphia and Paul Revere's silversmith shop in Boston are examples of the businesses that flourished in the rich northern towns. Many Northerners made their living at sea, either working the large numbers of merchantmen sailing across the Atlantic, or as fisherman, catching and then drying fish for the European market. Abundant sources of timber provided lumber for export and for an extensive shipbuilding industry. An upper class of wealthy merchants and landowners were very influential in the North, but their power was checked to a degree by a larger middle class than existed in the South. A more dynamic economy made for a more egalitarian society.

To do well on this question, be sure to follow all the directions! Provide a historically plausible thesis that addresses all aspects of the prompt. Your thesis should respond to and go beyond the prompt. Restating or paraphrasing the prompt is not an acceptable thesis. Use your historical analytical skills to construct your argument, emphasizing such aspects of the subject matter as cause and effect or change and continuity. Your thesis can be at the beginning or the end of your essay; it will not be counted if it is anywhere else. Put your response in a broader context, referring to historical factors preceding, following, or taking place at the same time as the subject of the prompt. Provide as much historical evidence as you can. You want to do this both to provide information that is relevant to the subject matter and also to support your argument. Finally, show a complex understanding of the subject matter of the prompt. You can do this in a variety of ways. For instance, you can connect this subject matter to similar historical events in another period. Other possibilities include highlighting differing perspectives on the subject matter, or exploring differing interpretations of the causes of the historical event that you are discussing. Relate this to your larger argument; an off-hand reference will not be counted.

Here is some information to help with this.

3. You could begin by talking about the rapidity of industrialization and urbanization in late nineteenth-century America. In 1865, the United States produced virtually no steel; by 1890, it was the largest steel producer in the world. Commensurate growth was seen in the cities. In 1860, no American city could boast a million inhabitants; in 1890, New York, Chicago, and Philadelphia all had more than a million inhabitants. Such rapid growth led to many problems, and American cities struggled to keep up with the paving and plumbing necessary to serve such masses of people. During the late nineteenth century, many cities were run by political "machines," highly organized operations that at their best ran with mechanical efficiency. At the top of the machine was the "boss." The boss often was not the mayor, preferring to exercise power behind the scenes. Political bosses took a very pragmatic, workmanlike attitude to politics. Richard Croker, leader of New York City's Tammany Hall, told a reporter that, "Politics is business." Machine politics could be very big business indeed, leading to famous examples of corruption. An earlier Tammany Hall boss, William Tweed, and his associates may have pocketed over $200,000,000 in city money. Machines more normally brought in money through their control of city contracts, taking payoffs from businessmen wanting to do work for the city. Much of this money went into paying for the army of sub-bosses and ward-heelers, who kept track of voters on the

local level. Another way of supporting a machine operative was to get him a job on the city payroll. Often, machine loyalists might have more than one job. Reformers frequently attacked the machines for their corruption, but they proved quite resilient, in large part because they retained the loyalties of voters. In an era before social security or a social safety net, the operatives of the machines often provided assistance to voters in a time of trouble, their reward being a vote at election time. The machines also helped acculturate immigrants, providing assistance to them when many Americans were denouncing them as a threat to American society. The flow of immigrants increased in the late nineteenth century. In the 1850s through the 1870s two million immigrants arrived each decade. In the 1880s five million arrived. The 1880s also saw a shift in the national origins of immigrants. Previously, most immigrants had come from western and northern Europe. Now they began to come from eastern and southern Europe, from places like Russia and Italy. Many were Catholic and Jewish, and in their clothing and culture, seemed more alien than previous immigrants. Anti-immigrant feeling was nothing new in the United States. The Know-Nothings had flourished in the 1850s, opposing the arrival of Irish and German immigrants. The American Protective Association was launched in 1887, and carried on the tradition of anti-immigrant and anti-Catholic agitation. Over 80 percent of the new immigrants settled in the cities of the North and Midwest. In 1890, one third of the population of Boston and Chicago, and one fourth of Philadelphia were foreign-born. Many of these immigrants lived in crowded ethnic enclaves such as the Lower East Side of New York. Machine politicians were not the only people to provide assistance to immigrants as they adjusted to their new country. The Roman Catholic Church grew dramatically with the influx of immigrants. By 1900, Catholics had become the largest denomination in America, with ten million congregants. The Church oversaw an extensive network of schools, hospitals, and homes for the indigent or aged. Similar developments occurred in the Jewish community. Protestants stepped into the urban mix with evangelists like Dwight Moody, and the liberal ministers of the Social Gospel movement. Idealistic reformers like Jane Addams established settlement houses in urban neighborhoods to assist immigrants. The immigrants joined with Americans moving into the city from the farm to create a vibrant popular culture that laid the groundwork for the mass media and mass entertainments of the twentieth century. People could get their news from the "Yellow Journals" that provided sensationalized headlines and stories, as well as popular features such as comic strips. Mass entertainments included professional sports. Baseball was becoming the national pastime. League play began in the 1870s, and fans could follow the fortunes of their favorite teams in the newspapers if they could not make it to the ballpark. Boxing was also a popular sport, and champions like John L. Sullivan and "Gentleman Jim" Corbett became famous. Also attracting patrons were spectacles such as circuses. In 1881, P.T. Barnum joined with James A. Bailey to put on one of the most successful and long-running circuses in American history, William "Buffalo Bill" Cody reached millions with his Wild West Show, featuring attractions like Annie Oakley, "Little Sure-Shot." Cody's vision of the west, with its dramatic displays of cowboys, Indians, and cavalry became the basis of the westerns that exerted such a popular hold for much of the next century. These and more highbrow intellectual attractions made the city an exciting and desirable destination, despite the many problems of urban America.

To do well on this question, be sure to follow all the directions! Provide a historically plausible thesis that addresses all aspects of the prompt. Your thesis should respond to and go beyond the prompt. Restating or paraphrasing the prompt is not an acceptable thesis. Use your historical analytical skills to construct your argument, emphasizing such aspects of the subject matter as cause and effect or change and continuity. Your thesis can be at the beginning or the end of your essay; it will not be counted if it is anywhere else. Put your response in a broader context, referring to historical factors preceding, following, or taking place at the same time as the subject of the prompt. Provide as much historical evidence as you can. You want to do this both to provide information that is relevant to the subject matter and also to support your argument. Finally, show a complex understanding of the subject matter of the prompt. You can do this in a variety of ways. For instance, you can connect this subject matter to similar historical events in another period. Other possibilities include highlighting differing perspectives on the subject matter, or exploring differing interpretations of the causes of the historical event that you are discussing. Relate this to your larger argument; an off-hand reference will not be counted.

Here is some information to help with this.

4. You could construct an argument making use of information that can include the following. The First World War saw the culmination of the Progressive Era's movement toward greater government regulation of the economy. The federal government took unprecedented steps as it mobilized the American people and the American economy for total war against Imperial Germany. The administration of President Woodrow Wilson and Congress financed the war through the sale of "Liberty Bonds" to the American people, and through steep rises in income taxes and taxes on corporate profits. A War Industries Board (WIB) coordinated the production of war materials, setting prices and allocating resources. A series of "war boards" supervised different aspects of the economy, such as fuel and railroads, which had come under federal control. Herbert Hoover headed the food board, encouraging Americans to conserve different types of foodstuffs. This organization of the economy had mixed results. Initially there was some confusion and missteps as the government sorted out its programs. The United States was still not producing all the military supplies and weapons that it needed when the war ended in November 1918, but during the brief period of the war the United States had made impressive gains in organizing its enormous economic potential. Very important for the future, businessmen and government officials had learned the advantages of working together, establishing a longstanding cooperative relationship between big business and government. In addition to organizing the economy, President Wilson attempted to mobilize public opinion during the war. He created the Committee on Public Information (CPI), headed by the journalist George Creel. The CPI worked to educate Americans about the war through books, pamphlets, posters, and movies. Although the original intent was to provide largely factual material, the CPI ended up producing a lot of overt propaganda. The government also acted to repress dissent. The Espionage Act of 1917 and the Sedition Act of 1918 essentially criminalized public opposition to the war. The Socialist leader Eugene Debs was one of many who went to prison for criticizing the war. The government fomented an atmosphere of hysteria that stigmatized all things German, leading to such phenomena as the renaming of sauerkraut as "liberty cabbage," and also promoted the suppression of radical groups like the International Workers of the World (IWW). This search for internal enemies eventually branched into the postwar First Red Scare. In large part because of the excesses of this attempt to regiment American opinion, there was a reaction against the wartime policies of Woodrow Wilson which resulted in the election of Warren G. Harding to the presidency in 1920, with his promise of a return to "Normalcy." Despite this reaction, elements of the wartime mobilization persisted, especially in the relationship between government and business, fostered in the 1920s by Commerce Secretary Herbert Hoover. The New Deal was influenced by the example of World War I. Once again the federal government intervened heavily in the economy. President Franklin Roosevelt and a number of his subordinates, such as General Hugh Johnson, the Head of the National Recovery Administration (NRA), were veterans of the First World War mobilization. The NRA,

with its attempt to set up industry codes, echoed aspects of the WIB. The mobilization of the United States for total war again in World War II unsurprisingly echoed that of World War I. The war was financed through a combination of loans and high taxes. The Office of Price Administration (OPA) worked to prevent inflation by controlling prices and wages. It also supervised an elaborate system of rationing resources and goods important to the war effort such as sugar, meat, rubber, and gasoline. A succession of federal agencies worked to coordinate industrial production. The War Production Board (WPB) was eventually replaced by the Office of War Mobilization (OWM). Despite this bureaucratic experimentation, the government successfully organized the American industrial base to produce massive amounts of war material, becoming the "arsenal of democracy" during the war. Though Roosevelt created the Office of War Information (OWI) to coordinate war information and propaganda, it never took on the importance of Creel's CPI, and the Roosevelt Administration studiously avoided launching the sort of political repression seen during World War I. The Roosevelt Administration did make one notorious concession to wartime hysteria. In 1942, it rounded up Japanese and Japanese-Americans living on the West Coast and sent them to internment camps. By the end of World War II, after years of expanding federal power, Americans had become used to the government playing an important role in their lives and in the economy. The overall success of the American war effort in World War I would foster a confidence in the abilities of government to meet challenges that would undergird the policies of later presidents such as John F. Kennedy and his New Frontier and Lyndon B. Johnson and his Great Society.

Scoring the Long Essay Question

TASKS	POINTS
Give yourself 1 point if you wrote a thesis that responds to the question with a historically plausible argument. You can't just restate or repeat the question. Your thesis can be expressed in one or more sentences in the introduction or conclusion of your essay.	
Give yourself 1 point if you put the question into a wider historical context. To do this, you should connect the topic of the question to events, developments, or processes that take place before, during, or after the period immediately covered in the question. A brief reference or phrase will not earn you this point.	
You can earn up to 2 points for providing evidence in your essay. Give yourself 1 point if you provided examples of historical information that are relevant to the question. This will increase to 2 points if you used well-chosen examples of historical information that support your argument.	
Give yourself 1 point if you used your historical analytical skills, such as identifying cause and effect, in constructing an argument that addresses the question.	
Give yourself 1 point if you demonstrated a complex understanding of the subject of the question, using historical evidence to modify, qualify, or confirm your argument. This understanding must be used to develop your argument, and it can't be merely a brief reference or phrase.	
TOTAL (6 points possible)	

AP U.S. HISTORY PRACTICE EXAM 1

Scoring Conversion

You can get a rough approximation of your score on the AP U.S. History exam. Use the answer explanations to award yourself points on the free-response questions. Then compute your raw score using the worksheet below. Finally, refer to the table below to translate your raw score to an AP score of 1 to 5.

Section I: Multiple Choice

Number of questions answered correctly (55 possible)   _____ × 1.31 = _____

Section I: Short Answer

Question 1 (3 points possible):   _____ × 4 = _____

Question 2 (3 points possible):   _____ × 4 = _____

Question 3 or 4 (3 points possible):   _____ × 4 = _____

Section II: Document-Based Question

Question 1 (7 points possible)   _____ × 6.43 = _____

Section II: Long Essay Question

Question 2, 3, or 4 (6 points possible)   _____ × 4.5 = _____

RAW SCORE: Add your points in the column above (180 possible):   _____

Conversion Table

RAW SCORE	APPROXIMATE AP SCORE
Low 110s to 180	5
Mid-90s to low 110s	4
Mid-70s to mid-90s	3
Mid-50s to mid-70s	2
Below the mid-50s	1

PRACTICE EXAM 2

Answer Sheet for Multiple-Choice Questions

1 Ⓐ Ⓑ Ⓒ Ⓓ	16 Ⓐ Ⓑ Ⓒ Ⓓ	31 Ⓐ Ⓑ Ⓒ Ⓓ	46 Ⓐ Ⓑ Ⓒ Ⓓ
2 Ⓐ Ⓑ Ⓒ Ⓓ	17 Ⓐ Ⓑ Ⓒ Ⓓ	32 Ⓐ Ⓑ Ⓒ Ⓓ	47 Ⓐ Ⓑ Ⓒ Ⓓ
3 Ⓐ Ⓑ Ⓒ Ⓓ	18 Ⓐ Ⓑ Ⓒ Ⓓ	33 Ⓐ Ⓑ Ⓒ Ⓓ	48 Ⓐ Ⓑ Ⓒ Ⓓ
4 Ⓐ Ⓑ Ⓒ Ⓓ	19 Ⓐ Ⓑ Ⓒ Ⓓ	34 Ⓐ Ⓑ Ⓒ Ⓓ	49 Ⓐ Ⓑ Ⓒ Ⓓ
5 Ⓐ Ⓑ Ⓒ Ⓓ	20 Ⓐ Ⓑ Ⓒ Ⓓ	35 Ⓐ Ⓑ Ⓒ Ⓓ	50 Ⓐ Ⓑ Ⓒ Ⓓ
6 Ⓐ Ⓑ Ⓒ Ⓓ	21 Ⓐ Ⓑ Ⓒ Ⓓ	36 Ⓐ Ⓑ Ⓒ Ⓓ	51 Ⓐ Ⓑ Ⓒ Ⓓ
7 Ⓐ Ⓑ Ⓒ Ⓓ	22 Ⓐ Ⓑ Ⓒ Ⓓ	37 Ⓐ Ⓑ Ⓒ Ⓓ	52 Ⓐ Ⓑ Ⓒ Ⓓ
8 Ⓐ Ⓑ Ⓒ Ⓓ	23 Ⓐ Ⓑ Ⓒ Ⓓ	38 Ⓐ Ⓑ Ⓒ Ⓓ	53 Ⓐ Ⓑ Ⓒ Ⓓ
9 Ⓐ Ⓑ Ⓒ Ⓓ	24 Ⓐ Ⓑ Ⓒ Ⓓ	39 Ⓐ Ⓑ Ⓒ Ⓓ	54 Ⓐ Ⓑ Ⓒ Ⓓ
10 Ⓐ Ⓑ Ⓒ Ⓓ	25 Ⓐ Ⓑ Ⓒ Ⓓ	40 Ⓐ Ⓑ Ⓒ Ⓓ	55 Ⓐ Ⓑ Ⓒ Ⓓ
11 Ⓐ Ⓑ Ⓒ Ⓓ	26 Ⓐ Ⓑ Ⓒ Ⓓ	41 Ⓐ Ⓑ Ⓒ Ⓓ	
12 Ⓐ Ⓑ Ⓒ Ⓓ	27 Ⓐ Ⓑ Ⓒ Ⓓ	42 Ⓐ Ⓑ Ⓒ Ⓓ	
13 Ⓐ Ⓑ Ⓒ Ⓓ	28 Ⓐ Ⓑ Ⓒ Ⓓ	43 Ⓐ Ⓑ Ⓒ Ⓓ	
14 Ⓐ Ⓑ Ⓒ Ⓓ	29 Ⓐ Ⓑ Ⓒ Ⓓ	44 Ⓐ Ⓑ Ⓒ Ⓓ	
15 Ⓐ Ⓑ Ⓒ Ⓓ	30 Ⓐ Ⓑ Ⓒ Ⓓ	45 Ⓐ Ⓑ Ⓒ Ⓓ	

AP U.S. HISTORY
PRACTICE EXAM 2

Section I

Time: 95 minutes

Part A (Multiple Choice)

Part A recommended time: 55 minutes

Directions: Each of the following questions refers to a historical source. These questions will test your knowledge about the historical source and require you to make use of your historical analytical skills and your familiarity with historical themes. For each question select the *best* response and fill in the corresponding oval on your answer sheet.

Questions 1–4 refer to the following quotation.

One of the rights which the freeman has always guarded with most jealous care is that of enjoying the rewards of his own industry. Realizing that the power to tax is the power to destroy and that the power to take a certain amount of property or of income is only another way of saying that for a certain proportion of his time a citizen must work for the government, the authority to impose a tax on the people has been most carefully guarded. ... A government which lays taxes on the people not required by urgent necessity and sound public policy is not a protector of liberty, but an instrument of tyranny. It condemns the citizen to tyranny. One of the first signs of the breaking down of free government is a disregard by the taxing power of the right of the people to their own property. ... Unless the people can enjoy that reasonable security in the possession of their property, which is guaranteed by the Constitution, against unreasonable taxation, freedom is at an end. ... With us economy is imperative. It is a full test of our national character. ... It is always the people who toil that pay.

—Calvin Coolidge, "Economy in the Interest of All," June 30, 1924

1. Which of the following political ideas *best* reflects the perspective of Calvin Coolidge in the passage above?
   A. Taxation is an effective means of redistributing wealth.
   B. Government should be limited.
   C. A bigger government can ensure social justice.
   D. Government has the final say on what people do with their property.

2. Which of the following presidents would be most likely to share Coolidge's sentiments?
   A. Franklin D. Roosevelt
   B. Lyndon B. Johnson
   C. Ronald Reagan
   D. Barack Obama

3. The ideas expressed above were influenced by which of the following?
   A. Widespread prosperity in the 1920s
   B. Widespread economic hardship in the 1920s
   C. The rapid growth of the welfare state in the 1920s
   D. Highly publicized antitrust prosecutions

4. In the passage above Coolidge is reacting against which of the following?
   A. The economic policies of his predecessor, Warren G. Harding
   B. The growing strength of radical politics in America following the Russian Revolution
   C. Populist agitation in the West
   D. The government policies of the Progressive Era

Questions 5–8 refer to the following image.

Theodor de Bry, "The Natives of Florida Worship the Column Erected by the Commander on His First Voyage," *Grand Voyages*, 1591

5. Which of the following most directly reflects the perspective of de Bry in the image above?
   A. The natives of Florida are primitive and superstitious.
   B. The natives of Florida are highly religious.
   C. The Europeans are unjustly exploiting the natives of Florida.
   D. Conflict is inevitable between the natives of Florida and the Europeans.

6. The image above is an expression of which of the following?
   A. European fear of native peoples
   B. European religious fervor
   C. European doubts about the value of exploration
   D. European curiosity about the wider world

7. The column erected by the commander signified which of the following?
   A. European intentions to convert the Native Americans to Christianity
   B. European desires for trade and new products
   C. European desires to establish political control over new territories
   D. European interest in sharing the culture of the Native Americans

8. European rivalries would lead to the French depicted above being driven from Florida by which of the following?
   A. The natives of Florida
   B. The Spanish
   C. The English
   D. The Dutch

Questions 9–12 refer to the following quotation.

Here is the case of a woman employed in the manufacturing department of a Broadway house. It stands for a hundred like her own. She averages three dollars a week. Pay is $1.50 for her room; for breakfast she has a cup of coffee; lunch she cannot afford. One meal a day is her allowance. This woman is young, she is pretty. She has "the world before her." Is it anything less than a miracle if she is guilty of nothing less than the "early and improvident marriage," against which moralists exclaim as one of the prolific causes of the distresses of the poor? Almost any door might seem to offer a welcome escape from such slavery as this. "I feel so much healthier since I got three square meals a day," said a lodger in one of the Girls' Homes. Two young sewing-girls came in seeking domestic service, so that they might get enough to eat. They had been only half-fed for some time, and starvation had driven them to the one door at which the pride of the American-born girl will not permit her to knock, though poverty be the price of her independence.

—Jacob Riis, *How the Other Half Lives*, 1890

9. Which of the following would be *most* likely to support the perspective expressed by Riis in the passage above?
   A. A supporter of Social Darwinism
   B. A Progressive
   C. A businessman
   D. An opponent of immigration

10. The situation faced by the young women in the passage above is *most* directly comparable to which of the following?
   A. American revolutionaries in the 1770s
   B. Slaves in the antebellum South
   C. Populist farmers in the 1890s
   D. Detroit autoworkers in the 1930s

11. Concerns like those expressed by Riis in the passage above led *most* directly to which of the following?
   A. Laws regulating the working conditions of women
   B. Restrictions on immigration
   C. Women's suffrage
   D. Antitrust legislation

12. Riis's work as an investigator of the lives of the poor can *most* directly be associated with which of the following?
   A. Yellow journalism
   B. Abolitionism
   C. The muckrakers
   D. Socialism

Questions 13–16 refer to the following quotation.

It is natural, it is a privilege, I will go farther, it is a right, which all free men claim, that they are entitled to complain when they are hurt. They have a right publicly to remonstrate against the abuses of power in the strongest terms, to put their neighbors upon their guard against the craft or open violence of men in authority, and to assert with courage the sense they have of the blessings of liberty, the value they put upon it, and their resolution at all hazards to preserve it as one of the greatest blessings heaven can bestow. ... But to conclude: The question before the Court and you, Gentlemen of the jury, is not of small or private concern. It is not the cause of one poor printer, nor of New York alone, which you are now trying. No! It may in its consequence affect every free man that lives under a British government on the main of America. It is the best cause. It is the cause of liberty. And I make no doubt but your upright conduct this day will not only entitle you to the love and esteem of your fellow citizens, but every man who prefers freedom to a life of slavery will bless and honor you as men who have baffled the attempt of tyranny, and by an impartial and uncorrupt verdict have laid a noble foundation for securing to ourselves, our posterity, and our neighbors, that to which nature and the laws of our country have given us a right to liberty of both exposing and opposing arbitrary power (in these parts of the world at least) by speaking and writing truth.

> —Andrew Hamilton, concluding argument, libel trial of newspaper editor
> John Peter Zenger, August 4, 1735

13. Which of the following *best* describes the significance of the Zenger trial?
  A. An important incident in opposing British taxation policy
  B. An early attack on the institution of slavery
  C. A landmark case concerning voting rights
  D. A landmark case concerning freedom of expression

14. Andrew Hamilton assumes which of the following?
  A. Americans have more freedoms than people in other countries.
  B. People in other countries have more rights than Americans.
  C. Natural rights are merely ideas that don't really exist.
  D. Rights are granted by the government.

15. The Zenger case can *best* be compared to which of the following?
  A. Abraham Lincoln's suspension of habeas corpus during the Civil War
  B. Government efforts to prevent the publication of the Pentagon Papers in 1971
  C. The trial of the accused Haymarket Square bombers in 1886
  D. The *Brown v. Board of Education* Supreme Court decision of 1954

16. Hamilton's success in the Zenger case *most* directly reflects which of the following?
  A. American desires for independence from Great Britain
  B. American rejection of Enlightenment ideals
  C. A long tradition of self-rule in the American colonies
  D. The weakening of economic ties between America and Great Britain

Questions 17–20 refer to the following cartoon.

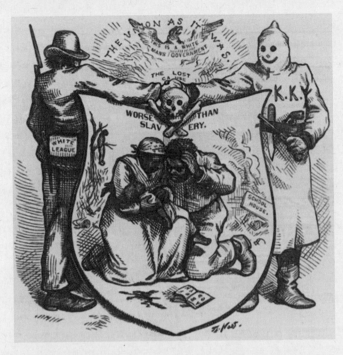

Thomas Nast, "The Union as It Was / The Lost Cause, Worse
Than Slavery," *Harper's Weekly*, October 24, 1874

17. Which of the following *best* expresses the perspective of Thomas Nast in the cartoon above?
    A. The Reconstruction of the South is going well.
    B. The government is not adequately protecting freed slaves.
    C. White people in the South need to stand together.
    D. The Reconstruction of Southern society was a bad idea.

18. The situation described in the cartoon above *most* directly resulted in which of the following?
    A. The passage of the Fifteenth Amendment
    B. The passage of the Homestead Act offering settlers free land in the West
    C. Efforts to create an industrialized New South
    D. The *Plessy v. Ferguson* Supreme Court decision

19. The Southerners in the cartoon above wanted a "Union" characterized by which of the following?
    A. Sovereignty centered in the federal government.
    B. An "American System" of internal improvements.
    C. Sovereignty centered in the states.
    D. The anti-nullification nationalism of Andrew Jackson.

20. The ideas in the cartoon above *most* directly reflect which of the following continuities in U.S. history?
    A. Debates about civil rights
    B. Debates about the use of military power
    C. Debates about gun control
    D. Debates about the role of political parties

Questions 21–24 refer to the following quotation.

Tonight, the daughter of a woman whose highest goal was a future for her children talks to our nation's oldest political party about a future for us all. Tonight, the daughter of working Americans tells all Americans that the future is within our reach, if we're willing to reach for it. Tonight, the daughter of an immigrant from Italy has been chosen to run for (vice) president in the new land my father came to love. . . . Americans want to live by the same set of rules. But under this administration, the rules are rigged against too many of our people. It isn't right that every year the share of taxes paid by individual citizens is going up, while the share paid by large corporations is getting smaller and smaller. . . . It isn't right that young couples question whether to bring children into a world of 50,000 nuclear warheads. That isn't the vision for which Americans have struggled for more than two centuries. . . . Tonight, we reclaim our dream. We're going to make the rules of American life work for all Americans again. . . . The issue is not what America can do for women, but what women can do for America.

—Geraldine Ferraro, Vice Presidential Nomination Acceptance Address, July 19, 1984

21. The nomination of Geraldine Ferraro for vice president was most directly a continuation of which of the following?
   A. The successful assimilation of immigrants to the United States
   B. The struggle for civil rights for ethnic minorities
   C. Increased economic and political opportunities for women
   D. The increasing democratization of the political nomination process

22. The political ideas expressed by Ferraro in the passage above *most* directly reflect those of which of the following?
   A. Colonial opponents of British taxation in the 1760s and 1770s
   B. Abolitionists of the antebellum period
   C. Republicans of the 1920s
   D. New Dealers of the 1930s

23. The ideas expressed in the passage above would *most* directly have strengthened which of the following during the 1980s?
   A. Opposition to the administration's arms buildup
   B. Efforts to deregulate many industries
   C. Efforts to reform the welfare system
   D. Support for the administration's cold war policies

24. Geraldine Ferraro can be most directly compared to which of the following women?
   A. Abigail Adams
   B. Sandra Day O'Connor
   C. Jane Addams
   D. Rosa Parks

Questions 25–28 refer to the following quotation.

These were the first emigrants that we had overtaken, although we had found abundant and melancholy traces of their progress throughout the whole course of the journey. Sometimes we passed the grave of one who had sickened and died on the way. The earth was usually torn up and covered thickly with wolf-tracks. Some had escaped this violation. One morning a piece of plank, standing upright on the summit of a grassy hill, attracted our notice, and riding up to it we found the following words very roughly traced upon it, apparently by a red-hot piece of iron:

MARY ELLIS DIED MAY 7th, 1845
Aged two months.

Such tokens were of common occurrence, nothing could speak more for the hardihood, or rather infatu-ation, of the adventurers, or the sufferings that await them upon their journey. ... We were late in breaking up our camp on the following morning, and scarcely had we ridden a mile when we saw, far in advance of us, drawn against the horizon, a line of objects stretching at regular intervals along the level edge of the prairie. An intervening swell soon hid them from sight, until, ascending it a quarter of an hour after, we saw close before us the emigrant caravan, with its heavy white wagons creeping on in their slow procession, and a large drove of cattle following behind. ... Many were murmuring against the leader they had chosen, and wished to depose him. ... The women were divided between regrets for the homes they had left and apprehension of the deserts and savages before them. ... As we left the ground, I saw a tall slouching fellow with the nasal accent of "down east," contemplating the contents of his tin cup, which he had just filled with water.

"Look here, you," he said: "it's chock full of animals!"

The cup, as he held it out, exhibited in fact an extraordinary variety and profusion of animal and vegetable life.

—Francis Parkman, *The Oregon Trail: Sketches of Prairie and Rocky-Mountain Life*, 1849

25. The situation described in the passage above led *most* directly to which of the following?
    A. Passage of the Homestead Act
    B. Passage of the Northwest Ordinance
    C. The *Dred Scott* Supreme Court decision
    D. Passage of the Indian Removal Act

26. The actions of the people in the passage above *most* directly reflect the influence of which of the following political ideals?
    A. Popular sovereignty
    B. Jacksonian Democracy
    C. Manifest Destiny
    D. Progressivism

27. The experiences of the people encountered by Francis Parkman can be *most* directly compared to those of which of the following?
    A. The Spanish conquistadors
    B. The Pilgrims
    C. The Apollo astronauts
    D. Cowboys on the first cattle drives of the 1860s

28. Which of the following had *most* directly anticipated and desired the movement described by Parkman?
    A. Benjamin Franklin
    B. James Madison
    C. Alexander Hamilton
    D. Thomas Jefferson

Questions 29–32 refer to the following quotation.

Our leaders talk about stopping aggression from the north, but this was a struggle among groups of Vietnamese until we intervened. We seem bent upon saving the Vietnamese from Ho Chi Minh even if we have to kill them and demolish their country to do it. As the native people survey bombed-out villages, women and children burned by napalm, rice crops destroyed and cities overrun with our military personnel, they are doubtless saying secretly of the Vietcong guerillas and of the American forces, "A plague on both your houses." . . . Stop the bombing, north and south, end search and destroy offensive sweeps, and confine our military action to holding operations on the ground. Bombing the north has failed to halt or seriously check the flow of troops to the south and may, in fact, have prompted a much greater war effort by Hanoi.

—Senator George McGovern, "The Lessons of Vietnam," April 25, 1967

29. Which of the following opinions from the 1960s *most* directly reflects the perspective of George McGovern's speech?
   A. Americans must maximize their technological edge in Vietnam.
   B. American bombing in Vietnam is step by step leading to progress in the war.
   C. American bombing in Vietnam is a failure.
   D. America must not give in to defeatism about the war in Vietnam.

30. The sentiments expressed in the speech above *most* directly influenced which of the following?
   A. The passage of the War Powers Act of 1973
   B. The Tet Offensive of 1968
   C. The resignation of Richard Nixon in 1974
   D. The emergence of a youth counterculture

31. The sentiments expressed in the speech *most* directly reflect which popular attitude that became widespread in the 1960s?
   A. The United States should embrace isolationism.
   B. The United States should use force to spread American ideals abroad.
   C. American commanders were not being given enough weapons in Vietnam.
   D. Government statements about Vietnam could not be trusted.

32. Political discord during the Vietnam War most closely resembled the political dissensions during which of the following?
   A. The Spanish-American War
   B. The Mexican War
   C. World War I
   D. World War II

Questions 33–36 refer to the following quotation.

On Being Brought from Africa to America

'Twas mercy brought me from my Pagan land,
Taught my benighted soul to understand
That there's a God, that there's a Saviour too;
Once I redemption neither sought nor knew.
Some view our sable race with scornful eye,
"Their colour is a diabolic die."
Remember, Christians, Negroes, black as Cain,
May be refin'd, and join th' angelic train.

—Phillis Wheatley, *Poems on Various Subjects, Religious and Moral*, 1773

33. The ideas expressed in Phillis Wheatley's poem *most* directly reveal the influence of which of the following?

A. The First Great Awakening

B. The natural rights theory of John Locke

C. British ideas about social hierarchy

D. Eighteenth century scientific racism

34. The sentiments expressed in Wheatley's poem *most* directly reflect which of the following continuities in U.S. history?

A. Debates over religious freedom

B. Debates over social justice

C. Debates over immigration

D. Debates over freedom of expression

35. The literary success of Phillis Wheatley led *most* directly to questions about which of the following?

A. The granting of political rights to women

B. The harsh treatment of pro-British Loyalists

C. The moral justification of slavery

D. The legitimacy of established churches in the states

36. The point of Wheatley's poem can *best* be compared to which of the following?

A. The Declaration of Independence

B. Jonathan Edwards's sermon "Sinners in the Hands of an Angry God"

C. The Seneca Falls Declaration of Rights and Sentiments

D. Martin Luther King, Jr.'s "I Have a Dream" speech

Questions 37–40 refer to the following quotation.

Wrong as we think slavery is, we can yet afford to leave it alone where it is, because that much is due to the necessity arising from its actual presence in the nation; but can we, while our votes will prevent it, allow it to spread into the National Territories, and to overrun us here in these Free States? If our sense of duty forbids this, then let us stand by our duty, fearlessly and effectively. Let us be diverted by none of those sophistical contrivances wherewith we are so industriously plied and belabored—contrivances such as groping for some middle ground between the right and the wrong, vain as the search for a man who should be neither a living man nor a dead man—such a policy of "don't care" on a question about which all true men do care—such as Union appeals beseeching true Union men to yield to Disunionists, reversing the divine rule, and calling not the sinners, but the righteous to repentance. . . . Neither let us be slandered from our duty by false accusations against us, nor frightened from it by menaces of destruction to the Government nor of dungeons to ourselves. LET US HAVE FAITH THAT RIGHT MAKES MIGHT, AND IN THAT FAITH, LET US, TO THE END, DARE TO DO OUR DUTY AS WE UNDERSTAND IT.

—Abraham Lincoln, Cooper Union Address, February 27, 1860

37. In his Cooper Union Address, Abraham Lincoln called for which of the following?

A. Northern voters to resist the demands of pro-slavery advocates

B. The seceded Southern states to return to the Union

C. More support for the war effort

D. Compromise with proslavery advocates

38. A member of which of the following political parties would have been most likely to support Lincoln's position?

A. Democrat

B. Republican

C. Progressive

D. Federalist

39. Lincoln and his supporters called for which of the following in 1860?

A. The abolition of slavery

B. Preventing the expansion of slavery into the western territories

C. Military action against the South

D. Strict enforcement of the Fugitive Slave Act

40. Lincoln's Cooper Union Address can best be compared to

A. the Declaration of Independence.

B. the Northwest Ordinance.

C. Franklin Roosevelt's "Arsenal of Democracy" speech in 1940.

D. William Jennings Bryan's "Cross of Gold" speech in 1896.

Questions 41–44 refer to the following quotation.

They ask us how we shall govern these new possessions. I answer: Out of local conditions and the necessities of the case methods of government will grow. If England can govern foreign lands, so can America. If Germany can govern foreign lands, so can America. If they can supervise protectorates, so can America. Why is it more difficult to administer Hawaii than New Mexico or California? Both had a savage and an alien population; both were more remote from the seat of government when they came under our dominion than the Philippines are to-day.

Will you say by your vote that American ability to govern has decayed; that a century's experience in self-rule has failed of a result? Will you affirm by your vote that you are an infidel to American power and practical sense? Or will you say that ours is the blood of government; ours the heart of dominion; ours the brain and genius of administration? Will you remember that we do but what our fathers did—we but pitch the tents of liberty farther westward, farther southward—we only continue the march of the flag?

—Albert Beveridge, "The March of the Flag," Indianapolis, September 16, 1898

41. In "The March of the Flag," Albert Beveridge supported which of the following?
   A. Populism
   B. War with Great Britain
   C. Constitutional reform in the United States
   D. The creation of an American overseas empire

42. Beveridge's speech was a response to which of the following?
   A. The purchase of Alaska
   B. The Mexican War
   C. The Spanish-American War
   D. World War I

43. The theme of Beveridge's speech can most directly be compared to which of the following?

   A. The Monroe Doctrine
   B. Containment
   C. Manifest Destiny
   D. The ideology of states' rights

44. The policy advocated by Beveridge foreshadowed which of the following?
   A. The rise of the United States to the status of a great power
   B. A period of growing isolationism
   C. A period of laissez-faire economics
   D. Growing support for constitutional strict constructionism

Questions 45–48 refer to the following quotation.

BECAUSE no People can be truly happy, though under the greatest Enjoyment of Civil Liberties, if abridged of the Freedom of their Consciences, as to their Religious Profession and Worship: And Almighty God being the only Lord of Conscience, Father of Lights and Spirits; and the Author as well as Object of all divine Knowledge, Faith and Worship, who only doth enlighten the Minds, and persuade and convince the Understanding of People, I do hereby grant and declare, That no Person or Persons, inhabiting in this Province or Territories, who shall confess and acknowledge One almighty God, the Creator, Upholder and Ruler of the World; and profess him or themselves obliged to live quietly under the Civil Government, shall be in any Case molested or prejudiced, in his or their Person or Estate, because of his or their conscientious Persuasion or Practice, nor be compelled to frequent or maintain any religious Worship, Place or Ministry, contrary to his or their Mind. . . .

> —William Penn, Charter of Privileges Granted by William Penn, esq., to the Inhabitants of Pennsylvania and Territories, October 28, 1701

45. Which of the following best describes the colony of Pennsylvania?

A. A charter colony in which the king granted a charter to a group of businessmen or colonists

B. A proprietary colony in which the king entrusted government to a proprietor and his family

C. A royal colony in which the king appointed the governor

D. An independent colony governed outside the authority of the king

46. William Penn was a member of which of the following persecuted religious groups?
A. Roman Catholics
B. Puritans
C. Quakers
D. Anglicans

47. Because of Penn's Charter of Privileges, Pennsylvania became

A. one of the most religiously diverse colonies in British America.

B. one of the least religiously diverse colonies in America.

C. notorious for witch hunting and popular superstition.

D. known for its hostility to traditional religious practices.

48. Penn's Charter of Privileges can be seen as a forerunner to which of the following?
A. The Declaration of Independence
B. The Fourteen Points
C. The Gettysburg Address
D. The First Amendment to the Constitution

Questions 49–52 refer to the following quotation.

The man who mounted the steps of the Capitol, March 4, 1801, to claim the place of an equal between Pitt and Bonaparte, possessed a character which showed itself in acts; but person and manner can be known only by contemporaries, and the liveliest description was worth less than a moment of personal contact. Jefferson was very tall, six feet two-and-a-half inches in height; sandy-complexioned; shy in manner, seeming cold; awkward in attitude, and with little in his bearing that suggested command. . . . His skin was thin, peeling from his face on exposure to the sun, giving it a tettered appearance. This sandy face, with hazel eyes and sunny aspect; this loose, shackling person; this rambling and often brilliant conversation, belonged to the controlling influences of American history, more necessary to the story than three-fourths of the official papers, which only hid the truth. Jefferson's personality during these eight years appeared to be the government, and impressed itself, like that of Bonaparte, although by a different process, on the mind of the nation. In the village simplicity of Washington, he was more than a king, for he was alone in social as well as in political pre-eminence. Except the British Legation, no house in Washington was open to general society; the whole mass of politicians, even the Federalists, were dependent on Jefferson and "The Palace" for amusement; and if they refused to go there, they "lived like bears, brutalized and stupefied."

—Henry Adams, *History of the United States During the Administration of Thomas Jefferson*, 1889

49. As the great-grandson of President John Adams, the historian Henry Adams might have been expected to be which of the following?

    A. Critical of the policies of Thomas Jefferson
    B. Supportive of the policies of Thomas Jefferson
    C. Critical of the Constitutional Convention
    D. More interested in the French and Indian War

50. Thomas Jefferson's victory in the election of 1800 was important because
    A. he was the first southerner to become president.
    B. it was the first time the presidency shifted from one political party to another.
    C. he believed it was necessary to go to war with Great Britain.
    D. he encouraged the rapid industrialization of the United States.

51. Although Jefferson believed that government should be small and limited, once in office he
    A. created a spoils system that bloated the size of the bureaucracy.
    B. laid the foundations of the welfare state.
    C. called for an ambitious program of road building and public works.
    D. vigorously exercised federal power in foreign affairs.

52. According to Henry Adams, the city of Washington in 1801 was
    A. the hub of American economic power.
    B. rapidly turning into the "Paris" of North America.
    C. still an underdeveloped cultural backwater.
    D. still under the control of the British.

Questions 53–55 refer to the following quotation.

Perhaps, however, I am more conscious of the importance of civil liberties in this particular moment of our history than anyone else, because I travel through the country and meet people and see things that have happened to little people, I realize what it means to democracy to preserve our civil liberties.

All through the years we have had to fight for civil liberty, and we know that there are times when the light grows rather dim, and every time that happens democracy is in danger. Now, largely because of the troubled state of the world as a whole, civil liberties have disappeared in many other countries.

It is impossible, of course, to be at war and keep freedom of the press and freedom of speech and freedom of assembly. They disappear automatically. And so in many countries where ordinarily they were safe, today they have gone. In other countries, even before war came, not only freedom of the press and freedom of assembly, and freedom of speech disappeared, but freedom of religion disappeared.

And so we know here in this country, we have a grave responsibility. We are at peace. We have no reason for the fears which govern so many other peoples throughout the world; therefore, we have to guard the freedoms of democracy.

— Eleanor Roosevelt, Address to the American Civil Liberties Union, Chicago, Illinois, March 14, 1940

53. In her speech, Eleanor Roosevelt alluded to the earlier threat to civil liberties created by which of the following?
A. World War I
B. The New Deal
C. The cold war
D. The Great Depression

54. An example of the threat to civil liberties that concerned Roosevelt was which of the following?
A. The Social Security Act
B. Executive Order 9066 interning Japanese Americans
C. The GI Bill
D. The baby boom

55. Roosevelt's concerns can most directly be compared to those of the people who debated which of the following?
A. The Gulf of Tonkin Resolution of 1964
B. The Voting Rights Act of 1965
C. The USA Patriot Act of 2001
D. The Affordable Care Act of 2010

Go on to Part B. ➔

Part B (Short Answer)

Part B recommended time: 40 minutes

Directions: Answer three questions. You must answer questions 1 and 2, and you can choose to answer either 3 or 4. Carefully read and follow the directions for each question. Some will refer to historical sources. These questions will require you to make use of your historical analytical skills and your familiarity with historical themes. These questions do *not* require you to develop a thesis in your responses.

Question 1 is based on the following passage:

Behold, then, the unlettered man of the West, the nursling of the wilds, the farmer of the Hermitage, little versed in books, unconnected by science with the tradition of the past, raised by the people to the highest pinnacle of honor, to the central post in the civilization of republican freedom, to the station where all the nations of the earth would watch his actions—where his words would vibrate through the civilized world, and his spirit be the moving star to guide the nations. ... The man of the West came as the inspired prophet of the West: he came as one free from the bonds of hereditary or established custom; he came with no superior but conscience, nor oracle but his native judgment; and, true to his origin and his education—true to the conditions and circumstances of his advancement, he valued right more than usage; he reverted from the pressure of established interests to the energy of first principles.

—George Bancroft, Eulogy on Andrew Jackson, 1845

1. Using the excerpt, answer A, B, and C.
   A. Briefly describe the historian and politician George Bancroft's assessment of Andrew Jackson.
   B. Briefly explain ONE historical event or development that supports Bancroft's assessment of Andrew Jackson.
   C. Briefly explain the perspective of someone opposed to Bancroft's assessment of Andrew Jackson.

Question 2 is based on the following passages:

It makes very little difference, however, where one opens the record of the history of the Indians; every page and every year has its dark stain. The story of one tribe is the story of all, varied only by differences of time and place; but neither time nor place makes any difference in the main facts. Colorado is as greedy and unjust in 1880 as was Georgia in 1830 and Ohio in 1795; and the United States Government breaks promises now as deftly as then, and with an added ingenuity from long practice.

—Helen Hunt Jackson, *A Century of Dishonor*, 1881

The settler and pioneer have at bottom had justice on their side; this great continent could not have been kept as nothing but a game preserve for squalid savages. Moreover, to the most oppressed Indian nations the whites often acted as a protection, or, at least, they deferred instead of hastening their fate.

—Theodore Roosevelt, *The Winning of the West*, 1889

2. Using the excerpts, answer A, B, and C.
   A. Briefly explain the perspective of Helen Hunt Jackson.
   B. Briefly explain the perspective of Theodore Roosevelt.
   C. Briefly explain ONE example of a development that supports the argument of one of the excerpts.

Answer EITHER Question 3 OR Question 4.

3. Answer A, B, and C.
   A. Briefly explain how ONE of the following was important in the formation of a distinctly American identity in the colonies.
      The Great Awakening
      The French and Indian War
      Resistance to the Stamp Act and other examples of British taxation
   B. Briefly explain how a SECOND of these options was important in the formation of a distinctly American identity in the colonies.
   C. Briefly explain how ONE of these events influenced the American Revolution.

4. Answer A, B, and C.
   A. Briefly explain how ONE of the following groups gained in rights and status during the twentieth century.
      Women
      African Americans
      Mexican Americans
   B. Briefly explain how a SECOND of these options gained in rights and status during the twentieth century.
   C. Briefly explain ONE example of how the experience of one of these groups was influenced by one of the others.

STOP. End of Section I, Part B.

Section II

Time: 100 minutes

Part A (Document–Based Question)*

Part A recommended time: 60 minutes

Directions: Use the documents to answer the question. You may want to spend up to 15 minutes outlining your response and 45 minutes writing the essay that answers the question.

Provide a thesis that responds to all elements of the question with a historically plausible argument. This thesis of one or more sentences must be in the introduction or conclusion.

Connect historical evidence supporting your argument to a broader historical context that reaches beyond the time frame of the question.

Use at least three of the documents to address the topic of the question.

Support your argument with evidence from at least six of the seven documents.

Support your argument by analyzing historical evidence that comes from outside the documents.

Base your analysis of no less than three documents on at least one of the following: the point of view of the author, the purpose of the author, the intended audience of the document, the historical context of the document.

Demonstrate a complex understanding of the subject of the question, using historical evidence to modify, qualify, or confirm your argument.

1. To what extent did the Supreme Court advance or inhibit Progressive regulation of corporations in the period 1885 to 1920?

Document A
Source: U.S. v. Debs, et al., 1894 (response to the Pullman Strike)

That the original design [of the Sherman Antitrust Act] to suppress trusts and monopolies . . . is clear; but it is equally clear that further and more comprehensive purpose came to be entertained. . . . Combinations are condemned, not only when they take the form of trusts, but in whatever form found, if they be in restraint of trade.

Document B
Source: U.S. v. E. C. Knight Company, 1895

Congress did not attempt . . . to make criminal the acts of persons in the acquisition and control of property which the states of their residence or creation sanctioned or permitted.

The contracts and acts of the defendants related exclusively to the acquisition of the Philadelphia refineries and the business of sugar refining in Pennsylvania, and bore no direct relation to commerce between states or with foreign countries. The object was manifestly private gain in the manufacture of the commodity, but not through the control of interstate or foreign commerce.

Document C
Source: Smyth v. Ames, 1898

By the 14th Amendment it is provided that no state shall deprive any person of property without the due process of law nor deny to any person within its jurisdiction the equal protection of laws. That corporations are persons within this amendment is now settled.

[The Court] adjudged that the enforcement of the schedules of rates established by the [Nebraska law reducing railroad rates] . . . would deprive the railroad companies of the compensation they were legally entitled to receive.

Document D
Source: Lochner v. New York, 1905

The act [state law limiting maximum hours of bakers] is not . . . a health law, but is an illegal interference with the rights of individuals, both employers and employees, to make contracts regarding labor upon such terms as they may think best. . . . Statutes of the nature of that under review, limiting the hours in which grown and intelligent men may labor to earn their living, are meddlesome interferences with the rights of the individual, and they are not saved from condemnation by the claim that they are passed upon the subject of the health of the individual whose rights are interfered with.

Document E
Source: Muller v. Oregon, 1908

The two sexes differ in structure of body, . . . in the amount of physical strength in the capacity for long-continued labor, . . . the influence of vigorous health upon the future well-being of the race, . . . and in the capacity to maintain the struggle for subsistence. This difference justifies a difference in legislation.

For these reasons, and without questioning in any respect the decision in Lochner v. New York, we are of the opinion that it cannot be adjudged that the [state law limiting the hours women may work] is in conflict with the Federal Constitution, so far as it respects the work of a female in a laundry.

Document F
Source: Standard Oil Company of New Jersey v. United States, 1911

The public policy has been to prohibit . . . contracts or acts entered into with the intent to wrong the public and which unreasonably restrict competitive conditions, limit the rights of individuals, restrain the free flow of commerce, or bring about public evils such as the enhancement of prices.

The combination of the defendants in this case is an unreasonable and undue restraint of trade in petroleum and its products moving in interstate commerce, and falls within the prohibitions of the [Sherman Antitrust Act].

Document G
Source: Wilson v. New, 1917

The effect of the [Adamson Act] is not only to establish permanently an eight-hour standard for work and wages as between the [railroad] carrier and employees affected, but also to fix a scale of minimum wages for the eight-hour day and proportionately for overtime.

Viewed as an act establishing an eight-hour day as the standard of service by employees, the statute is clearly within the power of Congress under the commerce clause.

Viewed as an act fixing wages, the statute merely illustrates the character of regulation essential, and hence permissible, for the protection of the public right.

Go on to Part B. ➔

Part B (Long Essay)

Part B recommended time: 40 minutes

Directions: Answer *one* of the following questions.

Provide a thesis that responds to all elements of the question with a historically plausible argument. This thesis of one or more sentences must be in the introduction or conclusion.

Connect historical evidence supporting your argument to a broader historical context that reaches beyond the time frame of the question.

Provide examples of historical information that are relevant to the question.

Use well-chosen examples of historical information that support your argument.

Use historical reasoning to construct an argument that answers the question.

Demonstrate a complex understanding of the subject of the question, using historical evidence to modify, qualify, or confirm your argument.

2. Evaluate the extent to which differing ideas about the nature of government shaped the emergence of political parties in the 1780s and 1790s.

3. Evaluate the extent to which reform movements played an important role in shaping American society from 1820–1860.

4. Evaluate the extent of social and political changes in the lives of women during the period 1900–1930.

STOP. End of Section II.

ANSWERS TO PRACTICE EXAM 2

Multiple Choice

1. B	15. B	29. C	43. C
2. C	16. C	30. A	44. A
3. A	17. B	31. D	45. B
4. D	18. D	32. B	46. C
5. A	19. C	33. A	47. A
6. D	20. A	34. B	48. D
7. C	21. C	35. C	49. A
8. B	22. D	36. D	50. B
9. B	23. A	37. A	51. D
10. D	24. B	38. B	52. C
11. A	25. A	39. B	53. A
12. C	26. C	40. D	54. B
13. D	27. B	41. D	55. C
14. A	28. D	42. C	

Count the number you got correct and enter this number on the scoring worksheet on page 476.

Explanations for the Multiple-Choice Questions

1. **B.** The political idea that *best* reflects the perspective of President Calvin Coolidge in the passage is that government should be limited. A limited government would be an inexpensive government. Hence Coolidge opposed heavy taxes on citizens. He believed overtaxation hurt taxpayers, took money out of the private economy, and encouraged wasteful government spending.

2. **C.** The president most likely to share Coolidge's sentiments would be Ronald Reagan. President Reagan also worked to limit the size of government and cut taxes. Reagan admired Coolidge and prominently displayed a portrait of him in the White House.

3. **A.** The ideas expressed by Coolidge were influenced by the widespread prosperity in the 1920s. Coolidge believed that the growing prosperity of most Americans was the result of keeping government out of the way of business and allowing people to keep more of their money by reducing taxes. His ideas proved popular with voters. Taking office after the death of President Warren Harding in 1923, he won election to the presidency in his own right in 1924. His Republican party kept control of Congress throughout the 1920s.

4. **D.** In the passage, Coolidge is reacting against the government policies of the Progressive Era. The Progressives greatly expanded the role of the government in the economy and in American life. This culminated in the policies of President Woodrow Wilson during World War I, when the government coordinated much of the economy and monitored what people said about the war. Following the war, there was a reaction against such control. Warren Harding successfully appealed to this sentiment with his call for a "return to normalcy" in 1920. Coolidge was Harding's vice president and continued his policies.

5. **A.** de Bry in the image reflects the perspective that the natives of Florida are primitive and superstitious. The image shows the Native Americans worshipping a column erected by the French explorers, indicating that they thought the Europeans possessed special powers. The Europeans tended to regard the natives of America as heathens who had to be Christianized and subjected to the tutelage of their more advanced civilization.

6. **D.** The image is an expression of European curiosity about the wider world. This illustration is one of many that de Bry made picturing the peoples of the New World. In addition to looking for lands to conquer and new sources of trade, Europeans were interested in learning more about the world. This desire for learning was inspired by the Renaissance and the Scientific Revolution.

7. **C.** The column erected by the French commander signified European desires to establish political control over new territories. The European powers competed to acquire new territories in the New World, which they hoped would be rich sources of valuable goods and trade.

8. **B.** European rivalries would lead to the French being driven from Florida by the Spanish. In 1564, French Protestants, called "Huguenots," built Fort Caroline, near modern-day Jacksonville. The following year Spanish forces from St. Augustine destroyed the settlement. The French retaliated with an attack of their own but were never able to reestablish themselves in Florida.

9. **B.** A Progressive would be most likely to support the perspective expressed by Riis in the passage. The Progressives were middle-class reformers interested in addressing the problems created by the rapid industrialization and urbanization of the United States during the first two decades of the twentieth century. Many Progressives worked to ameliorate labor conditions for workers.

10. **D.** The situation faced by the young women in the passage is most directly comparable to that of Detroit autoworkers in the 1930s. The autoworkers also needed better wages and working conditions. They staged famous sit-down strikes in 1936 and 1937 to win recognition of the United Auto Workers (UAW) union.

11. **A.** Concerns like those expressed by Riis in the passage led most directly to laws regulating the working conditions of women. During the Progressive Era, laws were passed

to protect women in the workplace. The great lawyer Louis Brandeis persuaded the Supreme Court to uphold a law mandating an eight-hour workday for women in *Muller v. Oregon* (1908).

12. **C.** Riis's work as an investigator of the lives of the poor can most directly be associated with the muckrakers. Muckrakers were Progressive Era journalists who exposed corruption and social injustice in American life. Examples of muckrakers were Lincoln Steffens, who wrote about urban political machines, Ida Tarbell, who documented the history of John Rockefeller's Standard Oil, and Ray Stannard Baker, who explored the living conditions of African Americans.

13. **D.** The Zenger trial was a landmark case concerning freedom of expression. Zenger was a newspaper editor who had published criticisms of the royal governor of New York. Brought to trial for seditious libel, the judge instructed the jury that the truth or falsity of what Zenger wrote was immaterial; the law held that printing unflattering commentary on a royal governor was enough to declare the defendant guilty. The defense lawyer Andrew Hamilton appealed to the jurors' love of liberty and asked them to oppose government tyranny. The jury voted to acquit Zenger. This case helped ensure freedom of the press and freedom of speech in colonial America.

14. **A.** Andrew Hamilton assumes that Americans have more freedoms than people in other countries. Hamilton appeals to the natural rights enjoyed by free men and to the liberties accorded to British subjects. He urges the jurors to vindicate these rights against arbitrary power "in these parts of the world at least," indicating a sense that Americans are freer than people living elsewhere.

15. **B.** The Zenger case can best be compared to government efforts to prevent the publication of the Pentagon Papers in 1971. Daniel Ellsberg, a former Defense Department official, leaked a secret Pentagon study of the origins of the Vietnam War to the *New York Times*. The Nixon administration went to court to stop the newspaper from publishing these documents. Ultimately, the Supreme Court upheld the right of the newspaper to publish the Pentagon Papers in *New York Times Co. v. United States* (1971). This decision was a strong affirmation of First Amendment protections for a free press.

16. **C.** Hamilton's success in the Zenger case most directly reflects a long tradition of self-rule in the colonies. Hamilton's argument to the jury assumed a lack of deference on the part of the jurors toward established authority. This reflected a century during which the colonies had been largely self-governing. Hamilton correctly expected that the jurors knew that they had rights and would feel free to defend them. This tradition of self-government would be very important during the political crisis leading to American independence.

17. **B.** The perspective of Thomas Nast's cartoon is that the government is not adequately protecting freed slaves. Nast was worried that Southern whites working through organizations like the Ku Klux Klan were returning the South to places where African Americans were oppressed. He notes that in some ways the situation is worse than it was under slavery, with the terroristic Klan lynching freedmen and burning schools.

18. **D.** The situation described in the cartoon most directly resulted in the *Plessy v. Ferguson* Supreme Court decision. *Plessy v. Ferguson* (1896) ruled that separate but equal facilities for whites and African Americans were constitutional. This court case reflected a retreat on the part of the government in protecting African-American rights in the South that began with the end of Reconstruction in 1877. Many in the North grew tired of trying to force Southern whites to accept African-American rights. While *Plessy v. Ferguson* paid lip service to equality, in reality Southern whites were able to impose Jim Crow laws on African Americans.

19. **C.** The Southerners in the cartoon wanted a "Union" characterized by sovereignty centered in the states. The doctrine of states' rights had been used before the Civil War to protect the institution of slavery. Following the end of Reconstruction, Southerners would invoke states' rights to justify the enforcement of Jim Crow laws.

20. **A.** The ideas in the cartoon reflect conti-nuities in debates about civil rights. Thomas Nast, at a late stage in Reconstruction, was worried about African-American rights. His cartoon was a plea for the enforcement of laws passed to protect African Americans, includ-ing the Thirteenth, Fourteenth, and Fifteenth Amendments to the Constitution.

21. **C.** The nomination of Geraldine Ferraro for vice president was most directly a continu-ation of increased economic and political opportunities for women. The women's move-ment of the 1960s was remarkably successful in altering people's expectations for women. Large numbers of women entered the work-force in the 1970s and 1980s and flourished in fields that had previously been largely closed to them. Ferraro's nomination was an emblematic first for women in politics.

22. **D.** The political ideas expressed by Ferraro in the passage most directly reflect those of New Dealers of the 1930s. Ferraro was a liberal Democrat. Like the New Dealers of Franklin Roosevelt's day, she believed that government could be used to help the ordinary in a coun-try dominated by the wealthy and big busi-ness. She opposed President Ronald Reagan's efforts to limit the size of government and deregulate business.

23. **A.** The ideas expressed by Ferraro would have most directly strengthened opposition to the administration's arms buildup. During the 1980s, President Ronald Reagan increased the size of the American military to carry on the cold war with the Soviet Union from a posi-tion of strength. Like many liberal Democrats, Ferraro opposed the size of this increase in military spending, preferring to spend money on domestic social programs.

24. **B.** Geraldine Ferraro can most directly be compared to Sandra Day O'Connor. In 1981, O'Connor became the first woman to serve on the Supreme Court, after being nominated by President Ronald Reagan. Like O'Connor, Ferraro was blazing new trails for women in the 1980s.

25. **A.** The situation described in the passage led most directly to the Homestead Act. Like the people Parkman met on the Oregon Trail, many Americans regarded the West as a land of opportunity. In 1862, Congress passed the Homestead Act. This law encouraged western settlement, giving people title to 160 acres of land if they lived on it for five years and made improvements.

26. **C.** The actions of the people in the passage most directly reflect the influence of Manifest Destiny. During the 1840s publicists popu-larized the idea of Manifest Destiny, that Americans would spread their democratic institutions across the North American con-tinent. This idea helped justify the Mexican War. It also helped inspire American settle-ment in the Oregon Territory, where the United States disputed a boundary line with Great Britain. Thousands of settlers followed the Oregon Trail to the Oregon Territory.

27. **B.** The experiences of the people encountered by Francis Parkman can most directly be com-pared to the Pilgrims. The people Parkman met suffered many hardships as they traveled west. The Pilgrims also suffered a great deal, including a starving time, before their colony began to prosper.

28. **D.** Thomas Jefferson had most directly antici-pated and desired the movement described by Parkman. Jefferson wanted to see a United States dominated by independent farmers. Land was necessary to fulfill this vision, so Jefferson was intensely interested in the West. Jefferson swallowed his constitutional scruples to purchase the Louisiana Territory in 1803 and then sent Lewis and Clark on an epic journey to explore it.

29. **C.** The perspective of Senator George McGovern's speech reflects the opinion that American bombing in Vietnam was a failure. Operation Rolling Thunder began in 1965 as a carefully calibrated bombing campaign designed to pressure the North Vietnamese regime to halt its support for its war against the South Vietnamese government. By 1967, it was becoming increasingly clear that bombing would not dissuade the North Vietnamese from carrying on the war. The American intervention into the war with a growing number of troops on the ground led the North Vietnamese to match this with a buildup of their own forces in South Vietnam.

30. **A.** The sentiments expressed in the speech most directly influenced the passage of the War Powers Act of 1973. Congress passed this law over the veto of President Richard Nixon. Hoping to prevent another situation like Vietnam where presidents involved the United States in a war without direct approval by Congress, this act required the president to notify Congress within two days of sending troops into combat. Unless Congress authorized the action, these troops would have to be withdrawn after 60 days.

31. **D.** The sentiments expressed in the speech most directly reflected the widespread popular attitude of the 1960s that government statements about Vietnam could not be trusted. As the war ground on without resolution, despite optimistic statements coming from the administration of President Lyndon Johnson, some commentators began to talk about a "credibility gap." Evoking memories of John F. Kennedy's political campaigning about a perceived "missile gap" with the Soviet Union, some now pointed to a gap between what the administration said and the truth.

32. **B.** Political discord during the Vietnam War most closely resembled the political dissensions during the Mexican War. Just as with Vietnam, there was significant opposition to the Mexican War. Many Americans thought it was an unjust war of aggression, and some thought it was intended to open up new territories to slavery. Prominent Americans who opposed the Mexican War included Congressman Abraham Lincoln and writer Henry David Thoreau.

33. **A.** The ideas expressed in Phillis Wheatley's poem most directly reflect the influence of the First Great Awakening. The First Great Awakening was a revival of religious fervor in the American colonies during the middle of the eighteenth century. It emphasized the need for salvation and a direct personal relationship with God. This religious movement spread to many slaves. Wheatley in her poem expresses her gratitude for her conversion to Christianity.

34. **B.** The continuity in American history most directly reflected in Wheatley's poem is debate over social justice. Wheatley makes a gentle case for human rights in her poem. She reminds her readers, almost exclusively white, that Africans can become Christians. The equality of all races in Christ could be a radical message in the 1770s.

35. **C.** The literary success of Phillis Wheatley led most directly to questions about the moral justification of slavery. Wheatley's critically acclaimed poetry contradicted racist assumptions that Africans were intellectually inferior. Wheatley, a slave who benefitted from an education, and who wrote poetry modeled on the best English forms, demonstrated that Africans, even slaves, possessed the same potential as white Europeans.

36. **D.** The point of Wheatley's poem can best be compared to Martin Luther King, Jr.'s "I Have a Dream" speech. Like King's speech, Wheatley's poem emphasizes the essential equality of all people and reminds readers that skin color should not be a barrier to unity. Just as King wanted all Americans to join together in equal enjoyment of their constitutional rights, so Wheatley urged all people to come together in Christian harmony.

37. **A.** In his Cooper Union Address, Abraham Lincoln called for northern voters to resist the demands of proslavery advocates. The Cooper Union Address was a long speech that enabled Lincoln to summarize his views in the wake of the *Dred Scott* case, his Senate race, and the John Brown affair. The success of this speech made Lincoln a leading contender for the Republican nomination for president.

38. **B.** A member of the Republican Party would have been most likely to support Lincoln's position. The Republican Party was created in 1854 in response to the passage of the Kansas-Nebraska Act, which repealed the Missouri Compromise and opened the possibility of slavery being established in territories where it previously had been barred. The Republican slogan was "Free labor, free land, free men."

39. **B.** In 1860, Lincoln and his supporters called for preventing the expansion of slavery into the western territories. Lincoln and the Republicans assured the South that, while they did not want slavery in the territories, they would leave it alone where it already existed. This did not reassure southerners who

believed that the institution of slavery would collapse if it did not expand.

40. D. Lincoln's Cooper Union Address can best be compared to William Jennings Bryan's "Cross of Gold" speech in 1896. Lincoln's success in clearly articulating the antislavery argument in the Cooper Union Address helped him win the Republican presidential nomination. William Jennings Bryan's fiery pro-silver "Cross of Gold" speech at the 1896 Democratic National Convention helped him win the Democratic presidential nomination by capturing the concerns of western and southern farmers who were being economically hurt by the "hard money" gold standard.

41. D. In "The March of the Flag," Albert Beveridge supported the creation of an American overseas empire. Beveridge, at the time in the midst of what would be a successful campaign for the U.S. Senate in Indiana, was one of a number of American political figures, such as Theodore Roosevelt and Henry Cabot Lodge, who believed that the acquisition of an empire in the Caribbean and in Asia would increase American economic and political influence in the world. They also believed that an empire would offer Americans a new frontier to replace the one rapidly disappearing in the west.

42. C. Beveridge's speech was a response to the Spanish-American War of 1898. In this war, the United States rapidly defeated the Spanish and acquired control of Cuba, Puerto Rico, Guam, and the Philippines. While there was general agreement that the Cubans would be given their independence, at the time of Beveridge's speech, there was an ongoing debate about what to do with the Philippines. Some argued that the Filipinos, who had risen against their Spanish rulers, should be given independence. Beveridge believed that the United States should govern the Philippines as a colonial possession. His view prevailed, and the United States purchased the Philippines from Spain; the American army then fought a war against Filipino forces from 1899 to 1902 before securely establishing the authority of the United States in the island chain.

43. C. The theme of Beveridge's speech can most directly be compared to Manifest Destiny. In the 1840s, many Americans believed that it was the destiny of Americans to carry the American flag and American institutions to the Pacific Ocean. Beveridge believed that it was the destiny of the United States as a rising power to plant its flag at outposts around the world.

44. A. The policy advocated by Beveridge foreshadowed the rise of the United States to the status of a great power. Victory in the Spanish-American War and the acquisition of a colonial empire made the United States a force to be reckoned with beyond the North American continent. Under Presidents William McKinley and Theodore Roosevelt, the United States exerted growing influence around the world. Under McKinley, the United States launched the Open Door Policy in China. Under Roosevelt, the United States mediated an end to the Russo-Japanese War of 1904–1905 and took part in the Algeciras Conference of 1906, settling a dispute between Germany and France over Morocco. Under President Woodrow Wilson, the United States would play a pivotal role in World War I.

45. B. A proprietary colony in which the king entrusted government to a proprietor and his family best describes the colony of Pennsylvania. The English King Charles II owed a large sum of money to William Penn's father. To satisfy the debt, in 1681, the king granted Penn a charter to a vast area of 45,000 square miles, which became the province of Pennsylvania. Penn and his descendants owned the colony until the American Revolution.

46. C. The persecuted religious group to which William Penn belonged was the Quakers. The Quakers were a group of Christians that emphasized the individual's direct experience of God. This brought them into conflict with the established Church of England. William Penn was imprisoned for his religious writings. He envisioned his province of Pennsylvania as a refuge for Quakers, where they could practice their religion in freedom. As proprietor, Penn would extend this religious freedom to all Christian groups.

47. A. Because of Penn's Charter of Privileges, Pennsylvania became one of the most religiously diverse colonies in British America.

In addition to people from England, groups of Germans settled in Pennsylvania seeking religious freedom. German Mennonites arrived in the 1680s, and the Amish settled in Pennsylvania during the eighteenth century.

48. **D.** Penn's Charter of Privileges can be seen as a forerunner to the First Amendment of the Constitution. The First Amendment prohibited the creation of an established, or official government, Church in the United States and guaranteed freedom of religion.

49. **A.** As the great-grandson of President John Adams, the historian Henry Adams might have been expected to be critical of the policies of Thomas Jefferson. John Adams was a Federalist, and Thomas Jefferson was a Democratic-Republican. The two men were bitter rivals in the election of 1800. Following his defeat, Adams declined to attend the inauguration of Thomas Jefferson. In later years, the two men reconciled and resumed their earlier friendship. Both former presidents famously died on the same day, July 4, 1826.

50. **B.** Thomas Jefferson's victory in the election of 1800 was important because it was the first time the presidency shifted from one political party to another. President George Washington had warned against political parties in his Farewell Address. Despite that, political strife between the emerging Federalist and Democratic-Republican parties grew fierce. At his inauguration, Jefferson made a plea for unity, saying, "We are all republicans, we are all federalists."

51. **D.** Although Jefferson believed that government should be small and limited, once in office, he vigorously exercised federal power in foreign affairs. Jefferson fought a naval war against the Barbary Coast pirate state of Tripoli from 1801 to 1805. He recommended the Louisiana Purchase despite his fears that such a purchase might be unconstitutional. Jefferson used troops to enforce his unpopular Embargo Act, which was passed by Congress in December 1807.

52. **C.** According to Henry Adams, the city of Washington in 1801 was still an underdeveloped cultural backwater. Washington was founded as a city in 1791. Congress met for the first time in Washington in 1800. That same year, President John Adams moved into the Executive Mansion, later named the White House.

The District of Columbia was officially organized as a territory under the control of the federal government with the Organic Act of 1801. In its early days, Washington was a very small place with few amenities, leading to Henry Adams's description of it as an "underdeveloped cultural backwater."

53. **A.** In her speech, Eleanor Roosevelt alluded to the threat to civil liberties created by World War I. During World War I, the federal government encouraged restrictions on civil liberties. The Espionage Act of 1917 set prison sentences for people who encouraged military insubordination or disloyalty. It also gave the postmaster general the power to confiscate publications that he deemed to violate the law. The Sedition Act of 1918 outlawed the use of "disloyal, profane, scurrilous, or abusive language" about the U.S. flag, government, and military. During the war, many people were imprisoned for violating these laws. The Socialist Party leader Eugene V. Debs was imprisoned for criticizing the war.

54. **B.** An example of the threat to civil liberties that concerned Roosevelt was Executive Order 9066 interning Japanese Americans. In the aftermath of Pearl Harbor, anti-Japanese feeling in California and fears that people of Japanese extraction might commit acts of sabotage led President Franklin D. Roosevelt to sign Executive Order 9066 calling for the forced relocation of 120,000 Japanese Americans living on the West Coast to camps elsewhere in the United States. Although the Supreme Court upheld the constitutionality of the relocation in *Korematsu v. U.S.* (1944), the U.S. government officially apologized in 1988 and paid each survivor $20,000.

55. **C.** Roosevelt's concerns can most directly be compared to those of the people who debated the USA Patriot Act of 2001. Following the Al-Qaeda terrorist attacks of September 11, 2001, Congress felt the need to strike a balance between imposing security and surveillance measures sufficient to protect the American public from further terrorist attacks while not sacrificing essential privacy rights and civil liberties. This led to a longstanding debate about the extent to which government electronic surveillance compromised the rights of American citizens.

Explanations for the Short-Answer Questions

Each short-answer question is worth three points. Give yourself one point for each part of the question (A, B, and C) that you get right. Then enter your score on the scoring worksheet on page 476.

1. **A.** The historian and politician George Bancroft sees Andrew Jackson as an embodiment of the West. Bancroft sees the West as untouched by the corruption of the more long-established, settled, and Europeanized East. As a product of the West, Bancroft regards Jackson as a child of nature, reflecting the virtues of an environment that produces people free from the stultifying manners and conventions of society. Bancroft's view of Jackson is heavily influenced by contemporary Romanticism. Similar ideas about the virtues of the "natural" man living on the frontier can be seen in James Fenimore Cooper's novel *The Last of the Mohicans*, 1826. Jackson's association with the West was also reflected in his reputation as a champion of democracy and the common man.
   B. Much of Jackson's early years were spent on the frontier in the Carolinas and Tennessee. As a man who lived through some of the wilder aspects of life on the frontier, Jackson became a notable duelist and Indian-fighter. Jackson's military activities as a commander against the Creeks, British, and Spanish during and after the War of 1812 helped secure the Western territories in the South, and acquired new lands for settlement. As president, Jackson would champion Native American removal to open up more land to settlers. A Jeffersonian in political philosophy, Jackson put himself at the head of the movement for an expanded franchise that became known as "Jacksonian Democracy." Jackson was the first president to come from the West. He promoted the "spoils system" in politics, which opened up government offices to ordinary men who were politically loyal. Jackson opposed any political or economic combination that struck him as representing illicit privilege, most notably the Second Bank of the United States which he ruined in his "Bank War."
   C. Members of the Whig party, which coalesced in opposition to Jackson's policies, would not have seen him as a champion of opportunity for the average man. The Whigs, led by men like Henry Clay, were more open to using the government to spur economic activity. Clay's "American System" called for tariffs to protect American industries, internal improvements to provide roads to help farmers get crops to markets, and a national bank to facilitate financial transactions. Whigs would have seen Jackson's opposition to internal improvements and the Second Bank of the United States as obstacles to ambitious and hardworking men getting ahead.

2. **A.** Helen Hunt Jackson was a novelist and reformer who publicized the injustices done to Native Americans. In this passage, she argues that the U.S. government has a long record of breaking treaties with Native American nations, furthering the interests of settlers greedy for land. She believed that the United States had always behaved dishonorably toward Native Americans.
   B. Theodore Roosevelt, at the time that he wrote this, was a historian and politician. He spent a few years as a rancher in the Dakota Territory. There he absorbed the attitudes of westerners concerning Native Americans. In his multivolume history *The Winning of the West* he dismissed criticisms of U.S. Native American policy, arguing that the Native American peoples were savages with no legitimate claim to lands that they lived on but had not improved through extensive farming and permanent settlement. A believer in Social Darwinism and contemporary theories of racial hierarchy, Roosevelt assumed that the Indians would inevitably disappear as they came into contact with America's Anglo-Saxon civilization. Their only hope of survival came from the efforts of the American government to protect them.
   C. There are many examples of broken treaties between the U.S. government and Native American tribes. In 1868 the Treaty of Fort Laramie created a great reservation in the Dakotas for the Sioux. In 1874, George Armstrong Custer led an expedition into the Black Hills that discovered gold. A gold rush ensued, bringing many miners into the Sioux

lands. The Sioux responded by going to war. This led to the 1876 Battle of the Little Big Horn in which Custer and the members of the Seventh Cavalry with him were killed. Despite this victory, the Sioux were soon defeated and lost more of their lands. Roosevelt would argue that the policy of placing Native American tribes on reservations, where they were often supported by the government, was evidence of the benign intentions of the United States, and that this offered the Native Americans the hope of a future as the continent was settled. Sometimes the best efforts of reformers hoping to help the Native Americans had unfortunate consequences. Legislators sympathetic to Native Americans passed the Dawes Severalty Act in 1887. The law was intended to help Native Americans assimilate into American society. Reservations were divided up, with heads of household receiving 160 acres of land to farm. Surplus reservation land was sold to fund schools intended to transform Native American children into Americans. This law intentionally weakened tribal society, but failed to effectively replace it. Many Native Americans ended up selling their land. By 1900, 50 percent of tribal lands had been sold. Conditions would not improve for Native Americans until the New Deal of the 1930s which attempted to restore tribal government.

3. **A, B.** The Great Awakening that began in the 1730s set off several decades of religious revivals in the American colonies. The preachers of the Great Awakening, such as Jonathan Edwards, George Whitefield, and Gilbert Tennant emphasized the dependence of individuals upon God's grace, and the need for the individual to develop a personal relationship with God. Many religious congregations split between the "New Lights" who embraced the revival, and "Old Lights" who preferred the traditional religious authorities. The Great Awakening was a phenomenon that united all the colonies. Many Americans contrasted the new religious fervor around them with the less Godly state of affairs back in Britain. The French and Indian War saw the American colonies mobilize large forces to assist the British in the war effort. By the end of the war, 20,000 Americans had served in the military.

The Americans cooperated in a joint effort that gave many young men like George Washington a more continental sense of American affairs. Following the conflict, Americans saw themselves as an important part of the growing British Empire. The resistance to the Stamp Act and other examples of British taxation was widespread throughout the American colonies. Opposition to the Stamp Act and other actions by Parliament forced the colonies to cooperate as never before. The 1765 Stamp Act Congress saw representatives from nine colonies meet to coordinate measures against the Stamp Act. Over time, organizations like the Sons of Liberty and Committees of Correspondence appeared across the colonies. In the crisis that followed the 1773 Boston Tea Party and the passage of the British Coercive Acts, the First Continental Congress met in 1774, bringing together such leaders as Patrick Henry, Samuel Adams, John Adams, and George Washington. Americans were increasingly thinking of themselves as a united people.

C. The Great Awakening weakened American's attachment to traditional religious authorities, making them also more inclined to question British political authority. The sense that Americans were a more religious people than the British also made them more inclined to strike out on their own. The French and Indian War helped prepare the way for the American Revolution by leading to the British financial crisis that led Parliament to attempt to tax the colonies. The defeat of the French removed the major threat to the Americans, and made British military protection less important. The political and military lessons learned in the war would be important in shaping the decisions of many American leaders during the War for Independence. George Washington and a number of other American military commanders were veterans of the French and Indian War and used the experience they gained there against the British. The acts of resistance to British taxation led directly to the American Revolution. Between the Stamp Act Congress and the First Continental Congress, Americans across the colonies grew used to coordinating their actions. The First Continental Congress created the "Association," an agreement to cease trading with Great Britain until the Coercive Acts were repealed. It also paved the way for the Second Continental Congress, which began meeting in May 1775. By then, fighting had begun outside Boston. The Second Continental Congress coordinated the American war effort, and in July 1776, declared American Independence.

4. **A, B.** The big battle for women at the beginning of the twentieth century was the struggle for suffrage. Carrie Chapman Catt led the mainstream National America Woman Suffrage Association. Alice Paul led the more radical Congressional Union. A number of states began to allow women to vote in state elections. The efforts of women to assist in the war effort during World War I overcame the last resistance to blocking women's suffrage. Congress passed a women's suffrage amendment which was ratified as the Nineteenth Amendment in 1920. Most women in the 1920s, such as the youthful "flappers," focused on personal self-fulfillment rather than politics, though women such as Jeanette Rankin, the first female elected to Congress, Nellie Ross of Wyoming and Miriam Ferguson of Texas, were elected governors in 1924, and Frances Perkins, the first female cabinet secretary, made notable contributions to public affairs. Alice Paul lobbied for an Equal Rights Amendment, though without success. During World War II, many women made important contributions to victory by working in war industries. "Rosie the Riveter" became a celebrated image. After the war, many women left these jobs as men returned from military service. Popular culture celebrated the woman as homemaker during the 1950s. Despite this, by the end of the 1950s, about 40 percent of women were working outside the home. This was a continuation of a growing trend in women's employment that had begun early in the century. In 1963, Betty Friedan published *The Feminine Mystique*, which argued that women needed to liberate themselves from the role of housewife. In 1966, Friedan helped found the National Organization for Women (NOW), launching what is now called "Second Wave" feminism, which worked to increase the influence of women in all aspects of society. The women's movement quickly saw many vic-

tories. Title IX of the Education Amendments in 1972 opened up unprecedented opportunities for female athletes at schools receiving federal money. The Supreme Court decision *Roe v. Wade* made abortion a right. Women rapidly moved into the workforce, a trend that was accelerated by economic problems in the 1970s. One defeat for the women's movement involved the Equal Rights Amendment, which passed Congress in 1972. At first seemingly assured of ratification in the states, it ultimately failed because of the opposition of conservative activists like Phyllis Schlafly, who argued that it would lead to drafting women into the military and unisex public restrooms. Despite this, women achieved many firsts in the 1980s. Sandra Day O'Connor became the first female Supreme Court Justice in 1981. Sally Ride became the first American woman in space in 1983. Geraldine Ferraro received the Democratic nomination for Vice President in 1984. African Americans at the turn of the twentieth century faced Jim Crow laws, legalized segregation in the South, and discrimination elsewhere in the United States. Booker T. Washington, the President of the Tuskegee Institute, argued that African Americans should focus on education and economic self-empowerment instead of immediately challenging segregation. He believed that increased economic power would eventually lead to full civil rights. W.E.B. Du Bois, a Harvard University trained historian, disagreed with Washington, and wrote that African Americans should strive for full social equality. In 1910 he was one of the founders of the National Association for the Advancement of Colored People (NAACP), which would become one of the most important and effective civil rights organizations. Around the time of World War I, many African Americans left the South in the "Great Migration" to northern cities, looking for work in war industries. This led to social tensions that sometimes erupted in race riots like those in Chicago in 1919. These new centers of African-American settlement also became the sources of cultural creativity, such as the Harlem Renaissance of the 1920s. Writers such as Langston Hughes and Zora Neale Hurston, and musicians such as Duke

Ellington won respect across racial lines. During World War II, more African Americans moved to the North and West seeking employment in rapidly expanding industrial plants. African Americans faced discrimination in war industries. A. Philip Randolph, leader of the Brotherhood of Sleeping Car Porters, threatened a march on Washington in 1941 to protest these conditions. President Franklin Roosevelt avoided this by creating the Fair Employment Practices Commission (FEPC) to ensure that African Americans were not subject to discrimination in the military and in defense work. The FEPC could not eliminate all discrimination, but it was an important precedent. During the war, many African Americans supported the "Double V" campaign—victory over the enemy overseas, and against racism in the United States. The NAACP kept up a legal campaign against Jim Crow laws in the South. The 1944 Supreme Court decision *Smith v. Allwright* declared all-white political primaries unconstitutional. In 1948, President Harry Truman, anxious to win African-American support in that year's presidential election, ordered the integration of the United States military. The 1950s saw the African-American civil rights movement make great strides. Thurgood Marshall, chief counsel for the NAACP, argued crucial cases before the Supreme Court. In 1950, the Supreme Court in *Sweatt v. Painter* ruled against segregated professional schools. In 1954, in *Brown v. Board of Education of Topeka, Kansas* the Supreme Court declared that segregated schools were "inherently unequal" and therefore unconstitutional, overruling the 1896 *Plessy v. Ferguson* decision and removing the legal basis of segregation. In 1955, Rosa Parks and the Reverend Martin Luther King Jr., led a successful campaign to integrate the buses in Montgomery, Alabama. The Montgomery bus boycott made Martin Luther King Jr., a nationally known civil rights leader. In 1957, when African-American students were prevented from enrolling at Central High School in Little Rock, Arkansas, President Dwight D. Eisenhower sent federal troops to protect them. Civil Rights Acts were passed in 1957 and 1960. These established a Civil Rights Commission and attempted to protect

African American voting rights. Martin Luther King Jr., founded the Southern Christian Leadership Conference (SCLC) in 1957. Other civil rights organizations followed, such as the Student Non-Violent Coordinating Committee (SNCC) in 1960. In 1960, students in Greensboro, North Carolina started the "sit-in" movement, sitting in a whites-only Woolworths lunch counter. Groups of black and white "freedom riders" rode buses into the south in an attempt to desegregate bus terminals. Many were attacked, and the Kennedy Administration had to intervene to protect them. President John F. Kennedy also had to protect James Meredith as he attempted to enroll at the University of Mississippi. The August 1963 March on Washington, with Martin Luther King, Jr.'s "I Have a Dream" speech, attempted to rally support for a new civil rights bill. Efforts to desegregate Birmingham, Alabama were met with violent action by police chief "Bull" Connor, who unleashed dogs and fire hoses on protestors. Episodes like this helped turn public opinion against the segregationists. President Lyndon B. Johnson pushed the Civil Rights Act of 1964 through Congress. This outlawed discrimination in public facilities and employment. The next year, the Voting Rights Act of 1965 made literacy tests illegal, and put the power of the federal government behind registering African American voters. The legal basis for discriminating against African Americans was overthrown by these laws. In the late 1960s, radical "Black Power" groups like the Black Panther Party promoted African American militancy and pride, but alienated many whites. By the 1920s, the Mexican-American population in the United States doubled in size as people fled the violence of the Mexican Revolution or looked for work in the United States. In the depths of the Great Depression, some Mexican Americans were deported, as local authorities in the Southwest attempted to protect jobs for white Americans. During World War II, demand increased for Mexican-American labor. Many Mexican Americans found work in war industries. The Bracero Program brought Mexican contract laborers into the United States to work in agriculture. Tensions between Mexican Americans and whites in Los Angeles,

California boiled over in the 1943 "Zoot Suit" Riots. After reports that Latino youths wearing gaudy "zoot suits" had insulted men in uniform, sailors from a nearby Navy base surged into Mexican-American neighborhoods and beat up young men wearing the distinctive clothing. The Mexican-American population continued to grow. In 1954, the government launched "Operation Wetback" and rounded up and deported up to a million illegal immigrants. In 1960, Mexican-American leaders formed the Mexican American Political Association (MAPA) to increase their political influence. Soon Mexican Americans were being elected to a variety of local, state, and federal offices. In 1965, Cesar Chavez formed the United Farm Workers to improve conditions for Mexican-American farm workers. His efforts brought the plight of poor Mexican Americans to national attention.

C. Early feminists were influenced by the gains African Americans had made during Reconstruction. They argued that if African-American men had the vote, white women should have it as well. The feminist movement was also influenced by the struggles of African Americans during the civil rights movement. Some female members of the civil rights movement joined the feminist movement. Feminists staged protests and marches modeled on those of the civil rights movement. The Equal Rights Amendment was an effort to gain a statutory victory akin to the Civil Rights Act of 1964. Cesar Chavez and Chicano activists were also inspired by the civil rights movement. Like Martin Luther King, Jr., Cesar Chavez emphasized nonviolence in his strikes and boycotts. Some Mexican-American activists imitated the African-American exponents of greater militancy and ethnic pride. Reies Tijerina led a group that occupied the Kit Carson National Forest to protest historic wrongs against Hispanics in the Southwest. "Brown Panthers" were modeled on the Black Panthers. *La Raza Unida* (The Race United) was founded to promote Hispanic interests.

Explanation for the Document-Based Question

To do well on this question, be sure to follow all the directions! Provide a historically plausible thesis that addresses all aspects of the prompt. Your thesis should respond to and go beyond the prompt. Restating or paraphrasing the prompt is not an acceptable thesis. Your thesis can be at the beginning or the end of your essay; it will not be counted if it is anywhere else. Put your response in a broader context, referring to historical factors preceding, following, or taking place at the same time as the subject of the prompt. Be sure to use at least six of the documents. You need to explain the historical significance of the documents; simply referring to or quoting them will not count for points. For at least three of the documents, explain how the point of view of the author, the intended audience, or the document's historical context is relevant to your larger argument. Bring in as much evidence beyond the documents as you can. Evidence that you use to provide context or to deepen discussion of at least three of the documents will not be applied to the overall outside evidence point; you can't double-dip on these evidence points! The more historical information outside the documents that you can provide, the better. Finally, show a complex understanding of the subject matter of the prompt. You can do this in a variety of ways. For instance, you can connect this subject matter to similar historical events in another period. Other possibilities include highlighting differing perspectives on the subject matter, or exploring differing interpretations of the causes of the historical event that you are discussing. Relate this to your larger argument; an off-hand reference will not be counted.

Here is some information to help with this.

1. You should begin with a discussion of the Interstate Commerce Act (1887) and Sherman Antitrust Act (1890). The Interstate Commerce Act attempted to regulate railroad companies. It required railroads to submit their fare schedules with the federal government and publicize their rates. The act created an Interstate Commerce Commission (ICC) to monitor the industry. The Sherman Act declared illegal all combinations "in restraint of free trade." It empowered the Justice Department to bring suit and break up such monopolies. However, these acts would have to pass the scrutiny of the Supreme Court. You could comment upon the composition of the Court during the period. You could explain how a conservative Court could thwart the efforts of reformers. You should discuss the labor movement during the Progressive Era. Several strikes occurred in this period, including the Great Railway Strike (1877), Haymarket Affair (1886), and the Homestead Strike (1892). You must examine the Pullman Strike (1894), in which railroad workers and the American Railway Union, led by Eugene Debs, crippled traffic in several states and territories. Many governors sided with the railroad companies by employing state troops to disperse the strikers. One notable exception was John Peter Altgeld, governor of Illinois. Railroad operators in Chicago appealed to President Cleveland and Attorney General Richard Olney to intercede on their behalf. The president ordered 2,000 federal troops to break up the strike. The Supreme Court further solidified the position of the railroad corporations by applying the Sherman Antitrust Act against unions that threatened free trade (Document A). In *E. C. Knight Company v. U.S.*, the Court further inhibited efforts to regulate corporations by putting manufacturing companies outside the purview of the Sherman Act (Document B). Thus, companies continued to form monopolies in various industries that fixed prices without competition. The Court undermined the Interstate Commerce Commission's authority to determine fair railroad rates by applying the "due process" clause of the Fourteenth Amendment to corporations (Document C). Progressives seeking to limit the hours of labor met with mixed results. In *Holden v. Hardy* (1898) the Court

affirmed the right of state legislatures to regulate maximum hours in the interests of workers' health. Seven years later, the Court again reinterpreted the Fourteenth Amendment to cast aside a state law. The Lochner decision asserted that legislation not directly related to health concerns violated the rights of workers (Document D). However, reformers gained a partial victory in *Muller v. Oregon* (1908), which sustained the legislature's authority to pass regulatory legislation to protect women's health (Document E). You might comment upon the double standard applied to men and women in the early twentieth century. You could refer to the Elkins (1903) and Hepburn (1906) Acts, which intended to further the federal government's ability to regulate railroads. Others might explain how presidential leadership advanced the cause of reform by briefly discussing Theodore Roosevelt, William Howard Taft, or Woodrow Wilson. You might touch upon how the Roosevelt administration implemented the Sherman Act in *Northern Securities Company v. United States* (1904) to set the stage for an examination of the decentralization of monopolies. The Court furthered its position by ordering the Standard Oil Company to break up its monopoly of the oil refining industry (Document F). You might compare the decision with the Court's response to Swift and American Tobacco. To conclude the essay, you could discuss how the Court endorsed the Adamson Act, which established an eight-hour day for interstate railway workers (Document G).

Scoring for the Document-Based Question

TASKS	POINTS
Give yourself 1 point if you wrote a thesis that responds to the question with a historically plausible argument. You can't just restate or repeat the question. Your thesis can be expressed in one or more sentences in the introduction or conclusion of your essay.	
Give yourself 1 point if you put the question into a wider historical context. To do this, you should connect the topic of the question to events, developments, or processes that take place before, during, or after the period immediately covered in the question. A brief reference or phrase will not earn you this point.	
There are 2 points possible here. Give yourself 1 point for providing the historical content of at least three of the documents to address the question. Give yourself another point if you supported your argument by using the historical content of at least six of the documents. You must explain the historical significance of these documents. Simply quoting documents does not count. To get the second point, you must relate the six documents to your argument.	
Give yourself 1 point if you used at least one piece of historical information that goes beyond the evidence in the documents. A brief reference to a piece of information will not earn a point. You must describe the how this historical information relates to the question. The historical information for this point must be different from information that you use to earn the point for placing the question in a wider historical context.	
Give yourself 1 point if you explained the point of view of the author, the purpose of the author, or a document's intended audience or historical context for at least three documents. You must explain how or why these are relevant for your argument.	
Give yourself 1 point if you demonstrated a complex understanding of the subject of the question, using historical evidence to modify, qualify, or confirm your argument. This understanding must be used to develop your argument, and it can't be merely a brief reference or phrase.	
TOTAL (7 points possible)	

Explanations for the Long Essay Questions

To do well on this question, be sure to follow all the directions! Provide a historically plausible thesis that addresses all aspects of the prompt. Your thesis should respond to and go beyond the prompt. Restating or paraphrasing the prompt is not an acceptable thesis. Use your historical analytical skills to construct your argument, emphasizing such aspects of the subject matter as cause and effect or change and continuity. Your thesis can be at the beginning or the end of your essay; it will not be counted if it is anywhere else. Put your response in a broader context, referring to historical factors preceding, following, or taking place at the same time as the subject of the prompt. Provide as much historical evidence as you can. You want to do this both to provide information that is relevant to the subject matter and also to support your argument. Finally, show a complex understanding of the subject matter of the prompt. You can do this in a variety of ways. For instance, you can connect this subject matter to similar historical events in another period. Other possibilities include highlighting differing perspectives on the subject matter or exploring differing interpretations of the causes of the historical event that you are discussing. Relate this to your larger argument; an off-hand reference will not be counted.

Here is some information to help with this.

2. You could begin with a brief discussion of the debate concerning the ratification of the Constitution. Anti-Federalists represented a significant number of people in the United States, perhaps even a majority, and their concerns that the new central government would prove as tyrannical as the British had been touched a chord. Crucial in winning passage of the Constitution was the promise that it would be amended with a bill of rights, a promise that James Madison kept when the new Congress met in 1789. The anti-Federalists demonstrated that there was a strong desire across the country for limited national government and a respect for local and states' rights. Thoroughly out of sympathy with such views was President George Washington's brilliant Secretary of the Treasury Alexander Hamilton. Dubious about the ability of the common man to rule, and convinced that the government should play a leading role in encouraging economic prosperity, Hamilton shocked many with his 1790 *First Report on the Public Credit*. In it, he called for the new government to pay off the debt of the United States at its full face value, and for the federal assumption of state debts from the Revolutionary era. The purpose of this was to establish the good credit of the United States, and to win the support of the propertied classes for the government. Longer term, the federal debt would become the engine for commercial development in the United States. Many southern states opposed the assumption of state debts because they were already paying off their debts. They feared that Hamilton's plans would favor the northern commercial states over the agrarian south. James Madison was concerned about full payment of the debt, because many original bondholders had been forced to sell to speculators at a steep discount and he did not want to reward such sharp dealing. In the end, a compromise was worked out whereby Hamilton's fiscal program went through and the new national capital was located in the South along the Potomac River. The next year, Hamilton proposed a national bank. The bank would be a place where the government could deposit its funds. The bank could also stimulate the economy by making loans and by putting into circulation a reliable supply of paper money. Washington asked his cabinet to state their opinions on the constitutionality of such a measure. Secretary of State Thomas Jefferson strongly objected. Taking a "strict constructionist," or literal reading of the Constitution, he argued that there was no mention of a bank in the founding document. He believed state banks could fulfill all the functions that Ham-

ilton desired. Hamilton countered by making a "loose constructionist," or nonliteral interpretation of the Constitution. He argued that the bank would further enumerated tasks of the government, and that the "necessary and proper" clause of the Constitution allowed the government to use implied powers to create institutions like the bank. Hamilton won the argument and the first Bank of the United States was chartered in 1791. But the constitutional disagreements between Jefferson and Hamilton were merging with sectional concerns and traditional worries about the power of the government to create two emerging blocs in the government. In 1791, Jefferson and Madison traveled to New York and New England and made contact with former anti-Federalists there. Newspapers for each side began editorializing against each other. The personal relations between Jefferson and Hamilton deteriorated. The coming of the French Revolution added a foreign policy dimension to the differences between the two camps. Jefferson favored the French in their quarrels with the rest of Europe, while Hamilton sympathized with their British antagonists. While both men favored Washington's Neutrality Declaration, Hamilton used the Citizen Genet affair to embarrass Jefferson. Hamilton's economic program was funded by a system of tariffs and excise taxes, including a tax on whiskey. Distilling grain into whiskey was the only way that frontier farmers could get their crops safely to a market, and they greatly resented the tax. In 1794, farmers in western Pennsylvania rose up in rebellion. They were suppressed by a military force led by Washington himself. Jefferson's supporters saw this as the repression of liberty and as an example of the way that Hamilton's program sacrificed the agrarian interests of the common man to the needs of the commercial elite. That same year foreign policy further divided the two sides. American shipping was caught between the British and the French as they waged a naval war against each other. American ships were being seized. Washington sent John Jay to London to work out an arrangement with Britain. The resulting Jay's Treaty was unsatisfactory. The British agreed to leave their posts in the American Northwest, something they would have to do anyway after Anthony Wayne's victory at Fallen Timbers. Jay won little in the way of commercial concessions. The British did agree to compensate Americans for seized ships, but Jay had to agree to the repayment of American debts dating to the pre-Revolutionary period. The treaty led to a firestorm of criticism. Southerners, who owed much of the old debt, were outraged, and again saw themselves as being subordinated to northern commercial interests. Jefferson's supporters attacked the treaty, while Hamilton defended it, believing that it was necessary to maintain good relations with Britain. The Treaty passed, but by the time Washington left office early in 1797, there were two clearly demarcated factions contending for power. Jeffersonians, known as Democratic-Republicans, distrusted a powerful government, supported a strict construction of the Constitution, and celebrated the common man and agrarian interests. Hamiltonians, known as Federalists, wanted a stronger central government, accepted a loose construction of the economy, and supported a mixed economy, with strong government support of commercial interests. These factions emerged more fully as parties during John Adams' term as President as a result of the X, Y, and Z Affair and the resulting troubles with France. In 1797, Adams sent a delegation to France to settle relations with that country. French representatives refused to negotiate until they received a bribe. This outraged the diplomats and public opinion at home. An undeclared naval war with France was fought at sea. At home, the Federalists attempted to use the anti-French feeling to crush their Francophile Democratic-Republican opponents. They passed the Alien and Sedition Acts, which were used to stifle opposition to government policy. Under the Sedition Act, editors defaming the government could be fined and imprisoned. The Democratic-Republicans responded with the Virginia and Kentucky Resolutions. The Virginia resolution was written by Madison, and Jefferson drafted the Kentucky resolutions. Both declared the Alien and Sedition Acts to be unconstitutional, and argued for state's rights. The Kentucky resolutions even argued that a state could nullify a law that it believe to be unconstitutional, a position later elaborated upon by John C. Calhoun. In the end, differences between John Adams and Hamilton led Adams to make peace, ending the crisis. In the election of 1800, Jefferson and his Democratic-Republicans would emerge victorious, setting up the first transfer of power between parties in American history. By this point, party politics had become a fixture of American political life, and differing interpretations of the Constitution would be an integral component of party ideology.

To do well on this question, be sure to follow all the directions! Provide a historically plausible thesis that addresses all aspects of the prompt. Your thesis should respond to and go beyond the prompt. Restating or paraphrasing the prompt is not an acceptable thesis. Use your historical analytical skills to construct your argument, emphasizing such aspects of the subject matter as cause and effect or change and continuity. Your thesis can be at the beginning or the end of your essay; it will not be counted if it is anywhere else. Put your response in a broader context, referring to historical factors preceding, following, or taking place at the same time as the subject of the prompt. Provide as much historical evidence as you can. You want to do this both to provide information that is relevant to the subject matter and also to support your argument. Finally, show a complex understanding of the subject matter of the prompt. You can do this in a variety of ways. For instance, you can connect this subject matter to similar historical events in another period. Other possibilities include highlighting differing perspectives on the subject matter or exploring differing interpretations of the causes of the historical event that you are discussing. Relate this to your larger argument; an off-hand reference will not be counted.

Here is some information to help with this.

3. You can construct an argument making use of information that can include the following. A variety of reform movements flourished in the United States in the period from 1820–1860. The Second Great Awakening began in Kentucky in the early 1800s. Initially a phenomenon of enthusiastic frontier camp meetings, this new religious revival soon spread across the country. The preachers of the Second Great Awakening fostered a vibrant evangelical Protestantism that emphasized the importance of personal conversion and an intense, often more openly emotional, relationship with God. One of the most famous evangelists of the Second Great Awakening was Charles Grandison Finney, a brilliant orator who abandoned a career in the law after being "saved." Many people touched by the Second Great Awakening found spiritual homes in the Baptist and Methodist Churches, but new religious groupings also appeared, such as the Millerites, or Adventists, who expected the imminent arrival of Jesus Christ. The Church of Jesus Christ of Latter-Day Saints, or Mormons, founded by the visionary Joseph Smith, emerged during this period of religious enthusiasm, though it was deemed heretical by more orthodox Christian Churches. Facing increasing hostility, the Mormons began moving to Utah in 1846. They were led by Brigham Young after Joseph Smith was murdered by a mob. The Second Great Awakening intensified the religious character of people in the United States. By 1840, nearly half of the population was formally connected to a church. Women played a prominent role in the Second Great Awakening, making up the majority of congregations, and actively supporting a growing range of charitable organizations. A "Benevolent Empire" of such organizations attempted to spread the Christian message by supporting moral reforms or missionary activity at home

and abroad. The American Bible Society (1816) and the American Tract Society (1825) were typical manifestations of the "Benevolent Empire," distributing Bibles and other religious writings everywhere in the United States. The temperance movement combined some of the religious fervor of the Second Great Awakening with a more strictly secular concern about the social cost of heavy drinking. The American Temperance Society appeared in 1826. The politician and businessman Neal S. Dow was the sponsor of the 1851 Maine Law that prohibited the sale and manufacture of liquor in that state. Prohibition remained a political issue throughout the nineteenth century. In this period, educational reform was spurred by the efforts of Horace Mann, who promoted public education for all children. Educators like Catherine Beecher established private schools designed for girls and young women. William H. McGuffey began publishing his phenomenally popular *McGuffey's Readers* in the 1830s. Large numbers of colleges, usually associated with religious denominations, appeared across the country. Oberlin College in Ohio began educating women as well as men in 1837. Efforts in these years were made to improve conditions in prisons. Alexis de Toqueville, the French author of *Democracy in America* (two volumes, 1835 and 1840), first visited the United States to study its prisons. Dorothea Dix became famous for her work to reform the treatment of the mentally ill in asylums. Various utopian communities sprang up in the United States. In 1825, Robert Owen founded a communal society at New Harmony in Indiana. The Oneida Community, established in New York in 1848, scandalized people by experimenting with "free love" and eugenics. Lucretia Mott and Elizabeth Cady Stanton began the women's rights movement by calling for women's suffrage. They helped organize a conference at Seneca Falls, New York in 1848 that issued a famous "Declaration of Sentiments" that demanded equal rights and the vote for women. Abolitionism grew in strength in the 1820s and 1830s. William Lloyd Garrison began publishing his abolitionist paper *The Liberator* in 1831. In 1833, Garrison, Lewis Tappan, and Theodore Weld founded the American Anti-Slavery Society. Abolitionists began an increasingly vocal campaign against slavery, infuriating many Southerners. Abolitionism was concentrated in the North, but some Southerners, such as the South Carolinian sisters Angelina and Sarah Grimke spoke out against the institution of slavery. African Americans like the escaped slave Frederick Douglass also joined the cause. In addition to agitating against slavery, abolitionists organized the Underground Railroad to help slaves make their way to freedom. The former slave Harriet Tubman helped "conduct" many African Americans along the Underground Railroad. Abolitionists were often very unpopular, even in the North. Garrison was attacked by a Boston mob in 1835, and in 1837 the abolitionist editor Elijah Lovejoy was murdered in Alton, Illinois. Despite this, the abolitionists succeeded in making slavery a major political issue, exemplified by the creation of the Liberty Party in 1844, and the Free Soil Party in 1848. Political abolitionism would set the stage for the emergence of the Republican Party in the 1850s.

To do well on this question, be sure to follow all the directions! Provide a historically plausible thesis that addresses all aspects of the prompt. Your thesis should respond to and go beyond the prompt. Restating or paraphrasing the prompt is not an acceptable thesis. Use your historical analytical skills to construct your argument, emphasizing such aspects of the subject matter as cause and effect or change and continuity. Your thesis can be at the beginning or the end of your essay; it will not be counted if it is anywhere else. Put your response in a broader context, referring to historical factors preceding, following, or taking place at the same time as the subject of the prompt. Provide as much historical evidence as you can. You want to do this both to provide information that is relevant to the subject matter and also to support your argument. Finally, show a complex understanding of the subject matter of the prompt. You can do this in a variety of ways. For instance, you can connect this subject matter to similar historical events in another period. Other possibilities include highlighting differing perspectives on the subject matter or exploring differing interpretations of the causes of the historical event that you are discussing. Relate this to your larger argument; an off-hand reference will not be counted.

Here is some information to help with this.

4. A starting point for you could be the evolving attitude toward women of the 1890s. The role of women for much of the nineteenth century had been dominated by the "cult of domesticity," which saw a woman's place as the guardian of the home and the keeper of moral and cultural values. This did not disappear entirely in the period from 1900–1930, but was already being modified by the turn of the century. The "New Woman" of the 1890s challenged older stereotypes of women as weak and passive. Symbolic of the "New Woman" was illustrator Charles Dana Gibson's "Gibson Girl," who was beautiful, athletic, and strong-willed. By the turn of the century, many women were receiving a higher education, at all-women's colleges such as Vassar or at coeducational institutions. A number of these women went into social work and became prominent progressive reformers. Emblematic of these was Jane Addams. A graduate of Rockford College, she cofounded Hull House in 1889. Hull House was a settlement house on the south side of Chicago that met many needs of the neighboring immigrant population. By the early twentieth century Addams was famous, and helped found the Progressive Party with Theodore Roosevelt in 1912. Many women were working outside of the home, most out of economic necessity, many by choice. Recent inventions like the switchboard and typewriter opened up new professions for women. The outbreak of war in 1917 opened up opportunities for women in the workplace, as they took the places of men called into the military. Although this movement into the workforce was not as massive as that of World War II, it was still significant, involving many thousands of women. For the first time, women were allowed into the American military. Many served as nurses. The contributions of women to the war effort proved decisive in convincing President Wilson, Congress, and the nation that women should get the vote. Critical in facilitating this was the work of Carrie Chapman Catt, leader of the National American Woman Suffrage Association. Congress sent the Nineteenth Amendment to the states on June 4, 1919, and it was ratified on August 18, 1920. American women would be able to vote in the 1920 presidential election. The 1920s was a time of contrasts for women. Margaret Sanger campaigned for birth-control. Alice Paul's National Woman's Party fought for an Equal Rights Amendment to the Constitution. Yet for many women, especially younger women, political struggle would not be a priority. The dominant image of females in the Jazz Age would be that of "flaming youth." Illustrator John Held's "flappers," with their bobbed hair, short skirts, boyish figures, cigarettes, and garter flasks, became the incarnation of the latest version of the new woman. Many women in the 1920s focused on the personal freedoms opening up to them in the postwar world. The woman of 1930 was very different from that of 1900, and in more ways than the amount of clothing that she wore.

Scoring the Long-Essay Question

TASKS	POINTS
Give yourself 1 point if you wrote a thesis that responds to the question with a historically plausible argument. You can't just restate or repeat the question. Your thesis can be expressed in one or more sentences in the introduction or conclusion of your essay.	
Give yourself 1 point if you put the question into a wider historical context. To do this, you should connect the topic of the question to events, developments, or processes that take place before, during, or after the period immediately covered in the question. A brief reference or phrase will not earn you this point.	
You can earn up to 2 points for providing evidence in your essay. Give yourself 1 point if you provided examples of historical information that are relevant to the question. This will increase to 2 points if you used well-chosen examples of historical information that support your argument.	
Give yourself 1 point if you used your historical analytical skills, such as identifying cause and effect, in constructing an argument that addresses the question.	
Give yourself 1 point if you demonstrated a complex understanding of the subject of the question, using historical evidence to modify, qualify, or confirm your argument. This understanding must be used to develop your argument, and it can't be merely a brief reference or phrase.	
TOTAL (6 points possible)	

AP U.S. HISTORY PRACTICE EXAM 2

Scoring Conversion

You can get a rough approximation of your score on the AP U.S. History exam. Use the answer explanations to award yourself points on the free-response questions. Then compute your raw score using the worksheet below. Finally, refer to the table below to translate your raw score to an AP score of 1 to 5.

Section I: Multiple Choice

Number of questions answered correctly (55 possible) _____ × 1.31 = _____

Section I: Short Answer

Question 1 (3 points possible): _____ × 4 = _____

Question 2 (3 points possible): _____ × 4 = _____

Question 3 or 4 (3 points possible): _____ × 4 = _____

Section II: Document-Based Question

Question 1 (7 points possible) _____ × 6.43 = _____

Section II: Long Essay Question

Question 2, 3, or 4 (6 points possible) _____ × 4.5 = _____

RAW SCORE: Add your points in the column above (180 possible): _____

Conversion Table

RAW SCORE	APPROXIMATE AP SCORE
Low 110s to 180	5
Mid-90s to low 110s	4
Mid-70s to mid-90s	3
Mid-50s to mid-70s	2
Below the mid-50s	1

abolitionist movement Movement dedicated to the abolition of slavery that existed primarily in the North in years leading up to the Civil War and consisted of both white and black members.

advertising age Term first used to describe America's consumer culture of the 1920s, when advertising began to influence the choices of purchasers.

affirmative action Policies that began in the 1970s to make up for past discrimination and give minorities and women advantages in applying for certain jobs and in applying for admission to certain universities.

affluent society Term used by economist John Kenneth Galbraith to describe the American economy in the 1950s, during which time many Americans became enraptured with appliances and homes in the suburbs.

Agricultural Adjustment Administration (AAA) Established by the Agricultural Act of 1932, a New Deal bureau designed to restore economic position of farmers by paying them *not* to farm goods that were being overproduced.

Agricultural Marketing Act of 1929 Act championed by Herbert Hoover that authorized the lending of federal money to farmers' cooperatives to buy crops to keep them from the oversaturated market; program hampered by lack of adequate federal financial support.

Albany Congress (1754) Meeting of representatives of seven colonies to coordinate their efforts against French and Native American threats in the Western frontier regions.

Alien and Sedition Acts Proposed and supported by John Adams, gave the president the power to expel aliens deemed "dangerous to the country's well-being" and outlawed publication and public pronouncement of "false, scandalous, and malicious" statements about the government.

Allied Powers Coalition of nations that opposed Germany, Italy, and Japan in World War II; led by England, the Soviet Union, and the United States. In World War I, the coalition consisted of France, Russia, and Great Britain. This group opposed the Central powers (Germany, Austria-Hungary, and Italy).

America First Committee Isolationist group in America that insisted that America stay out of World War II; held rallies from 1939 to 1941; argued that affairs in Europe should be settled by Europeans and not Americans and stated that the Soviet Union was a greater eventual threat than Nazi Germany.

American Colonization Society Formed in 1817, stated that the best way to end the slavery problem in the United States was for blacks to emigrate to Africa. By 1822, a few American blacks emigrated to Liberia. Organization's views were later rejected by most abolitionists.

American Expeditionary Force Official title of American army sent to Europe to aid England and France after United States entered World War I; army was commanded by General John J. Pershing.

American Federation of Labor (AFL) National labor union founded by Samuel Gompers in 1886; original goal was to organize skilled workers by craft. Merged with Congress of Industrial Organizations (CIO) in 1955.

American Indian Movement (AIM) Native American organization founded in 1968 to protest government policies and injustices suffered by Native Americans; in 1973 organized armed occupation of Wounded Knee, South Dakota.

American Liberty League Formed in 1934 by anti-New Deal politicians and business leaders to oppose policies of Franklin Roosevelt; stated that New Deal policies brought America closer to fascism.

American System Economic plan promoted by Speaker of the House Henry Clay in years following the War of 1812, which promoted vigorous growth of the American economy and the use of protective tariffs to encourage Americans to buy more domestic goods.

Anaconda Copper Company Large mining syndicate typical of many companies involved in mining in the western United States in the 1860s and 1870s; used heavy machinery and professional engineers. Many prospectors who found gold, silver, or copper sold their claims to companies such as this.

Anaconda Plan Critical component of initial Union plans to win the Civil War; called for capture of critical Southern ports and eventual control of the Mississippi River, which would create major economic and strategic difficulties for the Confederacy.

Anti-Federalists Group that opposed the ratification of the proposed Constitution of the United States in 1787; many feared that strong central government would remove the processes of government "from the people" and replicate the excesses of the British monarchy.

Anti-Imperialist League Organization formed in 1898 to oppose American annexation of the Philippines and American imperialism in general; focused the public on the potential financial, military, and especially moral costs of imperialism.

Anti-Saloon League Organization founded in 1893 that increased public awareness of the social effects of alcohol on society; supported politicians who favored prohibition and promoted statewide referendums in Western and Southern states to ban alcohol.

Appomattox In the courthouse of this Virginia city Robert E. Lee surrendered his Confederate army to Ulysses S. Grant on April 9, 1865.

Army-McCarthy hearings 1954 televised hearings on charges that Senator Joseph McCarthy was unfairly tarnishing the U.S. Army with charges of Communist infiltration into the armed forces; hearings were the beginning of the end for McCarthy, whose bullying tactics were repeatedly demonstrated.

Articles of Confederation Ratified in 1781, this document established the first official government of the United States; allowed much power to remain in the states, with the federal government possessing only limited powers. Articles replaced by the Constitution in 1788.

astrolabe Instrument that enabled navigators to calculate their latitude using the sun and the stars; allowed more accuracy in plotting routes during the Age of Discovery.

Atlantic, Battle of the Began in spring 1941 with the sinking of an American merchant vessel by a German submarine. Armed conflict between warships of America and Germany took place in September 1941; American merchant vessels were armed by 1942.

Atlantic Charter Fall 1941 agreement between Franklin Roosevelt and Winston Churchill, stating that America and Great Britain would support a postwar world based on self-determination and would endorse a world body to ensure "general security." U.S. agreement to convoy merchant ships across part of Atlantic inevitably drew America closer to conflict with Germany.

Aztecs Advanced Native American society located in central Mexico; conquered by Spanish conquistador Cortes. The defeat of the Aztecs was hastened by smallpox brought to Mexico by the Spanish.

baby boom Large increase in birthrate in United States that began in 1945 and lasted until 1962; new and larger families fueled the move to suburbia that occurred in the 1950s and produced the "youth culture" that would become crucial in the 1960s.

Ballinger-Pinchot Affair Crisis that occurred when William Howard Taft was president, further distancing him from Progressive supporters of Theodore Roosevelt. Richard Ballinger, Taft's secretary of the interior, allowed private businessmen to purchase large amounts of public land in Alaska. Forest Service head Gifford Pinchot (a Roosevelt supporter) protested to Congress and was fired by Taft.

Bank War Political battles surrounding the attempt by President Andrew Jackson to greatly reduce the power of the Second Bank of the United States. Jackson claimed the bank was designed to serve special interests in America and not the common people.

Bataan Death March Forced march of nearly 75,000 American and Filipino soldiers captured by the Japanese from the Bataan Peninsula in early May 1942; over 10,000 soldiers died during this one-week ordeal.

Bay of Pigs Failed 1961 invasion of Cuba by United States–supported anti-Castro refugees designed to topple Castro from power; prestige of the United States, and of the newly elected president, John Kennedy, was damaged by this failed coup attempt.

Bear Flag Republic Declaring independence from Mexican control, this republic was declared in 1846 by American settlers living in California. This political act was part of a larger American political and military strategy to wrest Texas and California from Mexico.

Beat Generation Literary movement of the 1950s that criticized the conformity of American society and the ever-present threat of atomic warfare; *On the Road* by Jack Kerouac, *Howl* by Allen Ginsberg, and *Naked Lunch* by William Burroughs were key works of the Beat Generation.

Berlin Airlift American and British pilots flew in food and fuel to West Berlin during late 1948 and early 1949 because the Soviet Union and East Germany blockaded other access to West Berlin (which was located in East Germany); Stalin ended this blockade in May 1949. Airlift demonstrated American commitment to protecting Western Allies in Europe during the early cold war period.

Berlin Wall Concrete structure built in 1961 by Soviets and East Germany physically dividing East and West Berlin; to many in the West, the wall was symbolic of Communist repression in the cold war era. The wall was finally torn down in 1989.

Bessemer steel First produced in 1856 in converter (furnace) invented by Henry Bessemer; was much more durable and harder than iron. Steel was a critical commodity in the Second Industrial Revolution.

bias No historical writing can be totally objective; observers are always influenced by either conscious or unconscious bias. Conscious bias might be a flattering biography of Lincoln written by an abolitionist in 1865, or an unflattering biography of Lincoln written by a southerner in the same year. Unconscious bias may be created by one's education, predispositions toward the subject, or even one's race or gender.

bicameral legislature A legislative structure consisting of two houses, this was adopted by the authors of the U.S. Constitution; membership of the states in one house (the House of Representatives) is determined by population, while in the other house (the Senate) all states have equal representation.

Bill of Rights Added to the Constitution in 1791, the first 10 amendments protected freedom of speech, freedom of the press, the right to bear arms, and other basic rights of American citizens.

Birth of a Nation Epic movie released in 1915 by director D. W. Griffith; portrayed the Reconstruction as a period when Southern blacks threatened basic American values, which the Ku Klux Klan tried to protect. The film was lauded by many, including President Woodrow Wilson.

Black Codes Laws adopted by the Southern states in the Reconstruction era that greatly limited the freedom of Southern blacks. In several states blacks could not move, own land, or do anything but farm.

black nationalism Spurred by Malcolm X and other black leaders, a call for black pride and advancement without the help of whites; this appeared to be a repudiation of the calls for peaceful integration urged by Martin Luther King, Jr. Race riots in Northern cities in mid-1960s were at least partially fueled by supporters of black nationalism.

Black Panthers Group originally founded in Oakland, California, to protect blacks from police harassment; promoted militant black power; also ran social programs in several California cities. Founded by Bobby Seale and Huey P. Newton.

black power Movement of black Americans in the mid-1960s that emphasized pride in racial heritage and black economic and political self-reliance; term coined by black civil rights leader Stokely Carmichael.

blacklist Prevented persons accused of being Communists from getting work in entertainment and other industries during the period of anti-Communist fervor of the late 1940s and early 1950s; some entertainers waited until the mid-1960s before working publicly again.

Bleeding Kansas As a result of the Kansas-Nebraska Act of 1854, residents of Kansas territory could decide if territory would allow slavery or not. As a result, both pro and antislavery groups flooded settlers into Kansas territory. Much violence followed very disputed elections in 1855.

bonanza farms Large farms that came to dominate agricultural life in much of the West in the late 1800s. Instead of plots farmed by yeoman farmers, large amounts of machinery were used, and workers were hired laborers, often performing only specific tasks (similar to work in a factory).

Bonus Army Group of nearly 17,000 veterans who marched on Washington in May 1932 to demand the military bonuses they had been promised; this group was eventually driven from their camp city by the U.S. Army. This action increased the public perception that the Hoover administration cared little about the poor.

Boston Massacre Conflict between British soldiers and Boston civilians on March 5, 1770. After civilians threw rocks and snowballs at the soldiers, the soldiers opened fire, killing five and wounding six.

Boston Tea Party In response to the Tea Act and additional British taxes on tea, Boston radicals disguised as Native Americans threw nearly 350 chests of tea into Boston Harbor on December 16, 1773.

Brown v. Board of Education 1954 Supreme Court decision that threw out the 1896 *Plessy v. Ferguson* ruling that schools could be "separate but equal." The ruling began the long and painful process of school desegregation in the South and other parts of America.

Bulge, Battle of the December 1944 German attack that was the last major offensive by the Axis powers in World War II. Germans managed to push forward into Belgium but were then driven back. Attack was costly to the Germans in terms of material and manpower.

Bull Moose party Name given to the Progressive party in the 1912 presidential campaign. Bull Moose candidate ex-president Theodore Roosevelt ran against incumbent president William Howard Taft and Democrat Woodrow Wilson, with Wilson emerging victorious.

Bull Run, First Battle of July 21, 1861, Confederate victory over Union forces, which ended in Union forces fleeing in disarray toward Washington. This battle convinced Lincoln and others in the North that victory over the Confederates would not be as easy as they initially thought.

Bull Run, Second Battle of Decisive victory by General Robert E. Lee and Confederate forces over the Union army in August 1862.

Bunker Hill, Battle of In June 1775, the British attacked colonial forces at Breed's Hill outside Boston; despite frightful losses, the British emerged victorious in this battle.

Calvinism Protestant faith that preached salvation "by faith alone" and predestination; desire by Calvinists in

England to create a "pure church" in England was only partially successful, thus causing Calvinist Puritans to come to the New World starting in 1620.

Camp David Accords Treaty between Egypt and Israel brokered by President Jimmy Carter and signed in early 1979; Israel agreed to give back territory in the Sinai Peninsula to Egypt, while Egypt agreed to recognize Israel's right to exist as a nation.

carpetbaggers Term used by Southerners to mock Northerners who came to the South to gain either financially or politically during the Reconstruction era.

Central Powers The alliance of Germany, Austria-Hungary, the Ottoman Empire, and Bulgaria that opposed England, France, Russia, and later the United States in World War I.

Chancellor of the Exchequer During the era prior to and during the Revolutionary War, this was the head of the department in the British government that issued and collected taxes. Many acts issued by the Chancellor of the Exchequer created great resentment in the American colonies.

Chancellorsville, Battle of Brilliant Confederate attack on Union forces led by Stonewall Jackson and Robert E. Lee on May 2 to 3, 1863. Union defeat led to great pessimism in the North and convinced many in the South that victory over the North was indeed possible.

Chateau-Thierry, Battle of One of the first 1918 World War I battles where soldiers of the American Expeditionary Force fought and suffered severe casualties.

Checkers Speech Speech made by Richard Nixon on national television on September 23, 1952, where he defended himself against charges that rich supporters had set up a special expense account for his use; by the speech Nixon saved his spot on the 1952 Republican ticket (he was running for vice president, with Eisenhower running for president) and saved his political career.

Cherokee Nation v. Georgia **(1831)** Supreme Court case in which the Cherokee tribe claimed that Georgia had no right to enforce laws in Cherokee territory, since Cherokees were a sovereign nation. This ruling by John Marshall stated that Cherokees were a "domestic dependent nation" and had no right to appeal in federal court.

Church of England Also called "the Anglican church," this was the Protestant church established by King Henry VIII; religious radicals desired a "purer" church that was allowed by monarchs of the early seventeenth century, causing some to leave for the Americas.

Circular Letter In reaction to the 1767 Townshend Acts, the Massachusetts assembly circulated a letter to the other colonies, asking that they work together and jointly issue a petition of protest. Strong-willed response of British authorities to the letter influenced the colonial assemblies to work together on a closer basis.

Civil Rights Act of 1866 Act that struck down Black Codes and defined the rights of all citizens; also stated that the federal government could act when civil rights were violated at the state level. Passed by Congress over the veto of President Andrew Johnson.

Civil Rights Act of 1964 Key piece of civil rights legislation that made discrimination on the basis of race, sex, religion, or national origin illegal; segregation in public restrooms, bus stations, and other public facilities also was declared illegal.

Civil Service Commission Created by the Pendelton Civil Service Act of 1883, this body was in charge of testing applicants and assigning them to appropriate government jobs; filling jobs on the basis of merit replaced the spoils system, in which government jobs were given as rewards for political service.

Civilian Conservation Corps (CCC) New Deal program that began in 1933, putting nearly 3 million young men to work; workers were paid little, but worked on conservation projects and maintaining beaches and parks. CCC program for young women began in 1937.

Clayton Antitrust Act of 1914 Act designed to strengthen the Sherman Antitrust Act of 1890. Certain activities previously committed by big businesses, such as not allowing unions in factories and not allowing strikes, were declared illegal.

cold war Period between 1945 and 1991 of near-continuous struggle between the United States and its Allies and the Soviet Union and its Allies; cold war tensions were made even more intense by the existence of the atomic bomb.

colonial assemblies Existed in all of the British colonies in America; House of Burgesses in Virginia was the first one. Members of colonial assemblies were almost always members of the upper classes of colonial society.

Columbian Exchange The exchange of crops, animals (as well as diseases), and ideas between Europe and the Western Hemisphere that developed in the aftermath of the voyages of Columbus.

Committee on Public Information Created by Woodrow Wilson during World War I to mobilize public opinion for the war, this was the most intensive use of propaganda until that time by the United States. The image of "Uncle Sam" was created for this propaganda campaign.

Committees of Correspondence First existed in Massachusetts, and eventually in all of the colonies. Leaders of resistance to British rule listed their grievances against the British and circulated them to all of the towns of the colony.

Common Sense Very popular 1776 publication in the colonies written by Englishman Thomas Paine, who had come to America in 1774; repudiated the entire concept of government by monarchy. After publication of this document, public sentiment in the colonies turned decisively toward a desire for independence.

Compromise of 1850 Complex agreement that temporarily lessened tensions between Northern and Southern political leaders, and prevented a possible secession crisis; to appease the South, the Fugitive Slave Act was strengthened; to appease the North, California entered the Union as a free state.

Compromise of 1877 Political arrangement that ended the contested presidential election of 1876. Representatives of Southern states agreed not to oppose the official election of Republican Rutherford B. Hayes as president despite massive election irregularities. In return, the Union army stopped enforcing Reconstruction legislation in the South, thus ending Reconstruction.

Concord, Battle of Occurred on April 19, 1775, between British regulars and Massachusetts militiamen. Almost 275 British soldiers were wounded or died; as a result, a wider conflict between the colonies and the British became much more probable.

Confederate States of America Eventually made up of 11 former states with Jefferson Davis as its first and only president; was unable to defeat the North because of lack of railroad lines, lack of industry, and an inability to get European nations to support their cause.

Congress of Industrial Organizations (CIO) Group of unions that broke from the AFL in 1938 and organized effective union drives in automobile and rubber industries; supported sit-down strikes in major rubber plants. Reaffiliated with the AFL in 1955.

conscription Getting recruits for military service using a draft. This method was used by the American government in all of the wars of the twentieth century. Conscription was viewed most negatively during the Vietnam War.

consumer society Many Americans in the 1950s became infatuated with all of the new products produced by technology and went out and purchased more than any prior generation. Consumer tastes of the decade were largely dictated by advertising and television.

containment policy Formulated by George Kennan, a policy whereby the United States would forcibly stop Communist aggression whenever and wherever it occurred; containment was the dominant American policy of the cold war era, and forced America to become involved in foreign conflicts such as Vietnam.

Continentals Soldiers in the "American" army commanded by George Washington in the Revolutionary War. Victory at the Battle of Trenton on December 16, 1776, did much to raise the morale of the soldiers (and convince many of them to reenlist). Also a term used for paper money printed in 1781 that was soon made worthless by inflation.

Contract with America (1994) Pledge by Republican candidates for House of Representatives; led by Newt Gingrich, candidates promised to support term limits, balancing the budget, and lessening the size of the federal government. In the 1994 Congressional elections, Republicans won both houses of Congress for the first time in 40 years.

convoy system System used to protect American ships carrying materials to Great Britain in 1940 and 1941; merchant ships were protected by American warships. Firing took place between these ships and German submarines, with American losses. Also used in World War I by the navy to allow American shipping to Europe.

Copperheads Democrats in Congress in the first years of the Civil War who opposed Abraham Lincoln and the North's attack on the South, claiming that the war would result in massive numbers of freed slaves entering the North and a total disruption of the Northern economy.

Coral Sea, Battle of the May 1942 American naval victory over the Japanese; prevented Japanese from attacking Australia. First naval battle where losses on both sides came almost exclusively from bombing from airplanes.

counterculture Youth of the 1960s who espoused a lifestyle encompassing drug use, free love, and a rejection of adult authority; actual "hippies" were never more than a small percentage of young people.

Coxey's Army Supporters of Ohio Populist Jacob Coxey who in 1894 marched on Washington, demanded that the government create jobs for the unemployed; although this group had no effect whatsoever on policy, it did demonstrate the social and economic impact of the Panic of 1893.

creationism Belief in the biblical account of the origin of the universe and the origin of man; believers in creationism and believers in evolution both had their day in court during the 1925 Scopes Trial.

Crittenden Plan (1860) Compromise proposal on the slavery issue designed to defuse tension between North and South; would have allowed slavery to continue in the South and would have denied Congress the power to regulate interstate slave trade. On the advice of newly elected President Lincoln, Republicans in Congress voted against it.

Crusades From these attempts to recapture the Holy Land, Europeans acquired an appreciation of the benefits of overseas expansion and an appreciation of the economic benefits of slavery.

Cuban Missile Crisis (1962) Conflict between the United States and the Soviet Union over Soviet missiles discovered in Cuba; Soviets eventually removed missiles under American pressure. Crisis was perhaps the closest the world came to armed conflict in the cold war era.

Currency Act of 1764 British act forbidding the American colonies to issue paper money as legal tender; act was repealed in 1773 by the British as an effort to ease tensions between themselves and the colonies.

dark horse candidate A candidate for office with little support before the beginning of the nomination process. James K. Polk was the first dark horse candidate for president in 1844.

Dawes Act of 1887 Act designed to break up Native American tribes, offered Native American families 160 acres of farmland or 320 acres of land for grazing. Large amounts of tribal lands were not claimed by Native Americans, and thus were purchased by land speculators.

Declaration of Neutrality Issued by President Woodrow Wilson after the outbreak of World War I in Europe in 1914, stating that the United States would maintain normal relations with and continue to trade with both sides in the conflict; factors including submarine warfare made it difficult for America to maintain this policy. Also declared by George Washington in 1793 to allow American merchants to trade with those on both sides of the French Revolution.

Declaration of Rights and Grievances (1774) Measure adopted by the First Continental Congress, stating that Parliament had some rights to regulate colonial trade with Britain, but that Parliament did not have the right to tax the colonies without their consent.

Declaratory Act of 1766 British law stating that the Parliament had absolute right to tax the colonies as they saw fit and to make laws that would be enacted in the colonies. Ironically, issued at the same time as the repeal of the Stamp Act.

deficit spending Economic policy whereby government spends money that it "doesn't have," thus creating a budget deficit. Although "conventional" economic theory disapproves of this, it is commonplace during times of crisis or war (e.g., the New Deal; post–September 11, 2001).

Democratic party Had its birth during the candidacy of Andrew Jackson; originally drew its principles from Thomas Jefferson and advocated limited government.

In modern times many Democrats favor domestic programs that a larger, more powerful government allows.

Democratic-Republicans Believed in the ideas of Thomas Jefferson, who wrote of the benefits of a limited government and of a society dominated by the values of the yeoman farmer. Opposed to the Federalists, who wanted a strong national state and a society dominated by commercial interests.

détente The lessening of tensions between nations. A policy of détente between the United States and the Soviet Union and Communist China began during the presidency of Richard Nixon; the architect of policy was National Security Advisor Henry Kissinger.

Dien Bien Phu, Battle of (1954) Victory of Vietnamese forces over the French, causing the French to leave Vietnam and all of Indochina; Geneva Peace Accords that followed established North and South Vietnam.

direct primary Progressive-era reform adopted by some states that allowed candidates for state offices to be nominated by the rank-and-file party members in statewide primaries instead of by the party bosses, who had traditionally dominated the nominating process.

dollar diplomacy Foreign policy of President William Howard Taft, which favored increased American investment in the world as the major method for increasing American influence and stability abroad; in some parts of the world, such as in Latin America, the increased American influence was resented.

domesticity Social trend of post–World War II America; many Americans turned to family and home life as a source of contentment. Emphasis on family as a source of fulfillment forced some women to abandon the workforce and achieve "satisfaction" as homemakers.

Dominion of New England Instituted by King James II in 1686. Sir Edmund Andros governed the colonies of Massachusetts, Connecticut, Rhode Island, New York, Plymouth, and New Hampshire as a single entity without an elective assembly; Andros was finally overthrown by militiamen in Boston in April 1689 (after the Glorious Revolution).

domino theory Major tenet of cold war containment policy of the United States held that if one country in a region turned Communist, other surrounding countries would soon follow; this theory convinced many that to save all of Southeast Asia, it was necessary to resist Communist aggression in Vietnam.

Double V campaign World War II "policy" supported by several prominent black newspapers, stating that blacks in America should work for victory over the Axis powers but at the same time work for victory over oppression at home; black leaders remained frustrated during the war by continued segregation of the armed forces.

Dred Scott **case** Supreme Court case involving a man who was born a slave but had then lived in both a nonslave state and a nonslave territory and was now petitioning for his legal freedom; in 1857 the Court ruled that slaves were not people but were property, that they could not be citizens of the United States, and thus had no legal right to petition the Court for anything. Ruling also stated that the Missouri Compromise, which banned slavery in the territories, was unconstitutional.

Dust Bowl Great Plains region that suffered severe drought and experienced massive dust storms during the 1930s. Because of extreme conditions many who lived in the Dust Bowl left their farms and went to California to work as migrant farmers.

Eisenhower Doctrine Policy established in 1957 that promised military and economic aid to "friendly" nations in the Middle East; the policy was established to prevent communism from gaining a foothold in the region. The policy was first utilized later that year when the United States gave large amounts of aid to King Hussein of Jordan to put down internal rebellion.

Electoral College Procedure outlined in the Constitution for the election of the president; under this system, votes of electors from each state, and not the popular vote, determine who is elected president. As was demonstrated in 2000 presidential election, this system allows a person to be elected president who does not win the nationwide popular vote.

Emancipation Proclamation Edict by Abraham Lincoln that went into effect on January 1, 1863, abolishing slavery in the Confederate states. The proclamation did not affect the four slave states that were still part of the Union (so as not to alienate them).

Embargo of 1807 Declaration by President Thomas Jefferson that banned all American trade with Europe. As a result of the war between England and Napoleon's France, America's sea rights as a neutral power were threatened. Jefferson hoped the embargo would force England and France to respect American neutrality.

Emergency Quota Act Also called "the Johnson Act," this 1921 bill limited immigration from Southern and Eastern Europe by stating that in a year, total immigration from any country could only equal 3 percent of the number of immigrations from that country living in the United States in 1910.

encomienda system American natives were given over to Spanish colonists, who in exchange for their labor, promised to "protect" them.

enlightenment Eighteenth-century European intellectual movement that attempted to discover the natural laws that governed science and society and taught that progress was inevitable in the Western world. Americans were greatly influenced by the Enlightenment, especially by the ideas of John Locke, who stated that government should exist for the benefit of the people living under it.

Enola Gay The name of the American bomber that on August 6, 1945, dropped the first atomic bomb on the city of Hiroshima, thus initiating the nuclear age.

environmentalists They broadly support the goals of environmentalism—a broad philosophy, ideology, and social movement that advocates preservation, restoration, and/or improvement of the natural environment by, in part, controlling pollution and protecting plant and animal diversity.

Era of Good Feelings Term used by a newspaper of the period to describe the years between 1816 and 1823, when after the end of the War of 1812 the United States remained generally free of foreign conflicts and when political strife at home was at a bare minimum (because of the collapse of the Federalist party).

Espionage Act World War I era regulation passed in 1917 that ordered severe penalties for citizens who criticized the war effort or the government. Mandatory prison sentences were also proclaimed for those who interfered with the draft process. Nearly 700 Americans were arrested for violating this act.

Essex Junto Group of Massachusetts Federalists who met to voice their displeasure with the policies of Thomas Jefferson during Jefferson's second term, and proposed that the New England states and New York secede from the Union.

Exodusters Large number of Southern blacks who left the South and moved to Kansas for a "better life" after Reconstruction ended in 1877; many failed to find satisfaction in Kansas because of lack of opportunities and open hostility from Kansas residents.

Fair Deal A series of domestic programs proposed to Congress by President Harry Truman that included a Fair Employment Practices Act, a call for government construction of public housing, an extension of Social Security, and a proposal to ensure employment for all American workers.

Farmers' Alliances After the decline of Grange organizations, these became the major organizations of farmers in the 1880s; many experimented with cooperative buying and selling. Many local alliances became involved in direct political activity with the growth of the Populist party in the 1890s.

Federal Deposit Insurance Corporation (FDIC) Passed during the first Hundred Days of the administration of Franklin Roosevelt, this body insured individual bank deposits up to $2,500 and helped to restore confidence in America's banks.

Federal Reserve System Established by the Federal Reserve Act of 1913, this system established 12 district reserve banks to be controlled by the banks in each district. In addition, a Federal Reserve Board was established to regulate the entire structure. This act improved public confidence in the banking system.

Federal Trade Commission Authorized after the passage of the Clayton Antitrust Act of 1914, it was established as the major government body in charge of regulating big business. The FTC investigated possible violations of antitrust laws.

Federalists During the period when the Constitution was being ratified, these were the supporters of the larger national government as outlined in the Constitution; the party of Washington and John Adams, it was supported by commercial interests. Federalists were opposed by Jeffersonians, who favored a smaller federal government and a society dominated by agrarian values. Federalist influence in national politics ended with the presidential election of 1816.

Feminine Mystique, The Betty Friedan's 1963 book that was the bible of the feminist movement of the 1960s and 1970s. Friedan maintained that the post–World War II emphasis on family forced women to think of themselves primarily as housewives and robbed them of much of their creative potential.

feminist movement Movement dedicated to the belief that women should have the same rights and benefits in American society that men do. Feminism gained many supporters during the Progressive Era, and in the 1960s drew large numbers of supporters. The National Organization for Women (NOW) was established in 1966 by Betty Friedan and had nearly 200,000 members in 1969.

Fifteenth Amendment Ratified in 1870, this amendment stated that a person could not be denied the right to vote because of the color of their skin or whether or not they had been a slave. This extended the rights of blacks to vote to the North (which the Emancipation Proclamation had not done); some in the women's movement opposed the amendment on the grounds that it did nothing for the rights of women.

Final Solution The plan of Adolf Hitler and Nazi Germany to eliminate Jewish civilization from Europe. By the end of the war in 1945, nearly 6 million Jews had been executed. The full extent of Germany's atrocities was not known in Europe and the United States until near the end of World War II.

fireside chats Broadcasts on the radio by Franklin Roosevelt addressed directly to the American people that made many Americans feel that he personally cared about them. FDR did 16 of these in his first two terms. Many Americans in the 1930s had pictures of Roosevelt in their living rooms. In addition, Roosevelt received more letters from ordinary Americans than any other president in American history.

First Continental Congress A 1774 meeting in Philadelphia at which colonists vowed to resist further efforts to tax them without their consent.

First Great Awakening A religious revival in the American colonies that lasted from the 1720s through the 1740s; speakers like Jonathan Edwards enraptured speakers with sermons such as "Sinners in the Hands of an Angry God." Religious splits in the colonies became deeper because of this movement.

flapper A "new woman" of the 1920s, who wore short skirts and bobbed hair and rejected many of the social regulations that controlled women of previous generations.

Force Act of 1832 Legislation that gave President Andrew Jackson the power to invade any state if that action was necessary to enforce federal law. The bill was in response to nullification of federal tariff regulation by the legislature of South Carolina.

Fordney-McCumber Tariff of 1922 Act that sharply increased tariffs on imported goods. Most Republican leaders of the 1920s firmly believed in "protectionist" policies that would increase profits for American businesses.

Fort Sumter Federal fort located in Charleston, South Carolina, that was fired on by Confederate artillery on April 12, 1861; these were the first shots actually fired in the Civil War. A public outcry immediately followed across the Northern states, and the mobilization of a federal army began.

Fourteen Points Woodrow Wilson's view of a post–World War I that he hoped the other Allied powers would endorse during the negotiations for the Treaty of Versailles. Wilson's vision included elimination of secret treaties, arms reduction, national self-determination, and the creation of a League of Nations. After negotiations, only the League of Nations remained (which the United States never became part of).

Fourteenth Amendment Ratified in 1868, this amendment stated that "all persons born or naturalized in the United States" were citizens. In addition, all former Confederate supporters were prohibited from holding office in the United States.

Franciscans Missionaries who established settlements in the Southwestern United States in the late 1500s; at their missions Christian conversion was encouraged, but at the same time Native Americans were used as virtual slaves. Rebellions against the missions and the soldiers sent to protect them began in 1598.

Fredericksburg, Battle of Battle on December 13, 1862, where the Union army commanded by General Ambrose Burnside suffered a major defeat at the hands of Confederate forces.

Free Speech Movement Protests at the University of California at Berkeley in 1964 and 1965 that opposed the control that the university, and "the establishment" in general, had over the lives of university students. Protesters demanded changes in university regulations and also broader changes in American society.

free trade The philosophy that trade barriers and protective tariffs inhibit long-term economic growth; this philosophy was the basis for the 1994 ratification by the United States of the North American Free Trade Agreement (NAFTA), which removed trade restrictions between the United States, Mexico, and Canada.

freedmen Term used for free blacks in the South after the Civil War. Freedmen enjoyed some gains in terms of education, the ability to hold office, and economic well-being during the Reconstruction era, although many of these gains were wiped out after the Compromise of 1877.

Freedom Rides Buses of black and white civil rights workers who in 1961 rode on interstate buses to the Deep South to see if Southern states were abiding by the 1960 Supreme Court ruling banning segregation on interstate buses and in waiting rooms and restaurants at bus stations. Buses met mob violence in numerous cities; federal marshals were finally called in to protect the freedom riders.

Freeport Doctrine Introduced by Stephen Douglas in the Lincoln-Douglas debates, the idea that despite the *Dred Scott* Supreme Court decision, a territory could still prevent slavery by electing officials who were opposed to it and by creating laws and regulations that would make slavery impossible to enforce.

Free-Soil party Political party that won 10 percent of the vote in the 1848 presidential election. They were opposed to the spread of slavery into any of the recently acquired American territories. Free-Soil supporters were mainly many former members of the Whig party in the North.

French and Indian War Called "the Seven Years' War" in European textbooks. In this war, the British and the French fought for the right to expand their empire in the Americas. Colonists and Native Americans fought on both sides, and the war eventually spread to Europe and elsewhere. The English emerged victorious, and in the end received all of French Canada.

Fugitive Slave Act Part of the Compromise of 1850, this legislation set up special commissions in Northern states to determine if an accused runaway slave really was one. According to regulations, after the verdict, commissioners were given more money if the accused was found to be a runaway than if he or she was found not to be one. Some Northern legislatures passed laws attempting to circumvent the Fugitive Slave Act.

Gadsden Purchase Strip of territory running through Arizona and New Mexico that the United States purchased from Mexico in 1853. President Pierce authorized this purchase to secure that the southern route of the transcontinental railroad (between Texas and California) would be in American territory.

Geneva Accords After the French were defeated in Vietnam, a series of agreements made in 1954 temporarily divided Vietnam into two parts (along the 17th parallel) and promised nationwide elections within two years. To prevent Communists from gaining control, the United States installed a friendly government in South Vietnam and saw that the reunification elections never took place.

Gettysburg Address Speech made by Abraham Lincoln at dedication ceremony for a cemetery for Union soldiers who died at the Battle of Gettysburg. In this November 19, 1863 speech Lincoln stated that freedom should exist in the United States for *all* men, and that "government of the people, by the people, for the people, shall not perish from the earth."

Gettysburg, Battle of The most important battle of the Civil War, this July 1863 victory by Union forces prevented General Robert E. Lee from invading the North. Defeat at Gettysburg, along with defeat at the Battle of Vicksburg during the same month, turned the tide of war firmly in the direction of Union forces.

Ghent, Treaty of (1814) Treaty between the United States and Great Britain ending the War of 1812; treaty restored diplomatic relations between the two countries but did nothing to address the issues that had initially caused the war.

Ghost Dances Religion practiced by Lakota tribesmen in response to repeated incursions by American settlers. Ghost dancers thought that a Native American messiah would come and banish the whites, return the buffalo, and give all former Native American land back to the Native Americans. Worried territorial officials had Sitting Bull arrested (he was later killed under uncertain circumstances) and killed another 240 Lakota at Wounded Knee Creek.

GIs Popular term for an American servicemen during World War II; refers to the fact that virtually anything worn or used was "government issued."

GI Bill Officially called "the Serviceman's Readjustment Act of 1944," this legislation gave many benefits to returning World War II veterans, including financial assistance for veterans wanting to go to college or enter other job training programs, special loan programs for veterans wanting to buy homes or businesses, and preferential treatment for veterans who wished to apply for government jobs.

Gilded Age, The Some historians describe the late nineteenth century in this manner, describing it as an era with a surface of great prosperity hiding deep problems of social inequity and shallowness of culture. The term comes from the title of an 1873 Mark Twain novel.

globalization Belief that the United States should work closely with other nations of the world to solve common problems; this was the foreign policy approach of President Clinton. Policies that supported this approach included the ratification of NAFTA, the United States working more closely with the United Nations, and "nation building" abroad. Many policies of globalization were initially rejected by Clinton's successor, George H. W. Bush.

Glorious Revolution English revolution of 1688 to 1689 when King James II was removed from the throne and his Protestant daughter Mary and her Dutch husband William began to rule. Reaction to this in the American colonies was varied: There was a revolt against appointed Catholic officials in New York and Maryland, and in Massachusetts the governor was sent back to England with the colonial demand that the Dominion of New England be disbanded.

gold standard Economic system that based all currency on gold, meaning that all paper currency could be exchanged at a bank for gold. Business interests of the late nineteenth century supported this. William Jennings Bryan ran for president three times opposing the gold standard, and supported the free coinage of silver instead.

"Gospel of Wealth" The philosophy of steel magnate Andrew Carnegie, who stated that wealthy industrialists had an obligation to create a "trust fund" from their profits to help their local communities. By the time of his death, Carnegie had given over 90 percent of his wealth to various foundations and philanthropic endeavors.

Grange Initially formed in 1867, the Grange was an association of farmers that provided social activities and information about new farming techniques. Some local Grange organizations became involved in cooperative buying and selling.

Great Compromise Plan drafted by Roger Sherman of Connecticut that stated one house of the U.S. Congress would be based on population (the House of Representatives), while in the other house all states would be represented equally with two representatives per state (the Senate). This compromise greatly speeded the ratification of the Constitution.

Great Migration Migration of large numbers of American blacks to Midwestern and Eastern industrial cities that began during World War I and continued throughout the 1920s. Additional workers were needed in the North because of the war and during the 1920s because of immigration restrictions. Blacks were willing to leave the South because of continued lynchings there and the fact that their economic situation was not improving.

Great Society Aggressive program announced by President Lyndon Johnson in 1965 to attack the major social problems in America; Great Society programs included the War on Poverty, Medicare and Medicaid programs for elderly Americans, greater protection for and more legislation dealing with civil rights, and greater funding for education. Balancing the Great Society and the war in Vietnam would prove difficult for the Johnson administration.

Greenback party Political party of the 1870s and early 1880s that stated the government should put more money in circulation and supported an eight-hour workday and female suffrage. The party received support from farmers but never built a national base. The Greenback party argued into the 1880s that more greenbacks should be put in circulation to help farmers who were in debt and who saw the prices of their products decreasing annually.

greenbacks Paper money issued by the American government during and immediately after the Civil War that was not backed up by gold or silver.

gridlock Situation when the president is a member of one political party and the U.S. Congress is controlled by the other party, causing a situation where little legislation is actually passed. This is how some describe the situation with President Clinton and the Republican-controlled Congress after the 1994 congressional elections.

Guadalcanal, Battle of Battle over this Pacific island lasted from August 1942 through February 1943. American victory against fierce Japanese resistance was the first major offensive victory for the Americans in the Pacific War.

Guadalupe Hidalgo, Treaty of Treaty ending the war with Mexico that was ratified by the Senate in March 1848 and for $15 million gave the United States Texas territory to the Rio Grande River, New Mexico, and California.

Gulf of Tonkin Resolution (1964) Congressional resolution that gave President Johnson the authority to "take all necessary measures to repel" attacks against American military forces stationed in Vietnam. Later, critics would charge, this resolution allowed the president to greatly expand the Vietnam War without congressional oversight.

Harlem Renaissance Black literary and artistic movement centered in Harlem that lasted from the 1920s into the early 1930s that both celebrated and lamented black life in America; Langston Hughes and Zora Neale Hurston were two famous writers of this movement.

Hartford Convention Meeting of New England Federalists in the closing months of the War of 1812 where they threatened that New England would secede from the United States unless trade restrictions imposed by President Madison were lifted. American victory in the war made their protests seem pointless.

Hawley-Smoot Tariff In response to the initial effects of the Great Depression, Congress authorized this tariff in 1930; this established tariff rates on imported goods at the highest level of any point in U.S. history. Some American companies benefited in the short term, although the effect on world trade was disastrous, as many other countries erected tariff barriers on American imports.

Haymarket Square Location in Chicago of labor rally called by anarchists and other radical labor leaders on May 2, 1886. A bomb was hurled toward police officials, and police opened fire on the demonstrators; numerous policemen and demonstrators were killed and wounded. Response in the nation's press was decidedly antiunion.

Head Start One of Lyndon Johnson's War on Poverty programs that gave substantial funding for a nursery school program to prepare children of poor parents for kindergarten.

heavy industry The production of steel, iron, and other materials that can be used for building purposes; great increase in heavy industry fueled the massive industrial growth that took place in the last half of the nineteenth century.

Hessians German troops who fought in the Revolutionary War on the side of Great Britain; Hessian troops were almost all paid mercenaries.

Historiography The study of history and how it is written. Students of historiography would analyze various historical interpretations and the viewpoints of historians. This field is not as concerned with historical events themselves as it is with how these events are interpreted.

holding company A company that existed to gain monopoly control over an industry by buying large numbers of shares of stock in as many companies as possible in that industry. The best example in American history was John D. Rockefeller's Standard Oil corporation.

Holocaust Historical term used for the extermination of 6 million Jewish victims by Nazi Germany during World War II. Much has been written on the reasons for the Holocaust and why it occurred in Germany.

Homeland Security Act of 2002 States that it is the mission of the Department of Homeland Security to prevent terrorist attacks within the United States, reduce the vulnerability of the United States to terror, and minimize the damage and assist in the recovery from a terrorist attack that might occur in the United States.

Homestead Act of 1862 Enactment by Congress that gave 160 acres of publicly owned land to a farmer who lived on the land and farmed it for two years. The provisions of this bill inspired hundreds of thousands of Americans to move westward in the years after the Civil War.

Hoovervilles Groups of crude houses made of cardboard and spare wood that sprang up on the fringes of many American cities during the first years of the Great Depression. These shacks were occupied by unemployed workers; the name of these communities demonstrated the feeling that President Hoover should have been doing more to help the downtrodden in America.

horizontal integration The strategy of gaining as much control over an entire single industry as possible, usually by creating trusts and holding companies. The most successful example of horizontal integration was John D. Rockefeller and Standard Oil, who had at one point controlled over 92 percent of the oil production in the United States.

HUAC (House Un-American Activities Committee) Committee of the House of Representatives that beginning in 1947 investigated possible Communist infiltration of the entertainment industry and, more importantly, of the government. Most famous investigations of the committee were the investigation of the "Hollywood Ten" and the investigation of Alger Hiss, a former high-ranking member of the State Department.

Huguenots Protestants in France, who by the 1630s were believers in Calvinism. Few Huguenots ended up settling in the Americas, as French officials feared they would disrupt the unity of colonial settlements.

Hull House Established by Jane Addams and Ellen Gates Starr in Chicago in 1889, this was the first settlement house in America. Services such as reading groups, social clubs, an employment bureau, and a "day care center" for working mothers could be found at Hull House. The Hull House model was later copied in many other urban centers.

Hun Term used in Allied propaganda during World War I to depict the German soldier; Germans were portrayed as bloodthirsty beasts. World War I was the first war where propaganda was used on a widespread scale.

Hundred Days The period from March through June 1933; the first 100 days of the New Deal presidency of Franklin Roosevelt. During this period programs were implemented to assist farmers, the banks, unemployed workers, and businessmen. In addition, Prohibition was repealed.

hunter-gatherers Early civilizations that existed not by farming but by moving from region to region and taking what was necessary at the time from the land; some early Native American tribes in northern New England lived as hunter-gatherers.

hydrogen bomb Atomic weapons much more powerful than those used at Hiroshima and Nagasaki; these were developed and repeatedly tested by both the United States and the Soviet Union in the 1950s, increasing dramatically the potential danger of nuclear war.

impeachment The process of removing an elected public official from office. During the Progressive Era several states adopted measures making it easier to do this. Presidents Andrew Johnson and William Jefferson Clinton were both impeached by the House of Representatives, but neither was convicted by the U.S. Senate (the procedure outlined in the Constitution of the United States).

impressment British practice of forcing civilians and ex-sailors back into naval service. During the wars against Napoleon. The British seized nearly 7,500 sailors from American ships, including some that had actually become American citizens. This practice caused increased tensions between the United States and Great Britain and was one of the causes of the War of 1812.

Inca empire Advanced and wealthy civilization centered in the Andes mountain region; aided by smallpox, Francisco Pizarro conquered the Incas in 1533.

indentured servants Legal arrangement when an individual owed compulsory service (in some cases only 3 years, in others up to 10) for free passage to the American colonies. Many of the early settlers in the Virginia colony came as indentured servants.

Industrial Workers of the World (IWW) Established in 1905, this union attempted to unionize the unskilled workers who were usually not recruited by the American Federation of Labor. The IWW included blacks, poor sharecroppers, and newly arrived immigrants from Eastern Europe. Members of the union were called "Wobblies," and leaders of the union were inspired by Marxist principles.

Influence of Sea Power upon History, The Very influential 1890s book by Admiral Alfred Thayer Mahan, which argued that throughout history the most powerful nations have achieved their influence largely because of powerful navies. Mahan called for a large increase in the size of the American navy, the acquisition of American bases in the Pacific, and the building of the Panama Canal.

initiative process Procedure supported by the Populist party in the 1890s by which any proposed law could go on the public ballot as long as a petition with an appropriate number of names is submitted beforehand supporting the proposed law.

internment camps Controversial decision was made after the bombing of Pearl Harbor to place Japanese Americans living on the West Coast in these camps. President Roosevelt authorized this by Executive Order #9066; this order was validated by the Supreme Court in 1944. In 1988 the U.S. government paid compensation to surviving detainees.

Interstate Commerce Act Passed in 1887, the bill created America's first regulatory commission, the Interstate Commerce Commission. The task of this commission was to regulate the railroad and railroad rates, and to ensure that rates were "reasonable and just."

Intolerable Acts Term used by anti-British speakers across the colonies for the series of bills passed in Great Britain to punish the Massachusetts colony for the Boston Tea Party of December 1773. These including the closing of Boston harbor, prohibiting local meetings, and mandatory quartering of troops in the homes of Massachusetts residents.

Iran-Contra Affair During the second term of the Reagan administration, government officials sold missiles to Iran (hoping that this would help free American hostages held in Lebanon); money from this sale was used to aid anti-communist Contra forces in Nicaragua. Iran was a country that was supposed to be on the American "no trade" list because of their taking of American hostages, and congressional legislation had been enacted making it illegal to give money to the Contras. A major scandal for the Reagan administration.

Iranian Hostage Crisis On November 4, 1979, Islamic Fundamentalists seized the American embassy in Tehran, Iran, and took all Americans working there hostage. This was a major humiliation for the United States, as diplomatic and military efforts to free the hostages failed. The hostages were finally freed on January 20, 1981, immediately after the inauguration of Ronald Reagan.

iron curtain In a March 5, 1946, speech in Fulton, Missouri, Winston Churchill used this term to describe the division that the Soviet Union had created between itself and its Eastern European Allies and Western Europe and the United States. Churchill emphasized the need for the United States to stand up to potential Soviet aggression in the future.

ironclad ship Civil War-era ships that were totally encased in iron, thus making them very difficult to damage; the ironclad of the Confederate army was the *Virginia* (it had been the *Merrimac* when it was captured from the Union), whereas the Union ship was the *Monitor*. The two ships battled each other in March 1862, with both being badly damaged.

irreconcilables After World War I, a group of U.S. senators who were opposed to a continued U.S. presence in Europe in any form. This group was influential in preventing the passage of the Versailles Treaty in the Senate.

island-hopping A successful American military tactic in the Pacific in 1942 and 1943 of taking strategic islands that could be used as staging points for continued military offensives. Increasing American dominance in air power made this tactic possible.

isolationism A policy of disengaging the United States from major world commitments and concentrating on the U.S. domestic issues. This was the dominant foreign policy of the United States for much of the 1920s and the 1930s.

Jay's Treaty of 1794 Treaty between the United States and Great Britain designed to ease increasing tensions between the two nations. The British did make some concessions to the Americans, including abandoning the forts they occupied in the interior of the continent. However, Britain refused to make concessions to America over the rights of American ships. Tensions over this issue would eventually be a cause of the War of 1812.

Jazz Age Term used to describe the image of the liberated, urbanized 1920s, with a flapper as a dominant symbol of that era. Many rural, fundamentalist Americans deeply resented the changes in American culture that occurred in the "Roaring 20s."

Jazz Singer, The 1927 film starring Al Jolson that was the first movie with sound. Story of the film deals with a young Jewish man who has to choose between the "modern" and his Jewish past.

Jesuits Missionary group who established settlements in Florida, New Mexico, Paraguay, and in several areas within French territory in North America. Jesuits were organized with military precision and order.

jingoism American foreign policy based on a strident nationalism, a firm belief in American world superiority, and a belief that military solutions were, in almost every case, the best ones. Jingoism was most evident in America during the months leading up to and during the Spanish-American War.

judicial review In the 1803 *Marbury v. Madison* decision, Chief Justice John C. Marshall stated that the U.S. Supreme Court ultimately had the power to decide on the constitutionality of any law passed by the U.S. Congress or by the legislature of any state. Many had argued that individual states should have the power to do this; the *Marbury* decision increased the power of the federal government.

Judiciary Act of 1801 Bill passed by the Federalist Congress just before the inauguration of President Thomas Jefferson; Federalists appointed by this bill attempted to maintain control of the judiciary by reducing the number of Supreme Court judges (so Jefferson probably wouldn't be able to name a replacement) and by increasing the number of federal judges (who President Adams appointed before he left office). Bill was repealed by new Congress in 1802.

Justice Reorganization Bill Franklin Roosevelt's 1937 plan to increase the number of Supreme Court justices. He claimed that this was because many of the judges were older and needed help keeping up with the work. In reality he wanted to "pack the court" because the Court had made several rulings outlawing New Deal legislation. Many Democrats and Republicans opposed this plan, so it was finally dropped by Roosevelt.

kamikaze pilots 1945 tactic of Japanese air force where pilots flew at American ships at full speed and crashed into them, in several cases causing ships to sink. This tactic showed the desperate nature of the Japanese military situation at this time. By July 1945, kamikaze attacks were no longer utilized, as Japan was running out of airplanes and pilots.

Kansas-Nebraska Act of 1854 Compromise legislation crafted by Stephen Douglas that allowed the settlers in the Kansas and Nebraska territories to decide if those territories would be slave or free. Bill caused controversy and bloodshed throughout these territories; in the months before the vote in Kansas, large numbers of "settlers" moved in to influence the vote, and after the vote (won by proslavery forces), violence between the two sides intensified.

Kent State University Site of May 1970 antiwar protest where Ohio National Guardsmen fired on protesters, killing four. To many, this event was symbolic of the extreme political tensions that permeated American society in this era.

Kentucky and Virginia Resolves Passed by the legislatures in these two states, these resolutions maintained that the Alien and Sedition Acts championed through Congress by John Adams went beyond the powers that the Constitution stated belonged to the federal government. These resolves predated the later Southern argument that individual states could "nullify" federal laws deemed unconstitutional by the states.

Kerner Commission Established in 1967 to study the reason for urban riots, the commission spoke at length about the impact of poverty and racism on the lives of urban blacks in America, and emphasized that white institutions created and condoned the ghettoes of America.

King-Crane Commission The American commission that went into various regions of the Middle East immediately after World War I to discover what political future was desired by residents of the region. It was determined that many did not want to be controlled by Britain and France, and saw the United States in a favorable light. Predictably, the British and French saw to it that the findings of the commission were largely kept quiet.

King William's War Colonial war against the French that lasted from 1689 to 1697; army from New England colonies attacked Quebec, but were forced to retreat because of the lack of strong colonial leadership and an outbreak of smallpox among colonial forces.

Kitchen Cabinet An informal group of advisors, with no official titles, who the president relies on for advice. The most famous Kitchen Cabinet was that of Andrew Jackson, who met with several old political friends and two journalists for advice on many occasions.

Knights of Labor The major labor union of the 1880s; was not a single large union, but a federation of the unions of many industries. The Knights of Labor accepted unskilled workers. Publicity against the organization was intense after the Haymarket Square riot of 1886.

Know-Nothing party Political party developed in the 1850s that claimed that the other political parties and the entire political process were corrupt, that immigrants were destroying the economic base of America by working for low wages, and that Catholics in America were intent on destroying American democracy. Know-Nothings were similar in many ways to other nativist groups that developed at various points in America's history.

Korean War (1950 to 1953) War in which American and other UN forces fought to stop Communist aggression against South Korea. U.S. entry into the Korean War was totally consistent with the U.S. cold war policy of containment. Negotiated settlement divided Korea along the 38th parallel, a division that remains today.

Ku Klux Klan Organization founded in the South during the Reconstruction era by whites who wanted to maintain white supremacy in the region. The KKK used terror tactics, including murder. The Klan was revitalized in the 1920s; members of the 1920s Klan also opposed Catholics and Southern and Eastern European immigrants. The KKK exists to this day, with recent efforts to make the Klan appear to be "respectable."

labor movement The drive that began in the second half of the nineteenth century to have workers join labor unions. Divisions existed in nineteenth-century unions as to whether unions should focus their energies on political gains for workers or on "bread and butter" issues important to workers. In the twenty-first century, unions have broad political powers, as most endorse and financially support candidates in national and statewide elections.

laissez-faire economic principles Economic theory derived from eighteenth-century economist Adam Smith, who stated that for the economy to run soundly the government should take a hands-off role in economic matters. Those who have favored policies such as high import tariffs do *not* follow laissez-faire policies; a policy like NAFTA has more support among the "free market" supporters of Adam Smith.

land speculation The practice of buying up land with the intent of selling it off in the future for a profit. Land speculation existed in the Kentucky territory in the 1780s, throughout the West after the Homestead Act, and in Florida in the 1920s, when hundreds bought Florida swampland hoping to later sell it for a profit.

League of Nations International body of nations that was proposed by Woodrow Wilson and was adopted at the Versailles Peace Conference ending World War I. The League was never an effective body in reducing international tensions, at least partially because the United States was never a member of it.

Lend-Lease Act Legislation proposed by Franklin Roosevelt and adopted by Congress in 1941, stating that the United States could either sell or lease arms and other equipment to any country whose security was vital to America's interest. After the passage of this bill, military equipment to help the British war effort began to be shipped from the United States.

Letters from a Farmer in Pennsylvania A 1767 pamphlet by Pennsylvania attorney and landowner John

Dickinson, in which he eloquently stated the "taxation without representation" argument, and also stated that the only way that the House of Commons could represent the colonies in a meaningful way would be for actual colonists to be members of it.

Lever Food and Fuel Control Act August 1917 measure that gave President Wilson the power to regulate the production and consumption of food and fuels during wartime. Some in his administration argued for price controls and rationing; instead, Wilson instituted voluntary controls.

Levittown After World War II, the first "suburban" neighborhood; located in Hempstead, Long Island, houses in this development were small, looked the same, but were perfect for the postwar family that wanted to escape urban life. Levittown would become a symbol of the post–World War II flight to suburbia taken by millions.

Lewis and Clark Expedition (1804 to 1806) Mission sent by Thomas Jefferson to explore and map the newly acquired Louisiana territory and to create good relations with various Native American tribes within the territory. Reports brought back indicated that settlement was possible in much of the region, and that the Louisiana territory was well worth what had been paid for it.

Lexington Massachusetts town where the first skirmish between British troops and colonial militiamen took place; during this April 19, 1775, "battle," eight colonists were killed and another nine were wounded.

Liberator, The The radical abolitionist journal of William Lloyd Garrison that was first published in 1831. Garrison and his journal presented the most extreme abolitionist views during the period leading up to the Civil War.

Liberty Bonds Sold to U.S. civilians during World War I. A holder who paid $10 for a bond could get $13 back if the holder held on to the bond until it matured. Bonds were important in financing the war effort, and celebrities such as Charlie Chaplin made short films encouraging Americans to buy them.

Little Bighorn, Battle of the (1876) Montana battle where Colonel George Custer and more than 200 of his men were killed by a group of Cheyenne and Lakota warriors. This was the last major victory by Native American forces over a U.S. Army unit.

London Company In 1603 King James I gave the London Company a charter to settle the Virginia territory. In April 1607, the first settlers from this company settled at Jamestown.

Lost Generation Group of American intellectuals who viewed America in the 1920s as bigoted, intellectually shallow, and consumed by the quest for the dollar.

Many became extremely disillusioned with American life and went to Paris. Ernest Hemingway wrote of this group in *The Sun Also Rises*.

Louisiana Purchase The 1803 purchase of the huge Louisiana territory (from the Mississippi River out to the Rocky Mountains) from Napoleon for $15 million. This purchase made eventual westward movement possible for vast numbers of Americans.

Lowell System Developed in the textile mills of Lowell, Massachusetts, in the 1820s. In these factories as much machinery as possible was used, so that few skilled workers were needed in the process, and the workers were almost all single young farm women who worked for a few years and then returned home to be housewives. Managers found these young women were the perfect workers for this type of factory life.

Loyalists Individuals who remained loyal to Great Britain during the years up to and during the Revolutionary War. Many who were Loyalists were from the higher strata of colonial society; when war actually broke out and it became apparent that the British were not going to quickly win, almost all went to Canada, the West Indies, or back to Great Britain.

Loyalty Review Board This were established in 1947 in an effort to control possible Communist influence in the American government. These boards were created to investigate the possibility of "security risks" working for the American government, and to determine if those "security risks" should lose their jobs. Some employees were released because of their affiliation with "unacceptable" political organizations or because of their sexual orientation.

Lusitania British passenger liner with 128 Americans on board that was sunk off the coast of Ireland by a German U-boat on May 7, 1915. This sinking caused outrage in the United States and was one of a series of events that drew the United States closer to war with Germany.

Man in the Gray Flannel Suit, The Early 1950s book and movie that compares the sterility, sameness, and lack of excitement of postwar work and family life with the vitality felt by many World War II veterans during their wartime experiences.

Manhattan Project Program begun in 1942 to develop an atomic weapon for the United States. The project was aided by German scientists added to the research team who had been working on a similar bomb in Germany. First test of the bomb took place in New Mexico on July 16, 1945.

Manifest Destiny Term first used in the 1840s, the concept that America's expansion westward was as journalist John O'Sullivan said, "the fulfillment of our

Manifest Destiny to overspread the continent allotted by Providence for the free development of our yearly multiplying millions."

Marbury v. Madison (1803) Decision of this case written by Chief Justice John Marshall established the principle of judicial review, meaning that the Supreme Court ultimately has the power to decide if any federal or state law is unconstitutional.

March on Washington Over 200,000 came to Washington for this August 1963 event demanding civil rights for blacks. A key moment of the proceedings was Martin Luther King Jr.'s "I have a dream" speech; the power of the civil rights movement was not lost on Lyndon Johnson, who pushed for civil rights legislation when he became president the following year.

Marshall Plan Plan announced in 1947 whereby the United States would help to economically rebuild Europe after the war; 17 Western European nations became part of the plan. The United States introduced the plan so that communism would not spread across war-torn Europe and bring other European countries into the Communist camp.

martial law During a state of emergency, when rule of law may be suspended and government is controlled by military or police authorities. During the Civil War, Kentucky was placed under martial law by President Lincoln.

Massacre at Wounded Knee December 28, 1890, "battle" that was the last military resistance of Native Americans of the Great Plains against American encroachment. Minneconjou Native Americans were at Wounded Knee Creek. American soldiers attempted to take their arms from them. After shooting began, 25 American soldiers died, along with more than 200 men, women, and children of the Native American tribe.

massive retaliation Foreign policy officials in the Eisenhower administration believed the best way to stop communism was to convince the Communists that every time they advanced, there would be massive retaliation against them. This policy explains the desire in this era to increase the nuclear arsenal of the United States.

McCarran Internal Security Act Congressional act enacted in 1950 that stated all members of the Communist party had to register with the office of the Attorney General and that it was a crime to conspire to foster communism in the United States.

McCarran-Walter Act of 1952 Bill that limited immigration from everywhere except Northern and Western Europe and stated that immigration officials could turn any immigrant away that they thought might threaten the national security of the United States.

McCarthyism Named after Wisconsin Senator Joseph McCarthy, the title given for the movement that took place during the late 1940s and early 1950s in American politics to root out potential Communist influence in the government, the military, and the entertainment industry. Harsh tactics were often used by congressional investigations, with few actual Communists ever discovered. This period is seen by many today as an era of intolerance and paranoia.

Meat Inspection Act Inspired by Upton Sinclair's *The Jungle,* this 1906 bill established a government commission that would monitor the quality of all meat sold in America and inspect the meatpacking houses for safety and cleanliness.

Medicare Part of Lyndon Johnson's Great Society program, this program acted as a form of health insurance for retired Americans (and disabled ones as well). Through Medicare, the federal government would pay for services received by elderly patients at doctor's offices and hospitals.

mercantilism Economic policy practiced by most European states in the late seventeenth century that stated the power of any state depended largely on its wealth; thus it was the state's duty to do all that it could to build up wealth. A mercantilist country would not want to import raw materials from other countries; instead, it would be best to have colonies from which these raw materials could be imported.

Merrimack Union ironclad ship captured by Confederates during the Civil War and renamed the *Virginia*.

Meuse-Argonne Offensive American forces played a decisive role in this September 1918 Allied offensive, which was the last major offensive of the war and which convinced the German general staff that victory in World War I was impossible.

Mexican-American War War fought over possession of Texas. The settlement ending this war gave the United States the northern part of Texas territory and the territories of New Mexico and California.

Middle Passage The voyage across the Atlantic Ocean taken by slaves on their way to the Americas. Sickness, diseases, and death were rampant as slave ships crossed the Atlantic; on some ships, over 20 percent of slaves who began the journey were dead by the time the ship landed.

midnight appointments Judicial or other appointments made by an outgoing president or governor in the last hours before he or she leaves office. The most famous were the judicial appointments made by John Adams in the hours before Thomas Jefferson was inaugurated as president.

Midway, Battle of June 4, 1942, naval battle that crippled Japanese offensive capabilities in the Pacific; American airplanes destroyed four aircraft carriers and over 200 Japanese planes. After Midway, Japanese military operations were mainly defensive.

Missouri Compromise In a continued effort to maintain a balance between free and slave states, Henry Clay proposed this 1820 compromise, which admitted Maine to the Union as a free state, Missouri to the Union as a slave state, and stated that any part of the Louisiana Territory north of 36 degrees, 30 minutes would be nonslave territory.

Model T Automobile produced by Ford Motor Company using assembly line techniques. The first Model Ts were produced in 1907; using the assembly line, Ford produced half of the automobiles made in the world between 1907 and 1926.

Molasses Act In the early 1700s colonists traded for molasses with the French West Indies. British traders wanted to reduce trade between the colonies and the French; in 1733 they pressured Parliament to pass this act, which put prohibitively high duties on imported molasses. Colonists continued to smuggle French molasses into the Americas in spite of British efforts to prevent this.

Monitor Union ironclad ship utilized during the Civil War; fought one battle against the *Virginia*, the South's ironclad ship, and never left port again.

Monroe Doctrine President James Monroe's 1823 statement that an attack by a European state on any nation in the Western Hemisphere would be considered an attack on the United States; Monroe stated that the Western Hemisphere was the hemisphere of the United States and not of Europe. Monroe's statement was scoffed at by certain European political leaders, especially those in Great Britain.

Montgomery bus boycott Year-long refusal by blacks to ride city buses in Montgomery, Alabama, because of their segregation policies. Boycott began in December 1955; Supreme Court finally ruled that segregation on public buses was unconstitutional. Rosa Parks began the protest when she was arrested for refusing to give up her seat for a white man, and Martin Luther King, Jr., was a young minister involved in organizing the boycott.

Morrill Land-Grant Act (1862) Federal act designed to fund state "land-grant" colleges. State governments were given large amounts of land in the western territories; this land was sold to individual settlers, land speculators, and others, and the profits of these land sales could be used to establish the colleges.

Ms. Founded in 1972 by Gloria Steinem, this glossy magazine was aimed at feminist readers.

muckrakers Journalists of the Progressive era who attempted to expose the evils of government and big business. Many muckrakers wrote of the corruption of city and state political machines. Factory conditions and the living and working conditions of workers were other topics that some muckrakers wrote about.

My Lai Massacre In 1968 a unit under the command of Lieutenant William Calley killed over 300 men, women, and children in this small Vietnamese village. The antiwar movement took the attack as a symbol of the "immorality" of U.S. efforts in Vietnam.

NAFTA (North American Free Trade Agreement) Ratified in 1994 by the U.S. Senate, this agreement established a free trade zone between the United States, Mexico, and Canada. Critics of the agreement claim that many jobs have been lost in the United States because of it.

napalm Jellylike substance dropped from American planes during the Vietnam conflict that horribly burned the skin of anyone who came into contact with it. On several occasions, napalm was "accidentally" dropped on "friendly" villages.

Nation of Islam Supporters were called "Black Muslims;" this group was founded by Elijah Muhammad and preached Islamic principles along with black pride and black separatism. Malcolm X was a member of the Nation of Islam.

National American Woman Suffrage Association The major organization for suffrage for women, it was founded in 1890 by Susan B. Anthony and Elizabeth Cady Stanton. It supported the Wilson administration during World War I and split with the more radical National Woman's Party, which, in 1917, began to picket the White House because Wilson had not forcefully stated that women should get the vote.

National Association for the Advancement of Colored People (NAACP) Formed in 1909, this organization fought for and continues to fight for the rights of blacks in America. The NAACP originally went to court for the plaintiff in the *Brown v. Board of Education* case, and Thurgood Marshall, the NAACP's chief counsel and later a Supreme Court justice, was the main attorney in the case.

national bank Planned by Alexander Hamilton to be similar to the Bank of England, this bank was funded by government and private sources. Hamilton felt a national bank would give economic security and confidence to the new nation. Republicans who had originally opposed the bank felt the same way in 1815 when they supported Henry Clay's American System.

National Consumers League Formed in 1899, this organization was concerned with improving the working and living conditions of women in the workplace.

national culture When a general unity of tastes and a commonality of cultural experience exist in a nation; in a general sense, when a country starts to "think the same." This occurred in America for the first time in the 1920s; as many people saw the same movies, read the same magazines, and heard the same things on the radio, a national culture was born.

National Industrial Recovery Act (NIRA) (1933) New Deal legislation that created the Works Progress Administration (WPA) that created jobs to put people back to work right away and the National Recovery Administration (NRA), who worked in conjunction with industry to bolster the industrial sector and create more long-lasting jobs.

National Labor Relations Board (NLRB) Part of the 1935 Wagner Act, which was a huge victory for organized labor. The NLRB ensured that factory owners did not harass union organizers, ensured that collective bargaining was fairly practiced in labor disputes, and supervised union elections. The NLRB was given the legal "teeth" to force employers to comply with all of the above.

National Origins Act Very restrictive immigration legislation passed in 1924, which lowered immigration to 2 percent of each nationality as found in the 1890 census. This lowered immigration dramatically and, quite intentionally, almost eliminated immigration from Eastern and Southern Europe.

National Security League Organization founded in 1914 that preached patriotism and preparation for war. In 1915, they successfully lobbied government officials to set up camps to prepare men for military life and combat. The patriotism of this group became more strident as the war progressed. In 1917, they lobbied Congress to greatly limit immigration into the country.

National Woman's Party Formed by Alice Paul after women got the vote, this group lobbied unsuccessfully in the 1920s to get an Equal Rights Amendment for women added to the Constitution. Desire for this amendment would return among some feminist groups in the 1970s.

nativist Nativist sentiment was especially strong in the 1920s. Nativism states that immigration should be greatly limited or banned altogether, since immigrants hurt the United States economically and also threaten the social well-being of the country. Nativist groups and parties have developed on several occasions in both the nineteenth and the twentieth centuries.

NATO (North Atlantic Treaty Organization) Collective alliance of the United States and most of the Western European nations that was founded in 1949; an attack of one member of NATO was to be considered an attack on all. Many U.S. troops served in Europe during the cold war era because of the NATO alliance. To counter NATO, the Soviet Union created the Warsaw Pact in 1955.

Naval Act of 1900 Legislation that authorized a large increase in the building of ships to be used for offensive purposes; this measure helped ensure the creation of a world-class American navy.

Navigation Acts of 1660 Measures passed by Charles II that were designed to increase the dependence of the colonies on England for trade. Charles mandated that certain goods produced in the colonies, such as tobacco, should be sold only to England; that if the colonies wanted to sell anything to other countries it had to come through England first; and that all trade by the colonies to other countries would have to be done in English ships. These measures could have been devastating to the colonies; however, British officials in the colonies did not enforce them carefully.

neoconservativism Modern American political philosophy that opposes big-government approaches to domestic issues yet favors an interventionist and aggressive foreign policy; most neoconservatives advocated American intervention in Iraq in 2003.

neoconservatives (neocons) Group who wanted to use American might to remake the Middle Eastern region into a democracy. Neocons believed that to accomplish this, Saddam Hussein had to be removed from power in Iraq.

Neutrality Act of 1935 To prevent the United States from being drawn into potential European conflicts, this bill said that America would not trade arms with any country at war, and that any American citizen traveling on a ship of a country at war was doing so at his or her own risk.

Neutrality Act of 1939 Franklin Roosevelt got Congress to amend the Neutrality Act of 1935; new legislation stated that England and France could buy arms from the United States as long as there was cash "up front" for these weapons. This was the first military assistance that the United States gave the Allied countries.

New Deal Series of policies instituted by Franklin Roosevelt and his advisors from 1933 to 1941 that attempted to offset the effects of the Great Depression on American society. Many New Deal policies were clearly experimental; in the end it was the onset of World War II, and not the policies of the New Deal, that pulled the United States out of the Great Depression.

New Deal Coalition The coalition of labor unions and industrial workers, minorities, much of the middle class, and the Solid South that carried Franklin Roosevelt to victories in 1936 and 1940 and that was the basis of Democratic victories on a national level until this coalition started to break up in the late 1960s and early 1970s. A sizable number of this group voted for Ronald Reagan in the presidential elections of 1980 and 1984.

New Democrat Term used to describe Bill Clinton and his congressional supporters during his two terms in office. A New Democrat was pragmatic, and not tied to the old Democratic belief in big government; New Democrats took both Democratic and Republican ideas as they crafted their policies. Some in the Democratic party maintained that Clinton had actually sold out the principles of the party.

New Federalism A series of policies during the administration of Ronald Reagan that began to give some power back to the states that had always been held by the federal government. Some tax dollars were returned to state and local governments in the form of "block grants"; the state and local governments could then spend this money as they thought best.

New Freedom policy An approach favored by Southern and Midwestern Democrats, this policy stated that economic and political preparation for World War I should be done in a decentralized manner; this would prevent too much power falling into the hands of the federal government. President Wilson first favored this approach, but then established federal agencies to organize mobilization.

New Frontier The program of President John Kennedy to revitalize America at home and to reenergize America for continued battles against the Soviet Union. Kennedy asked young Americans to volunteer for programs such as the Peace Corps; as he said in his inaugural speech: "Ask not what your country can do for you—ask what you can do for your country."

new immigrants Immigrants that came from Southern and Eastern Europe, who made up the majority of immigrants coming into the United States after 1900. Earlier immigrants from Britain, Ireland, and Scandinavia appeared to be "like" the groups that were already settled in the United States; the "new immigrants" were very different. As a result, resentment and nativist sentiment developed against this group, especially in the 1920s.

New Jersey Plan As the U.S. Constitution was being debated and drafted, large and small states each offered proposals on how the legislature should be structured. The New Jersey Plan stated that the legislature should have a great deal of power to regulate trade, and that it should consist of one legislative house, with each state having one vote.

New Nationalism The series of Progressive reforms supported by Theodore Roosevelt as he ran for president on the Progressive or Bull Moose ticket in 1912. Roosevelt said that more had to be done to regulate big business and that neither of his opponents were committed to conservation.

New Right The conservative movement that began in the 1960s and triumphed with the election of Ronald Reagan in 1980. The New Right was able to attract many middle-class and Southern voters to the Republican party by emphasizing the themes of patriotism, a smaller government, and a return to "traditional values."

New South Concept promoted by Southerners in the late 1800s that the South had changed dramatically and was now interested in industrial growth and becoming a part of the national economy. A large textile industry did develop in the South beginning in the 1880s.

Nez Perce Plains Native American tribe that attempted to resist reservation life by traveling 1,500 miles with American military forces in pursuit. After being tracked and suffering cold and hardship, the Nez Perce finally surrendered and were forced onto a reservation in 1877.

Non-Intercourse Act In response to the failure of France and Britain to respect the rights of American ships at sea, President Madison supported this legislation in 1809, which authorized trade with all countries except Britain and France, and stated that trade exist with those countries as soon as they respected America's rights as a neutral power. The British and the French largely ignored this act.

Northwest Ordinances Bills passed in 1784, 1785, and 1787 that authorized the sale of lands in the Northwest Territory to raise money for the federal government; these bills also carefully laid out the procedures for eventual statehood for parts of these territories.

NOW (National Organization for Women) Formed in 1966, with Betty Friedan as its first president. NOW was at first interested in publicizing inequalities for women in the workplace; focus of the organization later turned to social issues and eventually the unsuccessful effort to pass an Equal Rights Amendment for women.

nuclear proliferation The massive buildup of nuclear weapons by the United States and the Soviet Union in the 1950s and into the 1960s; in the United States this was fostered in the belief that the threat of "massive retaliation" was the best way to keep the Soviet Union under control. The psychological effects of the atomic bomb on the populations of the Soviet Union and the United States were also profound.

nullification The belief that an individual state has the right to "nullify" any federal law that the state felt was unjust. Andrew Jackson was able to resolve a Nullification Crisis in 1832, but the concept of nullification was still accepted by many Southerners, and controversy over this was a cause of the Civil War.

Ocala Platform Platform of the Farmer's Alliances, formulated at an 1890 convention held in Ocala, Florida. This farmer's organization favored a graduated income tax, government control of the railroad, the unlimited coinage of silver, and the direct election of U.S. senators. Candidates supporting the farmers called themselves "Populists" and ran for public offices in the 1890s.

Old Age Revolving Pension Plan Conceived by California doctor Francis Townsend in 1934, this plan would give every retired American $200 a month, with the stipulation that it would have to be spent by the end of the month; Townsend claimed this would revitalize the economy by putting more money in circulation. A national tax of 2 percent on all business transactions was supposed to finance this plan. A large number of Townsend clubs were formed to support this plan.

on the margin The practice in the late 1920s of buying stock and only paying in cash 10 percent of the value of that stock; the buyer could easily borrow the rest from his or her stockbroker or investment banker. This system worked well as long as investors could sell their stocks at a profit and repay their loans. After the 1929 stock market crash, investors had to pay these loans back in cash.

OPEC Acronym for Organization of Petroleum Exporting Countries, this organization sets the price for crude oil and determines how much of it will be produced. The decision of OPEC to raise oil prices in 1973 had a dramatic economic impact in both the United States and the rest of the world.

Open Door policy The policy that China should be open to trade with all of the major powers, and that all, including the United States, should have equal rights to trade there. This was the official American position toward China as announced by Secretary of State John Hay in 1899.

Operation Desert Shield After Iraq invaded Kuwait on August 2, 1990, President Bush sent 230,000 American troops to protect Saudi Arabia.

Operation Desert Storm February 1991 attack on Iraqi forces in Kuwait by the United States and other allied forces; although Iraq was driven from Kuwait, Saddam Hussein remained in power in Iraq.

Oregon Trail Trail that took settlers from the Ohio River Valley through the Great Plains and the Rocky Mountains to Oregon. Settlers began moving westward along this trail in 1842; by 1860 over 325,000 Americans had traveled westward along the trail.

Oregon Treaty Both the United States and Great Britain claimed the Oregon territory; in 1815 they agreed to jointly control the region. In 1843 the settlers of Oregon declared that their territory would become an independent republic.

Palmer Raids Part of the Red Scare, these were measures to hunt out political radicals and immigrants who were potential threats to American security. Organized by Attorney General A. Mitchell Palmer in 1919 and 1920 (and carried out by J. Edgar Hoover), these raids led to the arrest of nearly 5,500 people and the deportation of nearly four hundred.

Panama Canal Crucial for American economic growth, the building of this canal was begun by American builders in 1904 and completed in 1914. The United States had to first engineer a Panamanian revolt against Colombia to guarantee a friendly government in Panama that would support the building of the canal. In 1978 the U.S. Senate voted to return the Panama Canal to Panamanian control.

panic of 1837 The American economy suffered a deep depression when Great Britain reduced the amount of credit it offered to the United States. American merchants and industrialists had to use their available cash to pay off debts, thus causing businesses to cut production and lay off workers.

Paris, Treaty of The treaty ending the Revolutionary War, and signed in 1783. By the terms of this treaty, the United States received the land between the Appalachian Mountains and the Mississippi River. The British did keep their Canadian territories.

Pendleton Civil Service Act of 1883 Act that established a civil service system. There were a number of government jobs that were filled by civil service examinations and not by the president appointing one of his political cronies. Some states also started to develop professional civil service systems in the 1880s.

Pentagon Papers A government study of American involvement in Vietnam that outlined in detail many of the mistakes that America had made there. In 1971, a former analyst for the Defense Department, Daniel Ellsberg, released these to the *New York Times*.

Platt Amendment For Cuba to receive its independence from the United States after the Spanish-American war, it had to agree to the Platt Amendment, which stated that the United States had the right to intervene in Cuban affairs if the Cuban government could not maintain control or if the independence of Cuba was threatened by external or internal forces.

Plumbers A group of intelligence officials who worked for the committee to reelect Richard Nixon in 1972; the job of this group was to stop leaks of information and perform "dirty tricks" on political opponents of the president. The Plumbers broke into the office of Daniel Ellsberg's psychiatrist, looking for damaging information against him and totally discredited the campaign of Democratic hopeful Edmund Muskie.

pocket veto A method a president can use to "kill" congressional legislation at the end of a congressional term. Instead of vetoing the bill, the president may simply not sign it; once the congressional term is over, the bill will then die.

political machine An organization that controls the politics of a city, a state, or even the country, sometimes by illegal or quasi-legal means. A machine employs a large number of people to do its "dirty work," for which they are either given some government job or are allowed to pocket government bribes or kickbacks. The "best" example of a political machine was the Tammany Hall organization that controlled New York City in the late nineteenth century.

Populist party Party that represented the farmers who scored major electoral victories in the 1890s, including the election of several members of the U.S. House of Representatives and the election of one U.S. senator. Populist candidates spoke against monopolies, wanted government to become "more democratic," and wanted more direct government action to help the working classes.

Port Huron Statement The manifesto of Students for a Democratic Society, a radical student group formed in 1960. The *Port Huron Statement* called for a greater role for university students in the nation's affairs, rejected the traditional role of the university, and rejected the foreign policy goals that America was embracing at the time.

Postmodernism A recent trend in cultural and historical study that doubts the existence of absolute historical certainties. It is impossible to know, for example, what "really happened" in the past; therefore, how individuals observe and interpret the past becomes a valuable source of analysis. Postmodernists would also reject statements such as "democracy is best for all nations of the world," and would emphasize the study of various historical viewpoints.

Potsdam Conference July 1945 conference between new president Harry Truman, Stalin, and Clement Atlee, who had replaced Churchill. Truman took a much tougher stance toward Stalin than Franklin Roosevelt had; little substantive agreement took place at this conference. Truman expressed reservations about the future role of the Soviet Union in Eastern Europe at this conference.

Powhatan Confederacy Alliance of Native American tribes living in the region of the initial Virginia settlement. Powhatan, leader of this alliance, tried to live in peace with the English settlers when they arrived in 1607.

primary source Actual documents or accounts from an era being studied, these are invaluable to historians. Almost all true historical research involves analysis of primary source documents. Examples would be a letter written by Napoleon, an account of someone who knew Napoleon personally, or a newspaper account from Napoleon's time.

professional bureaucracy Government officials that receive their positions after taking competitive civil service tests; they are not appointed in return for political favors. Many government jobs at the state and national level are filled in this manner beginning in the 1880s.

Progressivism A movement that desired political and social reform, and was most influential in America from the 1890s up until World War I. Most popular Progressive causes included reforming city government, better conditions for urban workers, the education of newly arrived immigrants, and the regulation of big businesses.

proportional representation The belief that representation in a legislature should be based on population; the states with the largest populations should have the most representatives. When the Constitution was being formulated, the larger states wanted this; the smaller states favored "one vote per state." The eventual compromise, termed the Connecticut plan, created a two-house legislature.

proprietorships Settlements in America that were given to individuals who could govern and regulate the territory in any manner they desire. Charles I, for example, gave the Maryland territory to Lord Baltimore as a proprietorship.

Pure Food and Drug Act of 1906 Bill that created a federal Food and Drug Administration; example of consumer protection legislation of the Progressive Era, it was at least partially passed as a result of Upton Sinclair's novel *The Jungle*.

Puritans Group of religious dissidents who came to the New World so they would have a location to establish a "purer" church than the one that existed in England. The Puritans began to settle the Plymouth Colony in 1620 and settled the Massachusetts

Bay Colony beginning in 1630. Puritans were heavily influenced by John Calvin and his concept of predestination.

putting-out system The first textile production system in England, where merchants gave wool to families who, in their homes, created yarn and then cloth. The merchants would then buy the cloth from the families and sell the finished product. Textile mills made this procedure more efficient.

Quartering Act of 1765 British edict stating that to help defend the empire, colonial governments had to provide accommodations and food for British troops. Many colonists considered this act to be the ultimate insult; they perceived that they were paying for the troops that were there to control the colonies.

Queen Anne's War (1702 to 1713) Called "the War of the Spanish Succession" in European texts, pitted England against France and Spain. Spanish Florida was attacked by the English in the early part of this war, and Native Americans fought for both sides in the conflict. The British emerged victorious and in the end received Hudson Bay and Nova Scotia from the French.

Radical Republicans Group of Republicans after the Civil War who favored harsh treatment of the defeated South and a dramatic restructuring of the economic and social systems in the South; favored a decisive elevation of the political, social, and economic position of former slaves.

ratifying conventions In late 1787 and in 1788 these were held in all states for the purpose of ratifying the new Constitution of the United States. In many states, approval of the Constitution was only approved by a small margin; in Rhode Island ratification was defeated. The Founding Fathers made an intelligent decision in calling for ratifying conventions to approve the Constitution instead of having state legislatures do it, since under the system proposed by the Constitution, some of the powers state legislatures had at the time would be turned over to the federal government.

ration cards Held by Americans during World War II, these recorded the amount of rationed goods such as automobile tires, gasoline, meat, butter, and other materials an individual had purchased. Where regulation in World War I had been voluntary, consumption in World War II was regulated by government agencies.

realpolitik Pragmatic policy of leadership, in which the leader "does what he or she has to do" in order to be successful. Morality has no place in the mindset of a leader practicing realpolitik. The late nineteenth-century German chancellor Otto von Bismarck is the best modern example of a leader practicing realpolitik.

Rebel Without a Cause 1955 film starring James Dean exploring the difficulties of family life and the alienation that many teenagers felt in the 1950s. Juvenile delinquency, and the reasons for it, was the subtext of this film, as well as the source of countless other 1950s-era movies aimed at the youth market.

recall process One of a number of reforms of the government system proposed by Progressive era thinkers. By the process of recall, the citizens of a city or state could remove an unpopular elected official from office in midterm. Recall was adopted in only a small number of communities.

reconcentration (1896) Spanish policy designed to control the Cuban people by forcing them to live in fortified camps; American outrage over this led some politicians to call for war against Spain.

Reconstruction Act Plan of Radical Republicans to control the former area of the Confederacy and approved by Congress in March 1867. The former Confederacy was divided into five military districts, with each controlled by a military commander (Tennessee was exempt from this). Conventions were to be called to create new state governments (former Confederate officials could not hold office in these governments).

Reconstruction Era The era following the Civil War where Radical Republicans initiated changes in the South that gave newly freed slaves additional economic, social, and political rights. These changes were greatly resented by many Southerners, causing the creation of organizations such as the Ku Klux Klan. Reconstruction ended with the Compromise of 1877.

Reconstruction Finance Corporation Established in 1932 by Herbert Hoover to offset the effects of the Great Depression; the RFC was authorized to give federal credit to banks so that they could operate efficiently. Banks receiving these loans were expected to extend loans to businesses providing jobs or building low-cost housing.

Red Scare Vigorous repression of radicals, "political subversives," and "undesirable" immigrants groups in the years immediately following World War I. Nearly 6,500 "radicals" were arrested and sent to jail; some sat in jail without ever being charged with a crime, while nearly 500 immigrants were deported.

referendum process One of a series of progressive-era reforms designed to improve the political system. According to this referendum, certain issues would not be decided by elected representatives, but voters are called upon to approve or disapprove specific government programs. Consistent with populist and progressive era desire to return government "to the people."

religious right Primarily Protestant movement that greatly grew beginning in the 1970s and pushed to return "morality" to the forefront in American life. The religious right has been especially active in opposing abortion, and since the 1980s has extended its influence in the political sphere by endorsing and campaigning for specific candidates (e.g., during the 2004 campaign of President George W. Bush).

Removal Act of 1830 Part of the effort to remove Native Americans from "Western" lands so that American settlement could continue westward, this legislation gave the president the authorization (and the money) to purchase from Native Americans all of their lands east of the Mississippi, and gave him the money to purchase lands west of the Mississippi for Native Americans to move to.

Report on the Public Credit (1790) Report by Secretary of the Treasury Alexander Hamilton, in which he proposed that the federal government assume the entire amount of the nation's debt (including state debt), and that the federal government should have an increased role in the nation's economy. Many of America's early leaders vigorously opposed the expansion of federal economic power in the new republic and the expansion of American industry that Hamilton also promoted.

Republican party Formed in 1854 during the death of the Whig party, this party attracted former members of the Free-Soil party and some in the Democratic party who were uncomfortable with the Democratic position on slavery. Abraham Lincoln was the first Republican president. For much of the twentieth century, the party was saddled with the label of being "the party of big business," although Richard Nixon, Ronald Reagan, and others did much to pull middle class and Southern voters into the party.

reservationists This group in the U.S. Senate was led by Henry Cabot Lodge and was opposed to sections of the Versailles Treaty when it was brought home from Paris by President Woodrow Wilson in 1919. Reservationists were especially concerned that if the United States joined the League of Nations, American troops would be used to conduct League of Nations military operations without the approval of the Congress.

Resettlement Administration In an attempt to address the problems of Dust Bowlers and other poor farmers, this 1935 New Deal program attempted to provide aid to the poorest farmers, resettle some farmers from the Dust Bowl, and establish farm cooperatives. This program never received the funding it needed to be even partially successful, and in 1937 the Farm Security Administration was created to replace it.

Revenue Act of 1935 Tax legislation championed by Franklin Roosevelt that was called a "soak the rich" plan by his opponents. Under this bill, corporate, inheritance, and gift taxes went up dramatically; income taxes for the upper brackets also rose. By proposing this, Roosevelt may have been attempting to diffuse the popularity of Huey Long and others with more radical plans to redistribute wealth.

Revenue Act of 1942 Designed to raise money for the war, this bill dramatically increased the number of Americans required to pay income tax. Until this point, roughly 4 million Americans paid income tax; as a result of this legislation, nearly 45 million did.

revisionist history A historical interpretation not found in "standard" history books or supported by most historians. A revisionist history of the origins of the cold war, for example, would maintain that the aggressive actions of the United States forced the Soviet Union to seize the territories of Eastern Europe for protection. Historical interpretations that may originally be revisionist may, in time, become standard historical interpretation.

revival meetings Religious meetings consisting of soul-searching, preaching, and prayer that took place during the Second Great Awakening at the beginning of the nineteenth century. Some revival meetings lasted over one week.

Rio Pact (1947) Treaty signed by the United States and most Latin American countries, stating that the region would work together on economic and defense matters and creating the Organization of American States to facilitate this cooperation.

Roe v. Wade (1973) Supreme Court decision that made abortion legal (except in the last months of pregnancy). Justices voting in the majority in this 5-to-2 decision stated that a woman's right to privacy gave her the legal freedom to choose to have an abortion. Abortion has remained one of the most hotly debated social issues in America.

Roosevelt Corollary An extension of the Monroe Doctrine, this policy was announced in 1904 by Theodore Roosevelt. It firmly warned European nations against intervening in the affairs of nations in the Western Hemisphere, and stated that the United States had the right to take action against any nation in Latin America if "chronic wrongdoing" was taking place. The Roosevelt Corollary was used to justify several American "interventions" in Central America in the twentieth century.

Rosie the Riveter Image of a woman factory worker drawn by Norman Rockwell for the *Saturday Evening Post* during World War II. Women were needed to take on factory jobs that had been held by departing soldiers; by 1945 women made up nearly 37 percent of the entire domestic workforce.

Rough Riders A special unit of soldiers recruited by Theodore Roosevelt to do battle in the Spanish-American War. This unit was composed of men from many backgrounds, with the commanding officer of the unit being Roosevelt (after he resigned as assistant secretary of the navy). The most publicized event of the war was the charge of the Rough Riders up San Juan Hill on July 1, 1898.

Salem Witch Trials 120 men, women, and children were arrested for witchcraft in Salem, Massachusetts, in 1692; 19 of these were executed. A new governor appointed by the Crown stopped additional trials and executions; several historians note the class nature of the witch trials, as many of those accused were associated with the business and/or commercial interests in Salem, while most of the accusers were members of the farming class.

SALT I (Strategic Arms Limitation Talks) 1972 treaty signed by Richard Nixon and Soviet premier Leonid Brezhnev limiting the development of additional nuclear weapon systems and defense systems to stop them. SALT I was only partially effective in preventing continued development of nuclear weaponry.

salutary neglect British policy announced at the beginning of the eighteenth century stating that as long as the American colonies remained politically loyal and continued their trade with Great Britain, the British government would relax enforcement of various measures restricting colonial activity that were enacted in the 1600s. Tensions between the colonies and Britain continued over British policies concerning colonial trade and the power of colonial legislatures.

satellite countries Eastern European countries that remained under the control of the Soviet Union during the cold war era. Most were drawn together militarily by the Warsaw Pact. Satellite nations that attempted political or cultural rebellion, such as Hungary in 1956 or Czechoslovakia in 1968, faced invasion by Soviet forces.

Saturday Night Massacre October 20, 1973, event when Richard Nixon ordered the firing of Archibald Cox, the special investigator in charge of the Watergate investigation. Attorney General Elliot Richardson and several others in the Justice Department refused to carry out this order and resigned. This event greatly damaged Nixon's popularity, both in the eyes of the public and in the Congress.

scalawags Term used by Southerners in the Reconstruction era for fellow Southerners who either supported Republican Reconstruction policies or gained economically as a result of these policies.

Scopes Trial of 1925 Tennessee trial where teacher John Scopes was charged with teaching evolution, a violation of state statutes. The American Civil Liberties Union hired Clarence Darrow to defend Scopes, while the chief attorney for the prosecution was three-time presidential candidate William Jennings Bryan. While Scopes was convicted and ordered to pay a small fine, Darrow was able to poke holes in the theory of creationism as expressed by Bryan.

Scottsboro Boys Nine black young men who were accused of raping two white women in a railway boxcar in Scottsboro, Arizona, in 1931. Quick trials, suppressed evidence, and inadequate legal council made them symbols of the discrimination that faced blacks on a daily basis during this era.

Scramble for Africa The competition between the major European powers to gain colonial territories in Africa that took place between the 1870s and the outbreak of World War I. Conflicts created by competing visions of colonial expansion increased tensions between the European powers and were a factor in the animosities that led to World War I.

secession A single state or a group of states leaving the United States of America. New England Federalists threatened to do this during the first administration of Thomas Jefferson. Southern states did this in the period prior to the Civil War.

Second Continental Congress Meeting of delegates from the American colonies in May 1775. During the sessions some delegates expressed hope that the differences between the colonies and Britain could be reconciled, although Congress authorized that the Continental army be created and that George Washington be named commander of that army.

Second Great Awakening Religious revival movement that began at the beginning of the nineteenth century. Revivalist ministers asked thousands of worshippers at revival meetings to save their own souls. This reflected the move away from predestination in Protestant thinking of the era.

Second Industrial Revolution The massive economic growth that took place in America from 1865 until the end of the century that was largely based on the expansion of the railroad, the introduction of electric power, and the production of steel for building. By the 1890s America had replaced Germany as the major industrial producer in the world.

Second National Bank Bank established by Congress in 1816. President Madison had called for the Second Bank in 1815 as a way to spur national economic growth after the War of 1812. After an economic downturn in 1818, the bank shrank the amount of currency available for loans, an act that helped to create the economic collapse of 1819.

Second New Deal Beginning in 1935, the New Deal did more to help the poor and attack the wealthy. One reason Roosevelt took this path was to turn the American people away from those who said the New Deal wasn't going far enough to help the average person. Two key legislative acts of this era were the Social Security Act of May 1935 and the June 1935 National Labor Relations Act (also called "the Wagner Act)," which gave all Americans the right to join labor unions. The Wealth Tax Act increased the tax rates for the wealthiest Americans.

secondary source A historical account written after the fact; a historian writing a secondary source would analyze the available primary sources on his or her topic. Examples would be a textbook, a biography written today of Napoleon, or a new account of the Black Death.

Separatists Religious group that opposed the Church of England. This group first went to Holland, and then some went on to the Americas.

settlement houses Centers set up by progressive-era reformers in the poorest sections of American cities. At these centers, workers and their children might receive lessons in the English language or citizenship; while for women, lessons in sewing and cooking were often held. The first settlement house was Hull House in Chicago, established by Jane Addams in 1889.

Seventeenth Amendment Ratified in 1913, this amendment allowed voters to directly elect U.S. senators. Senators had previously been elected by state legislatures. This change perfectly reflected the spirit of Progressive-era political reformers who wanted to do all they could to put political power in the hands of the citizenry.

Sherman Antitrust Act of 1890 Congressional legislation designed to break up industrial trusts such as the one created by John D. Rockefeller and Standard Oil. The bill stated that any combination of businesses that was "in the restraint of trade" was illegal. Because of the vagueness of the legislation and the lack of enforcement tools in the hands of the federal government, few trusts were actually prosecuted as a result of this bill.

Shiloh, Battle of Fierce Civil War battle in Tennessee in April 1862. Although the Union emerged victorious, both sides suffered a large number of casualties in this battle. Total casualties in this battle were nearly 25,000. General Ulysses S. Grant commanded the Union forces at Shiloh.

Sioux Plains tribe that tried to resist American westward expansion; after two wars, the Sioux were resettled in South Dakota. In 1876, Sioux fighters defeated the forces of General Custer at the Battle of the Little Bighorn. In 1890, almost 225 Sioux men, women, and children were killed by federal troops at the Massacre at Wounded Knee.

sit-down strikes A labor tactic where workers refuse to leave their factory until management meets their demands. The most famous sit-down strike occurred at the General Motors plant in Flint, Michigan, beginning in December 1936. Despite efforts by company guards to end the strike by force, the workers finally saw their demands met after 44 days.

sit-in Tactic used by the civil rights movement in the early 1960s; a group of civil rights workers would typically occupy a lunch counter in a segregated establishment in the South and refuse to leave, thus disrupting normal business (and profits) for the segregated establishment. During sit-ins civil rights workers often suffered physical and emotional abuse. The first sit-in was at the Woolworth's store in Greensboro, North Carolina, on February 1, 1960.

Sixteenth Amendment (1913) Amendment that instituted a federal income tax. In debate over this measure in Congress, most felt that this would be a fairer tax than a national sales tax, which was proposed by some.

Smith-Connally Act of 1943 Legislation that limited the nature of labor action possible for the rest of the war. Many in America felt that strikes, especially those organized in the coal mines by the United Mine Workers, were detrimental to the war effort.

Social Darwinism Philosophy that evolved from the writings of Charles Darwin on evolution that stated people inevitably compete with each other, as do societies; in the end the "survival of the fittest" would naturally occur. Social Darwinism was used to justify the vast differences between the rich and the poor in the late nineteenth century, as well as the control that the United States and Europe maintained over other parts of the world.

Social Gospel movement Late nineteenth-century Protestant movement preaching that all true Christians should be concerned with the plight of immigrants and other poor residents of American cities and should financially support efforts to improve the lives of these poor urban dwellers. Progressive era settlement houses were often financed by funds raised by ministers of the Social Gospel movement.

Social history The field of history that analyzes the lives and beliefs of common people in any historical era. In American history, this field has grown dramatically since the 1960s. Social historians believe that we can get a more accurate view of the civil rights movement, by for example, studying the actions of civil rights workers in Mississippi than we can by studying the actions and pronouncements of leaders of the civil rights movement who were active on the national stage.

Social Security Act Considered by many to be the most important act passed during the entire New Deal, this 1935 bill established a system that would give payments to Americans after they reached retirement age; provisions for unemployment and disability insurance were also found in this bill. Political leaders of recent years have wrestled with the problem of keeping the Social Security system solvent.

Sons of Liberty Men who organized opposition to British policies during the late 1760s and 1770s. The Sons of Liberty were founded in and were most active in Boston, where in response to the Stamp Act they burned the local tax collector in effigy and burned a building that he owned. The Sons of Liberty also organized the Boston Tea Party. Samuel Adams was one of the leaders of this group.

Southern Strategy Plan begun by Richard Nixon that has made the Republican party dominant in many areas of the South that had previously voted Democratic. Nixon, Ronald Reagan, and countless Republican congressional candidates had emphasized law and order and traditional values in their campaigns, thus winning over numerous voters. Support from the South had been part of the New Deal Democratic coalition crafted by Franklin Roosevelt.

Spanish-American War War that began in 1898 and stemmed from furor in America over treatment of Cubans by Spanish troops that controlled the island. During the war the American navy led by Admiral Dewey destroyed the Spanish fleet in the Pacific, the American ship the U.S.S. *Maine* was sunk in Havana harbor, and Teddy Roosevelt led the Rough Riders up San Juan Hill. A major result of the war was the acquisition by the United States of the Philippines, which made America a major power in the Pacific.

speakeasies Urban clubs that existed in the 1920s where alcohol was illegally sold to patrons. The sheer number of speakeasies in a city such as New York demonstrated the difficulty of enforcing a law such as prohibition.

special prosecutor An official appointed to investigate specific government wrongdoing. Archibald Cox was the special prosecutor assigned to investigate Watergate, while Kenneth Starr was the special prosecutor assigned to investigate the connections between President Clinton and Whitewater. President Nixon's order to fire Cox was the beginning of the famous 1973 "Saturday Night Massacre."

speculation The practice of purchasing either land or stocks with the intent of selling them for a higher price later. After the Homestead Act and other acts opened up the western United States for settlement, many speculators purchased land with no intent of ever settling on it; their goal was to later sell the land for profit.

spoils system Also called "the patronage system," in which the president, governor, or mayor is allowed to fill government jobs with political allies and former campaign workers. Political reformers of the 1880s and 1890s introduced legislation calling for large numbers of these jobs to be filled by the merit system, in which candidates for jobs had to take competitive examinations. President Andrew Jackson began the spoils system.

Sputnik First man-made satellite sent into space, this 1957 scientific breakthrough by the Soviet Union caused great concern in the United States. The thought that the United States was "behind" the Soviet Union in anything worried many, and science and mathematics requirements in universities across the country increased as a result.

Square Deal The philosophy of President Theodore Roosevelt; included in this was the desire to treat both sides fairly in any dispute. In the coal miner's strike of 1902 he treated the United Mine Workers representatives and company bosses as equals. This approach continued during his efforts to regulate the railroads and other businesses during his second term.

stagflation A unique economic situation faced political leaders in the early 1970s, where inflation and signs of economic recession occurred at the same time. Previously, in times of inflation, the economy was improving, and vice versa. Nixon utilized wage and price controls and increased government spending to address this problem.

Stamp Act To help pay for the British army in North America, Parliament passed the Stamp Act in 1765, under which all legal documents in the colonies had to be issued on officially stamped paper. A tax was imposed on all of these documents, as well as on all colonial newspapers. The resistance to the Stamp Act was severe in the colonies, and it was eventually repealed.

Stamp Act Congress Representatives of nine colonies went to this meeting held in New York in October

1765; the document produced by this congress maintained the loyalty of the colonies to the Crown but strongly condemned the Stamp Act. Within one year the Stamp Act was repealed.

states' rights The concept that the individual states, and not the federal government, have the power to decide whether federal legislation or regulations are to be enforced within the individual states. The mantle of states' rights would be taken up by New England Federalists during the presidency of Thomas Jefferson, by many Southern states in the years leading up to the Civil War, and by some Southern states again in response to federal legislation during the civil rights era of the 1960s.

Stono Rebellion of 1739 Slave rebellion in South Carolina where over 75 slaves killed white citizens and marched through the countryside with captured guns. After the rebellion was quashed, discipline imposed by many slave owners was much harsher. This was the largest slave rebellion of the 1700s in the colonies.

Students for a Democratic Society (SDS) Founded in 1960, this group was part of the "New Left" movement of the 1960s. SDS believed in a more participatory society, in a society that was less materialistic, and in university reform that would give students more power. By 1966 SDS concentrated much of its efforts on organizing opposition to the war in Vietnam. The *Port Huron Statement* was the original manifesto of SDS and was written by SDS founder Tom Hayden.

suburbia The area outside of the cities where massive numbers of families flocked to in the 1950s and 1960s. Suburban parents often still worked in the cities, but the suburban lifestyle shared little with urban life. Critics of 1950s suburbia point to the sameness and lack of vitality noted by some suburban residents and to the fact that suburban women often had to forget past dreams to accept the role of "housewife."

Suffolk Resolves These were sent from Suffolk County, Massachusetts, to the meeting of the First Continental Congress in September 1774 and called for the citizens of all of the colonies to prepare to take up arms against the British. After much debate, the First Continental Congress adopted the Suffolk Resolves.

Sugar Act Another effort to pay for the British army located in North America, this 1764 measure taxed sugar and other imports. The British had previously attempted to halt the flow of sugar from French colonies to the colonies: By the Sugar Act they attempted to make money from this trade. Another provision of the act harshly punished smugglers of sugar who didn't pay the import duty imposed by the British.

supply-side economics Economic theory adopted by Ronald Reagan stating that economic growth would be best encouraged by lowering the taxes of wealthy businessmen and investors; this would give them more cash, which they would use to start more businesses, make more investments, and in general stimulate the economy. This theory of "Reaganomics" went against economic theories going back to the New Deal that claimed to efficiently stimulate the economy, more money needed to be held by consumers (who would in turn spend it).

Sussex Pledge A torpedo from a German submarine hit the French passenger liner the *Sussex* in March 1916, killing and injuring many (including six Americans). In a strongly worded statement, President Wilson demanded that the Germans refrain from attacking passenger ships. In the Sussex Pledge the Germans said that they would temporarily stop these attacks, but that they might have to resume them in the future if the British continued their blockade of German ports.

Taft-Hartley Act of 1947 Congressional legislation that aided the owners in potential labor disputes. In key industries the president could declare an 80-day cooling off period before a strike could actually take place; the bill also allowed owners to sue unions over broken contracts, and forced union leaders to sign anti-Communist oaths. The bill was passed over President Truman's veto; Truman only vetoed the bill for political reasons.

Tammany Hall Political machine that ran New York City Democratic and city politics beginning in 1870, and a "model" for the political machines that dominated politics in many American cities well into the twentieth century. William Marcy "Boss" Tweed was the head of Tammany Hall for several years and was the most notorious of all of the political bosses.

Tariff of 1816 An extremely protectionist tariff designed to assist new American industries in the aftermath of the War of 1812. This tariff raised import duties by nearly 25 percent.

Tax Reform Act of 1986 The biggest tax cut in American history, this measure cut taxes by $750 billion over five years and cut personal income taxes by 25 percent. Tax cuts were consistent with President Reagan's belief that more money in the hands of the wealthy would stimulate the economy. Critics of this tax cut would argue that the wealthy were the ones that benefited from it, as little of the money that went to the hands of the rich actually "trickled down" to help the rest of the economy. Critics would also argue that the national deficits of the late 1980s and early 1990s were caused by these tax cuts.

Taylorism Following the management practices of Frederick Winslow Taylor, the belief practiced by many factory owners beginning in 1911 (when Taylor published his first book) that factories should be managed in a scientific manner, with everything done to increase the efficiency of the individual worker and of the factory process as a whole. Taylor describes the movements of workers as if they were machines; workers in many factories resisted being seen in this light.

Tea Act of 1773 Act by Parliament that would provide the American colonies with cheap tea, but at the same time would force the colonists to admit that Parliament had a right to tax them. The Sons of Liberty acted against this measure in several colonies, with the most dramatic being the Boston Tea Party. Parliament responded with the harsh Coercive Acts.

Teapot Dome Scandal One of many scandals that took place during the presidency of Warren G. Harding. The Secretary of the Interior accepted bribes from oil companies for access to government oil reserves at Teapot Dome, Wyoming. Other cabinet members were later convicted of accepting bribes and using their influence to make millions. The Harding administration was perhaps the most corrupt administration in American political history.

Teller Amendment As Americans were preparing for war with Spain over Cuba in 1898, this Senate measure stated that under no circumstances would the United States annex Cuba. The amendment was passed as many in the muckraking press were suggesting that the Cuban people would be better off "under the protection" of the United States.

temperance movement Movement that developed in America before the Civil War that lamented the effect that alcohol had on American society. After the Civil War, members of this movement would become especially concerned about the effect of alcohol on immigrants and other members of the urban poor. Out of the temperance movement came the drive for nationwide prohibition.

Ten Percent Plan Abraham Lincoln's plan for Reconstruction, which would have offered full pardons to persons living in Confederate states who would take an oath of allegiance to the United States (former Confederate military officers and civilian authorities would not be offered this possibility). Once 10 percent of the citizens of a state had taken such an oath, the state could take steps to rejoin the Union. Radical Republicans in the U.S. Senate felt that this plan was much too lenient toward the South.

tenant farmers In the Reconstruction South, a step up from sharecropping. The tenant farmer rented his land from the landowner, freeing him from the harsh supervision that sharecroppers suffered under.

Tennessee Valley Authority Ambitious New Deal program that for the first time provided electricity to residents of the Tennessee Valley; the TVA also promoted agricultural and industrial growth (and prevented flooding) in the region. In all, residents of seven states benefited from the TVA.

Tenure of Office Act (1867) Congressional act designed to limit the influence of President Andrew Johnson. The act took away the president's role as commander in chief of American military forces and stated that Congress had to approve the removal of government officials who had been appointed by the president. In 1868, Johnson attempted to fire Secretary of War Stanton without congressional approval, thus helping set the stage for his impeachment hearings later that year.

Tet Offensive January 1968 attack launched on American and South Vietnamese forces by North Vietnamese and Vietcong soldiers. Although Vietcong troops actually occupied the American embassy in Vietnam for several hours, the end result was a crushing defeat for the anti-American forces. However, the psychological effect of Tet was exactly the reverse: Vietcong forces were convinced they could decisively strike at South Vietnamese and American targets, and many in America ceased to believe that victory was "just around the corner."

Thirteenth Amendment (1865) Amendment abolishing slavery in the United States and all of its territories (the Emancipation Proclamation had ended slavery only in the Confederate states). Final approval of this amendment depended on ratification by newly constructed legislatures in eight states that were former members of the Confederacy.

38th parallel The dividing line between Soviet-supported North Korea and U.S.-backed South Korea both before and as a result of the Korean War. American forces have been stationed on the southern side of this border continually since the Korean War ended in 1953.

Three-Fifths Compromise As the new Constitution was being debated in 1787, great controversy developed over how slaves should be counted in determining membership in the House of Representatives. To increase their representation, Southern states argued that slaves should be counted as people; Northerners argued that they should not count, since they could not vote or own property. The compromise arrived at was that each slave would count as three-fifths of a free person.

tight money Government policy utilized to offset the effects of inflation. On numerous occasions the Federal Reserve Board has increased the interest rate on money it loans to member banks; these higher interest rates are passed on to customers of member banks. With higher interest rates, there are fewer loans and other business activity, which "slows the economy down" and lowers inflation.

Timber and Stone Act of 1878 Bill that allowed private citizens to purchase forest territory in Oregon, Washington, California, and Nevada. Although the intent of the bill was to encourage settlement in these areas, lumber companies purchased large amounts of these land claims from the individuals who had originally purchased them.

Townshend Acts of 1767 Parliamentary act that forced colonists to pay duties on most goods coming from England, including tea and paper, and increased the power of custom boards in the colonies to ensure that these duties were paid. These duties were despised and fiercely resisted in many of the colonies; in Boston resistance was so fierce that the British were forced to occupy Boston with troops. The acts were finally repealed in 1770.

Trail of Tears Forced march of 20,000 members of the Cherokee tribe to their newly designated "homeland" in Oklahoma. Federal troops forced the Cherokees westward in this 1838 event, with one out every five Native Americans dying from hunger, disease, or exhaustion along the way.

Trenton, Battle of December 26, 1776, surprise attack by forces commanded by George Washington on Hessian forces outside of Trenton, New Jersey. Nearly 950 Hessians were captured and another 30 were killed by Washington's forces; three Americans were wounded in the attack. The battle was a tremendous psychological boost for the American war effort.

Triangle Shirtwaist Fire March 1911 fire in New York factory that trapped young women workers inside locked exit doors; nearly 50 jumped to their death, while 100 died inside the factory. Many factory reforms, including increasing safety precautions for workers, came from the investigation of this incident.

triangular trade system The complex trading relationship that developed in the late seventeenth century between the Americas, Europe, and Africa. Europeans purchased slaves from Africa to be resold in the Americas, raw materials from the Americas were exported to European states, while manufactured products in Europe were sold throughout the Americas.

Truman Doctrine Created in response to 1947 requests by Greece and Turkey for American assistance to defend themselves against potentially pro-Soviet elements in their countries. This policy stated that the United States would be ready to assist any free nation trying to defend itself against "armed minorities or . . . outside pressures." This would become the major American foreign policy goal throughout the cold war.

trusts Late nineteenth-century legal arrangement that allowed owners of one company to own stock in other companies in the same industry. By this arrangement, John D. Rockefeller and Standard Oil were able to buy enough stock to control other oil companies in existence as well. The Sherman Antitrust Act and the Clayton Antitrust Act were efforts to "break up" the numerous trusts that were created during this period.

Turner Thesis Published by Frederick Jackson Turner in 1893, "The Significance of the West in American History" stated that western expansion had played a fundamental role in defining the American character, and that the American tendencies toward democracy and individualism were created by the frontier experience.

Twelfth Amendment of 1804 Amendment that established separate balloting in the Electoral College for president and vice president. This amendment was passed as a result of the electoral deadlock of the 1800 presidential election, when Thomas Jefferson and his "running mate" Aaron Burr ended up with the same number of votes in the Electoral College; the House of Representatives finally decided the election in favor of Jefferson.

U-2 American reconnaissance aircraft shot down over the Soviet Union in May 1960. President Eisenhower initially refused to acknowledge that this was a spy flight; the Soviets finally produced pilot Francis Gary Powers, who admitted the purpose of the flight. This incident created an increase in cold war tensions at the end of the Eisenhower presidency.

Uncle Tom's Cabin 1852 novel by Harriet Beecher Stowe that depicted all of the horrors of Southern slavery in great detail. The book went through several printings in the 1850s and early 1860s and helped to fuel Abolitionist sentiment in the North.

unicameral legislature A government structure with a one-house legislature. As written in the Articles of Confederation, the United States would have a unicameral legislature, with all states having equal representation.

United Farm Workers Organized by Cesar Chavez in 1961, this union represented Mexican Americans engaged in the lowest levels of agricultural work. In 1965 Chavez organized a strike against grape growers that hired Mexican-American workers in California, eventually winning the promise of benefits and minimum wage guarantees for the workers.

U.S. Forest Service Created during the presidency of Theodore Roosevelt, this body increased and protected the number of national forests and encouraged through numerous progress the efficient use of America's natural resources.

Universal Negro Improvement Association Black organization of the early 1920s founded by Marcus Garvey, who argued that, however possible, blacks should disassociate themselves from the "evils" of white society. This group organized a "back to Africa" movement, encouraging blacks of African descent to move back there; independent black businesses were encouraged (and sometimes funded) by Garvey's organization.

unrestricted submarine warfare The German policy announcement in early 1917 of having their U-boats attack all ships attempting to land at British or French ports, despite their origin or purpose. Because of this policy, the rights of the United States as a neutral power were being violated, stated Woodrow Wilson in 1917, and America was forced to declare war on Germany.

U.S.S. *Maine* American ship sent to Havana harbor in early 1898 to protect American interests in period of increased tension between Spanish troops and native Cubans. On February 15 an explosion took place on the ship, killing nearly 275 sailors. Later investigations pointed to an internal explosion on board, but all of the muckraking journals of the time in the United States blamed the explosion on the Spanish, which helped to develop intense anti-Spanish sentiment in the United States.

Valley Forge Location where General Washington stationed his troops for the winter of 1777 to 1778. Soldiers suffered hunger, cold, and disease: nearly 1,300 deserted over the course of the winter. Morale of the remaining troops was raised by the drilling and discipline instilled by Baron von Steuben, a former Prussian officer who had volunteered to aid the colonial army.

vertical integration Type of industrial organization practiced in the late nineteenth century and pioneered by Andrew Carnegie and United States Steel. Under this system all of the various business activities needed to produce and sell a finished product (procuring the raw materials, preparing them, producing them, marketing them, and then selling them) would be done by the same company.

Vicksburg, Battle of After a lengthy siege, this Confederate city along the Mississippi River was finally taken by Union forces in July 1863. This victory gave the Union virtual control of the Mississippi River and was a serious psychological blow to the Confederacy.

Vietcong During the Vietnam war, forces that existed within South Vietnam that were fighting for the victory of the North Vietnamese. Vietcong forces were pivotal in the initial successes of the Tet Offensive,

which did much to make many in America question the American war effort in Vietnam and played a crucial role in the eventual defeat of the South Vietnamese government.

Vietnamization The process begun by Richard Nixon of removing American troops from Vietnam and turning more of the fighting of the Vietnam war over to the South Vietnamese. Nixon continued to use intense bombing to aid the South Vietnamese efforts as more American troops were being pulled out of Vietnam. In 1973, a peace treaty was finally signed with North Vietnam, allowing American troops to leave the country and all American POWs to be released. In March 1975, North Vietnamese and Vietcong forces captured Saigon and emerged victorious in the war.

Virginia Plan A concept of government crafted by James Madison and adopted by delegates to the convention that created the U.S. Constitution; this plan proposed a stronger central government than had existed under the Articles of Confederation to prevent too much power being placed in the hands of one person or persons. The plan also proposed that the powers of the federal government be divided among officials of executive, judicial, and legislative branches.

VISTA (Volunteers in Service to America) Program instituted in 1964 that sent volunteers to help poor Americans living in both urban and rural settings; this program was sometimes described as a domestic peace corps. This was one of many initiatives that were part of Lyndon Johnson's War on Poverty program.

voluntarism The concept that Americans should sacrifice either time or money for the well-being of their country. A sense of voluntarism has permeated America during much of its history, especially during the Progressive Era and during the administration of John Kennedy ("ask not what your country can do for you—ask what you can do for your country"). President George W. Bush called for a renewed sense of voluntarism in the aftermath of the attacks of September 11, 2001.

Wade-Davis Act Congress passed this bill in 1864 in response to the "10 Percent Plan" of Abraham Lincoln; this legislation set out much more difficult conditions than had been proposed by Lincoln for Southern states to reenter the Union. According to Wade-Davis, all former officers of the Confederacy would be denied citizenship; to vote, a person would have to take an oath that he had never helped the Confederacy in any way, and half of all white males in a state would have to swear loyalty to the Union before statehood could be considered. Lincoln prevented this from becoming law by using the pocket veto.

Wagner Act Also called "the National Labor Relations Act," this July 1935 act established major gains for organized labor. It guaranteed collective bargaining, prevented harassment by owners of union activities, and established a National Labor Relations Board to guarantee enforcement of its provisions.

war bonds Also called "Liberty Bonds," these were sold by the U.S. government in both World War I and World War II and used by the government to finance the war effort. A person purchasing a war bond could make money if he or she cashed it in after 5 or 10 years; in the meantime, the government could use the money to help pay its bills. In both wars, movie stars and other celebrities encouraged Americans to purchase war bonds.

War of 1812 War between the British and Americans over British seizure of American ships, connections between the British and Native-American tribes, and other tensions. Treaty ending war restored diplomatic relations between the two countries.

War Industries Board Authorized in 1917, the job of this board was to mobilize American industries for the war effort. The board was headed by Wall Street investor Bernard Baruch, who used his influence to get American industries to produce materials useful for the war effort. Baruch was able to increase American production by a staggering 22 percent before the end of the war.

Warren Commission The group that carefully investigated the assassination of John F. Kennedy. After hearing much testimony, the commission concluded that Lee Harvey Oswald acted alone in killing the president. Even today many conspiracy theorists question the findings of the Warren Commission, claiming that Oswald was part of a larger group who wanted to assassinate the president.

Warsaw Pact Defensive military alliance created in 1955 by the Soviet Union and all of the Eastern European satellite nations loyal to the Soviet Union; the Warsaw Pact was formed as a reaction against NATO and NATO's 1955 decision to invite West Germany to join the organization.

Washington Conference of 1921 Conference where the United States, Japan, and the major European powers agreed not to build any no more warships for 10 years. In addition, the nations agreed not to attack each other's territories in the Pacific. This treaty came from strong post–World War I sentiment that it was important to avoid conflicts between nations that might lead to war.

Watergate Affair The break-in into Democratic campaign headquarters was one of a series of "dirty tricks" carried out by individuals associated with the effort to reelect Richard Nixon president in 1972. Extensive efforts were also made to cover up these activities. In the end, numerous government and campaign officials spent time in jail for their role in the Watergate Affair, and President Nixon was forced to resign in disgrace.

Webb Alien Land Law (1913) California law that prohibited Japanese who were not American citizens from owning farmland in California. This law demonstrates the nativist sentiment found in much of American society in the first decades of the twentieth century.

Webster-Hayne Debate (1830) Senate debate bet-ween Senator Daniel Webster of Massachusetts and Senator Robert Hayne of South Carolina over the issue of state's rights and whether an individual state has the right to nullify federal legislation. Webster skillfully outlined the dangers to the United States that would be caused by the practice of nullification; this debate perfectly captured many of the political divisions between North and South that would increase in the 1830s through the 1860s.

Whig party Political party that came into being in 1834 in opposition to the presidency of Andrew Jackson. Whigs opposed Jackson's use of the spoils system and the extensive power held by President Jackson; for much of their existence, however, the Whigs favored an activist federal government (while their opponents, the Democrats, favored limited government). William Henry Harrison and Zachary Taylor were the two Whigs elected president. The Whig party dissolved in the 1850s.

Whiskey Rebellion Many settlers in Western frontier territory in the early 1790s questioned the power that the federal power had over them. In 1793 settlers in the Ohio territory refused to pay federal excise taxes on whiskey and attacked tax officials who were supposed to collect these taxes; large numbers of "whiskey rebels" threatened to attack Pittsburgh and other cities. In 1794 President Washington was forced to send in federal troops to put down the rebellion.

White Man's Burden From the poem of the same name by Rudyard Kipling, this view justified imperialism by the "white man" around the world, but also emphasized the duty of the Europeans and Americans who were occupying new territories to improve the lives of those living in the newly acquired regions.

Whitewater The name of the scandal that got President Bill Clinton impeached but not convicted. Whitewater was the name of a real-estate deal in Arkansas that Clinton and his wife Hillary Rodham Clinton were both involved in; opponents claimed the actions of the Clintons concerning Whitewater were illegal, unethical, or both. Independent Counsel Kenneth Starr expanded the investigation to include the suicide of Clinton aide Vincent Foster, missing files in the White House, and the relationship of President Clinton with a White House intern, Monica Lewinsky.

Wilmot Proviso In the aftermath of the war with Mexico, in 1846 Representative David Wilmot proposed in an amendment to a military bill that slavery should be prohibited in all territories gained in the treaty ending that war. This never went into law, but in the debate over it in both houses, Southern representatives spoke passionately in defense of slavery; John C. Calhoun even suggested that the federal government had no legal jurisdiction to stop the existence of slavery in any new territory.

Woodstock Music Festival (1969) Event that some perceive as the pinnacle of the 1960s counter-culture. 400,000 young people came together for a weekend of music and a relative lack of hassles or conflict. The difficulty of mixing the 1960s counterculture with the radical politics of the era was demonstrated when Peter Townshend of the Who kicked Abbie Hoffman off the Woodstock stage.

Works Progress Administration (WPA) New Deal program established in 1935 whose goal was to give out jobs as quickly as possible, even though the wages paid by the WPA were relatively low. Roads and public buildings were constructed by WPA work crews. At the same time, WPA authors wrote state guidebooks, artists painted murals in newly constructed public buildings, and musicians performed in large cities and small towns across the country.

writ of habeas corpus Allows a person suspected of a crime not to simply sit in jail indefinitely. Such a suspect must be brought to court and charged with something, or he or she must be released from jail. Abraham Lincoln suspended the right of habeas corpus during the Civil War so that opponents of his policies could be contained.

Yalta Conference Meeting between Stalin, Churchill, and Roosevelt held two months before the fall of Nazi Germany in February 1945. At this meeting Stalin agreed to assist the Americans against the Japanese after the Germans were defeated; it was decided that Germany would be divided into zones (each controlled by one of the victors), and Stalin promised to hold free elections in the Eastern European nations the Soviet army had liberated from the Nazis. Critics of the Yalta agreement maintain that Roosevelt (he was only months from his own death) was naïve in his dealings with Stalin at this meeting, and that Churchill and Roosevelt essentially handed over control of Eastern Europe to Stalin.

yellow journalism This method uses accounts and illustrations of lurid and sensational events to sell newspapers. Newspapers using this strategy covered the events in Cuba leading up to the Spanish-American War, and did much to shift American opinion toward desiring war with Spain. Some critics maintain that many tactics of yellow journalism were used during the press coverage of the Whitewater investigation of Bill Clinton.

Yorktown, Battle of The defeat of the forces of General Cornwallis in this battle in October 1781 essentially ended the hopes of the British for winning the Revolutionary War. American and French troops hemmed the British in on the peninsula of Yorktown, while the French navy located in Chesapeake Bay made rescue of the British troops by sea impossible.

Zimmermann Telegram January 1917 telegram sent by the German foreign minister to Mexico suggesting that the Mexican army should join forces with the Germans against the United States. When the Germans and Mexicans were victorious, the Mexicans were promised most of the southwestern part of the United States. The British deciphered the code of this telegram and turned it over to the United States; the release of its content caused many in America to feel that war against the Germans was essential.

BIBLIOGRAPHY

To get the perfect 5 on the AP exam, you should read this study guide thoroughly. In addition, read all of the assignments your teacher gives you from the textbook. She or he will undoubtedly give you primary source readings and additional readings; these are also critical to your success. Remember, the more you read about American history, the more prepared you will be for the exam!

On this page, I have also included a number of topics that you will study in an AP U.S. History course and books that have been helpful to me in studying each particular topic. This is a totally subjective list; your teacher would probably recommend other books for some of the topics. Nevertheless, if you feel weak in a particular subject (or if you want to learn more about it) read all or a part of the books I have recommended. I am confident that you will not be disappointed.

The Age of Jackson: *Waking Giant: America in the Age of Jackson* by David S. Reynolds (Harper, 2008).

America and World War I: *The Illusion of Victory: America in World War I* by Thomas Fleming (Basic Books, 2004).

The American Revolution: *The American Revolution: A History* by Gordon S. Wood (Modern Library, 2003).

The Civil Rights Movement: *Eyes on the Prize: America's Civil Rights Years, 1954–1965* by Juan Williams (Penguin, 1988).

The Civil War: *Battle Cry of Freedom: The Civil War Era* by James M. McPherson (Oxford University Press USA, 2003).

The Clinton Era: *The Natural: The Misunderstood Presidency of Bill Clinton* by Joe Klein (Broadway, 2003).

The Cold War: *The Cold War: A History* by Martin Walker (Holt Paperbacks, 1995).

Colonial Settlement and the Environment: *Changes in the Land: Indians, Colonists, and the Ecology of New England* by William Cronon (Hill and Wang, 2003).

The Constitution: *A Brilliant Solution: Inventing the American Constitution* by Carol Berkin (Harvest Books, 2003).

The Early Republic: *Empire of Liberty: A History of the Early Republic, 1789–1815* by Gordon S. Wood (Oxford University Press USA, 2009).

Early Industrialization: *What Hath God Wrought: The Transformation of America, 1815–1848* by Daniel Walker Howe (Oxford University Press USA, 2007).

George Washington: *His Excellency: George Washington* by Joseph J. Ellis (Vintage, 2005).

The Gilded Age: *America in the Gilded Age* by Sean Cashman (NYU Press, 1993).

The Great Depression: *The Forgotten Man: A New History of the Great Depression* by Amity Shlaes (Harper Perennial, 2008).

The Late Nineteenth Century: *The Republic for Which It Stands: The United States during Reconstruction and the Gilded Age, 1865–1896* by Richard White (Oxford University Press USA, 2017).

The Late Twentieth Century: *Restless Giant: The United States from Watergate to Bush v. Gore* by James T. Patterson (Oxford University Press USA, 2005).

1920s: *New World Coming: The 1920s and the Making of Modern America* by Nathan Miller (Da Capo Press, 2004).

The 1930s and World War II: *Freedom from Fear: The American People in Depression and War, 1929–1945* by David M. Kennedy (Oxford University Press USA, 1999).

1950s: *The Fifties* by David Halberstam (Ballantine Books, 1994).

1960s: *The Sixties: Years of Hope, Days of Rage* by Todd Gitlin (Bantam, 1993).

1970s: *It Seemed Like Nothing Happened: America in the 1970s* by Peter N. Carroll (Rutgers University Press, 1990).

Origins of the Civil War: *The Impending Crisis, 1848–1861* by David M. Potter (Harper Perennial, 1977).

Native American History: *Indigenous Continent: The Epic Contest for North America* by Pekka Hamalainen (Liveright Publishing Corporation, 2022).

The Post–World War II Era: *Grand Expectations: The United States, 1945–1974* by James T. Patterson (Oxford University Press USA, 1996).

Progressivism: *A Fierce Discontent: The Rise and Fall of the Progressive Movement in America, 1870–1920* by Michael McGerr (Oxford University Press USA, 2005).

The Reagan Era: *Transforming America: Politics and Culture During the Reagan Years* by Robert M. Collins (Columbia University Press, 2006).

The Reconstruction Era: *Reconstruction: America's Unfinished Revolution, 1863–1877* by Eric Foner (Harper Perennial Modern Classics, 2002).

The Revolutionary Era: *The Glorious Cause: The American Revolution, 1763–1789* by Robert Middlekauff (Oxford University Press USA, 2005).

The Settlement of the American Colonies: *American Colonies: The Settling of North America* by Alan Taylor (Penguin, 2002).

Slavery: *Slavery and the Making of America* by James Oliver Horton and Lois E. Horton (Oxford University Press USA, 2006).

Thomas Jefferson: *Thomas Jefferson: Author of America* by Christopher Hitchens (Eminent Lives, 2005).

U.S. Foreign Relations: *From Colony to Superpower: U.S. Foreign Relations since 1776* by George C. Herring (Oxford University Press USA, 2008).

Westward Expansion: *The American West: A New Interpretive History* by Robert V. Hine and John Mack Faragher (Yale University Press, 2000).

The West in the Nineteenth Century: *Dreams of El Dorado: A History of the American West* by H.W. Brands (Basic Books, 2019).

World War II: *The American People in World War II: Freedom from Fear, Part Two* by David M. Kennedy (Oxford University Press USA, 2003).

WEBSITES

There are literally thousands of sites on the web where you can get valuable information on aspects of American history. Historical figures, historical events, and historic sites all have websites with specific information; in addition, there are hundreds of websites with a vast variety of information and resources on topics of U.S. history. If you want to start somewhere, I would recommend two sites. One is a University of Delaware Library site, entitled "Internet Resources for U.S. History." This is found at University of Delaware's "Websites for U.S. Ed: The periods are used on the page itself: http://guides.lib.udel.edu/c.php?g=85352&p=549115. History" page and the Internet Public Library's "United States History" page.

Do some more exploring, and you will be utterly amazed at what you can find. In addition, go to your state and local historical society sites; here you will find information about the connections between the history of your town and state and the larger historical themes that you have studied in your AP U.S. History class.

5 Steps to Teaching AP U.S. History

TEACHER'S MANUAL

Patrick Hinson

Blythewood High School, Blythewood, South Carolina

Thanks to Greg Jacobs, an AP Physics teacher at Woodberry Forest School in Virginia, for developing the 5-step approach used in this teaching manual.

Introduction to the Teacher's Manual

It has never been easier for teachers to access a variety of resources to use in their AP United States History classrooms. Teachers do not have to rely primarily on the traditional textbook anymore. Today's teachers can take advantage of a myriad of websites, videos, and other digital platforms, many of which are teacher created and free to access. In addition, the College Board provides invaluable resources for AP U.S. History through the AP Classroom.

Over the years I have observed that AP teachers can easily become overwhelmed by an excess of teaching materials and resources that are available. I recommend starting with a few solid resources to build your class around for the year. As you continue to teach the course and reflect, you will be able to monitor and adjust the resources that work best for you and your students.

This book is one of the core resources that all AP U.S. History teachers can build their classes around. It is teacher and student friendly and describes in straightforward language what a student needs to be successful on the AP U.S. History exam. It also provides a review of all the key concepts, multiple-choice questions and free-response questions, and practice exams.

This teacher's manual takes you through the five steps of teaching AP U.S. History. These five steps are:

▶ Prepare a strategic plan for the course

▶ Hold an interesting class every day

▶ Evaluate your students' progress

▶ Get students ready to take the AP exam

▶ Become a better teacher every year

I'll discuss each of these steps, providing suggestions and ideas of things that I use in my class. I present them here because over the years, I found that *they work*. You may have developed a different course strategy, teaching activities, and evaluation techniques. That's fine; different things work for different teachers. But I hope you find in this teacher's manual something that will be useful to you.

Prepare a Strategic Plan for the Course

The AP U.S. History Course and Exam Description (CED) created by the College Board is located at **https://apcentral.collegeboard.org/pdf/ap-us-history-course-and-exam-description**. It lays out a suggested scope and sequence for the AP U.S. History class. The suggested pacing keeps you on track to cover the material prior to the AP exam. I also suggest following the CED's sequence of introducing the free-response questions (FRQs) to students. The suggested sequence of staggering the introduction of short-answer questions (SAQs), long-essay questions (LEQs), and document-based questions (DBQs) allows students to master the skills needed to be successful on each of these.

It is very easy to get bogged down in topics that we as teachers may be more interested in. The CED gives some flexibility on the amount of time spent on each period, but I would suggest in your first few years of teaching the course to follow the CED pacing as closely as possible. Remember that you must also include your assessments in this pacing. Most of my assessments take two class periods: one class period for multiple-choice questions and one class period for free-response questions—SAQs, LEQs, or DBQs.

A good general rule is to have covered through Period 5 (Reconstruction) by the end of the first semester. Some teachers may choose to move a little faster to allow more time for in-class review at the end of year. I like to make sure that in the first semester I have set aside enough time to focus on test-taking skills such as going over multiple-choice questions and FRQs in more detail than we will in the second semester.

The following chart shows the periods and the time suggested for each unit. The number of class periods is based on a typical 45-minute class. If your school follows a block schedule or other atypical schedule, you need to adjust the pacing to fit your class needs. Please note that the periods often overlap into multiple chapters.

TOPICS	PACING	5 STEPS TO A 5 (Most periods cross over into multiple chapters.)
Period 1: 1491–1607	8–9 class periods	Chapter 6, pp. 77–83
Period 2: 1607–1754	14–15 class periods	Chapters 7–9, pp. 84–109
Period 3: 1754–1800	17–18 class periods	Chapters 9–11, pp. 100–133
Period 4: 1800–1848	17–18 class periods	Chapters 12–14, pp. 134–168
Period 5: 1844–1877	17–18 class periods	Chapters 14–18, pp. 155–216
Period 6: 1865–1898	18–19 class periods	Chapters 16–20, pp. 179–228
Period 7: 1890–1945	21–22 class periods	Chapters 19–25, pp. 217–317
Period 8: 1945–1980	20–21 class periods	Chapters 25–28, pp. 302–356
Period 9: 1980–Present	8–9 class periods	Chapters 28–31, pp. 343–392

As you plan your year, make sure to come up with a structured, organized plan for review. Some teachers like to leave two to three weeks of dedicated review time just before the test. Around six weeks before the exam, I like to have my students start exam review outside of class (including after-school review sessions) using my review videos on VoiceThread and a detailed, structured plan of what to review each of these weeks. There is no right or wrong way to approach the exam review. However, it is imperative that you find what works best for you and your students. Your review schedule and review materials should be developed and organized in a manner that will not overwhelm students who also may be reviewing for other AP exams.

STEP 2

Hold an Interesting Class Every Day

The best way to make sure that students are successful in AP U.S. History is to make sure that students are engaged in your daily lessons. I feel the foundation of engaging lessons starts with detailed planning. This will take more time during your first few years of teaching the course, but you will find that once you have the foundation of your lessons created, you will have more time to make adjustments from year to year. I follow the same schedule daily but with different activities.

▶ **Bell ringer.** I like to use varying strategies and activities for the first five minutes of class each day. This may include working on one AP-released multiple-choice question, writing a thesis sentence from an AP prompt, or using the historical thinking skills to analyze a primary source. Sometimes these bell ringers are from previous units/periods that allow for review, and sometimes they are from the previous night's reading.

The *5 Steps to a 5 AP United States History: Elite Edition* of this book provides additional questions that can be used in your class. It contains activities and questions that require five minutes a day. While they are primarily intended to be used by students studying for the test, you can use these as daily warmups in your course. To do this, you can refer to the following table that organizes these questions and activities by unit.

UNIT	QUESTIONS/ACTIVITIES IN THE ELITE EDITION
Period 1: 1491–1607	1–7
Period 2: 1607–1754	8–29
Period 3: 1754–1800	22–42
Period 4: 1800–1848	43–63
Period 5: 1844–1877	57–92
Period 6: 1865–1898	72–106
Period 7: 1890–1945	93–144
Period 8: 1945–1980	137–166
Period 9: 1980–Present	160–180

▶ **Big ideas.** I like to call the class lecture or discussion our "big ideas." I give students a weekly agenda that allows students to know what we will be covering each day in class; this lets students be better prepared. Students are given a copy of my textbook notes along with the big ideas that we will cover in class. These include essential questions and primary source analysis from the reading and VoiceThread videos. Students know the expectation is that they will be called on to lead the discussion on these big ideas and primary source analysis. This allows the teacher to be more of the facilitator who creates an atmosphere where students are engaged and accountable.

▶ **Historical thinking skills/primary sources.** I like to close class by taking the information we have covered and having students apply it to a primary source that we did not go over in the discussion of big ideas. I let students work individually or in small groups using the AP U.S. History historical thinking skills found in the CED (cause and effect, compare and contrast, and change and continuity). I make sure to vary the source by sometimes giving students a political cartoon or a photograph instead of a written source. It will take you a few years to build up your bank of these primary sources, but it will be easier each year you teach the course. I feel it's important for students to have the same element of surprise that they will feel on the AP exam by analyzing documents (or other sources) they have not seen before. I often use these same documents on our quizzes and tests to make sure students are actively engaged.

The primary sources, classroom activities, and videos/documentaries that you decide to use in your course should be guided by the AP U.S. History Key Concepts found in the CED. It can be overwhelming to find these primary sources; Google is always a great place to start, and I would recommend working with your media specialist at your school. These are some of the primary sources, documents, and videos that I like to use for each period.

UNIT	RECOMMENDED ACTIVITIES
Unit 1, **Period 1:** 1491–1607	▶ Graphic organizer of the Columbian Exchange ▶ Compare-and-contrast activity on European exploration ▶ Las Casas and Sepúlveda class debate ▶ SAQ introduction on how the North American Native Americans adapted and transformed their environment ▶ CED-based historical thinking skills activity ▶ Cause and effect ▶ Compare and contrast ▶ Change and continuity
Unit 2, **Period 2:** 1607–1754	▶ Activity on how geography affected the development of the New England, Middle, and Southern colonies ▶ Timeline activity on the origins and development of African slavery and its introduction into the New World ▶ John Winthrop's *City on a Hill* activity ▶ Graphic organizer that compares and contrasts the New England, Middle, and Southern colonies politically, socially, and economically ▶ LEQ introduction—historical context and thesis activities
Unit 3, **Period 3:** 1754–1800	▶ Graphic organizer on steps toward American Revolution ▶ Declaration of Independence activity ▶ Loyalist or patriot class debate ▶ Venn diagram comparing and contrasting the Articles of Confederation with the Constitution ▶ Federalists versus Democratic Republicans activity ▶ DBQ introduction—change and continuity after the American Revolution
Unit 4, **Period 4:** 1800–1848	▶ Graphic organizer on foreign policy leading up to the War of 1812 ▶ SAQ practice—secondary sources on "The Revolution of 1800" ▶ Market revolution map activity ▶ DBQ introduction—causes and effects of antebellum reform movements
Unit 5, **Period 5:** 1844–1877	▶ Map activity on manifest destiny ▶ Graphic organizer on causes of the Civil War ▶ Civil War amendments activity ▶ LEQ activity—change and continuity after the Civil War
Unit 6, **Period 6:** 1865–1898	▶ Causes of the end of the Plains Indians' way of life activity ▶ Graphic organizer of the major Western economic sectors ▶ Robber baron versus captain of industry class debate ▶ Jacob Riis *How the Other Half Lives* activity
Unit 7, **Period 7:** 1890–1945	▶ Populism/Progressivism activity ▶ WWI graphic organizer ▶ SAQ activity on causes and effects of the Great Depression ▶ New Deal graphic organizer ▶ Compare and contrast WWI and WWII activity ▶ Decision to drop the atomic bomb class debate ▶ DBQ activity—compare and contrast US imperialism with Manifest Destiny

(continued)

UNIT	RECOMMENDED ACTIVITIES
Unit 8, Period 8: 1945–1980	▶ Cold War graphic organizer by decades ▶ Women's rights graphic organizer by decades ▶ Civil rights graphic organizer by decades ▶ Class debate on the Vietnam War and the Domino theory ▶ Watergate activity ▶ DBQ activity—change and continuity as a result of the post–WWII Civil Rights Movement
Unit 9, Period 9: 1980–Present	▶ Graphic organizer for Presidents Reagan, Bush, Clinton, Bush, and Obama ▶ 9/11 activity ▶ Globalization activity ▶ Clinton/Trump impeachment activity

On the actual AP test that students will take:

▶ 4 to 6 percent of the exam will relate to issues concerning Period 1.

▶ 36 to 59 percent of the exam will relate to issues concerning Periods 2, 3, 4, and 5.

▶ 30 to 51 percent of the exam will relate to issues concerning Periods 6, 7, and 8.

▶ 4 to 6 percent of the exam will relate to issues concerning Period 9.

Many teachers are worried when their AP class doesn't get to the present day. As you can see, only 5 percent of the test is on material after 1980; therefore, not making it all the way to present-day events will not have a major impact on student scores.

STEP 3
Evaluate Your Students' Progress

Multiple-Choice Questions

The multiple-choice questions comprise 40 percent of the AP exam. It is important to work with your students on how to break down the type of multiple-choice questions they will see on the AP exam. Most of your students will not be used to multiple-choice questions that are based on a stimulus (primary/secondary text, political cartoon, graphs/charts, and so on). It is imperative that a large portion of your multiple-choice questions be stimulus based. You can find examples of these in AP Classroom, Problem-Attic, and the NY Regents exams. I also use the primary sources covered in class when I create the multiple-choice questions used in tests, quizzes, and so on. We spend time in class working on how to eliminate detractors and to focus on the key words in the questions. I often ask students to come up with their own multiple-choice questions for bell ringer activities or for homework.

Free-Response Questions (FRQs)

The FRQs account for 60 percent of the AP U.S. History exam. This can be further broken down by type of question:

▶ Short-answer questions: 20 percent of the exam

▶ Document-based questions: 25 percent of the exam

▶ Long-essay questions: 15 percent of the exam

Short-Answer Questions (SAQs)

I introduce the SAQs to students beginning with Period 1. I start with the SAQs found in AP Classroom and in *5 Steps to a 5* that are not stimulus based. These questions are usually more manageable and build confidence in your students. I then move on to the SAQs that use a political cartoon, photograph, chart, or graph and finish with the SAQs based on two secondary sources. In my opinion, you will find that students will struggle the most with the secondary-source-based SAQs. You can help students with this by incorporating these secondary sources into your class as often as possible. By the end of the first semester, I try to make sure that my students feel comfortable with all three types of SAQs.

Long-Essay Questions (LEQ) and Document-Based Questions (DBQ)

I then introduce the LEQs before beginning to tackle the DBQ. Introduce students to the rubric for the LEQs found in the CED. I recommend making your own student-friendly rubric that students can understand more clearly. Scaffold the LEQs by teaching students how to write the introduction paragraph by working on historical context and writing a thesis. Once you feel comfortable that students have mastered historical context and the thesis, move on to the analysis and evidence portion of the rubric found in the CED. The most important skill you can help your students with is making sure their analysis and evidence supports the argument in the thesis. Similar to the SAQs, I like to make sure that students feel comfortable with the LEQ rubric by the end of the first semester.

When students are reasonably comfortable with the LEQs, you can move on to the DBQs. If they have mastered the basics of the LEQs, then they should have the foundation to tackle the more challenging DBQs. From the LEQs, students should already be able to write the introductory paragraph of historical context and be able to construct a thesis. If students have mastered the rubric used for the LEQs, the rubric for the DBQs will not be that difficult for them. Introduce the DBQs by only using a few documents at a time; this will make it easier for the student and for you to give feedback. We often look at sample DBQs found in the AP Classroom and in *5 Steps to a 5* as bell ringers and small-group work.

I strongly encourage you to have students look at examples of student work that earned the point on the rubric and those that did not earn the point, and to be able to recognize why or why not the point was earned/not earned. You can find samples in both *5 Steps to a 5* and in the AP Classroom. I have found this is where the "lightbulb" comes on for many students who struggle with the FRQ portion of the exam.

Get Students Ready to Take the AP Exam

One of the best ways to get your students ready for the exam is to continue to review material throughout the course. I make sure that every lesson includes connections to material we have covered in the past, as well as topics we will cover in the future. I also use the bell ringers to look at multiple-choice questions and FRQs from material we have previously covered. This helps prepare them for the "shock" of working with content we're currently not covering.

Teachers will have many different approaches for exam review. I would suggest finding what works best for you and your students. Successful review plans are organized, structured, manageable, and have student buy-in. Most of your students will be taking other AP classes and reviewing for these exams as well, so make sure your reviews take this into consideration.

Many teachers cover the material at a pace that allows for in-class review for three or more weeks, and this is great if it works for you and your school's schedule. I have found personally that my students struggle with that pace, and I prefer to leave only two weeks for in-class review. But I break down the exam review into *out-of-class review* and *in-class review*.

Out-of-Class Review

I continually stress throughout the year that my students have been successful on the exam, and that this success is largely in part to students' commitment to the out-of-class review. For many students this will be their first AP exam, and they may not be prepared for how to study for an assessment that covers a large amount of material.

I share with my students and parents a Google document and calendar that starts the out-of-class review seven weeks before the exam. We spend minimal time reviewing Periods 1 and 9, but for each of the seven other periods, I create review units that have links to the following:

▶ The pages in *5 Steps to a 5: AP U.S. History* that they need to cover. It is ideal that each student be provided a copy; however, if this is not possible, students can access the online Cross-Platform Edition (see the back cover for information).

▶ VoiceThread videos that I create for students to watch that correspond with Google slides created for each of these review units. I also create a study guide for each video.

Then we do an in-class quiz once a week on the review unit assigned for that week. It consists of multiple-choice questions from the AP Classroom. You can also use *5 Steps to a 5* as a source for questions. We go over the explanations as to why the correct answers are right and why the detractors are incorrect.

In addition, to ensure that the out-of-class review is going well, I do the following:

▶ I stay after school one day per week in case any students have specific questions. I limit these sessions to one hour and do not reteach the information, but rather focus on material they may be struggling with. If your students are taking multiple AP exams, you will find that they may miss some days; it is helpful to record these sessions on Google Meet for those students.

▶ I help facilitate student study groups where students can help each other. This helps those students who may be reluctant to reach out on their own to other students to form these groups.

▶ I e-mail parents each week to remind them of the review schedule and to remind them to use encouragement to help lower test anxiety.

Finally, if students have access to *5 Steps to a 5: AP United States History,* they have the option of taking the two full-length practice exams found at the end of the book and scoring themselves.

In-Class Review

Although there are only two weeks of in-class review time, I use that time wisely. Because students are reviewing content outside of class, I focus on the questions they will encounter on the exam. As I mentioned earlier, I give a weekly multiple-choice quiz in class. In class, we also look at potential SAQs, LEQs, and DBQs found in AP Classroom. If you have large classes, you may find it more manageable to look at responses together as a class, analyzing what would and would not earn points according to the rubric.

Two weeks before the exam we begin spending some time in class on test-taking strategies for the multiple-choice questions and the SAQs, the LEQ, and the DBQ. The key strategies are listed in the chart that follows:

Multiple-Choice Questions	▶ Students should underline the key parts of the question itself. I encourage my students to answer the question mentally before they look at the potential answer choices. ▶ Eliminate the detractors! Students should almost always be able to eliminate two of the detractors. ▶ Students should not get bogged down with a particularly hard question. Students should do the best they can with a challenging question and then move on. Students should answer the question and flag it in case there is time to revisit.
Short-Answer Questions	▶ Make sure you understand what the question is asking you to prove and that you provide supporting evidence to support your answer. ▶ The first SAQ question will consist of two secondary sources, which may require additional time to read. This question is usually going to ask you to identify different points of view. ▶ The second SAQ question will consist of a political cartoon, chart, or graph. Be sure to practice with different types of stimuli. ▶ SAQ Questions 3 and 4: these questions will not contain a stimulus and are often the most manageable of the SAQ questions. Remember that you're only choosing one of these questions. Don't spend too much time deciding between the two questions; pick the question that you can provide the most evidence for. ▶ Make sure you keep track of time for pacing! You have 40 minutes, which works out to around 13 minutes per SAQ. Remember that the first SAQ may require a little more time than the others.
Document-Based Questions	▶ Don't let the DBQ intimidate you! Think of the documents as resources that will help provide evidence to prove your thesis. ▶ Make sure you let the reader know which document you are sourcing. ▶ Remember that when you source the documents as resources that will help prove evidence to support your thesis.
Long-Essay Questions	▶ You will have three LEQs to choose from. Do not take too long in choosing among the three questions. ▶ Make sure that you keep track of the time that you have left and finish strong.

In addition, I require students to take one practice exam out of class for a grade at the beginning of the two-week in-class review period. I offer two Saturday sessions and one day after school for students to take a practice exam. If students choose to take more than one practice exam, I offer extra credit. I use the practice exams found on AP Classroom and have students complete the multiple-choice section and a DBQ. I let students see the SAQs and LEQ that were on that particular exam but do not require them to complete them. Students should be able to complete the SAQs by this point, and if they can write the DBQ, they will be able to write the LEQ. I have large classes, and this gives me time to grade the DBQs with feedback before the exam. If you have smaller classes, you may choose to give the entire exam if you feel you will have time to grade all the FRQs with feedback.

After the practice exam, we go over the frequently missed multiple-choice questions in class. We also look at trends in the type of stimulus used for the frequently missed questions. Were they political cartoons, graphs/charts, secondary/primary texts? This determines how much time we spend on each of these. We also look at student examples of the DBQ that earned the rubric points and those that did not. Finally, we look at the SAQs and LEQs that the students were not required to complete and work through them together as a class.

STEP 5

Become a Better Teacher Every Year

If you're teaching AP U.S. History for the first time, make sure to remember that building your course will be a process. Try not to get overwhelmed! Work unit by unit mastering the content and building your major assessments. You will find that each year will get easier after you have the core of your class built.

Start this process by attending an AP Summer Institute (APSI) that will go into much more detail about the structure of the exam and how to build your course. Attending the APSI will allow you to build your syllabus with the help of veteran teachers and beginning teachers as well. You will make lasting connections with other teachers that will allow you to collaborate about best practices on pacing and textbook selection. Reach out to other AP teachers at your school or in your district that can help you navigate AP Classroom and the AP daily videos and practice questions.

Reflect each summer about what worked well and what did not. I have found that making major changes to the course during the year is difficult for both the teacher and the student. Work on the areas that you feel you can improve on the most. Most teachers find building assessments and pacing to be the most challenging areas of the course.

Make sure you work on building relationships with your students and parents. AP students and parents are also under the stress of the exam. Effective communication about class expectations and assessment dates will help build these relationships.

Make sure that you don't let the pressure of pass rates discourage you. We would all like all of our students to earn a 3 or higher on the exam, but each school has its unique circumstances and challenges. I also make sure that my students know that a test score does not define them. For many students who are taking an AP class for the first time, earning a 2 can demonstrate significant growth.

For all AP teachers, the Chief Reader's Report released after the conclusion of exam scoring each year is a vital resource to help you see the breakdown of scores and on which topics students scored well or poorly. You can also utilize AP Classroom to see the breakdown of your own students' scores and how well they did on multiple-choice questions from each unit. This can often lead to adjustments in the way you teach certain topics or the amount of time spent on those concepts or skills.

I would encourage any AP U.S. History teacher to take advantage of becoming a reader for the College Board if you have the opportunity. In my opinion, this is the best professional development to best prepare your students for the FRQs.

Additional Resources for Teachers

Make sure to always use the College Board's CED for the course that is found at **https://apcentral.collegeboard.org/courses/ap-united-states-history/course.**
If the topic is in the CED, it will be on the AP test. If the topic is not in the CED, it is out of the scope for the course and will not be tested.

Videos

I have organized these by periods. I have found that students like the consistency of the Gilder Lehrman Institute of American History review videos that come with a study guide, followed by one of the many individual themes offered under each time period. There are many more, but these are some of my favorites. Also, do not forget that AP Classroom has videos for every topic.

Period One

▸ The Gilder Lehrman Institute of American History AP US History Study Guide, Period One: 1491–1607

▸ Crash Course US History video 1: The Black Legend, Native Americans and Spaniards

Period Two

▸ The Gilder Lehrman Institute of American History Study Guide, Period Two: 1607–1754

▸ Crash Course US History video 2: Colonizing America

Period Three

▸ The Gilder Lehrman Institute of American History Study Guide, Period Three: 1754–1800

▸ The Gilder Lehrman Institute of American History AP US History: *Slavery and the American Revolution*

▸ Crash Course US History videos 5–7 (you probably will not be able to go over all of these; pick and choose which ones you feel will best help your students)

Period Four

▸ The Gilder Lehrman Institute of American History Study Guide, Period Four: 1800–1848

▸ The Gilder Lehrman Institute of American History: *The Idea of America: Reflections on the Birth of the United States*

▸ Crash Course US History videos 9–15 (pick and choose which ones you feel will best help your students)

Period Five

▸ The Gilder Lehrman Institute of American History Study Guide, Period Five: 1844–1877

▸ The Gilder Lehrman Institute of American History: *Backlash Against the Fugitive Slave Act*

▸ Crash Course US History videos 16–22 (pick and choose which ones you feel will best help your students)

Period Six

▸ The Gilder Lehrman Institute of American History Study Guide, Period Six: 1865–1898

▸ The Gilder Lehrman Institute of American History: *America's Emergence as a Global Power*

▸ Crash Course US History videos 23–26 (pick and choose which ones you feel will best help your students)

Period Seven

- The Gilder Lehrman Institute of American History Study Guide, Period Seven: 1890–1945

- The Gilder Lehrman Institute of American History: *The Progressive Era*

- Crash Course US History videos 29–36 (pick and choose which ones you feel will best help your students)

Period Eight

- The Gilder Lehrman Institute of American History Study Guide, Period Eight: 1945–1980

- The Gilder Lehrman Institute of American History: *What Are the Legacies of the Civil Rights Movement?*

- Crash Course US History videos 37–43 (pick and choose which ones you feel will best help your students)

Period Nine

- The Gilder Lehrman Institute of American History Study Guide, Period Nine: 1980–Present

- The Gilder Lehrman Institute of American History: *America at the End of the 20th Century*

- Crash Course US History videos 44–47 (pick and choose which ones you feel will best help your students)

Websites

- Khan Academy has student activities broken down by the periods in AP U.S. History. https://www.khanacademy.org/humanities/ap-us-history

- The Gilder Lehrman Institute of American History has topics broken down by all the themes for AP U.S. History. https://www.gilderlehrman.org/history-resources

- New York State Regents offers practice multiple-choice questions broken down by themes in US History. http://www.nysedregents.org/

- The National Archives is a great resource of primary and secondary sources to practice AP historical thinking skills. https://www.archives.gov/historical-docs

- History Central is another student-friendly website with theme-based primary and secondary sources. https://www.historycentral.com/USHistory.html